Nathaniel Hawthorne

Foreword

This remarkable work of criticism is not only one more volume on Hawthorne: it is a highly significant one, because it testifies to the universality of him whom Henry James, in his acute little book on Hawthorne in 1879—in a series called "English Men of Letters"—had called "the most valuable example of the American genius." It is also a profound, almost scientific, study of the creative process in letters and in the arts. Freud, Jung, Bergson, Bachelard are drawn upon to provide clues to the mystery of imagination at work on subconscious images and dreams. Hawthorne is set beside Melville and Thoreau, but also beside Dostoevsky, Gide, Lawrence, Faulkner. The perspective is much broader than in the usual academic studies on an American author. The literary progenitors of one who was a poet in his tales and novels are not altogether neglected: Spenser, Bunyan, the Shakespeare of *A Midsummer Night's Dream*. The symbol of Oberon, the magician, the dweller in fairyland, recurs as a leitmotiv in the book. But the perspective is clearly that of today, and Hawthorne, cruelly neglected and maligned by his contemporaries, is envisaged with the hindsight afforded by the twentieth-century writers of America and of France, even more than he fascinated by cruelty, persecution, intolerance, sexual repression. This abstract volume, while not unmindful of the style, language, and imagery of Hawthorne, of his skill as a storyteller and, in a few cases, as a novelist, set out to reach beyond and behind literature to the psychology and the aesthetics of artistic creation. Such a design, and the allusive writing which it required, as well as a lavish recourse to abstract generalizations, rendered the translator's task unusually arduous. It is also bound to irk more traditional critics, who prefer summarizing plots, discussing characters, analyzing technical devices to the elucidation of the process through which a work of art comes out of a discontented, morbidly introspective, torn man. It may be that the question of why and how a man of genius creates can never be clarified. Kierkegaard, whose striking similarities to Hawthorne have not escaped M. Normand, warned once: "In a sense, not even God in His heaven understands genius." But the audacious attempt had to be made; it is made here with modesty, though with much firmness, and with a minimum of psychological jargon.

Hawthorne, and Melville, and indeed Walt Whitman (whom Hawthorne never mentioned) had been known to the French relatively early and in the lifetime of those writers, when they were still ignored or scorned in Puritan America. Henry James found it advisable, in his volume of 1879, fifteen years after the novelist's death, to defend him repeatedly against the eminent French critic Emile Montégut, who had, in 1860, entitled his essay on Hawthorne "A Pessimistic Novelist." The French have always been puzzled by the gloomy view of life which seems to be held by almost all the writers of the English-speaking New World, Emerson excepted, and most blatantly of all by the one whom they would like to imagine as perpetually cheerful, Mark Twain. For a time, their view was summarily dismissed as that of a foreign nation which had had the poor taste of acclaiming Edgar Poe, the paragon, according to Aldous Huxley, of "vulgarity in literature." But their high estimation of Poe as a critic and theorist of poetry and a storyteller, can no longer be condescendingly rejected by Anglo-Saxon critics. The small, bellicose, but clear-sighted *Studies in Classic American Literature* by D. H. Lawrence, published in 1923, slighted at first on this side of the Atlantic, eventually served as an eye-opener to many students of American letters. It was, after all, Melville, who had been strangely drawn to solitary and misunderstood Hawthorne, who had coined the now famous phrase on "the power of blackness" and pointed to the weird force which that power derived "from its appeals to that Calvinistic sense of innate depravity and original sin, from whose visitations . . . no deeply thinking man is always and wholly free." Harry Levin, who used the phrase as the title of his incisive study of Hawthorne, Poe, and Melville, called his first chapter "The American Nightmare." According to less polished observers of the American scene, the nightmare has only become more hideous

NATHANIEL HAWTHORNE

AN APPROACH TO AN ANALYSIS OF ARTISTIC CREATION

BY JEAN NORMAND

TRANSLATED FROM THE FRENCH BY DEREK COLTMAN

THE PRESS OF CASE WESTERN RESERVE UNIVERSITY

CLEVELAND AND LONDON · 1970

Nathaniel Hawthorne: Esquisse d'une Analyse de la Création Artistique, by Jean Normand, copyright © 1964 by Presses Universitaires de France.

English translation, by Derek Coltman, copyright © 1970 by The Press of Case Western Reserve University, Cleveland, Ohio 44106.
Standard Book Number: 8295-0151-7.
Library of Congress Catalogue Card Number: 70-84494.

To J.-B. Fort

through being now "air-conditioned" and haunting an affluent population freed from Calvinism and worshipping technology.

A reinterpretation of Hawthorne, however, had to wait for the publication of many of his notebooks, letters to and from friends, a precise knowledge of the moods and feelings of New Englanders in the first half of the last century. M. Normand is fully up-to-date on the scholarship which has accumulated around Hawthorne, the Transcendentalists, the flowering of New England, and the more seamy and sordid side of life in Massachusetts and Maine then. Hawthorne never shared in the heroic adventures of his countrymen who were trying to develop the West or in the idealism of those who sensed a Civil War approaching and hailed the inevitable struggle for the abolition of slavery. He was addicted to solitude, to long walks in the dark, to dreaming, and, as his compatriots would say today, determinedly anti-social. "He is a lion, a bear, a tiger," Emerson said of him. After a sickly childhood and a strange affection of one of his legs, which had seemed to stop growing, he became indeed an athlete and he sought the company of woodcutters, masons, sturdy workers on the docks of Salem when he was employed by the Customs there. He did not care much for intellectual companionship, there or later in England, when his college friend Franklin Pierce, having become president of the United States, sent him there and to Italy as consul.

But a creator is almost always a man divided against himself, unable in practical life to come to terms with his inner conflicts, oscillating in his dual polarity and finding a temporary unity only when projecting his torments into imaginary creatures. He realizes that some of the anguish which corrodes him, and of the venoms which he secretes, will cease to appear monstrous to him if he succeeds in having his readers share them with him. M. Normand analyzes with rare delicacy the worship of his sickly mother by the little boy Nathaniel, her sole "God-given" male child, which is the meaning of Nathaniel in Hebrew. The father had died from yellow fever in Dutch Guiana in 1808, when the child was only four. The family, after having once been prosperous and surrounded with public esteem (in the seventeenth century) had declined and become impoverished. The family tradition had it that a curse, once uttered by a witch dying on the gallows, had brought about its demise. The Gallows Hill in Salem was one of the spots to which dreamy Nathaniel repaired often in his solitary wanderings. His mother, crushed by the loss of her husband, lived sequestered upstairs in her room, melancholy and too much of a Puritan to show or to express to her children her feelings for them. No wonder if the boy felt gloomy himself, fearful of love and of woman, realizing at the same time that he had what he himself termed "a feminine cast of mind" and was endowed with "the tremulous sensitiveness . . . of the most finely organized woman." He was prone to lethargy and "sluggishness," as he called it, liked to indulge his dreams and knew that he had to create in order to escape passiveness and to give voice to the other facet of his true self, the poetical, "Oberonian" side of his nature. The myth of Oberon, of which his French biographer makes constant use, happens to be a convenient one, since Oberon had been the nickname given Hawthorne in college by his friends, and he used it as a pseudonym in one of his early stories. When his "Oberonian" personality failed him and his sense of elation deserted him, as when he was deprived of his position with the Salem Custom House and maligned by envious enemies, he swung to the other pole of his dual nature and fell into fits of depression and sterility. His last years were indeed barren and mournful. His creative vigor was dried up.

There is nothing commonplace or facile in M. Normand's book, no display of erudition for erudition's sake, no dallying with the anecdotic side of exterior biography. The titles of his chapters are subtle and enigmatic. The tone of the critic is often poetical, and it should be when dealing with a novelist who had a poet's delicacy and fancy. Hawthorne, Henry James concluded in his study of him, was both a moralist and a poet, but not completely either: "the moralists are weightier, denser, richer, in a sense; the poets are more purely inconclusive and irresponsible. He combined in a singular degree the spontaneity of the imagination with a haunting care for moral problems." M. Normand follows with patience and ingeniousness what he calls the arabesques of Hawthorne's conscience, the labyrinthine paths through which his creative gift had to travel before he could exteriorize and transmit to imaginary characters his obsessive sense of guilt. His study is a thematic one, and his chapters on the present captured in the past, on the remorse of Hawthorne's conscience, on his nostalgia for the lost Eden and his narcissism of sin, offer a penetrating psychoanalysis of an author who, in other times, might have been drawn to psychoanalysis himself. He alluded often to the many letters which he received "from spiritual invalids." Those tormented souls sensed a kindred spirit in him.

M. Normand is a psychologist intent upon discovering, not in the abstract how all creators proceed, but as one of them, in a certain natural setting and a certain cultural milieu, dreadfully alone as an American artist could be in the first half of the last century, created. But that case study is constantly related to that of other creators, in America and Europe. Hawthorne as an artist was even more original. The final chapters on his imagery and on the almost cinematic play of light and shade, of reality and symbol, while bordering at times on paradoxes and making the novelist almost too "relevant" to the anxieties and tastes of modern youth, are revealing and original. E. A. Poe, who could be a very acute critic, had remarked on "the profound undercurrent" running under the seemingly smooth flow of a clear, restrained style. Henry James, less discerning in this case, judged the symbolism of Hawthorne, his play upon the invisible reality made visible by art, to be a fault. It becomes mechanical, he declared, and "grazes triviality." We know better or think otherwise today, in an age which has restored allegory to a high estate in poetry and fiction. "I can never separate the idea from the symbol in which it manifests itself," admitted casually a character in one of Hawthorne's stories. M. Normand's aesthetic speculation on the enigma of creation, now placed within the reach of a larger number of American readers, is another proof of the hold, upon continental Europeans, which American imagination has on them. Not even Emily Brontë or Thomas Hardy, not even Dickens in his most visionary moments, has fascinated the continental Europeans as Poe, Hawthorne, Melville, and their most authentic successor, Faulkner, have done.

HENRI PEYRE

Preface to the American Edition

To write—and we must believe that writing always tends, in some way or other, to put life on the level of language (otherwise would one start literature over again as one does history?)—is to be present in one's written word.

People have seen fit to say that my biography of Hawthorne was in reality a self-portrait. The writer who labeled my work thus[1] knew quite well that the act of writing, whatever the degree of impersonality the author may seek, is essentially different in nature from even the most complicated operation of an electronic brain. Every piece of writing is the reflection of a human being, and is thus autobiography. And Marguerite Yourcenar was quite conscious, as she wrote the *Memoires d'Hadrien*, of making her own portrait.

If I had to do my book over again today I do not believe that I would write it in a very different way. The method, the exposition would be perceptibly the same. Perhaps I would put into it a little more of what I know of myself in the light of experience; a little more of the insights that creative awareness has given me in the course of repeated new readings and the continuous effort of personal creation in the areas of the essay and the poem;[2] a little more of what I have learned from the contradictions, the violences of this world, torn apart by irresolvable conflicts, and from the new dangers, the precarious hopes that it contains.

Intuitive analysis (which by itself leads, through the imagination as much as through critical examination, to the center of the problem

---

[1] Robert Merle (Prix Goncourt, 1948), author of *La Mort est mon Métier*.
[2] *Poèmes de Mai*, illustrés par l'auteur (Editions Mic Berthe, 1969).

xiii

of creation) is as valuable, as necessary to the age of space conquest as it must have been at the period when man was beginning the exploration of his inner dimensions through religion and later, when he was continuing this exploration through psychoanalysis: an exploration conducted through all time, with the same stubborn energy, by all creative minds, mystical or not, whether poets or rationalists. All these investigations, which preceded scientific investigation and are still its contemporaries, are indispensable for the balance of psychic forces at the level of humanity as a whole. They have a permanent reality; they are witnesses to the permanent youth of the mind, even in its deepest pessimism. If despair is a modern sickness, this is not simply the result of chance. And must we blame for this the poet, the thinker, or rather the anti-human devices which the technicians of oppression force upon us? Hell, like paradise, is a province of our physical universe as well as of our consciousness. Hawthorne, coming after Dante and before Céline and William Burroughs, knew this. The deliriums of *Naked Lunch* could just as easily have been nourished from the deadly perfumes of Doctor Rappacini's garden.

To make of Hawthorne a writer and a witness of our own time is no artifice or trick to enlist under the banner of superficial modernity or to give borrowed luster to a classic author of the golden age of American letters; nor is it, (as one might affect to believe) to draw him onto dubious ground in bad company—that of Gide, I believe, being no more disgraceful than that of Melville. The reproach that one is uprooting an author from his place and period has meaning only in the case of those authors whose reach, as it were, is limited only to their own provinces. There are no such limitations when one talks of Faulkner, Conrad, Strindberg, whose true contemporaries are Aeschylus, Racine, Shakespeare, themselves modern, most fully modern, because they have always retained their youth, their truthfulness, something that believes that the world can and must change, that man is not at the end of his development, is not finished for all eternity, but still is in the making. Modern, they require no sanction, because of the virtue that they have of continuing to exist in us—modern, through the inquietude that they carry within themselves, which came to them from the farthest reaches of their humanity and which, meeting our own inquietude, perpetuates them in our own humanity. Something in Hawthorne is akin to these prodigies—who are in fact men of the very most normal sort, that is the most fully human and those who would be encountered most frequently if our education were not so grievously incomplete and did not turn us into cripples. To obtain this fertile consciousness, all too rare, the creator of itself and of the man of the future on new bases of love at last understood, "reinvented," realized, has required, up till now, quasi-miraculous circumstances. Hawthorne is a textbook example of the uncertain creative success. His creative being was born through a conjunction of singular chances, evolved, enlarged against odds, given its time of triumph, allowed to decline, and at last to disappear before the man who had given it a refuge did. It is well to isolate this fragile creative being, to strip from it pitilessly (except insofar as they illuminate it) all the elements that injured it, that cast it into gloom. A new study of Hawthorne should push even further this policy, to espouse more exclusively the cause of Oberon—not the "gothick" puppet so often evoked, but the poet, the precursor, the psychologist of the depths. Being haunted by sin could not by itself explain the complexity of stories such as "My Kinsman, Major Molineux," "Young Goodman Brown," "Ethan Brand," "The Minister's Black Veil," and *The Scarlet Letter*, in which there are, inextricably mingled in the same dream, an Adamic experience in reverse (from innocence to the knowledge of evil): a tragic crisis of growth, a perverted, sadistic—in the magnificent sense of the word—experiment, and an esthetic experience. It is inquietude that makes the poet, in the modern sense, the Haunted Mind, hexed as well as tormented by a capricious and corrosive music which leads him without rest, without mercy, into the enchanted labyrinth of wonder and nightmare. Thus it had been with Coleridge, was with Isidore Ducasse in Hawthorne's own time, and would soon be with Pierre-Jean Jouve and Jean Genet. And the poet who sees into the blackness is the father of the psychoanalyst as he is of the alchemist and the warlock. He goes to the furthest depths of the "cavern" to awaken the Minotaur, the Serpent, the Dragon, to seek out the mystery of the "Terrible Mother" or to snatch away the secret of the tyrannical Father, of the eternal Despot. He is the provoker, the stealer of fire and of the Carbuncle, the sworn enemy of the mothers who guard the realm of shadows and of the jealous God. He is the protean explorer, the Ariel who defies all the laws of gravity, the demiurge who seizes with impunity hidden matter, forbidden keys. Finally, he is the one who climbs again into the light of day, who, unveiling his discovery, makes it shine with a thousand facets, making it give up its manifold and ambiguous message, and who exposes himself to hatred, to contempt, and sees himself often refused human rights by his fellow men. It is he who spares no one, himself included, who suddenly projects with subtle art the images of his hallucinatory cinema into the sleeping consciousness. The play of shade and light is for him the most fascinating spectacle; it favors the ambiguity thanks to which allegorical rigidity yields to psychological complexity. Hawthorne was very likely saved as a writer by the guilty pleasure that he took in his interior cinema.

This Hawthorne, in his purest, wildest essence, of marvellous tenderness and disturbing cruelty, is the Hawthorne I wish to portray—he who anticipates the giddiness of the modern consciousness, its frenzy, its rage to live, its race toward death, its convulsions in the darkness, its last sunburst of disintegration: what an apalling possible transposition—in the near future, perhaps—of *The Scarlet Letter*!

To depict in strong colors horror, despair, degradation, is still to perform a "work of life," to bear witness. Among the signs of ill omen of our times, there is one that should make us pause and think: the need, which we find in ourselves all too easily, to imagine the man of the future as a paragon of balanced temperament, emotional and intellectual, inaccessible to all passion, all revolt, but capable, under the guidance of cold reason, of genocidal acts. But what if our scientific progress should finish with a terrifying regression of humanity? For the antagonism as well as the harmony of opposites, as Jung demonstrates, the natural aggressive pulsations, as Lorenz believes, are necessary to life and do not inevitably give rise to evil. On the other hand, the denial of natural instincts and imaginative aspirations is a sure means of giving birth to evil in the most frenzied forms. There is sometimes in pure scientific thinking a strange blindness whose seriousness Hawthorne foresaw. Art and imagination must counterbalance these tendencies toward the absolute rule of the intellect. The heart and the mind must remain, or become, connected spheres. Abstract thought will devour itself if it destroys its roots. Poetry has, from the beginning of time, been the cry of alarm uttered by the instincts and the imagination—the angel and the beast (almost always divided, like Oberon and his double: the frightened or unchained beast of Goodman Brown and the angelic child for whom death has the transparency of a dream)—against the systematic and repressive mind. Art has always been an oneiric festival, a ritual and an exorcism of the instincts, but also a revolt against the excesses of the Law that considers only the theoretical being, or in other words, the skeleton! The difficult, pathetic, tortured revolt of a Hawthorne against a world without love is a victory, precarious, to be sure, but precious. It remains as a sign, ambiguous but rich in promise, on the uncertain road of our momentary or far-distant liberty.

Jean Normand
Clermont-Ferrand
November 7, 1969

Acknowledgments

I should like to begin by thanking all those who have helped me in my task: First, M. Fort, to whom this book is dedicated as an expression of my gratitude for the instruction, the moral support, and the example he has given me;

the "Commission Franco-Amèricaine d'Echanges Universitaires" in Paris, thanks to whose generosity I have been enabled to continue my research outside France, especially at Harvard;

the American Council of Learned Societies, which enabled me to spend a whole year studying in the United States, and whose director for American Studies, Mr. Downar, together with Mr. Turner and Miss Liang, was of inestimable aid both to my family and myself;

the teaching staff of Harvard University, particularly Messrs. Freidel, Davidson, Levin, and Lynn;

Professor Norman Holmes Pearson of Yale;

Mr. Randall Stewart, for the documents he sent me;

President J. S. Coles of Bowdoin College;

Miss Margaret Lathrop, who has succeeded in making "Wayside" into the secure haven for the memory of Hawthorne's life and times that it is today;

my friend Edmond Volpe of the City College of New York, who so kindly helped me to adapt certain passages of my work into English with a view to publishing them in article form;

the staffs of the Widener and Lamont libraries at Harvard, of the New York Public and Pierpont Morgan libraries in New York, of the Salem Essex Institute, of the Odéon and Benjamin Franklin American libraries in Paris, of the American Cultural Center in Tours, of the university libraries of the Sorbonne, Rennes, and Lyons, and of the Bibliothèque Nationale and the British Museum;

M. Le Breton, who supervised this work for many years with patience and understanding, whose criticisms directed my efforts toward the essential problems involved, and thanks to whom I was able to improve my method;

Henri Peyre, who generously reviewed the French edition;

Lastly, it is impossible for me to refrain from expressing my particular gratitude to my wife and constant partner in this project, who typed most of the manuscript and who, apart from the many helpful suggestions she was able to make, was always a source of comfort and encouragement.

Contents

toward the unknown, toward progress, and of the perpetual braking action of tradition. American classicism, because of the combination of this given impulse and its favorable terrain, was to be an "Adamic" classicism, the expression of a long-established tendency finally liberated by the physical, emotional, and intellectual experience of a new genesis.

This is why America cannot see its literature except through the process of its own development. The American experiences a difficulty in envisaging the artist as an individual. He poses the problem of creation in terms of social and national consciousness. That art may be a personal affair between the artist and the world is a notion that, generally speaking, escapes him. Yet the writer recreates his environment just as much as his environment creates him: it is no longer possible to see the South in the same way since Faulkner, and the same may be said of New England since Emerson, Hawthorne, Thoreau, and Dickinson. The European is not always attuned to their "Americanism," and his contemporary in Boston also has difficulty in imagining the American adventure of a Thoreau or a Hawthorne to the full, since those adventures were too solitary. And yet, if you keep going beyond Concord, on into the Massachusetts hills, you will find yourself, as you would have done three hundred years ago, in the midst of impenetrable forests. Primitive America is still there, and the possibility of adventures on the borders of the nonhuman world still exists—just as the problem of the transplanted consciousness still exists, the consciousness which, face to face with the unknown, becomes troubled, readapts itself, projects itself into the future, turns back on itself, and re-examines itself in a perpetually snowballing struggle toward awareness.

This psychological phenomenon, inseparable from introspection, is exemplified in its purest state by Hawthorne, who assimilated his America as no one had done before him, and who gave back to it, in his own very individual way, all that he had originally received from it. The inner landscape produced by this alchemy superimposes itself, even without our being conscious of it, upon the external landscape. There is a Hawthorne landscape just as there is a Lamartine landscape or a Faulkner landscape. Concord, where the Indian summer is so marvelously sensual, where the "October contrast," to use M. Le Breton's phrase, is so much more penetrating than elsewhere, doubtless belongs just as much to Emerson and Thoreau as it does to Hawthorne. But Raymond, Maine and its Nordic, deserted lake with that noble and barbaric name, the Sebago; the silence-wrapped White Mountains, where everything takes on a strange remoteness from reality; Tanglewood, where mythology and music meet: these are Hawthorne's fiefs and present us with multiple images of his private, closed worlds. Walking across those hills, with their ripening fall colors blazing before their burial under the winter snow, one understands better the irresistible attraction they were able to exert upon the imagination of a man always so strongly drawn back to that solitude of his, peopled with seductive images, so tempted to lose himself in it, to bury himself in it, far away from kith and kin, and absorbed totally and forever in the primitive landscape that his mind had at first reflected, then transformed and stylized, and finally recreated in the form of a moral and psychological panorama. Elsewhere, on the coast especially, modern life has swept Hawthorne's world away: in Salem, between a power plant and an airfield, there is nothing but a neighborhood of old wooden houses rotting in their own dirt. But the sky over Boston and its suburbs, the most crowded in the world, where the lights of passing airliners blink at night above the flickering neon signs and drive-in movie screens, is still capable of blindingly irrational eruptions. One can still imagine, beneath the abrupt and rocky slope of Gallows Hill (today a high school's playing fields), the terror that gripped those condemned to die as they glimpsed the gibbet silhouetted up there against that haunted sky. Down near the harbor, the ironic, the bewitched, House of the Seven Gables, angular, theatrical, as in the novel that bears its name, presents its jutting angles like sentinels to the floodlights. Black, it seems to be emerging freshly tarred from the sea. On the other side of the garden stands the house where Nathaniel was born, now a faded red; at Raymond, the house, like an abstract sculpture carved from snow, where the summer holidays were spent; at Lenox, the purple-brown "shanty" by the side of its magic lake; at Concord, the Old Manse, greyish green with a hipped roof; and, also at Concord, the Wayside, yellow ochre, like a whimsical structure made with a toy building set: all of them built of wood and justifiably thought of as "haunted," stamped as they all are with the Hawthorne seal in their rustic appearance, their secretive atmosphere, and the sites on which they stand. There still exists a subtle resemblance between the man and the places where he lived.

A great deal has been written about the scenes of Hawthorne's life and work by zealous admirers, but their admiration has too often been paralyzed by an unfortunate fetishistic respect.[1] The same criticism could be applied to many of the biographies. It must be admitted at the outset that to find out the exact truth about Hawthorne is not an easy task. He himself takes pleasure in mystifying us, assumes poses, feigns inscrutability and lack of ambition, obscures his own traces by burning manuscripts, letters, documents. And in addition to his own sabotage there are the cuts made by Sophia Peabody, the deformations inflicted upon certain texts by his son Julian Hawthorne, and the apocrypha. At this point one is bound to pay tribute to the invaluable work done by Randall Stewart on the *Notebooks* and by Davidson on the posthumous works, thanks to which it has become possible to correct the mutilated and mysteriously veiled image that Hawthorne's contemporaries would have liked to leave us. Elizabeth Peabody, among others, displayed a particular talent for creating little pockets of secrecy in her brother-in-law's private life.[2] As for Julian Hawthorne, he introduces melodramatic and legendary elements at every opportunity in his account of his father's life.[3] Cantwell, another biographer with a taste for the sensational, sees treachery and dark shadows everywhere. Reacting against these tendencies, the "realist" critics have attempted to pass sentence on all such "romantic" fantasies and set up, in the end, the figure of a presentable Hawthorne, healthy in body and mind, full of good sense, and a respectable member of society, a complete stranger to both emotional complications and the agonies of creation. Randall Stewart, for example, brings forward a fearsome compilation of facts, and Wagenknecht a profusion of anecdotes, in order to draw for us the portrait of a man "normal" to the point of incredibility, which was their indirect way of publicly giving the lie to all the Edgar Allen Poes and other Baudelaireans, and of discrediting that least understood of human types, the artist.

There is no lack of pretexts for making Hawthorne into one of those "immortals" never tainted by the vice of introverted "morbidity." By dint of concentrating exclusively on the civil servant, on the responsible father, on the consul, on his connections, and by minimizing the most revealing admissions, by distorting their import or pretending not to see it, it is possible in the end to do away with the writer and his embarrassing testimony in order to substitute a character more in conformity with the wishes of the "average" reader and possessing, moreover, the necessary "social motivation."[4] The notion that a total extrovert could have written *The Scarlet Letter*, whereas even *Leaves of Grass* was the work of a "social misfit," does not seem absurd to those who explain art with reference to all that is foreign to it. For the irrelevant and the external always mislead by their sheer quantity. Mallarmé was never a poet for more than a few hours a day: a quantitative biography would be unthinkable in such a case. But Hawthorne's life was a perpetual compromise between his art and his public, utilitarian activities, so that the quantitative biographers feel that they are justified in declaring themselves to be the sole sources of "objectivity" —which in turn leads them to claim that they have definitely refuted all previous and hasty judgments based merely upon impulse, the better to reject any attempt at qualitative interpretation.

Yet it is only insofar as one takes the secret tendencies and hidden contradictions of the man into account that one can draw any "portrait of the artist"—in this case, that of the Oberon about whom the "realists" do not wish to hear.

Hawthorne, in his role as a sort of foil for Poe, has scarcely proved much of a temptation to psychologists. We find a few snatches of psychoanalysis in various studies, but that is all.[5] Yet there is sufficient material in the struggle between the man and his diverse tendencies for a work that could be set beside Jean Delay's book on Gide. Such is not, however, the opinion of McKiernan, who, in his study *The Psychology of Hawthorne*,[6] brushes aside the problem of his subject's personality with suspicious haste. On the other hand, one ought to avoid any literal imitation of Marie Bonaparte's psychoanalysis of Poe, since the obsessions residing within the artist, even if he is their victim, serve him as pretexts and points of departure—which does not mean, as Hoeltje would have it,[7] that there exists a direct and permanent correspondence, even on the psychic level, between the life and the work, since some of the very deepest blueprints for the latter were formed even before the awakening of consciousness. Hawthorne knew, just as Baudelaire did, that "genius is nothing but the recovery of childhood at will." Everyday life has its own particular rhythm, and so does creation. It is not raw images of the external world that man, and a fortiori the artist, simmers in his memory, but "elaborated" images, images that bear the same relation to everyday reality that the sap of a tree does to mere water—or, in Hawthorne's own language, "allegories." The majority of individuals do nothing with these images; they content themselves with adjusting them so as to make them fit in with the "norm" of the collective vision. Some, the poets, make them the object of their study, work on them, and organize them till they have made them into a work of art. Such works have their own history, one that stands in an indirect relation only to the external events of the writer's life. And the true history of the artist is, in the last resort, the inner history of his images, of the seeds of creation that have inhabited him. To say how the carefree Nathaniel became the haunted Oberon, to sketch the mental history of Hawthorne the writer, such is the object of the psychobiography with which this book begins.

Hawthorne has been abundantly studied and variously interpreted. But French critics, since Dhaleine's rather charming but also slightly prim book, have paid little attention to his work, though Régis Michaud, Charles Cestre, Pierre Brodin, Julien Green, M. Le Breton, and J.-J. Mayoux have, it is true, devoted some memorable pages to it. In England, it seems paradoxical that D. H. Lawrence's resoundingly successful book on the American classics has excited so little emulation. In Germany, in Scandinavia, in Italy,[8] we find merely sporadic outbreaks of interest. Hawthorne criticism flourishes almost exclusively on the soil in which the works themselves have their roots, the diversity of the interpretations that have sprung up being an eloquent testimony to its richness.

Certain of Hawthorne's mannerisms have the gift of attracting the sympathy of the moralists, while certain of his themes contrive to attract the thunderbolts of the censorious. It is a singularity of this writer's fate that he remains today, as he was a hundred years ago, both a great favorite among preachers and a bête noire among the prudish,[9] even though his reputation has known such spectacular highs and lows. After the books piously dedicated to his memory by his children and his friends, the parsimonious praises meted out to him by his celebrated contemporaries, the blindness of the Shakespearian critics, the prejudices of the feminist critics, Hawthorne was subjected to the Transcendentalist floodlighting directed on him by Moncure D. Conway—the reflections of which are to be found in Dhaleine and Van Wyck Brooks—and then to the eclipse engineered by the "realists," before he was able, after the Depression and on the eve of World War Two, to break through the obscurity concealing him and to shine anew, not because of a renewal of interest in some sort of vague literary symbolism,[10] but because the allegory in his work has authentic psychological roots. In his lifetime Poe's articles alone, long before James, Woodberry, and Paul Elmer More, succeeded in giving the exact measure of Hawthorne's talent, by situating it on the only terrain where discussion of it has any true meaning—that of art. After the penetrating intuitions of Woodberry and James, however, criticism of Hawthorne from the artistic point of view tended to take refuge in a mere concern with technique, in an exclusive insistence on the meaning of symbols, so that the psychoesthetic complexity of the works was in danger of having the secret of its substance obscured rather than revealed by the light of such analyses. However, Leland Schubert did do some extremely intelligent pioneering work in this field, demonstrating in advance the futility of any attempt to reduce Hawthorne to mere neo-Gothicism, as Pierce and Jane Lundblad[11] tend to do. Fogle's interpretation, "The Light and the Dark," is talented but does not go to the heart of the problem: the substance of the darkness is not made tangible enough. Davidson's study of the last phase is also remarkable, but too limited, since it does not take us deeply enough into the living matter of the works. There is no lack of historical, or even philosophical interpretations, whether we go to the first biographers or to the studies by Herbert Schneider and Perry Miller on American civilization and thought. Roy R. Male depicts Hawthorne's tragic vision in the light of Protestant pessimism, and the Reverend L. Fick his evangelical conception of the universe. Stein analyses his Faustian aspirations, and Levin comes back to the Melvillian conception of a genius possessing "the power of darkness." All these works open up perspectives for us, but none of them organizes the available material around a central point of view.

Though subjected to such a variety of exegeses, Hawthorne is nevertheless not a "popular" author. Though esteemed in his own day by a certain number of cultivated people, he was never able to earn his living by his pen, whereas fashionable women novelists were able to achieve considerable financial success. Literary success is too often based upon misunderstandings. Given sufficient "wrong reasons," even Faulkner can achieve a certain commercial success. But for a lack of such reasons, Conrad Aiken, one of the greatest twentieth-century American poets, whose voice in the *Preludes* is that of an atomic-age Milton, remains in obscurity. Hawthorne lacked all the external factors that were necessary to guarantee success in his lifetime: because he was not an abolitionist—or pro-slavery—or a Transcendentalist, or a trumpeter of America's glories, he seemed retrogressive. Turned in upon himself, a discreet and disturbing analyst of the inner self, he seemed too private a writer, even though his inner vision of the world, like his art itself, was that of a precursor. He appeared at the wrong moment, and even today the movies, which he invented on a literary plane, do not do him justice. (Film-makers do not think of Hawthorne, but of film technique, that source of new novelistic forms, not of poetic literature, the disregarded mirror of human consciousness, the source of true cinema, not to mention the real American world, which is able to nourish the fantastic element of *The Scarlet Letter*, with its natural marvels, or to provide the whirlwind cutting and shifting of images of a vast advertising display in Dos Passos' *U.S.A.* trilogy.) In Europe, Hawthorne does not seem "representative" enough. Everyone has heard of James Fenimore Cooper, of Harriet Beecher Stowe, of Pearl Buck, but how many have heard of Wallace Stevens? As Jean Paulhan says, there are "the bad books that everyone reads and the good ones that no one reads." And though Hawthorne has won a certain following of late, *The Marble Faun* is often read with more pleasure than *The Scarlet Letter* because it makes possible that "turning back of time" that every American dreams of. This preference of the public for the minor works of great authors is, of course, a frequent phenomenon.

Though Hawthorne is now generally recognized to be one of the founding fathers of American literature, his true stature has begun to be apparent only very recently, at a time when we have already passed the centenary of his death. Nevertheless, there are still a few dissenting voices to be heard: one critic refuses to give *The Scarlet Letter* any more than a grade of $A-$,[12] and Von Abele sees Hawthorne as no more than a pusillanimous artist whose endeavor added up in the end merely to painful failure, the causes for which he seeks in the contradictions within the writer himself, forgetting that every artist suffers from this same disharmony between his inner self and the world, and is bound to create despite, and with, that disharmony inside himself, without knowing whether he is right or wrong to do so. If, in Hawthorne's case, there is in the end a lack of integration, this is to be explained by a breakdown in the balance of power between the conflicting tendencies in his inner self. In a general fashion, however, the importance of his work is scarcely disputed. Moreover, the quality of his art is such as must recommend itself from the very outset to any reader sensitive to the magic of form. And this classicism in his style, this discreet, finely shaded use of language, devoid of dazzle and exaggeration, apparently abstract and emanating as it were from a mind in safe detachment, contributes to the misunderstanding which has come to hang over this writer like a sort of curse, since a lack of literary finish—ever since it was decided that Whitman represents its transmutation into sublimity—is now taken as a form of liberalism of the spirit. So that Hawthorne has come to be classed by the critical establishment among the reactionary "aristocrats"[13]—except when he is viewed, as he is by F. O. Matthiessen,[14] as a frustrated "realist" who has disguised himself as an allegorist in self-defense, the better to attack the established order.

It is, in fact, the moral rather than the social order that Hawthorne is concerned with attacking. He is fascinated by the world of hidden monsters (Montégut saw this quite clearly as early as 1852),[15] the deep-buried symbols of our most irrational and most inadmissible propensities—the outward and visible forms of the hideous being only the concrete sign indicating the existence of those little-known forces, emphasized by Jung, whose unleashing may plunge the entire world into darkness. The approach of the Second World War, the rise of Nazism, of racism established as a state religion (a religion whose seeds are still alive today) were to justify the "pessimism"[16] which had once proved so deleterious to Hawthorne the prophet of disaster. The American consciousness—and that of the whole world—was shaken awake by these terrifying experiences to face a nightmare from the abyss. The tragic element so firmly rooted in reality by the possibility of total destruction by nuclear fission no doubt enables us to turn back today with increased sympathy to such disturbed and disturbing works of art. No, Emile Montégut was right, Hawthorne "does not reassure" us:[17] he wants us to become aware of the pitiless and tragic depths of our being. That is why his works are numbered among those with a curse upon them. And just as there is the attempt to conceal the artist behind the official persona, so there have been ingenious attempts, using certain plausible appearances, to gloss over his true riches and display what are in fact his pinchbeck qualities: the moralizing piety, the bigoted obsession with sin, the satanic temptations, the bric-a-brac of witchcraft, the cerebral allegory as opposed to the imagery of the heart, the fluttering despair of all those shadows unable to find a way in to the drama of life: all the reassuring aspects of his work. Yet they all, of course, have their place in Hawthorne's spectrum, a spectrum much darker and also much more luminous than people suspect, and, above all, than they wish to admit. We do not dare to look Hawthorne's world in the face, for fear of seeing our own features mirrored there, for fear of seeing that his world is a resemblance of the great horror inside us from which we are escaping and which religion tries to convert into a horror of ourselves—in vain, for the circle of fascination with evil closes around us as it did around Ethan Brand. Man's despair is condemned to seek other issues. Hawthorne, walking with Goodman Brown into the forest, opens up unforeseen vistas, and that is a sure sign of a work that belongs to the future, of a work whose analysis demands the most complex methods of investigation. The different levels of meaning presented by the great texts around which at any given moment the whole sum of human experience accumulates reveal themselves to be ever more and more numerous from age to age. The Bible, Dante, Shakespeare are not the same in the twentieth century as they were in the sixteenth: they are richer, and they will be richer still a century from now.

It is therefore possible to attempt a reinterpretation of Hawthorne yet again: the analysis of the Oberon side of his personality has still to be made, that of the inner processes of his creation has scarcely been touched upon, and, lastly, that of Hawthorne's world, the world he created, is also still incomplete. To pose the problem in all its complexity and extent does not necessarily imply, however, an expectation of resolving it in any definitive way. What it does imply is calling into question criticism's methods of investigation and positing the existence of material other than merely "literary" material in the traditional sense. Lacking direct experience of creation, we must be initiated into its psychology. The works of Jung, Bergson, Bachelard, and Jean Delay provide an inestimable stimulant in this respect. They enable us, better than the work of many specialists in literary questions, to place Hawthorne, as far as his temperament is concerned, among the great intermittent creators (Gide, Strindberg, Dostoevski) and, as far as his imagination is concerned, among the great family of poetic fabulists that includes Boccaccio and Andersen, Bunyan and Faulkner. Attempting to situate, to define, Hawthorne as an artist, as a type of creator, also means posing, with reference to a single individual, the whole problem of creation.

The method of analysis must be neither too simplistic nor too rigid. It will be scientific insofar as notions of pure psychology will be indispensable to it, and poetic insofar as tangible proofs must be supplemented by intuition, or simply brought out by it as a watermark is brought out by holding it up to a strong light. The advantage of the psychopoetic method over systematic, dogmatic methods is its flexibility: it permits the attempt to follow the windings of an artist's thought or of the labyrinth of his works without endangering their structures or doing violence to their spirit, providing them, on the contrary, with an unrestricted area of possibilities. It also permits the application of precise scientific notions, without necessitating the use of a tedious and offensive technical vocabulary, while following from an imaginative as well as an objective point of view the development of certain typical psychological figurations. The return to the mother and the quest for the father, the two opposing and complementary processes of the Oberon persona, are as much poetic themes as psychological ones. The same is true of the rivalry between the masculine psyche and the feminine psyche, a central nexus in America's hidden drama, which, as D. H. Lawrence has pointed out, attains an intensity in Hawthorne unexampled among his contemporaries and equalled only in the works of Strindberg. O'Neill, Arthur Miller, Salinger, Albee, and Updike seem, each in his own way, to have returned to the "witness" abandoned by Hawthorne in the race through which the masculine being seeks his freedom, and which in our day has become a race into space. The American male, jealously keeping the conquest of the cosmos to himself, is but a new incarnation of the pastor in *The Scarlet Letter* fleeing from the influence of the flesh: an unforeseen—yet as inevitable as it is striking—manifestation of Puritanism reaching a sphere of activity scarcely hoped for even by the bigotry of a Mather.

Hawthorne's works, whose vistas become ever broader as America and the world evolve, are as much a body of prophecy as they are the re-creation of a self and of a personal past—and are therefore, for the same reasons that hold good in Faulkner's case, poetic works. The process of the mind wishing to understand them must therefore itself be poetic, intuitive. There must exist an active, dynamic sympathy between author and critic during the course of a "slow reading" of the sort recommended by Bachelard. And any reader who has attained a certain degree of conscious sympathy with Hawthorne becomes aware of being drawn into a dialectic of depth, of inwardness and outwardness, into a linking of closed worlds that open momentarily, then close again, communicating with one another like rooms with secret passages between them, or lakes connected by underground streams. It might well be that this is merely a matter of optical illusion, an empty game of hide-and-seek. But, in fact, it is the natural and necessary procedure of a mind projecting its structures and reproducing its movements in artistic creations. In Hawthorne, more than in any other writer, the works are the mirror of the mind's gestures. Interlocking structures, spiraling, enveloping movements, themes that overlap with one another, organisms nesting one within another, multiple solutions and choices, contradictory realities beneath a single surface appearance, labyrinthine sentences: on every level the same gestures, the same dynamic. Moreover, it is of little importance which aspect of the work one studies, the demonstration itself must always confine itself within the work's own spheres in order to adapt itself sufficiently closely to Hawthorne's own movement, Hawthorne's own processes, Hawthorne's own spiritual arabesques. In short, we must attempt our analysis from within.

J. N.

Part One
OBERON

· I ·
The Hieroglyphs

I. NATHANIEL

On July 4, 1804, the little town of Salem was awakened by salvos of artillery. A quarter of a century earlier, everyone would have supposed that the English fleet was attempting a landing. In fact, what was going on was merely a Federalist demonstration with a procession of the Salem cadets in red uniforms, fanfares, cheering, fireworks, and a solemn parade of notables, magistrates, and ministers.[1] In Union Street, a little street not far from the harbor, on the fringes of Salem's least reputable neighborhood, where the taverns stayed open all night catering to smugglers, thieves, and sailors on shore leave, little Nathaniel Hathorne had just come into the world. Half a century later, he would be recognized as possessing some little genius, but the Federalists who had thus unwittingly acclaimed his birth, and the burghers of Essex Street, equally inimical to him as a man, would still be a long way from naming their main street Hawthorne after him;[2] the only honor they would perhaps think of doing him would be to tar and feather him. Yet it was to the sound of a cannon salute that Consul Hawthorne was to leave America for England.

In that dawn of the nineteenth century the American nation had only very recently succeeded in winning its independence. The Union had been in existence scarcely more than twenty years and still comprised only seventeen states. That number was to have been swelled by nine more in 1837, when Hawthorne's *Tales* were first published,

3

and by yet another eleven by the time of the novelist's death in 1864. The purchase of Louisiana from France in 1803 had opened up the possibility of the Union's expansion to the west; the "frontier," still so close, was to be pushed back. Before the election of Thomas Jefferson in 1801, there had been only two previous Presidents: George Washington and John Adams. Hawthorne was to see fourteen Presidents succeed one another in the course of his life, from Jefferson to Lincoln. Industry was still in embryo: the American economy was based, as it always had been, on trade with England and on the slave trade and slave labor. The railroad era was still in the future, and the great canals linking the Atlantic ports and the Mississippi basin by way of the Great Lakes still had no existence other than as projects. The Erie Canal, begun in 1817 by De Witt Clinton, would not be open to navigation until 1825, the year when Hawthorne emerged from college, torn between the demon of literature and that of travel.

And while the United States was struggling to be born, the little port of Salem was sinking into extinction.[3] After its Colonial splendor and its trade in spices, rum, and slaves,[4] after having surrounded itself with an aura of legend in the eyes of the Indies and Africa, after having been the rival of Nantes, of Amsterdam, of Boston, of Bilbao, it was now, with first the cessation of the slave trade, then the embargo, then the War of 1812, to experience decline, ruin, abandonment. Grass would sprout on the deserted wharves, and the great houses of the Forresters, the Derbys, the Crowninshields[5] would be shuttered up with their pasts inside.

Nathaniel Hawthorne belonged to that aristocracy of American New Englanders who had ancestors and who were able to say exactly where on the soil the "old country" the cradle of their family was sited and to quote the date upon which the first immigrant of their line set foot on the shores of the New World. The particular site, in this instance, was Hathorne Hall, Cheshire, Macclesfield Hundred, Winslow parish;[6] the ancestor was William Hathorne,[7] who disembarked in the Massachusetts Bay Colony in 1630, the same year as John Winthrop.[8] A soldier, a magistrate, and a great clearer of forests, he made war against the Algonquin tribes, conquered the wilderness, and laid the foundations of the colony's theocratic society. He was one of that race of intolerant Puritans who meant to remain masters, after God, of the land they had chosen. Hawthorne was to preserve with great care a copy of a letter in which Major William Hathorne, standing out against the orders of Charles II, appears as an intrepid defender of liberty.[9] Born on July 4, under the sign of Independence, Nathaniel was almost bound to dedicate a cult to the memory of such an ancestor. William Hathorne's name, however, can also be construed as a synonym for persecution. For the great early Puritans, of whom John Endicott, the hero of *Twice-Told Tales*, has remained the prototype, the ideal of "purity" went hand in hand with political and religious "purging," even if the purging had to be carried out by fire and sword.[10] William Hathorne's "pitiless severity" toward the Quakers is still famous.[11] His son, Judge John Hathorne, flourished at the period when New England was "purging" itself in Salem by hanging and burning its witches. Later, the Hathornes slipped from positions of high office into oblivion. Was this the result of a curse hurled upon them by a witch from the scaffold, as ancestral tradition had it? Hawthorne himself claimed to believe this legend, and perhaps, obscurely, he really did. When we meet the Hathornes again, in the late eighteenth century, they have become seafaring folk. Daniel Hathorne, known as Bold Daniel, "the sternest man that ever walked a deck,"[12] was a privateer during the War of Independence. He emerged from it a ruined man. His son Nathaniel, captain of a seagoing vessel, was married in 1801 to Elizabeth Clarke Manning. He had three children by her: Elizabeth, Nathaniel, and Louisa.[13] In 1808, Captain Hathorne died of yellow fever in Dutch Guiana. His brother Daniel having been wrecked in 1805, the Hathornes disappeared from the seafaring world and ceased to belong to the Salem aristocracy. They were left with no heritage but the family curse and a future with little promise of glory.

For Nathaniel, the curse manifested itself in the first place as the void left within him by the memory of a mysterious friend once glimpsed by chance during a ship's call, and whose insufficiently defined image would never enable him to represent to himself in any satisfactory fashion the father, the protector he was always to lack. He piously preserved a logbook kept by this vanished figure during a voyage to the Far East, a sort of testament bequeathing to the boy a nostalgia for the sea, for travels, and for those exotic paradises with their strange blooms that Puritanism had laid beneath its ban. This small black book, whose nautical expressions became so many incantatory formulas which the boy repeated to himself aloud and copied out in the margins,[14] with which he intoxicated himself so deeply that he even spoke of sailing away and never coming home,[15] thus betraying his obscure desire to identify himself with the dead man, this little handwritten volume is a symbol, doubtless unrecognized by the future writer but nevertheless real, of his profound vocation. By seeking a talisman in those rhythmically repeated and copied words he was already, even at that age, unwittingly enclosing the actually experienced adventure within the magic circle of the library.

The Manning house, which gave onto Herbert Street, "a tall, ugly, old, grayish building"[16] to which Mrs. Hathorne retired with her children, was densely populated with uncles and aunts: "four uncles and four aunts, all . . . unmarried."[17] Nathaniel immediately found himself surrounded by a feminine court. It was a beautiful child with blond hair, blue eyes, and "with broad shoulders," that Elizabeth Peabody often saw playing in the garden.[18] Being the only boy, he was the most spoiled of the three Hathorne children, especially since he was also of delicate health and subject to frequent illnesses.[19] This meant that his attendance at school was irregular, even though the schools he did go to were, according to his sister, the best in Salem.[20] His uncles also helped in his education, as did Mr. Manning his grandfather, an arms maker by trade and always willing to retell the odyssey of the first immigrants. Nathaniel's tutor, and that of his sisters, was Robert Manning, a distinguished pomologist and the owner of the finest orchards in the district. He was a man possessed of both wealth and good sense, though not without wit and given to sarcasm. Perhaps it was partly to Robert Manning that Hawthorne was to owe his sense of humor and the irony that he later fashioned into a weapon, as well as that love for trees which bursts from every page of the *American Notebooks*.

The education of the Hathorne children was, according to Elizabeth, a fairly liberal one: "We were the victims of no educational pedantry. We always had plenty of books, and our minds and sensibilities were not unduly stimulated."[21] We have only to compare this with the education thrust upon the child Mozart, forced into an unremitting study of music and the sciences by his father and forbidden all games at the age of seven, or that of Edgar Allan Poe, an orphan without father or mother, who had been turned by the age of six into a strutting little figure on a tabletop proposing toasts to tipsy gatherings. Hawthorne lacked the precocity of Rimbaud, of Mozart, or of Longfellow, who published his first collection of poems at the age of twelve. Endowed with great vivacity of mind and body, he was both handsome and intelligent, his sister Elizabeth has told us, but, she continues, "if he had been educated for a genius, it would have injured him excessively."[22] Nathaniel was to be neither a seven-year-old composer, nor a "seven-year-old poet."[23] His attitude toward his public remained that of a child, whereas that of the very young Mozart was as ambiguous as that of his audiences: he felt bearing down upon him a sort of astonishment that is not admiration and in which tenderness has almost no part, so that the already formed artist was made to suffer equally with the child, the child that was ignored at the expense of the "dwarf," the performing animal, the freak. There was nothing like that in Hawthorne's life, no premature career, no sufferings or effort disproportionate with his years, no adult brain crushing the growing child.

One wonders what sort of education Nathaniel would have had if he had been taken in by his father's family. The Hathornes had a reputation for being much more austere in their Puritanism than the Mannings,[24] and Captain Hathorne himself was a "silent, reserved, severe man,"[25] who may well have proved a man of extremely rigid educational principles. No one, however, was ever to replace for Nathaniel the vanished father whose rough discipline he would have accepted with joy and who would have made a sailor out of him. Later, he attempted to compensate for the paternal strength and authority he had lacked as a child by turning to the Puritans of the colonial period. So that the father image in his mind always tended to be somewhat confused with the somber silhouette of his Puritan ancestor.

Left for the most part to himself, Nathaniel experienced "a grievous disinclination to go to school."[26] He became a confirmed truant, seeking out his education in the countryside. On a farm, not far from Salem, lived his cousins the Fosters.[27] And near their house, which stood at the foot of a hill shaped like a whale, was a well where Nathaniel used to amuse himself by looking at himself in the water and making echoes. Benjamin Foster let his farm go to wrack and ruin, beat his wife, and finally left her for a mistress. Amstis Foster, tall, thin, and withered, had the physical appearance of a witch. Nathaniel used to escape from the house with his cousins up to the top of the hill, a sort of Wuthering Heights moor where the children could play in the ruins of the mansion "Browne's Folly,"[28] their shouts lost in an atmosphere of unreality.

There were also expeditions on the Salem-Boston stagecoach, run by the Manning Company, the owners of which were Nathaniel's uncles. The bright colors, the bustle of the arrivals and departures, the skill and agility of the coachmen, all combined to clothe the coaches in an aura of glamor equal to that of the ships that were now entering Salem harbor less and less frequently, for this was the period of the embargo. Nathaniel became a mascot for the Manning Company coachmen and was taken for rides with them up on the high driver's seats, from which the spectacle of the high road, of nature, of life was so much more visible. From the top of those wheeled towers his gaze, like a movie camera, followed the scenes, the incidents, the dramas, the play of light and shadow all around. Nathaniel the vagabond, and Nathaniel the writer too, was to remember all those impressions. At this age his imagination was still no more than a complement to physical activity. Esoteric games of fantasy, meditative amusements were not the dominant feature of his first childhood. Indeed, his carefree temperament and his irresistible tendency to mockery,[29] everything—were it not for the void left by his father's death—seemed to be guaranteeing him immunity from the anguish that was later to give birth to the writer.

II. THE BIRTH OF OBERON

It was during the year 1813 that the accident happened. One day, in the school playground, while playing a sort of baseball called at that time "bat and ball," he hurt his foot. The causes of the accident still remain unexplained. "There was no visible wound," Elizabeth writes,[1] "but after a while his foot stopped growing like the other." All sorts of empirical remedies were tried; they even went as far as pouring cold water on the foot from an upstairs window, while he stuck his leg out of another window on the ground floor.[2] Nothing did any good. Nathaniel still limped. Drugs, surgical apparatus, orthopedic boots introduced a strange new world of paraphernalia into his life: a new relationship was established between his invalid's body and exterior objects. A nightmare had taken real shape at his bedside: rigid, grimly angular instruments, as ill-favored as creatures blasted by a curse, were in daily contact with his flesh, and his deformed body tended to become identified with them. Even though he experienced no physical pain,[3] suffering had already taken up residence inside him. As the months, then the years went by, Nathaniel came to believe that he would never get better; he became convinced that he would die before he was twenty-five.[4] There was a moment when it was thought he was cured, but then, Elizabeth tells us,[5] he was attacked by another illness that took away the use of all his limbs. Polio perhaps? Yet he was to display uncommon agility as an adolescent. Whatever it was, however, this illness was to have a profound and lasting effect on him. The original accident occurred at an age when children undergo a physiological revolution. But in Nathaniel it was the psychological revolution that was to prove infinitely more important. This dramatic halt forced upon a life still scarcely begun, this total idleness imposed upon an individuality still in formation, was heavy with consequences, with threats and promises. Those three years spent living an abnormal life were to lead to the abnormal development of a single dominant faculty.

For months, the limits of Nathaniel's life were those of the Manning house. His walks consisted of no more than a few steps on crutches in the garden next to that of the old house now standing empty on Union Street. Most of his time was spent lying down, reading, and immersed in endless daydreams. Through the window, he saw only roofs, among them the gambrel roof[6] of the house where he was born. Perhaps the young invalid lay still dreaming of the enormous loft in which he used to play at inventing ghosts and terrors for himself. Perhaps those specters, those imagined monsters, came back to him again, their forms and colors intensified by the atmosphere of unreality now maintained around him by his inaction and his early initiation into allegorical literature. And those images were finally, perhaps, to become superimposed upon the images of other lofts, of other secret rooms peopled with dark or seductive shadows, and so finally to assume color and volume in the mind of the artist and achieve significance in the imaginary sphere.

Cut off, deprived of contacts with the outside world, Nathaniel was nevertheless the center of a tiny universe: he would have been its tyrant if the Manning clan had set as great store by "genius" and the caprices of children as, for example, their neighbors the Peabodys did.[7] But in fact, without going so far as to agree with the old Puritans that children were "vipers," and that they must be whipped in order to drive the devil out of them,[8] the Mannings certainly paid more attention to defects than to talents, though that did not prevent their little Hathorne cousin being more coddled and adulated than ever by a court of admiring women, stroked and kissed by his aunts, his sisters, and their neighbors. Later on, the young author was to dream of experiencing a like success as a writer, but he was obliged to content himself with imagining it. As a child, his sympathy went spontaneously to all things beautiful. Because the dressmaker who made his clothes had a homely face he flew into tantrums in order not to go to his fittings.[9] When rough-mannered housewives came to ask after his health he would have nothing to do with them. If the "ogress" of the neighborhood, with her shrew's voice,[10] tried to take him into her arms he was seized with panic. He could not even bear her to look at him.[11] Ugliness in a woman filled him with unease and revulsion, as though he were faced with a monster engendered by magic and endowed with a power of casting spells. He was always to prefer "fairies" to "witches." And among those who were there to watch over him there was one fairy, the most beautiful of them all, all of whose love he would have liked to possess, and yet to him the least real of all, his own mother.

In the midst of that household of fourteen people, Mrs. Hathorne, if we are to believe the legend,[12] remained always in her room, took all her meals alone, and left the care of her children to an old serving woman. Still only twenty-eight, beautiful and cultivated, she might well have expected a great deal out of life still. But she chose to play the part of the sequestered widow who sacrificed herself with "all but Hindoo self-devotion to the manes of her husband."[13] Elizabeth Peabody has left us a formal portrait of her at the age of sixty, one not without tenderness or grace, in which she appears "as if she had walked out of an old picture, with her antique costume, and a face of lovely sensibility and great brightness."[14] To imagine what she must have been like thirty years earlier is to experience to some small extent the fascination she must have exercised over her son. A letter he himself wrote at the age of sixteen, when he was about to leave for Bowdoin, reveals the extent of his fixation upon her: "The happiest days of my life are gone. Why was I not a girl, that I might have been pinned all my life to my mother's apron?"[15] This tendency to identify himself with a girl is still to be found in the adolescent, together with a markedly feminine sensibility and a nostalgia for maternal protection. The Oedipus aspect, though veiled, is also to be observed: the need of a mother who is love in all its forms. It is probable that this was precisely the origin of that misunderstanding between them referred to later in his *American Notebooks*: "I love my mother; but there has

been, ever since my childhood, a sort of coldness of intercourse between us, such as is apt to come between persons of strong feelings, if
they are not managed rightly."[16] The impression of distance created
by the archaic atmosphere of Elizabeth Peabody's portrait is perhaps
a reflection of reality. Always slightly withdrawn into her grief, Mrs.
Hathorne presented her young son with the image of a mother somehow removed and far off, a mother seen in a dream, a "ghost of a
mother," a "thinnest fantasy of a mother."[17] It was not hardness on
her part that repelled his affection, but rather her Puritan inability to
display any tender feelings; it was not any sullen gloom in her that
forbade spontaneity of feeling, but rather a smiling passivity that
showed like indifference. In her presence, Nathaniel felt ashamed of
his natural impulses, of his gaiety, of his carefree attitude. This im-
passivity was as much a product of upbringing as of temperament, and
it was passed on to Hawthorne as much by daily contagion as by inheritance. But he had also inherited from his father—who beneath a
cold exterior had concealed the Hathorne's secret violence—an ardent
temperament that was later to make him loathe the cyclic recurrence
of those torpid states during which he was to feel himself indifferent to
everything, and also, on the other hand, to fill him with a desire to
penetrate to the heart of everything that sleeps and tries to make itself
into a blank surface: water, mirrors, portraits, the faces of living men,
as closed as death masks. Moreover, his mother's reticence was interpreted by the child as a symbol of rejection, a symbol with which the
person never became completely fused, but which was the point of
departure of a psychic and esthetic blueprint. His mother was always
to remain for him the sealed-up source of affection, the padlocked
paradise. Tall, with "a peculiar and striking beauty,"[18] dark-haired,
with deep gray eyes, she was always to remain for him the image of
the ideal woman that he was several times to believe he had found
again, but in whom he was to seek in vain to stir up any emotion. The
mother with whom he was unconsciously in love was to make him
dream of finding a maternal beloved. And it was also from her, in fact,
that he had received his "sensitiveness, and his capacity for placid
enjoyment":[19] a heredity that is insufficient, if we limit ourselves to
what we know of it,[20] to explain his talent. Should we then attribute it,
this talent, to the good use to which Nathaniel put his illness and his
solitude? Perhaps, on condition that we recognize the existence in him
of a seed that had not existed previously either in the Hathornes or in

the Mannings, and which began to develop when brought into contact with stylized human images and images of impossible action. It was the gaps in his life's reality that summoned legend to fill the void around the imaginative child's bed; it was the gaps in his emotional life that created within him the emotion-charged myths, the ineffaceable symbols needed to fill them.

For it would be impossible to insist too much upon the importance of signs, in the hieroglyphic sense of the word, in the life of a child destined to become a creator of imaginary beings. For Rimbaud,[21] his mother was the white vowel *E*, immaculate, imperious, "crushing the cow-parsley"—an object of possible hatred—the angel with "the blue gaze—that lies!"[22] For Hawthorne, his mother was the first letter in his allegorical alphabet, a black hieroglyph, the gloom of a life that wishes itself over and done with, unexpressed affection, an austere and "badly managed" love imprisoning a child's heart inside a maze of contradictions. And both the absence and the existence of that sign lead on to a symbolic quest: Rimbaud's directed at erasing the mother from the field of consciousness, at eliminating the feminine sign from his world, at being at last the creator without a mother, at forging his own sign for himself—*"alchimie du verbe"* and the *Saison en Enfer*; Hawthorne's at finding the absent father once more and creating the ideal mother himself, with his own hands—the great hieroglyph of the Scarlet Letter. But always, superimposed upon the model of the woman to be loved, there was to be the primary silhouette of classical tragedy, stylized in its hieratic attitude, forbidding all re-entry into the maternal paradise that the artist was so painfully struggling to reconquer, only, in the end, to reject it. It was precisely at the period of his boyhood illness that Hawthorne felt the need of feminine consolation. But a Puritan mother, even an affectionate one, was bound to refuse all sentimental indulgence. And for American Protestants, displays of emotion and self-pity were things left strictly to Irish Catholics, Jews, and Negroes. Disappointed in his expectations, and even ashamed of them, the child hardened his heart, turned away from the mother's breast on which he was not able to weep, and cast himself into an emotional exile that would leave him free to go in quest of his cold and masculine father image. Can this be the same happy child we hear of from Elizabeth, when she writes, not without a certain retrospective jealousy, of her young, privileged, idle brother, entirely given over to the agreeable occupations of his imagination?[23] Shouts and laughter came up to him from the street, from the gardens. For him too, life had begun as a thing of games, of childish rivalries; he had had strength, skill, and intelligence on his side; he would have been a leader, a twelve-year-old captain and adventurer. Now, he was out of the running. And from the direct cause of his accident, from some urchin's possible vengeance, he thought his way back to the witch's curse on his ancestor, and on all the Hathornes: "God will give you blood to drink!"[24]

All the legends and stories of the past he had heard, all the echoes of the world that was still so close and yet so inaccessible, flooded in upon him and organized themselves around this theme of isolation, of an evil spell, of the curse that was cutting him off from life, a feeling that he was never, throughout his life, able to shake off. The witch herself had been reincarnated in order to torment him: the ogress with her evil eye was the representative of all the repulsive old hags who grimaced around his bed and even in his dreams. In this atmosphere of sorcery, accounts of the War of Independence and of Jackson's recent victory over the English at New Orleans paled beside the epic of the Puritan past and the flaming arabesques of the world of superstition and allegory. Young Nathaniel was well aware that he would never be a soldier, or a sailor, or an explorer, that he would never earn a place in New England history in any heroic capacity. Nor had he even the consolation of feeling himself the obscure martyr of some great cause, like Ilbrahim, the ten-year-old Christ with whom he was to seek to identify himself later on.[25] His sufferings were useless. They could be nothing, in the last analysis, but a punishment. The great Puritans of the past were not only his models, they were also his judges. It was not only as a pilgrim to the tombs of his family's heroes, but also as a sinner that he turned his gaze back to his forefathers. In an obscure way, it seemed to him that he had offended his dead father, for had he not, after all, taken his place in the world of the living? Disturbed by this thought, his conscience was perpetually returning to face the tribunal of his ancestors. And yet, were those judges themselves not guilty too? So that he was forced to bear not only the weight of their reprobation but also that of the curse which had been handed down, from generation to generation, to all the descendants of that first ancestor, the persecutor. The injury from which he was suffering was the physical mark of that curse in his flesh. The words hurled from a scaffold had continued their trajectory through the years to overtake him: the deserter attempting to escape the influence of the past, the deserter who, had he been too careless of such things, would have become the poetaster, the fiddler evoked with contempt in that dialogue of the dead which figures in the prologue to *The Scarlet Letter*.[26] The Judge's crime had fallen upon the head of the orphan: the chain had been re-established, and "the bloody footstep" was re-traceable from Nathaniel back to his colonial ancestors, and even as far as the origin of man, as far as the Fall. Thus, for Hawthorne, original sin was always to be fused in a sense with the crime of Cain, with the first murder: sin was always to be scarlet in color. Sex and murder, both symbolized by blood, met in the original wound of sin. The tragedies of Leonard Doane and Reuben Bourne spring wholly from this seed.[27] The young Hawthorne saw his accident as a punishment for the incest and the murder of which he imagined himself guilty. A contradictory punishment, since it was the witch who was avenging herself and the father who had been offended. And it also seems as though Nathaniel saw himself as being persecuted as a "witch" by the judges before whom he was to be tried as a "murderer." Having stood up to accuse himself before the tribunal of his peers, far from finding himself treated as one of them, he found himself treated as a felon, an excommunicate, a heretic. Stretched on a bed of Procrustes where his limbs were gradually losing their symmetry, he was experiencing the dungeon, the chains, and the pillory all at the same time. And the torture he underwent then was to return in obsessive form toward the end of his life.[28] Wishing to present himself as a guilty prisoner, he found himself becoming more and more a victim. As a victim of the witch, he was expiating the crime of his ancestors. As a victim of the Puritan inquisition he found himself wronged in the integrity of his being, for he was being refused both his spiritual heritage and his enjoyment of life at the same time. His wound was the wound that kills the hero whose feet have the lightness of wings, that nails spirits to the earth: Achilles' heel, the feet of Mercury, the feet of Ariel, pierced by the poisoned dart. Hermes, the messenger of the gods, has become Prometheus on his rock, Ariel venting his groans within the cloven pine, imprisoned by Sycorax. This captive Ariel, this wounded Ariel, is Oberon, the spirit of the air burdened with darkness and bound down by accursed powers. By a supreme irony, the gay and lively sprite has been crushed beneath Bunyan's fardel. And with a fierce effort of pride he takes up the challenge; he sets out on his pilgrimage, on his progress, bearing the burden of responsibility.

III. THE PILGRIM IN THE REALM OF IMAGINATION

At the time of Nathaniel's birth, religious fanaticism had ceased to flourish in New England. The Hathornes, once intolerant Puritans, had become Unitarians.[1] The only point upon which Mrs. Hathorne displayed any intransigence—devout though she was[2]—was that of Sunday activities. In particular, she forbade all reading other than that of religious works. Yet Sunday was already at that time a day most people spent amusing themselves,[3] and the young Nathaniel, judging the austerity of the measures that seemed to him to ruin his holidays excessive, held John Wesley responsible for the dull tasks inflicted upon him in the name of piety.[4] One winter evening, he snatched up a bust of his enemy, filled it with water, and left it like that, head downwards, in the garden. He saw himself as subjecting Wesley, in effigy, to the ordeal by cold. But Wesley's head remained uncracked and Nathaniel's efforts were in vain. He was to have more success later in life when subjecting many a doctrinaire to the same sort of ordeal: their theories he did succeed in exploding.

Despite all this, the boy's taste for reading became a veritable passion, encouraged perhaps by a Dr. Worcester, who came every day to hear him recite his lessons.[5] By the time he was six, *Pilgrim's Progress* was one of his bedside books. Shakespeare, Milton, Pope, and Thomson were all very soon familiar to him, as was Spenser's *Faerie Queene*.[6] The stories and chronicles of the colonial age introduced a distant reality into his dreams, but it was allegory, and in particular "Bunyanesque" allegory, that stamped its mark upon the smallest objects of his restricted world: his favorite cats were named Apollyon and Beelzebub.[7] Shakespeare also contributed to this poetic atmosphere with which he surrounded himself: "My Lord, stand back and let the coffin pass,"[8] he would declaim in order to drive the importunate away or summon up his fantasies. He had in fact built up a certain store of passwords, of cabalistic formulas, in order to facilitate his entry into a world apart, the world of legend, which is also the world of books. He could remain reading in an armchair for hours on end without raising his head once. When ill he often read lying on a bed or on the floor. He also invented "wild and fanciful stories"[9] that were genuine explorations as far as he was concerned; he could send himself into a sort of ecstatic trance by repeating to himself over and over again that he would never return[10] from those regions he took such pleasure in describing. When he was tired of literature he would play with his cats, revealing a fertility of invention that was already very "Hawthornesque." He built platforms, bridges, tunnels, whole labyrinths out of his books,[11] then sent his kittens on winding and complicated itineraries through these constructions, hugely enjoying their expressions, their appearances and disappearances, while he himself lay on the carpet, his eyes on a level with his castles, his pyramids, and his cities. And that tiny universe down on the floor, bounded by the walls of a room, could become immense. He was to return to it later, and though he never reproduced it he did make use of its dimensions. Without yet being aware of his vocation, the little Nathaniel, coddled by his family, surrounded by books and cats, had no other substitute for outdoor play and expeditions into the woods but games of this sort and imaginary voyages. To look out of a window is to dream of flying away. But his wings had fallen from his shoulders, and if he wished to find them again it was within himself that he had to look. This world of the haunted mind became more necessary to him than the other, against which he armed himself with the weapons of contempt and rancor, and which was his prison. His only ways of escape led inwards: mirrors, portraits, the pages of books—all so many openings inviting him to plunge deeper into the chiaroscuro regions of legend and consciousness, where all gestures are ambiguous, all masks reversible, all objects ungraspable. In such half shadow, in slanting beams, at the margins of mirrors, between the lines of his Milton or his Spenser, Oberon began to weave the first circles of his dance. The magician, caught in his own spell, was recognizing himself in the looking glass.[12] His vision was no longer a direct thing, but something filtered, a play of spotlights, a transformation scene rather than simple perception. Nathaniel gave himself up to the spectacle of a historical diorama, and discovered his affinities with the great Puritans of the past. Even though he did not approve of them, he admired them; he set them in the center of his consciousness as a symbol: they represented the virile principle of his race, his spiritual heritage, and the patriarchal tradition. Thus imprisoned by his ancestors, the young Hawthorne was to turn his back on the moral and religious developments of his own time. Though labeled a Unitarian because all his family were Unitarians,[13] he was only interested in the theocratic society of the Mathers.[14] Jonathan Edwards'[15] "tongue of fire" was still echoing in his ears a half century after it had ceased to speak. Nevertheless, the Wesleyan influence represented by Whitfield had certainly brought elements of emotion and imagination to the art of preaching that had hitherto been forbidden by the theological austerity of Puritanism: the minister in *The Scarlet Letter* was to be more Wesleyan than Puritan. With Jean-Jacques Rousseau, the European age of the Enlightenment had brought into being a moral romanticism founded on a belief in the natural goodness of man, thus permitting a reorientation of religious thought toward more consoling prospects. Instead of being alone with his burden of sins, man once more became a creature able to communicate with the divine through nature and through his heart. According to the Unitarian doctrine, which had crystallized these tendencies in the late eighteenth and early nineteenth centuries under the influence of William Ellery Channing, not only is God one but man is good and carries the seed of his own regeneration within him. Thus, the earthly life was no longer wholly cut off from the celestial sphere; nature was no longer the labyrinth in which Satan and his helpers set their traps; the human heart was no longer that noisome cavern which could be rendered acceptable to God only by the streams of grace: we are watching the dawn of Transcendentalism.

Hawthorne, instead of embracing these new beliefs, remained with his eyes fixed on the past. The awareness he enjoyed of his solitude and of his condition as a victim of fate was not exempt from a secret pride, even though it had nothing in common with sectarian fanaticism: it was not into the theological sphere that he transposed his ancestral beliefs but into the sphere of imagination. His Puritanism is at the same time narcissistic, contemplative, and esthetic. This tendency is brought out most clearly by comparisons. Bunyan experienced prison when already a mature man, and the ordeal fortified the believer in him. He turned author in order to defend his faith; art to him was an irrelevancy. With Milton, on the other hand, faith was the vehicle of a poetic determination that both preceded it and went beyond it. And we find Emerson,[16] a pastor's son whose whole environment seemed to be orienting him toward the ministry, turning instead to literature for a career. The closest parallel with the young Hawthorne's

experience, however, is that of his Danish contemporary Søren Kierkegaard.[17] Yet solitude was to turn the one into a philosopher and the
other into a novelist. Wherein did the difference lie?

Kierkegaard, being a delicate child and the pupil of a tyrannical and
puritanical father, was easily detached by him from reality, and his
physical impulses in particular were always to remain weak, which is
far from being the case with Hawthorne, the descendant of robust
pioneers and sires. Whereas Hawthorne was a young but wounded
animal languishing at his inability to escape from himself, Kierkegaard was a hothouse plant. And the existence of evil was revealed to
him in the form of a shock. His father told him how once, when keeping his sheep as a child, devoured by hunger, he had stood on top of a
rock and cursed the Lord: a dramatic gesture that was to remain
forever in the son's mind as a symbol and turn him into the meta-
physician-poet of anguish and despair. The violation of Hawthorne's
consciousness by guilt was less obvious and more subtle. He knew
that his ancestors too had offended God, but no one ever gave him a
description of the precise act that called down the curse upon them.
The semilegendary ancestors that he had chosen to be his judges, being
figures of history and tradition, always remained at a certain remove,
and it was his imaginative nature that turned him into their accomplice
in its search for sensations. The Puritan heritage, in him a still un-
tapped reservoir with no communicating channel into the social sphere,
was to find its outlet in the esthetic sphere. Kierkegaard's soul, on the
other hand, was totally violated, kneaded out of the very substance of
sin itself. There was nothing left for it to do but plunge into a despairing quest. And its despair was at the same time a certainty, the man's
reason for being, and his truth. Whereas Hawthorne was not absolutely at one with his anguish. He was able to play upon it like an
instrument even while he was suffering from it. It was a source of
myths for him and included a parallel strain of skepticism. For him,
the Giant Despair[18] belonged as much to the world of fable as to that
of moral experience, and when he trembled it was as much in the role
of spectator as in that of victim. What makes Hawthorne and Kierkegaard alike is the existence of their inner adventures. But the progress
of the latter is ontological and theological, that of the former psychological and esthetic. One was obsessed by sin made flesh in the harsh
light of Judgment, the other by an ambiguous guilt kept continuously
in doubt by the play of flickering shadows. Kierkegaard had no further
choice to make; Hawthorne was always forced to go on choosing. The

first had a tragic destiny, the second a dramatic one. Kierkegaard became a philosopher by dint of clinging to his anguish;[19] Hawthorne became a novelist by detaching himself from his,[20] in order to encompass it in all its ambiguity. On the one hand we find implacable logic, on the other perpetual contradictions. Kierkegaard is always one in his dialogue with his self. Hawthorne is always two.

There is no doubt that the religious and moral uncertainty concealed beneath Hawthorne's characteristic tendency to mystification originated in the double trauma brought about by his father's absence and his mother's apparent indifference. Finding himself unable to dispel this inner unease, maintained as it was by inaction and cultivated by his imagination and reading, the child gradually found ways of turning it to some use.[21] For as we have seen, the most fascinating game he was able to invent in his sickroom was precisely that of conjuring up the ghosts of his past, of himself participating in their legend, and allowing himself to be haunted by his ancestors by offering himself— as much out of moral curiosity as out of a need for self-punishment—as a sharer in the curse laid upon them. Was he searching for expiation, for pleasure, or for an atmosphere? Was he trying to purify himself, to escape from himself, or to hew himself out a dream-castle in a fantasy world? His works are there as an answer to those questions—and what an ambiguous answer! If the young Hawthorne darkened his own horizon so deliberately in this way, at a time when the moral and religious climate around him was lightening, it was not solely in order to take pleasure in his own noble sadness or to offer himself up as a sacrifice, but also in order to make his own an entire historical period whose characters had struck his imagination and to borrow its dramatic colors: intenser and darker than those of any other, and the wellspring of his style. The Bible and Bunyan served him more as a foundation for daydreaming than for meditation, and theology was less important to him than allegory. In the closed world of the early Puritans he was able to rediscover his own cloistered universe, his own labyrinth of contradictions, and the dark cave of his own heart.

IV. LESSONS FROM NATURE

When the young Nathaniel emerged from his forced withdrawal from the world he was twelve years old. He rediscovered Salem as though recognizing a past dream in present reality. The world he had never

ceased to imagine was there before him, materialized in the wooden
Colonial houses, those precarious monuments of historic American
Puritanism. But now that he was strong again Nathaniel had better
things to do than pursue his former invalid's dreams: the vagabond in
him was thirsty for wide open spaces, the young savage aspired to lose
himself in nature. And it so happened that Mrs. Hathorne did in fact
own a country house at Raymond, Maine, near Lake Sebago. She
went to spend the summer there with her children, and then, two years
later, made it her permanent residence.[1]

Not a church or a school for leagues around:[2] these were real holidays for Nathaniel. He hunted, fished, and scoured the countryside
with a gang of other young rogues: he was getting his own back. "The
country roundabout," G. E. Woodberry tells us, "was wilderness, most
of it primeval woods. The little settlement, only a mill and a country
store, and a few scattered houses, lay on a broad headland making
out into Sebago Lake, better known as the Great Pond, a sheet of water
eight miles across and fourteen miles long, and connected with other
lakes in a chain of navigable water; to the northwest the distant horizon
was filled with the White Mountains, and northward and eastward rose
the unfrequented hill and lake country . . . presenting a vast solitude."[3]
A Canadian, almost Nordic landscape, still unspoiled today, in which
the young Hawthorne was to live like a savage. There was also Pulpit
Rock, so called because of its shape, from which Apostle Eliot[4] may
once have preached to the Indians, a cliff renowned as a "lover's leap,"
and also some prehistoric paintings:[5] in short, a rich store of objects
immediately assimilable by a mind already oriented toward the interpretation of signs.

The young Nathaniel consigned his impressions to his first notebook.[6] To him, everything was new, everything was an enchantment.
He felt the need to express himself, to prove to himself anew the very
existence of so many marvels: the lake where he went canoeing or even
swimming, when his mother wasn't watching—the streams—Crooked
River, in which H. Jackson, Jr. was drowned—the mountains, "splendid old Rattlesnake," Frye Island, "like a monstrous raft," the animals, the fish, the snakes, and the game—the people: farmers, hunters,
hoboes, Robinson Cook, the little Quaker, Samuel Shawe, who went
down into the well instead of "Widow Hathorne's son" because the
latter's life was esteemed too precious. Surrounding Raymond, he
found a ready-made microcosm that answered to all his inclinations,

a small society in which he was king, a landscape whose vistas were made for escape, a universe at once withdrawn and at the same time opening onto the wide open spaces of water, earth, and sky. Nature was present there in all its various forms, domesticated as well as wild, from the virgin forests beyond the vast expanse of the lake out to the mountains rearing their regularly receding peaks into space, though without ever crushing the tiny human archipelago below. Hawthorne was to imitate this natural distribution of water, wood, and mountain into successive or concentric zones in his own interior microcosm. And the still inviolate elements of this wilderness presented him with the image of a fenced off world—quite the opposite of the overpopulated city that Boston was to be for him—the image of a multiplicity of tiny private universes, lakes and hills, hamlets and valleys, all so often reproduced later in his works, the foundations of which were already being silently established. The adolescent was now beginning to take shape within the wild child, and tendencies forgotten in the ardor of childish games were reasserting themselves. He would plunge alone into the forest, armed with his carbine. What a trophy if he were able to bring back a bearskin![7] At least once he spent the night in a log cabin where there was "half a tree" burning in the hearth, watching the flames flicker up the chimney toward the stars.[8] Fire was always a magnet to his imagination. In Salem he went to watch all the fires that broke out[9] and remained, a fascinated spectator, gazing at the flames and the bustling firemen, to the great indignation of some. One intriguing detail: he used to send his sister out to investigate the fires and tell him whether they were worth getting out of bed for!

In winter he loved skating on the lake by moonlight: the silence, his own speed, and the vague brightness around him gave him the impression of being no more than a shade in an unreal world. He was well aware of his own strength, however, and would have nothing to do with the sort of flimsy sentimentality that he used to parody in doggerel verse. He was not yielding to a fashion, he was experiencing a personal, spiritual vertigo. Alone with nature he felt himself living more intensely, as though his whole being were being extended and ramifying out into the elements; without his conscious knowledge, he was trapped in an enchanted circle. He was absorbing nature, but nature was also absorbing him. He would have to escape from it in order to depict it properly, as he had finally escaped from his sickroom and its phantasms. A cursed solitude, a "cursed habit," for among those woods and hills, even as he was thinking of himself as being as free as a bird of the air,[10] he was building his own prison. Such were the expressions he himself used when lamenting his fate toward the end of his life, forgetting that the curse came from further back, and that nature had merely been the accomplice of his own secret tastes.

However, he had not yet learned shyness, or how to be ashamed of himself, of his idleness, of his talent. He would have to return to "civilization" in order to contract that disease. At this point, the time had come to think seriously of returning to his studies. He therefore went back, much against his will, to Salem, where he was entrusted to the care of a private tutor named Benjamin Lynde Olivier, who was the first to recognize his pupil's exceptional gifts and succeeded, at the expense of a few months' cramming, in bringing him up to the standards set for college entrance. Olivier, a Salem attorney, enjoyed the possession of a genuine laboratory: mirrors, microscopes, lens grinders, apparatus for experiments in physics, a telescope, an electrical machine lay here and there cluttering up the corners of his rooms.[11] Thus the young Nathaniel found himself daily penetrating into the study of the alchemist who was to reappear clothed in the lineaments of so many characters in his tales.[12]

During the afternoon, he worked as a clerk for the Manning Company. No more wandering where he willed through the woods. He could not even find time to read as much as he would have liked. Scott and Godwin were his gods at the time. But where was he to find time for writing? No one can be a clerk and a poet at the same time, he wrote to his mother.[13] Nevertheless, he managed to throw off verses in the taste of the day with great facility, and it was this very facility of his that disappointed him. Only his mother, and his sister Louisa, who was his collaborator on the family "Spectator,"[14] were kept informed of his projects. Elizabeth had too caustic a wit, and the young Nathaniel had no wish to make himself the butt of her irony. Later, when he had mastered his art, he was to take pleasure in showing her his works and hearing himself praised by her. For Elizabeth's approval, even when tinged with reluctance, was of far more use to him than that of even the best-informed of critics.

At this point, however, there was no example of artistic vocation in his own environment; he sensed that no one, perhaps not even his mother, would encourage him in such a course. The embarrassment, the shame that chills and exasperates the artist surrounded by Philis-

tines and turns him into a failure or an iconoclast, had entered his
soul. Even when he met his peers later on, he was never quite sure of
his rightful place among them. There was not a single musician, not a
single singer, not a single poet, not a single rhymester, not a single
actor in his whole family! What was he doing trying to crash the gates
of the world of art?

It was part of his nature to take pleasure in clandestine activities:
the role of conspirator was not without a certain charm for him and
he even took a humorous enjoyment in it. The first society he founded,
the "Pin Society,"[15] was a parody of the legal world. He had a taste
for ceremonial, for administrative phraseology, for procedural formali-
ties,[16] for titles,[17] for words with double meanings, for enigmas, secret
codes,[18] clandestine activities, and mystery. The collaboration between
brother and sister had a touch of freemasonry about it; they were the
initiates, the only two, and it was this fact that gave their literary complicity the savor of a forbidden fruit. Hawthorne was particularly
anxious that his uncle Robert, who looked upon his nephew as a good-
for-nothing, should not get to know of these illicit activities. His letters
at this time seem fairly adequate proof that he had no great love for
the Mannings: "I hope, my dear mother, that you will not be tempted
by their entreaties to return to Salem to live. You can never have so
much comfort here as you now enjoy. You are now undisputed mistress of your own house."[19] For the son himself was clinging to Raymond with desperation: it was the symbol of his happy adolescence.
Whereas in Salem, he was in constant conflict with his grandmother
and Manning aunt, both miserly and shrewish women. He could not
bear to see his mother falling under the influence of her brothers and
sister again and at the same time losing Manning's Folly.[20] The Mannings probably made the Hathornes feel their dependence on them,
and Nathaniel became bitter on this score. He did not want their
charity. Possibly the strain already existing between mother and son
was aggravated by these family squabbles and Nathaniel's want of
"gratitude" toward his benefactors. He certainly did not let this stop
him going to college, however: his training as a writer depended on it.
But the family's attitude was that if he went to college then he must
choose a profession worthy of the name he bore. He would owe it to
himself to become a lawyer, or a doctor, or a pastor. But was it up
to the Mannings to interpret the wishes of the Hathorne ancestors?
In fact, Nathaniel never at any point abdicated his right to self-

determination, not even to those ancestors themselves; his soul, in exile among them though it was, never yielded itself up entirely to their discretion. He was not to be their messenger, their continuer, but their interpreter, their portraitist. Had he believed in predestination, then his name alone—Nathaniel being the Hebrew equivalent of the Latin *deodatus*,[21] gift of God—might have led him to accept that he was destined for the priesthood. This may indeed have been his mother's secret wish, but he rebelled in advance against such a thought: "A minister I will not be."[22] In reality, his choice was already made: "What do you think of my becoming an author, and relying for support upon my pen? . . . How proud you would feel to see my works praised by the reviewers, as equal to the proudest productions of the scribbling sons of John Bull."[23] And there was a postscript to the letter adjuring his mother not to show it to anyone else. Mrs. Hathorne may have lived in fear of having her son taken from her by the sea, for he had, after all, frequently expressed a desire to sail away from her. She could not experience the same apprehensions at the idea of a literary vocation, since its adventures and perils, on the surface at least, belong only to the world of fiction. Moreover, in becoming a writer Nathaniel would be able to remain near her, and that, in her mother's heart, secretly burning with a passionate love for this son of whom she already had reason to be proud, was what she most desired. Nathaniel for his part, already dreaming of conquering the world with his pen, was determined not to vegetate forever in one place, whether as a lawyer, a minister, or a writer, and certainly not in Salem![24] Yet it was to Salem that circumstances, and perhaps some obscure attraction, were to draw him back.

· 2 ·
Oberon and the Storyteller

I. THE CASTLE OF INDOLENCE

It was in October of 1821 that Hawthorne entered Bowdoin College.
Built at the end of the eighteenth century[1] near Brunswick, Maine, in
hitherto unsettled territory, Bowdoin was still unknown. Engravings of
that era depict a "quad" in the middle of an immense meadow on the
banks of the Androscoggin, a torrent already disfigured by industry and
used for floating lumber down from the forests.[2] Again, Hawthorne was
confronted with a landscape of Nordic legends, poems, and sagas.
The students were all pure New Englanders,[3] countrified, solid, and
needy. President Allen, a pious and strict Congregationalist minister,
was not well liked.[4] The strict discipline imposed by the college's
Draconian regulations[5] was ill suited to any student with an independent and indolent temperament: up at dawn, prayers in chapel,
an hour's private study before breakfast, lessons from nine till midday
and from two till five, prayers before dinner; no games, no leisure time.
Moreover the rules were enforced by what amounted to a strict penal
code.[6] Hawthorne fought back against this system, sometimes with
open rebellion and sometimes simply with inertia. He was one of the
pillars, if not the founder, of the Pot-8-O'Club,[7] which used to meet
in one of the town taverns and was in fact a group of hearty young
drinkers with nothing of the literary club about it. The members' con-

25

tributions were in the form of smuggled food and wine rather than essays or poems.[8] The Hawthorne who frequented the Pot-8-O'Club —the same character who later on used to attempt to forget himself in the crowds and the atmosphere of inns or fairs—was not regarded by the faculty as by any means a model student. The offenses for which he was penalized are eloquent enough testimony in themselves to this fact: staying out all night, neglecting his recitation, uselessly prolonging a Sunday walk, going to a tavern on Saturday night,[9] absence from Sunday service, and lastly, having played cards. President Allen wrote to his student's family. Nathaniel pleaded guilty, but to his sisters at least he insisted on taking the responsibility for his actions, claiming that he would feel dishonored if he had merely been tempted into them by another.[10] In fact, he was very much afraid of being expelled. It is extremely likely that he had incurred one of the public admonitions that the President himself reserved the right to administer when he so chose. Of all the thunderbolts censors are empowered to wield, social anathema was without doubt the one most likely to strike the young Hawthorne's imagination: the useless and the idle, like other malefactors, are punished with ostracism. Even though he had never betrayed his honor—the ideal of the "gentleman" was as much a standard of conduct at Bowdoin as at Harvard or Oxford—was he ever going to become a useful member of society? His uncle was extremely doubtful on this score, which only made his nephew proclaim his lack of ambition the more openly. He affected an idleness and a love of mediocrity that were incompatible with his secret hopes, asserting that his only desire was "to plod along with the multitude."[11]

Nevertheless he created a sensation upon his arrival at Bowdoin, though not, it is true, by his learning but by his physique and his character. Tall,[12] slender, broad-shouldered, he had inherited his mother's delicate features and gray eyes,[13] sometimes dreamy, sometimes piercing; moreover, he had strong, well-made hands, as apt for throwing as for delicate sculpting[14] or handling the heaviest tools. His "walk was square and firm,"[15] his "figure somewhat singular, owing to his carrying his head a little on one side."[16] It is possible that what some people thought of as an indolence of movement was in fact produced by a weakness of the spine caused by his childhood illness, though his strength and agility were a matter of admiration to all who met him: he was able to walk for hours without becoming tired, to climb trees with a rapidity that was still amazing his children when he was over forty, and to do a standing jump as high as his shoulder. A century later he would have been a college high-jump champion.[17] His moral prestige was equally great. He seems to have inspired both friendship and respect, even fear, not only on account of his strength and virile good looks but also by his vitality, the mischievous or disturbing fantasies of his poetic mind, and the mystery that seemed always to hover around him. By turns open and secretive, mocking and melancholic, capable both of spectacular rages and of "the delicacy, the tremulous sensitiveness . . . of the most finely organized woman,"[18] such was the Oberon[19] in whom Emerson was to see a quasi-mythological figure as he went skimming on his skates with all the lightness of a sylph and the majesty of a specter down the Concord River,[20] as well as an essentially feminine mind.[21] Hawthorne is as much a mystery to us physically as he is morally: to some he appeared frail, his body weighed down by a massive head; to others he seemed athletic and physically formidable. In the same way, some describe him as taciturn, others as exuberant. Even allowing for an element of Romantic attitudinizing in the Oberon persona,[22] both aspects seem equally true. There were two Hawthornes: the fulfilled Oberon, happy to be alive and to be admired, and the unfulfilled Oberon, weighed down with a head too heavy for him, in search of himself, full of doubts—the raw material of Fanshawe. Complex as he was, the conflicting elements of his being were rarely in perfect balance, which was one of the reasons why he created a mask of inscrutability for himself. His moments of energy and enthusiasm were always followed by phases of depression. He needed long periods of rest and inactivity between his periods of physical and intellectual hyperactivity. These passive states, which might last for days or weeks, enabled him to preserve his energies intact and build up fresh reserves. Oberon the enchanter was able to live quite happily with the magician Indolence,[23] director of that fecund leisure so ruthlessly banished from Bowdoin by President Allen's cane. Leisure could well have been the allegorical inspiration of the Athenians, with whom Hawthorne was always pleased to associate himself; whereas Study would have been that of the "learned Thebans," among whom were Longfellow and Gorham Deane, the Louis Lambert of Bowdoin[24] who was to be carried off by tuberculosis and overwork in 1825. Though he did not quite share his friend Pierce's outright loathing of study, Hawthorne did, as he himself said, "prefer to nurse his own fancies."[25]

The hours stolen from "declamation," an exercise that made him feel ridiculous and pilloried, and sometimes from his prayers, were doubtless partly devoted to the laborious acquisition of his skill as a writer.[26] To others, he often appeared to be doing nothing. Yet he disliked being disturbed in this apparent idleness.[27] An affectation of idleness is, of course, one of the attitudes of the dandy. For there was also the Hawthorne in his elegant, blue, brass-buttoned suit dazzling the freshmen with his extravagance, and running up debts, simply for pleasure, in order to give himself a foretaste of dissipation, just as he frequented gamblers and hard drinkers out of bravado. If we are to believe his friend Bridge,[28] handsome though Hawthorne was, as well as being a good dancer and a brilliant conversationalist, there was nothing of the Lovelace about him. Perhaps there was an unconscious homosexual element there, masked even from Hawthorne himself by his Puritan upbringing.[29] He also had the dandy's taste for paradox and reluctance to give way to emotion. He refused to let himself be moved by Kean as Lear, even though he himself admitted that "it was enough to have drawn tears from millstones."[30] Behind the dandy there is always the Puritan.

The caprices of friendship are as strange as those of love. Oberon's friends were all rather prosaic creatures: Horatio Bridge the future businessman, Franklin Pierce the "politician," and Jonathan Cilley the social climber. All three were Democrats, so Hawthorne too became a Democrat, in sympathy. But what mattered much more to him than any political consideration was the moral—and occasionally material—support that his friends were to bring him in his career as a writer. At least one of them sensed the direction of that career from the outset. The young Horatio, fascinated by Hawthorne, professed a passionate admiration for him that never ceased to embarrass the shy Oberon. Nevertheless, Horatio's openness and generosity eventually gained the confidence of this reticent Hamlet, preyed upon by his recurrent fits of anxiety. A tormented creature, reluctant to be such, Hawthorne felt the need of simple friendships, of companions who would take him out of himself, complement his own temperament, reassure him, and be content to admire his talent without attempting to explain it to him. Moreover, he belonged to no literary circle. To know that there did exist a few chosen spirits in the community, among whom the brightest was Longfellow, was enough for him. He had no desire to approach them, to become acquainted with them, to discuss things with them, or to talk about his own projects. It was always to be the same with him. All he needed was to know that he was not completely alone. Longfellow's example was a stimulus to him, even though he was not conscious of it, for Longfellow, when he spoke of young American literature, was expressing aloud what Hawthorne himself was thinking in a whisper.[31] His first works of any value seem to have originated during his time at Bowdoin,[32] but he preferred to work on without witnesses, without publicity. He needed to weigh everything for himself, and he needed silence in order to listen to his own voice. Whereas Longfellow could declaim his verses in public, success for Hawthorne was a question of private communication. He needed his audience to be won over in advance. Consequently, when he wanted to try out the power of one of his tales on a listener he would take aside a friend he could be sure of. And is that not what he is really doing in all his prefaces? It was in the secrecy of a college room, or safe amid the complicity of untamed nature during some expedition along the Androscoggin, that Oberon confessed his illicit activities to his friend Horatio.[33] Longfellow was already officially "the Poet," but Hawthorne was still nothing, nothing, that is, other than the mysterious Oberon, apparently concealing a strange hidden hoard of intellectual and physical resources to which he himself had no key. Moreover, his rightful place was already taken. He was perfectly able to content himself with eighteenth place in his class in 1825,[34] but he could never consent to be ranked second in the sphere of literary competition, especially when the faculty selected the precocious author of a bad novel, who was to have no future, as the writer most worthy of discoursing on the writer's craft![35] Ashamed of his first poetic stammerings and doubting whether he would ever find an audience ready to listen to his tales, he remained silent. Doubtless there was also, mingled with his resentment, an obscure wisdom, an instinct. But the storyteller was to wait a long time before achieving fame.

II. THE WIZARD OF HERBERT STREET

Back in Salem, Hawthorne shut himself up in his room. Any other budding writer would have gone to Boston or New York; he preferred to continue his apprenticeship in solitude. This is another of those contradictions with which his life is filled: he did not like his uncles, he loathed Salem, and he was tormented by a thirst for freedom, yet he returned to all that he longed to escape from, for his need of a maternal haven was profound. At Bowdoin, he became homesick almost as soon as he had arrived. He even went so far as to use moral blackmail in order to go home again before the official end of the term: he wrote to his sister saying that it was so long since he had seen the place where he was born that he felt sick almost to death. He told her he was afraid that if he were not allowed to go home very soon his health might suffer seriously.[1] And now that Bowdoin was behind him, even though his aspiration was to fly with his own wings he still needed security, home comforts, feminine attention: his long illness had conditioned him to such things once and for all. He was not one of those who go to sea, who do any job that comes along, who leave home without money, travel all over the world and live their works in action before sitting down to write them. He was one of those who live them from the very outset in imagination. And this was also the reason he refused to show himself in society: it would have been a waste of time for him. Since there was nothing, on his own admission, that he feared as much as his sister Elizabeth's sarcasms, why should he go looking for jibes elsewhere, in the drawing rooms of the rich Salem middle-class families[2] who were so contemptuous of the Hathorne's poverty? The feminine audience so dear to the young author was constituted for Hawthorne in the first place by his family circle. He found it natural that his lady admirers should forgo society in order to provide him with a faithful public, since he too was renouncing it in order to become a writer worthy of the name. In his mind, Louisa and Elizabeth were the guardians of his still obscure works, the women perhaps that he depicted as the moved listeners to the story of Alice Doane,[3] and whose faces were doubtless superimposed on other female faces: for he was soon to feel the need of new and different Egerias. He had no intention of allowing himself to be drawn into the torpor of family life and of abandoning himself to the domestic spell of solitude and celibacy.[4] The desire to escape was always there, the vagabond was bound to awake.

Even in the midst of his own family he was still a being apart. He worked alone in his room, in "this dismal chamber" where "FAME was won."[5] And whether that room did really look out on Union

Street, as the entry in his notebook suggests, or whether this was a lapse of memory—whether Hawthorne did remain in the house on Herbert Street or in fact cross the garden to the "family manor," populated with his earliest memories[6]—it was nevertheless a fact that he had rediscovered the realm of his imagination. And the lapse of memory, the unfulfilled intention, would still be as revealing as the act performed: for Hawthorne, the world of fiction began on the threshold of the house where he was born.

Even in the Manning household, it was into the atmosphere of his happy childhood, of the time before his illness, that he plunged back at this time. He wished to be on his own home ground in order to confront the phantoms of his past again. The artist had to be free, to belong to his creations alone. That is why it would have been as senseless in his eyes to conform to the ideal of a self-made society as to write according to the dictates of his ancestors. Perhaps adding a letter to his name was a way of freeing himself from their tutelage, of putting himself at a certain distance from those Hathorne forefathers in order to examine them more clearly as characters in a legend, of turning their curse away from himself while continuing to draw upon his ancestral sources with impunity. But could he seriously dream of writing the epic of the great traders of his home town—as a companion piece to the legend of the great Puritans[7]—without incurring the punishment meted out to all artists who are unfaithful to their work? Hawthorne was not to be the American Chatterton: the Salem Philistines were not to reap the glory of having reduced him to silence either by hunger or slander. In the event, the "poet" of Salem caused remarkably little stir in that town, once turned topsy-turvy by its witches. The only things that anyone could lay at the "wizard" of Herbert Street's door were the seeming idleness with which he appeared so content[8] and a certain contempt for social conventions. But in order to be suspect it is enough simply not to be the same as others. If he had lived in 1692, when Judge Hathorne's reign was at the height of its rigor, Nathaniel would have been called to account for the very least of his actions. How did he spend his time? It was clear that he was sponging off his mother, he, a young man who had been to college and could become a lawyer or a doctor. One of his sisters could be seen almost daily on her way to the Athenaeum to fetch books for him.[9] Was it magic he was studying with such application? He left the house very little, during the day at least. Whereas he was to be seen out walking at the most un-usual hours, this "wizard," leaving the house at dusk,[10] with the agility of a Goodman Brown[11] on his way to the Sabbath, threading his way through the town's narrow streets, mingling for a moment with the lower classes, and then passing on through the suburbs into the open country. All this could not but seem strange to honest minds whose lack of imagination was always prone to make them believe in fantasies, provided they presented themselves as the small change of backbiting and witchcraft. Why in the devil's name should Widow Hathorne's son go out walking in the twilight like that in so mysteri-ous a fashion? What companions was he meeting on these expeditions, this young man who never visited anyone in Salem itself,[12] apart from a few rogues, radicals, porters, coachmen, and tavern haunters?[13] Though magic was losing its power over men's minds, the threat of drink, gambling, and debauchery was, on the contrary, in the ascen-dant. Julian Hawthorne later expended a great deal more zeal than the cause warranted in order to restore his father's reputation to that of a pillar of the league of temperance.[14] But the slanders did not stop there. It was even said that this unworthy offshoot of the Hathornes, who was never seen in church, could well have been arraigned in sermons a century earlier as a living illustration of sin against the Seventh Commandment! Such was the real explanation of his noc-turnal expeditions, it was said: he went to visit that fisherman's daugh-ter at Swampscott, five miles away, and then came back early in the morning to collapse into bed, worn out with the excesses of his lust. Did he not, after all, go and spend several weeks with this Susan, this "mermaid," one summer, and without leaving any address?[15] Was that any way for a gentleman, for a Hathorne to behave?

During the winter of 1830, the whole town was thrown into a great agitation by the murder of Joseph White, one of Salem's richest merchants. The sons of some of the town's best families were impli-cated in the affair. Salem was back once more in its days of supersti-tious fury: bands of vigilantes were formed, strangers were arrested,[16] Daniel Webster presided at the Supreme Court. That great man's famous speech on the guilt of the criminal had nothing to teach Haw-thorne on a subject that the young writer understood instinctively better than anyone. But the affair as a whole plunged him into a flood of irrational emotion and collective frenzy. A whole sensational epoch had been reconstructed to haunt him. His contemporaries were evidently no kinder of heart than his ancestors or today's lynchers of Negroes. In 1835, when visiting Cheever, his former Bowdoin acquaintance, in prison, even though such an action had not the merit of affronting public opinion—Cheever was in fact so overwhelmed by messages of sympathy that he received visits only by appointment![17]— Hawthorne genuinely felt himself to be the persecuted man's brother. He was one of those who, because they despair of ever being like other people, need to feel the vague hostility of society weighing down upon them, need to be and to create against and in opposition to the rest of the world. This was the only stimulus he had at hand, in fact, since his first works aroused no echo in the world. It seemed to him that he would never again be able to escape from Salem, and his bitterness against the town where he was born increased still further. He considered it responsible for his obscurity. While feeling a desire to become a part of the "multitude," at the same time he was "conscious of being utterly unlike every one else . . . he began to withdraw into himself."[18] He began to experience the painful feeling of having been left behind by all the others in his generation.[19] The "same dream of life hopelessly a failure!"[20] was to pursue him to the end. There was always the same recurring nightmare: he was back on a school bench apparently for time without end[21] and without having moved forward a single step.

There were, however, times when he was "happy—at least, as happy as I then knew how to be,"[22] when he was visited by visions of the past that would allow themselves to be captured. At those times, his home town was no longer the Salem of 1830 but the Salem of a legendary era floodlit by his own imagination.[23] His walks out to the Neck, along the deserted beaches, up to Gallows Hill, where the bonfires were lit for Guy Fawkes night on November 5, his visits to the old wooden houses with their clustering gables, like that belonging to his aunt Susan Ingersoll, so "proud of being proud" of her aristocracy,[24] took him back at every step to his childhood, led him ever deeper into the labyrinth of Salem in its colonial days, that abundant wellspring from which he drew his early works. On certain evenings, when the weather was bad, his artistic curiosity and other obscure inclinations led him to seek out a different kind of solitude, that provided by the night, by the cold, by the rain, and the wavering and distant lights around him gave him the feeling of being lost at sea, yet still linked by tenuous threads to the land:[25] an image of his own situation with regard to humanity. If he went out during the day it was always in order to find the shortest route to the most propitious lonely spot available, which was usually somewhere by the edge of the sea.[26] But there were days of sunlight and popular festivity when he felt a need to live in the present. On fine summer mornings he would rush out at dawn and dive into the waves. And yet the sea, which was always the cradle of his deepest awareness, never became one of the major themes of his work. His own missed vocation, and the image of his father's ship, the *America*, rotting in harbor, prevented him from ever singing the exploits of the privateers.[27] It was toward those who cleared the forests and built the colony on land, not toward the great seafarers, that the novelist was drawn. Even the need for movement was a form of contemplation with him. Sometimes he would get up before dawn in order to go out and stand on the bridge over the North River, near the tollkeeper's cabin, and watch the carriages, the horsemen, and the people on foot pass by:[28] this was the frustrated vagabond's way of participating, though as a motionless and musing spectator, in the bustle of the world. Sometimes he would hurl himself into the maelstrom of the crowd. As soon as any sort of gathering began to take place he would leave the house and join it.[29] He went out to acclaim Jackson as he rode into Salem in 1833, not out of political fanaticism but out of a love for the picturesque and crowds.[30] He was disappointed when all there was to see was a small detachment of militant Democrats. Being in a crowd enabled him to participate anonymously in events without any demands being made upon him. And for that reason he liked crowds. But as soon as a crowd took him to itself and tried to make him play some role in it, he loathed it. What he wanted was to be able to remain isolated while being in the middle of it, as he could with nature and in his own room: a need for quietness, for mystery, and also an inherent defeatism that could only be counterbalanced by his need for experience and for success.

III. THE VAGABOND

Hawthorne was always possessed by a wanderlust. He would have liked to visit every region of the globe, he tells us, though with the exception, he adds wryly, of the Poles and Central Africa. These particular restrictions are all the more significant in that it is the "Solitary Man"[1] who rejects those desert places. Travel, for Hawthorne, was always to mean communicating with his fellow men. Far from contenting himself, like Thoreau, with country life and very limited excursions, he dreamed constantly of long journeys of exploration and escape. Once a year, as he himself tells us, he used to make an excursion of several weeks, during which he drew as much profit from life as other people do in the course of a whole year.[2] Stagecoaches still stimulated his imagination as much as they had in childhood. The first railroads were still only being used for the transportation of mining products; whereas the Erie Canal had been open to navigation for many years, the first section of railroad connecting Boston to the Great Lakes was not to be completed until 1831.[3] It was therefore either by stagecoach or by steamboat that our wanderer, during this eve of the modern industrial era, went visiting other parts of America. These journeys often present problems of chronology, however, since the earliest entry in Hawthorne's notebooks dates from 1835.[4] Moreover, a study of the tales and sketches for which these excursions were the principal source is of no great help in the matter, since such material consists for the most part of collected fragments, sometimes rewritten and combined with later additions after the destruction of works whose original proportions we do not know.[5] The only definite facts that remain after eliminating this material, therefore, are two terminal dates: that of Hawthorne's leaving Bowdoin and that of the failure of *The Story-Teller*.[6] It is during this ten-year period (1825–1835) that we must situate some of the journeys that were most important in the young writer's formation.

Even though no reference can be found to any journey beyond Lake Champlain, there can be no doubt that Hawthorne did see Niagara: one only has to read the pages he devotes to it. He also alludes to travels of even greater scope,[7] but all we can know with any degree of certainty are the dates of his less ambitious expeditions, through Connecticut and New Hampshire for example, and that of his stay at Crawford Notch,[8] all of which, when arranged in a chronological table,[9] enable us to envision a possible alternation between long and short trips. There were three periods during which Hawthorne may have undertaken his really long journey, apart from the expedition to Crawford Notch, and there is nothing that definitely proves he made it only once. Having left Bowdoin in 1825, his big desire must have been to make a first voyage up the Erie Canal, continuing as far as his financial means would permit. Perhaps he waited until 1826 or 1827 to put this plan into execution, in which case he must have gone at least as far as Niagara.[10] The two years following he restricted himself to accompanying his uncle Samuel on the latter's regular summer horse-buying expeditions. The following summer, that of 1830, had probably been chosen as the one for a "grand tour"; moreover, having meanwhile entered into relations with Goodrich, Hawthorne had a little money.[11] Circumstances were therefore favorable for a further long voyage of escape. The vagabond dreaming of journeying up to Canada through the lakes and the mountains[12] may well have been Hawthorne himself, traveling through Connecticut in 1829 and meditating on journeys of even wider scope. This leaves 1833 and 1834. The summer of 1833 was the one he spent at Swampscott. On the other hand, 1834 was a year of great literary hopes, and he may well have tried to slip on his seven-league boots again in order to put the finishing touches to *The Story-Teller*. Quantitatively speaking, the 1832 expedition would not have furnished sufficient material for a work that leads us to presuppose a great variety of experiences at different times.[13]

The vagabond who turned his back on Salem and its sequestered life was still the same Oberon, concerned with seeking in nature and the world's bustle an image of his own self, as well as realities that would take him out of himself. The adolescent, freshly turned out of his university mold, asleep on the side of the road;[14] the young Canterbury Shaker,[15] returning to the world with his sweetheart; the wandering bard escaping from his family;[16] the pilgrim storyteller dreaming of being the American Homer:[17] were all different aspects of the same vagabond. And the traveler asleep by the spring was continuing Oberon's dream; the Shaker running away with his pretty Miriam drank from the spring of his origins before resuming his way;[18] and the storyteller, deep in his Bible by the brink of the welling water, looked down at the stranger in black who resembled him like a brother.[19] Thus it was that the vagabond, retreating from the glaring sunlight, from the dust and the tumult, turning aside into the shade of the woods, rediscovered his other self in the wellspring of his being. In reality they were both one: like Oberon in his solitude, the vagabond on the road was always double, and the journey—a manifestation of the spirit of enterprise as well as of the imagination—always remained one of the great themes of Oberon's musings. Whereas the one went out in search of bustling highways, of populous cities, of democratic companionship and cosmopolitan crowds, the other was always drawing him back to untamed nature, to lonely vistas, to ruins. And what enchanted Oberon could also exert its seduction over his companion at the same time, and, inversely, what amused the vagabond also diverted the poet. They were companions and accomplices, and from this double vision they shared, from their perpetual dialogue, there sprang a particular way of understanding both the concrete and the intangible, a multiple, realistic, and poetic interpretation of things.

Hawthorne the vagabond would have liked to see everything; but it was always Oberon who laid down the itinerary in depth and led him, willy-nilly, toward the spots that haunted him. There were several escape routes out toward the hills and lakes. But the most tempting of all was the one through the White Mountains, for it passed through Raymond, the site of his happy adolescence, and then plunged into the most fragmented section of the Appalachian range before continuing on toward the Canadian border. The road drove into the foothills along the Saco River. The mountains, a closed, compact, natural tract broken up into tiny parcelled-off worlds, bore a strange resemblance to the soul of their visitor, which they moved to ecstasy with a perpetual revelation of multiple dimensions. Being an indefatigable walker, Hawthorne probably did this part of the journey on foot[20] in order to feel himself more at one with nature. The pass through the White Mountains was for him the strait gate that enabled him to enter the secret world,[21] made in the image of his own awareness, where horror and beauty lay asleep.[22] The height of the peaks, their names,[23] and their shapes spoke to his soul; he was in an enchanted, allegorical world where great faces of stone reared their stern profiles above secluded lakes.[24] It was nature's task to answer the poet's expectations and confirm his inner vision. The cave of the Regicide Judges at West Rock was inadequate: there was not even room to bury a dead cat in it.[25] Hawthorne felt the need for natural caves worthy of men's own depths and curiosity.

Hawthorne, being a solitary traveller, enjoyed finding himself in the evening one of a circle of guests around an inn fire, a familiar and magical circle providing a charm against the darkness, against the cold, against solitude. His sleep was cradled in that night's valley, protected by ramparts or threatened by overhanging precipices.[26] During these evening hours around inn fires he may have heard many stories of avalanches, of Indian raids,[27] of various legends. Perhaps he sometimes improvised a story himself, if he found himself among simple people—he was mistrustful of city folk—and if there was a reasonably pretty girl among their number. But the vocation of itinerant storyteller was no more than a whim with him. The vagabond almost always spoke louder within him than the storyteller or the seducer.

As he left the mountains once more, the highway and the steamboat routes led him back down to the plains and the cosmopolitan cities there. After living among ravines and torrents, he felt that he was coming down to the sea again when he saw Lake Champlain[28] in the violet half-light of the setting sun: there, the New World was still the insubstantial image of a promised land. This district, which was where the war against the French had largely been fought, is still a mine of documentary information for the historian,[29] and it is still easy, when visiting Burlington, Montreal, and the old Fort of Ticonderoga,[30] to find material for dreams and to conjure up uniformed tableaux and processions from that embattled past.

The teeming cities around the Great Lakes, where Yankees, English, Indians, French Canadians, Irish, Scots, Italians, Swiss, and Poles live crowded cheek by jowl, that vast frontier fairground they still form might well be the chosen territory for a wandering bard of today. In Rochester,[31] then a mushrooming town created by the Canal, a Vanity Fair in which lotteries made and unmade fortunes daily, the teeming crowds of visiting trappers, of fur dealers, of tattooed savages, of speculators, would have been a Barnum's dream public.[32] Hawthorne, in the very depths of his nature, felt a repugnance for histrionics. But though he would have been ashamed to appear as a showman or performer himself, the role of spectator fitted him like a glove. Any spectacle, any eye-catching motion, any show of vitality awakened an echo in him. Everything was of interest to him: the garish colors, the shouts, the general clangor, the overblown gesticulations, the drum rolls, the blaring processions, the military parades, the dogfights, the tavern choruses, the daredevil acrobats, the diorama exhibitors,[33] outbreaks of fire at night, or the arrival of a Democrat general. And if there had still been executions for witchcraft, then he would have gone to those too, just because he loved to stand and stare. Which is also the reason he never grew tired of traveling. Yet there always also existed, alongside the active spectator within him, the lover of sensations, the passive spectator. His attitude oscillated continually between participation and contemplation. Those slow canalboat journeys[34] drew the images past his eyes in tranquillizing cadences: bargemen and their families on their slow-moving houses, a black boat drawn by three Indians, a joyful boatload of Swiss immigrants, the unhealthy face of a housewife at the window of a house, a brief comic interlude—the absent-minded schoolmaster cracking his forehead against the low arch of a bridge.[35] How is one to photograph a face personifying poverty[36] through the windshield of a Ford or Pontiac moving at sixty miles an hour? But Hawthorne, because of the methods of communication of his age, was still an eighteenth-century traveler. The rhythm at which he recorded images was still the same as that at which Johnson, Fielding, and Sterne recorded them. But his vision was already a cinematographic one: not a speeded-up vision, of which the railroad was to provide him with a concrete image, but the slow motion that rocks the nomad in his wagon.

Hawthorne the traveler reveals himself in his true duality when faced with Niagara. The falls had already been a symbol in his mind for a long while. A Niagara disfigured by industry could only be loathsome in his eyes. While Oberon is[37] deploring the presence of rude men in such a sublime place, the vagabond dallies a while to watch the Canadians bargaining with the ferryman for his contraband liquor, even though the falls are thundering there above his head, even though Oberon is growing impatient—even though he is the very first to try to conceal his enthusiasms, flirtatiously delaying the moment at which he finally presents himself, all dressed up, in front of the great falls.[38] Here, we are seeing a literary dandy personality, an offshoot of Oberon, embracing and containing the double personality of Hawthorne the traveler. Yet the artist, who is also Oberon's offspring, in the profoundest sense, and the wanderer, is in no way involved in these poses: he moves about, searching out all the various viewpoints, absorbing the landscape with each and every sense. Like Chateaubriand, he wants to look up at the falls from their base; he has a solid series of steps at his disposal, whereas Chateaubriand, of necessity, had to use a clumsy ladder of vines. But in order to receive the baptism of the falls one must be in a state of grace. It was through his ears, at dead of night, that Oberon was finally able to communicate with Niagara. Everything that connected the spectacle to the present destroyed the ideal relation: the sublime exists only in the absolute.

Where Chateaubriand saw himself lost in his wonder, Hawthorne forgot himself in the object of his contemplation. His vision was less theatrical and more penetrating. And if the demon of romanticism did come by chance to tempt him, then the mocking vagabond sent it packing with a jest.[39]

Having seen Niagara, Hawthorne would have liked to continue his journey on into the Far West.[40] The wanderer in him was never satisfied. His peregrinations through New England and the Great Lakes region had already covered a territory more than half the size of France. These journeys of escape in young manhood prefigure the longer journeys of his maturity, but if Hawthorne had been able to visit England and Italy at the time of his "Niagara" period his work would doubtless have been very differently affected, enriched and modified by a greater diversity of experiences, a greater multiplicity of comparisons. In that case, instead of the Hawthorne we know we should have had another James. Speculation to one side, however, the fact is that his European experience, coming after the great creative period, at the period of his domestic troubles, occurred too late in the day. The only map that Hawthorne was to read clearly with his instinct and his intuition was that of his early escapades from Raymond and of the vagabond's later travels, with its network of streams, its spreading lines of beaten earth roads and secret paths, the labyrinth of its forests and valleys, its caves, its lakes, its mountains, its towns, like the allegorical map that Bunyan had once used to work out the theme of Christian's pilgrimage. All the itineraries of the writer's inner labyrinth are represented on this map, sometimes deep in shade, sometimes flooded with light: he had only to walk into its landscape and he was already following Endicott, Hester, or Dimmesdale through its byways, so closely had his summer journeys intertwined with the dreams and tales of childhood to form the secret background fabric of his work.

IV. THE LABYRINTH

Hawthorne explored a world into which he projected his own memories and private preoccupations as he went along. His journeys took on the colors of his own consciousness. And the consciousness of the vagabond poet was always accompanied by an unquiet conscience. He may have believed himself free—but was he really so? He was pursued by disguised emissaries of the old Puritans, by austere representatives of his family tradition and society. The storyteller meets the minister on his journey,[1] an embodiment of conformist morality. He is also afflicted by a repressive guardian, the Reverend Thumpcushion.[2] Wherever he goes, the young nonconformist is only out on parole. Even though his intent in escaping from the maze of customs he had been brought up in was not to seek out new ways of being and thinking, but simply to see what there is hidden beneath appearances, he was none the less a traitor to society, for he was refusing to play the game. He had therefore forfeited all his rights, his identity, indeed all reality, and even in his own eyes. An exile among the "Calibans," with their deeply imbued principles, he belonged to no recognized category. A writer's work appeared so little like work to the eyes of the Salemites! The artist, for those pious utilitarians and industrious sermonizers, was a man of very little weight either in this world or the next, one with no grasp either on the real or the spiritual sphere, and one who, since he produced no measurable commodity, had no claim to any share of worldly goods—apart from a mouthful of bread and a glass of water[3]—and still less of one to heavenly rewards, since he must without any doubt be of "the Devil's party."[4] But Hawthorne was no utopian. He did not expect a ready-made society that would accept him without conditions and erect statues to him in his own lifetime. All he asked was to have his own place in society as it was, the right to fulfill his function as an artist among the people he was depicting, and who—they and their forefathers—were necessary to him just as they were or just as the painter saw them, not as they believed themselves to be—hence the misunderstanding. That was his place, his "true place" in the world.[5] And he was no more able to achieve it in Boston than he had been in Salem. Boston, to which he moved in 1836, and which was for him the great city, the labyrinth in which young Robin was lost, through which his relation Major Molineux,[6] covered in tar and feathers, paraded his disgrace one rioting night, the former capital of the province in which the Governor's Palace still stood,[7] the Babylon of New England where the grandson of Puritans did not scorn to drink his wine and smoke cigars,[8] was no more than a vast and rather ugly conurbation in which he worked himself to death editing the *American Magazine* and a *Universal History*.[9] The publisher, Goodrich, who had for years been feeding the best of Hawthorne's work into the *Token* at very low rates, seemed to have no intention of ever paying him. Hawthorne finally quarrelled with him, and commented "that this world is as full of rogues as Beelzebub [one of his cats] is of fleas."[10] A cleverer man would probably have got more out of Goodrich. Hawthorne, with his distrustful, sarcastic air,[11] managed to be a thorn in his side, but whether held back by modesty or pride could never bring himself either to demand his due or break the yoke altogether. Instead, he withdrew into saturnine stoicism and little by little adopted an attitude of failure. There is no lack of examples of men of value with touchy characters who have managed to get themselves treated as undergraduates in this way by clever and important men, not to mention women.

Aside from his literary disappointments, Hawthorne was also feeling sexually deprived. He was thirty-three, and neither fame nor love had come his way. It may have been true that he was more handsome than Lord Byron,[12] but what can a young man tormented by scruples do, even when he is loved? The Swampscott "mermaid" may well have given herself to him only in her literary form.[13] And Hawthorne's Don Juanism consisted more in enjoying the promise of love than in love itself: a smile exchanged with a beautiful, unknown, white-armed woman on the canal, an idyll mapped out in the mind, feelings never disclosed. One significant trait: when he depicts himself in the persona of Oberon in amorously inclined company he is always with several young girls[14]—sometimes indeed he merely admires them from a distance[15]—whereas the vagabond prefers to address himself to a single female,[16] even though he does not follow up his advantage. This is partly a question of literary fashion, which then forbade both undress and any sexual realism, but also a behavioral revelation. The provocations of a fairly pretty and whimsical little devil, an eighteen-year-old brunette[17] left him quite cold, even embarrassed him perhaps. Having realized that he was falling in love with Mary, his landlady's daughter in Thomaston,[18] and sensing that she loved him too, he saw to it that they separated, very melancholy and solemn.[19] The whole of Hawthorne is to be seen there. The two personalities of his youth, and of his whole life, enter into opposition as soon as he is under pressure to move outside of himself. The vagabond makes the first steps, but Oberon quickly turns tail and then beats a retreat. This is why he could not experience "a young man's bliss," the possession of the beloved.[20] The role of Paris, awarding the golden apple to the most beautiful competitor, was very much to his taste.[21] But completing his conquests filled him with fear. Hence the quest for compromise. The storyteller takes a sensual pleasure in the emotion stirred up by his words in his female listeners: to find "the well-spring of their tears"[22] is also to find the path to their hearts. He took pleasure in this atmosphere of veiled sensuality in which talent often elects to show itself. And the pleasure he experienced in the midst of such a swarm of listeners, flattering him and mocking him at the same time—whether in reality or in imagination—is strangely ambiguous. His sensibility was an extremely complex system. And this very complexity was able to make him believe in the insensitivity of which he sometimes accused himself.[23] Mistrusting his own emotions as he did, he always retreated back into his inner self: out of a vain concern for an illusory purity, the purity of a void, his Puritan narcissism laid an embargo on all impulses from the heart. And so, caught in this trap of purity, he considered himself as much a criminal because of his insensitivity as because of his sensuality. And though we do find him sometimes treating his memories of past love with cruel humor, as in the case of the sugar heart, a gift from the "mermaid," which he deliberately crunched up before a witness,[24] his cruelty was exercised above all against himself. Being incapable of accepting the joys of love without uneasiness or remorse, he felt a need to punish himself for having loved, as well as to invent diabolical female figures to justify his renunciation—and perhaps to secure a pardon for himself by becoming their victim. Hawthorne had within him a Holofernes in search of a Judith.[25] He was very near giving way to this tendency when he met Mary Silsbee.[26] Abused by lying confidences, he provoked his friend O'Sullivan to a duel, whereupon the latter revealed the "Ophidian Armida"[27] to him at last in her true colors. Arming himself with a willed scorn for this Lady Eleanore,[28] he managed to repress a passion that was threatening to destroy him, and with him his work. He was obliged to learn how to make use of these fascinations that suddenly seized him in order to master the dark forces that had made him a creator. Studying the passions with an unmoved heart, however, is hardly the usual way to achieve strong descriptions of them, and such detachment led to the rejection of humanity symbolically expressed in "David Swann." The philter of solitude is as pernicious as Armida's own: the result was an Oberon bewitched in another manner, languishing by the wayside on life's road,[29] a victim both of his own concern for purity and of his fear of becoming calloused by constant contact with the multitude[30]—a fear in complete contradiction with the democratic tastes of the vagabond and those tendencies of his imagination which, though they led him away from the beaten tracks of life, did not in fact make him avoid reality. Urged on by his curiosity, by his thirst for knowledge, by his need for secrecy, he took pleasure in losing himself, in merely marveling, without a thought at first about his loneliness; he pursued experience from discovery to discovery, and when he wanted to retrace his steps, it was too late. The undergrowth had grown up behind him and become trees, the paths were grown over, there was no way out any more.[31] He no longer had any guides to follow, except for the light of the dream he was pursuing, which led him continually back to the heart of the labyrinth in which he was lost, like Goodman Brown in the forest: his own prisoner, locked in a dungeon and unable to find the key that would free him from it. Even if the door had in fact been open, he tells us himself, he would have been afraid of venturing outside.[32] His own cry was that he had never in fact lived, but only dreamed his life.[33]

And perhaps he was still only dreaming when he thought he was creating: that was the tragedy in the labyrinth. In reality, there were several labyrinths, one superimposed upon another, interlocking to form an inextricable complexity: the maze of the virgin forest, of illicit excursions; that of his adventures behind the picaresque events and the scenery of the highway; that of his incoherent gropings, his baffled desires, his contradictory approaches, all occurring in counterpoint with his journeys along the traditional and reputedly normal routes. The irreplaceable richness of a singular personality. A poverty-stricken richness though, since it was both a perpetual torment and prized only by himself. His sensibility, so fertile in surprises, disconcerted others; his intelligence worked by caprice, and seemed alien both by its nature and its detachment. It was more and more as a stranger that he returned to his retreat, to Salem, the inevitable center of the world,[34] to his obscurity, to his uselessness. Despite all his efforts to rid himself of his consciousness of failure, he still always found himself in the situation of the pariah, of the accused. His summer escapes merely increased the extent of the labyrinth whose central dungeon, with its bolts and invisible bars,[35] was his own self.

The summer of 1836 was spent in editing the *American Magazine*.

Perhaps for the first time, he was unable to take a vacation. He continued work until September on the enormous compilations that were to make Goodrich's fortune without bringing any profit to himself. *The Story-Teller* the year before had been a failure. Lacking the money to attempt a second edition, feeling himself to be "the obscurest man of letters in America,"[36] it seemed to him that all he could do now was to burn all he had ever written and choose another profession. It was during October of this year that Bridge received a letter from Hawthorne couched in a tone of "detached despair." "I fear," Bridge replied, "that you are too good a subject for suicide, and that some day you will end your mortal woes on your own responsibility."[37] He then urged Hawthorne to come and join him in Boston. For at the time when he wrote those words Bridge was already in correspondence with Goodrich, without Hawthorne's knowledge, over the publication of *Twice-Told Tales*.

Oberon always had need of intermediaries. During the course of his journeys, the vagabond with his worldly wisdom always knew how much a horse should cost, always knew the latest news, could talk horses with coachmen, shop with a tradesman, theater with an actor, and was therefore able to serve the poet as guide and steward. So that Oberon, who held the keys to the hidden spheres, could sail under the flag of the vagabond, who likewise possessed the open-sesame to certain social spheres. But just as the first was Hawthorne's communicating, joyful consciousness, so the second was his unhappy consciousness, a consciousness he would have been glad to disown. Consequently he tried to make fun of it, to take his revenge on it, or to boast about it.[38] But it was all labor lost. Oberon never ceased to accompany him. If the student in black went before the storyteller to the spring, that was because he was its guardian: he had already drunk from it, had been the first to drink from it, so that he was at once enriched and appalled by the secret he now possessed, and the Bible whose pages he sat turning was a symbol of his knowledge, an alchemical symbol wrenched up from the strange and anguished depths he had discovered, not knowing now whether he should turn back from them or plunge further in. But, once left to rely solely on his own strength, there was soon nothing left for Oberon to do but burn his books.[39] Broken and sick, he returned to the society that he had betrayed in his quest for truth, confessed his heresy, and was at last reconciled in death:[40] a respectable form of suicide. Such was "Oberon's Progress." Happily, however, Bridge's providential intervention, by opening a window for his friend onto the world and by restoring him once and for all to himself and his work, spared Hawthorne the necessity of playing out the fictional destiny of his ill-starred self in reality, or of resorting to any such extreme solution.

·3·

The Artist and His Evil Geniuses

I. CONTACT WITH THE WORLD: EARTHLY PARADISE

To the obscure author, success seems bound to present itself as a total change of environment, a renewal of the world and the self, the birth of an ideal relation between the soul and reality, the advent of true harmony in the world, the solution of all problems, an assurance of continuity for the creative afflatus. But once the intoxication of this first contact with celebrity had passed, Hawthorne was obliged, for all his ambition, to recognize the modest proportions of his book's success. The voice calling out to him was not the thunder of a triumphal entry but "a still small voice,"[1] and having answered that summons, he had found nothing in the world that was preferable to his former solitude,[2] nothing of such a nature that it could change his financial situation or his attitude to life. On his own confession, he could not continue for very long in his circumstances as they were then.[3] The horizon had cleared, but this only meant that he could perceive the restrictions of his world the better. The only conclusion he had been able to come to was that his situation was still one of waiting, and that he was doomed to perpetual half success. This prospect filled him with exasperation in advance. Where was the fame that was to enable him to find his new

47

being at last, that of the triumphant poet crowned by a unanimous people? Once more his Oberon double was to serve as a scapegoat. It is as though he had only been waiting for the moment of his emergence from obscurity in order to begin complaining more bitterly than ever, not only in his letters but later in his prefaces too,[4] of his lack of contact with reality. His disappointment caused him to neglect and despise the singular and secret aspects of his individual experience and to see only the nocturnal and negative side of that labyrinth. Everything positive and luminous now appeared in his eyes to be entirely on the side of ordinary existence. Everyday reality became an inaccessible ideal:[5] there was a sort of breakdown in his psychological contacts. He had no idea himself how wise this division of his time between reality and his work was. To live like everybody else was of no use to him, except during holiday periods, when he acted as an intermediary, but above all as a spectator, of other people's activities. And the summer of 1837 was to be particularly fertile in a variety of experiences. In Augusta, he watched the Irish laborers at work on the dam his friend Bridge was building, rubbed shoulders with the immigrants' homely, foulmouthed wives, exchanged ideas with a young and cultivated Frenchman,[6] examined the territory bordering the river with a surveyor's eye, and made sociological observations on the laborers' living quarters, their poverty, and the numbers of their offspring. He was astonished that Bridge could threaten several families with the demolition of their cabins simply for having stolen a few fence posts:[7] he too would have liked to be rich, but he did not feel that he had a landowner's soul. With Cilley, at Portsmouth naval base, he mingled with the officers, visited the ships, and talked politics. He no longer thought about literature at all. He was rediscovering the masculine complicity he had known earlier as an adolescent at college, though among mature men and charged with a greater significance, which was now to encourage him in a more virile attitude with regard to women, at least on a literary level: for the notebooks of this period, so fertile in amorous emotions, teem with entries of a sensual kind. It was the period of his idyll with Mary Trott. Just as Hawthorne became more discreet, more elegiac, more and more the secretive Oberon when he was in love, so he became more capable of frankness, joviality, and Fielding-like comment when he was not—so much so that he reacted to the loose behavior of an adulterous slut as though he saw it as farcical rather than tragic.[8] Sensuality vies with realism in his portrait of Mrs. Harriman with her pale skin, her swelling breasts, full of milk for a little brat of a three- or four-month-old girl,[9] in the picturesque simplicity of his depiction of a young giantess with a virginal air,[10] and in the poetry of his image of a young madwoman who seemed to him like a statue of melancholy and beauty.[11]

There were two types of women that interested him particularly: one pleasure-loving and haughty, the other witty and high-spirited. The oriental charms, the queenly carriage of Elizabeth Gibbs[12] fascinated him more than he himself judged seemly, and the bewitching tactics of the little "demons" whose teasing he so much enjoyed might well have been able to subjugate him completely if he had not had his memories of those other demons in the city, dressed in scarlet.[13] What disturbed him even more was that the Esthers, the Cleopatras,[14] clothed in all the seductions of the flesh, had the same stature, the same eyes, the same glamor as his mother, so that the haven of tenderness was also a trap baited with sensuality. Which was why Oberon fled from the very women whom he desired the most and who embodied his ideal. The blond angel type with an air of gentle authority, to whom he tended to subject himself in his imagination, in reality and on the sexual plane, had little attraction for him. Like the ethereal, languishing type it was an allegorical and literary image. Yet his distrust of the flesh, by making him shy away from sensual pleasure, was always pushing him toward such frigid angels. Before long, chance, love's powerful ally, was to spare him the embarrassment of this invidious choice.

The Hathorne house was originally separated from that of the Peabodys by no more than a garden. The children of the two families had played together at one time, then shortly afterwards lost sight of one another. It was not until 1837 that Elizabeth Peabody, by now imbued with the theories of the Transcendentalists but as ever a lion hunter, recognized in the author of *Twice-Told Tales* her erstwhile little neighbor with the curly locks, now the handsome and famous Nathaniel Hawthorne. The surprise must have been considerable, since in 1836 she was still under the impression that the author of these anonymous stories was an old Quaker who had renounced the prejudices of the sect. But as soon as she knew the truth she did not rest until the Hathornes had accepted her invitation and she had lured the "lion" of Salem from his lair.

And so, after repeated approaches on the one hand and much hesitation on the other, the Hawthornes finally appeared in the Peabody drawing rooms. But Elizabeth was swiftly obliged to give up any hope of winning Nathaniel's love. Having done so, she seems to have then made it her task to interest him in her sister Sophia, who spent all her days up in her room like an invalid. How could he fail to perceive in this recluse the one woman in the world made to understand him, since he was himself the man who understood better than any other both the pains and joys of solitude? A perusal of Sophia's diary revealed to Hawthorne the delicate, slightly precious talent of a cultivated young girl whose life was apparently wholly confined to the soul. He might, upon reflection, have discerned a certain narrowness in this excessively transparent mind, and a certain self-esteem in such stubborn moral elevation. But if he found himself trembling in the face of this miraculous purity it was because he was already planning, perhaps with anticipations of delight, to yield himself up to such an angelic "liege-lady."[15] His curiosity, and the feeling of sharing a hidden world with the mysterious Sophia, finished the task of demolishing his inner barriers. He felt that she inhabited a world similar to his own; a little kindly help from his imagination, and there she was, as at home as though she had always lived there, had always had the key to it, in the heart of his own secret domain. And he even believed he held the key to her world as well. All of which excited him even more over the game.

One evening (we are in the spring of 1838)[16] Sophia came down into the drawing room wearing a white dressing gown. Hawthorne rose to his feet and fixed her with an intense gaze, how intense he himself did not even realize.[17] The introductions over, conversation was resumed, and every time Sophia made a remark in her gentle, quiet voice, he stared at her with a piercing gaze that took in the whole of her being: she had the gray eyes of his beloved mother,[18] the same frail lines as the "mermaid," the pallor and voice of an angel. It seemed to him that he himself had conjured her up in his own inner sphere, where her voice awakened disturbing echoes. She completed his universe, completed the man himself, was an answer to all his contradictory desires. As an angel, she required his subjection, as an invalid she required his protection. For Sophia, despite her Victorian reticence, was conquered. Hawthorne had found what he wanted most, perhaps, in life: to be loved meant to exist in someone else's eyes and for someone else, to exist at last truly, thanks to love, thanks to its joys and the obligations it creates. There had been a time when he believed he had imagined everything,[19] and now he found himself face to face with the heart's realities where before there had been only fantasies, simulacra, repressed caprices. Mystery and surprise had stirred him to wonderment: for the first time, he gave himself wholly. Once invited to enter his secret world, Sophia would be able to play the role of Ariadne and guide him back out of his labyrinth, wrest him free from his solitude, perhaps in order to draw him into her own world, peopled with Transcendentalist myths. That would be an outcome not without its danger, since the realm of love is also Circe's palace,[20] where the lover runs the risk of finding himself distressingly metamorphosed—in this case into a proselyte of the misty theories made fun of in "The Hall of Fantasy,"[21] and it is also the dwelling place of the angel who demands that man shall plight his troth to the mirage of purity. Sophia was the feminine link connecting these two allegorical extremes. Thanks to her, Hawthorne was to discover that a human being—a woman—cannot be reduced to the idea that a man—a Puritan—conceives of her, and that purity can exist also in a carnal union. To conceive of flesh without sin is to rediscover innocence. It seemed as though Hawthorne was at last trying to shake off the yoke of that "tacit law,"[22] imposed upon his family by their curse, which had hitherto constrained him to bottle up his feelings and renounce all attempts to fight free of his inner self.[23] It seemed as though he was trying to banish all obsession with "crime and punishment"[24] from his mind so that he could yield at last to an imperious need for happiness.

Obstacles appeared, however. Apart from his mother's silences, there were complications created by Elizabeth Peabody, who had not in fact given up the idea of marrying Hawthorne herself.[25] She was using her sister, whom she supposed incapable of ever marrying on account of her incurable infirmity,[26] as a bait to keep the writer by her side, and she was also counting on his gratitude for all the work she was doing on his behalf in Boston literary circles. Hawthorne, caught in the toils of a veritable Cousine Bette, saw his secret engagement being prolonged indefinitely: Sophia was to have much more difficulty overcoming her sister's resistance than Phoebe her cousin Hepzibah's.[27] Hawthorne's excursion in 1838 therefore has very much the appearance of a flight intended to avoid any violent outbreak of feeling, and of a period of delay that would enable him to think things over a long way from his former acquaintances.[28] There may also have been an element of coquetry in this disappearance, for Hawthorne always took a malicious pleasure in extracting the subtlest possible nuances from his sensibility. When he came to say goodbye to Sophia, looking radiant we are told, he announced that he was not going to give anyone his address and that he was thinking of changing his name, so that if he should happen to die no one would ever find his grave.[29] This may have been a joke, but one cannot help reflecting that it came from the mouth of the man who wrote "Wakefield" and who was to go away to die, twenty-five years later, far from all his family. In reality, he was giving himself a respite, standing back from things for a while in order to contemplate his new found happiness the better.

When he left Salem, Hawthorne was leaving behind him not only those he loved but also his disappointments and his griefs. The idyll with Sophia had not been wholly unclouded; there had been Cilley's death[30] and Bridge's ruin[31] as well. It was the Oberon of the black days who plunged into the Green Mountains, not the carefree vagabond.

The steep-sided valley from Pittsfield to North Adams was scattered with various kinds of factories and mills, where the working girls were chained all day long to their tasks. Across the mountain torrents, dams; in the cliffs, marble quarries. In all the places where the Indians had fished and hunted there were now the hideous scars of the white man's work. Despite himself, Hawthorne became interested in these first symptoms of our industrial leprosy: he found a sort of picturesqueness in these "artificial establishments . . . set in the midst of wild nature."[32] The remark is still an artist's, but it does betray another concern all the same: that of utility. Similarly, this solitary walker was also, in his own way, both a geologist and a speleologist before his time: when he wanted to explore a cave, he had no hesitation in stripping his clothes off and swimming into it.[33] While at North Adams, he became interested in the lawyer Haynes's soap factory, in the manufacture of lime in the big, twenty-foot high, round kilns,[34] and above all in the fiery spectacle the place presented at night, the vigil around a sort of domesticated volcano. The Hawthorne we encounter here is once more the man who loves crowds: markets, countrymen meeting to vote on the building of a road, funerals—the awful sound of the earth on the coffin—circus performances. The diorama man was his great favorite: his hairy brown hand, disproportionately magnified by the diorama, was that of Destiny freezing the scenes of history in their tracks.[35] This aged German, forever traveling to and fro across America, was in fact the Wandering Jew. But it was above all the lantern itself, and its power to isolate and magnify particular and revealing details, that fascinated the artist. In the same way, his eye (which according to the one-armed Haynes was that of a hawk)[36] could pierce to the depths of consciousness, magnifying even the minutest stains. Can such a judge's gaze truly express tenderness? One doubts it sometimes. As for instance when he prophesies, so impassively and scientifically, the probable career of little Joe, from tavern to poorhouse by way of the jail.[37] Is this lack of sympathy due to a cruel, imaginative self-indulgence or to a defense mechanism? Haynes's horrible wounds, sustained in an accident at work and leading to amputation of one arm, the hundreds of girls working like hopeless Danaides in the factories, the obsessive presence of machines and engines, everything in the place contributed to his vision of the machine as a monster endowed with an evil spirit. Coldly, he describes a nightmare steam engine that tears off arms and legs and heads, that seizes a girl by her hair and scalps her, then finally snatches up a man and crushes him.[38] He keeps the horror he feels inside himself, and his hardness of manner is often the result of a shock to his sensibility. What good can tender, gentle poets really be in this world? Their tears are useless. "Tender lover or tough love," which is preferable, he asks himself?[39]

Back in Salem again, Hawthorne became concerned with finding himself a job of some sort. He was tired of being a mere ornament, he says. To have a plot of ground that was completely his, big enough to turn around on and to be buried in,[40] such, if we are to believe him, was his present ambition. Does this mean that he was ready to renounce his art in order "to gather gold, and till the earth, and set out trees, and build a house"?[41] He wanted to have something to do in the material world, he said.[42] His desire to start a home was making him more inclined than ever to idealize everyday life. Thanks to the influence of Elizabeth Peabody, who knew how to include politicians among her trumps,[43] in January of 1839 Hawthorne was appointed inspector of salt and coal cargoes in the Boston Custom House. His incautious desire had become reality. Nevertheless, with a novice's enthusiasm he shared his pride with Sophia: at last he had his burden to carry like other men, he had the right to count the "sons of toil" among his brothers.[44] He believed he had discovered the secret of emotional stability in physical fatigue,[45] and that it was sweat, rather than thought, which entitled one to claim the rights of a man among men. So that now, as well as the Puritan censor, Oberon had another companion in the "realist" who despised the futility of art, in the utilitarian Aminadab,[46] the Caliban who secretly countermines the work of the alchemist of the word, the earth-spirit in league with the spirit of doubt and discouragement as well as with social appearances and with the myth of purity—all of them conspiring to paralyze him.

Hawthorne had never been so obsessed by purity as he was now: on his own admission, he could not even open a letter from his beloved without first having washed his hands;[47] reading it surrounded by other people would have been sacrilege in his eyes.[48] He took pleasure in imagining Sophia as a pure spirit who had deigned to become flesh out of love for him.[49] If the tales written at this period lack passion,[50] it is because he was putting all his fire into his letters, which were not entirely free at times of the hyperbolic jargon then used to express noble sentiments.[51] This obsession with purity was also confused in Hawthorne with an organic need for fresh air. One April day, the wind brought him the "effervescent" freshness of the sea. This breeze, not breathed in advance by a hundred thousand pairs of lungs,[52] was for him yet another emanation from the heavenly "dove," existing as he did in clouds of anthracite dust and among sweating dockers. In a letter to her, he tells her of the certainty he had reached of Christian's burden having been coal.[53] Before long, the Custom House was nothing in his eyes but one of those "dark dungeons"[54] in which monsters and giants keep men in gloomy servitude.[55]

On January 1, 1841, he handed in his resignation. This was precisely the period at which Transcendentalism was beginning to be the intellectual rage of Boston.[56] The entire Peabody family was infatuated with Emerson. For Sophia, he was a demigod, the greatest genius who had ever lived—and the most complete.[57] Hawthorne had veered from Charybdis into Scylla: scarcely liberated from the "dungeon" of the Custom House he was already being drawn into the dark cave of the Transcendentalist oracles. The Peabody library was the receiving agency for subscriptions to the loan launched by Ripley for his phalanstery, Brook Farm, and the Peabody drawing room was the classroom, the Transcendentalist seminary where adepts of the new doctrine were initiated into German. Hawthorne allowed himself to be pressed into these ranks for a while. But he had no more real talent for languages than he had for music, and he preferred to continue his cultural education alone and in his own way. In April, he decided to join the Brook Farm community.[58] He hoped to be able to find some means of subsistence at West Roxbury and to set up a home there with Sophia. He also entertained the illusion that farm work would prove propitious to meditation. This pastoral idyll at Brook Farm began for Hawthorne with a blizzard and a bad attack of influenza, but once his health and the fine weather had returned he set enthusiastically to work, though without taking any part in the intellectual activities of the educational part of the Institute[59] whereby members could become acquainted with the philosophies of Kant and Spinoza, the poetry of Dante, or the music of Beethoven and Mozart.[60] He wrote to Sophia describing his exploits as a tyro farmer, how he milked his cows with fear and trembling,[61] chopped wood, smashed the hay-chopping machine with righteous vehemence,[62] and worked in the "gold mine"[63] by which he meant the dungheap. There were also endless jokes about Margaret Fuller's "transcendental heifer,"[64] which were his facetious way of getting back at her rampant feminism. Brook Farm was a wonderful field for observation: an entire fauna of reformers, utopians, and charlatans was represented there. There were the dreamers, the doctrinaires, the profiteers, and the con men.[65] There were the pseudo-ministers, the pseudo-writers, the spies, the agitators. The "pastoral" side of the venture was still being maintained: Margaret Fuller herself was still determinedly playing the shepherdess. For Emerson, Brook Farm was never to be anything more than a fancy-dress picnic in which he had been cast as the sage.[66] Hawthorne, on the other hand, was content to play a mere spectator,[67] which naturally rendered him somewhat suspect, especially since he was given to fraternizing with the neighboring farmers, who made no effort to restrain their sarcastic comments at the community's expense. He made enemies, not because he passed judgments, but simply because he would analyze other people's actions. He was unable to be an uncritical accomplice, to help maintain the community's illusions; he remained detached, and was therefore looked upon as a turncoat. Before long, the air of "Blithedale"[68] seemed to him quite unbreathable, and it was a great relief to him when he finally left Brook Farm and found himself free once more to enjoy nature on his own—free once more to think and feel.[69] His curses were laid above all upon forced labor, which he now thought of as a scourge upon the world.[70] Willy-nilly, he was now forced to admit that the artist too is a specialized worker, that his work requires his entire being and energies, despite the fact that it also necessitates a deep and extensive experience of the human condition. But in art, experience must never become a substitute for the work itself.

Meanwhile, Nathaniel and Sophia's love, reduced for so long to speaking the language of the angels, was now aspiring to speak the language of the flesh. The effusions in their letters had failed to appease the lovers' longings,[71] while making it fairly clear that their sensuality was merely seeking another way of exchanging caresses in these amorously mystical expressions—caresses as necessary for keeping love alive as leaves are to the life of the tree.[72] The experience that was to count most now was one of the affections and of the flesh: "Indeed, we are but shadows; we are not endowed with real life, and all that seems most real about us is but the thinnest substance of a dream —till the heart be touched. That touch creates us—then we begin to be—thereby we are beings of reality and inheritors of eternity."[73] It was not solely the "Eve without sin"[74] that Nathaniel loved in Sophia but also that other, the "naughty Sophie"[75] whose nature also had its demands.

Despite his repugnance for hypnotism, which seemed to him to be a violation of the human individual's "holy of holies,"[76] Hawthorne agreed, in the hope of hastening their marriage, to allow Sophia's migraines to be treated by magnetism—mesmerism and spiritualism were then at the height of their fashion—but he insisted that the session should be a short one and that it should not entail his fiancee's total spiritual abandonment, no matter how briefly, to the power of a stranger. For Hawthorne did in fact take this scientific form of witchcraft seriously. It frightened him, and the psychologist in him was envious of its practitioner's power to sound his patient's consciousness, while he was also jealous, as a man, of the intruder who could thus coldly appropriate the soul of his soulmate. This nightmare of psychic rape fascinated him and reawakened former esthetic projects still dormant within him.[77]

After their marriage on July 9, 1842, Nathaniel and Sophia went to live at Concord, in the Old Manse recently made available by the death of the Reverend Ezra Ripley. What a difference from the mock Eden of Brook Farm! In that beautiful garden, now left to run to seed, only a short period of daily labor would suffice to enable them to enjoy the fruits of the earth. For Nathaniel, true son of the Golden Age, much preferred the spontaneous gifts of Providence[78] to the rewards of toil. His whole being was enmeshed in a dream of Eden: the scent of the ripe fruit hanging in the light and sap-laden air, the dull thud of a great apple blown down by a gust of wind,[79] the sweetness of life, the contentment of loving, all these were its odors, its echoes, its image rediscovered in reality. Nathaniel and Sophia were the new Adam and Eve[80] of Concord's golden Indian summer, where the serpent seemed to have no place. Eden's first couple were regenerated in the newlyweds by the bright newness of their love. Even guilty love was henceforth to have its dignity, its "own consecration."[81] If love turns the earth into a paradise, must the earth not therefore be holy? As he continued to discover the reality of happiness, so Hawthorne began to wonder whether renunciation of earthly joys is not in fact the greatest of human follies.[82] To live, to enjoy life,[83] that, he now discovered, was his true vocation. Never, he claims, had they been as happy, never had they possessed such capacity for happiness.[84] And Sophia was his accomplice in creating this Edenic myth. Because of her feminine nature, it was she who was most profoundly affected by their amorous bliss: buds, flowers, running streams, everything spoke in her with the language of fecund nature.[85] And answering the woman's sparkling stream of joyous celebration there came the man's deeper and wider river of joy.[86] But, for him happiness was beginning to be a theme for meditation and deeper concern. He found now that there was more to tremble at in the aspect of felicity than in that of affliction, since the latter is terrestrial and finite, whereas the former is the very stuff and substance of eternity, so that even spirits still embodied in flesh are able to conceive its awfulness.[87] Happiness, Claudel says, is a strong prison:[88] but that is the woman's conception of it, not the man's. The man, preoccupied with the progress of his becoming, cannot give himself up to happiness for very long. And Hawthorne was such a man: his senses, his sensibility, urged him to enjoy the present, but an ever vigilant sense of inward unease forbade him to linger long in it. Imagination is credulous, the mind mistrustful: nothing can be had for free, everything has a reason, a price, and is part of some natural, divine, or diabolical plan. Such was the mechanism of the masculine, Puritan uneasiness that would have been destructive in its effects had the heart not been "touched," the soul not weighed down with new scruples founded upon human kindness.[89]

Three happy years went by in this way. It does one good to live as though this world were Paradise,[90] was Hawthorne's comment. But he also added that it is good to stand aside from one's happiness in order to contemplate it.[91] And though he complained of Sophia's absences,[92] he too felt the need to escape from time to time. Sometimes this meant a few days spent in Salem, sometimes long expeditions through the countryside—on occasion with Thoreau, who used to moor his boat at the bottom of their garden where it followed the line of the river. He took pleasure in feeling that he could always continue to choose between his former "twilit" life and the one he was leading at present. He was one of those who play at losing themselves with the knowledge that the way back remains always open. He often indulged himself in this way, on a physical level, during his walks. But alas, it was more difficult to attain true solitude at Walden and Sleepy Hollow than at Raymond. There was no time at which Hawthorne was forced to be so wary of the Transcendentalist threat: he had only to enter a glade inviting him to rest and meditation to discover it already occupied by Margaret Fuller, stretched out on the grass; whereupon he was obliged to undergo a formal repetition of that inexhaustible lady lecturer's "conversations."[93] Or else it would be Emerson, appearing round the turn of a path, a book in his hand, or the ebullient Ellery Channing suggesting a boating party. Even the very ravens seemed to be croaking propaganda for some doctrine or other.[94] The whole countryside was haunted. Moreover, the untouched nature he had once known was soon to be no more than a memory: the whistle of locomotives now pierced the very heart of the woods,[95] the discordant shriek of mechanical progress, archenemy of dreams. And what Hawthorne required of nature was precisely the serenity of the Sabbath,[96] a serenity capable of endowing collected thought with its own solemn rhythm. He loved Sunday as a day of rest, even though he never went with Sophia to church,[97] simply because it provided him with that same possibility of quiet recollection, that same solemnity so propitious for meditation. He also loved to relive his schoolboy escapades, which enabled him, despite the enslaving influence that man exercises upon man, to rediscover the freedom he had known as a child:[98] that oneiric feeling of independence one can enjoy by absenting oneself from the world and allowing oneself to drift outside the bounds of time. No earthly paradise without a holy leisure, without divine idleness—the felicity of the pumpkin in the sun[99] no longer tainted with the least unease. For unease, like conscious life, is intermittent, and sometimes gives way, though not without irony, to a careless joy; and then one can persuade oneself, like those antic worshippers at the maypole,[100] that the earth is Paradise in reality. Cradled by the heavenly stream—the torpid and muddy Concord—Hawthorne was storing up reserves of warmth, of joy, of images, of psychic energy.[101] But by lantern light, on a July night,[102] the river could also assume a hellish aspect, as when it was being dragged for the corpse of a young girl, a suicide drawn up from its bed on the end of long boathooks, her body swollen with its waters, her limbs stiff, her face puffed and bleeding. The men of the search party tried to keep her arms down along her body with their hands and feet, while the drowned girl "purged" herself through her nose. No languid Ophelia here! Yet that nightmare river glittered with such beautiful reflections as he rowed back on summer evenings toward his house, the fixed star that enabled him to set his course, or as his feet and thoughts wandered along its banks—that river, as sinuous as his own mind, was soon to be an object of regret, for he was to forced to leave Concord[103] before publishing the delicate and occasionally disturbing fantasies of *Mosses from an Old Manse*.

II. CONTACT WITH THE WORLD: THE PILLORY

In April of 1843, Hawthorne went to Salem on a pilgrimage to the "solitary chamber" and, apparently, to thumb his nose at Oberon, since he refers ironically to all the other pilgrims who will doubtless come to pay their tribute of veneration in that same room for centuries to come.[1] The new Adam, so sure of his triumph, nevertheless still carried within him the forebear he was mocking. And indeed, in October 1845 we find him back there, penniless, Sophia pregnant with their first child, Una, his only refuge the house on Herbert Street, and on the verge of the most Oberon-like discouragement. Once more it was necessary to use political influence to obtain the appointment as Customs Inspector that he took up late in August 1846.[2] Once again he took his new duties very much to heart. At first, being useful still seemed to him a happy change. But would he be able to resign himself, even in order to provide his family with a subsistence, to spending his entire life being no more than an efficient machine? He divided his time between the Custom House and the nursery.[3] Becoming a father, though it plucked hitherto unsounded chords in his being, also forced him to limit his ambitions and threatened to reduce him, like so many other men, to mediocrity. He adored his children, but he sometimes found them an encumbrance too, since he no longer had even a single room in which to be alone. While waiting for the day when he would have his own study, his favorite occupation was to take notes in the nursery, a new field of observation for him, and one lacking in neither the picturesque nor the unexpected. The little Una, an extremely highly strung child, was sometimes excessively affectionate, sometimes shockingly insensitive. She had fits during which she was like one possessed and suffered from tics, as though some monster had taken hold upon her spinal cord and brain[4] and was squeezing the flesh on her face. Her parents had absolutely no control over her. Her father simply observed her, completely helpless, but fascinated by this "elf" that seemed to be no human child.[5] His observations, which are those of a moral psychologist, are in strict contrast with the sentimentalism to be found in Sophia's letters.[6]

Hawthorne was over forty. He was poor and he was ashamed of it.[7] His talent had not been confirmed by a corresponding worldly success. Sophia did not complain, but she did leave him often, on various pretexts, in order to go and rest at her mother's. Was she perhaps one of those wives who prefer their childhood and maiden's memories to their homes?[8] During these absences, the husband found the loneliness in his house unbearable. At least once, he wrote telling her of his unhappiness at having to go to bed without her, and appealing to her to come back.[9] It was the cry of an abandoned lover, but also a cry of fear. Marriage had created a new habit in him: he counted on Sophia to drive away from his bedside the anxieties attendant upon a solitude that now possessed no positive virtues in his eyes, but had become a source of unhappiness and terror. But adversity and injustice were soon to produce a salutary stiffening of his attitude by confronting him with a fresh form of isolation, that of disgrace.

In the November presidential election, the Democrats were beaten by the Whigs, and on June 8, 1849, Hawthorne was relieved of his duties.[10] Confident in his own integrity, he protested. Whereupon the Whigs, loosing the full force of their fury against him, transformed the termination of his appointment into an ignominious dismissal. He was accused of corruption and political activities incompatible with his post; his pieces of literary criticism published in the *Salem Advertiser* were referred to as pamphlets; he was accused of having been seen making ill-advised demonstrations on the public highway during the torchlight procession celebrating Independence Day; he was crushed, in short, beneath a whole conglomeration of lies and absurdities that were only given weight by the authority of a minister, the Rev. C. W. Upham, "a smooth, smiling, oily man of God,"[11] and that of the mayor of Salem, Nathaniel Silsbee, father of the grudge-bearing Mary. All the mediocre minds of the district, those who were jealous of Hawthorne, those who hated him, and even some former friends, such as "that pitiable monster Connolly,"[12] rushed to join the pack. These were the tortuous minds that were to confirm the existence of certain monsters that had until then only writhed confusedly in the half-darkness, but which at this point took on clearer forms, threatening, deformed like the Serpent. From this mass of moral deformities there later emerged the grimacing features of Chillingworth.[13]

Despite all his efforts, Hawthorne did not succeed in achieving his reinstatement. He no longer had either credit or friends in the proper places. His name had never been so much on people's lips, it is true, but they spoke it only in order to mock and muddy it. Yet there was no danger of his being forgotten. His enemies were to be the first to read his next book: the ways of fame are sometimes full of strange quirks and twists. It was in fact Hawthorne's original intention to avenge himself by writing a biting satire, by choosing a victim, then pouring into his heart a little drop of venom that would make him writhe before the grins of the multitude:[14] the punishment of Hester in the pillory, which happened to be also his own. His concern over his mother's health, then her death on July 31, intervened, however, to prevent the immediate execution of this project. He had not expected to be overwhelmed when he entered the dying woman's bedroom, for the coldness of their relations had only increased over the years. Moreover she had never accorded Sophia more than a token acceptance. Yet he found himself forced to his knees at her bedside by his emotions; his eyes filled with tears that he tried in vain to restrain, and he burst into sobs. It was, he himself said, assuredly the darkest hour that it had ever been given him to live.[15]

During this period his resistance was being undermined by extreme expenditures of nervous energy, by his indignation, by violent grief, and by perpetual worry. He fell ill, and it was feared that he had contracted a brain fever.[16] This was perhaps the first shock wave heralding the premature deterioration in his health that was to follow. But for the moment, at the very point when his reason might have been expected to give way, this series of shocks seems to have had the effect of reawakening his creative energies. For it was this moment, seemingly the least favorable possible for such a thing, when he was without resources, surrounded by enemies, only just risen from his sickbed, that he chose to write his masterpiece. It is possible to wonder, taking a contrary view, whether circumstances had not in fact conspired to force him to write it. As for Sophia, she was apparently bearing up under adversity better than a man.[17] At a time when his grief and exhaustion reawakened in Hawthorne the need for a maternal presence, it was to her he instinctively turned in his search for the mother he had so recently lost. He felt a need, at this painful period of his life, to recreate for himself the myth of woman as a being at the same time protective, heroic, and tender-hearted.

It was not until his novel was finished that Hawthorne returned to the satirical work he was burning to write. His bile and anger had cooled off somewhat in the meantime. And with his mind recently delivered of a great work, he no longer felt the need to throw his entire resources into the attack. The end result was "The Custom House," his ironic introduction to *The Scarlet Letter*, in which the "venom" he had spoken of earlier is very much diluted, though still present in sufficient quantity to provoke a fresh wave of resentment against him. To make fun of highly-placed persons, to treat the stupidity of his fellow citizens with irony, to denigrate the town where he was born[18]— there could be no doubt that all this constituted the most heinous of all crimes. They would have preferred imprecations, or fury. He had not even done them the honor of complaining. As he wrote to Bridge, he felt only unlimited contempt for them all. He realized that his preamble to the novel had caused the biggest upheaval in Salem since the days of the witch hunts, and felt he would be lucky if he managed to escape from the place without being tarred and feathered. He added, however, that he would be glad if they did tar and feather him, since it would be such a novel distinction for a man of letters, and considering how incompetent his judges were in literary matters he would hold such a punishment to be a greater honor than a crown of laurels.[19]

The "martyr's crown"[20] did not sit ill on Oberon. And if we also add that the novel itself was taken as a confirmation of his reputation for immorality, it will be appreciated what his situation in Salem must inevitably have been from then on, spied upon by the descendants of former witch hunters, by the witches themselves—all those old hags who made scandal and gossip their daily diet—by sly schoolgirls stifling their giggles as they read his book,[21] and by all the pious church-goers and self-proclaimed defenders of morality. He was the criminal waiting to be lynched, the condemned man in his pillory, the heretic, and the witness. Every artist, be he a Bunyan or a Gide, has always within himself, as Baudelaire claims, the counterpart to his inverted vocation toward Satan, which is a vocation toward saintliness. He has two ways before him that will lead to that goal: the sacrifice of his art in the name of purity (the "Wisdom of a Louis Racine"), or the sacrifice of self in the cause of his art. Hawthorne did not feel himself worthy of either of these sacrifices. He was afraid that he possessed neither sufficient purity nor sufficient strength. Only a child, Ilbrahim, could have the one, only a woman, a mother, could have the other. But he himself, he felt, by choosing the path of art, had not only re-nounced the purity of the child through ambition but also succeeded in avoiding the burden of existence. He had been lulling himself with a double illusion however, for now he found himself an object of persecution without having "the right to be a martyr."[22] It was not a simple question of moral scruples: he was not merely a man wanting to be a saint yet too much afraid to smash the necessary idols; he was a tormented creator wishing to enrich his poet's fame with the dignity of the man who has suffered in his own person. To choose the one is usually to renounce the other. The result was that Oberon was to play the role that so attracted him, which he was not certain of being able to perform in reality, in imagination only. His esthetic sensibility was moved in sympathy with the martyr's tragic fate; the poet bore the saint, the hero within him—he created them, but he did not seek out their sufferings in reality. His sufferings were of another kind: Haw-thorne, like all poets, was a martyr to his own contradictions.

In April of 1850 Hawthorne left Salem, never to return. A few weeks later he arrived in Lenox, in the middle of the Berkshires.[23] Exhausted, drained by fever, he moved into the "red shanty"[24] that Sophia was to transform into a charming little home decorated with reproductions of old masters.[25] He was in no state to go back immediately to writing. Moreover the hot weather was no help. He devoted himself to the manual labor necessitated by the state of their house. He joined his children at their play, made Lilliputian boats,[26] windmills, and kites for them, took charge of their physical education, and transformed their expeditions through the countryside into a perpetual adventure, inventing myths and fables as they went along. Enchanted woods, mysterious echoes,[27] dragons, hydras, chimaeras, demons, and giants:[28] a perpetual contest of classical mythology with Bunyanesque allegory. The vagabond of those earlier summer expeditions began to revive, and with him the whole man's health and joy in living. The Berkshires were the vacation meeting place of many writers, artists, actors, critics, and publishers from Boston and New York. Bryant had a house a few miles outside Lenox. Melville, though Hawthorne was still unaware of his presence so close by, was at Pittsfield. Lowell and Holmes were both staying temporarily nearby, as were Fields, the publisher of *The Scarlet Letter,* and the painter Ehniger, who had illustrated it.[29] One fine August day, while out on an excursion, Hawthorne met Melville.[30] They immediately conceived a mutual sympathy for one another. For the first time, among all Hawthorne's friendships, one can truly speak of an affinity. Melville, with youth on his side, perhaps saw the elder writer right away as not merely a friend but also a father.[31] He also had the glamor of his travels about him and awakened in his host a passion that he had been obliged to repress for many years, a passion for the sea.[32] For Sophia, Melville was always to remain a south seas savage disguised as a civilized man, "Mr. Omoo,"[33] brandishing an imaginary club, as well as being the man with the "veiled," fascinating eyes that seemed to take in everything,[34] which proves that he and Hawthorne were of the same race, that of the seers and inquirers. Hawthorne was enchanted by his new guest, but this *enfant terrible* was to prove somewhat of a Rimbaud to his Verlaine.

During the course of a prolonged absence on Sophia's part, Hawthorne became closer than ever to his new friend. They were free to indulge, during their walks, or else lying in the fresh-smelling hay, or sometimes late into the night, in endless philosophic and literary wanderings, which were almost certainly not limited to considerations on "temporality and . . . eternity," but in which the physical and psychological trials of Melville's Pierre without doubt played their part.[35] Hawthorne must have felt in some way restricted by his situation as a married man, otherwise why do we find no mention of Melville in the Notebooks when their author was willing to use up so many words on the subject of Julian and his bunny?[36] We are forced to recall that Sophia always read her husband's diary, and that Hawthorne even wrote certain portions of it at her request;[37] this is perhaps one of the reasons why the Notebooks contain so little that is "intimate." Doubtless Hawthorne had nothing to hide from his wife, but every artist, simply because he is an artist, leads a double life. Hawthorne had his family life, his more or less settled social position, and also his secret life, where the imaginary, the unexpected, and the illicit had the upper hand. And Sophia, of course, was on the side of conformism and the conventions. She would have had difficulty in understanding the exigencies of a contradictory sensibility in need of nourishment and sensations. It was this element of sensation that Melville was now providing: his enthusiasm, his rejection of conformism—forcing the older man to "swim for his life"[38]—his talent, even his affection: "Whence come you Hawthorne? By what right do you drink from my flagon of life? And when I put it to my lips—lo, they are yours and not mine. I feel that the Godhead is broken up like the bread at the Supper, and that we are the pieces."[39] From this paradisaic idea of brotherhood, Melville then goes on to declare his adoration of the "archangel."[40] Nathaniel is for him what Sophia had been for Nathaniel: "The divine magnet is on you, and my magnet responds. Which is the biggest? A foolish question—they are One."[41] This identification with his friend, his mystical sensuality, and the passionate tone of his protestations all seem to indicate a homosexual element in Melville's feelings, and the "flagon" is as much the symbol of some dark, Lethean draught as it is of eternal life. Did Hawthorne feel it his duty, as the Consul did later on when the drunken minister was brought to him,[42] to deliver a sermon? Did he reply to the appeal of a "damned soul" with mere coldness?[43] His nature, as we know, was such that he tended to stiffen and withdraw when his emotions were stirred. But it is a fair wager that he was afraid of yielding to pity, or to some even more fearful demon. Was Melville the wicked angel come to destroy all the good angel's work, to tempt the master he admired, the man he idolized, to draw him away into some adventurous quest of a spiritual and sensual absolute? Had Hawthorne—who had already replied to Melville in advance in "Ethan Brand"—not been provided at home with a stability more or less favorable to his art, had he been, like Melville, unhappily married,[44] driven to compensate for the void left by love with friendship, then he might have become a precursor of Gide's Immoralist. It is certainly true that Oberon was always open to the temptation of an esthetically pleasing fate: flight from all possible refuge, the tearing up of all roots—Narcissus walks in the steps of the anchorite but all he finds in the wilderness is his own emptiness. Hawthorne had long since imagined Oberon's return.[45] It was in the peace of a settled home, in the somewhat tedious atmosphere of set habits and a circle of secure affections, that he was best able to pursue his troubled dreams. Beyond that, he was content to offer up no more than an occasional sacrifice to Wakefield's demon, symbolically at least, when he went to Washington on business[46] or to the Isle of Shoals on vacation.[47] And even those escapes he chose to interpret as opportunities for embellishing the image of his own home from afar.[48] The solitary adventuring that had become Melville's only possible path could no longer be anything more for Hawthorne than a diversion, at least on the surface—for the last flight of all was later to throw a most disturbing light, in retrospect, on even his most harmless escapades.

Melville was a meteor in Hawthorne's life. Whereas Bridge and Pierce were to remain his traveling companions to the very end of the road, Ishmael the sailor, after those fine Berkshire days, after the brief meetings later in Liverpool and London, was to disappear for good over his horizon.[49] Hawthorne had in fact loved him, that friend whom he judged more worthy of eternal life than most of us,[50] but he was held back by the shame of having witnessed the birth of an inadmissible passion of which he himself was the object—the shame of not having been able to respond to that despairing cry.[51] And his secret, elder brother ambition, that of helping, of protecting his young friend, had been thwarted.[52] Indeed, if we go back to that "red shanty" period, it seems rather to have been the younger writer who took the recognized author under his wing, proclaiming his talent to the world, calling him the equal of Shakespeare,[53] even providing him with material.[54] If we think back to the bittersweet tears that Hawthorne shed when he received Hillard's check in Salem, at a time when he felt himself abandoned by everyone else,[55] it becomes possible to suspect that Melville's very generosity had in fact reopened that wound to his self-love. Moreover, the author of *Moby Dick,* far from being relegated to the rank of Hawthorne's disciple, might well have proved the master of the man who wrote *The House of the Seven Gables*,[56] had it not been for *The Scarlet Letter*. His genius was bolder; he had lost none of the fire of his adolescence. Hawthorne, on the other hand, was sensing the approach of maturity, of the age when famous mediocrity is tempted to stoop a little in order to accommodate the social framework with which it likes to feel itself surrounded. For Hawthorne had now become a man with a certain weight in the world: his financial situation had improved, his reputation was assured, and he was now the father of three children.[57] Were all his efforts now to be bent more and more toward a reconciliation with the values he had always questioned? His dream was to buy a house by the sea. But that dream was not to be realized: circumstances, his own restless temperament, and his failing health, were henceforth to make of him a perpetual traveler—not the joyful or melancholy vagabond of former days, but an aging nomad unable to find a resting place.

III. THE NOMAD: OBERON AND THE NONARTIST

Overcome by the stifling summer heat, Hawthorne fled from the Berkshires, which he had now come to loathe with all his soul.[1] Possibly he was already experiencing the first symptoms of the great intellectual and physical fatigue that was lying in wait for him.[2] Hawthorne after 1850 is already no longer Hawthorne. And he was to become less and less so. The painful ordeal of being pilloried in Salem and suffering a bereavement at the same time did doubtless screw up his sensibility and imagination to the pitch necessary for the production of his masterpiece, and in this sense *The Scarlet Letter* is, as it were, Hawthorne's *Crime and Punishment,* since his creative temperament, like Dostoevski's, drew its energy from adversity. Nevertheless, those successive shocks to his nervous system and the creative act itself did in fact exhaust him. His moral and psychic reserves had been reduced. That one fearless leap into the void apparently shook the foundations of his whole consciousness. He was never again either able or willing to put into any book what he had put into the tragedy of Hester. The energy contained in *The House of the Seven Gables* is already of a lesser order. The satirical portrait of the Judge[3] is no longer any more than a distant echo of his inner torment. The meeting with Melville, a new ordeal, a new "temptation," involved still further psychic expenditure. Was he to let himself be won over by the younger man's example? Should he go on to explore his genius to the very limit? Or should he remain on the side of security? Even though his choice was already made in advance, the renunciation was not without bitterness. Unable to follow his demon, he was bound to let him go, that image of his own youth, his own talent, yet without being able to forget him. At West Newton, not far from the site of Brook Farm, he wrote his *Blithedale Romance*.[4] Once again, we meet the magician who had always haunted him. Should we see him wearing the features of Melville this time? Is this Westervelt, so handsome and so perverse, the friend he loved too much? In the presence of this unpredictable, Mephistophelian stranger, Coverdale is a timorous Oberon refusing all risks. This splitting of the artistic personality, accompanied by a degradation of the creative animus,[5] is symptomatic. The character of Coverdale, the "minor poet,"[6] is a prophetic portrait of Hawthorne himself, the artist in decline who can no longer find the keys to his kingdom. The pinchbeck daring of *The Blithedale Romance* draws us on continually, further and further into the labyrinth of a no more than mediocre tragic nightmare. It is an unhappy, distressing mediocrity too, if we look closely at what it conceals.

From then on, always unsatisfied, already aging, Hawthorne was to seek for himself everywhere but in his own art, with a sort of furious disappointment. Seeing himself caught up in a banal involvement with social appearances, like all those other people from whom he nevertheless felt himself to be so different, he denied himself as an artist and reacted, under pressure from his touchy temperament and with paradoxical exaggeration, by devaluing his secret self, exalting his social self, and plunging into the world of politics. He even became an antiliberal, as though in an unconscious reaction against the position taken up by other writers and intellectuals of the day, almost all of them abolitionists. Having returned to Concord, he bought the Alcott house there, which he then rebaptized "Wayside,"[7] thus making it into a symbol of his own particular position by the side of life's road.[8] In this ideal spot, so much in conformity with his own longings, he was unable to get back to work, and Pierce's nomination as Democratic candidate for President finally provided him with the excuse he needed in order to neglect it. He wrote on his own initiative to offer his services,[9] and gave up work on a "romance"[10] in order to write a biography of the future President, which he nevertheless declared that he had undertaken much against his will.[11] In the same way, he was still proclaiming his disinterestedness[12] at a time when the question of his being made a consul had already been broached: the contradictions of a man who was no longer at peace with himself, a man who was casting around for subterfuges that would enable him to avoid looking himself in the face. Ordinary duplicity has nothing to do with this affair. Hawthorne's apparent hypocrisy was in fact caused simply by a need to conceal the true reasons for his undertaking and also by his secret remorse at allowing himself to be seduced into it. Less sure now than he had once been of his artistic vocation, he was aspiring to a place alongside the kind of men who had a hold on reality, men who counted, who carried weight in the world, who had succeeded, who were happy, and whom facts proved to be in the right. These were the true heirs of the great colonial ancestors. How could those hewers-down of forests, those builders, those austere politicians disown their industrious and efficient descendants, the Yankees? Was Hawthorne, worn out by his struggle, about to justify both Puritan authoritarianism and utilitarianism as well as the new "Young American" nationalism?[13] It is at this point that the contradictions that are the mark of his character become so startlingly apparent, and such a source of confusion. Hawthorne, an admirer of the champions of American independence, he who had deplored the fact that Sanders,[14] the defender of oppressed peoples, should not have been appointed to the post of American consul in London, now appeared to have gone over to the reactionary side on the question of abolitionism, so that his compatriots were led, and are still led, to judge him severely. Yet his "feelings" on this matter were not always in accord with his "principles."[15] It must be pointed out that in political and social matters Hawthorne was governed by ethical considerations, or even, like Baudelaire,[16] by esthetic ones. His reactions differ according to whether he was attempting to affirm his moral opinion or whether he was giving way to the profound sensitivity that was part of his true temperament.[17] His hidden tenderness of heart was always allied, it is true, to a ruthless irony, and when it was smarting from disappointments it could transform itself into an astonishing hardness of heart. His attitude with regard to Jews reveals an unavowed attraction in conflict with a feeling of resentment. The Puritan, the "aristocrat" in him loathed a certain traditional image of the Jew (Shylock, Judas);[18] whereas the sensualist and the artist secretly adored the beauty of Judith and of Miriam, that daughter of his last creative flame.[19] For such an irrational antagonism to exist, there must have been a repressed attraction at work. The Jewish temptress reveals the Semitic threat: a piece of Puritan sophism that adds a hint of antisemitism to sexual distaste,[20] thus killing two birds with one stone. Hawthorne allowed himself to be caught in this trap only because of the psychological disintegration that was diminishing and humiliating him. The nonartist was taking his revenge on the sensual and liberal writer by becoming a Puritan and a conservative. The bitterness of no longer being able to create, and so to liberate his instincts, exteriorized itself with him, as it did with Barrès— though to a lesser degree—in the form of hate. And yet the Hawthorne who found the reformers at home so intolerable proved to be a philanthropist during his time at the Liverpool consulate:[21] he denounced the abuses and cruelty prevalent on board American ships with great force.[22] Yet his efforts remained in vain, his letters unanswered. He was mortified by this.[23] Here was yet another reason for refusing to take any interest in abolitionism,[24] which in his eyes was no more than empty theorizing—for slavery has many roots, innumerable forms, and can never disappear until man himself does;[25] moreover, for him slavery was above all a form of moral subjection, an enslavement of the mind.[26] This aspect of human servitude never ceased to preoccupy him, but the by now defeated artist was no longer able to forge his major theme into an instrument for his own deliverance.

At this period of his life, because of his inability to create, Hawthorne needed surrogates. The persona who had already tried so many times in his life to take the center of the stage now reappeared, more seductive than ever: Oberon's eternal companion, his ally and his worst enemy, the erstwhile vagabond. Older, able to speak from experience, perceiving that Oberon had played out his part and was already fading back into the wings, diminished and full of self-doubt, the vagabond-turned-consul asked nothing better than to take his place in order to act, to travel, and to cull new riches. At the age of fifty, and thanks to Pierce,[27] Hawthorne was now at last able to realize the dream of his childhood—a visit to England—and also that of his premature old age—an excuse for not writing! He became quite clearly another man. Literature was now his past, and perhaps one day, who could say, it might become merely his hobby.[28] As for the present, he intended to live that to the full. He and his family boarded the steamboat *Niagara* at Boston. The harbor cannon fired a salvo in his honor:

Europe was to greet Hawthorne the consul—Hawthorne the writer had ceased to exist.

Having left for the Old World as though setting out to discover a new one,[29] Hawthorne, absorbed by his new duties, entirely taken up with his many social obligations, was cut off from his bases, wholly deprived of the environment in which his art had flowered, as it were divorced from his own creative consciousness. Only the England he had imagined while still in America could have inspired him; once he arrived in the real England he was no more than a foreigner among foreigners. Worse, he was also a foreigner in the realm of art, lost in the London and Manchester art galleries, and lastly, the supreme form of exile, a foreigner in the kingdom of his own creation. One also has the impression, moreover, that he was deliberately trying to forget his literary persona, to disguise it, so much did the idea of being an object of curiosity fill him with horror,[30] and so little did contact with English writers seem to matter to him.[31] Why pose as a great author when one no longer has any talent? Though that would certainly have been no stumbling block to the "mob of scribbling women"[32] at whom he unleashed his sarcasms. One of these women, Delia Bacon,[33] did however manage to find grace in his eyes, and even had work published at his expense. A strange contradiction. Was he in love? By no means. She was hardly a pretty woman.[34] Did he think he had unearthed a genius? Even further from the mark.[35] She had simply known how to appeal to his chivalrous feelings and flattered his vanity.[36] He was allowing her to perform moral extortion at his expense, and at the same time was unable to resist the temptation of playing the magnifico: it was a way of affording some distraction to both his sensibility and his creative faculties. The inactive writer needed his compensations too—so Hawthorne became a giver of advice, a redresser of wrongs, a patron.

Though he had exhausted his vein and became a public figurehead, an official irked by his own dignities and a tourist encumbered by his family,[37] Hawthorne nevertheless expended just as much energy as before upon his flagging genius. In order to revive it, or in order to neutralize it? The prodigious accumulation of notes with which he continued to stuff his notebooks often takes on the character of propitiatory rites intended to reawaken his sleeping energies, or of a conscientious inventory in which the artist, even the realist, is less apparent than the civil servant. And on top of that, there are also the reflections of the moralist to make things more turgid still. The memory of Oberon's brightly flaming contributions had become unwelcome to him. Oberon had deserted him, and Hawthorne had not forgiven him for it. That profoundly and wildly imaginative being who had once been himself was no longer to his taste:[38] a reaction brought about by rancor, by something that was already almost despair, as his ill humor, his disenchantment, and his lassitude show. Under pretext of living, of acting, of continuing his cultural education, he was running away from himself. Dragged by Sophia from museum to museum, from ruin to ruin, from church to church, he found himself preferring the more curious exhibits of the British Museum[39] to all Turner's watercolors put together. His passion for bustling streets[40] reached its paroxysm in London: he felt the need, more than ever before, to lose his identity, to forget in the anonymity of a crowd the artist he had once been. The abnormal beings, the monsters,[41] the flotsam of crime and vice that inspired him with a "reprehensible"[42] sympathy were a source of fascination inviting him once more to recognize his share of responsibility in the face of suffering and ugliness. During a visit he made to a hospital, a scorbutic child clung to him in despair; he was shattered by the experience.[43] Yet emotion, realism, and art were finding it more and more difficult to find free expression in him. Where Dickens gathered his rich harvest of sociological and anatomical documents, where Baudelaire drank the dark lees of human misery in order to distill them into poems, Hawthorne took notes out of duty and without any genuine purpose, in order to give himself the illusion of writing without having to confront the real problems that writing involves. That was why the realistic novel he continued to dream of was never to be written. And conversely, "The Ghost of Dr. Harris"[44] is nothing but an empty phantasmagoria that does nothing to express the inward nightmare once experienced so intensely by Wakefield and Goodman Brown.

Hawthorne had wasted his time in England, and he knew it. In January of 1858 he set out to explore the Continent. It was a sullen and feverish traveler who crossed France—an "arctic region"[45]—on his way to Italy that winter, the rest of which was spent, rather wretchedly, in an icy apartment in Rome. His mind and his senses were blunted. He could not even raise an interest in the carnival. Yet the heady atmosphere of Italy and its artistic masterpieces did not try their powers upon him wholly in vain: the man who had once, in Concord, celebrated his pagan love for nature in authentic paeans[46] could not remain entirely untouched by those landscapes over which the authentic spirit of mythology had blown. But there, on that earth impregnated with paganism, he did not dare to abandon himself as he had in the bosom of the land where he was born. And already his heart was beating less and less strongly in response to the caresses of air and sun, in answer to the rhythm of the elements. Strength, beauty, and youth were all no more. The demigod had given place to the man. It was a sad meeting, that of Praxiteles' Faun and the aging Oberon, prefiguring that between Ishmael and the Antinoüs.[47] His adolescent self sprang to life again before his eyes in that noble marble body. This tête-à-tête between two legendary creatures was the artist's last dream: all the personas of his genius were present at that twilit meeting in which his pagan nature and his uneasy conscience were mingled.

As spring warmed the earth, as Rome began to reveal its captivating charms, the Hawthornes were regretfully obliged to leave it in order to avoid its fevers, to escape from the marshy lowlands up into the hills. Landscapes drenched in sun, olive trees, sheer rocks, cities rich in Renaissance treasures, disturbing and picturesque crowds, swarms of yelling beggars, an idle nomad existence: for Hawthorne, this was to be one of the most exclusively sensual, one of the "brightest and most uncareful interludes" of his life,[48] the prelude to his luminous stay in Florence. The latter began with a rather social period at the Casa del Bello. But even their meetings with the Brownings proved disappointing. Sophia and Mrs. Browning were able to meet on the common ground of spiritualism, but no real exchange took place between the two writers. Whereupon Hawthorne was seized once more by his old need for solitude. He rented the villa Montauto,[49] a former nobleman's residence with battlements and loopholes, perched on top of a hill and surrounded by vineyards. From the top of the crenelated tower one could look down onto Florence. Hawthorne often stayed up there alone in the evenings to meditate. The charm of Italy began to do its work: a certain paganism, tinged with melancholy, had begun to flow in his veins; fertile associations began to form. The mildness of the climate, the myths and fables, the cult of beauty—was Hawthorne about to follow in Goethe's steps, advancing toward a serene maturity, reconstructing his artist's personality in accordance with a renewed wisdom based upon the classical model? Fate was not to give him time.

Scarcely had the Hawthornes returned to Rome than their daughter Una contracted marsh fever. She was thought to be doomed. Hawthorne was prostrate. His natural pessimism, abetted by the profound nervous fatigue that had been undermining him[50] and that had perhaps already affected his heart,[51] turned to despair. He could not rid himself of an obsessive awareness of death.[52] With all his strength he began to curse Rome, that necropolis, that cadaver gnawed by worms. These feelings strengthened and exasperated his Protestantism: from sickness of body to sickness of soul is but a step. From then on he had but one thought: how to escape from Italy. The journey into beauty had been nothing but an illusion, a guilty weakness of the spirit. Guilt, punishment: the vicious circle was closing around him.

All Hawthorne's efforts to renew his inner self by travel had proved as vain as those he had made to forget it. Both Europe's past and Europe's novelty merely gave him back the image of certain Puritan prejudices and of the secret preoccupations that had always been with him. Catholicism,[53] it seemed to him, was admirably adapted to the needs of the human heart. The practise of confession[54] particularly interested the psychologist in him, even though it was repugnant to the Calvinist. He nevertheless believed that religion needed new blood[55] and that it was in any case a strictly personal affair.[56] Protestantism could scarcely go further. He could accept no intermediary between himself and his God—Dimmesdale's cry[57]—especially if that God was nothing but the torturing doubt within him, the overwhelming awareness of a tragic fatality that rules the universe and is reflected in art. In the deepest recesses of himself, Hawthorne expected nothing. He had never had any hope to sustain him in affliction, only a despairing stoicism: the loss of his parents, of his talent, and soon perhaps of his daughter, were simply inevitable and irreparable misfortunes.[58] They struck at his very vitals, as he himself wrote.[59] The world, which had been composed for him originally of moving contrasts, was now darkened: the supreme powerlessness[60] of the creator, even the divine creator, who cannot preserve his works from ruin, and who finally comes to doubt that he ever did create. To be, even to be God, is to be alone and ephemeral, a more or less brilliant accident in the great chaos, to throw out a few sparks, then die into darkness. Hawthorne's inward sky, once a region of bright flame, had turned to ashes. He could no longer see any light in the darkness.

Helpless in the face of this void within him and the meaninglessness of his strange, wandering life,[61] he began to identify himself more and more with all those who lacked hearths and homes: all vagabonds had become interesting to him, he wrote.[62] At no point had he ever been so close to the exiles and outlaws of this world; at no time had he ever been more imbued with social prejudices. At no point had he ever been in closer contact with poverty; at no point had he ever been more directly involved in the human comedy than in London, in Rome, and in Florence. In a word, at no time had he ever been more torn apart by his own contradictions or less capable of making use of them. After his return to the United States he was to feel even more of an exile than ever. And indeed, even the return itself was somewhat lacking in enthusiasm for a man who had exalted nationalism to the point of absurdity in his *English Notebooks*,[63] and who had reproached himself with betraying his country because he had left it at a time when the Union was threatened.[64] Here again, the intellectual convictions, the acquired ideas were at odds with his instinct. America had become unrecognizable in his absence: the Civil War was imminent. Hawthorne declared himself for the abolitionist North,[65] though more out of attachment to his place of birth than out of any ideological conviction. The great America that he was never to know seemed to him too vast. New England was quite enough for him,[66] if he could only find his place in it again. Once back in Concord, it was in vain that he shut himself away on top of the tower that now rose above the roof of "Wayside,"[67] he was forced to submit to the evidence: he had nothing further to say. For two pins he would have gone off to fight, in order to give himself the illusion of reliving his youth[68]—though there had been nothing of a military nature in that—or rather, in order to seek the swift death that he was longing for at that time[69] and so deliver himself from the care of his futile labors. His natural horror of violence was only transformed into warlike patriotism[70] as a result of his artistic impotence—just as his "innate" antipathy for the police[71] was transformed into a nostalgia for authoritarian order by his despair at not being able to stem the disorder reigning in his own mind.

The world and the America he had known were no more. His visit to the *Monitor*[72] completed the transformation of his vision of the future into a nightmare in which one's most frightening dreams became everyday realities. He could not tell how far even his own monsters were anticipations of history. He saw himself, and his work as well, excluded from the world of the machine. He had no idea that men would return to his own "chimaeras" in order to explain some very real monstrosities to come. His eyes remained fixed upon the image of an America that had vanished, a past that he could no longer "possess." The time when, by means of his magic art, he had been the sovereign of his own particular kingdom, the explorer of *his* America, was now as distant, psychologically, as the colonial period. In those days he had been able to create his heritage—the only way of possessing it truly—while at the same time remaining dispossessed by reason of his descent from the ancestors who had incurred the family curse. That contradiction had not been very important: his creative powers had held the balance. But now, unlike Barrès, he could not even identify himself with the dead, with his country's sacred soil. Did he even have a native soil, in the ordinary sense of the term? And besides, again unlike Barrès, his nature was such that however great the void within him he could never require slaughter and butchery in order to satisfy it. When Hawthorne appeared on a platform beside ex-President Pierce, on July 4, 1863, it was not in order to launch a call to arms—the occasion was in fact a demonstration in favor of peace—but in order to answer the call of friendship, even at the risk of appearing a traitor in the eyes of the northerners, which was in fact the case when his last book appeared with its dedication to Pierce.[73] There is a paradoxical heroism in that unpopular act, an act which was to make him a pariah, consign him to a tragic solitude, and hasten his death.

Abandoned by almost all his friends, painfully affected by both the absurdity and the inevitability of the Civil War, Hawthorne was aware, even as the press unleashed its insults upon him, that he had only a short time left to live. His drooping, Italian-style moustache, his mane of grey hair, his deeply sunken eyes all combined to emphasize his expression of haunted melancholy.[74] It was the statue of this broken old man that was to usurp the marvelous Oberon's place in his native town.[75] Shut out from the world of his youth and imagination, the feeling of exile he was experiencing was in fact a mortal illness. Neither Concord nor any other place in the world could from now on give him back the keys to that hidden world in which he had been fully himself. The magic sphere was broken: Oberon was condemned to a slow suicide. Aware of the tragic void within him, he nevertheless fought savagely on. The effort was so painful, so futile, that eventually he could no longer bear to hear literature discussed at all in his home.[76]

For the fallen writer, writing was the torture of Tantalus. The manuscript of *Dr. Grimshawe's Secret*[77] enables us to achieve some idea of that hell of aborted creation. The illness gnawing him from within was mysterious—as it were "negative."[78] Moreover he refused to let himself be examined. Only travel, he believed, could do him any good. With Ticknor as a companion, he left home determined to take ship for Cuba. The two friends were obliged by bad weather to stay for a while in Philadelphia, where Ticknor contracted pneumonia and died after only a few hours. Death had made a mistake;[79] Hawthorne had the impression of being involved in a sinister farce. He returned home alone, having aged ten years in only a few days. There was no one to meet him at the station and he was forced to make his way back to "Wayside" on foot, arriving there exhausted and soaked with sweat, his face ravaged and frightening to look at.[80] He no longer had the strength even to sit up, and remained some time in a state of stupefied prostration; his eyes were blank, and yet restless, his air desperate and broken. Dr. Holmes, pretending he was merely paying a friendly visit, attempted to make him give some details as to the exact nature of his illness and subsequently diagnosed a disease of the alimentary canal. Modern methods would doubtless have revealed a cardiac condition— coronary thrombosis[81] or angina pectoris. In any case, Holmes knew that Hawthorne was doomed. Whereas Hawthorne himself believed— or pretended to believe—that a change of air was his only hope of improvement. Pierce, faithful as ever, offered himself as a companion. It was as though the two old men who left to take the train on May 12, 1864, were re-enacting the gesture of those two pathetic figures in *The House of the Seven Gables*, attempting to escape their past.[82] They made their way toward the region of lakes and hills that had been Hawthorne's true native land all his life—the land of his own creative fantasy. Making their way up into the White Mountains, perhaps with the expectation of reaching Crawford Notch, the two friends stopped off at the little town of Plymouth. Hawthorne seemed to be having more and more difficulty in walking and using his hands. Was it paralysis or a heart attack?[83] However, on the evening of May 18 he went off to sleep peacefully enough. Between three and four o'clock in the morning of the nineteenth, Pierce went into his friend's room, and upon touching him discovered that he was already cold. That was how Hawthorne died, at the age of sixty, in the completest solitude, his last thoughts, his torments, his doubts, and the mystery of his genius locked up forever in his heart.[84] The vagabond's last escapade was also the last caprice of Oberon, whose country, beyond birth and death, remains the country that he himself invented, the one inhabited by Hester, Endicott, and Ilbrahim.

CONCLUSION

The Contradictory Personality

A mystery to his contemporaries, Hawthorne's personality is still an enigma today. In the perpetually retouched portrait of him painted for us by his critics and all those who knew him—whether friends or enemies—there is not a single feature that does not magnetically invite its contrary. Like all those who attempt to conceal themselves from other people's curiosity and do not take the trouble to construct a solid façade for the outside world, he has been judged in extremely various ways. Some have found him interesting, others disturbing, others antipathetic. And since his behavior was in its very essence contradictory, since he appeared by turns to be sociable and charming or lacking in self-confidence and social poise,[1] insensitive or impulsive, effeminate or virile, a dreamer or a realist,[2] one begins to wonder where the real Hawthorne is. Are we dealing with a protean joker with a delight in mystification? Or was he perhaps a case of multiple personality, unable to make a choice between his conflicting selves?[3] He had so many different aspects: the enchanter, the dandy, and the robust utopian; the insouciant good-for-nothing, the sensual pagan, and the Puritan; the man of letters, the dry joker, and the civil servant; the individualist, the solitary, and the lover of crowds. None of those personas was Hawthorne, but he carried them all inside him; they all, by turns, did service as masks for his deepest self, and veiled "the abyss of his nature."[4] For the man of shadows, the unpredictable duke of dark corners, did exist. A hypocrite, or a mind verging on lunacy, one might say. In fact, an uneasy spirit condemned to a perpetual quest of himself, forever torn between the male and female poles of his being.

Hawthorne himself was dissatisfied with this ambiguous self that could never impose a wholehearted masculinity upon itself. While apparently, and unsuccessfully, leading a man's life, he felt and imagined things in a feminine way. Despite, and in direct conflict with, his animus, he was attempting to realize himself in a feminine mode, even to the point of losing himself in a superfemininity. The synthesis of these tendencies proved difficult indeed: the unfulfilled artist, the creator with his eclipses lay wholly in that hiatus. The arbitrary conventions governing the relations between the sexes and codifying their differences did nothing to simplify matters. In the sick child brought up almost wholly by women the anima came to dominate the animus. The imprisoned man acquired feminine reflexes. The fact was a source of irritation to him, but this conditioning nevertheless opened up horizons that he could not prevent himself from exploring, even though there were inhibitions forbidding the anima to release its full energies.

The house in which the child Nathaniel lived through those sequestered years was the mold in which his "mind and character were formed."[5] The depressions of his temperament made this womb-like absorption ever more unavoidable. There were two stages in this formation: the first, the passive stage, was that of childhood, the second, more active, was that of adolescence and the years of "apprenticeship," during which he alternately fought his way free of that early upbringing by affirming his independence and deepened its impress by self-imposed solitude and meditation. By the time he went to Bowdoin his personality was formed. The psycho-physical complex that was to constitute his inner self was in place, once and for all, and was to continue functioning henceforth, though not without capricious aberrations, in an alternating mode—with constant advances and retreats, highs and lows —as an intermittent internal generator of energy.[6] The artist, like the athlete, can be delicate. Hawthorne's creative power, the robustness of his art, had as its foundation a mental organization as delicate as Owen Warland's masterpiece.[7] Oberon the artist was a demigod hyperconscious of his mortality, perpetually unfulfilled, frustrated, tantalized by the talent that alternately beckoned and fled from him. His creative euphorias and depressions, his nervous releases and recuperations obeyed no laws of logic. Inspiration could come to the writer at the most unforeseen moment, and sterility strike in the very heat of work or at a time when he ought to have been perfectly happy. During his honeymoon, for instance, Hawthorne was infuriated by the "sense of imbecility"[8] that took hold of his mind. It was during these periods of "torpidity of intellect"[9] and body that he used to deplore the lack of reality in his existence and his incapacity to grasp what was real. Hawthorne's lament that he had only dreamed of life echoes Kierkegaard's words when he cried out to be given a body.[10] Hawthorne, of course, had in fact been given an athlete's body. Yet even his need for muscular activity gave way to a distaste for all effort during those periods of depression that are the price all sufferers from such recurrent attacks of psychological and physiological debility must pay for their weak nervous constitutions. Hawthorne was a victim of the same capricious temperament that was also a constant source of sudden spiritual subsidences in Gide,[11] Amiel, and Jean-Jacques Rousseau. The sense of "imbecility" that Rousseau, like Hawthorne, writes of from firsthand knowledge was produced by the same psycho-physical state described by André Gide as a "withdrawal of the sap."[12] This is an admirable image that tells us a great deal about the feeling of inadequacy that accompanies these phenomena and also about the wealth of awareness available to the sufferer the rest of the time. For individuals of this type, when gifted, are not merely unstable neurotics but intuitive beings, explorers of the hidden self, as Gide was, as James and Hawthorne were. It is nevertheless impossible to gloss over the negative, privative character of such constitutions, for the unpredictable and demoralizing periods of lowered psychic and nervous energy also entail the repression of emotional impulses, indecisiveness, and an inhibition of all effort. In Hawthorne's case, the active periods never lasted very long, and every undertaking was followed by doubts and equivocations. How many opportunities did he miss of acting, of loving, of reaching out for success? When the "withdrawal of sap" was total, he withdrew into solitude, not in order to meditate but in order to hide, for at such times he felt himself to be in a state of inferiority, of lowered resistance, of imbecility, incapable of attempting to live life, of expressing his feelings, sometimes even of experiencing any. To keep up a conversation became impossible for him. He spoke in an "irresolute"[13] voice, groped for words, sometimes even chose them badly:[14] symptoms of paramnesia perhaps,[15] doubtless bound up, if so, with his unsociability, each reciprocally intensifying the other. Hawthorne's shyness in society went back to his childhood and his years at college.[16] It was bound up with the deepest tendencies of his personality, both psychological and artistic. Custom requires that one should not erase one's spoken discourse. But the requirements are quite different in the realm of the written word, where the search for improvement is a law even for the most highly gifted. Hawthorne was essentially a man of the written word and feared the ordeal of speech. Though when moved by sympathy or indignation he could nevertheless display a most persuasive or vehement eloquence upon occasion. He was no more just a man with weak nerves than Dimmesdale was.[17] The healthy blood provided by the vagabond made Oberon a better animal than many poets. There was a genuine force of nature latent in him that occasionally awoke, as magnificent and astonishing in his moments of anger[18] as in his moments of creation, a force that came from his anima as much as from his animus.

Hawthorne was the man of all contradictions, each of his tendencies, whether inhibited or expressed, being a possible Hawthorne. And yet, though threatened on the one hand by Oberon's narcissism, which could have led to madness, and on the other by the dissociation of consciousness that was finally to lead him into a deadend of failure, divided, torn apart, forever his own double,[19] he did nevertheless manage to effect a miracle of unstable and paradoxical mental balance that would have been useless for anyone else. This miracle consisted in the association of his two dominant personalities, one drawing together his deep and hidden tendencies, holding a monopoly of all his scruples and inhibitions as well as of his imagination and directing itself inwards, the other drawing together all his active, sociable, nomadic tendencies, holding a monopoly of all his common sense and initiative and directing itself outwards, the two together capable of combining their efforts, of forming an alliance between his somatic and nervous energies in order to effect the transition from the sphere of everyday to the esthetic sphere. The region of the consciousness in which the work of art is contemplated is not that of everyday concerns, and the rhythm of life within it is different even from that of the seasons. Hawthorne the writer may have taken account of happiness and unhappiness, of hot and cold—the winter may have sharpened his faculties and summer dulled them[20]—but his periods of creation often occurred, nonetheless, out of season or at apparently unlikely times. The mythological tales were a summer inspiration. As for the demon behind *The Scarlet Letter,* could he, on the surface, have chosen a more unlikely moment to make his demands? It was in the midst of crises that assailed him with self-doubt, at times when he was despairing of himself, denying himself, confessing himself defeated in the secrecy of his lonely room—tortures inflicted upon him by his own "fancy"[21]—that some of his finest tales struck root. The monsters of his nightmares were a torment to him, but they also set his powers of invention in motion. So that Hawthorne, both constitutionally and on account of his "haunted" mind, must be placed within the category of obsessive artists. Without going as far as homicidal madness, like Van Gogh or Verlaine, he nevertheless carried lodes of wealth within him that were also seeds of disintegration. The obsession that subsumed all his contradictions, moral as well as esthetic, was that of purity and impurity. The notion of purity—a religious notion from which he drew his mistrustfulness, his lucidity, the motives for his moral withdrawals and rejections—by insinuating itself into his art in the form of a debased "Puritanism" also introduced the spirit of censure that eventually rendered that art barren. Art needs impurity; it must accept everything, embrace the totality of the being, make use of the entire life-material available. All truly honest artists recognize the necessity for a heavy psychological burden of antagonistic and morbid tendencies in order to give the mind's constructions substance. Hawthorne's esthetic conscience was in direct opposition to his moral conscience. Instead of functioning in accordance with a simplistic set of antitheses it followed the sinuosities of the life process itself, transposed into the dimensions of art. The irreconcilable elements of his life, sources of distress on the everyday level, were made to balance and complement one another in the process of creation. The everyday personality was scattered, fragmented—the creative consciousness, male and female, active and passive, was one.

But this balance was a precarious one. Before long, the conditions that made it possible could no longer be met. As Hawthorne grew older, so he had more and more difficulty in making contact with the Oberon whose fertile imagination enabled him, without effort, to bring him into harmony with himself: a little peace, a little leisure, intense labor upon a page where all the anguish and love of one man's life were concentrated—these were enough to change the dimensions of being and reality, to transport them onto another level where everything was possible. The reign of impossibility began when the writer lost his power to deal with his own incompatible tendencies. Torn apart by his contradictions, Hawthorne tensed, tried to fight them, and was destroyed by them. Moreover, his physical and psychological nature as well as his creative nature had always proceeded by means of successive forward leaps and suddenly imposed halts. Such a rhythm is exhausting both for the physical constitution and for the mind. This would explain the premature wearing out of his athlete's constitution and the even more rapid exhaustion of a fecund talent. Yet that talent, at once powerful and precarious, seeking to consolidate its unstable equilibrium by yoking itself to other and antiesthetic tendencies, only to be finally devoured by them, that talent was nevertheless the living principle thanks to which Hawthorne, however much he may have lamented the fact, enjoyed the privilege of being himself. For the real Hawthorne, the only Hawthorne, was Oberon, the eternally youthful elf, ironic and ardent, tender and cruel, filled with equal wonder and despair by the ambiguity both of his inner self and of the reality he saw before him. It is rare indeed for a being so noble in appearance, and so gifted, to love himself so little, to sacrifice himself so totally to a prosaic double. Who would now remember the member of Brook Farm, the Salem customs inspector, or Consul Hawthorne, if it had not been for Oberon, the poet, the storyteller, the magician?

Part Two

THE SPHERES

CREATION

· 1 ·
The Library

I. CULTURAL FORMATION

Oberon, the melancholy and mocking spirit, was always seeking everywhere for the image of those alternately somber and luminous spheres
through which his imagination traveled. Among them, there was one
in which he found confirmation of their existence on the esthetic level
and in which it became possible to conceive endless new ones: the
library. From his very earliest childhood Hawthorne spent many long
hours in the company of books. Though it is in fact difficult to measure the exact extent of his cultural background since, unlike Gide for
example, he left behind no critical works or notes on his reading. So
that although the records of the Athenaeum[1] do provide us with information as to the number and nature of the works he read over a
certain limited period, it is only from the shape of his work as a whole
and his style that we can tell to which great literary family he belonged. A man's culture is not to be measured by the amount of literature he consumes. It depends upon the quality of that literature and
the manner in which he absorbs it; it extends to his way of thinking
and writing and even to his mode of being; it is incorporated into the
individual's very life to the point where it modifies, or at least clarifies,
its direction. It therefore has value as a conditioning factor, it sets the
individual's mind on the path it is obscurely seeking. And even then
the mind must still isolate, in the mass of knowledge it has absorbed,
the specific nutriment that is most suited to it. If it does find it, then
the work of acquisition will not stop and will be completed sooner or

87

later by an act of creation. Hawthorne required his reading to provide him with documents, and above all—at that time the works he read must be of a poetic character—with fertile seeds.

In early nineteenth-century New England there was hardly any other way of acquiring culture besides books. From childhood, everything was directing Hawthorne's imagination and sensibility toward literature and literature alone. No other path offered itself to him as a way of satisfying his inclinations and exercising his talents. For him, fiction was a haven, a veritable movie house of the mind. Reading as a means of instruction, on the other hand, was always repugnant to him. At Bowdoin, his reading was voracious but disconnected.[2] The teaching of a man like Samuel P. Newman, a man of great culture and taste who cared deeply about the beauty of English prose, or of T. C. Upham,[3] who told his students ex cathedra that "the object of a poet's study is the human heart," could scarcely have left a young man of Hawthorne's stamp indifferent. The curriculum at Bowdoin represented, for those days, a considerable accumulation of knowledge in various fields.[4] Apart from the traditional humanities, theology, and philosophy, we also find the natural sciences, anatomy, mathematics, cosmography, hydrography, and also the rudiments of physics and chemistry—in short, enough to provide the all-round gentleman with a general panorama of the world and nature.[5] Though Hawthorne was by no means outstanding in all fields,[6] he did nevertheless acquire a smattering of most of the learning available in his day, and his creative intelligence, even without his knowing it, seized upon such rudiments of medicine, mineralogy, or chemistry as were to prove useful later on to his particular ends. His mind was not that of a Paracelsus, even less that of a neo-Scholastic,[7] even though he always retained a poetic conception of science, but rather a naturally selective one that looked upon knowledge as its plunder and was already transmuting what it could assimilate. Too much learning would have been a burden to it, too little would have starved its energy and blunted its acuity. Hawthorne needed a happy medium between knowledge and ignorance. More than that, it was essential for him that there should remain zones of ambiguity in his mind, regions of uncertainty that would permit an interplay of probability and fancy. There was nothing systematic in his intellectual progress, but rather an instinctive forward impulse that led him to neglect the Greeks and Romans somewhat at the expense of the great English classics, or even the "gothick" novelists.[8] His affinities as well as his vocation were clarifying themselves. He read and educated himself in order to become a writer. The sphere of knowledge was for him a convenient retreat in which he was protected from the bustle of outside activity and was able to commune with the great men whom he already looked upon as his precursors.

Perhaps the young Hawthorne daydreamed more than he read.[9] But a certain minimum of active reading is still necessary in order to awaken the instinct of imitation. Participation in literary works can even become a fever and translate itself into gestures, into action. The extreme example is Don Quixote. The young Hawthorne was as intoxicated with what he read as with his own inventions. So that reading, for him, became a sort of foretaste of creation. He lived on terms of intimacy with the great works even in childhood, and it was not long before he was taking pleasure in imagining his own ranged up there among all the other world classics, a whole shelf of books with "Works of Hathorne" printed on their backs.[10] Ambitious folly, perhaps, for the works with which he lulled his dreams and which had such an air of familiar, household objects in their material envelopes, those books, when the mind sought to penetrate them and the stirred imagination to explore their real dimensions, seemed to have proceeded from some empyrean far beyond reach. To dream of having Milton, Shakespeare, and Johnson one day as one's peers is to attempt to equal the gods. Yet even the most timid men, if they have talent, may dare as much in thought. Why should an American not attain to the stature of his English models? The day was to come when he would no longer read them simply for pleasure but in order to study them in depth and search out their secrets. An "artistic study" of novels and various other works[11] is a further step, after active reading, toward creation itself. Like Ronsard and Gide, both of whom shut themselves away in order to read, Hawthorne too had his reading bouts, during which it was his sisters' task to provide him with a constant supply of literary victuals. He devoured everything that came to hand: novels, poetry, plays, chronicles, memoirs, sermons, essays, travel books, old newspapers. But the titles that recur are all works of the imagination—with Racine and Voltaire competing not unfavorably with Swift[12]—the works that he was to read later to his children[13] and which never ceased to stimulate his creative faculties. Hawthorne's reading was more notable for its depth than its extent. Indeed, there were some particular pieces that he read specifically in order to induce a poetic frame of mind: a certain Dryden poem on solitude[14] for example, when reread at dawn, could lend its tone to a whole day of meditation.

Any choice entails omissions. Whereas he seems to have had a fair acquaintance with Florian, Schiller, and Lamartine, for example, he seems never to have read La Fontaine, Goethe, or Victor Hugo. Though our only source of information in the matter is the list compiled by the Essex Institute, Hawthorne may well have read a great deal that does not appear on it. It is probable, for instance, that he knew Balzac,[15] and he himself tells us that he had read Rabelais.[16] On the other hand, it is more or less certain that he knew nothing of Russian or Scandinavian literature. As for his personal library, it was never to comprise more than 500 volumes,[17] for he was not rich enough to be a bibliophile.[18] But it is not unlikely that he could well have obtained most of the new publications via his sister-in-law, who kept a bookshop in Boston and would have asked for nothing better than to make sure he read everything published by her Transcendentalist friends and initiate him into German literature.[19] Whatever the truth of the matter, it is certain that Hawthorne always returned to the English classics that had enchanted his long years of solitude. So that he certainly owed them a pilgrimage.

As a complement to his reading, however, that pilgrimage came rather late in the day. And when confronted with the places made famous by the masters of the past, Hawthorne's point of view changed. The masters, he discovered, had needed their former distance to reveal their true stature; familiar objects reduced them to everyday proportions. Not that Hawthorne took pleasure in smashing idols. He simply wanted to be able to touch their human reality with his own fingers. In the event, Shakespeare's house seemed to him rather shabby for such a genius.[20] And his bust was even more disappointing still: it was the man it depicted, in his vulgarity, not the poet but the Stratford burgher, cunning and fond of his food.[21] Such visits palpably added nothing to Hawthorne's literary culture[22] and merely encumbered his mind with useless memories. In everything to do with Johnson, on the other hand, Hawthorne displayed a veritable fetishism, touching the stair-rail of the Temple staircase[23] and meditating in the market place at Uttoxeter where the great man had done his solemn penance.[24] As a child, Hawthorne had been greatly struck by this proof of such spectacular humility in such a giant,[25] and doubtless

Dimmesdale's public confession was suggested to him by that incident.[26] This beautiful and touching story,[27] as well as the hero's gesture in the novel, must be counted as belonging in the first place to the library.

The pilgrimage to the sources was a closed circuit: the itinerary was exclusively a literary, not a topographical one. As, for instance, the journey into the Burns country: Dumfries, Mauchlin, Mossgiel, Kirkalloway. In the testimony of stones, of objects, of places, it was Burns's physical presence that Hawthorne was seeking. The vigorous ghost[28] of that son of the soil drew his sympathy, and so, like a magician, he conjured Burns up in his own sphere: the ploughman poet, the singer of the soil and carnal love, the devil's fiddler calling the witches to dance in the kirk—whereupon our Salemite waxed indignant, but only for the sake of form, for the Scotsman's satanic humor pleased him extraordinarily, to such an extent that he insisted on going one better and introducing the character of an apostate priest celebrating a Black Mass in the Lord's own temple.[29] Thus the artist, instead of being absorbed by his models, absorbed them. They began by furnishing him with suggestions, with themes, and then, little by little, those borrowed themes were dropped in favor of his own personal ones. In other words, the new writer used his predecessors in order to develop his own personality inside the mold they had left him. In the end, having created his own mold, it often happened that he recognized unexpectedly in reality, not the forms and types that he had once extracted from it with the aid of his masters, but his own. When he saw an old antique dealer, for instance, in Boston, England, he recognized him as his own Collector[30] in the flesh. Twenty years earlier he would have said Shylock or the Wandering Jew. Similarly, in Arezzo, the well in front of Petrarch's house reminded him of the town pump,[31] not the well of truth. For the writer moved in a library that was very much his own, one in which the first place was occupied by those authors who had influenced him, whose works had eventually taken on the colors of his own imagination, a library tending more and more to be lined first and foremost with his own personal works.

For Hawthorne, everything referred back to the library. The theater, which at that time had no national characteristics, was for him simply an illustration of English literature. Not the stage itself, the world of backstage intrigue, not even that of dramatic art, but Shakespeare, the middle-class drama, the "gothick" melodrama, and farce:[32] all so many authors, genres, works. Hawthorne's dramatic criticisms in the *Salem Advertiser* are significant in this respect. He had a total lack of indulgence for the actors and accused them of betraying a literary ideal.[33] But as soon as Shakespeare was no longer in question, the stage, if we are to believe his own notes,[34] held much less interest for him than the audience, and he found much more pleasure in resting his eyes upon a young woman giving suck to her child than upon the actresses. A paradoxical Puritan reaction: it is better to be moved by a natural object than by theatrical puppets. In Shakespeare, though, we are able to recognize our own everyday nature and humanity, but magnified even in their evil, which requires a corresponding effort from the actor. Hawthorne's criticisms of the bad interpreters of Shakespeare he saw were the judgments of a moralist and a writer. An even greater crime against literature was the fact that the plays had been expurgated. *Lear* was given in the emasculated Nahum Tate version, and *Richard III* in that of Colley Cibber.[35] It would decidedly have been better to turn the theaters into lecture halls.[36] To Hawthorne, literature was the art of arts, the art to which all others seemed bound to contribute and pay homage, and he could not bear to see it thus betrayed.

The library is incomplete, however, without the museum. Unfortunately, the fine arts were not held in very high esteem in the little town of Salem. Even in Boston, in 1839, an exhibition of statues at the Athenaeum raised a wave of moral indignation.[37] It is nevertheless true that one of Hawthorne's first and most lively esthetic impressions was produced by an engraving after Michelangelo representing the three Fates, in which he perceived the cold severity of expression typical of Puritan allegory.[38] The great masterpieces, in this domain even more than in that of letters, remained the prerogative of the Old World. Hawthorne did, it is true, see a few paintings by Benjamin West[39] and Washington Allston, but he was to spend his whole life in total ignorance of Whistler, though the latter was born only a few miles from Salem in 1834.[40] He had scarcely any acquaintance with painting at all before his journey to Europe, except through reproductions in books, and possibly thanks to the Bowdoin engravings collection.[41] But is it possible to speak of painting where there is no color, no light? What Hawthorne saw at home were drawings rather, illustrations of Biblical scenes or literary classics, and as such part of the province of literature. For Hawthorne, the museum was never any more than a minor annex to the library, and one to which books were the key.

It was to books that Hawthorne turned in order to document himself, not merely upon art, but also upon trades, techniques, and all sorts of curious minor subjects. He looked upon the museum first and foremost as a collector's cave. In the Museum of the Salem East India Marine Society,[42] he encountered the counterpart of that literary bric-a-brac contained in the dictionary he pored over during his illness[43] and in the magazines of the day, in which miscellanea and curious information always abounded, a fashion to which he himself was to conform as an editor[44]; the extreme of this was represented by Madame Tussaud's and the Barnum museum.[45] All his life, Hawthorne was to retain a taste for rare objects, for talismans to protect and guide the artist through the labyrinth of his secret world. Indeed, many of his works were to be constructed around such fetishes, almost all of which belong to the cabalistic tradition.[46] The truth is that outside of literature Hawthorne looked upon art as a form of magic.[47] The procedures of the painter or the sculptor were always to be in his eyes somewhat akin to those of the sorcerer, and the museum a sort of palace of illusion in which figures and faces were always about to spring to life, and pictures about to become enactments of dramas and tragedies.[48] Paintings also belonged to history for him, as well as to the sphere of alchemy. All the books on art that he may have read[49] could do nothing to alter this. It was in vain that Sophia decorated his study with engravings, for him they were always to remain merely Biblical, allegorical, or mythological scenes. And Sophia's selection, since she had been a pupil of Allston, was essentially literary and Transcendentalist. Beside Corregio's Madonna and Raphael's Transfiguration, a present from Emerson, she had also hung Claude Lorrain's Golden Calf and a da Vinci Madonna, as well as a view of Lake Como.[50] Hawthorne certainly admired such Madonnas a great deal, though not as works of art but as women, as spiritualized representations of motherhood, such as his own portrait of Hester was to be.[51] Like Sophia, he saw only the subject. But whereas she looked for a representation of the ideal in such paintings, he was always seeking to see an example of humanity ennobled by a spark of the ideal. In short, what Hawthorne looked for in religious pictures was what he always looked for in his fellow men. He never judged them as pictures.

The most accessible form of art to a man whose esthetic education is incomplete is doubtless architecture, which in its form is more closely allied to the structure of the written work. The classical tradition had always delighted in evoking the majestic monuments that Hawthorne was to see for himself in Rome, the Romantic tradition in depicting the ruins, the castles, the Gothic cathedrals,[52] with which he had become familiar through his reading of Scott and the specialists in the "gothick" novel. He was equally sensitive to the beauty of the former and to the picturesqueness of the latter. There was a secret affinity between his mind, seeking to reduce its own contradictions to harmony, and those Roman remains, just as there was a concrete affinity between his exuberant yet austere imagination and Gothic architecture: scale, nobility of line, a fancy both aerial and grotesque in its details, mysterious and twilit effects,[53] the revelation of an inner light.[54]

It was not until his journey to Europe that he was able to perceive that the world's museum of painting and sculpture was in no way secondary to the library as a depository of riches. Moreover this belated revelation was distressing to him, for he was no longer young and his mind had difficulty in assimilating the novelty of such a discovery. The man who had once delighted in vestiges of the past, in the oddity of chance collections, now longed to see all such things disappear, all the paintings, statues, mummies, pottery, coins, the entire heritage of the centuries whose weight was such a crushing burden to the mind.[55] To tell the truth, his own mind had never been able to accommodate itself to the past except in small doses: he could cope with one simple region of the past, his own native region, but not with the past of the world, of whole races, of civilizations. In Manchester, he didn't know where to put himself upon entering the art gallery. He had not yet learned how to look at paintings. He peered at them as though they were books printed in minute print: his way of seeing things was that of the reader or the anatomist. So it is scarcely surprising that he could make out nothing but "blotches, dabs of the brush"[56] without any meaning. Even though he did succeed in educating his eye a little,[57] the world of color and pure form was to remain closed to him. Neither the diaphanous wonders of Turner[58] nor the Italian primitives[59] had anything to say to him. What he looked for in a portrait was expression, pathos, the hidden drama of a Beatrice Cenci;[60] what interested him in a still life was the materiality of the objects,[61] the microscopic precision that he found in the work of the minor Dutch masters.[62] The portrait, in fact, was always the genre he preferred, for there the painter's and the writer's art approach closest in their search for a maximum of psychological intuition. Hawthorne, fascinated by the hidden life of painted portraits, was to have himself painted several times,[63] as though in order to penetrate his own secret. To do him justice, it must be said that he did succeed, once the charm of Italy began to take its effect, in attaining a certain degree of esthetic intelligence, and given a suitable frame of mind he was eventually able to bring his intuition into play when faced with the great masterpieces.[64] Rubens, who had at first left him cold,[65] in the end revealed the sanguine generosity of his colors.[66] He began to make comparisons, notably between the Flemish painters and Raphael, who seemed to him to represent the opposite poles of painting:[67] the minute realism and the unrealism between which he himself was divided. But an esthetic education is not easily acquired when the moral and psychological reflexes have already been fixed a long while, and Hawthorne's approach to sculpture is yet another proof of this.

For him, it was an outworn art, one that no longer corresponded to the realities or customs of modern life.[68] And then, how could a sculptor possibly achieve the expression of delicate feelings, how could he render the metamorphosis of Daphne in Apollo's embrace pleasing to the eye,[69] how could he make a statue blush![70] Though the Laocoön did affect him as a powerful allegory of man's struggle and anguish.[71] It was perhaps a moral emotion that enabled him to achieve such a beautiful formulation of that group, which he perceived above all as an oceanic swelling of muscles and coils.[72] And the whiteness of the marble itself, its spiritual and abstract quality,[73] seemed to him ultimately precious in itself, thereby reconciling him to the nudity of certain statues. Confronted with the Venus de Medici, instead of a pagan goddess he perceived the modest femininity of a Beatrice, a femininity that disturbed him so much that he was obliged to go to great lengths in order to endow her with virtues capable of exorcizing from her seductiveness the slightest hints of sin.[74] Though reduced to indignation by the indecency of the Fornarina[75] and Titian's voluptuous Magdalene,[76] he was unable to condemn the Venus, and indeed was determined to rehabilitate her nudity. In his heart of hearts, for he was an artist before all else, Hawthorne was naturally obliged to love beauty for itself. All the same, his admiration was in fact fetishism.

To him, the Venus was not a statue but a woman. And eventually this romance was to end on a strangely cold note of goodbye.[77] By some singular reversal, the Venus, his love at first sight, was to become no more than a lump of marble. Our sensitivity to works of art is no more continuous than their creation. It can cease to be stirred. It can also be transferred to new objects. Hawthorne, as he left Florence, was carrying his own *Faun* within him, and like all artists in a period of gestation he preferred his own work to any other.

It was because of this preference, as much as out of his desire to belong only to himself, that Hawthorne remained on the periphery of the influences prevalent in his day. His attitude at Bowdoin was to be maintained throughout his life. Esthetic and theoretical discussion played very little part in his education and cultural formation. Moreover, during his early years as a writer Boston itself was still very much on the periphery of the artistic world, which began, geographically, in New York.[78] True, Hawthorne was aware of American literature's being on the march, but he himself was not much concerned with being a standard bearer or spreading theories and slogans. His nature drove him to work in the shadows, not to agitate in the glare of publicity. He stayed in his own province, vegetating, aware that Irving, Bryant, and Poe were drawing the whole country's intellectual energies around them. Irving, the first great American storyteller, was the only one of these who really influenced him. But it did not occur to him to become Irving's disciple, and much less his protégé.[79] For one thing, he eventually became very tired of the perpetual comparisons between Irving and himself,[80] and secondly, Irving had the defect of not being truly American. Transatlantic literature seemed condemned, in fact, at that time, either to imitation or to works of edification. Hawthorne also avoided the pseudo-intellectual society of Salem itself, which meant all those who frequented the drawing rooms of the Silsbees and the Whites, where Byron and Southey were the only names to conjure with and where only Channing and Upham[81] were prized. Later, when the literary center of America moved north and Boston and Concord entered into their period of effervescence, Hawthorne stood aside, an ironic spectator, watching all the would-be intellectuals gravitate into orbit around a great "original thinker,"[82] like so many flesh and blood goblins, bats, and owls, coming to burn their wings in the light of truth.[83] As for Hawthorne himself, he asked for nothing from Emerson as a philosopher.[84] Though it is true that a number of neo-Platonic banquets were held at the Old Manse: Emerson provided the ambrosia and the nectar, Thoreau the music of the spheres,[85] rites and symbols to which Hawthorne himself lent no credence. He felt even more ill at ease in the gay whirl of literary society. Hawthorne the consul and cultural representative yawned his way through the London parties he attended, stiff with boredom.[86]

This is not to say that he was not concerned with making Europe more aware of American literature, but that was something he did in private conversation rather than by means of lectures, recommending his friends to read Thoreau or Lowell (though for some reason omitting to mention Whitman), while at the same time he spoke in favor of various minor writers, in particular certain lady novelists, who doubtless seemed to him more representative,[87] even though he himself held them in abomination. For it is only too true that on the level of international exchange even literature is no more than a product to be exported. Hawthorne was to meet neither Dickens nor Thackeray in London, but there may have been a secret feeling of relief mingled with his disappointment. His comments on the writers he did meet were restricted to comments on their physical appearance or everyday behavior: Tennyson's Indian gait[88] and neglected appearance, Leigh Hunt's cordiality and distinction of manner,[89] the Brownings' conjugal happiness.[90] He rarely set himself up as a critic or analyst. His criticism took the form of simple choice, his analysis remained unexpressed, and he does not seem to have felt the need to spur himself on perpetually, like Poe, with diatribes and comparisons. His critical intelligence, far from being a separate faculty continually demanding satisfaction, was strictly subordinated to his creative intelligence; he never exercised it except indirectly, merely making use of the deductions he had made when writing, in order to achieve an effect or avoid a weakness. If he had committed himself to doing so, then he would retire into the aloof impartiality of the library to write a note on some particular historical genre with reference to a contemporary author, but he would rarely venture to comment more directly unless he felt it his particular duty to recommend some book by a friend.[91] His critical faculty only became acid or aggressive when he sensed that the integrity of his thought was being violated by an alien kind of thought. This was an automatic defense mechanism particularly apparent when he was faced with the threat of feminine and reformist writing. Indefatigable lady lecturers, prolific women novelists, and people of ideas all frightened him; they were tedious and tiring machines whose perpetual agitation was ultimately sterile. He preferred the restfulness of people without pretensions or theories who refrained from asking him to take up attitudes all the time and who left him to enjoy the caprices of his own fancy in peace. For Oberon's fief always remained that of the undefined borderland between thought and art, the chiaroscuro zone of personal search, not the bright circle lit by the glare of collective fireworks. He needed no more than a reflected light from the various intellectual centers of his day in order to bring his secret work to fulfillment. His cultural background was always to remain more or less the same, and despite its quantity, all that he assimilated so belatedly in Europe brought him little profit as a writer. It was during his youth that the only cultural reserves upon which he was ever able to draw were constituted. Culture for culture's sake left him indifferent. Unlike Sophia, he was unable to give every work of art the precise amount of admiration it deserved. The creative intelligence cannot accept everything. It is by nature selective and partial. It will refuse quite ruthlessly anything that is an encumbrance to it, whereas it will absorb and make its own any substance whatever that it can make use of in order to nourish and renew the forms of its own art. To create means always, in fact, to create differences.

II. THE GREAT TRADITIONS

At the time when Hawthorne was thinking of becoming a writer, the literary ideal of his contemporaries would have been to possess an American Shakespeare, or Milton, or Spenser.[1] And it was precisely those writers who were in fact his open-sesame to the world of the imagination, to the universe of secondary realities that soon became as naturally accessible to him as that of the primary ones. This is why he borrowed themes, atmospheres, and symbols from them so freely and ingenuously. Even the names of his characters often have a literary origin. Roderick Elliston recalls Smollet and Southey.[2] Dr. Heidegger refers back to Pope,[3] despite the Existentialist overtones the name has today. Wakefield makes us think of Goldsmith,[4] Priscilla of Spenser,[5] and Beatrice of Dante.[6] Donatello is the name of a sculptor;[7] Phoebe and Zenobia are figures of classical antiquity;[8] Hester and Hepzibah, of Biblical antiquity.[9] Among those from whom Hawthorne drew his earliest nourishment, the masters of allegory take pride of place. But at the same time he was becoming familiar with the great storytellers, among whom Cervantes and Fielding introduced the picaresque note, while the historical chroniclers and novelists provided him with local colors and backgrounds. And lastly, Johnson and Swift initiated him into the notion of relativity and the manipulation of irony. Thus his work was contained in advance, in certain of its essential lines, within the bounds of Oberon's library.

Since reading was for Hawthorne a compensation, what he required of it was fiction, transportation to other worlds. He did not like "true stories."[10] In the beginning, what he delighted in above all was the fantastic, the unreal. So that his mind entered early into the confining and magic circle provided by the tradition of poetry and romance. There is no doubt that it was the vast allegorical tapestries of Spenser and Bunyan that produced in him that inner dazzlement, as it were, that decides the vocation of the painter or the poet: for it is to be found everywhere in his work, that silken and seductive interweaving of the primitive themes of medieval and Renaissance literature, which is not merely a means of decoration but also an endlessly unwinding story, not frozen and austere like theological allegory but shimmering with the inspiration of life, with color and movement, obeying the curves of its own sinuous decorations, contrasting with the shadows and the halts imposed upon it by law or destiny. The seed of the future "romancer's"[11] art is already there.

Hawthorne's true preference was not for the Arcadian frivolity to be found in the masques of *The Blithedale Romance*,[12] but for the serious though overburdened fancy to be found in Spenser.[13] He was particularly fascinated by magic, and it would be true to say that he became familiar with the Faust theme through the works of the allegorists rather than through Marlowe or Goethe. The black magic exercised by Archimago, who can even influence his victims in their dreams,[14] is the alchemy of those who violate others' consciences. The masques of Furor and Jealousy,[15] and the even more gargoylish succubi, goblins, and necromancers of the "gothick" novel[16] prefigure Hawthorne's own hating hearts, female demons,[17] and fatal heroines. On the other hand, there is Oberon's and Prospero's white magic: the powerful glamor of art. And the graces of the pastoral, of *l'Allegro* and *Il Penseroso*, which are to be found revived in so many pre-Romantic works, are also there to give their cool highlights to his backdrops.

The knightly tradition, one closely associated with allegory, was what gave its epic momentum to this decorative drama, the only kind of theater that really spoke to Hawthorne's soul. Valiant knights, damsels in distress, lovers torn apart, transformed, and reunited—surrounded with its glamorous aura of adventure, arms, and love, the Arthurian cycle, from Malory to Edwin Arlington Robinson, has never ceased to fertilize the poetic imagination. In the background of *The Blithedale Romance*, which consists wholly of veils and masks, we glimpse the resurrections and transformations of Florimelle and Marinel.[18] There is also a Spenserian aura surrounding Donatello,[19] whose ancestor was a sylvan deity. Guyon and Acrasie,[20] Jason and Medea[21] all live again in Giovanni and Beatrice.[22] And the Forest of Error is also the forest where Hester and her lover lose themselves. As for the Cave of Despair,[23] that we find everywhere, for it is a symbolic archetype. There, Hawthorne is not in fact imitating, he is simply reworking a universal theme. It was only later on, when his own faculty of invention was growing weaker, that he was to return to the passage about the cave and transpose it, point by point, into *Dr. Grimshawe's Secret*.[24]

In both Milton and Bunyan, the courtly, allegorical, and love elements were all combined in a religious argument. The Puritan ideal and the symbolical ideal found a common meeting ground in their works. So that Hawthorne was presented with a ready-made solution: art charged with symbolic implications. The couple of Milton's Paradise is always there in the background of Hawthorne's idylls, and no adultery is ever consummated except with the Serpent, who always recurs in the guise of the "demoniacs."[25] Satan's gesture of rage is reproduced by many of the latter.[26] One might say that Milton and Bunyan, Bunyan especially, were Hawthorne's true Bible, the Bible of an artist more than of a believer. Theological works were useful to him only as sources of information. He preferred parables to abstract religious thought. In his tales, he was to transpose even his own meditations into dramatic form. Themes or quotations of purely Biblical origin are rare with him, whereas there are a great many themes taken indirectly from the Bible, allusions to Bunyanesque allegories, and paraphrases of the *Pilgrim's Progress*. For Hawthorne, Bunyan was the source par excellence of Christianity's supernatural elements. His mind adopted the processes of dramatic symbolism quite instinctively. There were so many occasions when he made reverent pilgrimage to the House of the Interpreter,[27] where Christian

discovers the portrait of his future guide—a prophetic picture reproduced later on in another context[28]—where he sees the glowing
fire of grace, that image of the affections that soften genius's solitude,[29]
where the Gospel, in the likeness of a young girl, purifies the house of
the soul in the way that Phoebe lets light into the House of the Seven
Gables.[30] The nourishment that Hawthorne drew from Bunyan was
not "spiritual," but poetic. He enjoyed being carried along by the
simple and powerful momentum of all the great allegories, and they
all helped to awaken the storyteller's instinct in him. The *Iliad*, the
Odyssey, the *Arabian Nights, Gulliver's Travels*: all have the basic
structure of ceremonies, ritual celebrations, processions. The kind
of adventure they contain is less a succession of peripeteias than a
journey, a cycle, an excursion, a narrative scheme to be found not
only in Homer, Chaucer, and Bunyan, but also in Fielding, Smollet,
Scott, and Irving. For Hawthorne, all adventures referred back in the
end to Christian's "progress." Bunyan's topography reappears spontaneously to surround Hawthorne's own protagonists: the Slough of
Despond,[31] the Valley of Humiliation,[32] and the Valley of the Shadow
of Death.[33] Doubting Castle is the same place as Dimmesdale's cell.[34]
The Lethean air of the Enchanted Ground is the same air as that
breathed by David Swan and by the central characters in *The House
of the Seven Gables*.[35] The Delectable Mountains are recognizable in
Monte-Beni,[36] and the By-Way to Hell is there in Hawthorne the
storyteller's mind whenever he has to evoke men's illicit deeds.[37] So
great was Bunyan's hold over Hawthorne's mind that he was eventually obliged to exorcise it by parody.[38]

Superimposed upon this basic allegorical blueprint we then find a
series of variants drawn from romances, picaresque novels, and
humorous works. The adventures of Panurge, Don Quixote, Gil Blas,
and Roderick Random are by no means foreign to those of Hawthorne's vagabonds. And "philosophic" travels, such as those of
Gulliver and Micromegas, reappear discreetly in "The Great Carbuncle."[39] The supernatural beat of the German ballad also recurs,
transmitted through the later "gothick" literature to haunt both Fanshawe and Goodman Brown, the former walking in the footsteps of
Melmoth the Wanderer,[40] the latter apparently carried to his fate by
Bürger's courser.[41] In response to these combined accretions, Hawthorne's narrative line acquired its particular sinuosity, its particular
rhythmic modulations; the storyteller learned how to use his art in

evoking movement, the better to highlight a deceptive immobility and pierce its mystery, a process that led him to make an ever increasing use of halts and to give more and more weight to his rests.

Moreover, the detail and the color used to clothe this basic narrative line are also largely of bookish origin, since Hawthorne's curiosity about the past of his native region turned him early into something of a historian. Stories of crime and war added still further brutality to an evocation of the persecutions and superstitions of a ruthless age in which the atrocities committed in the Old World[42] were equal in their horror to those of the Indians and to the savagery of a Mrs. Duston.[43] From witchcraft and crime to "gothick" horror is but a step. The tradition of cruelty, continually fed by barbarian invasions, Roman circuses, and executions, goes even farther back than the legend of the Atridae, back to the genocide found in the Old Testament and in later times; after providing so valuable a source of material for the Elizabethan theater, it then went on to absorb the products of criminal and macabre literature before finally producing the "gothick" novel, which consisted of a mixture of debased allegory and supernatural narrative allied to the merely sensational. Hawthorne did not take long to perceive its limitations, and consequently, as a writer, refused to sacrifice everything else merely in order to produce mechanical thrills of horror. Only Poe was able to use that particular form as an artist. Hawthorne, the collector of curiosities, was interested in the bric-a-brac of the "gothick" novel only insofar as he could transpose it onto another level: moral, psychological, symbolic. Rusty coffers, parchments, poisons, melodramatic monks, and deformed gnomes with demoniacal laughs were to him nothing but transformable "commodities."[44]

For Hawthorne, the romantic, the horrible, and the picturesque could never embrace the totality of reality and the human experience. He needed another dimension added to them all: tragedy. Imbued with the spirit of his ancestors, he was conscious of the gravity conferred upon any individual destiny by an awareness of guilt or predestination. In Bunyan, more even than the allegory, it was the image of the ordeal in itself and its set stages that fascinated him. The man shut up in a dark cage because he had sinned against the light of the world[45] doubtless seemed to him the image of himself, the invalid imprisoned in his room. And it was easy, too, for him to identify his own doubts with those of Christian when flung into his dungeon by the

Giant Despair.[46] But Bunyan's just man in the pillory[47] was, upon reflection, very quickly relieved of his burden.[48] Whereas Hawthorne was not so easily rid of his, and his anguish, sprung from the very ambiguity of his nature, became the instrument upon which he was to play as an artist. All Hawthorne's heroes are also pilgrims, but they all knock upon the Interpreter's door in vain: there is no guide for them, and no certainty. This very modern aspect of the nobility and wretchedness of man was revealed to him by Shakespeare more than anyone else. So that we often find his heroes confronted with a terrible alliance of implacable destiny and crushing predestination. His human dramas were to be dominated by a metaphysical necessity and a poetic fatality at the same time. The Greek tragic writers and Racine were also perhaps present at the conception of certain of Hawthorne's heroines, and had some influence on the ineluctable progress of the guilty and the persecuted in his works toward their fates.

The artist is left weaponless if he has no discipline to support his creative effort. The Puritan dialectic, with its clear-cut contrast between good and evil, provided Hawthorne with an extremely rigid infrastructure, even though it also maintained a constant, though salutary, disquiet of soul. As for the system of symbols employed by the Mathers to interpret the world of phenomena, of signs and meteors,[49] the codification of prodigies, magic recipes,[50] and cases of witchcraft into weighty tomes,[51] these provided much food for the imagination, though not for the intelligence. It was a spirit of unfettered enquiry, backed up by the firm Calvinist method of "strict investigation,"[52] that alone encouraged in Hawthorne the tendency to probe men's hearts and to explore so many divergent paths, an attitude that led him away from the rigorous procedures of theology toward a position nearer to the skepticism of Montaigne,[53] and that certainly differentiates him from the German philosophers of the time and their disciples. It was not Kant, Hegel, Fichte, or even Carlyle that Hawthorne cultivated but the English and French eighteenth-century philosophers.[54] He did not draw upon the same sources as the Transcendentalists, though he shared with them a cult of nature acquired in his case from Rousseau[55] and the Romantics,[56] and was led by his contemplative tendencies to commune with them in a vague neo-Platonism that nevertheless failed to satisfy him completely because it was an oversimplification of the problem of life.[57]

This is why, leaning on the one hand upon Calvinism, which revealed the world and human nature to him as a battlefield of contradictory forces, he also relied upon Johnson, Swift, and Voltaire, who enabled him to escape from the level of Manichean duality onto that of relativity. Their detachment and irony also added further nuances to his interpretation of the world. He was even able to draw upon Swift's "nasty" fables[58] as a source for his own parables. The Yahoo section of *Gulliver's Travels*, for example, contributed to "The New Adam and Eve,"[59] and Swift's abstract imagination enabled the author of "Hall of Fantasy"[60] to raise the theme of collecting to a philosophic level. Similarly, the philosophy of clothing in *Tale of a Tub* is to be found in *The House of the Seven Gables*. Lastly, Hawthorne's cosmic and microscopic vision was developed as much by his frequent commerce with *Gulliver's Travels* as by his acquaintance with *Paradise Lost*. Thus, in his own way, Hawthorne was a summation of European literature. Having early found the masters that awakened the deepest echoes in him, he remained faithful to them, and they led him on a voyage of discovery, both of himself and of his art. Within the broad decorative lines of the allegorical arabesque we find engraved innumerable microcosms and scenes from Hawthorne's traveling diorama.

Hawthorne did not conceal from himself the fact that any mind, however rare, is never alone of its kind, and that in the domain of the library thoughts may "take root" and intertwine without their authors ever having known one another.[61] The works of the past are the common reservoir upon which everyone may draw. Hawthorne was perfectly willing to recognize the debts he owed to his predecessors, but he was no more concerned with making a show of erudition than he was with disguising his borrowings. For he had a horror of literary patchwork. What he borrowed he made his own: in his crucible foreign elements changed their properties and natures. He never quoted the authors he took from, except indirectly or in the form of amalgams.[62] For the intoxication of erudition he substituted the incantatory intoxication of formulas tirelessly repeated and repeated until they give sudden birth to a new image. The only pedantic vein we find, and even then it is humorous too, is in his student letters and his very early works. Unconscious imitation? No: parody and pastiche. The "Spectator," whose name alone is evocative of a whole tradition, is more a satire of contemporary Boston newspapers and periodicals than an imitation of Addison. It was simply the child Hawthorne's way of amusing himself, this falling in with the taste of the day by writing essays on hackneyed themes, pieces of "gothick" or sentimental verse, and parodied advertisements.[63] The writer, like the musician, must learn to play his scales before composing in earnest.

In the early works, Hawthorne's discovery of his themes and placing of the personal elements are closely dependent upon the elements drawn from the library. The young writer's art, as well as his thought, required a framework. It seems to be true, however, that Hawthorne found his formula and his balance in the very first stories he wrote. Though the same cannot be said where the novel is concerned, we may well wonder whether *Fanshawe* and a few shorter pieces of which nothing has been preserved[64] did not in fact constitute the sum of his youthful gropings. His apprenticeship seems to have been conducted all in the mind, by osmosis.

Except for the poems, *Fanshawe* is the only work in which Hawthorne is manifestly seeking himself and leaning heavily upon his predecessors. Though even this imitation is calculated: what we are faced with here is a purposeful experiment; not the desperate divagations of *Dr. Grimshawe's Secret*, but a consciously controlled combination of elements, carried out by a lucid and ironic mind, with the purpose of "precipitating out" his personal themes. The atmosphere of the tale is Chaucerian, Fieldingesque, and "gothick," and the tempo of the narrative is that of Walter Scott. The best part of the action is provided by the rides: the tradition comes from so far back, clothed in all the glamor of the *chansons de geste* and European aristocracy, to which the student, newly initiated into horseback riding, was particularly susceptible, to say nothing of the luster added to nocturnal chivalry by the "gothick" novel. The temptation to mix ancient romance with modern sensationalism was too strong. The black and white distinction between good characters and bad characters, the good genius and the demoniac seducer circling around a conventionally beautiful object of desire, certainly does not foreshadow the future master of ambiguity, but there are times, as in the deathbed scene,[65] when he seems to be groping his way toward avenues that will eventually lead him beyond the merely macabre to a discovery of those secrets that a man might wish to carry with him into the grave. The work as a whole, however, is little than a series of outlines, seeds, possibilities. A cluster of elements, some of them already exploited with consummate art,[66] seems to have been assembled in order to conduct an experiment. Nothing is explored deeply, even though the symbols of the precipice and the cavern[67] have a tendency to attract all the rest of the material into orbits around them, and even though the theme of the procession—a borrowed one—can already be distinguished standing out from the unfamiliar, wild background of upstate Maine. There exists in the book all the latent power of a true creation[68] in the poetic tradition of romance, an extension of the world of the great epics transposed onto a provincial American level. For Hawthorne intended his art to have firm roots.

· 2 ·

The Quest
for Reality

I. FRIVOLOUS ART AND SERIOUS ART

Everything predisposed the young Hawthorne to daydreaming, to un-
focussed diversions of the mind and senses. His very temperament
inclined him to a passive enjoyment of every instant as it came, and
there were occasions when he found himself longing for nothing better
than a purely vegetative life.[1] But art in the form of passive enjoyment
of things, or in the form of mere diversion, could never have satisfied
him. Hawthorne meant to be an artist without making any sacrifices
to the frivolity of art. Ultimately, there was only one form of art that
was not contemptible in his eyes, the art of writing, and perhaps,
within strict bounds, that of painting: both rely upon a well-defined
technique and attempt to elucidate a meaning from the materials they
employ. But music, the least illustrative of all the arts, had nothing
to say to his intelligence. It was merely a diversion for the senses, an
accompaniment for the dance, for processions, or for the words of
hymns—when it was not lending its strident notes to the encouragement of debauchery. Hawthorne was wholly ignorant of what the
faithful interpretation of a great musical work can be. The Handel
Society[2] was scarcely more than an annex of the church. Everything
conspired to discourage him, even to prevent him from listening to
the great composers.[3] His head filled with the rhythms of poets like

107

Spenser and Shakespeare, he was doubtless shocked by the bad instruments used or understandably dissatisfied by the tinkling harmonies of music boxes.[4] Though one does wonder whether it was not vexation that underlay his attitude when he claimed to have absolutely no ear[5] or refused to go and hear Jenny Lind,[6] for he was appreciative of organ music.[7] But when present at a public concert he was paralyzed by the fear of showing his emotion. He had to be alone in order to lose himself in the music, or else have religious meditation as an excuse for being moved. Though even so, to associate art and religion too closely seemed to him a suspect indulgence. And any form of art that did not either represent or symbolize seemed to him futile. Consequently he was led to condemn music, for he conceived of it in terms of imitation and expression, spheres in which its means are limited: proof that art acquires true dignity only insofar as it does not imitate. Instinctively, Hawthorne knew this, even though he lacked imagination of the musical or purely poetic kind.

At that time, the poet was the writer par excellence, and Hawthorne's favorite models were poets: poets whom he never had the presumption to parody in doggerel verse in the way that he parodied the lesser, pinchbeck Romantics. The great poetry of his models he incorporated into his prose, for the lyric temperament was something he lacked. Verse for him was merely an empty form: he did not possess the inspiration to fill it. What good would it have done him to whip himself up into an ecstasy by inventing a "Sylphide"? Though he expressed an almost religious admiration for the melancholy Una[8] and the modest Perdita,[9] he was wholly a stranger to such Romantic transports as those of Chateaubriand's René. The "fair yet fearful guest" of one of his "gothick" songs[10] is nevertheless the anima whose yoke he longed for. The lyric strains of love, as opposed to the theme of guilty love, were to remain in Hawthorne always strictly on a literary plane. The flights in his letters to Sophia are mostly pure rhetoric. It is not until he approaches the theme of solitude, of secret communications and inner dimensions, that his prose becomes electrically charged, that it becomes incantatory and magical.[11] Literature expressing the writer's own emotions he found repugnant, and sentimental verse especially. To be a poet like Milton would have a meaning. To be one in the sense of writing posies for calendars had none. It would be better even to go in for the "gothick" fashion. To indulge in laments or imprecations in order to be in fashion was for him unthinkable. If fiction there was to be, at least let it be complete: at least the short story and the novel had the advantage of making no mock show of confession and of providing the writer with a more inscrutable mask. But prose and the impersonal narrative also have their traps: no author can escape from his work, and any attempt at self-disguise may sometimes end in self-betrayal. This is why Hawthorne, the writer ashamed of writing, chose a scapegoat which he could use as a screen and which he could abandon to the reader's severity: the rhymester, the "fiddler," the mountebank. It is with apparent delight that he consigns "wits and poets" to the scourge of the Puritan provost,[12] and treats them as foolish visionaries,[13] fantastical, irresponsible ne'er-do-wells who sing much as the grasshopper in the fable sings. Coverdale, the "minor poet,"[14] is scarcely better treated: he is a pallid sort of creature who applies himself to his art without any conviction, and we recognize in him the author of the prefaces who does not believe in his own work, who depreciates it and minimizes himself.

The inspired poet, the poet who inhabits Shakespeare and Milton, the poet of "The Great Stone Face,"[15] did not deign to frequent Hawthorne; the fact was painful to him, made him feel unworthy, caused him to seek to punish himself for his own mediocrity. His temperament forbade him to indulge in any sustained enthusiasm, in the pugnacious ardor of a Milton, that "great poet" with "iron sinews."[16] What did he amount to when set beside that Samson of literature? Hence that cry, "I hate poetry":[17] the confession of the disappointed poet. He had the feeling of having been only half endowed by the Muses, of having been given his share of fancy but not the creative imagination that gives color, warmth, and vigor to an artist's work, so that his work, he believed, was characterized by wanness, coldness, and insignificance.[18] He despised the gifts he possessed and exaggerated the importance of those he lacked: Hawthorne, the dreamer, the poet of the half-light, had no clear awareness of his own strength, and often mistook it for weakness.

Moral strength seemed to have been embodied once and for all in the Puritan theologians, preachers, and legislators. The artist's strength was of a different nature. It impinged neither upon the artist himself nor upon the world; it was mysterious and concealed: it was in this sense that it was spiritual[19]—one could never be certain of possessing it; its manifestations were always intermittent, and its very capriciousness was its own condemnation, morally. Such were certainly the feelings of the theocrats whose rigid system of thought claimed to lay down laws applicable even to untamed nature. Their influence was one that made itself felt even more by means of spoken eloquence than through the written word. In Hawthorne's day—and Hawthorne was a great reader of sermons[20]—the supreme tribunal was still the pulpit. Those who, like so many statues, symbolized immortality in his eyes had been the defenders of a faith, of a truth—or of an error. In his mind, the imposing figures of men like the Mathers and Jonathan Edwards were superimposed upon the ideal of the modern writer as he himself wished to embody him: they had set the tone for a possible American literature, dictated their moral attitude to America's young authors, and, above all, planted in those authors' minds the seeds of a fertile disquiet. Hawthorne himself, full of that disquiet, longed to rediscover the "tongue of fire" that moves men's hearts and souls. But the instrospective element in his nature was too strong; what he retained from his moral inheritance was above all the useless part, a fact that led him into superfluous detours, into censurable transgressions in which art and psychology were allowed to gain the upper hand over the ethics and reality. This was why he felt himself to be inferior both to the Puritans and to the realists, and why he tried to replace the melancholy Oberon with the Storyteller, a figure partly bard and partly preacher. There is a fundamental incompatibility between the depiction of truth and moralizing that he could not avoid being aware of. The *reductio ad absurdum* of his proposal to rework Byron and Shelley in accordance with Victorian taste[21] makes this clear. He would be a storyteller, since the fable, the narrative, was the art form to which he was most sensitive, but, whether he was dealing with an adventure or an apologia, it was the journey accomplished by his imagination that was the primary attraction for him. Hawthorne certainly wished to be serious in his art, but not to indulge in works of moral edification. And the narrative form enabled him both to be an artist without having to display his inner self or indulge in vain ornaments and also to be serious without actually delivering a sermon: he was able to assimilate and harmonize both the high notes of adventure and the graver notes of moral concern. So that the moralist was satisfied while still allowing Oberon his due, and Oberon, in his turn, was content to allow free play to the observer: an observer who was also a poet.

II. THE HIDDEN OBSERVER

After his long periods of being shut off from the world, Hawthorne was burning to renew contact with outside reality: at such times he was in an extremely receptive state, sensitive, in the photographic sense of the term, to every chance impression. In the writer, as in the painter, the visual sense is the most acute: reflections, patches of color, shadows and beams of lights, snapshots of gestures and faces seem to absorb his entire being; even sounds capture the attention of the eye with their ability to heighten images even further. Hawthorne's sensitivity to sounds and smells in the pure state was only secondary, and functioned only during his periods of passivity: it was when he was dreaming with half-closed eyes that he became aware of the tinkling of a bell, the distant whistle of a locomotive,[1] or the smell of wood smoke.[2] Generally speaking, he was slow to receive impressions from the outside world.[3] He needed time to bring his sensibility into harmony with reality. His senses were often directed inwards or in a state of torpor;[4] they needed a long time to "warm up," like some complicated and capricious form of recording apparatus. Moreover his capacity for recording sense impressions was limited. He could not tolerate large doses of a reality sufficiently variegated as to lead his eye astray, and even less of a hostile, aggressive, noisy reality. Indeed, he required a more or less extensive period of preparation before being able to deal with any reality. To confront it without such preparation meant plunging headlong into chaos. And Hawthorne did not like being caught unawares; he had no wish to be reality's plaything. On the contrary, it was his aim to understand it, to dominate it, to organize it beneath his gaze. It was his nature to be a spectator, not an actor, whether it was a question of simple enjoyment or a matter of serious concern.[5] Yet this was the same man who was forever clamoring for closer and closer contacts with the world, the same artist who wanted to fashion his work out of reality!

Reality for Hawthorne, however, was never what he perceived at first glance. He was always much more concerned with what was concealed beneath surface appearances than with objects themselves. It was the reflection, the blueprint that held his eye,[6] which was that of an "anatomist" as much as of an idealist. He always felt that he could catch the defects in reality's armor better in mirrors, that he could perceive the vistas of a superreality through the attenuated appearance they provided, lit by a light that was, as it were, filtered through the reality, revealing its spectral or internal image. All of which did not prevent him from being exceedingly mistrustful of anything that lacked "substance," which meant to him anything that avoided everyday reality and tried to blindfold the mind. These attitudes were complementary: sometimes he was contemptuous of reality, sometimes he would cling on to it for fear of losing his footing. Once more we find a compromise solution to these contradictions: the contact was to be intermittent, "withdrawals" always alternating with "sallies." And just as there were two explorers in him, so there were to be two spectators—one active, curious, and ferret-like, the other detached, ironical, and contemplative—sometimes operating with the former under the mocking gaze of the latter, sometimes in mutual harmony, but in either case forbidding the artist himself to plunge into the scrimmage, to lose himself in reality and then fight to find himself again as Melville and Whitman did. Had he taken part in the expedition to the South Seas, sailed the seven seas, tried his hand at every trade, then this subtle and precarious harmony between his inner self and the world would have given way to a simpler, more unified vision —and the poet's eye to a merely utilitarian organ. In Hawthorne's personality, as in his art, everything was founded upon dualities. On the coal ships in Boston, in the fields of Brook Farm, he seized and molded reality with his own two hands. But he felt that such experiences were in opposition to his deeper nature, to his "real Me,"[7] that they deprived his mind and senses of their freedom,[8] of their true, airy mobility. In Whitman the robust laborer was one with the poet, and the transition from reality to poetic vision was effected through physical contact. In Hawthorne, there was a separate level of transition at one remove from reality; sensation, such as that of Wordsworth, no matter how fertile it proved to be, had at the same time to be reflection. Reality had to wait a while before being allowed to penetrate deeper into consciousness. It had to be tamed before it could be invited into the secret recesses of Hawthorne's being: reality, like light, had to be sifted before it could serve as food for his art. He

needed protective screens about him, which is why he would sometimes retire from company and hide himself away behind curtains and
hangings.[9] He was always on the lookout for discreet observatories
that would serve him in the office of a camera obscura: the tree that
Coverdale used as an accomplice[10] from which to watch the tragedies
of life unseen; the village steeple from whose summit this Paul Pry
of ours felt that he was pulling the strings of a human puppet show;[11]
all those shady spots just off the highway and those belvederes from
which the poet gazed down at valleys below; the solitary chamber in
which Clifford was seized with vertigo at the sight of the procession
beneath[12] and in which Holgrave, the daguerreotypist, fixed the images
he saw upon the sensitized plate of his mind:[13] all so many intermediary zones between the inside and the outside—the threshold of
the "cavern."[14] Neither too far away nor yet too high above the circle
of earthly sympathies to make him no longer a part of them,[15] Hawthorne wanted to be invisible and yet present everywhere at the same
time, to mingle with everything without being bound by anything, "to
fly" where the breeze wafted him,[16] like a wandering spirit, active and
passive in equal measure, free, and yet still a prisoner in his body.[17]
Wherever he went in the world, around him there were always the
walls of an imaginary chamber that made a screen between him and
the external world and created a zone of calm in which his sensibility
could run in its own closed circuit. Instead of coming out of himself
he let the world come to him, then passed its elements through a filter
that transmuted them into an assimilable form, that modified them as a
stained glass window does the light.[18] He would re-enact a scene inside
himself even as it was taking place before him, and would only allow
himself to be convinced by the mental representation of the reality
that he himself had made. The camera obscura meant that his imagination could take flight in safety; it enabled him to penetrate the substance of objects and beings by surprise: ultimately, that camera obscura was his own mind, the meeting place of all his images, whether
of reality or revery.

At the same time, this filtering vision of his impoverished reality,
and the atmosphere of his own consciousness became rarefied because
of it. His covert, oblique stalking of reality was an ultimately disappointing tactic, and yet the only one he was able to adopt. Though
it enabled him to keep his distance, it enabled reality to do the same.
He did not want to scare it off, but might it not be said that he annoyed

it by taking so many precautions? The mistrustful, calculating observer provokes an answering coquetry in nature:[19] she may refuse to unveil herself to the hunter who seeks to catch her unawares.[20] Hawthorne tried to finesse with reality, pretending not to look, employing mirrors and peepholes[21]—the result was a veritable game of hide-and-seek, a ballet in which every figure was based upon the wiles of disguised lovers and the tantalizing flights of the coquette. Two-faced reality[22] was playing a double game with him. She would give him to believe that she existed, and then, when he tried to grasp her, she would take on another face, or faint away. It was a waste of time to pull off her masks, one could never tell what form one was embracing, or which symbol to choose: the plant, the woman, or the serpent?[23] There was no definite reality, only a multiple and protean reality absolute only in its ambiguity. It was seductive, deceitful, disquieting, tantalizing, ephemeral, unapprehendable—in a word, unreal.

Hawthorne found the unreality of reality's reflections deeply attractive, but this other, ironic kind of unreality gave him a sense of frustration. What is desirable in revery is detestable when one is trying to fix the elements of one's art—no matter how tenuous its substance —and even more unacceptable in the struggle for existence. Necessity leaves no room for ambiguities. Hawthorne, like other mortals, had experienced the necessity of single and immediate choice, the kind of choice that excludes everything else, that reduces reality to a single aspect, that hardens and impoverishes it quite as much as unrealistic contemplation can, if not more. So that, from no matter what angle he approached it, the overriding impression he had of reality was of its insufficiency, its uselessness to the artist. When he complained of his lack of material,[24] he was complaining of the void that the world left within him when it slipped from his grasp and refused to fulfill his expectations. Does this mean that the relation between the artist and the world is a purely quantitative one? The artist's primary requirement is that the world should exist for him, the artist, and for art, not outside of art—for what he needs is a superabundance of material at which he can hack and from which he can discard without fear, from which he can draw as copiously as those Victorian realists whom Hawthorne so much admired, Dickens, or Trollope, who had an entire world at their disposal in order to fill each and every page, like those fabled giants who once used to move entire countries about, inhabitants and all.[25] But he, Hawthorne, was unable to accommodate

such wealth.[26] His particular vision of the world reduced him to remaining content with only a little: he had the demoralizing feeling of
being poverty-stricken. And there can be no joyful creation except
for the artist with the whole universe in his bank.

III. THE NOTEBOOKS

In order to remedy this poverty, Hawthorne periodically made attempts to re-educate his eyes, to rediscover direct perception. Hence
his recourse to the diary, to his notebooks: a diary that was in fact a
sketchbook, very different from those of Emerson and Thoreau, for
though the entries were those of a moralist they were much more those
of a Puritan psychologist than of a Transcendentalist, and above all,
those of a "romancer."[1] His first attempt in this line dates back to his
childhood.[2] After that, we have to wait until 1835; though it is quite
possible that he made use of notebooks long before that date. The
"Sketches from Memory" and the "Fragments"[3] certainly contain material from preliminary studies. As for the descriptions in *Fanshawe*,
they were also probably taken from life. We know, in fact, that Hawthorne burned numerous manuscripts before 1837, among them several finished works; he would have found it even easier to burn mere
notes. On the other hand, it may well have been that he was more
inclined to take mental notes during this period than written ones.
But from 1837 onward, he decided that everything was to be written
down—and kept. During his travels abroad, he made it a duty to make
entries in his notebooks with scrupulous regularity, despite his fatigue
and distaste for the task.[4] The volume of these notebooks was to increase in inverse ratio to that of the works proper, so that ultimately
it came to be larger than that of the novels. To look to reality for
reassurance is also, however, to seek for reassurance against it, to ward
off the possibility of invasion. Hawthorne's notebooks thus represent
an effort to combat his tendency to a passive enjoyment of daydreaming by attempting to constitute in his memory and in his notes a précis
of the riches existing in the outside world. And in doing so, perhaps
he would succeed in identifying reality, in exorcizing it. In that case,
his notebooks would provide the intermediary he needed between
himself and things, thus enabling him to remain free and to devote
himself wholly to his work. His vision of the world had not changed,

it was still the same filtering screen, still intellectual, still full of disquiet. His mind still kept up its strict patrol of the frontiers, but that did not prevent some measure of brute reality from being smuggled through.

STYLIZED REALITY

The natural procedure of the observer, when he emerged from the library, was to refer everything to the blueprints his reading had fixed in his head. His eyes were sensitized in advance to certain forms, certain colors, certain gestures. His long musings and hours of reading in his sickroom had taught him how light could be used poetically. The colors he saw were those in Thomson's[5] landscapes or those in the somber or sumptuous clothing of legendary heroes, and his preference went to the slow majesty of processions rather than to the frantic motion of machines. He was drawn in the first place to everything that could be immediately related to the forms and lines already stylized by art. A tree with a Virginia creeper growing up it[6] was not merely vegetable but also an allegorical arabesque. The entrance to a cave[7] or a wood was also the door to some legendary or infernal world. Paths, bridges, and inns all had a historic patina conferred upon them by Walter Scott and a picaresque connotation provided by Fielding. A face, according to circumstances, could be that of a classical goddess,[8] of an allegory, of an elf,[9] or of a witch. Animals, plants, and people all became objects of a moral stylization. Pigs were men whose beastliness had taken concrete, allegorical form.[10] Plants were moral ideas: the impurity of water lilies,[11] the crabbed eccentricity of old trees.[12] Even houses became legendary personages: the blackened Roman palaces threw dark looks at one another like aged Puritans.[13] As for machines, they became monsters, related in some way to deformed living creatures.[14] In short, Hawthorne's immediate interpretation of reality was spontaneously poetical and magical.

His eye could not tolerate disparateness. When confronted with diversity, he always sought to establish a unity, a frame of reference. The tapestries and sculptures of St. Mary's Hall immediately connect with a descriptive plan of the Governor's Hall[15] whose origin is to be traced back to Spenser's enchanted castles. His travelers, his itinerant dentist,[16] his country doctor wending his way on horseback through the hills,[17] his itinerant performers, his caravans of animals,[18] all have other and invisible horsemen and vagabonds for company provided

by a long tradition from Chaucer to Irving: they are all part of the
great human pilgrimage, of the world's great carnival. All human
activities had a meaning, a function drawn from allegory or romance.
Smiths, ferrymen, tollgatherers,[19] musicians, peddlers, coachmen, inn-
keepers,[20] all entered, still clothed from head to toe in the tawdry costumes of their picaresque forebears, into this new Hawthorne territory, where they were to take up their positions in accordance with a
new esthetic order. The Dutchman at North Adams was catalogued
as an avatar of the Wandering Jew even before he made his contribution to the symbolism of fate in "Ethan Brand."[21] Hawthorne's aim,
whether conscious or not, was to organize the whole of reality into a
coherent microcosm in which nothing would be beyond his control.
Whenever he found himself embracing the vast and motley expanse
of the outside universe with his gaze, then the allegorical landscape
he carried within him was immediately projected upon it. The panorama from the top of the Green Mountains[22] presented him with the
same changing checkerboard as that viewed from the Scottish High-
lands or the Apennines.[23] Even the Italian landscape itself had to be
interpreted in Bunyanesque terms, its hills transformed into so many
armed giants,[24] except when they became the viewpoint from which
Florence shone in splendor like the heavenly Jerusalem.[25]

In order to elevate reality to a state of perfect coherence, nothing
seemed more legitimate to Hawthorne than to retouch and complete
it. This was precisely what he did during the course of his geological
expeditions up the Green Mountain river beds: at such and such a
spot a "marble arch" must once have formed a natural bridge.[26] He
was constantly obliged to discover, to abstract, or to invent forms that
would correspond with what he expected of nature, and in particular,
those arabesques, those curves that would outline the subject in a
pictorial, dramatic, or moral sense. His eye tended to complete any
curves he perceived in rudiment, to extend them till they became enveloping, closed in upon themselves, like the microcosm that he superimposed upon external reality: arches, gateways, niches, valleys, all
presented their treasures as though in goblets[27] and multiplied themselves beneath his gaze. Not that he corrected and organized nature
as a geometrician, an engineer, or a strategist would: there was no
question of his devastating a site in order to build bridges and dams
across the rivers, or fortresses on its peaks. The bridges, the dams,

the ledges, the ravines were already there; all that was necessary was to perceive them, to reveal the essence of the form, the blueprint behind the reality. As for life, he for his part would have liked to imprison that in abstraction too, but it demanded a more flexible mold, one that he was eventually to find, thanks to the intuition that later led him on from the realm of allegory into that of psychology. Hawthorne's esthetic purpose did not fail to be akin to neo-Platonism, especially when Sophia's hand is apparent in his notebooks,[28] with the one difference that his idealist procedure is not that of a Nirvana-directed contemplation, but one of perpetual experiment.

THE REALITY OF THE LABORATORY

Hawthorne employed stylized forms as reference points, as a framework or armature that would enable him to take in and capture other, more numerous elements. However large the amount of plunder he brought home, it was not the totality of the real world he had at his disposal but only reality as his eye saw it, isolated from its context: a laboratory reality, iron filings already magnetized into a pattern—not the random samples collected by the naturalist but an alchemist's ingredients. He carefully circumscribed his field of observation, then imprisoned his reality under glass so that he could study its restricted ecology at his leisure. He needed selected elements, particular conditions. Whereas Whitman labored in a vast workshop upon the rawest of raw materials, Hawthorne had to have ground already cleared and carefully picked samples to work upon. It was as though an assistant, some Aminadab[29] or other, set up his experiments for him beforehand, spiriting away all superfluous and unwanted objects before the master magician's entrance upon the scene. Hawthorne then concerned himself with nothing but the restricted area in which the experiment was being carried out: the caves of the Hudson, a transparent pool of water,[30] or the light and shade of a thicket. Every landscape became a model that he used in the same way as Leonardo da Vinci used his machines when experimenting with perspectives or light. Similarly, human beings were always studied in a well-defined atmosphere and community: their reactions were observed in isolation, beneath glass. Filled as his mind was with memories of the hills, the woods, the lakes of Raymond, of primitive life in the villages of Massachusetts and Maine, conditioned by the psychological experiences undergone in childhood, he always needed at least one of those elements in order to undertake a work. That was why he went back every summer to visit his natural laboratory of lakes and hills.

The various compartments of the landscape he had imprinted upon his memory were for him so many crucibles, which he used, in his fashion, as a scientist. He exercised his faculties of observation by poring over their geological curiosities, the stratified rocks, the potholes,[31] the concave and convex erosions of the riverbanks[32]—by setting himself engineering and architectural problems—by examining the plants and insects with a naturalist's eye. The experiments were for the most part imaginary: the construction of edifices, the moving of mountains, the trajectories of projectiles[33]—or else were reduced to the mental repetition of a particular phenomenon: the fall of an apple brought about by the weight of its ripeness,[34] the formation of islands and continents as a flooded river withdrew from the surrounding land, the microscopic reproduction of a cosmic phenomenon.[35] It was not scientific laws that he drew from these observations but poetic formulas: we are in the universe of an experimentally inclined philosopher who is playing at giving himself an illusion of godlike power over organic and inorganic nature.[36]

The pleasure he derived from such spectacles and experiments sprang even more from what he himself put into them than from what was merely given in them. As he pored over this limited universe of his, he was able not merely to survey it but also to organize it, to people it, to light it as his fancy dictated. Whether he lay in wait for a light effect, for the passing of a carriage, or for a group of persons to gather, it was always in a spot especially designed for such a purpose by nature or art: the side of a road, the entrance to a bridge or cave, a public square, a lonely valley. And it is as though he did not merely wait for such meetings and spectacles but actually produced them in some way. All his experiments were dictated by his own psychological and esthetic inclinations. In the compartmentalized universe made in the image of his own mind, every partition, every natural wall poses not only a topographical problem but also, and simultaneously, the problem of secrecy and communication. The thread of Ariadne in this labyrinthine universe is the water omnipresent in it, bursting over the walls like a fluid intelligence, tumbling in cascades,[37] sawing its way through rocks,[38] opening up a water path[39] and distant luminous perspectives,[40] hewing out natural staircases,[41] and sometimes halting behind a dam to form a still pool like some deep and secret lake of consciousness.[42] Everything, in the last resort, is referred back to the inner level of existence, everything returns to the cave of the human mind and heart, the crucible of thought and art.

THE DOCUMENTS

Though Hawthorne's researches into reality often assume the character of arbitrary games or experiments, this does not mean that his direct perception ever ceased to demand its rights or that his need for raw, unprocessed material did not continue to manifest itself. However, reality in its truly raw state never revealed itself to the observer in him, even in his "realist" guise: it was the reality of everyday life with which he was confronted and which enabled him to communicate. The Raymond notebooks teem with entries that reveal a spectator amused by a comic incident or filled with pity by a tragic death in a blizzard.[43] In the Augusta notebooks it is still the same sympathetic principle that holds sway. Hawthorne also needed to see and to feel the same things as other people, to appreciate things according to their market value, their weight, or their usefulness, to see sheep as the shepherd saw them,[44] fields as the peasant saw them,[45] to look at people as his contemporaries and fellow countrymen, not merely as they appeared to him in the vistas of allegory or as figures in a pastoral. This was his way of struggling out of himself and into the circle of other people's existences; such as that of a child, his son, whose games he evoked not as an adult but by becoming a child himself, or that of a wretched creature coming to beg for his help at the consulate.[46] Hawthorne's capacities were not limited solely to analysis and abstraction; he was also able to live experiences other than his own by means of sympathy: a faculty indispensable to the storyteller, to the novelist.

The two modes of vision were, in fact, complementary, and frequently coincided, with the participating vision—at the outset less highly developed than the contemplative vision—playing the role of auxiliary. After 1837, a change took place: Hawthorne's vision became increasingly directed toward the outside. Circumstances obliged him to pay much less attention to the fears and repugnances encouraged by the habits of his hitherto excessively well-regulated life. Deprived of his refuge, driven out from his tranquil observatory, Hawthorne saw all his plans toppled and brought to naught—but at the same time the content of his universe underwent a renewal, an outcome that was at once an advantage and a danger. His vision acquired a tendency to confuse itself with action. But the maintenance of his esthetic equilibrium required that his vision should only become externalized in order the better to achieve a subsequent reinternalization, enabling the raw material of reality to be perceived as poetic reality. This meant that all a priori abstract structures had to be dismantled: the observer had to be as unprepared as possible, yet ready to seize upon any and every chance clue. Which meant that everything became new again, everything could be felt, touched,[47] and redefined afresh. Instead of organizing material in advance, it was now a question of participating in a new interplay of sometimes very ancient themes, created by things themselves with the mind as an accomplice, or of interpreting what had never before been written about. All this often reduced Hawthorne to contenting himself with mere inventory.[48] The essential now was to extract the most diverse elements as rapidly as possible without forcing them into any category, to look first of all for variety: an inverse and complementary process to his original method, and one that developed the rapidity, precision, and efficacy of his observation.

Hawthorne was thus able to take refuge in the diversity existing within the unity provided by allegory and psychological obsession. He piled up detail upon detail, sometimes out of enthusiasm, sometimes out of duty. It was as though he were attempting to carry over the very decorative motifs and stones of the monuments into his notes,[49] the individual members of each crowd, the leaves on the trees, even the very twigs he saw floating in a river[50]—as though he wanted to gather every single element of the world together, even down to the very tiniest crumbs of reality, so that he could then fit them all together again like a jigsaw puzzle. His eye became a faceted mirror reflecting a reality fragmented into elements of microscopic size.[51] When these elements were of the same nature and could be fitted into the same frame they constituted a microcosm. When they were disparate they formed nothing but an arbitrary collection that had no ability to reconstitute the illusion of reality. Because of this, Hawthorne attempted as much as possible to enclose his collections, even the least homogeneous of them, within a restricted and precisely defined circle. As soon as he had a tiny, neatly circumscribed universe at his disposal, one that he could call his own, then he felt at ease, and the arrangement of elements within it could take place of itself, in accordance with lines of force always more or less related to his broad symbolic schemes. On the Isle of Shoals[52] everything fitted for him into frames naturally akin to those of his own mind—the picturesqueness, the economy, and the demography of the island combining naturally into the harmonious whole he desired. Documentation, in order to be useful, had to cease to belong to reality and become the exclusive property of the artist.

It was no longer the forms and types of the library that Hawthorne was making his own, but things, faces, figures, gestures not yet fixed by art, and to which he had reserved for himself the task of giving a style:[53] an old Shaker pouring out cider for his guest,[54] a fat woman sweating inside her black clothes,[55] a New Yorker, even his walk betraying his city origin, taking out a subscription to an abolitionist newspaper,[56] the intellectual Negro avoiding punishment with his clowning[57] —naval officers,[58] customs officials, politicians; puddlers stripped to the waist tipping out their molten metal;[59] Italian priests, French soldiers, Confederate prisoners.[60] So many human documents, rudimentary no doubt from the psychological point of view, but rich in a multiplicity of possible meanings.

Despite the interest he displayed regarding the modern world, Hawthorne did not consider it worth his while to gather evidence about everything in it. The expansion of America toward the West and "frontier life," for example, left him indifferent, as did the great business and financial enterprises, the great commercial epic that was to fire Dreiser's enthusiasm, as well as the primitive life that was to fascinate Jack London and Faulkner. Negroes, as Negroes, held no more real interest for him than the Indians, despite their sufferings, the intensity of their physical life, and their pictorial qualities. Ultimately, he found it less repugnant having to deal with the raw material of nature than with insufficiently refined humanity, especially when its mentality was foreign to him. This incapacity to make use of a large section of reality was paralleled by a similar incapacity to use most of the documents that he himself had amassed precisely in the hope that they would serve to enrich his work. For with Hawthorne, creation depended upon the organizing power of his poetic vision and the penetrative power of his interiorized experimental vision: the exteriorized vision performed no more than a complementary and compensatory function; though this did not exclude a certain sense of reality, often perceived through the mediation of symbols. The long looks he took at the world, and the exercises he set for his eyes, did provide Hawthorne with a better grasp of external things and enabled him to make progress in the direction of realism, just as his introspection enabled him to make progress in the direction of poetry, though without always being able to reach that goal. For he was seeking, despite himself, to crystallize his materials and his dreams, to transform them into fixed and frozen elements, while his eye, serving as a go-between for the haunted mind within, was piling up wealth upon wealth inside its cave —that cave which was to become, thanks to a particular form of psychic energy, the womb of Hawthorne's creation.

· 3 ·

The Creative
Consciousness

I. THE CREATIVE ENERGY

The instinct of creation is universal, and its manifestations are the inner self's supreme form of affirmation. When frustrated, it manifests itself as destruction, which is creation's complementary instinct and also its inversion. The child that is prevented from doing what it wants will smash, rip, demolish instead—as the young Nathaniel wanted to see the bust of Wesley burst. Nevertheless, creation in the child, even the child prodigy, is merely a spontaneous impulse. Similarly, the adolescent expresses his emotions in poems he does not stop to revise, like the doggerel verses that the young Hawthorne sent to his sister. And the adult with a hobby will paint on Sundays in order to satisfy a tormenting need to express himself occasionally in some language other than a strictly utilitarian one. Hawthorne's way of providing a distraction for his creative faculties was to make model windmills and animals for his children,[1] just as he also improvised stories for them.[2] In doing so he was satisfying his instinct in the way that a manual worker whose job is actually making things can do. He secretly envied such immediate and anxiety-free forms of creation.[3] He burned to model solid materials with those big powerful hands of his:[4] physically, he was a sculptor, the artist made to struggle with

124

clay, with wood, with metal, with stone, and who often demanded of the writer that he should be allowed to take flesh.[5]

For every artist, being sensitive in many ways, is tempted, at least at the outset, by several means of expression. Bewitched though he was by the magic of words, Hawthorne was nevertheless not insensible to the magic of sounds and colors. The writer is also a painter and a musician, the composer also a poet. Certain artists, like Leonardo da Vinci, retain this varied sensitivity all their lives; others, like Théophile Gautier, change their vocations. Hawthorne, being endowed with a strong visual imagination, was for his part drawn toward painting.[6] It was not solely the means put at his disposal that decided his ultimate direction, however, but rather the profound psychological demands that guided his hand and made him prefer, in the end, to hold a pen rather than an engraver's tool or a brush. Thus, though his hands were made to seize and knead material substances, to create hard and tangible things, Hawthorne was destined to caress only shadows. But his body remained in contact with the real world and always remembered it when his mind forgot it: for physical rhythms also have a part to play in constituting the psychic reserves necessary for the generation of creative energy. The muscular rhythms of the athlete as he leaps or throws are recorded in the memory and can be played back later on to the poet, transformed by the slow alchemical processes of the brain.[7] This transformation can only take place at leisure, for the consciousness must assimilate time as well as its other materials. Hawthorne was aware that he needed time to feel and think,[8] a trait that brings him even nearer to the authors of the eighteenth century.[9] Reflection and distance, and therefore leisure and solitude, a silent and secret activity that from the outside must look very like idleness,[10] were thus his primary conditions for fertile work.

Hawthorne never attempted to shroud himself in the mystery with which pseudogeniuses surround themselves in their spotlit retreats. He gave no one thanks for disturbing his meditations. The more he was experiencing difficulties the more he avoided tedious intruders, as though he were already carrying some unfinished "Kubla Khan" within him. This was why he used to shut himself away for days on end,[11] why he chose deserted paths to walk in,[12] and why, toward the end of his life, he spent whole days walking to and fro, absorbed in thought, on the hillside behind the house in Concord. He had a horror of anything that might interrupt him, that might change or jolt the train of his thoughts. One has only to listen to him inveighing against the custom house, against Brook Farm, against the consulate.[13] However strong his desire may have been to share the common lot of men, it was always at the price of a kind of mutilation that he succeeded in fulfilling it, by sacrificing his inner, artist's self, like Owen Warland[14] when he despairingly resigns himself to being no more than a cog in the great movement of utilitarian society instead of remaining the thinking, imaginative, and sensitive being[15] for whom the world is a pretext for producing works of art. To be free was for Hawthorne an imperious necessity, the very condition of his creativity: free, absolute master of his time—free to convert time into a temporary eternity[16] during which his mind could feel invulnerable, indestructible.[17]

Nothing conjures up eternity better to the mind than solitude and silence. In his room in Salem, Hawthorne found the solitariness and even the exact quality of boredom that suited him. There was no one to distract him, not even his mother or his sisters, in that house where everyone lived as though in separate cells. Ignored by the world, counting on no one but himself to give meaning to his sequestered life, he had no choice but to give himself up entirely to his task and to seek both within himself and in the objects that surrounded him a total complicity. Material environment and everyday objects also have their role to play in the production of works of art. That gloomy room on Herbert Street could not hope to see the same images as were later to bloom in the sunny air of the Old Manse or in the red shanty with its decorative pictures and carpets—which does not mean that the first stories all took their colors from that solitary Salem chamber, or that all those in *Mosses* took theirs from the luminosity of the new Eden. It simply means that the writer's awareness became impregnated with the places where he lived, that it could take on color or atmosphere from an environment that was itself already colored by his memories, though without taking it over color for color, shadow for shadow, form for form. During the writing of *The Blithedale Romance*, West Newton became impregnated with the atmosphere of Brook Farm as Hawthorne recreated it, not as he may have recognized it there. And though it is not a matter of indifference to know, in view of the importance that the theme of the belvedere assumes in the work, that *The Marble Faun* was conceived in the first place on top of a tower, we must not therefore expect to find the campaniles of Florence in that novel, but rather the aeries of Hawthorne's own particular microcosm. Color, lights, shadows, and forms are only there in order to impress themselves upon the consciousness that then transforms them into energy, or, less frequently, in order to crystallize a tendency, a profound theme. As the years passed, so Hawthorne sought to surround himself with an ever more elaborate apparatus for the stimulation of his creative faculties. Whereas a single bare room was able to contain all the talismans he required in his youth, the tower constructed above "Wayside" at such expense, the study perched like an aerie up in the sky, was not to witness the birth of a single work. It was stiflingly hot up there in the summer, icy in the winter: there was no longer any beneficent season for the aging Hawthorne. For him, the hot season[18] had always been the closed season too, the season during which he impregnated himself passively with reality, as though with sunlight, and replenished his reserves. In the heyday of his talent, it was always the cold season that brought him his inspiration, blowing the dormant fire within him into flame by its very contrast, just as it gives the winter hearth its true and radiant value. It was then that the secret heart of the artist began to melt, that the flow of his work was released again in abundance. He needed the first frost to color his imagination as it did the leaves.[19] The bright autumn glow filled him with panic and poignant feeling; all that glowing red on the threshold of the Arctic night sang in him like a line from *Macbeth*. The Birthmark was perhaps a minute maple leaf the color of blood.

A fleeting impression may sometimes attain an unsuspected importance, awaken an undreamed of echo in the artist's mind. But circumstances do not always produce the effect one might expect of them. In Hawthorne's case, for example, love and happiness, though they increased his epistolary production, seemed to put a brake on his creativity. Elizabeth was convinced for her part that happiness was of no value at all to her brother, which was not entirely true, for all changes require time to bear fruit. Had he remained a bachelor, Hawthorne would certainly never have written *The Scarlet Letter*. That he was able to write it in the center of a political storm and while overwhelmed with domestic worries is one of the paradoxes of literary history. Without money, without friends, sapped by his grief, by illness, by shame, he withdrew into himself and surpassed himself.[20] Not only did he draw upon all his available resources, he even converted what should have been prostrating him into an additional source of energy: the more the work was endangered the more it demanded to be created. The paradox of *The Scarlet Letter* shows to what an extent the creative consciousness can turn anything into the fuel it needs to attain its ends: joy, pain, love, distress, humiliation—if the "turmoil" boiling within it subsided "in the process of writing,"[21] that was because it had found a use for them. It cannot better be described than as omnivorous: a consciousness that in seeking to appropriate everything to itself, to make use of everything, even its sufferings, even its own crimes, is aspiring to a flawless unity and to unlimited power, such domination and hegemony being no more than a means for it to achieve its end: the work. The universal type of genius—Goethe or Byron—tends by means of a constant rivalry between art and sexuality, politics, and science, to make creative activity into a continuous form of activity of which art is only one manifestation among others. Whereas with obsessive, possessed types of genius—Beethoven or Van Gogh—it is, on the contrary, the exclusive manifestation of an intermittent creative energy.

Hawthorne stands halfway between these two extremes. Instead of advancing on all fronts at the same time, like Goethe, or throwing his entire being into his art, like Cézanne, he compartmentalized his activities in the same way as he did his personality: for him, there was a time for loving, a time for acting, a time for creating—and there existed inside him the self that loved, the self that acted, the self that created. This does not mean that all interaction between them was necessarily excluded, but the tendency was there, and a suitably Puritan one too, for purity admits of no mixtures. The sexual element appeared to Hawthorne as a source of perturbation.[22] He denounced as dangerous the illusion that makes the artist see woman as an ally.[23] Moreover there was an instinct that almost always led the excessively vulnerable artist to limit the role of love, to circumscribe its psychological ravages, to make it into a means, not an end.[24] The worst of all catastrophes for him would no doubt have been to win the heart of a woman incapable of understanding him,[25] a woman who would have insisted upon his sacrificing his art to his love, and then to his family: hence the myth of the infant monster that destroys the artist's work.[26] Yet, emotional complications and family responsibilities, it must be said, were less prejudicial to Hawthorne as a poet, in the event, than his terms as an administrator, for he was unable to be a customs officer or a consul in the way that Faulkner was later to be a postman.[27] In addition, he also suffered as an artist from his own sudden bouts of vitality, which led him into a desire for action, urging him to deny and dissipate the mirage of creation.[28] For James, on the other hand, there could never be any question of such a dispersion: Don Juanism and action were both equally impossible for him[29]—he could only be either an artist or a dilettante. Moreover he had private means, which meant that he was no more distracted from his literary projects by the need to earn his living than by that of satisfying other inclinations. Hawthorne's situation, on the other hand, was rendered much more precarious by the dispersion and arbitrary compartmentalization of his artistic personality. He needed a great deal of vigilance and will power on the one hand, and a very sure instinct on the other, in order not to let his Oberon double escape beyond recall or else to sacrifice him to a love for order. He had to keep watch on him, recall him, ceaselessly recreate him.

This state of division in a consciousness that particularly needed to muster all its energies in order to perform a single task is to be explained by Hawthorne's particular psychological make-up.[30] His artistic self tended to overflow into the rest of his personality much less than is the case with many other writers. It was not that he harbored any doubts about his vocation in his heart of hearts—for it is by no means true that he had entered upon his chosen path without enthusiasm[31]—it was simply that he yielded more than others, because of his mental constitution, to an inevitable inclination among those who create, that of abandoning himself to the obscure forces of the void, of nothingness. For it is true that every artist carries within him a something that is always surreptitiously negating and destroying him.

The creative consciousness is not organized and armed for its task in a continuous fashion, once and for all, as the moral consciousness sometimes is. The mind has its periods of low vitality, its dead seasons as well as its periods of energy. And the artistic temperament will add a tortured, suffering affectivity to these organic fluctuations. The poet, the painter, the composer, whatever his creative powers, lives with the perpetual threat of sterility, of becoming just a man with no talent. A fertile mind is a "haunted" mind in all possible ways: it is haunted by its personal superstitions, by its visions, and by the sense that its gifts are precarious and may at any moment be withdrawn. Hence the exasperation inherent in the artist's awareness of time, and that tragic sense of a race against time in what we call creation.[32] The depressive states that follow his periods of afflatus have the effect of reminding him how fragile his gifts are, a realization that leads him to discouragement, to despair, and consequently whips up his energies anew and forces him always to create a fresh and ever more imperious necessity. To create is in reality to survive. To renounce creation is to die. Hawthorne could have explained it all better than anyone, the Hawthorne who one day, seeing himself condemned to obscurity, having lost all faith in himself, and being brought face to face with the gravity of the artistic adventure, wrote to a friend: "I am a doomed man, and over I must go."[33] It is not the pangs of despised love that makes an artist think of killing himself, it is despair over his work;[34] yet the more it evades him the tighter he tries to grasp it, the more he clings on to it like a lifeline. It is probably true that each of the crises that threaten to destroy him also lead to a rebirth of himself to himself by stirring up a fresh revolution, a fresh ebullition of his psychic elements. Then the exhausted mind is numbed by a beneficent torpor that makes possible the process of sedimentation, the hidden labors of the unconscious, and the restoration of the energy that has been lost.[35] The consciousness needs sleep and oblivion[36] in order to prepare for its rebirth. Hawthorne, always subject to fits of nervous lethargy,[37] at once restless and indolent, often felt the need to withdraw into himself, to hibernate, to sleep a great deal.[38] He looked upon sleep as a necessary interruption, a salutary halt in the world's frantic, forward march. For agitation without repose,[39] the labor of an intelligence constantly directed toward the outside world has nothing in common with the labor of creation.

Corresponding to this intermittency of energy and activity, there was Hawthorne's comparable intermittency of production. Empty periods and fertile periods often alternated in regular waves that followed the writer's inner psychological rhythm, the latter coinciding in its turn with that of the seasons insofar as Hawthorne's creative forces sensed in them a complicity often neutralized or negated by various traumas. This rhythmic expenditure and recharging of his energies seems to have continued quite regularly in Hawthorne's case over a number of years; it seemed as though no accident could ever interrupt this organic rise and fall presiding over the birth of his works.[40] Though we must take care not to confuse creative energy and quantitative production: such and such a series of sketches or children's stories, even though they may have required more actual labor, in fact entailed a much less intense expenditure of energy than a short work like, say, "Ethan Brand," which was written during a lean period. But above all, the wave of fertility had its "caprices," which is to say its own individual rhythm—the seasonal rhythm serving merely as a reference. The consciousness took the external temperature into account in the matter of creation, but without always conforming to it, sometimes prolonging its efforts beyond what appear to be the normal limits —hence the out-of-season works such as the mythological tales— sometimes withdrawing its forces before the usual moment: aside from the normal gaps, there are also unexpected ones, lacunae that can be measured in months, as for example after the failure of *The Story-Teller* or during the custom house period.[41] The interrupted current was nevertheless restored every time by a miracle of creative continuity. Hawthorne always found his way back to his basic rhythm, his binary rise and fall, his alternation between fecundity and torpor: a natural rhythm, but not nature's rhythm. It does not follow from this, however, that it is sufficient for the artist merely to rely upon the periodic return of a mysterious and intermittent inner energy. Despite all appearances, the artist does not wait for inspiration, he summons it, provokes it—he lives, and acts, in anticipation of its coming.

II. THE CREATIVE WILL

The artist, unlike the dreamer constituting the reverse side of the poet's personality, is not divided between the real and the imaginary, but between the world and his own work. The dreamer is a renunciating being who limits himself to the contemplation of what he will never write. The artist intends that his dreams shall become real: the work, that is his sole aim. Even though he may appear to forget it, to negate it, he lives in order that it shall exist, and already in what it will be. The psychic dynamic of creation is one of the most typical manifestations of the human impulse toward the future: forces from the very furthest regions of the consciousness mass in front of the work, draw it toward them, and provide it with the magnetic symbol[1] without which the will is powerless, and which dictates to the mind its policy of alternately concentrating and liberating its energies. Hawthorne was quite determined to "do nothing against [his] genius,"[2] an

elliptical formula that is to be interpreted positively as well as nega-
tively, and in the strongest sense: to do everything that would encourage the flowering of his talent, and not merely to avoid impeding it.
The artist must will himself to be an artist, must work to become himself, begin that work over and over again, as often as circumstances
require, begin his preparation for that struggle by "breaking off customs"[3] that will engender facility or torpor, "shake off spirits ill-
disposed"[4] that might leave him a prey to doubts and the temptation
to betray his vocation, and "meditate on youth,"[5] the starting point,
the foundation upon which everything must be built. One is reminded
of Gide's intellectual rules.[6] The artist has to create himself with his
own two hands. Not in order to turn himself and his life into a work of
art and, like Wilde, to create an esthetic façade for himself, but on the
contrary, in order to pour his life into his work—work and life
welded into one block, not merely reflections one of the other. It is
within himself that the artist lives his artist's life, it is in the universe
of his work that he becomes himself. For his art's sake, not for the
world's, Hawthorne imposed an almost monastic rule upon himself
in his retreat: he wrote in the morning principally, and in the early
afternoon,[7] sometimes without a break; the evening was given over to
reading.[8] It was a demanding discipline, but not a rigid one. If the
weather was too fine to stay indoors, then he went out without remorse
to take advantage of the sun and the countryside.[9] The greatest danger
for the artist is that because he is being continually faced with the same
images, the same problem, he may become bored by his own work and
end up counting the lines like a prisoner counting his own steps.[10]
Solitude can become a cage, and creative activity transformed into
mechanical movement can take on the character of a punishment, a
curse. We have only to compare the obstinate striding to and fro of
the old man on his hill above "Wayside" with the unfettered gait and
fancy of the Salem vagabond: on the one hand the stubborn persistence
of the novelist at the end of his resources, forced to the edge of spiritual bankruptcy, and on the other, the purposeful design of a man in
full possession of his talent. In order to remain fruitful, the mind must
have a flexibility, a fluidity that it is deprived of by the abuse of rigid
working methods. Hawthorne in decline subjected himself to his own
authoritarianism at the expense of his failing faculties. The mature
man knows when to discipline, when to spur on, and when to moderate

his genius; he does not brutalize it, he encourages it, advises it, trains it. Hawthorne, though a regular and methodical worker, loathed forced labor, and even more so if it had to be done with the head rather than the hands.[11] He knew, in any case, that he could not exceed a given measure in this respect, and that it was essential to know when to stop if he was to continue again later at peace with his work. When he demanded an effort from himself it was because he knew the energy was there. Whereas the actor can rely on his director and the athlete on his trainer, the artist is his own and only trainer and judge: this is the fearsome solitude and responsibility of art from which many recoil. The creative mind is not an "absent" mind, and even less an oppressed one—it is, we must repeat, a "haunted" mind. Always concentrated on its task of creation, it must make certain its self-imposed rules become the means to canalize its hidden energies, not ways of dispersing or exhausting them.

This discipline is first and foremost a rhythmic framework intended to guarantee a continuity of the creative flow. Hawthorne was obliged, in particular, to learn how to make the most of the absences, the vacations his genius was prone to. Instead of using his energies in trying to fight back against his torpor, as he attempted to do on certain summer days at the Old Manse,[12] he generally allowed himself to be carried along until the moment came when he was able to seize the initiative again. And even the ability to wait implies a kind of discipline. Just as he used deliberately to delay the moment of experiencing a pleasure, of looking at a view, so he used to delay the instant at which he consented to make use of an idea or employ a given detail. But this waiting was neither coquetry nor distrust. It was dictated either by the psychological necessity of allowing the consciousness to pass from a minor into a major mode, or by the esthetic necessity of allowing the object sufficient time to take on its authentic meaning and take up its position at the required distance and in the required perspective. He refused to translate his sudden inspirations, his vision of the moment[13] into written form right away, preferring to put off until tomorrow the gesture that might prove to have frozen a fleeting and still malleable thought prematurely. The written sign, far from helping the mind to react, tended to paralyze it, whereas this ability to restrain his impulses increased their vigor, enabling him to think ahead, to consider all the possibilities, to plan exactly how to use his available energy in advance, with the result that when the right moment came he was able to pour everything evenly into the mold without spill or waste.

All this implies the acquisition of artistic virtuosity through a perpetual education of the senses, an incessant forging of the mind in order to make it into a precision tool. Hence the importance of mental exercises: reading—which a Gide did pencil in hand, while Hawthorne took his notes in his head—and reflection and variations upon given themes: all the juggling, all the "scales" that a writer is able to perform in his mind, even if only in order to amuse himself with possible ambiguities, trying all the alternatives, all the possible combinations of pictorial, dramatic, or absurd elements,[14] envisaging all the hypotheses, all the explanations—a game that was to become tragic later on, when the "haunted" mind had become the prisoner of its own mechanisms. In the last resort, the notebooks are a huge compilation of stylistic exercises that were to be the starting point of the various series of sketches,[15] but also, and above all, a storehouse of "germs," and of the palpable traces left by a labor that the artist liked to keep reminders of, even if he did not actually make use of the material accumulated. These preparatory labors, whether in the concrete or the imaginative sphere, were intended as an aid to the mind, whose function was to give substance to its own revery, to develop its acuity, its skill, its power to provide precise images, as also to exercise its strength by essaying its powers of organization on groups of disparate objects. Thus we find numerous passages in the notebooks indicative of a determination to attempt poetic and philosophical constructions.[16] The writer was inculcating in his mind a plasticity that would enable it to adjust itself to innumerable forms, reflexes that would guarantee the rapid mobilization of its forces when required, and a tonus that would maintain it perpetually upon the verge of creation, ready to make use of its faculties, its energies, and its reserves of material. Now, the coordination of all these elements is often difficult to effect: even the best organized consciousness does not function at any given point like a machine; it does not achieve its unity and arrive at its ends except at the price of innumerable false starts—a sign of the artist's perseverance and stubborn resolve. In Hawthorne's case, if we consider these tentative stages first of all from the outside, by examining the stages in the composition of certain works from a strictly chronological point of view,[17] we find a definite series of false starts, pauses, and fresh attempts. He had particular difficulty, it seems, in actually beginning his works. If we accept that Hawthorne began writing *The Scarlet Letter* on September 27, 1839,[18] and not immediately after his dismissal from the customs, as legend would have it,[19] then we are obliged to take into account a number of unfruitful attempts made before that date. And in the first place we must consider "Ethan Brand," that "tooth ill-drawn" whose roots had begun to grow again,[20] and also, very probably, a series of vain attempts during the actual custom house period, at a time when everything was encouraging him to take the present as his theme rather than the past.[21] Though less laborious, getting *The House of the Seven Gables* under way was still a tricky matter. Hawthorne's first attempt occurred in August:[22] labor in vain; the season was not yet favorable, and he was scarcely able to do more than "seize the skirt of ideas and pin them down."[23] With the fall, a first thaw took place,[24] but in November he was once again complaining of his slow progress.[25] In December, as a further proof that the seasonal rhythm of his production had no inevitable regularity about it, we find him once more blocked, tangled up in his own ideas, incapable of judging what he had done or of saying what he had to do.[26] As for *The Marble Faun*, the project was conceived in Rome,[27] then taken up again in Florence at the same time as the sketch for the "English novel,"[28] but Hawthorne was even then not working on it for more than one or two hours a day;[29] he was unable to achieve any momentum. The second draft, made at Redcar, also seems to have been a painful business: the comments in his notebooks[30] provide evidence both of his disappointment and of that perseverance which, in the "last phase," was to become a savage doggedness. These perpetual reworkings of his interrupted works underline not only the intermittent quality of his creative functions but also a tendency to push back the goal to be attained, to raise it higher and higher as each new level was reached. The work is an ideal that the creative will is pursuing. And in order to attain an ideal one is obliged to engage in hand-to-hand fighting with reality, with the material from which one is attempting to create.

Hawthorne began by organizing his material from a distance before he kneaded and modeled it directly, before he endowed it with a form. He began by constructing, sketching, and erasing in his head, in depth, on all the multiple levels of his mind, the richest of all palimpsests: though this by no means prevented him from erasing things on paper too. A great deal of ingenuity has been expended in depicting Hawthorne as the distinguished man of letters, of the type who never soiled his hands with making rough drafts,[31] with actually slopping his precious poetic material about like a bricklayer, a writer who wrote without blotting a single line, under the dictation of his Muse—or else as a domesticated genius sitting beside the hearth, swathed in a dressing gown presented to him by his model Victorian spouse, embroidering some kind of sampler for which he carried the "pattern" in his head. Both images are sentimental and false. It would be nearer to the truth to depict him as the absorbed, preoccupied child wiping its pens on its sleeve,[32] or as an artisan at his trade, treating the ink as a raw material to be scooped up and pressed into place to repair some error.[33] Doubtless he never produced rough drafts in the way that Pascal or Balzac did, but it is difficult to believe that "Ethan Brand," his "chapter from an abortive romance,"[34] so laboriously composed on its author's own admission,[35] was not the end product of several versions, and perhaps the product of the condensation of several hundreds of pages.[36] In the same way, the ultimate version of *The Scarlet Letter* was in fact preceded by at least one preliminary sketch, the germ that Fields mentions.[37] And *The House of the Seven Gables* did not see the light of day until it had been through the stage of "the wildest scribble of a first draught."[38] In the case of *The Marble Faun*, Hawthorne himself explicitly admitted that it involved a period of "planning and sketching"[39] and that it involved "a larger amount of scribble than either of my former romances."[40] As for the notebooks, they contain a great many preliminary sketches where no attempt has been made to achieve any unity or polish in the details.[41] The belief that Hawthorne wrote without rough drafts is therefore based upon legends, and upon a double illusion: an artist necessarily alters, because he is in search of himself, but he does not always keep his sketches. We must not forget that Hawthorne was a great destroyer of manuscripts. Many writers keep their rough drafts as witnesses of their efforts, as fetishes. Hawthorne, on the other hand, burned them: whereas the "notes" retained the glamor and prestige of reality in his eyes, his first drafts were merely badly made, deformed beings that he preferred to consign to oblivion. Not that he was attempting to conceal the fact that creation requires ungrateful labors, but since for him the work was an ideal, the tools he used to realize it had no interest for him in themselves. It never occurred to him, in consequence, that he might find a means on

this level to reconcile his esthetic inclinations and his democratic inclination, as Whitman did, by celebrating the work of his brain as
well as that of his muscles, the secretions of his intelligences as well as
those of his glands.[42] So that Hawthorne was in fact placing his activity
above the common level. Without admitting it to himself—and Sartre
himself sees this as one of the artist's inevitable tendencies—he was
divinizing it: neither the sweat, nor the gross matter of which it was
made, was to have a share in it. His efforts, his failures, and his anxieties, bearing as they did upon the human condition, would in any
other profession have given him the joy of communicating with his
fellow men. But being a writer he did not wish to employ any but the
private means that make possible perfect creation. In the name of art's
"purity" he would have been ready for any and every ingratitude
toward his own humanity, even at the cost of storing up remorse for
himself and cursing his "allegories," had not his instinct told him that
it is impossible to attain to the supreme activity of the mind without
the intervention of physical and psychic elements that he thought unworthy to be mentioned—elements isolated behind the veil of symbols,
forming the very substance of the unconscious, and ultimately enabling
the fertile germs to flower.

III. THE GERMS

We must distinguish in Hawthorne between the periods of preparation during which the unconscious alone was at work, the periods of
invention when the germs were multiplying, the periods of sedimentation during which he allowed them to develop, and lastly, the periods
of creation proper, during which he put his long-meditated projects
into execution. Until he was about forty, his head always teemed with
ideas of which some succeeded in reaching maturity but of which a
much greater number were lost. In creation, as in biology, superabundance is a necessity. The inventive period par excellence was Hawthorne's youth, during which his psychological and moral themes took
shape: the majority of the germs date from before the "Old Manse"
years.[1] The reflections we find in the notebooks between 1835 and
1842 are probably those which the author enunciated to himself men-
tally, or in a murmur, as he went on his walks through the countryside
or meditated in his room:[2] they are the voice of the creative conscious-

ness at last become audible, at last articulated. All the future works depended upon these brief and unexpected spurts of inspiration, which were the products of a slow process of mental and sensorial impregnation later released by a moment of quietude or some chance incident. At such times, the unconscious, crammed with its myriad collections of impressions, threw out sudden discharges of energy, bright flashes. Whereupon the alerted mind sought to grasp hold of them, fix them, and make use of them: here is something that needs to be looked into, that requires thinking out, that might be made into a symbol[3]—the writer was attempting to set the complex machinery of creation into motion, and in order to do so made use of incantatory and mnemonic techniques.

The germs were first of all the product of certain resurgences in the passive consciousness, of shocks awakening dormant echoes. A shrewish, wrinkled face, a handsome looking man with false teeth,[4] an old woman alone in a vast house,[5] a traveler on a deserted road, and the mind flowed back to its sources. After that, a moment's absent-mindedness, an accident, any vacancy of the consciousness would suffice: the face or object would suddenly rise to the surface, an idea would spring into being, even in sketch form, and the object or face would become the symbol of it. A gesture, a pebble thrown at his own shadow,[6] and the whole cycle of narcissism had begun again. Or else it would be a dream: a mountain and the cries of suffering humanity rising up from the valley[7]—one of those dreams of archetypal origin (during which the unity and the division of the dreamer's being are involved simultaneously) which, having led the consciousness in a certain direction, are then recovered by it and thrown back into its esthetic crucible: in this case to be molded into an allegory. In Hawthorne's case, one can easily imagine other dreams containing the things that haunted him and with the power to give rise to literary themes, in particular the pillory, the scarlet woman (dream of divorce),[8] the labyrinth (dream of school).[9] As for the dream of the burned grass revealing the imprint of his own body and dotted with green shoots,[10] that is the Adamic dream, the Metamorphosis dream par excellence, the dream we find echoed in "Earth's Holocaust" and "The New Adam and Eve."[11] It is interesting to note that among Hawthorne's literary projects we find one for using a dream as the starting point of a story.[12] Memories from the library also rise up again quite often in the same way. Sometimes a simple name: Pearl,[13] the music of which, harmonizing with Biblical associations, summoned up the image of a heroine; or else the evocation of Dr. Johnson's penance at Uttoxeter,[14] which caused the theme of the guilty man in the pillory to spring up afresh in his mind. On occasion, even lapses of memory became of use: when hesitating between a feminine and a masculine allegory for vengeance and evil we find Hawthorne suddenly changing from feminine to masculine within the same sentence.[15] Instead of Lady Eleanore, who was to return and claim her rights when circumstances were more favorable,[16] it is suddenly Chillingworth who is standing there, so that before borrowing from external reality, Hawthorne began by drawing upon the secret storehouses of his own consciousness. The germs he owed to reality were only a condensation of his meticulous observations. When he had an abundance of materials, of characters, of situations, of settings at his disposal[17] he was unable to deal with them right away. In order to make use of them, it was first essential for him to express everything in a single formula; then he might eventually extract a small work from them. But it was rarely that the deep organic principle was in operation while the materials were actually being accumulated. The moment of meeting could only be fortuitous. As a general rule, the teeming elements of reality had to recede and give way to a condensed core that might, if all went well, become a fertile germ in the hands of the biologist-magician.

The first condition necessary for the germs to become fertile was that they should be swept up in the deepest currents of Hawthorne's consciousness, the obsessional currents that all flowed into one great dominant theme: that of the solitary and guilty human heart, the sheaf that contained all the others bound within it—the past, the inheritance, the curse, alchemy, all of which were then subdivided and given their particular places on the level of the works themselves. These currents, perpetually swelled by fresh provender, maintained by both the interest and the anguish they aroused, only rose into particular prominence at irregular intervals, borne up to the surface again by the upward eddies, some of them continuing indefinitely in the consciousness, others, for want of sustenance, being reabsorbed into the night of the unconscious: these themes may themselves be considered as germs, though with possibilities vast enough to be qualified as generic.

The theme-currents were not oriented from the outset in any definite fashion. They formed tangles waiting to be unraveled. Thus the idea of heritage and aristocracy was at first intertwined with that of the curse and solitude.[18] Later, secondary themes, such as mesmerism[19] and the antiquities of Salem[20] were to direct Hawthorne's consciousness back once more toward the notion of the curse, a movement finally resulting in *The House of the Seven Gables*, whereas the theme of inheritance was eventually to abort in *Dr. Grimshawe's Secret*. Or else we begin with a vague seeking after solitude[21] that is eventually transformed into the quest for happiness, and finally into the symbol of the impossibility of happiness in love.[22] So that several themes have had to be sacrificed in order to allow the development of another, single one: having dallied for a while with the problem of happiness in love, Hawthorne returned to his deeper preoccupations. Conversely, a particularly magnetic current may draw a great many individual germs into a single pattern: the themes of vengeance,[23] hypocrisy,[24] and penitence,[25] of the violation of conscience, of moral torture and degradation,[26] all reveal an obsession with the relationship between the solitary man and the man who spies on him, between the defendant and the judge, between the victim and the executioner, which Hawthorne, no doubt unconsciously, was led to link up with the theme of adultery, of sexuality. It was to take many years for the graft to "take," which it did finally thanks to a particular and pre-eminent germ around which everything could at last be structured. The second step toward creation was thus the channelling of the various currents, a process that could not take place without the intervention of catalysts. As adjuncts to the generic seeds, therefore, there were also the necessary specific germs, the male germs.

These germs could remain buried for a long while without their specific properties becoming apparent. That of the bloody footprint was to remain dormant for ten years.[27] The incubation period for the scarlet letter was to be still longer: it appeared for the first time in "Endicott,"[28] but it still had not attained the value of a germ. It was not until five years later that Hawthorne was to isolate it and store it away in his notebooks.[29] His creative consciousness was unable to seize immediately upon the first spark that presented itself. It was obliged to wait upon the effects of time and of those subterranean currents whose unpredictable resurgences were the certain signs of vitality in the germs they bore along within them. Current and germ needed time to adapt to one another—so that the germ, by impregnating itself with the waves of the consciousness in which it floated, could become positive. The specific germs functioned like ganglia, discharging their own

energies back from time to time into the deep currents by which they
had been charged, drawing whole zones of the consciousness into their
fields of force, creating an organization, a psychic structure where
ordinarily there was nothing but vague desires, unconscious aspirations, disorder and confusion. These germs were almost all images, or
objects—those that the poet-observer had extracted from reality, the
imaginative reader from his books, or the dreamer from his memory.
They were the concretizations of unconscious preoccupations, and
were often superimposed upon signs as old as the secret books of the
alchemists: hieroglyphs like the letter A, fetishes (the black veil, the
mirror, the ring).[30] Sometimes on the other hand, they were objects in
everyday use (the banquet table,[31] the town pump[32]), natural emblems
(tree, butterfly, spring),[33] artifacts, or monuments. Whatever their
nature or form, they were always talismans. Even when they had no
existence as objects, they became real and living for the imagination.
One can understand why his museum of oddly assorted objects should
have been so important to Hawthorne: it was his storehouse, the place
where he accumulated the disparate bric-a-brac of which only a few
elements, without his knowing how, were destined to become radio-
active. For one glowing hieroglyph, for one obsessive and active fetish,
there were untold numbers of knickknacks and dusty antiques piled up
in that junk-room of his.[34] Hawthorne seems always to have started
from the infinitely small,[35] from a single cell, a nucleus[36] in order to go
on and build a body, a work in which the germ always remained em-
bedded like a "birthmark,"[37] a blazon[38] that kept its brilliancy and
hardness at the heart of the shadows and reflections built up around
it. And these germs still remained living and active even after they
had produced their fruits,[39] for the themes they had brought to a
momentary stage of crystallization continued to evolve,[40] to produce
fresh extensions of themselves as new elements became available. The
artist may thus be defined first of all as a generator of "germs." Though
this does not mean that the generative faculty is sufficient to explain
the work of art, for the same faculty also exists in the novelette writer,
and can also often function copiously in great writers without any
fruitful result,[41] so that it cannot be used as a measure of creative
fecundity, the only proof of that being the use to which the selected
germs are put—which presupposes that there must also exist in the
consciousness a directing will and a subterranean continuity.

The use the artist makes of them depends in the first place upon the conjunction of the generic and the specific germs. At the outset, the organic development is generally apparent in the form of explicit or implicit association: the scarlet letter, for example, is implicitly opposed to both the white letter of the angel and the black letter of alchemy, while the green letter[42] appears spontaneously to provide the flower with leaves borrowed from the sea—which tells us something of the deep regions from whence it sprang, this most ambiguous plant in the entire Hawthornian flora. These associations were part of the very texture of the consciousness, and therefore of the substance of the generic germs. It took only the slightest shock for them to appear and draw objects, words, and ideas together in the most banal, or the most surprising manner. The relationship was based upon the principle of attraction—the magnet and the filings[43]—and repulsion. The elements could thus belong to opposing signs—blood and ice[44]—or the same sign—crime and guilt. Sometimes they were opposite, like good and evil, sometimes closely connected, like purity and defilement, and in an irreversible way: the relationship in that case was moral and allegorical. Sometimes the attraction and repulsion were simultaneous or ambiguous: the relation in that case was psychological and esthetic. The natural preference of Hawthorne's mind was for essentially poetic ambiguity—the human face and the stone face[45]—sometimes in disquieting forms—evil in good, good in evil[46]—the essential being that choice should remain possible. Ambiguity and freedom of choice were alone able to introduce an esthetic dimension in the blueprints being prepared, to allow the necessary play between the elements seeking to form a unity, and to make further development possible.

In Hawthorne, at the origin of those germs that were destined to develop, there was always a static (moral) element and a dynamic (psychological and esthetic) element, each counterbalancing the other.[47] They could not evolve in isolation. Thus a color, a light effect, an anecdote could not take on the value of a germ except within a simultaneously moral and psychological context: red in that of suffering and sin, rays and shadows in that of the heart's contradictions. Pure allegories[48] and attempts at wit[49] were alike condemned to sterility. Whatever, in advance eliminated all ambiguity also halted the creative process. A fertile current meeting a static element could result in a sudden and premature crystallization in the form of a maxim, a moral formula or a sketch.[50] Once the germ had been fixed in this form no further fertile encounter could occur.[51] It had to free itself again before it could enter into a fresh association. Thus the theme of sincerity returns in dramatic form,[52] having meanwhile acquired, through a chance contact, a dynamism that it had not possessed in isolation. The rule, it seems, was that the ethical element had to be vivified by the esthetic element, while conversely, the poetic impulse had to be braked and controlled, the beauty of the work ballasted, by an existential, moral gravity. This could not happen unless the static element was first of all made flexible enough to become a suitable receptacle for the living element, from which we may deduce the structure of the developed seed, which had now reached the symbol[53] or formula state and comprised both a psycho-esthetic kernel and an allegorical or moral outer envelope. If the envelope was too rigid, then the seed could not continue its evolution. If it remained flexible, then development by association, by ramification and proliferation was still possible.

This psychoesthetic dynamic was brought into particular play whenever the mind was set on a scent, thus permitting the formation of a chain of fresh relations—or the re-establishment of existing connections along lines already laid down—by reviving a current as old as the consciousness itself. Thus the eddying wind, gently drawing the autumn leaves round with it,[54] evoked the movement of the serpent and perhaps became the coils of the escaping reptile in Roderick Elliston's garden.[55] Or else it was a vein to be exploited: that of the blind man exploring the world,[56] that of childish experience,[57] of existence experienced as successive installments,[58] life as an intermittency, the artist's own life rhythm become the object of conscious experiment. Nothing stimulated Hawthorne's psychic dynamism as much as experimentation, for curiosity was one of the most powerful motive forces of his cerebral activity. What would happen? Hawthorne never restrained his impulse toward hypothesis:[59] he imagined perilous relationships—an immoral creature in the heart of a virtuous family;[60] crimes; a "philosopher" injecting sin, like a virus, into a Negro slave;[61] sacrileges; a poisoning with sacramental wine.[62] He was always seeking out sensations to stimulate his creative functions: there was something of Nero in this stirrer-up of anthills.

Inventing a story is also a form of experimentation. And it took very little to spark off a narrative line in Hawthorne's head. A pile of abandoned logs immediately summoned up a dead woodcutter.[63] But though there was a dramatic framework there it lacked a psychological framework to give it substance, or if there was one, it was in the vein of "Roger Malvin's Burial,"[64] and Hawthorne decided it would be pointless to repeat himself. A tame raven following a stagecoach[65] suggested the "gothick" corpse theme. The same theme in Faulkner's hands was to become *As I Lay Dying*. Hawthorne could do nothing with it because he lacked the appropriate symbol, or moral formula. The problem, therefore, was to introduce that pre-existing symbol into a dramatic context. Sometimes the plot was present in the symbol from the very start, especially if the symbol was a character: that of the inexperienced young man suggested his development toward maturity,[66] or else a series of bungled adventures;[67] the persecuted child summoned up the circle of persecutors:[68] thus a "central"[69] scene took shape from which all the others then developed, often by simple multiplication, as with the scenes of the pillory, the room, or the death in the ancestral chair.[70] The symbol became a sighting point, a magnetic center of attraction; it was frequently an object of curiosity, of admiration, of scandal—such as the black veil, the pink ribbon, the carbuncle, or the pool in the hills,[71]—that became the concrete symbol of an obsession. Conversely, it could also be a hidden or distant object, and in that case, instead of the gathering of a crowd we have the procession. In "The Lily's Quest," the image of the temple, perpetually receding, is an invitation to pursue it.[72] Just as the ideal point beyond the earthly life summons us to a pilgrimage toward eternity.[73] Thus the symbolic image, while remaining identical to itself, imprinted a new dynamic upon the current carrying it that could become a narrative or poetic framework.

The decisive factor in the development of the germs was often of a personal nature. The caprices of a weak nervous constitution are sufficient to explain why certain subjects, some of them very tempting, were unable to come to anything: for example the blind man theme, one with a peculiarly Hawthorne flavor, and also one that seems to have been a real preoccupation with him.[74] There were also some that were too big. The Resurrection,[75] for example, is a theme for a Michelangelo or a Milton, but it tends to paralyze the disturbed, Oberon type of creator. Conversely, certain experiences and certain shocks make him return with passion to germs long since buried. The example of the Letter and the pillory is typical in this respect: both of them started off, in effect, as no more than picturesque objects at the center of already organized scenes.[76] They did not become the centers of a whole dramatic framework until placed in a sufficiently rich psychological context: in other words, it was necessary for the germ to become personal.[77] After having himself undergone the ordeal of the pillory in a moral context, Hawthorne was ripe to deal with the themes of guilt, persecution, and hypocrisy necessary to engender the indispensable concentration-camp atmosphere. The central scene was already found, the protagonists already defined in their most intimate reality. Another germ that was only waiting for the necessary psychological shock to become active was that of the dead man in "The Cursed House."[78] The shock in this case was the feeling of liberation Hawthorne experienced upon leaving Salem, the house of the past in which—in the guise of the dead Judge—he was leaving his enemies blasted by an immanent justice[79]—the ancestral house abandoned to the guardianship of an elder sister, and haunted by his self of days gone by, while he took Hepzibah and Clifford with him. The theme of liberation is the essential motive force of the novel, and the feeling of relief he experienced in writing it was the deep cause of his preference for *The House of the Seven Gables*.[80] As for *The Blithedale Romance*, that owed its origin in part to a coincidence. Returning to a spot close to the site of Brook Farm, Hawthorne was revisited by his fancy-dress self during that Transcendentalist pastoral: an excellent opportunity to make use of his vituperative feelings toward reformers and modernity. It is possible to see the adventures of Zenobia and Priscilla as being in fact an allegory of what might happen to his own daughters in a world of such deceptive appearances. The theme of veils and masks, of penetration and violation, proved stronger than all the others at this point and awakened a germ that had long been lying dormant: the episode of the drowned girl in the river at Concord.[81] Memory, when used by the writer, becomes anticipation. It is as though Hawthorne was guided by a presentiment[82] toward that final scene in which Zenobia's soul, having been stripped naked, seeks to shroud itself in a Lethean veil. In Europe, a whole series of shocks was necessary to produce *The Marble Faun*: the sense of foreignness, the light, the contrasts—memories of Arcadia mingled with those of Roman orgies—a whole world of sensations and reminiscences combined to stimulate the mind of the writer obsessed with Edenic beauty and a lost innocence. Moreover the statue of the Faun produced a genuine case of esthetic love at first sight: the novelist seized upon it as a symbol of his primal self, and then, beginning from the Golden Age, he made his way a second time along the path to knowledge in the hope of discovering his ultimate self. If the development of the esthetic germs was indeed linked at this point to a particular way of feeling and reacting, then the act of creation itself must also have been, to the utmost degree, a personal act.

IV. THE ACT OF CREATION

Creation is not a conjuring trick. Nor is the artist's skill one intended for public exhibition. The presence of spectators is necessary to the improviser[1] and the actor, and is scarcely likely to disturb the artisan who fashions objects according to a given pattern. But it would throw the true creator's processes entirely out of gear. The artist feels as much repugnance at observing himself at his work as he does at talking about it: the secrecy of the marriage bed—creation is not an act to be watched. Sometimes Hawthorne leaves it to the reader to imagine everything himself,[2] sometimes he disguises the truth, denies the existence of any depths, any hidden force[3] within himself, and asserts that he has an "abhorrence" of mystery[4]—a deliberate attempt to put us off the track, so that he need not yield up his inner self, even though he was sometimes tempted to do so, as certain pieces bear witness.[5] Conscious of his singularity, Hawthorne defended himself by denying it[6]—for in that tiny area where all minds overlap, truly personal subjects have no meaning. As for exchanging professional secrets with his peers,[7] that he looked upon as being, like critical analysis,[8] a violation of the mind. The privilege of creation cannot be shared. Hawthorne always kept his artist's activities decently hidden, and when the long awaited impulse manifested itself in him he was merely following his natural bent when he sought to concentrate its energy rather than disperse it in words.

Whether the artist seeks inspiration in the teeming profusion of reality or in the silence of a retreat, it is a question, sooner or later, of making a pact with the world, of each agreeing to keep the proper distance—so that the images and sounds of external reality no longer constitute anything more than a background contributing to the creation of a favorable environment, even becoming totally absorbed into it. In this way, in accordance with the principle of the U-tube, the indispensable balance between exterior and interior is established. In the mind at rest, a reconciliation of all its tendencies occurs. Instead of contradicting one another they become ready to enter into harmoniously achieved alliances or oppositions; action and reflection, ethical and esthetic no longer clash, but seek a ground of agreement upon which to build together. Creation requires unity in the normally divided consciousness—a unity in multiplicity that cannot be brought about suddenly, by crystallization or mutation: the artist must remain for a long while in the posture of creation before being able to accomplish the act itself.

The creative consciousness proceeds gropingly at first: it has the world to remake. Hence the sensation of stupidity the artist feels in the face of his material, in the face of his work. This state of confusion is one of the prices the creative temperament has to pay. But the cause of this chaos is a superabundance of riches,[9] not the intellectual debility of a Clifford Pyncheon.[10] Just as certain crises activate the distillation of ideas, so the whirlwind of sudden images annihilates the mind incapable of pinning them down. One may suppose that Hawthorne was at first, like Dimmesdale,[11] the victim of visions which he subsequently reduced to order. In order to achieve dominion over the movements of his thought he had first of all to attain the zone of twilit calm where waiting was possible. It was in this half passive attitude between vigil and sleep[12] that the haunted mind was able to grasp the messages apparently converging upon it from the depths of space, able to hear the beating of muffled rhythms, see forms rise and vistas open before it. Which does not mean that we must consider Hawthorne as having been literally a nocturnal writer, even though he did doubtless write during the night on occasion, impelled by inspiration.[13] If he remained awake at night it was above all in order to profit from the obscure and silent atmosphere in which images spring up as though on a screen, in which his themes would start their secret song. No words as yet. Just directions, relationships, figures attempting to give themselves outlines. Still groping, he sought to tap the veins he sensed rising to the surface, and with a prompt, subtle, bold finger, like some surgeon of the invisible world, without damaging a single fiber, established his connections, drew together his threads, and carefully set up his delicate devices, frailer than any of those woven or embroidered webs we use as symbols for the creations of the mind.[14] Owen Warland's butterfly is in reality an image of the impalpable machinery of the creative consciousness and the tenuous web of inner creation, not of the work of art.[15]

The mind's gestures are uncertain at first. It is only through the in-

termediary of the body and the observation of external movements
that they acquire any precision. For if gestures of the mind are possible
they are so only by analogy, physical rhythms being transformed into
psychic rhythms. And conversely, the exterior gestures of the artist
are psychic energy transformed into mechanical energy. Which means
that a master's sketches may well tell us more than his finished work,[16]
for in the former we are seeing the outline of the creative gesture itself.
Pascal's rough drafts suggest the shifts and equivocations of a metaphysical mind, Hawthorne's handwriting[17] conveys the flow of an apparently tranquil and regular current. In reality, many of his letters
have a tendency to close in upon themselves (the *l*, symbol of the
self), to form loops (*j, g, f*), and upon closer examination we perceive
a succession of links, each word imprisoning an entity, a substance, a
secret. The erasures effected by spreading ink with the finger are equivalent to the painter's method of scraping off his still-wet paint. The
touching of objects, of fetishes:[18] the gesture of one blind in the dark.
And the mechanical divisions of a graph or a piece of needlework[19]
correspond to the gesture of dividing up or trimming raw material—
and also to that of penetration into the resisting object. All these gestures are, in fact, to be found in the interior process of creation too,
which implies the presence not only of interior organs but also of
interior senses and objects: for the artist is a man for whom the world
of the imagination exists and for whom it is even more real than
the other.[20]

The primal gesture of creation is that of prehension. The imagination renders objects palpable by its evocation of them, and arms itself
with organs of prehension sometimes tentacular in their strength. Hawthorne found his way around his inner universe to a large extent by
touch: manipulation of hard and compact materials, assaying of dense
blocks, fingering of tenuous veils, finger-tip appreciation of stuffs—the
rich, silky, sensuous clothing of Hester, of Zenobia, of Beatrice. Our
Puritan was a fetishist with female garments: to touch them in imagination was to grope his way toward the secrets of the flesh and the soul.
To touch the material of the Letter was little by little to feel Hester's
heart beating beneath it. All Hawthorne's fetish germs were made to
be carefully polished[21] and caressed. He began by trying to possess
objects through his sense of touch, and quite often it was in this roundabout way that he attained his vision: the mere contact of two hands
seeking one another in the darkness makes up for the lack of all the

other senses,[22] and similarly, the mind touches the object and illumines it.[23] In order to "see," Hawthorne needed darkness.[24] For he could not grasp objects effectively except through veils, through the mystery with which he surrounded them in advance and which alone spurred him on to examine them from every aspect and in depth. Hawthorne used shadows in order to make light spring forth, confused the trails he followed in order to find himself again, and created closed spheres in order to penetrate them. The detective,[25] the explorer, and the experimenter all had to be satisfied in this process. Probing, burrowing, penetrating[26]—those, just as much as the act of enclosing, of encircling, that preceded them, were the activities, the creative gestures that were specifically Hawthorne's own, that gave his work its stamp and mold. So that his creation was in fact a gesture of the mind.

It was as though the creator had to warm the elements at his disposal in his hands in order to activate their growth and their transmutations. This was, literally, the "magic touch."[27] Hawthorne's instinct for creation was not merely a need to express himself and to experiment; it was also the urge to transform, to give life. The germination of plants,[28] the unfolding of leaves and flowers, the emergence of insects,[29] and the birth of children were all so many concrete images urging the artist back to his work. It was at the moment of Una's birth that Hawthorne returned to the problem of creation with "The Artist of the Beautiful" and "Drowne's Wooden Image."[30] The artist's gestures tended to produce a fertilization of his inner world, in the first place by activating the germs within so that they released their radiations of energy: heat, light, pollen, all symbolized by the bright spangles on the butterfly's wing.[31] The mind was seeking to fill, to create a magnetic field in the waiting space where the materials of creation were piling up. The materials, concentrated inside the mind as it contracted and folded in upon itself, began to ferment, became explosive, and cried out for a dilatation of the whole consciousness. The stored material was "snowballing" inside, not by mere accumulation but by multiplication, till it had constituted a whole, an organism, a being—and then it burst, or faded: the sheaf of fire in "Earth's Holocaust," the unfolding of strange vegetations, or the melting of a snowman.[32] Creation, in Hawthorne's case, was also the growth and explosion of the self in the effort to go beyond itself. To create was to aspire to replace the world by the mind creating the world.

Like his personality, Hawthorne's work hesitated in the midst of multiple possibilities. In biology, mutations are the exception. In art, changes and remoldings in the course of the genetic process are the rule. The living organism finds its way gropingly, imperceptibly toward its definitive form.[33] The conscious work of art alone, knowingly upsetting the order of its part, seeks its own plan. The mind must "lubricate [its] object" for a long while,[34] knead it carefully, set it aside, return to it, perform transpositions: an intermittent but relentless and untiring labor. No one who has not attempted it can ever become aware of the existence of creation's cogs, which can only be brought into play if they have been positioned in advance. There are those who believe themselves to have labored as artists and who have contented themselves with a mere simulacrum. There are several degrees in creation, degrees of intensity, degrees of authenticity. Imitation is only a form of creation powered by sympathy,[35] an act of mystical love lost in a great work. Hawthorne showed clearly enough the difference he made between his own productions and the artistic triflings of his wife when he left certain domestic or everyday fields entirely to her.[36] Sophia, though she may have believed herself to be an artist,[37] was merely an amateur capable of bringing off a pretty piece of lady's work, either in painting or in prose, but not of creating a true work of art. Hawthorne was also well aware that his own creations were not all produced on the same level. In the twilit atmosphere with which he surrounded himself, the inner mirror often remained "tarnished";[38] the images he stirred on such occasions were mere cold ashes, and everything to which he attempted to give life remained torpid and lacked any vitality of tone,[39] with the result that he was not far from extending those characteristics to everything he produced.[40] How many incompleted acts before the "wall of ice" between the author and his subject was at last thawed![41] And then the illusory satisfaction of writing in an unimpeded surge after a flash of inspiration! It was better, after all, to be forced to dig, to burrow into his own mind as though into the earth in order to wrest from it, however laboriously, a glittering stone[42] that might perhaps be the Great Carbuncle itself,[43] to wrench from his wretched brain, however painfully, a glowing allegory[44] that might prove capable, like the Dragon's Teeth,[45] of germinating in the field of consciousness and of opening springs in it that would gush forth in sparkling abundance.[46] This plenitude in the act was the manifestation of genius. But it did not come until it was ready, and it was for its sake alone that the entire apparatus of creation was deployed.

If the world of daydreams offers no resistance to the imagination it is because the imagination is content with vague ideas. In creation, the images need to be detailed and precisely modeled. The floating faculty must be transformed into specific organs, into tools, into precision instruments: Alice Vane's brush, Drowne's graving tool, Robert Danforth's hammer and anvil, Hester's needle, Owen Warland's fingers, Aylmer's retort,[47] all lend their invisible aid, while powerful and discreet machines set vast constructions into place: strength and delicacy, an alliance at which Hawthorne himself marveled[48] and which was necessary for his inward labors. He stood at last in the center of the spreading net he had so stubbornly woven. What was later to be a lethal web[49] was at this point a magnetic fabric of threads that vibrated to his touch. The world he had for so long sought in vain to construct inside him had for this moment become a perfect sphere within which he reigned as master, yielding himself up to an intense activity in which magic entered into harmonious conflict with mechanics, geometry with fancy. The momentum, the interest that his mind then excited within itself, was prodigious. The emotion caused by creation became the summation of all the emotions previously experienced and now transformed into a new emotion: not pity, not terror, not love, not hate, but a vibration esthetic in kind, shaded with tenderness, with amusement, with sadness, with abstract anger, and which, at its paroxysm, produced a feeling of dominating both the organic and the inorganic world. At this stage, even the greatest efforts cost nothing; his mind was able to surpass itself, to expend itself and multiply itself at the same time. Nothing had any weight. Everything disposed itself, transposed itself, was raised by its own power, was borne along. It was the activity of play raised to an incalculable power, all the elements of his consciousness taking part in it, habits, phobias, moral principles all caught up in the heart of the effervescing psychic mass, losing their paralyzing tendencies or their rigidity in order to serve as an infrastructure for the constructions taking shape. Though art may be a gamble there is nothing gratuitous in it, for the artist is staking his very being in order to achieve the liberation of his haunted self, the discovery of a new relation between man and the universe and of a significance in his acts and his destiny never before brought to light. This discovery is at the same time a spectacle,[50] that of the birth of a being, of a world for which the creator is responsible and which he models, organizes, and transmutes at white heat. The apogee of creation is characterized by omnipotence. No one knows "the secret of [his] powers" before having been through this experience:[51] it is the lyric state, the state that Goethe spoke of as being drunk without wine, and in which everything is possible. At such times the creative mind, enveloped in its own creation, pours outwards in an impetuous torrent, full of its own strength, its fantasy, its demon. The inner energy is transformed into a will toward outward projection; images and rhythms are poured into the waiting mold—in Hawthorne's case the narrative, become poem: inspired and savage[52] utterances which, as opposed to writing that is dead, cause the thoughts to leap upward in answer—a perpetual exchange between the moving, changing text of the consciousness and the linear text, milestoned like a road, like a map, of the written page.[53]

This perfect osmosis only occurred at intervals. Whereas the creative forces in the work of nature never abandon the gestating creature as it bathes in the abyssal warmth of the womb, human works, external as well as internal, are built up, destroyed, then built up again by successive tides. When the wave withdraws the work is deserted: nothing remains but the manuscript, splotches of color, an inert block. A fresh thawing of the consciousness must take place before the writer or the painter can rediscover the paths by which he reached that spot and press further on. The most ungrateful labor is that which must be done in the chill pause between two creative waves, for nothing is more difficult than to recast what has once been poured into a defective mold. To rediscover, to recreate that mold every time, that is the artist's perpetual anxiety.[54] It is only in the act of total creation that he takes full possession of his work, that he conceives its form not in the abstract any more but in the concrete, and is able to surpass himself at last in inspiration.[55]

V. THE INNER DIMENSIONS

It may be said that the artist exists as an artist thanks to a particular organ that has come into being within him without his knowledge, of whose existence he is more aware than other men but which he is perpetually afraid of losing because of its capriciousness, and which must seemingly be indefinitely and continuously recreated—an organ that functions only intermittently, that in which the poetic faculty resides and that reveals strange vistas to the mind—vistas which he will increasingly desire to explore to their depths. This being so, the dimensions of the external world, considered as a system of references, become inadequate and, in the form of utilitarian space and time, unacceptable. The writer is first of all obliged to create an inner space and time that will serve him in the office of a relative, flexible infinity and eternity that is renewable at will, an environment in which the total self can flower as if within himself. This is why the poetic organ must be exercised as a muscle is exercised, for it alone is capable of creating those conditions. Hawthorne began cultivating the faculty of concentration in himself from his early childhood. Illness, in certain privileged cases, is a happy accident, as with Montaigne and Pascal, for it teaches the senses to direct themselves inwards, and it is within himself that the poet sees and hears: otherwise how could we explain the blind Milton's visions, or the deaf Beethoven's music?

There are rituals that aid the mind in rendering itself sensitive to these inner dimensions. Gide sat down at his piano or selected an appropriate book to read. Steinbeck listened to records. Hawthorne, sometimes with the aid of physical exercise,[1] sometimes by mental concentration, also used to take his distance from external time and space in order to penetrate into the imaginary room of the haunted mind, using as his open-sesame the half-light of dusk, the glow of coals,[2] or the blue tinge of moonlight,[3] whether he was conjuring up a beloved face,[4] contemplating a work of art,[5] or communing with the forms born of his own imagination. This adjustment to a twilight and shade was so natural with him that he could even perceive the sun as the reflection of a copper kettle[6] in a Dutch interior. His vision was very prone to assume an intimate, restricted, archaic character; whereas in bright daylight, surrounded by boundless space and teeming reality, he was seized with vertigo. For him, light had always to be mingled with shadow, immensity bounded, the present remembered. It was within the circle of surrounding hills, of a bay, or of the horizon that he inscribed his space; within a forest, within a house, within a cloud[7] that he enclosed it. Infinity for him was closed, bathed in the light of a legendary eternity, that of the stained glass window.[8] And his secret, inner universe was interfused with that infinity, as the past with eternity.

Inner space is as vast or as limited as we wish. The external world is perpetually sending the artist's mind back, like an echo, into his imaginary world, and that imaginary world shrinks or dilates according to whether the soul is in need of a retreat or enthusiasm, love, or creation is giving it wings,[9] enabling it to extend itself, to deepen itself of its own accord.[10] But whether the mind desires to expand so as to fill the entire universe or to withdraw into itself, it does not absent itself or take possession of the space involved other than in imagination, a fact that ultimately enables it to win on both scores, since the creative imagination is endowed with the faculty of disposing at will, either simultaneously or alternately, of both the universe it breaks through all obstacles to occupy and the space it creates for itself beyond reality. This spatial arrangement is often to be found reproduced in Hawthorne's work, particularly when the escape theme reappears in the form of a subterranean journey[11] or when the explorer of the real world is being accompanied by his Oberon double, whose presence imparts an inner quality to the reality being explored,[12] and even more so in the relationships between the communicating spheres. Shadow and light, inner self and outer world all interpenetrate one another, so that the cave, the interior cosmos, reflects the colors and the forms of the outside world,[13] like an eye that has become, in its turn, a projector and is able to people the entire universe with its images in the manner of a magic lantern. Any image is at the same time both interior and projected, and the ground of all creation, as of all thought, is a double space, at once concave, reflected, and reflecting (cave and mirror), and also convex, penetrated and measured by an imaginative flight: which is why Hawthorne was able to bridge the distance separating him from his fiancée and how his inquisitor characters are able to transport themselves from their lairs into the very minds of their victims.[14] It is never, therefore, a question of real space, but of an imaginary, poetic, nongeometric equivalent. The ambiguity of "inside" and "outside"[15] may express itself, as Bachelard pointed out,[16] as a defeated bafflement in a mind deprived of its "geometric homeland," as the anguish of claustrophobia and agoraphobia combined, the expression of which, in Oberon's terms, is the specter walking through Broadway dressed in its shroud.[17] On the esthetic level, this ambiguity—which can only be explained by the pre-existing ambiguity between dream and reality and by the identification of the being with the objects it evokes[18]—is nowhere more clearly apparent than in Hawthorne, where it is related to a fundamental interiority.

There are always two zones in Hawthorne's inner space: a luminous zone and a shadowy zone, reversible and interpenetrating, since day and night are simply the reflections of those psychological colors whose combination was to prove the supreme source of Hawthorne's most characteristic effects. This inward space, with its ability to light up or grow dark at will, could also make itself rarefied or condensed, shrink or expand, in the same way. We find it softening into moonlit nocturnes,[19] coagulating into a dark forest night,[20] solidifying into the cave from which the petrifying water flows,[21] stiffening to form an architectural structure,[22] contracting as it makes contact with frigidity,[23] only to become fluid once more under the influence of warmth and heart-dilating sympathy:[24] there are as many physical images as there are transformations of the mind. Plasticity, together with the gift of metamorphosis, was the essential quality of Hawthorne's consciousness. If it had hardened, all movement, all thought would have stopped. It chose fragility, agility, instead of hardness, putting itself at the mercy of those periods of depression during which, sinking down upon itself, it seemed stratified, reduced to two thin dimensions,[25] incapable of supporting any inner sphere. It seemed destroyed forever—then there it was, reborn: it accepted such vulnerability only in order to be more free, to take support from what was attempting to overwhelm it, in order to nourish its wavering thought with its own anguish. It re-formed itself without cease around the embryo that it brought back to life, into which its energy had already been incorporated like a yeast, and which invited the consciousness to close in and envelop it. It was at this point that the consciousness assumed the shape of a womb with multiple inner dimensions, directing all its fluids in from its periphery toward the central germ. It became an independent organ in which both time and matter were made to form a closed circuit within a space that was now a sphere.

Just as the hidden space was preceded by a void, so the time of consciousness was bound in by a current of external temporality. There is a time of composition and a time of creation. The first is to the second what the zone of retreat is to the inner sphere. And the ephemeral character of the creative act makes it essential that it should be constantly repeated, which in Hawthorne's case was not possible without a long period of even, uninterrupted, linear time, a period of "monotony"[26] during which the impulse was recreated out of its own momentum. The length of these fertile periods was given to him in advance by the slow rhythm of the approximately seasonal waves upon which his production was broadly based. The composition of the novels was to take appreciably the same amount of time as the most abundant groups of stories, which is to say a period of from five to seven months, though broken up into two or three sections.[27] The stories individually only required from three to six weeks,[28] but if Hawthorne had several on the ways at the same time, as seems probable, they may have each been spread over several months, the creative process occurring in brief and intermittent spurts—a rhythm which Hawthorne maintained over a period of twenty-five years, and from which he was to have difficulty in disentangling himself when adapting to the continuous narrative form. The longest period of sustained work could never, in his case, exceed four months, and the maximum of daily effort was nine hours: a record established by *The Scarlet Letter*.[29] The artist treated time like a canal, and divided it up into set distances to suit his temperament: he could never go very far beyond the limits of these calm reaches, all of equal depth, which were specifically measured off to fit the rhythm of his creative energy. Having these massive units of time at his disposal, he was able at any given moment to transfer a sufficient quantity of it into the closed spatial circuit within his inner sphere. The time of composition was merely the environment in which the time of creation was suspended. Similarly, the outer void protected the womb against shocks.

The time that was inserted in this way within the sphere took part in the whirlpool movement of all the other inner elements and became an energy producer. All the enclosed momentums, curving back upon themselves, entered into the gravitational orbit. The inner space was a solar system in which the planets were symbols and images, the lighter ones revolving around those more dense than themselves: the pillory, the fire,[30] the maypole,[31] the mountain, the tower.[32] This explains the circular movement of many of the works, the excursion, the tour of the arena,[33] the perpetual returns. And it was this interior movement that gave time its psychosymbolic scale. The revolution of the sun and moon around the House, the star hanging like a rapacious bird of prey above the sinning woman,[34] the interminable night of the tortured heart, all were slowed down, halted, or accelerated at the will of the consciousness. Time in the pillory is stagnant, burdensome, whereas it is devoured by the frantic flight through the forest. And the town clocks are rarely in agreement with the inner timepieces of Hawthorne's characters,[36] for the latter are marking off a personal time, moments uniquely theirs, those of inspiration,[37] of expiation,[38] of deliverance,[39] of death.[40]

Not only is it permissible to make use of these notions of gravitation and solar revolution, but other astronomic phenomena may also be recognized, by analogy, in this "inward sky": conjunctions, quadratures, eclipses, meteors—all occurring, not at mathematically calculated intervals, but arranged by an imaginative prescience akin to astrology.[41] Dimmesdale's star, entering into conjunction alternately with those of Chillingworth and Hester, is obeying a psychological law, not a mechanical fatality. The appearance of the meteor that coincides with a total eclipse of the minister's soul is foreseen: Hawthorne keeps it in reserve, a mere glimmer until the moment when he allows it to explode into the sky.[42] It is thus the movements, the very lightning flashes of the consciousness itself that are transcribed in the representations that the mind creates for itself, even those made on the written page.

These movements are also transcribed as plays of light and shade. And in the "inward sky,"[43] everything follows the laws of refraction just as it does those of gravity. Gestures, sounds, light beams, all are reflected back by mirrors, by walls, by facets, by obstacles. Hence the continual barrage of crossfire, of echoes,[44] of ricochets, of atoms dividing and uniting as their increasing heat gives them mobility. With Hawthorne, creation took place in an atmosphere of inward fascination, a fascination existing both between the elements themselves and between the consciousness and its own labors. We shall see that all the internal exchanges, psychic and esthetic, were based upon this principle, which is not without analogy to that of communication. Everything here proves that the inner dimensions were of an imaginary order, even though we are obliged to represent them to ourselves by means of mathematical symbols. And the consciousness that cannot conceive the world without a "ballasting of geometry"[45] will press that ballasting into the service of psychology as soon as it delves into itself with an intent to create rather than to abstract. The artist's geometry presents figures in perpetual evolution, like reflections in moving mirrors whose curves are always imperceptibly changing as the magician places and displaces them before the forms he is evoking.[46] The psychological space in Hawthorne's work, even more than the physical space, overflowed the containing frames of intelligence. Its dimensions expressed the consciousness's contradictory and cyclic life, the impulses of the creative spirit, its great leaps from one extremity to the other of its domain, its plunges into the depths, its soaring returns to the peaks. As Ariel, Hawthorne flew in the luminous, starry, or misty air;[47] as Oberon, he plunged into underground forests.[48] He was ceaselessly being summoned to first one, then the other of the inverse poles of his inner vertical dimension.[49] Like a Doctor Faustus, he transported himself by magic across the ocean,[50] or became a meteor and spanned a whole hemisphere. This mobility is evidence of the fluidity and vitality of his consciousness. Once it vanished, the mind was left chained in its dungeon to gnaw itself away and perish.[51] It was the fundamental motive power of the desire for psychological and esthetic investigation, and of the power to accomplish it, without which Hawthorne could not create. He had no choice but to undertake his perpetual explorations—but the itineraries to which he returned were always the same. The map of his inward world was inextricably fused with that of his first imaginary journeys as an invalid child and with that of his Bunyanesque pilgrimages as a young man.

In order to construct for himself a universe whose dimensions would assure him of the freedom essential to the creative act, Hawthorne therefore began by repossessing that childhood sphere, the sphere containing the origins of his thought, of his being, and of his art. He enclosed himself within it and then, within its walls, sought to perpetuate the movements of the inward life, the cyclical movements whose recurrences had the character of a private fatality, and of which Hawthorne's individual psychology and even his ethics bore the stamp. For Hawthorne, creation *in utero* was more than an artistic necessity: it was a psychological, almost a physical need. To recreate the conditions of creation also meant, for him, to make his way back to the original maternal refuge, to the womb—which made him a child-creator, sheltered by the womb within which he deployed all his adult powers and resources. This was why he persistently sought to identify himself with the mother, to lose himself inside her: an attempt that would have doomed his talent to failure if the memory of the father had not also been present to disturb his Lethean quietude—for the "haunted" mind, androgynous in its complex texture,[52] transformed itself into a womb in order to perpetuate its creative principle, which was not exclusively male, as the descendant of the great Puritans would have wished, so that the artist was always prone to blame himself for his lack of participation in the divine work,[53] for his failure to continue it[54] as his forefathers had attempted to do. But for Hawthorne, deprived of his father so early, God was a distant being and as if absent from his creation, aloof in an eternity whose threshold there could be no daring to cross.[55] As the artist in his inward sphere awaited the arrival of his characters, so God in his infinity awaited the souls of men. But at no point did the two spheres overlap. Communication could take place only through intercessors, through angels—through women. But did the female Christ, whether Hester or Hilda, fulfil her mission? Hawthorne returned to his solitude, to his fertile doubts. The artist's work is a work apart, one that must be sufficient unto itself, that must redeem itself and redeem its author.

· 4 ·

Work,
the Self, and
the World

I. THE DEVIL'S MANUSCRIPT

As long as the work is in gestation, or in the early stages of its genesis, it belongs wholly to its author. The artist, pregnant with his project, seeks increasingly to interiorize his gestures. At the same time, however, the work tends to free itself from its matrix as it takes shape, struggling to exteriorize itself, to exist in the world. It becomes for its author the object of concerns that are no longer solely esthetic but also affective or social. For now, instead of the work depending upon him, he is beginning to depend upon it, upon the form it is taking despite himself in the light of day, and upon the vistas it opens up. Having ceased to be fused with the inner self of the artist and become an individualized object, it begins to exert a fresh fascination upon its creator. The work always transforms its author into a Pygmalion, whether he fears or admires it, whether he falls in love with it or comes to detest it. Hawthorne even pretended after the event that he had found the just-finished manuscript of *The Scarlet Letter* in a loft. Yet he could not see that closed book from which his mind had now withdrawn other than in the burning glow of the fetish from which it had emerged.[1] Even when the poetic fever had passed, the words that had

160

flowed from his pen still gave off for him sensual warmth, a perhaps demoniac phosphorescence, a disturbing magnetism that was still acting upon him as he wrote his introduction. Those throbbing pages were still able to move him to the point of making his voice quiver and his eyes fill with tears.[4] The work of others could also produce the same effect on him sometimes: a Thackeray novel could draw tears from his eyes, as a Greek tragedy could from Gide's.[3] The artist is also a being whom books, paintings, and music can touch more directly than other men, and for specifically esthetic reasons. There exists a sympathy, a complicity between him and all works of art—which does not exclude a sensation of unreality, of frustration, for a manuscript is as "delusive as moonshine":[4] one must have the text in print before being able to judge a work sanely, which is to say, before being able to see it as a work, and not simply as a fleshly extension of the self. The reactions of publishers are quite different in kind. For Goodrich, Hawthorne's manuscripts were so much inert matter: it was their marketable value that interested him; the art in them—and he was incapable of perceiving any but superficial merits—was an irrelevancy. First came the rejection of *Provincial Tales,*[5] then the sabotage of *The Story-Teller*: printed without order, stripped of the picturesque and anecdotal elements that were intended to frame it, the work was disfigured.[6] Hawthorne felt that he had been betrayed. So many sacrifices, so many mutilations doubtless forced upon him by the need to please his publishers, not to mention the cuts that he made in "Monsieur du Miroir" and "The Seven Vagabonds" in order to please his fiancée.[7] All of which resulted in his actually feeling ashamed of his best stories, some of which were to remain moldering away in magazines for many years, in great danger of being forgotten.[8] To add insult to injury, having succeeded in inspiring him with a revulsion for his own work, Goodrich assigned him to the most degrading task of all for a writer—that of compilation. For months on end, with a sort of fury, he devoted himself to the amassing of the literary pabulum that was to absorb and distort his talent.[9] Germs already in existence, themes such as that of the petrified man,[10] were diverted from their true destination in order to serve in an article on "The Preservation of the Dead" or on bells.[11] Though in the midst of a normally propitious season—the spring—Hawthorne was condemned to let the superabundance of his energies overflow into such drudgery and to pillage his own work in order to fill the pages of an educational anthology. "The Canterbury Pilgrims" and "The Great Carbuncle" were the origins of "Ancient Pilgrims" and "The Rainbow."[12] One of the only themes that took concrete form during this period of forced labor was that of fire worship[13]—and Hawthorne had been carrying the germ of that in him since childhood. Meanwhile, his energy was all being consumed without the slightest artistic or material gain.[14] He was not one of those who become rich from their pen.

Is it astonishing, therefore, that his disappointment, his exasperation, and his loss of all confidence both in himself and in others should have turned him against his artistic self and against his work? All his manuscripts filled publishers with repugnance. Therefore they must be bewitched: they were possessed by the Devil! Whereupon, despairing of his cause, he burned them all as an auto-da-fé: *The Seven Tales*, *Fanshawe*, *The Story-Teller*, to say nothing of all the letters and rough drafts.[15] "The Devil in Manuscript" and "Earth's Holocaust" express the same frenzy, that of the author who destroys his own work. A destruction that was simply an inverted form of creation—a love-hate —an act that is never anything but an external simulacrum, an exorcism. For in the depths of his heart and his consciousness the work remained, like a poison,[16] like a flame of enthusiasm or rage,[17] like a promise of reconquest:[18] though the losses sustained were nonetheless irreparable. Perhaps, among those *Seven Tales*, there was another of the same quality as the "Hollow of the Three Hills," so much admired by Poe.[19] And in the *Story-Teller* disaster it was an entire aspect of Hawthorne's work that was threatened with oblivion. Since his intention had been to compose his stories into a continuous cycle, like those of Boccaccio and Chaucer, making use of the two aspects of his own personality—which were much less strongly contrasted in the version ultimately published—he was often to be tempted to resuscitate his Storyteller personality.[20] The framework of the book seems originally to have comprised a narrative and geographical element, at times semi-autobiographical, and a moral element as well.[21] The itinerary was very probably that of his own summer excursions, and the *Sketches from Memory* perhaps give us some idea of the original plan of the work.[22] As for the complete arrangement of the work and how its parts were to be linked, it is scarcely possible to do more than suggest, with the aid of such elements as have been preserved and with the utmost reservations, an idea of what it was to be.[23] There is reason to suppose, however, that the manuscripts destroyed were above all the drafts and sketches from life—the equivalents of "notes," since the notebook itself had not yet become a sacred depository in Hawthorne's own eyes —and also the tales of the vagabond. In any case, the Oberon vein was almost certainly predominant. And it was also the one that bore the finest fruits.

These fruits were not much enjoyed by the public. To some they seemed insipid, to others suspect. Being all twice- or even thrice-told tales,[24] they caused little stir, until the day when the author of "The Gentle Boy" also became that of *The Scarlet Letter*. The defenders of a threatened morality, the censorious,[25] the prudish,[26] and even certain ministers,[27] all leagued together in order to provide Hawthorne with a *succès de scandale*. Truly, neither George Sand nor Shelley had ever imagined anything so immoral.[28] According to these spirits, blinded by their own concern for appearances, young American literature had to be pure, just as the young American soul had to be white.[29] Hawthorne saw and painted black.[30] This faculty for plunging into the dark night of the consciousness, this "great power of blackness,"[31] alarmed the public. Even though sometimes tempted to become a participant in the illusion of his contemporaries' ideals, Hawthorne could not prevent himself from seeing darkness even at high noon.

This is why his work was, to use Poe's expression, "damned": not so much because of the "faint praise"[32] it received, or because of the lukewarm climate in which it developed,[33] but because it appeared absolutely out of its time. There was then no psychological, esthetic, or moral background that would enable it to be placed in its true perspective. If we add to the contempt and lack of awareness shown by the general public for the persecutions of the Salemites, then it is hardly astounding that Hawthorne's pen should sometimes have distilled the gall and venom of satire,[34] and that he should have taken revenge upon his enemies, as Dante, Michelangelo, and Dryden had, by immortalizing their scoundrelly behavior in his works.[35]

The pen, that most cutting of all weapons, is also the most perverse of tools. Neither the hand nor the mind can afford to trust it. Hawthorne was even reduced to cursing this "abominable little tool."[36] Though that was at a time when he had reached the final stage of his writing career, which is revealed to us in all its distressing details by the bewildering *Grimshawe* manuscript, that agonized set of variations on the theme of impossible creation.[37] In it, in its agonies of impotence, we surprise an artist in decline, animated by a frenzied, obstinate desire to create[38] even though his faculties are no longer capable of response.[39] Instead of the joy of creation, torture.[40] He wrote it all down: the discontinuous, hacked off, incoherent story of his characters, the corrections, the reflections, even his exclamations of rage, of disappointment, of despair.[41] The multiplication of hypotheses had ceased to be a useful source of ambiguity and become a sterile mechanism.[42] The work had become a diabolical trap, a bewitched mirror. It drained the writer's brain, it sucked his very substance from him. He was killing himself working for a succubus, trying to fill an insatiable void. Oberon, the enchanter attempting to continue his spellbinding after the allotted hour, was caught in his own trap. The web he constantly saw before him,[43] the concrete symbol of which was the inextricable manuscript in which he was tangled and stuck, that web was the very fabric of his creative consciousness, a fabric he himself had woven, thread by thread, and which now, stiffening around him, was binding him and strangling him.[44] The sphere's cycle was completed: we now behold the creator himself imprisoned in a petrifying cave,[45] a cave in which, surrounded by the bric-a-brac of his museum and the shattered machinery of his art, he is threatened by madness.[46] Even though he attempted to disguise the truth from his family, despair was closing in on him, a perpetual irritation snarled inside him. When his daughter Una confessed to him that she wrote stories he received the confidence with a face that surprised her, with a harshness that shocked her;[47] he forbade her absolutely to write, rediscovering in that flash of anger the authoritarianism, the intransigence of the Puritan patriarchs. He wanted to keep the privilege, within his family, of being the sole artist and creator; above all, he did not wish the name of Hawthorne to be added to those of the dozens of other female writers already cluttering the American scene. The American genius was still in his eyes that of the great male ancestors, now dethroned by feminism. But could Hawthorne still invoke a past that had lost its meaning for him? He had been cut off from it by events, and frustrated by the same blow of an entire future. What he needed was a long rest, a long, oblivion-bringing sleep—for he had always desired to live his life by installments[48]—a respite that would have permitted him to adjust his mind to a world in convulsions, a world teeming with horrible realities that his own intuition had nevertheless already surpassed on the psychological plane. But could he, by some sudden mutation, become a Whitman? The truth was that his cycle had been accomplished, that he no longer had anything to say, and that, being no longer able to bear the void that was replacing the creative power within him, he was attempting to deceive himself—Laocoön locked in an exhausting and pathetic struggle with his Athena. Hawthorne was a typical example of the artistic personality that has developed from a single psychic nucleus, flowered, and is then doomed to disintegration.

II. UNION AND DIVORCE

Just as there are exchanges between the consciousness and the external world before the process of creation, so there exists a reciprocal communication between the consciousness and the work as it is created. The work demands all the energies, all the resources of the personality that is carrying it. And that personality must adapt itself to the work's presence and model itself upon it. The work becomes a second consciousness that borrows the structures of the first. This double, this new being will then go on to live its own, independent life, leaving the exhausted, dispossessed artist to experience the prostration that succeeds a fever,[1] the void that follows a harvest, so that he would often renounce all attempt to renew the experience, were his unconscious being and his physical being not in league against such an outcome, and were there not always left, after each creation, a secret store within him that is the pledge of a possible rebirth. Though the work is created at the expense of the self, the self is in its turn regenerated by the work, and even created by it. For Hawthorne, pursuing the composition of *The House of the Seven Gables*[2] to the bitter end and giving himself up entirely to the devouring demon of *The Scarlet Letter*, also meant attempting to renew his own being. "The poem must write its poet," Alain Bosquet says. Creation demands that the poet shall each time raise himself above the level of his everyday self. It is, as Wagner put it, lifework, a perpetual renewal of the being through successive works.

Each work draws diverse currents toward itself and constitutes a point of convergence, a nexus where the creator's art and personality are both thrown back into the melting pot. We cannot, in Hawthorne's case, speak of a genuine evolution. The data of his art and self remained the same from the beginning of his life to its end. Everything rested upon the complex formed by the Oberon aspect and the social, communicating aspect of his very individual genius. He scarcely seems to have experienced artistic immaturity,[3] apart from his first novel. He is himself even in the very first stories. We can scarcely even talk of adolescence, or if we do then we must make it clear that it was in some sort a period of prematurity. There was nothing childish, nothing wild and whirling or groping, in the progress of his art. It is only from Oberon's dandyism,[4] from the resurgence of the orphan theme,[5] from the romanticism of the solitary genius[6] that we can divine the presence of a personality suffering from some lack, from some insufficiency that he himself is playing upon rather than being the plaything of, and without which he would not be an artist, since the work has been called into being precisely in order to compensate for it. A creation based in this way upon such intimate preoccupations could only have resulted from the attainment by the artistic personality—in this case the Oberon persona—of its fulfillment.

With physical and emotional maturity, the new Adam came into being. His adolescent narcissism, his feeling of having been abandoned, his personal obsessions receded into the background leaving the center of the stage to the grown man's moral, social and intellectual concerns.[7] This was no more than a lull, however. Optimistic themes and the Edenic myth of the prosperous and immaculate young American couple could not truly inspire him:[8] they were reassuring surface images hiding the anguished abysses still lying beneath. The artistic personality is a compromise between appearances and a sensed truth. Art, however, refuses to be any sort of compromise, or to pursue any other ends than its own. Hawthorne knew that he had to have a theme that was absolutely pure, even if it were also infernal—pure, even if that meant incorporating all the corruptions of the heart in its flow, so obstinate would be his journey in search of art's truth. He was not to rest until conjugal happiness and misery had furnished him with that theme. And there followed those two successive descents—"Ethan Brand" and *The Scarlet Letter*—in which all the Oberon themes burst forth in unprecedented splendor. Hawthorne was at last fully himself, and his creation had carried him both to the oceanic deeps and to the summit of his being. Yet this latest work of his seemed foreign to him after the event,[9] excessively somber,[10] and abstracted from some nightmare. He felt doubts as to whether it could have been in his nature to produce such a monster. One could swear that being forced to recognize himself in the author of his masterpiece filled him with

fear. This story from the depths of the past was also, from the artistic
point of view, a leap of half a century into the future.[11] Yet he himself
does not seem to have been concerned with the psychological originality of what he had just written. Stupefied by the dark tone of the
story, alarmed by its deliberately experimental character, he was convinced that the work was altogether too personal, that he had betrayed
himself, in short, which in his eyes constituted both a moral and an
esthetic sin. He had been unable to control his actions,[12] and that dis-
tressed him, not because he had exhibited his clumsiness as an artist,
but because he had gone so much further than his hopes. In the depth
of his consciousness there floated a face that he could never forget,
that of the sacrilegious monster. He had always known that this
violator of souls was there inside him, but he had never seen it so close
to the surface before. Partly driven by his own bitterness, he had
probed into the heart of man without pity. And it had been not only
a form of reprisal against his fellow men, and a violation of his own
heart, but also and equally an act of instinct. He had taken all the
unspeakable feelings, all the pains and foul spots of man's consciousness and made them his own—locked them up inside him. And then
he had probed down to fetch them out again, so as to offer them as a
spectacle, to set them loose amongst the crowd.[13] Now, he felt remorse: though that did not prevent him from remaining perpetually
fascinated by that same abyss for the rest of his life—and when he
evoked the abyss of "gothick" absurdity,[14] was it not in reality the
abyss of the soul he was thinking of?—though without ever again
daring to descend into it, despite his constant hovering on the brink.

Is this, in fact, the reason why from then on Hawthorne was always
attempting to be something other than what he was, to write otherwise
than he actually wrote,[15] to be a realist, to repudiate his former self,
which was not, he told Fields, "very much to [his] taste,"[16] and to
consign all his "allegories" to the flames? All delusions, for there was
never to be any other artist in him than Oberon.

After that descent, he wanted to get to the surface again, to breathe,
to see the light. Yet the sun of *The House of the Seven Gables* is even
paler than the contained fire of *The Scarlet Letter*. Despite himself, it
was still the shadows, the dark crannies of the House that he insisted
on exploring. And even in *Blithedale* it was not the golden delights of
those optimistic theories that interested him, but the darkness behind
the veils.[17] The last phase was to be one long and vain attempt to dig

his way back to those buried wellsprings. Meanwhile, the heyday of his maturity was squandered upon fancies brimming with talent but without any real import, such as the mythological tales, and he finally turned his back upon his vocation when he entered politics. He had worked out his vein—so be it. It is also evident that he was running away from himself. There are those who will claim that he had become aware of the fact that his genius was threatening to lead him irremediably away from the common path, that he was about to lose his footing in the real world, to cease to belong to his own age, to be deprived of all human contact, of all sympathy, while also forfeiting the moral support of his ancestors[18]—of all prospects the one that would best explain why, sensing that he had become a precursor, he repressed his impulsion toward the future and seemed to be prepared to halt the progress of time in his work in order to preserve his roots. A satisfactory explanation, on one condition: that Hawthorne was a timorous artist. Why did he give up the project of writing—in "the *Scarlet Letter* vein"[19]—the story of Agatha suggested to him by Melville, especially since the latter's *Moby Dick* must have been sufficient assurance that he was not alone in his explorations of the forbidden depths? Unless that was, precisely, the reason. A bad reason that enabled him, like all the previous ones, to avoid working his way back to the primary cause. Hawthorne had left his new being behind in the melting pot of *The Scarlet Letter*: in creating him, the poem had devoured him. The new Oberon, quite different from the new Adam, had not had time to strike firm root in him. He committed the fatal error of beginning to write merely from the impulse of his own momentum, as though the superabundance of energy liberated by one creation of the first order were sufficient to nourish a second. Instead of following his inner fire, he began to follow the light of common day, of reality,[20] which he believed to be more in conformity with his nature,[21] and which led him to produce a series of novels that are no more than a sugar-coated expression of his genius. After that, he was to devote the remainder of his life to a quest for the vainest of mistaken paths, a quest from which the mind, assuming with ever increasing authority its role of censor and intellectual antagonist, was constantly trying to exclude the imagination in order to drive it into the parallel but dead-end paths of the Oberon universe, the traps of Hawthorne's slowly petrifying moral maze. Constantly haunted by his deepest inner self, but always choosing those paths that would lead him away from

it even as he sought to rediscover it—for the part of him now undermined and ill with disappointment and lassitude was already asking
nothing better than to be rid of it—Hawthorne rushed half willfully
into the bankruptcy of his talent. Creation, though a long-term labor
—for work and artist form a couple, not merely for a furious and
brief copulation but for the lengthy marriage presupposed by the
possibility of a growth, a development—does not exclude the possibility of divorce. Thus Rimbaud, for example, repudiated his muse
soon after emerging from adolescence. The aging Hawthorne, about
to decline into premature old age, could no longer oblige his to serve
him. Just as the artist within him reached maturity with great rapidity,
so that same artist was to destroy himself with equal speed. After the
brief reawakening of the *Marble Faun*, Hawthorne the artist was no
more than a shadow of his former self. He was to have been an adult
genius for twenty-five years, having scarcely known an adolescence.
Though at an age when demons normally lose their energies, he had
nevertheless succeeded in experiencing the burning torment, the wild
flights of a Poe or a Melville. But what he was to be deprived of was
the Olympian old age of the patriarch-creator, of whom James was to
prove the American prototype.

Yet Hawthorne did not believe in his own maturity, or rather, his
maturity as an artist did not satisfy him. He felt the lack of a maturity
as a man of action. To be an artist, a nonrealist artist, sheltered by his
art, that was to remain a child, a minor. He provided the "realists"
with their most telling argument against himself. He discounted entirely the too precarious strength that made possible the inward transpositions and the oneiric fidelity that also constitute a "realism." Unlike
Rousseau, he could not be content with his art and his self.[22] The
artist's nature, "winged" though it may be,[23] appeared to him nonetheless as unstable. Where Baudelaire conceived a bitter pride in his
possession of it, Hawthorne lamented his, and looked upon the majority of the poets he met as ill-formed creatures: Tennyson, whom
it would be easy to take for "a madman";[24] Leigh Hunt, so sensitive
and secret;[25] W. C. Bryant, a torpid mind for whom the world "lacks
substance,"[26] all of them recall his own Clifford, that mutilated image
of himself, a caricature spawned by the masochism of an artist perpetually poised for self-destruction.

If the Oberon-artist could not resign himself to his infirm condition
as an impotent poet, then he became a criminal. Whereupon it was

the turn of the sorcerer, the moral pervert, the hypnotizer, the alchemist[27] to impose his rights. So that art tended to become akin to
sacrilege, to sexual crime,[28] to the crime of Lucifer and the Titans.
The sexuality that is a desire to save, to perpetuate, or to lose one's
being in or with another and the knowledge that is a will to power or
to destruction both meet in artistic creation. There exists in all creation
a vocation toward the libido—for Hawthorne, toward Hester, the
frustrated wife who desires a child[29]—and toward excess—for Hawthorne, toward Ethan Brand—as well as a tendency to do violence to
the work and to allow oneself to be done violence by it, while the moral
consciousness simultaneously attempts to escape the consequences of
these perilous urgings on the creative consciousness's part. So that art,
in the last analysis, is an illicit activity, at least for an artist like Hawthorne, in whom imperatives and interdicts were both indelibly
stamped. His poetic demon experienced an upsurge of enthusiasm in
braving them that was quickly paralyzed by his sense of guilt. The
most powerful motive force of his art was that toward the revealing of
the unspeakable, and yet, precisely on account of this tendency, he
felt himself doomed to reprobation unless he agreed to devote himself
to literary anodynes. If only he could make himself into a "realist"!
But that path was never to be anything more for him than a way of
escaping his temptations, not a vocation. He was even ready to try
convincing himself that the esthetic sense is superficial, and therefore
superfluous; that it has no moral value because it can exist just as
easily in criminals.[30] One more excuse to avoid using his secret weapons, though he did not extend his condemnation quite so far as to
apply it to literature. No doubt he was remembering that it had taken
generations of Puritans to produce the seed that had flowered into his
own tormented, scrupling, artist's soul. Was he, in short, the shame or
the crown of his line? He was never able to decide. Hearing his "genius" spoken of seemed to him a derision.[31] Though this in no way
prevented him from insisting upon his position as a writer (and even
using it to solicit administrative posts), from proclaiming his intention
to live from his pen,[32] or from declaring himself a citizen of the world
of art.[33] In which case, why his doubt about having heard the call of
the "still small voice,"[34] why his fear of following his vocation through
to the end? Would he have treated his genius so slightingly for ten
years[35] if Oberon had not abandoned him? And his reincarnation in
the Faun was, upon reflection, derisory: the once all-compelling cre-

ator of the cinema of the mind now seemed unable to see anything that touched upon creation other than from the outside; he was merely wasting his time inspecting artifacts, all wholly alien to his work, instead of seeking to penetrate deeper into the mystery he had undertaken to sound. Then came sterility: at which point Hawthorne seems to have rediscovered, caught in a last despairing undertow, the true importance of his adolescent's vocation. What if it was the work alone that counted? What if it required, and rightly required, the artist's entire being? The work, once betrayed, takes a terrible and mocking vengeance on the artist who abandons it and will not believe in it: in its turn, it rejects him, evades him, turns to unreality, becomes inaccessible. Had he ever created a genuine work? Had he been an artist? Had his talent been no more than an illusion?[36] This supreme doubt of the dying Beethoven may also have been Hawthorne's.

III. COMMUNICATION

The halt that the artist imposes upon time, his deliberate exclusion of all that occurs around him while he is creating, does not stop the real progress of events. From that moment when he has chosen to close the account of his dealings with the world he is allowing himself to be left behind by it, so that the creating being is in the same situation as the being waiting to be born. He too, it seems, has a delay to make up for—an impression that Hawthorne was to retain all through his life[1]—whereas in reality he has moved ahead of the world, since he has to wait for his contemporaries to catch up with him, since his true public has still to appear. The artist and his work do not always attain fame together. There are certain poems, certain romances, now part of the common store of human memory, that have left their authors behind in obscurity. Nor does an artist's work necessarily reach posterity in its entirety. In Avignon, Hawthorne was surprised to discover that he was the author of but a single work: *The Wonder Book*.[2] Even today, for Europeans and even for his fellow Americans, he is still only the author of a single book: *The Scarlet Letter*. It is the book that is famous, rather than the author. It is books that are admired, not whole bodies of work. Often, indeed, it is merely an oral version, or a repeatedly heard title that is adopted as a symbol, repeated like a slogan.

Certain works have their titles as it were indelibly printed upon them, a sign, a name, a letter—a fact of which Hawthorne was the first to suggest taking advantage, since he asked for the letter *A* to be printed red on black, on the cover of his first edition,[3] as much for a publicity gimmick as a heraldic motif. Others, like literary bastards as it were, present themselves to their authors without any names. As was the case with *The House of the Seven Gables* and *The Marble Faun*, for which Hawthorne thought up dozens of possible titles.[4] For it is as though the author has not fully recognized and completed his work until he has baptized it: to give it a name is to define it, perhaps for ages to come. When Hawthorne reverted to his first title for *The House of the Seven Gables* it was because he sensed that the work could never truly be itself unless it bore that name, like a ship or a stately home. The title of a work is always a coat of arms.

The profound longing of the artist is not so much to make all things beautiful in order to live in a wholly harmonious world[5] as it is to create formulas that will stamp reality with the impress of his art, to refashion nature in the image of his thought, to transform the world into a work of art, to make it a personal museum. In a community of artists, each artist would therefore have his own particular museum from which the works of the others would be excluded:[6] the city of beauty would be a city of rivalry and "schools." In which case, would the man without any esthetic pretensions not be the person best able to make contact with works of art, when they are the sincere expression of a truth?[7] Hawthorne would have liked to have created in sympathy with the general public,[8] to have been acclaimed, as Yevtushenko is today, to have known at last one blaze of glory.[9] Illusion. The general public did not possess the sensitivity he attributed to it; it was not even responsible for the quality of its emotions—emotions that those with the necessary astuteness make it their business to provoke. But Hawthorne, alas, had nothing of the "ubiquitous quack" about him.[10] His first concern was with what he carried inside him, with the means of rendering it communicable without denying himself in the process. And that concern led him to take the strait gate of art: instead of newsworthy brilliance, discreet chords that scarcely rose above the threshold of hearing. His inward themes could reach the ear of a lazy public only with great difficulty.

Is it the fault of the work if it does not immediately awaken admiration? Or that of the world? An esthetic emotion requires both a spectator and an object, the first in a certain disposition of mind,[11] the second standing in a certain light. Which is why the work cannot, after all, be wholly released, wholly abandoned to itself in the world. There must exist a certain degree of distance or mystery if we are to be touched by it; the soul must be prepared for the encounter. Hawthorne welcomed none but chosen visitors into his inner library. So that the ideal reader was for him a friend, a confidant, and, as with Baudelaire, an accomplice[12] whose enlightened sympathy was his recompense for the mockery of the multitude.[13] He therefore interiorized his communication with others—he interiorized the world afresh in order to communicate with it. For the world whose progress lags behind that of the mind has no coin with which to repay the artist's gift.[14] The artist must find his recompense within himself, in his own secret certainty.

In his own lifetime Hawthorne never found his place in the world in which he was creating, on the basis of which he built up his works, usually by reaction. The anonymity that was forced upon him and the pseudonyms his artist-self was obliged to assume[15] did indeed make him the obscurest writer in America.[16] And even the modest renown he was later able to enjoy was founded for the most part on misunderstandings. It was the moralist, the lay preacher,[17] the poet of the graceful fancies that were being honored in him. And it was the innocuous embroideries of Mrs. Sigourney that provided the standard for judging the merits of the "Night Sketches,"[18] the "gothick," even the flamboyant qualities of Mr. Pierpont[19] that were often the chance criteria of a reader's appreciation of "Young Goodman Brown." Or else he was extravagantly praised for all the wrong reasons,[20] as when he indulged in the sentimental facility we find in "Little Annie" or "The Town Pump,"[21] the latter story eventually being pressed into service, in tract form, as temperance propaganda! Then, the Transcendentalists, taking over "The Celestial Railroad," almost the only one of Hawthorne's works that Emerson deigned to honor with his approval,[22] the reason being that he saw it as a pamphlet. Generally speaking, the author of *Twice-Told Tales* was recognized as possessing grace, fancy, but not much force:[23] in short, in an age when literature was being invaded by women, an essentially feminine talent. Meanwhile, Hawthorne was consumed with fury at having to watch a damned mob of scribbling women[24] reaping a harvest of easy popularity at his expense, while the most enlightened critics of the age were for their part awaiting the appearance of the male genius, America's poetic Jupiter,[25] that same figure whom Hawthorne himself saluted as the master genius of the age,[26] though without risking giving him a name—perhaps, who knows? for fear of cheating himself out of first place. One might have supposed that it would have been his upon the appearance of *The Scarlet Letter*, but that masterpiece was greeted, in the event, mostly with shouts of scorn.[27] *The House of the Seven Gables*, applauded enthusiastically by Melville, Whipple, and Chorley,[28] awakened no echo whatever in the circles that created American opinion at the time. Hawthorne was held in high esteem neither by the prudish,[29] the reformists, nor the neo-Platonists. Emerson was of the opinion that his work had "no inside to it,"[30] and abolitionist opinion forced his rising fame into a new eclipse the moment his *Blithedale Romance* appeared, in such a very unfortunate conjunction with his panegyric of a supporter of slavery.[31] In the end, it had to be Whitman, whose personality and esthetic program were at the antipodes of Hawthorne's, who, though wholly unknown to his idol, protested against this oblivion and proclaimed Hawthorne to his blind and deaf contemporaries as the prophet Elijah of the New World, "the first Poet, the first Historian, the first Novelist, the first Tragedian our country has produced."[32]

Even though he was already, in some people's eyes and even in England, a classic in his own lifetime, Hawthorne could never quite succeed in believing in himself. He even went so far as to choose a mentor, in the person of Whipple,[33] whose advice he asked like the greenest novice. (Racine, too, used to have Père Bouhours correct his work.) Despairing of ever being recognized, even after his death, he offered up a very strange prayer during a visit to Westminster Abbey, in the Poet's Corner: that those who had tried, even in vain, to scale the peaks of art should all nevertheless find their places on Parnassus.[34] And he, would he be among the crowds of poor relations or at the high table? Pathetic humility of a writer who was nevertheless not unaware of his value, but whom his nature always inclined to doubt, to excuse himself in all his prefaces for the defects, the tameness, and the insignificance of his works![35] He excused himself, but he was also, indirectly, accusing. He was putting himself on trial, but was he not also expecting to be vindicated—at least on appeal? For we must remember that he was of the opinion that all works of art not irreplaceable should be destroyed when their little day was over,[36] leaving only the masterworks behind. In reality, however, even the masterworks themselves were seen to disappear, whereas the most absurdly minor productions lasted as long as the Laocoön,[37] at least in the case of sculptures and inscriptions. The frescoes, the paintings, the statues of past masters now peeling, rotting, shattered—what more desolating spectacle for an artist?[38] Even the most beautiful of works may cease to speak to men—and its death is also the ultimate death of the artist who created it. So that even the very greatest artist cannot be sure of posterity.

Yet it was upon posterity nevertheless, willy-nilly, that Hawthorne was obliged to rely. For it is equally true that popularity is perhaps not essential to the fate of a durable work.[39] If he had enjoyed the blaze of great fame, Hawthorne would have produced more, shown himself more brilliantly to the world, given lectures, but would he have been so individual, would he have taken the trouble to delve so deep—would he, in short, have been Hawthorne? His work had come before its time, and he had to reconcile himself to that fact. The encouragements he received had no application to the present: though he found himself celebrated in London[40] in 1834, that was no more than an assurance as to the future. The approbation of Poe,[41] the enthusiastic praise of Melville—who incautiously compared him to Shakespeare[42]—are proof of this. The sobriety and sureness of his art brought him to the notice of connoisseurs and of his peers—though even they could reverse their judgments[43]—without imposing it upon the general public. It was as though he were being kept in reserve. Communication was to take place for him in the inner space of the library, as it were outside time.[44] His work, in other words, was going to have to drag him into fame behind it. The finished work was to develop in a time and a space particular to itself, those of its own becoming, and thus, as it grew more distant, and despite its eclipses, was to reveal its author's true stature. Hawthorne's profoundness of theme and artistic orginality were bound to escape his contemporaries. It took the development of psychoanalysis and the movie to reveal them fully and to establish how much more they contained than mere fantasy and allegory. It is only now that we are able to measure the importance of the path he cleared, a path that leads on the one hand to Stephen Crane through his obsession with darkness and monsters, and on the other toward Faulkner through his haunted perception of time, while also springing from sources deep in our past, leading back as far as Bunyan and Spenser.

THE THEMES
· I ·
The Past

I. HAWTHORNE'S USE OF TIME

As with Faulkner, Hawthorne's themes are all direct functions of time. A writer's themes emanate from the deepest regions of his consciousness, and Hawthorne's consciousness may be defined as one that lived in the past, a past in which psychological time, progressing backwards, became the poetic time of memory, as opposed to the poetic time of anticipation. His consciousness was one of reflection, not projection. To reflect, for Hawthorne, meant to make himself into a mirror in order to attempt the rediscovery of a lost world, a heritage of which the poet in him was never sure. And that is why he was a poet, why he created. All the gaps left in the present by the bankruptcy of former dreams demanded to be filled. Poetic creation, a deferred, contemplated form of action, is also, as opposed to immediate action, a return through time to the origins of the being, and, for Hawthorne, to the sources of the consciousness in its totality.[1] He wanted to know. But his own feeling of unworthiness was sufficient to make him recoil from such a task, and equally, moral certainty would have meant the futility of any esthetic research. This was why he took up an intermediate position, between the moment of the world's origin and that time of vast confusions, the present: the historical period of the origins of the American nation, of American Puritanism, of the settling of his ancestors in New England, all of which he made into his own private past, his refuge and his observatory in time. Just as Hawthorne needed a

176

mirror in space in order to surprise the flaws in things, so he liked to use time as a rear-view mirror with which to reduce the vistas of past ages to order. Whereas Faulkner, carried by time as though by a vehicle, turned his back on the future[2] and waited for his images to be projected on the screen of the past, Hawthorne, at the margin of life's current, seems to have looked in at time as though through a window, or through the opening of a magic lantern,[3] watching its events unfurling in images tinted with psychological archaism inside a box. This explains the resemblance between the daguerreotype of the judge and the portrait of the ancestor.[4] The sun, however objective its light, when it penetrates into the camera obscura becomes the sun of the past. For it was always in vistas from the past, through the atmosphere of a clearly defined period, that Hawthorne saw his historical movies projected. Often, the allegorical procession of the past invaded the present: the ancestors returned to mingle with the living,[5] and pilgrims from the age of Bunyan traveled on a nineteenth-century businessman's train.[6] Or else we find modern folk in fancy dress, as in the Roman carnival[7] or at Brook Farm, where the community members amuse themselves in the course of a picnic by bringing the mythological gods back to life, mingled with figures from Spenser.[8] And what if those same people, back in their everyday clothes, were in fact ancestors in fancy dress? With what facility the bearded Puritan, with his dark cape, his sword at his side, becomes for a moment the Judge, with his fashionable sidewhiskers, with his dazzling white neckcloth, with his gold-knobbed cane.[9] These masques emphasize the importance of the past in our life, and the precarious reality of the present. A procession of Hawthorne's contemporaries, without wigs or pointed hats, without anything picturesque about them, without mystery, only took on any meaning if he could model it more or less on the pomp of an ancestral procession, so that, when glimpsed during the course of a political demonstration led by a band,[10] or passing through the gallery of the Hall of Fantasy,[11] it could assume, at a sufficient distance, a certain majesty. For the present can be lost in the past, just as new images of the world are soon effaced in the speed of a railroad train.[12] As in Faulkner's universe, the past in Hawthorne's universe makes the hegemony of temporality wholly a reality. The descending vista of "Main Street" presents us with the image of a prophetic past[13] in which everything is contained in advance. Essentially, it embraces only one epoch, an epoch that is always the same: Hawthorne lived imaginatively in the time of the Puritans in the same way that the French Classicist writers lived in the age of the Greeks and the Romans. He lived in it in order to construct a past of his own out of it—a past that was no more that of the Mathers than Corneille's was that of Augustus —and also his true present, that of his acts, of his enduring and ever-present works.[14] What is and what will be only exist through the agency of an anterior and indestructible reality—a reality that germinated at the moment time began and has been ripening with it ever since. Present day reality, in Hawthorne's eyes, was therefore inevitably tinged with archaism.[15] For him, time had almost the same value whether one journeyed up its stream or down it: is not everything the past in relation to eternity? If so, then the past, which encloses the whole of temporality, is nothing other than the place of man's exile.

Thus imprisoned by time, Hawthorne made himself its explorer, and the anxiety always alive within him drove him to seek for ways of escape. But how to escape from the past while also remaining faithful to it? The riches he mined from it were irreplaceable, but the burden it imposed upon him was oppressive. The divorce became certain at the moment when Salem, a symbol of his colonial and family past, became untenable for him:[16] the curse that lay upon him had finally come home to roost.[17] Whereupon the past became fused with the nightmare present: once a powerful tree, the tree of life, it had now become no more than a "giant's dead body."[18] Would Hawthorne attempt to live and think in the here and now in order to avoid being crushed beneath a heap of ruins? Instead of running away he locked himself up in his room: he wrote *The Scarlet Letter*. The diatribe against the past was not to come till afterwards, when the mine had already been exploited. And when he did attempt to enter into more direct contact with his own age it was as though he were doing so in order to discover a means of access to the future,[19] with the hidden purpose of slipping unobserved to the very frontiers of the beyond, since it is the future that opens the doors of eternity to us.[20] Yet even when he took that path it was still the past he came back to, caught in the circle, the descending spiral of time curving back in upon itself[21]—a circle with its diameter tangent to eternity at the point where past and future meet,[22] the present serving merely as a transition,[23] both salvation and perdition being situated at the meeting point of the two extremes.[24] Hawthorne, a voyager in time, forward on the path of progress as well as backward on his pilgrimage to revisit the cradle of his race, was in search of his ancestral home.[25] For him, the future tended to be merely the realization of hopes from the past. Though the man might deny that past, the writer, on the other hand, was obliged to make it his true home or perish.

For Hawthorne, to live in the past did not merely mean to go out collecting examples of local color but to penetrate back into the ancestral consciousness that was so intimately mingled with his own. To tell the truth, he had only one central theme, that of consciousness, whose essential dimension was precisely the time from which all his other primary and secondary themes proceeded before being developed into two parallel cycles, each of which had a different kind of time corresponding to it. The Oberon cycle developed in the deeper time of moral and psychological realities, the Storyteller cycle in the time that is a vehicle for action, an agent of chronological relations: the cycle of secret communications is opposed that of direct communications. They both continue throughout all his work, counterpointing one another—*The Story-Teller* would probably have been the most typical example in this respect[26]—or interpenetrating one another. That one is exterior and the other interior in no way alters the fact that they stem from the same source. Despite certain appearances, it is always Oberon who calls the tune, only allowing his vagabond companion free rein in order to draw him back later into the hidden and recessed regions of dream and memory. In almost all the great works it is Oberon who is dominant. When the complementary vein takes the upper hand, it is because Hawthorne has moved away from his inner, personal, provincial bases in order to venture upon some rather unfamiliar terrain where he cannot be himself. The Storyteller's cycle, and its disparate elements taken from reality, had to be carried, if not absorbed by Oberon's cycle. When two themes occur together, it is the deeper that always carries the day. The number of Oberon tales in relation to that of the sketches is significant in this respect. And the *Letter* had to be written before the *House*, the private story before the picturesque story, before the satire and the intellectual theories. The "English novel," conceived before the Italian novel, had to yield pride of place to the *Faun*, the symbol of the elixir to that of the Fall, the "gothick" to the psychological.[27] It is true that the Storyteller's themes are always to be found intermingled with the Oberon themes, but stylized in such a way as to take on an allegorical value that gives them the necessary distance. Thus the theme of the journey and conquest of the world, from Fanshawe's wild ride to Redclyffe's pilgrimage, via Ethan Brand's excursion, the supernatural movements of the alchemist and the witches, Clifford and Hepzibah's escape, and the tribulations of Kenyon and Donatello,[28] all these "processions" are motivated by deeply buried causes. And all invariably lead back to a migration of the consciousness, to the quest for a lost sphere—the past, Eden, an ancestral home—or else to the exploration of a hidden sphere—the self, the human heart; these spheres all reciprocally engender and envelop one another, and all proceed from a single sphere made up of spheres within spheres—the Oberon self. The deepest themes, all interdependent upon one another, often develop out of a single germ, which is in the first place that complex self: consciousness of the self and consciousness of sin, indissociable from one another and soon leading to a consciousness of the rending conflict engendered by the joy and the horror of being in the world, and then, achieving the synthesis, consciousness of the moving, colored, poignant images that finally produce the poem, the tragedy—all these modes of consciousness overlapping, their nexus occurring in the realm of time, in the past, at the root of the artist's personal anguish. Hawthorne's undertaking was based upon his will to convert all instants of temporality whatever into past time, to annex them to his own private past, to make each work an instant of Hawthorne-time, outside of time—and among those instants, each eternal, we find both the noon and midnight of the Puritan mind.

II. THE PRESENT IN THE PAST: THE DEBITS AND
CREDITS OF MODERN AMERICA

The present is the past's worst enemy. It is in the name of modernity that we scorn what is outdated, obsolete. Hawthorne did not forbid himself that attitude: we find Holgrave coming to live in the House of the Seven Gables simply in order to find fresh fuel for his hatred of the Pyncheons and of the prejudices and abuses they embody, in order to watch an entire past of injustice crumble before his eyes,[1] while life, with the march of time, withdraws from those timeworn walls as though from a wreck: soon, the proud Pyncheon home will be like the ruined church rotting beside the railroad track.[2] The decline of the European type of aristocracy was implicitly inevitable in the development of the American nation. But the Puritans, though they may have been the heroes of colonial independence, had nevertheless betrayed the ideal of democratic simplicity and that of individual liberty. The severity of their way of life did not stop them entertaining dreams of dynastic power.[3] And liberty—a thing apparently not incompatible in their eyes with inquisitorial intrusions into others' private lives[4] such as those of the Judge into his cousin's affairs,[5] or those of Hawthorne's personal enemies into his—was something much resembling an iron cage.[6]

Meanwhile, however, modern American society was in its formative stages. The rise of the middle classes, of the artisans, the shopkeepers, the small farmers—the Maules, the Danforths, the Hollingsworths, the Silas Fosters[7]—was beginning to make itself felt. There were penniless and resourceful men, like Holgrave, the man of all trades,[8] not to mention such opportunists and charlatans as Westervelt,[9] or the shady politicians, who were soon to create a new aristocracy, one based upon luck, success, and money, while the reformers were simultaneously attempting to realize an impossible social utopia. The time of disillusionment was at hand: whereupon our Democrat-individualist turned his eyes back toward the good old times. So that we should not be astonished at finding his tales and romances concerned more with an aristocratic than a democratic society. Hawthorne's real characters, those he studied in depth, belong to the liberal professions in which the Puritans had so distinguished themselves. They are ministers like Dimmesdale and the Reverend Hooper, magistrates like Judge Pyncheon, doctors like Chillingworth and Rappacini. Even the artists, such as the painter of the Prophetic Pictures and Holgrave, have the preacher's, the anatomist's, the lawyer's turn of mind. Often, the author leaves us in ignorance as to his characters' professions, but all the evidence usually indicates that they belong in most cases to the rich, or at least the educated classes. They are people of leisure: they have the time to ask themselves questions about their inner lives, to cultivate psychological idiosyncrasies, and to pore over their pasts.

Hawthorne is less the painter of his time than that of the moral evolution of his country, which he renders palpable by making himself the echo of contemporary realities as they struck and disturbed him. It was in his depiction of certain failures and certain unnatural effects

that Hawthorne went furthest in his own "prophetic picture" of
America, a field in which he was a precursor of both Dreiser and Dos
Passos. Among the human wrecks, Uncle Venner still belongs to a
semipastoral world, in which poverty still retains its human shape
and has not yet become a condemnation without hope of appeal.[10]
Old Moodie, the bankrupt,[11] however, is already much closer to the
shattered machines, the hoboes of America in the twentieth century.
For the blame for the modern world's misery had to be laid at the door
of the mechanical utilitarianism that was destroying man's true heritage, nature. Though the Puritans, imbued with their faith in a super-
nature, were wary of it, the Transcendentalists, on the other hand,
exalted it. Emerson made it a symbol of all wisdom.[12] And Thoreau
was violent in his protests against the false progress that was compli-
cating everything, instead of simplifying it, and polluting the source of
all life and all purity.[13] Hawthorne, for his part, saw modern science
as a survival of ancient witchcraft: since its roots lay in the very lowest
of human instincts it was bound to people the world with monstrous
shapes. With the help of the machine, man was now able to realize
certain of the ancient magicians' dreams, such as that of abolishing
distance: in the flight of the two "suspects," the two "owls," the
railroad becomes a substitute for the witch's broom.[14] And electricity
was capable of even more false miracles than alchemy. What chiefly
fascinated Hawthorne in the sphere of scientific discoveries and inventions, however, were the developments in communications and the
transmission of messages,[15] together with the bringing to light of the
phenomena of magnetism in the domains of physics and psychology:[16]
the passing of a current through solid bodies, galvanism, and, of course,
mesmerism, the science applied by the magician Westervelt that later
improves on the rudimentary hypnotic methods of the wizard Maule.[17]
Everything that concerned the functioning of the mind or psychic exchange, anything that seemed to provide a way of probing further into
the consciousness, even phrenology,[18] was of interest to him. In this
field, the concerns of the artist coincided with those of the scientist.
Though their paths very soon began to diverge, for nineteenth-century
science was apparently intent upon pursuing the mechanistic path so
heavily criticized by Bergson,[19] whereas art and psychology were to
base themselves upon organic conceptions.[20] Transcendentalism's inability to give a soul to the age's scientific civilization is an expression
of the divorce that had occurred between an ideal founded upon an

ancient humanism and the demands of a world tending to become more and more dehumanized.

The reformers of the age were also men with minds conditioned by rigid concepts: they were attempting to interpret the universe and regenerate man with theories based upon an idée fixe, without any awareness of the way in which their narrow viewpoint was perverting their good intentions and frequently making them into no more than useless martyrs. The example of Hollingsworth is particularly striking in this respect.[21] Hawthorne had a tendency to reduce philanthropy to its most extreme and absurd forms:[22] one cannot save humanity by sacrificing everything to the re-education of criminals, but only by attacking the roots of criminality—since each one of us is potentially guilty, in thought or in fact—and its material causes. Hawthorne was by no means convinced that it was possible to tear out those roots by eliminating whatever it was in the social structure that fed them. An example of conservatism upon artistic grounds: evil was his domain, his fief, his reason for existing and creating, so he defended it without even daring to admit as much to himself and put all his faith—not without a certain hypocrisy—in time, in hope.[23] The reformers, by doing violence to the course of events, could only destroy his world—as the Civil War eventually did. To destroy a world, however bad, is to destroy both the memories and the hope it contained. The living must surround themselves with their dead, put down their roots into an earth heavy with memories, rich with bones. Only then will their lives be sufficiently ballasted with the weight of past generations to take on body and substance. But Hawthorne, reduced in the end to making use of an artificial past, was to fail where Faulkner, thanks to the availability of historical raw materials ready-made for his purpose, was later to succeed.[24] The return to the "motherland" is simply a return to the womb of time.[25] The obstinacy of the Judge besieging the House has much in common with the obsession of Redclyffe and that of Sutpen in *Absalom*.[26] Even Holgrave the radical does not leave the House of the Seven Gables except in order to move to another.[27] So powerful is the magic of the past that the blackest of misdeeds, linked with the great crimes of the perpetrator's ancestors, acquires a horrible stature that justifies it. The Judge, because of his very iniquities, is a true continuer of the Pyncheon line, a status to which neither Clifford nor Hepzibah can lay claim, and Miriam, the displaced person, invokes the illustrious murderers who have covered Rome in blood before her—a retrospective method of providing the slaying of the Model with imaginary godfather-ancestors.[28] But the utopian communities had neither roots nor past. The failure of Brook Farm, like that of Oneida[29] and Fruitlands,[30] seemed to demonstrate the practical impossibility of founding a society upon new foundations—religious, socialist, Fourierist—if it is cut off from its foundations in time. How chimerical the utopian's creation is, even compared with that of the artist, which is founded upon living, even if intangible, realities, and not upon a superficial agitation of the mind.[31]

The nationalist and optimistic members of the Young America group were also betraying these fundamental realities, since they were attaching themselves to the ideal of material and moral appearances that was destined to aggravate the prevailing confusion of values even further. America, the land of the chosen, the new Eden, the land of destiny[32] whose very prosperity was a sign of divine benediction: such was the myth that was then being created by the growth of American influence in the world and the discovery of yet further wealth in the Western territories. America was already beginning to thunder out the formulas that expressed its new-found faith, that faith so cruelly ridiculed by D. H. Lawrence:[33] success, wealth, and morality, they were all the same thing. Ultimately, idealism was to be measured by material opulence. Judge Pyncheon was already the living embodiment of this paradox.[34] Less virulent than Thoreau, since he was compelled by his situation to show greater respect to the requirements of social convention, Hawthorne was nevertheless not kind to utilitarianism,[35] to the worship of the machine,[36] to wealth and the pursuit of an illusory happiness.[37] Though he defended the prestige of his country when abroad, we must not therefore conclude that he had contracted the "Yankee" mentality.[38] Though he believed that American democracy represented the future,[39] he did so mainly out of opposition to the English aristocratic social structure and for idealistic reasons. In reality, he was aware that the future had already been compromised by partisan passions and conflicting interests: the theorists were advocating opposing recipes for realizing America's earthly paradise—one side was planning a white man's paradise based upon Negro labor, the other that of racial fraternity. And together they were in fact paving the way to hell!

Eden had to be sought for elsewhere or otherwise. "Talk of heaven! ye disgrace earth!"[40] was Thoreau's cry, a cry echoed a hundred years later by Henry Miller.[41] Hawthorne himself expressed his total disapproval of budding Americanism in his "New Adam and Eve" parable[42] and in "The Procession of Life." America was trying to be the paradise of a new Adam without a past,[43] and that was why it had become possible to accuse it of having no soul.[44] But Hawthorne, unable to play along with the transcendental, utilitarian, or moralizing strains of contemporary optimism, felt himself to be more or less a traitor to his own age. Surrounded by his contemporaries, all confident in the spiritual value of their prosperity, he had the feeling of being an armored Puritan in the midst of a crowd of maypole dancers.[45] Regretfully, without pharisaic triumph, he embodied the deep consciousness upon whose shallower margins the consciousness of those around him, forgetting its roots, was busying itself with superficial futilities. Hawthorne, though a traitor to modern America, was faithful to another America, that of his ancestors.

III. THE ANCESTRAL EPIC

Hawthorne's historical consciousness was awakening at a time when the Declaration of Independence was little more than half a century old and the possibility of a continental hegemony stretching from the Atlantic to the Pacific still merely a vague dream. Hawthorne, who always considered himself above all a citizen of New England, had no ambitions to be the historian of a whole continent after the manner of Francis Parkman.[1] Though he informed himself upon his country by means of journeys and extensive reading,[2] it was always in order to return to Massachusetts in the time of the Puritans. Innumerable details concerning the traditions, manners and customs of foreign countries lay sleeping uselessly in his Notebooks, including those that were intended for use in his "English romance," despite the fact that England, from which both the Pilgrim Fathers and the Winthrop fleet had, after all, sailed, never ceased to attract him. It was in the Puritans, who were quite as intolerant as their persecutors, that Hawthorne, despite their narrowness of mind, saw America's true greatness as lying. The epic of the New World began with the emigration of the first settlers.[3] Hawthorne, however, never bothered to depict the sailing of the Mayflower,[4] probably because he thought of it as being irretrievably the province of facile, gushing verse. As for the rough life of the early colonial era, he limited himself to representing that in only a few,

highly-colored, panoramic glimpses. It was contrary to his tastes to insist upon the crushing material difficulties that ate up the physical and
even the spiritual energies of the pioneer farmers and hunters, who were
obliged to live, like cavemen, in burrows roofed with turf,[5] or like
nomads in huts imitating the Indians' tepees.[6] Even their struggles
with the redskins awoke very little interest in him. It would doubtless
have been easy enough for him to thrill his readers with re-creations of
the perilous atmosphere that reigned in those isolated hamlets on the
fringes of the forest,[7] or with descriptions of such incidents as Mrs.
Hutchinson's cruel death among the Indians.[8] But the Indian Wars,
that formed the whole framework and substance of Cooper's novels,
were accorded scarcely more than brief allusions by Hawthorne.[9]
Neither the "noble savage" nor the fine, primitive animal was to find
any favor in Hawthorne's eyes, no matter how attractive the Indian
epic may have been to Chateaubriand or Longfellow.[10] To Hawthorne,
the historian-moralist, Indians were scarcely more than picturesque
scarecrows—when their abuse of firewater was not inciting them to
riotousness.[11] He was much less revolted by the genocide perpetrated
by his race in the New World than he was by the persecutions of the
Quakers. Although he criticized the early settlers for their racism,[12] he
considered the Indians wholly devoid of moral and psychological
subtlety, which was why, despite their stoicism, he despised them and
refused to tolerate either the romantic aura in which some writers attempted to clothe them or their supposedly admirable barbarism.[13]
Moreover, when he seized upon Mrs. Duston's odyssey[14] it was because
it enabled him to show primitive violence in an even more unfavorable
light when displayed by a woman born of a reputedly civilized race.
Consciousness in a rudimentary state held no more interest for him
than rudimentary forms of society. This is why he chose to write about
New England society during an era when it had become sufficiently
consolidated to permit the development of the individual consciousness
and to confront adversaries more suited to the stature of a great nation.

    As a historian, Hawthorne concentrated above all upon America's
struggle for independence. In the history of the United States that he
wrote for children,[15] he limited himself to sketching this struggle only
in its broadest outlines, without bothering to go very deeply into its
causes. He was not overfond of describing feats of arms:[16] his purpose
was to depict, not a vast military fresco, but the triumph of a great
national and democratic idea over tyranny. The forces of oppression

were provided by England, the country from which the early settlers
had emigrated to freedom. However, the fact that the British yoke
eventually became intolerable was solely due to certain overzealous
representatives of the Crown, such as Sir Edmund Andros,[17] Edmund
Randolph, who abrogated the colonies' charter,[18] and Lieutenant Governor Hutchinson,[19] whose dream was the establishment of a hereditary
aristocracy after the British model, or to lower-ranking military men
such as Captain Preston, who was responsible for the Boston massacre.[20] Confronting the oppressors—whether they were as far away
as King George himself and Archbishop Laud, or actually occupying
the country like Sir William Howe at the head of his regiments[21]—
were the champions of liberty. And first among these were the great
Puritans: Winthrop, Dudley, Bellingham, Endicott, Leverett, and
Bradstreet,[22] all of whom are to be found in the person of the Grey
Champion,[23] the spectral figure who represents America's political and
religious aspirations. Endicott was the one who, in Hawthorne's eyes,
best incarnated the spirit of independence allied with Puritan intolerance. A very robust man, of unbreakable energy, he was made for
the New World[24]—whereas Lady Arbella, that pale flower of the
English aristocracy, withered and died after only a few weeks of colonial life.[25] A fierce partisan of the right of Massachusetts to autonomous rule and of his fellow believers' right to freedom of worship, he
was nevertheless brutal in his repression of the slightest quirk of independence in others.[26] He is the epitome of American Puritanism: impatient of an alien yoke, yet a persecutor at home; laying claim to
democratic principles, yet totalitarian and repressive. For Puritan
liberalism was always to be accompanied by an authoritarianism that
effectively negated it, as the Body of Liberties indicates.[27] These characters were well suited to the times in which they flourished, the age
of the Mathers, the very structure of whose theocratic societies was to
make possible the collective frenzy of the witch hunt.[28]

Above Puritan virtue, above its strength, Hawthorne placed the
charity of the Apostle Eliot who devoted his life to missionary work
among the Indians and to translating the Bible for their use.[29] But the
fact remained that New England's stability rested not upon evangelical
gentleness but upon military successes and moral severity. Hawthorne,
however attracted he may have been by the great Puritan past, was at
the same time repelled by the tyranny that accompanied it. Should he
smash his idols, and make the people into the true hero of indepen-

dence? Hawthorne loved the warmth of common humanity and the goodness of simple people, but he mistrusted the instincts of the mob.[30] And in the end, he was unable to do without great men, even if they were Cotton Mathers and Endicotts.[31] Though he saw the wrath of the people, "a thousand-fold more terrible than the wrath of a king,"[32] as the expression of the national and democratic genius, he had no wish to see it used as a pretext for the unleashing of men's passions. He would have liked to see the entire American people maintaining at all times and in all circumstances the dignity that he himself lent to the crowd around the pillory in Governor Bellingham's day.[33] The same tendency drove him to depict the human being once transplanted to the New World in poetic terms. The entire race has become more refined, and the women in particular have a distinguished bearing to be observed even in the lower classes.[34] Even the peasants have lost something of their primitive rusticity.[35] Hawthorne seems to have been set upon discovering an American elite, and at every level of society. He always remained fundamentally aristocratic in spirit. This is why, helped by the lapse of time, he was able to be equally moved by the greatness and virtues of the adversaries of independence as he was by those of its defenders.[36] Moreover, this also enabled him to exalt the latter even further: the nobler the enemy the more glorious the success. And were the settlers not, after all, fighting against people of their own race and blood?[37] Those modern Americans who counted Royalists and Nationalists among their ancestors were able, by 1840, to lament the fate of those defeated in 1776: Judge Oliver, torn between his love for New England and his loyalty to the Crown,[38] the old Tory whose return to the motherland was equivalent to exile,[39] Esther Dudley, faithful to the phantoms of the monarchy, who piously preserved the memory of the former governors.[40] All were figures made dear to Hawthorne by the discretion of their suffering—tragedy and torment lurking beneath polite and formal exteriors. History and life, like art, had to have a style, which also implied a certain ceremoniousness—Puritan, Elizabethan, even Spanish—a court etiquette that can be found even in the pomps of democracy. It would have been easy enough for Hawthorne to take such scenes of glaring horror as the Boston Massacre[41] or the heart-rending pathos of the Acadian deportation[42] and use them to compose great bravura set pieces. He preferred to pass over them in order to return to the great, austere figures of America's champions, democracy's artistocrats. Aloof in the center of his canvas stand those who represent not only liberty but also authority. For Hawthorne, the embodiment of both was the man whose majesty he revered as worthy of a throne: Washington.[43] Franklin, on the other hand, was already a little too "Yankee" for his taste.[44] Washington was the link between the Puritans, whose work he brought to completion, and the Democrats whose duty it was to preserve it. He was the last representative of the great ancestors and the first modern hero. Hawthorne, a historian in the epic sense of the term, knew how to single out the most striking episodes in his story and present them in separate frames so as to give his fresco the epic touch: Endicott rending St. George's cross from the colony's flag with a blow of his sword,[45] Wolfe charging across the Plain of Abraham at the head of his troops,[46] or Richard Dana under the Liberty Tree, demanding that Judge Oliver take the anti-Royalist oath.[47] He was in fact writing a history in pictures, the history of a past that was then still tangible.

IV. THE TRAGIC RETROSPECTIVE

Hawthorne certainly loved the picturesque, but he loved even more the freedom he experienced when playing at bringing ghosts back to life. His interest became a passion when he was able to set the drama, the tragedy of the past into living motion. In Salem, he seems to have lived as though in a museum where personal memories stood elbow to elbow with historic remains. Gallows Hill reared up in his path like a perpetual reproach, while such and such an aristocratic home reminded him constantly that his family too had once been rich and influential. In his eyes, the old houses had a humanity, a life, that was lacking in the new ones. They had a personality, a style, a legend: governors' houses,[1] ship-owners' houses, old taverns,[2] almost lordly houses in the Tudor or Jacobean styles, with Gothic, Flemish, or Italian decorations.[3] Built of wood, they embodied the very labors of those who had first cleared the virgin forests. Their sharp gables evoked the hats of the old Puritans who built them, and their austere gaze: the streets still seemed to be haunted by their somber bustle, or suddenly about to fill with a crowd in holiday clothes. There were costumes, suits of armor, coats of arms[4] still symbolizing the ancestors' dream of power. Hawthorne, true collector that he was, gathered together a veritable storehouse of accessories that were later employed in his historical reconstructions in the form of sketches,[5] pictures,[6] processions,[7] reviews, and panoramas of the past.[8] He went instinctively to the telling, pictorial detail—and even more so to the dramatic one. Local superstitions, witchcraft, and Puritan punishments provided him with his favorite themes. The earliest settlers, convinced that God took a particular interest in the destiny of a country where they intended living according to His Commandments,[9] saw signs, favorable or ill-omened, on every side, sometimes heralding a battle,[10] sometimes an epidemic, sometimes the death of a saint[11] or the coming of a liberator. This latter sign often took the form of the specters that the Elizabethans were so fond of introducing into their plays as instruments of prophecy or justice: the Grey Champion, for instance, or the Angel of Hadley.[12] They also tended to see portraits come to life or change their expressions: warnings of imminent change or catastrophe.[13] Hawthorne took pleasure in bringing these ancestral beliefs back to life in all their "majesty."[14] He took even more pleasure in evoking certain others in their most fantastic aspects: the exploits of witches, their grotesque and lascivious dances, their flights up chimneys,[15] their incantations and evil spells,[16] the devilish practices of wizards, their hypnotic power,[17] their sorcery, their curses,[18] their black masses,[19]—all the monstrosities produced by the presence of the devil when invoked by magic: the evil eye, possession,[20] fetishism, idolatry, ritual crimes, satanism.[21] From the modest village witch[22] up to the learned alchemist[23] and the heretics, the devil possessed the souls of a whole ascending chain of emissaries who pursued the work of the great Destroyer in the Creation.

At that time, however, the theocratic social edifice that had been built up was considered to be sacred. The wizard, a recognized enemy in the theological sense, was soon to become one in the political sense also.[24] This is the nexus of the historical tragedy in which Hawthorne's ancestors played such a bloody role. Both persecuted and persecutors stand out of their own accord as natural protagonists. On one side the supposed enemies of the state and religion, the Quakers, the apostles of nonviolence, and on the other, the judges, the ministers, the provosts. Opposite Endicott, the Mathers—father and son—and Judge Hathorne, there stood, not only the adventurers such as Morton,[25] but also heroines like Ann Coleman[26] and Mrs. Hutchinson,[27] who had the moral stature of a Hester Prynne. The Salem witch hunts mark the apogee of the Puritan persecutions. The trials took place in an atmos-

phere of hatred and passion in which the voice of reason was unable
to make itself heard.[28] After the supposed crimes of the so-called
witches there followed the very real crimes of an entire population.
The public executions excited the crowd into a ferocity that was only
aggravated by the curses of their victims,[29] and the raging thirst for
blood that resulted was eventually succeeded by a feeling of collective
guilt. What if the "witches" were actually martyrs?[30] Would they prove
to be intercessors or accusers on the Judgment Day? This terrible doubt
still had the power to grip Judge Hathorne's descendant in a vise of
anguish, and might perhaps have driven him in another age to offer
himself up as an expiatory victim. The only way left for him to take
the ancestral sin upon his own head[31] was to make use of both crime
and remorse in the creation of a work of art. Though the young Hawthorne may at one time have considered entering a community of
Shakers,[32] that was no more than an imaginary gesture of renunciation,
though one that he was later able to recall and use when writing "The
Canterbury Pilgrims": the only reparation that he could in reality, as
an artist, offer to the sect once persecuted by his forefathers. Not that
even the tragedies of Sophocles had any power to wash away the blood
the Atridae had shed. Nor could the stories of Ilbrahim, Alice Doane,
Hester Prynne, and the Pyncheons ever wipe out the abominable deaths
of Giles Corey and Martha Hunt.[33] They simply effect an esthetic and
emotional conversion capable of touching the hearts of those now alive.
And they also bear witness: neither blood that is shed nor injustice are
forgotten. Art does not justify those who have killed and tortured.

Whether he wishes it or no, the artist contracts a debt both toward
preceding generations and toward his own time, since it is they who
furnish him with the materials for his visions of horror as well as
beauty, with the opportunities to express indignation, to shudder, to
sympathize, to admire, or to hate. The memory of those "Puritan
Punishments"[34] could not but excite feelings of repulsion and shame in
a "poet" descended from a Puritan judge, and that is perhaps the reason
why he sometimes presented them as though they were disturbing and
bizarre buffooneries, strangely akin to the quirky extravagances of the
witches and to certain human caricatures,[35] not as atrocities perpetrated upon living beings who were deserving of pity and sometimes
young and beautiful. The pillory, of the kind that imprisoned both the
neck and the hands of its victim,[36] the stocks that immobilized the legs,[37]
the ducking stool, which was used for scolds,[38] the whipping post,[39] and

the gallows, all sprouted like so many poisonous mushrooms in front of the prison and the church.[40] The shrew with her tongue in a cleft stick,[41] the heretic with cropped ears,[42] the burglar branded with a red-hot iron,[43] the man with a noose around his neck[44] are all grotesque figures, not pitiable or tragic ones, and serve as a foil to the beauty of the woman with the red Letter[45] whose crime, in those days, was punishable by death.[46] The rigor of the laws, the disproportion between punishments and faults committed, that is one of the essential features of the period Hawthorne so frequently depicted for us. Better to commit an injustice than to disturb the established order. From these teachings, Hawthorne, though he insists on the right to "do wrong" within certain limits,[47] nevertheless retained a belief in the necessity of certain severe punishments, provided that they were inflicted without hatred and without cruelty.[48] He was on the side of Puritan dignity,[49] not that of fanaticism and oppression.[50] And in this respect the moralist was in agreement with the artist. Without the great punishments, without the death penalty and the great crimes for which it was the retribution, there could be no tragedy: just as, without martyrdom, life lacked a supreme beauty. There had to be examples, there had to be symbols to excite the creative imagination. The tragedies, the legends, the high deeds of the past were a standard for the actions, the events, the works of the present. As related in the chronicles, as they had been handed down by popular, word-of-mouth tradition, they already possessed the aspect of a well-directed spectacle mounted to produce a particular effect, imbued with an austere dignity even in their more amusing moments,[51] and providing a strong contrast with the motley bustle of the modern world. As he grew older, so Hawthorne became more and more attached to material objects, to relics for their own sake, to the tangible inheritance rather than to the atmosphere recreated. His bric-a-brac from the past was to become a collection of tourist's fetishes. But that petrified past, even when it was ceasing to be an artistic talisman and becoming more and more exclusively a charm against death, always remained for Hawthorne, right to the end, a moral fetish: the symbol of an imaginary heritage, outside of time.

· 2 ·
Conscience: The Guilty Quest

I. THE ORPHAN

Hawthorne was to search all his life for the father of whom he had been deprived. The pilgrimage into the past on which he was forever setting out was the pilgrimage of the orphan in quest of the parent.[1] He often undertook explorations of his own restless conscience, using his fictional creations as a cover. Heir to the sins of his ancestors, the orphan carried a sinner inside him. He also carried an innocent, a son of martyrs[2] or a son betrayed by fanatical parents.[3] In contrasting the young, deformed Puritan to the gentle Ilbrahim[4] Hawthorne was expressing a duality that was also his own: the double vocation that existed inside him as a solitary and invalid child—one toward the angels, the other toward satanism.

This sense of having been abandoned, felt by the orphan-victim, could turn to mysticism and a call to martyrdom. Ilbrahim, the child-like Christ, dies for his persecutors as Alyosha in *The Brothers Karamazov* is willing to do.[5] Exposed to the rigors of a winter world, he carries in his own heart the love to which his mother's heart is closed.[6] But in recreating his own inner drama, Hawthorne did not identify himself with the angelic orphan alone, but also with the deformed orphan[7] who revenges himself out of a hatred caused by lack of love, the little monster who possesses the young Hawthorne's own ironic intelligence[8] and even, despite his youth, the diabolic intelligence of Ethan Brand.[9] The Hawthorne hero was defined from the very outset as being essentially a deserted hero, one without support, without a guide—an orphan. He was therefore almost always to prove a young being for whom maturity is an ideal beyond his grasp. Oberon; Fanshawe; Alice and Leonard Doane;[10] Dimmesdale, vainly invoking his mother's shade,[11] or Hester, the image of her aged parents;[12] Hepzibah and Clifford imploring their heavenly Father;[13] Pearl, whom the minister does not dare to acknowledge as his child;[14] Zenobia and Priscilla, the daughters of a bankrupt;[15] Hilgrave and Phoebe, last offsprings of two warring families;[16] Miriam who has no country; and Hilda in exile[17]—all of them orphans either in the literal sense or else in the wider meaning of the term, whether because they have offended against their parents[18] or because they have become alien to the world in which they live, to their age,[20] or to the God of their ancestors.[21] To be abandoned and to be cursed are more often than not synonymous, though the reactions they provoke in their victims are very diverse. There are the resigned victims, like Hepzibah and Moodie,[22] the rebels, like Holgrave, who take a stand against the past,[23] Zenobia, who cannot accept her condition as a woman,[24] and Miriam, whom the continual reminder of her sin drives mad.[25] There are those who sell themselves to the devil, like Goodman Brown and Ethan Brand.[26] There are the failed saints, like Dimmesdale, who allows himself to be destroyed by his sense of guilt,[27] and Hilda, whose sterile virtue is no more than a form of moral cowardice.[28] All feel themselves unworthy. The sometimes obscure, sometimes blinding memory of a crime forbids their return to the house of their birth. The father, though rarely actually present in Hawthorne's stories, is nevertheless, like the mother in O'Neill, a dominant dramatic figure. A distinction is imposed between the legal representative of paternal authority, an insupportable caricature of the vanished or ideal father—the minister who acts as godfather rather than father to young Robin,[29] the young vagabond's guardian,[30] the adoptive father[31]—and the symbolic archetype, whether appearing as the main character of the story,[32] as the Great Stone Face,[33] or as the House.[34] Whereas the former group are by no means immune either to ridicule (Parson Thumpcushion),[35] or to degradation (Major Molineux),[36] the latter are generally untouchable. The great ancestral figures are the only ones before which one may, without humiliation, acknowledge oneself to be guilty, as though before the gods—fallen gods, accursed gods. The truly dominant figure is nevertheless that of the mother. In *Fanshawe*, the dying woman surrounded by "witches" assumes a prominence that betrays in the mind of the young writer an anguish that was not to receive its justification until long after, when the moment came for the real death of Mrs. Hathorne, whose ghost we may dimly perceive in the agonies of Dimmesdale's tormented soul. Moreover, the maternal archetype is also embodied at the same time—and in a much more fleshly and living fashion than the paternal archetype—in the majestic figure of Hester,[38] to be reflected again later in the person of the luxuriant Zenobia,[39] and then becoming increasingly rarefied until it is no more than a frigid emanation of the Virgin to whom Hilda devotes a pallid form of worship tinged with Transcendentalist spirituality.[40]

Hawthorne's sons and daughters do not seek to identify themselves to the same degree as O'Neill's with the father and mother as persons, but rather to find their way back to the image of the archetype[41] that the father and mother reflect—an image that for Hawthorne always remained masculine.[42] This explains the metaphysical prominence of the father at the mother's expense, though it does not alter the fact that the earthly mother is called upon to play a role in relation to Hawthorne and his characters that the father could never lay claim to, for she accompanies the son much further on his path through life, and then, even after her death, is still beside him in the person of his wife. Lacking an earthly father, the orphan searches for a fixed star,[43] and it is a woman's hand that points it out to him. But that hand, like Miriam's or that of the scarlet woman,[44] may also lead him astray from the path to his heavenly Father's house and set him on the road to that of the infernal father, the corrupter, sometimes in an incestuous sense.[45]

In the same way, the offense against the father—real or symbolic—is also often sexual in nature, which for a Puritan conscience makes it as serious as murder, with which Hawthorne does in fact associate it on more than one occasion, as he also associates it with witchcraft. The guilty son was to be for him, as for Dostoevski,[46] a murderer—or a wizard—and also, as for Faulkner,[47] guilty of incest. Leonard Doane[48] loves his sister Alice and kills a rival who bears an exact resemblance to his father: a double incest complicated by murder. Young Reuben Bourne,[49] who leaves his wounded companion to die in the forest, only to go on and marry that companion's daughter, Dorcas, becomes guilty of an almost identical offense, one that Dimmesdale repeats, in his turn, by taking away from Chillingworth—his symbolic, satanic father—the young wife who could be his daughter: a double incest again, aggravated on both sides by witchcraft.[50] Sexual crimes and crimes of blood are also reflected in all the rites of the black mass. The union of the young couple in the flicker of the burning pine torches is akin to those rites, and Young Goodman Brown himself may perhaps be secretly united to an incestuous sister who is also the mistress of the Dark One, her pink ribbon[51] possibly signifying, like Rappacini's poisonous plant,[52] the consummation of a union that is either too natural or else wholly unnatural.

The guilty daughter becomes in the same way a witch, a female demon. The heroine of "Hollow of the Three Hills," whose parents die dishonored by her sin, turns to magic for its fatal aid.[53] Prudence Inglefield reduces her father to despair and rushes deliberately to her own doom.[54] It was at the time of his troubles with Mary Silsbee, then of his contacts with Margaret Fuller,[55] that Hawthorne, as he made a closer acquaintance with the female nature and the feminist question, began to discover the female rebel, the destroyer of men already latent in his imagination. Hester Prynne, who deserts the conjugal bed, was also capable of defying the Governor,[56] as Ann Hutchinson might have done at that time. Miriam, like a Strindberg heroine, sees man as the hereditary enemy and the father as the source of evil.[57] As for Zenobia, she despises a father without authority and transfers her admiration to Hollingsworth, the man of strength, only to be let down eventually by him as well.[58] Since he saw the drama of the modern American woman so clearly, it would not even have been surprising if Hawthorne, a half century before Dreiser, had given us a Sister Carrie. Although he remained very much of his time when dealing directly with sexuality, his investigations go beyond the traditional sociological and psychological boundaries and plunge the reader, even without his knowing it, into the broad stream of human evolution.

Though the punishment of the rebel son avenges the father and restores his absolute authority, as the death of Reuben Bourne's son does—Isaac sacrified to a God more implacable than Abraham's[59]— the same is not true of the retribution exacted from the guilty daughter, which restores no luster to the fallen patriarch who may perhaps have sinned with her. There is an abyss between the admired father, who is the apparent repository of wisdom and sexual dominion, and the scorned father, who acknowledges his weakness when subjected to fleshly temptation or adversity—between Endicott, whose quiet strength has such a magnetic attraction for the young captive who later becomes his spiritual son,[60] and Governor Hutchinson, flouted by his niece,[61] or Old Moodie, so pitifully similar to Old Goriot in his humility before his daughters.[62] The father who commands awe is the embodiment, not only of the idea of the family but also of the national destiny and religious revelation. The humiliated father is the embodiment of failure, or moral and social bankruptcy, or else is identified with some unpopular cause. He has denied his private god[63]—or has he simply let fall the mask of the mere appearances that inspire respect? When success becomes the accepted sign of strength, or even of moral value, then woe to the bankrupt: in the age of utilitarianism such an unhappy hero will not even find an Antigone to console him. Once defeated, the American male is a totally denuded Lear rather than an Oedipus. The rising tide of voracious appetites in the younger generations, especially the women, though masked by the angelic myth by which even Hawthorne sometimes allowed himself to be duped, as well as the need felt by the Puritan male, as he became increasingly less sure of himself and his truths, to find an ever more secure support in his wife, while at the same time repressing her libido in other ways, until the day when all his authority had passed to the distaff side—all this explains the onset at this time of a veritable subversion of the father's position and a debasement of the paternal archetype. The modern woman, a new Minerva sprung fully armed from the American male's head, was destroying that anemic race of Victorian heroines[64] in front of whom man had become accustomed to parade his proud strength and whom he needed to convince of their own weakness so that he could subjugate them. And this modern Minerva had not only beauty and physical and moral strength,[65] but also intellectual power to use for her ends. Before long, man took fright and began trying to fight free of the tyrannical love, the insatiable appetites that he had aroused in his companion. Whereupon he turned once more to the wan Victorian miss: but Hollingsworth, having sacrificed Zenobia to Priscilla, then found beneath the latter's conventional helplessness the spirit of an inflexible Nemesis.[66] Hawthorne was one of the first[67] to give forceful expression to the profound antagonism between the sexes in modern life. Carrying this drama within his own person as he did, it is possible that he could see the lengths to which it would eventually go, and refused, in consequence of that knowledge and despite a strong temptation to the contrary, to subordinate everything to the feminine ideal, to the maternal archetype.

The most evident consequence of the absence, of the abdication or the destitution of the father, is that the "orphans" are not able to reach their maturity. How could they without a father's help? The emancipation demanded by the sons, and even more so by the daughters, is in danger of condemning them to a perpetual adolescence, to an irreparable psychic imbalance such as we observe in Zenobia and Miriam. An individual, like a people, must fight in order to win his independence, otherwise he will never attain to anything but the most precarious maturity. He must fight against whoever formed him and gave him birth, as New England did against the Old, as Holgrave does against tradition, against those authoritarian forces that can only play a positive role in the growth of beings and nations to the degree in which they make themselves instruments of education and not of repression—the effect of repression being to stifle natures that are generous (Hester) or tender (the young couple in "The Lily's Quest"[68]) or weak (Hepzibah and Clifford) and to develop only those natures that resemble it, or resolutely oppose it, though at what cost!—a tragic mode of education that dooms mankind to unhappiness. In addition to authority, as well as in its absence, the adolescent must invent himself another enemy, the devil, who is in fact no one but himself, the embodiment of the evil or rancor he bears inside him. Such is the aspect often assumed by the quest for the absent father in the darkness of a maze in which the mind wanders in its own confusion, beckoned to on every hand by contradictory symbols. For the young Lord of the May, the choice between the apostate priest and the Puritan is simple and without ambiguity.[69] The same cannot be said, however, of Young Goodman Brown, standing between the Black Man and the man officiating at the black mass;[70] or of Robin between the two-faced monster[71]—which embodies in itself alone what the preceding examples divided between them: sin in all its blackness and purple sin,[72] the two poles of the mind's inward vertigo—and the distinguished demon who is an extrapolation of his own artful and success-starved spirit, anxious to wean him away from his profounder self;[73] or, lastly, of Giovanni between Baglioni, the earthy sneering devil and Rappacini, the demon of excess.[74] Since he lacks any other, the infernal father presses down upon the orphan like a destiny: Westervelt, the modern

Comus,[75] who magnetizes Priscilla and leads Zenobia to her ruin; the disturbing Model, always at Miriam's heels[76]—like a necessity; the Black Man, who escorts young Goodman Brown to the sabbath, and whose influence weighs upon Pearl from her earliest childhood;[77] the demon that love places in the way of Donatello,[78] whose ancestors availed him nothing in his voyage of self-discovery. Hawthorne waited until the end of his life to write his *Wilhelm Meister*. But he had never in fact ceased to pore over the problem of man's education—an education that was never finished, always being begun afresh—that could add up finally to mere disintegration, as with Ethan Brand, but that could also lead to self-discovery, as in the case of young Robin, in whom the shock of disillusion at the degradation of his symbolic father awakened the sense of his own strength,[79] of his personal "independence." For there could be no true education in Hawthorne's eyes other than one that taught man his individual responsibility, his solitude in the face of good and evil,[80] that experience which every man must go through on his own. Whoever goes in search of consciousness must pay that price.

II. THE NARCISSISM OF SIN

The way to self-discovery lies through an awareness of personal culpability, a realization that responsibility is incumbent no longer upon the father alone but upon each son individually also. Everyone must take his share upon himself. Any individual who believes himself to be innocent is merely masking his own inner truth and yielding to the demon of appearances. Hawthorne's heroes prefer to abandon themselves to their inner demons. Far from being content merely to share Adam's burden, they feel themselves predestined for evil. Whereupon they determine to live their lives as guilty consciences: it is as though they find in their sin not only their inheritance but also their vocation, their reason for being, and the proof that their souls are alive.

This guilt, though often masked at first, is a secret disease that gradually becomes acute and agonizing to the point of tearing animal cries from Dimmesdale's breast[1] and driving Miriam to hysterical and crazed behavior.[2] The cause of so much suffering, however, is, generally speaking, imperceptible, impalpable. If we except the execution of Maule and the murder of the Model,[3] there is no obvious crime in any of Hawthorne's works that would be given space in a news-paper.[4] Usually, the crimes are legal ones, as in the case of the Judge,[5] hypothetical, like Miriam's, or purely moral ones, as in the cases of Reuben Bourne, Ethan Brand, or Chillingworth. Even Donatello's crime, the only one that is really circumstantiated, is presented in a strangely doubtful light. The typical Hawthorne crime is an ambiguous and secret crime, one that has no physical reality. The act of violence is done in the recesses of the soul. Often, indeed, it is anterior to the action, and even to the birth of the main characters—immemorial, as in *The House of the Seven Gables.* Even Dimmesdale's adultery seems as far away as the original sin. It is always, as it were, the same sin that we encounter, the same conscience successively embodied in dif-ferent offenders, or even more than one at the same time, each one add-ing a variation to the original crime as it spreads like oil through time and space till it has affected the entire human race: the Judge, at a distance of several generations, dies of the same illness as the Colonel, the Governor Hutchinson, who was not even present at the Boston Massacre, is nevertheless choked by the blood of those martyred there.[6]

A seed planted in the soul from the beginning, the crime in Haw-thorne is also, like that of Strindberg's Maurice,[7] a crime of intention—like those we see filing past in "Fancy's Show Box"[8]—an evil, per-verted, bloody thought that leaves its stain upon the soul,[9] the black stain of the moral crime, indelible, corrosive, and more irremediable than the red stain of the committed crime. A criminal intention is annihilated by the act. But the twisted thought, on the other hand, goes on living without ever achieving satisfaction, and no forgiveness can ever reach in to it. So that evil seems to live in man like a virus that has found a favorable host. Lady Eleanore's smallpox is in reality pride.[10] The man ill with sin is incapable of conceiving what health of soul is. Trapped in a vicious circle of evil he plunges inward into himself, hypnotized, in quest of the forgotten misdeed or the sin still to be committed. A detective of his own concentration camp of con-science,[11] fascinated by this inner adventure, he sets off in pursuit of a double—or even several—stalks him, tracks him, while he himself is also being flushed and pursued, at once hunter and hunted. Good-man Brown surprises the pious churchmen at the witches' sabbath, but he is himself surprised by the Black Man.[12] Dimmesdale, following in the tracks of the penitent he would himself like to be, is himself spied upon in the midnight dark by Chillingworth.[13] All these consciences, wandering in their own darkness, sleep ill, spending their whole time spying upon one another. Aware that they are rotting inwardly, their only consolation is in the spectacle of the corruption they perceive around them. They cannot tolerate any appearance of self-content in others. A quiet conscience is merely a conscience asleep. Those with unquiet minds are driven by their torments to awaken, and sometimes to terrify those around them: the Reverend Hooper, attempting to make all his parishioners share his vision of the world, conceals his face behind a black veil.[14] Roderick Elliston, by means of moral radioscopy, is able to detect a serpent in the bosoms of all his fellow men, and he derives a bitter pleasure from the knowledge.[15] Hester Prynne quivers with a perverted joy when she recognizes her "sisters"[16] among even the most innocent seeming of women. In this way there is established a brotherhood of the guilty that is founded, not upon mutual sympathy, but upon horror and contempt—the contempt of Caligula[17] establishing the reign of inhumanity. When the only possible joy becomes that of despising someone else as much as oneself, then the earth becomes a place of humiliation and torture: hell. For Hawthorne's tormented characters, hell is not an abstraction, but a living, present, permanent reality, without any means of escape. For it is not enough merely to increase the number of criminals in order to justify oneself, or to play the judge in order to be absolved.[18] The judge in Strindberg's *Advent*, the lawyer in Camus' *The Fall*, and even more so the minister in *The Scarlet Letter*, are illustrations of this truth. The first two do succeed by skillful sophistry in placing themselves above their fellow men. But the minister, called upon to censure the adulteress, is crushed by his own unworthiness.

The offender, discovering his solitude, conceives a horror of himself. Whether he feels himself to be inferior or superior to others, the Hawthorne hero is a being apart, an excommunicate. Sometimes, like Wakefield, he himself feels that he is in quarantine.[19] To be above others, below them, or apart from them[20] is still to be wretched. Hawthorne establishes a natural bond between the poet, the reformer, and the criminal.[21] To be guilty is to be alone. Inversely, to be alone is to be guilty. To be isolated from others like a plague carrier, to be imprisoned like Clifford for a crime one has not committed[22] is enough to make an innocent man assume the attitude, the gestures, the reflexes of the truly guilty, of the convicted, of the prisoner who shrinks from the light and others' eyes,[23] who sees nothing but accusers, jailers, judges, and executioners on every side. Here again it is possible to make a comparison between Strindberg's *There Are Crimes and Crimes*, Camus' *The Fall*, and *The House of the Seven Gables*.

If moral solitude always produces the "unease" in which no soul can preserve a sense of its innocence,[24] then all solitude considered from without is ambiguous, since it appears as a dissimulation. Is it out of pride or out of humility that the Man of Adamant cuts himself off from others?[25] Is the man who shuns society and hides himself away a criminal or a saint? Does the black veil conceal an unspeakable crime or the pallor of the just man who is appalled at the sins of others?[26] Dimmesdale's flock assume that he must be conversing with the angels alone in his monastic cell,[27] while his doctor imagines it more probable that he is conjuring the devil. In solitude and silence good is transmuted into evil:[28] dissimulation becomes simulation; solitude and untruth become inextricably one, thus rendering necessary the aid of illusion, which in turn engenders moral confusion. The noble façade of his house, his immaculately white neckcloth, the ostentatious geniality of his grimace are all so many appearances that the Judge employs to dazzle the eyes of the world,[29] to such an extent that he succeeds in creating the world in his own image: both become mere appearances, façades and facets reflecting one another like the small-paned windows of the old colonial houses,[30] till the dazzlement is such that everyone forgets the absence of the essential. And the inner void is the cause of the impossibility of being true. "Be true! Be true! Be true!" Hawthorne cries.[31] But how? How can we show ourselves as we are, and in our worst light,[32] if even what is worst in us is negative? Who will dare to proclaim his nothingness?—not the fascinating metaphysical abyss but the "nothing" that does not even call out for scorn. To stick to one's lie is a question of social life or death, the only form of death that the would-be saint fears. He has felt God shrink to the dimensions of his own society. Revelation turned inside out: no further possibility of flight, no salvation other than in untruth. The soul and the world are both withered by the knowledge: the terrible effect of absence when man creates the desert inside himself.

And absence is always the absence of love. The man crushed by guilt, like the man possessed by the spirit of titanism, is incapable of loving, because he creates God in his own image and then attempts to propitiate Him, the first by the mortifications inflicted upon him by an excess of sufferings that do nothing to regenerate him,[33] the second by seeking to unite himself with Him by means of the intelligence, like the hermit with the adamantine heart.[34] For him, purity is no more than a nullity of the heart. And it is by the same path that Ethan Brand, striving to rival the divine intelligence, stirs in him the demoniac intellect.[35] The divorce between heart and mind[36] is in Hawthorne's eyes the source of all moral and psychological conflicts and monstrosities. Hester, abandoned by her lover to bear the burden of their shared crime alone, reduced to stifling all her emotional aspirations, plunges into intellectual speculation,[37] whereas Dimmesdale experiences all the more remorse for having yielded to his passion because his fundamental Puritanism forbids him listening without automatic mental reservations to the reasons of his heart.[38] There are many examples of characters who refuse to listen to those reasons, either because they confuse love with sin—the gloomy, black-veiled minister who rejects his betrothed in order to live with ghosts,[39] the man with the petrified heart who excludes from his desert retreat the one woman who attempts to tear him free from it[40]—or because they wish to pollute or dam up a spring from which they may not drink—Lady Eleanore carrying scorn, hatred, and death in the folds of her cloak,[41] Roderick Elliston made venomous by a secret jealousy,[42] or Ethan Brand making a pastime of driving those who love him to despair.[43] All of them believe that they are free because they are exempt from the disease of loving. All are in reality immured within their own caverns—their petrified hearts—plague carriers. The seed of sickness unto death,[44] of the unpardonable sin,[45] is precisely emptiness of heart. He who sins out of love or hate, even a murderer like Donatello, will be saved, for he has only committed one single act, but the man who, without being guilty in fact, bears within him the soul of all crimes, without love and without hate, can never be redeemed. The most wretched of men,[46] as the most damnable, is the one who knows no sympathy—the "stranger" ever ready to betray his fellow men to the profit of the common enemy—or truth. Hawthorne, though he was wont to brush aside ordinary emotional considerations, nevertheless convicted himself upon the same grounds as all of his despairing and demoniac characters who give themselves up to gratuitous crime in the belief that they are performing scientific acts. Neither sexual errors, nor adultery, nor even incest, can compare to the sacrilege of the man who violates another's consciousness.[47] Chillingworth, who penetrates without scruple into the sanctuary of the human heart,[48] does at least have the excuse of jealousy, but Ethan Brand is seeking merely to satisfy his intellectual sadism, to prove the existence of his own liberty by the monstrosity of his acts, by sowing the seeds of evil and causing them to multiply in the obscure crannies that he is able to discover in even the simplest souls.

All these creatures possessed by this narcissism in sin, not content with multiplying its image around them, also seek to perpetuate it in themselves: they dream of an eternity spent in the sterile contemplation of their own deformity, and Puritan gloominess is transmuted in them to the absolute sadness of Satan. In fact, it is death that the drinker of the elixir of life takes into himself.[49] So that we find Hawthorne, like Dostoevski, ratifying the words of the Gospel: "He that findeth his life shall lose it."[50] No artifice, above all no mutilation, can ever render life "really alive," only the fusion of heart and mind, and the final gift of the being purified by the ordeal of life and the fire of passion. To cure sin with love,[51] that is the remedy Hawthorne proposes. For only then will pity be able to perform its office beside the judgment seat.[52] And suffering ought finally to bring back love. Such is the meaning of the ordeal that breaks Alice Pyncheon's pride,[53] of the life of frustration led by Hepzibah with her unwrinkled heart,[54] and of the experience undergone by little, carefree Phoebe, who through contact with the wretchedness of others attains emotional maturity.[55]

The miracle of the heart does not always occur. Hilda, faced with Miriam, recoils instead of opening her arms,[56] and Dimmesdale, at the point of death, shrinks from Hester's embrace.[57] Neither of them believes in salvation through the heart, and the coldness and terror they respectively betray create an uneasy contrast with the young sculptor's need for love and the passion of the woman who wears the Letter. From the emotional point of view they are non-committal: they never really give themselves. They pay no more than lip service to the notion that they are part of humanity and hardly even believe in the possibility of a brotherhood of the guilty.[58] They are too thoroughly convinced of their having destroyed their Eden—and not only theirs but that of others as well[59]—to be able to believe in a reconciliation. Even when they finally ask, as Dimmesdale does, for the sanction that restores the pariah's right to belong, it is without any total adherence to the notion in their heart but solely because they are adhering to the letter of the law in their heads.[60] Donatello, the pagan, is much nearer to Christian acceptance than either Dimmesdale (the minister) or Miriam. The reluctance of Hawthorne's heroines in their sacrifices, as well as the coldness of their charity, provides food for thought. Can it be that the heart of woman is not, after all, the heart of hearts—love itself? Does it perhaps conceal the supreme form of pride, the utmost form of egoism?

The egoism that manifests itself in the narcissism of purity, as well as in that of sin—which is inseparable from pride—that is the form of possession that must be exorcized above all else. It is egoism that makes the self into a sealed-off sphere,[61] that imprisons man within the skin of the beast, whether swine or serpent.[62] In order to liberate himself the individual must plunge into the heart of humanity,[63] lave himself in the regenerating stream of fraternity. The desire man is given after a criminal act to communicate with his fellow men and redeem himself, that is the "good fortune" that the Fall represents for him:[64] evil causes him to discover forces inside himself that he can use to go beyond himself.[65] Sin, instead of hardening him, ought to soften his heart,[66] to render it fertile, to sow in it the seed of a love stripped of all pride. Humility, Gide wrote, opens the gates of heaven, whereas humiliation opens those of hell:[67] that is the tragic distinction between the noon confession and the midnight confession in *The Scarlet Letter*. Dimmesdale standing on the scaffold in the darkness feels himself, between his daughter and his mistress, becoming a link in the great chain of beings,[68] but his confession in the daylight, under the whole town's gaze, was to be no more than a reflex action brought about by his fear,[69] a convulsive clutching at salvation *in extremis*. The reticence of his Puritan heart traps the minister in a vise of torturing doubt: though he is wresting himself free from the certainty of hell, he is still not taking with him any certainty of salvation. Though this does not alter the fact that his readiness to suffer reduces the zeal of his torturer to naught, as the faith of the Quakers did that of their persecutors.[70] Dimmesdale, an unwilling martyr, needed to be provoked to the utmost extreme before he could consent to bear witness in his own person to the guilt of mankind.[71] Since shame had come to preponderate over love in his soul he could be neither a saint nor a

Christ. And this failed Christ also cheats the woman with whom he sinned of her opportunity to be a saint. It is the reticence stifling their hearts that renders sainthood inaccessible to Hawthorne's heroes.

III. EDEN

The effect of fatalism in evil and narcissism in sin is that man is bound to go on feeding himself upon the substance of darkness. Nevertheless, there does exist one glimmer that indicates the existence of another sphere—the sphere of light. The dark bedroom in which Hawthorne saw his mother die communicated, by means of a heavily curtained window, with the sunny garden where the child with blond curls was playing.[1] The stagnant heart of the House opens up on holidays to the joyous world around it.[2] The shadow in which Miriam struggles contains the light that burns on the tower and is intended, even as it fades, to feed her hope.[3] But in the sphere where Hester and the minister carry the burden of their sin, the light is an emanation of the night:[4] we are in an autonomous universe from which all escape for the soul is impossible. And yet, the more improbable the existence of Eden is, the more the human heart dreams of it without admitting it. This forcible negation of light that we find in *The Scarlet Letter* is a cry of revolt, a retreat into satanic opposition: "Let the black flower blossom as it may,"[5] since the flower of Paradise can never bloom.

This flower symbolizes the lost heritage, the object of the individual or collective quest of all Hawthorne's guilty, wretched, orphaned, obsessed heroes and heroines. So that human life in Hawthorne's eyes always assumes the air of a pilgrimage, a procession.[6] It is the quest for a talisman like the Great Carbuncle,[7] whose imaginary glitter can attract a whole population of visionaries and chimera chasers—for a miraculous plant like the tree of the Hesperides,[8] for a rare flower like the one that sprouts on the path of the adulteress and her fairy child[9] or the one that Zenobia wears at her breast.[10] This quest is often confused with that for love and happiness. The flower of Eden,[11] symbol of the lost Paradise, the flower of memory—which is not blue, as Bachelard so rightly pointed out,[12] but blood-red—is a flower of flesh.

Thus the nostalgia for paradisiac joys is accompanied by a deep mistrust that leads back once more to the narcissism of sin. The heady flower, the tempting fruit cannot but be poisoned since they disturb the senses. When Hawthorne, in a fit of optimism, envisaged the moral progress of mankind as an "ascending spiral curve"[13] had he forgotten the Serpent he had introduced into the Garden of his new Adam? The Serpent grows with the tree, and the woman with the poisonous plant.[14] The feminine tree is suspect[15]—that maternal tree we meet later on in *Desire Under the Elms*:[16] it is the tree of *Paradise Lost*, the tree-serpent. Hawthorne needed the symbol of the virile man-tree that resisted the poison—the kind of tree that had dry bark, a rough texture, and glossy leaves,[17] the Puritan champion's coat of mail—the paternal tree with its venerable shade and gigantic trunk.[18] The garden full of unctuous and flaccid plants, even more treacherous than the withered Eden behind the House of the Seven Gables,[19] is the Eden of evil triumphant on the sexual level. The beauty of Beatrice is a poison,[20] because it disturbs Giovanni, the young "Puritan" who resembles young Robin[21] like a brother. A paradise where one is tempted in such a way cannot be pure. It is a false Eden, wholly manufactured by the devil, and one that must be destroyed, just as it was necessary to destroy the pagan paradise that still stubbornly struggles to revive— despite all the efforts of the Puritans to fell the phallic May Day emblem, to wither the blooms of immodesty, to scourge a humanity so recalcitrantly obstinate in its quest for happiness by means of the flesh, and blast all nature, in short, with their anathema. But in Hawthorne's heart, for all that, the worship of nature remained very much alive: "the poor old earth,"[22] its joys, and its sun. Eden blooms anew for each human being.

Hawthorne for his own part almost always made it into a private, secret garden surrounded by a wall—Roderick's or Rappacini's.[23] Like his hell, Hawthorne's Eden is an individual place, bounded by the heart sphere in which each character's original theological drama is played out. The human heart, a battlefield for God and the Demon in the Gothic imagination, was for him more familiar with Satan than with the saints. Celestial messengers venture rarely into this melancholy Eden. The "angels" are either as aloof as Hilda or as swiftly neutralized as Alice.[24] Phoebe alone, being an extrapolation of Sophia, is able to drive back the evil one temporarily on one sector of the front.[25] Everywhere else, he has the field to himself. The messengers of hell live in the very closest intimacy with their victims, like Chillingworth with Dimmesdale.[26] Man in Hawthorne's works often gives the impression of being alone with his familiar demon, his devilish twin.

And the couple in Hawthorne also has its infernal chaperone. The original triangle—Adam and Eve and the Serpent—is formed again and again in obedience to the barren geometry of fate: Leonard Doane, his sister and his rival; the couple in love and the jealous ghost; Goodman Brown, Faith, and the Black Man; Giovanni, Beatrice and the doctor; the Lord and Lady of the May and the apostate priest; Dimmesdale, Hester and Chillingworth; Hollingsworth, Zenobia, and Westervelt; Donatello, Miriam, and the Model.[27] Holgrave and Phoebe are not truly united until the Judge's death[28]—and who can say that the ghost of the repulsive but fascinating seducer[29] will not return to insinuate his shadow between them, and that their idyll will not end in the nightmare of the forest? In this universe of parted couples, of couples irremediably separated by ghosts, by remorse, by hellish visions, the happiness of lovers is impossible.

These beings hurled toward one another by desire and passion do not really believe that their impulses, that their union can bring the earthly Eden back to life again. Their evil genius tells them that they do not carry the seed of it within them. By a metaphysical Malthusianism, the man gnawed by sin is doomed either to unproductive narcissism or to a quest for the impossible. All Aylmer's tragedy lies there, for what he attempts to do is to create perfect beauty by abolishing the birthmark that is also the mark of sex.[30] Rappacini, for his part, would like to be the father to a race pure in its evil. His daughter Beatrice, whom he has tried to wean away from the springs of nature, is killed by her discovery of human love.[31] Hawthorne's characters do not know how to live with their imperfections: they poison the principle of all joy in themselves with their despair at not being angels—or devils. They destroy themselves by attempting to realize their condition in the abstract and the eternal. Which means that they abandon their human reality in order to become allegories.

What place could there be for a child in this world of abstract and obsessive adults? What can become of him, a new "orphan," between parents haunted solely by the thought of sin and the inaccessible? Those who feel themselves abandoned do not believe in posterity; their children, like them, will have no expectations either in this life or the next: such is Hester's private conviction.[32] So that the home cannot exist. The house in which it is born can never be a nest, a paradise to the child, only a wretched and transitory place to lay its head. Instead of warmth and affection, cold and insecurity. The home, that image of earthly happiness celebrated in the *Mosses*,[33] usually appears as the flickering reflection of a distant ideal.[34] Despite the fact that he had himself set up a happy home, Hawthorne continually returned, whether he wished it or not, to his own experience as a lonely child tormented with adult cares.

So that even though he writes lovingly of children in his less austere tales, and eventually, with time and the help of circumstance, might have learned the art of being a grandfather—if we may rely upon the strange figure of Doctor Dolliver[35] as evidence—it should still cause us no surprise to find so few children in his serious works, and such maturity in those he does describe. Little Joe already carries within him the drunkard that he is to become,[36] just as Ned Higgins is already the future shrewd businessman.[37] As for Pearl,[38] she is not merely a woman from earliest childhood—the woman of the future[39]—but also an elfin messenger, the glowing link of carnal passion, dressed in crimson velvet, between the minister and the woman of sin, the beam of light joining hell and heaven.[41] But from what region does she come in reality? Was it the Black Man[42] or the Divine Father that sent her?[43] Has she come to lead her earthly father down to the paradise of sin or up toward that of recovered innocence? Whereas in Strindberg the child is an instrument of salvation,[44] in Hawthorne it is no more than a wild rosebud on the path that the female Christ may possibly follow.

Is not Ilbrahim the herald of this being, whose grace, delicacy, and languor are those of a virgin martyr as much as of a child Christ?[45] The idea of Christ reincarnated in a woman was subsequently to become more and more clearly defined in Hawthorne's mind.[46] Yet how could he make Christ of the female sex without desiring him carnally? Sacrilege. So that a compromise began to take shape in his consciousness: since he was obliged to forbid himself all sensual love for the divine female messenger, he turned his attentions to the woman of flesh in order to deify her, though without giving her the actual name of Christ, but secretly calling her beloved and mother.

If there was one image that demanded above all others to be embodied in Hawthorne's works, it was undoubtedly that of the mother-mistress. Returning to his deepest emotional obsessions, to the memory of his Puritan mother and the perfidious beloved,[47] he created, as compensation for what they had withheld, an ideal anima in whom there flowered in abundance all the affection he had not known in childhood, a figure to whom the bewitching Armida lent her seduction and the beauty queen of Martha's Vineyard her royal bearing.[48] This dazzling creature, exercising that same awful sexual fascination that he believed he had exorcised in creating Lady Eleanore and later Beatrice, reappeared, more captivating than ever, and in his heart he enshrined her as an idol. To give himself utterly up to her, to fly with her to the ends of the earth[49] would have been to enter Eden once again. For Hawthorne, the way of salvation was unconsciously the way back to the womb, as it was to be later on for O'Neill, though in a more conscious fashion. The disappearance of the human race[50] which makes possible the birth of the new Adam and the new Eve, is equivalent to an absorption, a redeeming transmutation of mankind by the womb—the Jonah story on a universal scale. The union of the son with the mother-beloved thus finds its own consecration in itself.[51] It is Hester, the woman, who utters the liberating word when Hawthorne allows his secret desires to speak. By means of a sexual and emotional alchemy, the Hawthorne hero, like Marlowe's Faust,[52] is seeking to become the regenerate Adam, worthly at last of his eternal heritage. But linked and opposed to this emotional alchemy there is also a cerebral alchemy. In addition to the heart's heritage, there is also the heritage of the mind, dreaming of recovering its plenitude, of regaining ideal wisdom: not the "rediscovered childhood"—which is the source of love, and, provided it is grasped by an adult, of poetry[53] —but the perfect maturity that is a forgetting of the womb, an intellectual rejection of both the female Christ and the poetry of the heart. One of the unconscious reasons for Aylmer's "crime" may well be this rejection—which is at the same time a negative recognition—of the redemptress. And Ethan Brand's experiment could well, and even more probably, have the same meaning.[54] Hawthorne burned in public what he worshipped in secret. For his emotional self, Hester was a divine incarnation, for his reasoning mind she was a woman whose reforming powers had failed.[55] What his heart exalted his intellect decried. And when he went on to paint his satirical portrait of Zenobia, whose emancipation led, not to happiness, but toward the new female egoism,[56] despite all his overt emphasis on the demystification of the new woman, he still retained his nostalgia for that same feminine ideal. But the gradual progress toward the false angel and the new Delilah had begun. After Hester, Phoebe indicates a return to his old mistrust with regard to hidden desires and fantasy values. Hilda, whose icy whiteness eliminates all possibility of a desire to return

to the womb in the virgin worship she inspires,[57] forbids any rediscovery of the Eden of the senses. Then comes the reappearance of the
carnal woman as an instrument of man's fall: Miriam, initiating Donatello into the mysteries of sin, and Sibil Dacy, Septimius Felton's fatal
Egeria.[58] Thus, invincibly, the male mistrust of the womb and his
bitterness against it springs back to life. The egocentric and creating
animus, dreaming of its own, original intactness, is psychologically a
being without a mother, a being that wishes to owe its life to no one
but itself and intends to provide its own salvation.

Bitterness toward the motherland is precisely one of the psycho-
social phenomena characteristic of the American colonial age. The
settlers were exiles who wanted to forget their emotional and historical
past. They could not succeed in erasing the impress of that past entirely, but their conscious will was directed toward forging a new
metaphysical and national destiny for themselves with their own hands,
and even toward inventing a new past. This accounts for the formation
of the myth of the new Eden[59] and the American Adam that we find
later on in Steinbeck and Henry Miller,[60] that Hawthorne took it upon
himself to express explicitly during his Old Manse period,[61] and that
runs through a great many of his other works like a hidden watermark:
the May Day lovers, the young married couple of the Carbuncle mountain, the couple in love who set out to discover the world, the "young
Americans" of *The House of the Seven Gables*, even Giovanni and
Beatrice, all carry the Adamic dream within them.[62] Children of the
future—and imaginary—Golden Age, who dream of immortal youth
like Clifford in his second childhood,[63] like Miriam attempting to re-
cover her innocence[64] and succeeding only in ruining an innocent—a
youth as illusory as that of the elixir drinkers, as poisonous as that of
the alchemist's daughter,[65] an impossible urge to go back—a mirage
of progress: they are all more or less acknowledged children of the
intellectual thirst for power, as well as being the creations of the heart's
emotional alchemy.

· 3 ·

Conscience: Its Psychology

I. THE FIRE IN THE DARKNESS

The depths of the self, when dreams or remorse lead us down into them, can be made to reveal their intense and teeming life. Hawthorne could scarcely be unaware of this, since he held the sense of guilt to be the open-sesame of man's consciousness, the reality that for all its secrecy nevertheless determines our entire moral existence,[1] a thing that the rigid principles of Calvinist determinism alone are insufficient to explain. The problems of the soul were for Hawthorne of a psychological order.[2] Heaven and hell—particularly the latter—are realities of the conscience. And the nocturnal tribulations experienced by explorers of that forest are not merely allegories but also an illustrated psychology both of the obsessions that lie in the unconscious and also of a metaphysical quest. The blackness with which Puritanism clothed everything—when it did not make it the actual substance of things— was the color upon which the imagination of Hawthorne the storyteller fixed in earliest childhood. It hypnotized and absorbed him. The "power of Blackness" that Melville recognized in him[3] proceeded from this initial obsession. He was not content merely to give the external universe a tragic meaning by draping it with the inward shadows of "Innate Depravity":[4] if he cast a veil over the face of the world and its inhabitants[5] it was in order that the light, once their mystery had

212

been revealed by this rubbing of darkness, should be able to etch into them and show them in greater clarity. The veil here is an emanation of the "secret blackness"[6] hidden behind appearances. Though the color is an allegorical sign, the substance of blackness is a psychological reality whose varying layers must be pierced—a task at which Hawthorne was adept, thanks to his "cat-like faculty for seeing in the dark."[7] He was attempting to put his finger, not upon an ethical absolute, but upon a concrete moral existence. The truth of consciousness lies not in its certainties but in its gropings, in the tentative progress achieved by doubt and anguish, by indecision, and by error, through the darkness of a contradictory maze. It is via the moral conscience that Hawthorne penetrates into the psychological consciousness. He makes use of allegorical figures in order to picture it to himself in a more precise fashion, and it sometimes happens that these figures are also psychological archetypes, hereditary images that every individual modifies, and which serve as stocks for the grafting of new myths. The cave, varying in its degree of depth, through which one advances in semidarkness or pitch darkness toward a central brightness,[8] is one of the most familiar images in psychoanalysis. And the house is often equivalent to the cave,[9] for it also can contain a labyrinth similar to the maze of streets and paths through which one winds one's way at twilight, driven on by a feverish curiosity, despite the terror the shadows all around inspire.[10] Hawthorne discovered that this labyrinth, through which he wandered in company with Bunyan and Spenser, was also the lair of the archetypes and monsters that were haunting him. He found the superficial self as unrewarding as Kierkegaard did[11]—as we can tell from his story "Feathertop."[12] And he perceived the social self as being essentially a mere mask: Dimmesdale has a minister's dress, a minister's eloquence, a minister's facial expression —but has he a minister's soul? And above all, can we be reduced to our social selves? The extroverted self is either an imposture[13] or else it is the sign of a personality insufficiently deeply developed and therefore in need of external compensation. It takes only a little solitude and melancholy to transform Phoebe, a creature of the outer light, into a real woman.[14] The individual—the soul—cannot develop fully except in shadow. The consciousness too needs its womb.

The sphere of darkness is thus the first retort that the alchemist of the soul sets up for his purpose. Into it he introduces the light of his mind, in order to surprise the monsters lurking there. He also knows that his gaze must remain veiled if he wishes to know the true secret of the shadows: the inward fire, the hidden principle of the soul's life that flickers sometimes in his eyes,[15] but more often than not dissimulates itself. The guilty man flees from the sunlight, and the sunlight itself flees from him, as it does from Hester and Dimmesdale.[16] But he cannot escape the secret glow that murders his sleep.[17] An astrologist in reverse,[18] he makes his way down toward the underground fire, toward the carbuncle shining amid the coal,[19] toward the hellish star that reveals him to himself and that reveals others to him in the same light of suffering or in the same red and sinister glow. Goodman Brown discovers all his fellow citizens assembled at the black mass in the crackling blaze of a forest fire[20] and Robin sees his nocturnal procession by the flicker of torches.[21] Dimmesdale is blinded by the growing dazzle of the meteor, which is an emanation from his own inward torture chamber.[22] Lit by such flickering fires in the darkness, the theme of the descent into hell and nightmare takes on a greater clarity.[23] It was upon his return from the forest, from the Far West of the mind, from the frontier territory of the soul, that the poet—like the haunted minister[24]—still a prey to the terror and the blinding dazzle of what he had seen, experienced inspiration.

Nightmares in Hawthorne are generally characterized by the intrusion into the consciousness of monstrous paternal and maternal apparitions. For Hawthorne, as for Blake, terror took human form.[25] And his characters share their creator's obsessions. Lost children, wandering spirits, they make their way along darkened paths, through gloomy streets and dismal corridors,[26] stalked by giants, by devils, by witches, by living portraits, by images of criminal ancestors and ogresses that all suddenly become masculine and feminine symbols of the Tempter. For Hawthorne, the devil is much more likely to turn himself into a man or a woman than into a poodle. Allegory and metaphysics in his work are both clearly seen to be rooted in psychology. The darkness of the temptation of Saint Anthony is also the night of Dionysiac orgies, and the capital sins are more than symbols, they are acts performed in a dream. If Robin encounters Pride in the labyrinth of the city streets, that is because pride already possesses him and is attempting, like a hellish and smoldering fire, to break loose.[27] If he encounters Lust,[28] that is because she is already inside him and is seeking satisfaction under cover of the darkness. For the hellish fire is also the sexual fire: pink ribbons, red dresses, purple blossoms—all symbols of venery.[29] It presides over the initiation of the young couple in the forest,[30] takes the form of a devouring reptile in the jealous breast,[31] and that of an inner cancer working its way little by little to the surface in that of the adulterer.[32] Its only antidote is the ideal fire of love[33] and the light of heaven. When he uncovers his ulcerated breast to the sunlight, Dimmesdale is fighting fire with fire. The Prometheus complex is present in all the "sons" who dream of rivalling the "father," whether on the sexual plane, like Dimmesdale, or on the level of creation, like Rappacini. And the Empedocles complex is its corollary. Ethan Brand, hypnotized by the fire he has made it his pastime to play with, tries to identify himself with it, which also betrays a will toward transmutation. Instead of psychoanalysis, there is an exorcism of the fire, accompanied by a form of fetishism.

The inverse of fiery exaltation is the descent into the underworld. Darkness, the mother of fire, can also extinguish it. The dialectic of ignition and extinction is inherent in the consciousness. It is also a dialectic of the womb as Meleager's firebrand makes us aware. Annihilation by extinction, by suffocation, is a womb-nightmare. Prison, house, the past—they are all lethal wombs for Clifford.[34] And the female monsters are all child and man eaters: the ogress; the titaness;[35] Medea, the witch in alliance with the dragon—the female dragon; the Sphinx, prepared to eat Jason up;[36] Circe the enchantress, whose lovers awaken imprisoned in a womb-like skin.[37]

Yet it is this same prison—this refuge—that the lost children of the shadows, shivering and weeping, so long for. It is less the brightness of the flames that many of them are seeking than the warmth of the breast that Dimmesdale, for instance, rediscovers for an instant with Hester,[38] the gentle touch that brings oblivion, in which the being consents to its annihilation in order to rediscover its vigor. The path to maturity and the light beyond passes through the protective shadow that lulls the child, as well as through the terrifying shadow where the smoldering fire lies. The quest for the father thus passes through the womb, in which the questing being sometimes forgets his purpose. The sexual fire, brought to a paroxysmic blaze by contact with the beloved, then dies down in the arms of the mother in order to be reborn, purified—and above all revivified—before returning to the creative fire. The spark stolen from the father is finally restored to him—the spark of life, either infernal or celestial, that first issued from the primal fire. It is by its very nature double, it is the ambivalent act, that of the ambiguous God, Hawthorne's God, who with one and the same gesture creates darkness and light, good and evil,[39] twin brothers both endowed with an equal vigor. The very metaphysical origin of life was Manichean in Hawthorne's eyes. The Promethean fire was therefore also the creative Manichean fire in the sphere of good and the sphere of evil. It was above all the Dionysian fire of life lived in its profound contradictions, not a fire purified in accordance with a theoretical ethics—a fire flaming with both masculine and feminine values to an intense degree—the raging fire of the animus and the lambent fire of the anima—of which human bodies, their symbolic homologues, are the receptacles. Like Doctor Faustus, the adulterous minister seeks out womb-like crucibles —his cell, the forest, and dark, which have their counterparts in Marlowe as the earth, the ocean, and the cloud[40]—and woman herself, the sexual crucible in whose womb he has imperfectly sublimated himself, and from which, nevertheless, he wishes to tear himself free:[41] for Dimmesdale the Puritan, to think of love after death would be to renounce God.[42] Ethan Brand, on the other hand, like Septimius Felton, goes to the crucible where the burning phallic emblem rules, and rediscovers the myth of the Phoenix. Hawthorne's psychology usually only frees itself from metaphysics and allegory in order to become, in some sort, alchemy.[43]

II. SYMPATHY AND THE VIOLATION OF THE CONSCIOUSNESS

In Hawthorne, the psychic dynamic, both introvert and extrovert, springs from the contradictory tendencies polarized by the paternal and maternal archetypes. The interferential effects of good and evil, guilt and innocence, solitude and communication, form a highly Puritan network of complexes. These contraries are the poles of attraction and repulsion that determine the dialectic of sympathy and antipathy. The criminal has a nostalgia for innocence that also inspires him with the temptation to sully it. When Dimmesdale is tempted to defile the child's, the young girl's purity, it is the purity of the mother he is attempting to reach and blast.[1] And innocence is always fascinated by crime, especially if it is clothed in a paternal prestige—that is Miriam's whole tragedy[2]—so that guilt and innocence each becomes a psychic stimulant for the other. Their presence in a single individual creates an internal dynamic that usually ends by taking the form of torture: for Hawthorne, a living conscience can only be a torn conscience. This is of course the eternal allegorical combat between the forces of good and the forces of evil—but it is also the conflict between the forces of life and the forces of death in the lists of the consciousness. Whoever lives that drama with true intensity, whatever the power of bewitchment or narcissism over him, is unable to remain imprisoned within himself, self-sufficient, like the petrified man,[3] but is instead driven to search for himself in others, to question the universe and his fellow men with love, with hate, with anguish. The soul's profound duality alone explains the necessity for exchanges between "spheres" that would otherwise remain autonomous and separate.

These exchanges are psychophysical in nature—sexual as much as they are spiritual—and Hawthorne, who was very much of his time in this regard, would have liked to disencumber them of all excess of carnal impurity. They had less to do with the alchemy of the senses, it seemed to him—or did he want to persuade himself so?—than with the galvanism, the magnetism of telepathy.[4] Though he did not stop at a psychoelectric interpretation; it was more that he was aware that this new science that gave him the opportunity to yield to the demon urging him to "intellectualize the blood"[5] had a kinship with occultism and magic. Science provides the artist with images only; it does not offer him keys, as the Naturalists claimed, prepared as they were to reduce psychology to chemistry and biology.[6] Hawthorne, for his part, sought to transpose even the "fleshy effulgence"[7] given off by the Judge onto the level of nerves and radiations. Contacts are often made without hands, lips, or breasts touching.[8] But the psychic fluid is itself physical, and the abstract fluid that Hawthorne the psychologist uses as an intermediary takes on a sensual density upon contact with the matter of consciousness. The true writer follows his intuition, even though he may be in part a dupe of fashion and moral superstitions. He is never a total traitor. Magnetism in Hawthorne is the sign that conveys not only the impinging of radiations emitted by the mind, but also the communication of the heat that is passed from body to body in a crowd, within a family group under the same roof, or between individuals as diverse as those gathered together in the Blithedale common room.[9] Hawthorne's experimental formula, as with the majority of novelists, is the couple: it is when the "magnetic chain"[10] is shortest that the current reaches its maximum intensity. A single spark can then express, without the help of the slightest gesture or the slightest physical contact, the boiling rage of a passion, sexual upheavals, or the inevitability of a crime: the gaze is enough—that of the man who hates,[11] that of the lover,[12] that which seals the fate of the Model[13]—the radiation that emanates from the face of a loved woman,[14] the aura of a sensuous body,[15] or that of a demoniac being.[16] In every case we are dealing with a mutual fascination that makes two consciousnesses into two interdependent and connected vessels.

Sympathy is the open-sesame that allows the fluid to pass from one consciousness into another. A veritable osmosis takes place through the ear, and even more so through the eyes, which are windows opening upon symmetrical worlds, and behind which there are elves, goblins,[17] demons, and will-o'-the-wisps hiding, flitting, and spying on one another. The inward fire rises from the deeps of the being and seeks a corresponding spark in other eyes. Clifford's never shine so brightly as in Phoebe's presence.[18] Thus the secret images in those "artesian wells"[19] mount up to meet images proceeding from other sources, and the path that the hypnotic, exploratory gaze will take, in the opposite direction, has already been opened up. The being jealous of his self's integrity needs no more than that to make him regard all sympathy with suspicion.[20] And what is one to say of love, which requires that there should be no limits to the fusion of the beings concerned! The "transported" soul leaves its place vacant. What stranger might not enter at such times? Love is always more or less a form of sorcery, a spell, as soon as one places oneself on the sexual plane.[21] Gervayse, Dimmesdale, Hester, Miriam, Zenobia, they are all literally spellbound, all comparable to Alice Pyncheon, who was not only possessed by the wizard Maule but also forced by him to prostitute herself.[22] Holgrave, the descendant of a fortuneteller, falls in love with a Pyncheon.[23] But being also a moral heir to the Puritans he restrains himself from using his magnetic fluid, or in other words his power of sexual fascination, because he senses that the demon of hate might take advantage of the paths that the gentle persuasion of love would open up.[24] For the Puritan, love is not only a physical violation but also a psychical one, such as those inflicted upon Alice and Priscilla.[25] And is Chillingworth's hatred not also a strange kind of love—so much solicitude for an abhorred rival—one almost feels it is Dostoevski's eternal husband all over again. Yielding to the enchantment of love means giving oneself up to the Tempter just as surely as if one yields to the fascination of hate, for love and hate are the two faces of sin.

It is not simply by chance that the doctor, the artist, and the minister play such a preponderant role in the body of Hawthorne's work.[26] They all belong to the same intellectual family: they all have the same close concern with the complex machinery of the inner life. Whether he is a painter,[27] a clockmaker like Owen Warland,[28] a sculptor like Drowne and Kenyon,[29] a poet like Coverdale,[30] an alchemist like Aylmer, Rappacini, and Chillingworth,[31] a sorcerer like Maule or Westervelt,[32] or a preacher like the Reverend Mr. Hooper or Dimmesdale,[33] Hawthorne's intellectual is above all an "anatomist," simultaneously akin both to the Puritan, whose concern for the health of his soul entails its ceaseless examination, and to the demoniac inquisitor. Their field of activity, whatever their situation in life, is essentially the human soul. It is there, in the cavern of the heart and mind, that they set up their laboratory. Their meditations over the crucible are merely an image for inward meditation and moral exploration. The saint's cell and the alchemist's cabinet communicate with one another:[34] though their activities are opposed from the ethical point of view, they are complementary from the psychological point of view.

The "keen, cool, interested"[35] mind of Hawthorne the observer is to be found also in all his violators of others' consciousnesses. The instinct toward such violation is stimulated in them by the existence of a torment, a secret of which they wish to find the reciprocal complement in others. They are all first fascinated by their victims and by psychic phenomena, and that is why they themselves have powers of fascination, even though they are not all mesmerists. The investigation does not always take place on the same level, or by the same means, or from the same point of view. Chillingworth's eyes slice into Dimmesdale's soul like a scalpel:[36] his gaze penetrates the wound, but does he see anything other than the wound? The anatomist of evil constructs his notion of the personality according to the unhealthy elements he isolates within it: he does not replace those elements in their general psychic context. His intention is to verify his a priori belief in depravity, as Alymer's is to verify his in purity, not to make a psychological discovery. He will use any means to produce the proof of what he believes the truth to be, for without that proof the whole structure will collapse, his world will lose its meaning. That is what happens to Chillingworth when Dimmesdale eludes him.[37] Tricks, blackmail, persuasion, violence, treachery, the inquisitor will stop at nothing. The Judge, for instance, is certain that Clifford knows the secret of the lost inheritance. It is pure perversity that makes him refuse to divulge it:[38] torture would make him do so.[39] It is in the same spirit that Chillingworth "tends" his patient, subjecting him to precisely the treatment likely to create those symptoms in him that the doctor wishes to find. So that it is the method of investigation that actually brings about the psychological reality. The experimenter subjects the subject to violence and suggestion until he becomes the being whose guilt will justify the means employed: he begins by making the person he wants to make vomit into a sick man—methods worthy of the witch-hunters themselves.

A more subtle method consists in rendering the consciousness transparent. This is employed by the violator endowed with extreme intellectual finesse who is aiming at total psychic possession. He wishes to know the other to his very depths; to drain him dry. His behavior is that of the succubus, his partner's that of the incubus. At this level, psychic exchanges are more exhausting and more degrading than physical, sexual excesses—as witness the moral disintegration inflicted upon his victim by Chillingworth. The destructive process, however, does have its obstacles to overcome all the same. In order to sap them, the succubus begins by effacing his own personality, by making himself the persecuted person's double, so that the latter, believing himself in the presence of a mirror self who is there to console and understand him, allows the pernicious fluid to pass into him under cover of this mask of sympathy. Already, under the charm of a confidant all too skilled at identifying himself with his victim, Dimmesdale is being lulled into numbness, yielding to the sweetness of abandoning himself to brotherly solicitude.[40] Not that he does not know what to expect from his doctor, from the demon seeking to putrefy his soul or blast it with barrenness, uniting the sadism of corruption to that of purity in evil; but he experiences a bitter delight in betraying himself—as though in a dream it seems to him—and in feeling the other's gaze searing into him like a corrosive. If his masochism were not held in check by a reflex of self-defense, he would let himself be wholly subjugated by the invader, by the hostile serpent seeking to occupy all the vital centers of his consciousness.

In accomplishing such a transfusion of psychic fluid, the invader runs the risk of losing his own identity or of finding nothing but himself. In consequence, fearing that he may be thwarted and scorned, or perhaps become a victim himself, he remains on the frontiers of the consciousness that he is aiming at plundering from attic to cellar. He often contents himself, like Maule and Westervelt, with annihilating all power of refusal in the other, and with putting him or her—like the haunted mind[41] preyed upon by its own cruel associations—into a secondary state of consciousness and making him dream aloud, much as a modern psychiatrist might do.[42] In this way he obtains an oral and imaged transcription of the hidden reality, which is precisely what the laboratory psychologist is seeking. Chillingworth is a past master in the art of stage-managing shocks, of creating profound upheavals that will surge up and exhaust themselves at the surface in the form of quivers across the face, clenchings of the hand,[43] or explosions of anger betraying a mad inner panic.[44] Holgrave's lack of considerateness when discussing the Pyncheons in front of Phoebe[45] is also a means of exercising the ascendancy he has won over her from the very outset. Psychic violation is a masculine privilege, which is as much as to say, a prerogative of the father. It is only in the presence of the father that one accuses oneself, that one confesses. This is masochism, of course, but a masochism attempting to free itself of sexuality. The masochism in relation to the mother, to woman, although manifest in Gervayse and Kenyon, is mingled with sadism in Holgrave and the Model.[46] None of them commits himself entirely, not even Gervayse, who in the end gives way to the need he feels to triumph over his tormenting temptress.[47] In fact, in order to escape from feminine (maternal) domination, man (the son) would rather choose to give himself up to the executioner (the father). By deliberately giving himself up to the pillory Dimmesdale is of course escaping from his satanic father, but he is also escaping from the domination of the woman he loves, from love the quest for the absolute, from love the cerebral torment—from the love of Pearl, the interrogator, the demanding woman to be, the future destroyer of the masculine psyche.[48]

These subtle or frenzied probings, motivated by a desire to understand or to possess, permit those who make them to verify the existence of psychic depths, but they do not enable them to measure those depths. And above all they do not provide a knowledge of the consciousness in its plenitude, in its freedom and multiplicity: they reveal only a truncated consciousness, a watched, a spied-upon consciousness. The artist sees more deeply than the mesmerist, the loving tyrant, or the man who hates. There is in his "ministry" something religious, because he holds the unhappy consciousness to be sacred.[49] He also sees things broadly, and upon multiple levels. He is, like Holgrave, a radiologist of the mind who proceeds, not by hypnotism, but by imagination, to an inward scrutiny in his darkroom. He photographs secret images instead of physical features, and from those images he creates psychological portraits.[50] In the same way, the painter's eye penetrates to the very depths of his sitter's soul. And it is the soul he paints—in all its beauty and ugliness—not the face. The prophetic pictures bring to light an unconscious driving force in the soul of an Othello unaware of what he is.[51] Just as the sculptor sees through the marble, inside the roughhewn block itself, the hidden form,[52] the face, the already living body,[53] performing a radioscopy on the inert matter he works with, so the novelist performs a radioscopy on his human material. In the clay from which Kenyon has modeled his Cleopatra, Hawthorne sensed inward passions fermenting like a yeast, and behind impassive masks he perceived the inner procession of memories.[54] He himself had his memory of that electric and sensual contact with Hester, the statue of flesh that he in his case had sculpted from within.

III. PSYCHOLOGICAL CREATION

The artist has no use for oppressed and captive souls, since he is able to recreate them all with the magic of a universal sympathy and because he possesses a faculty for limitless self-division. It is a grave sign of impotence if he cannot see himself as though he were someone else,[1] become someone else, and, conversely, see others as so many avatars of himself. He must therefore possess a rich, luxuriant consciousness, one capable of containing all human contradictions. Without unquietness of mind there can be no impulse toward others, and in consequence, no fertile return into the self: no creation. All art proceeds from the dialectic of the divided soul, whose energy is able to flow in a wholly unpredictable manner to either its negative or positive extremes. Creation takes place in opposition to the forces that drive man to abandon himself to his demons, to destroy himself by satisfying his deepest desires—those desires that are too convincingly depicted in Ethan Brand, Dimmesdale, Zenobia, and Miriam not to have originated in their creator. This is the artist's sheet anchor: to be able, at privileged moments, even if he is one day doomed to be wrecked entirely, like Poe or Verlaine, to convert these forces into powerful allies. Even in Hester, the energy she brings to her passion finds esthetic employment, which for her, since she is not granted redemption,[2] is a compensation. Whoever is capable of sin is capable of creation: the creative faculty is indissolubly linked with a practical or an intuitive knowledge of evil. Pearl's spirit of mischief is also a creative spirit.[3] When Puritanism confuses the one with the other its tendency is to drain the soul of its fertility without uprooting the evil in it. The "angel," content with its own abstract purity, is sterile[4] and therefore does not escape sin. Hawthorne the poet was always to set less store by such negative forms of consciousness than by the kind of living consciousness given to bursting its banks, whether openly or in secret, and that, like his own, was able to project itself in a thousand shapes, change, and proliferate.

The wonderment of the artist when faced with living beings, men, women, children, those enigmas,[5] is added to the scientific interest of the psychologist. Psychological creation relies upon a dialectic of the heart and mind. Certain characters are created by sympathy, others by antipathy—can Hilda's existence be explained without a hidden resentment on her creator's part?—but all owe their life to the author's psychological interest in the realities, even the unpleasant ones, of the consciousness. The psychological varieties that the novelist-poet applies himself to describing are all imagined homologues of the various aspects of his own inner self. Whereas the realist describes his characters from the exterior, without wishing to admit to himself that he is only following his intuition—without which he would be unable to distinguish any prominent features—Hawthorne describes his from the inside, and refuses to apply himself to any objective analysis of individuals whose moral substance seems to him insufficiently dense, forgetting that he needs only to study their particular cases thoroughly enough, as Balzac and Dostoevski do, to make them become interesting. His principal characters are, as we have seen, aristocrats. Moreover, their moral existence takes precedence over their social existence. Consequently it is futile, apart from a few exceptions,[6] to concern ourselves much with his "models," in the physical sense of the term. In his case, there can scarcely be any question of anything other than psychological models, which, by fusion with the various aspects of his own personality, finally produced the "types" that the reader later qualifies as "Dickensian," or "Balzacian," or "Hawthornian." Hester was born from the fusion of several figures in a single dream.

Hawthorne quite evidently projected his own self into his characters. In his tales, there is generally a single character to synthesize the writer's personality or to represent one of his aspects, as Robin, Gervayse, Wakefield, and Endicott do, except when he remains a simple two-dimensional figure like the ambitious young man,[7] or hardens into a symbol like David Swan. These are not true characters, but individualities tending to become closely identified with their creator, a process that in the best tales permits a sort of interior monologue—as in "Young Goodman Brown" or "Ethan Brand." At the same time, using his narcissistic element, Hawthorne was creating the hermaphrodite apparent in Giovanni[8] and continuing its existence in the later Edenic couples. But both these processes precluded the appearance of contrasted characters before Hawthorne's novel-writing period—except perhaps in "Rappacini," in which we find two individualized embodiments of the father both disputing the other's claim to the same son. After "Ethan Brand," Hawthorne attempts to give all the elements of his self a greater solidity by embodying each one in a separate character. He evolves from a poetic psychology to a dramatic psychology. Instead of merely an alter ego of the artist or the isolated Edenic couple, we have successive combinations and confrontations.[9] The conflicts and attractions that before tended to be limited to the two sexes or to remain on the level of psychological symbolism are extended to individual temperaments. Whereas the youthful Hawthorne was content to project his own nervous, rather than full-blooded, temperament into his heroes, the mature Hawthorne felt the need to dissociate these two elements, which tended increasingly to exist in a state of equilibrium. So that we find him creating oppositions between these two masculine types, the nervous and the sanguine, between Rappacini and Baglioni, Ethan Brand and Bartram, Clifford and the Judge, Coverdale and Hollingsworth, though not without an awareness of the fact that such arbitrary oppositions do not conform with nature. Which is why he adds a suspicion of sensuality to Clifford, a touch of spirituality to Hollingsworth, and creates an even subtler mixture in Donatello and Kenyon, the one being more mercurial, the other more placid, though his most brilliant synthesis still remained the one he had achieved in Dimmesdale. The differentiation of the female characters, as we have seen, is closely linked with a definite metapsychology: on the one hand the frigid angels, on the other the sensual demons, but all of them perverse, whether in virtue or in vice, intent upon molding man to their wishes and refusing to be molded by him. There are few women in the traditional European sense of the term, young girls like Susan and Phoebe[10] waiting to be revealed to themselves by their lovers—above all very few women who have not emerged fully armed—armed against him, in accordance with his desire—from Hawthorne's sexual imagination, which tended more to passivity than aggression, and who are not female doubles of their creator in the same way as the male characters are his masculine doubles.

The increased number of characters in Hawthorne's novels is dependent upon more serious reasons than the simple law of contrasts, however. The use of the quaternary formula[11] in particular is not based solely upon dramatic requirements. It seems to have been sketched out for the first time in "Rappacini": opposite the figures of the father and the son there stands a female figure capable of capricious division: Beatrice and her "sister" the poisonous plant. The formula becomes even clearer in *The Scarlet Letter*: two masculine natures, one intellectual and sadistic, the other imaginative and masochistic, stand as counterparts to two feminine natures, one carnal and maddening to the senses, the other elfin and bewildering to the mind. Only the androgynous self of the creator could have given birth to such a symmetrically androgynous flowering of characters, just as it was the source of the Oberon-hermaphrodite. But in discussing Hawthorne, is it sufficient to say that, in *The House of the Seven Gables* for example, his animus[12] is split between the enterprising daguerreotypist and the inert Clifford, while his anima is embodied simultaneously in the young girl and in the old woman? If the division merely took place in this way, horizontally, there would naturally be many intermediate figures occurring between the extremes. Thus the realist, who identifies himself with all human beings by imitation, immediately turns them into characters. Whereas Hawthorne identifies himself with only a few particular individuals capable of reflecting his own essential tendencies, since it is those tendencies that give meaning to the images and novelties provided by experience. It is the primary image of the mother, of the widow, that places Hepzibah in her true psychological perspective, as it is that of the young and beautiful mother we find reflected in Phoebe. Similarly, if the image of the poet in *The Blithedale Romance* summons up that of the practical reformer, and Zenobia's sexual luxuriance the ectoplasmic fragility of Priscilla, it is because Hawthorne was haunted by an ideal of manhood that he felt to be unattainable and by an ideal of femininity that he felt to be contradictory. We are thus always dealing with a variation upon a single psychological archetype, or around a dominant psychological preoccupation, in accordance with a quaternary formula that tends to reproduce itself in all the novels, a fact that certainly seems to indicate in every case a definite quadripolar projection—the creative self splitting into an animus and an anima which then in their turn undergo a similar division.[13] Thus in *The Scarlet Letter*, Hawthorne's animus, with its will toward creation and domination, becomes the alchemist whose anima is the witch-child, the child of magic, the "soror mystica"[14] while the novelist's anima becomes Hester, whose animus is the minister, the character who, like his creator, feels a deep need for the mother-beloved. There are as many arrangements of this quadripolar situation as there are groups of characters. If Hawthorne's animus felt the need to be an artist and a wizard, then it became Holgrave, whose anima is the young girl, Phoebe, whom he enchants. But his anima, having already experienced the glory of passion in its scarlet apparel, underwent an eclipse and donned the black garb of Hepzibah, whose unmanly animus took the form of Clifford. Then, wishing to reaffirm itself, it became Zenobia, with Coverdale as her animus and swooning lover. As for Hollingsworth, he fails in his would-be embodiment of the supermasculine and is eventually absorbed by the frail Priscilla. The animus attempts to take the upper hand again in Kenyon, but is swiftly neutralized by Hilda, while the anima re-embodied in Miriam completely subjugates the innocent Donatello. The cycle of novels taken as a whole, while heralding the triumph of the American woman, seems also to be consecrating that of the anima in Hawthorne himself. The position of the animus is weakened in the three works that follow *The Scarlet Letter* by the appearance of a fifth protagonist: the Judge, the magnetizer, the Model. Instead of retaining the masculine, creative, patriarchal figure's ambiguity, he separates off its satanic element by extrapolating from it an essentially allegorical character: he destroys with his own hands the psychic unity and richness he was dreaming of and imperils the meaning of his work, justifying in advance the criticism advanced by James, who was to perceive nothing more in *The Marble Faun* than a tissue of "picturesque conceits."[15]

This defect becomes even more evident in the posthumous novels, in which Hawthorne was unable to rediscover his former self, and in particular that duality of the anima that is sometimes so forcible a characteristic of his work.

Hawthorne's psychology is a thing of perpetual scission and fascination. Two by two, or alone with their author, or with their own images, the characters achieve their precision of outline by means of symmetry and reflections. One is justified, with Hawthorne, in talking of a maieutic method whose instrument is the mirror. As well as being an esthetic accessory, the mirror is also the inner eye that multiplies, reanimates, or summons up images. Itself a creator of the unexpected, it also enables us to be spectators at the psychological birth of beings. Hester in the pillory is born of the gazes in which she is reflected. She is created daily in the image of the Letter as it is reflected in the eyes of her daughter;[16] even the polished metal of the armor and the water of the stream enter into the conspiracy.[17] Dimmesdale is not simply attempting to overcome his flesh with the ascetic discipline he imposes upon himself: his fasts, his vigils, his fascination with his own image in the looking glass,[18] even his flagellation, are all means of provoking fantasies, hallucinations, psychological scission. He employs the mirror as a means to breed new selves out of a narcissistic ecstasy: even his mother's ghost is an ectoplasmic product of his own ego.[19] Other characters attempt to grasp the being of their dreams in the fountain or well of their childhood. The vision that wells up in the fountain,[20] the "shifting phantasmagories" in Maule's well,[21] the naiad brushing the Faun's lips,[22] are all resurgences of some primal being returning from an "anteworld."[23] Every face seeks its mirror, its reflection, its double, in order to explain itself to itself; every individual given to introspection attempts to find the way back to the source of his dreams, to grasp both the purest and the most tormented images of his being in their emotional and hidden life. This is why so many of Hawthorne's characters have a primarily oneiric existence: Goodman Brown, Wakefield—not to mention the various incarnations of the father and the mother. In the absence of living models for Pearl, he need only have searched in his dreams to find her there: the witch-girl, like the Black Man, was an oneiric reality from which no heir to the Puritan tradition could possibly have escaped. And the best proof of this is the fact that Hawthorne took pleasure in describing his own daughter in terms that a theologian from the age of witch hunts would not have been ashamed to acknowledge.[24] Pearl filled a void in her universe: everything was calling her into being, to incarnate herself in that suffocating sphere inside which her tormented parents dared to meet only in secret. And Reverend Hooper, in spite of the guarantee offered for the authenticity of the character by a reference to historical fact,[25] is purely and simply a figure from a nightmare, surely. Clifford himself, imagined by Hepzibah as a child lost in the maze of a dream,[26] must have first appeared to his creator as a child-self, helpless and lost in a world of adults and pain, for does he not in fact make him into an aging adolescent?[27]

The growth of these apparitions is not ectoplasmic, as it is in Poe. The psychic growth of Hawthorne's creations follows a pattern derived rather from the vegetable kingdom. The silhouettes we first see dancing in the flames of the fire or sketching their outlines in the glow of the moon do not remain as shadows or will-o'-the-wisps.[28] They take on substance, they expand and unfurl like plants. For Hawthorne, man's vegetable double did exist. We have only to remember how many of his heroes have a tree as a natural companion[29] or are born under the sign of the forest.[30] Each of them has roots that plunge into the darkness, into the humus of existence in which all their tendencies unite. The Hawthorne hero is an Antaeus rooted in the maternal earth, like Hollingsworth, whose strength evokes the oak, or Donatello the primitive man—and also a prisoner of his own roots. The dungeon of the solitary self is a hardened, subterranean womb from which the conscious being despairs of escaping, like Clifford imprisoned in the somber House calling upon his lost youth.[31] These rooted beings also have branches that aspire, with the vehemence of desire and passion, toward the caresses of the light.[32] When he compares love to a plant with many leaves,[33] Hawthorne is enclosing within a single image an entire aspect of the psychic life and poetic oneirism. Puritan austerity, however, is meanwhile attempting to strip the human plant of its thirsty branches and all unnecessary foliage. When he has his young captive's curls cut off, Endicott's intention is to prune him of his natural and superfluous graces and forestall the useless efflorescence of psychological and esthetic complications. He kills the budding poet so that the future leader may develop.[34] To blast the emblems of fertility is to risk drying up the sap of life. The enormous, cracked, scorched, ineradicable trunk to which the weak, the parasites cling— Clifford and Hepzibah clinging to the ancestral elm as Alice's posies cling to the House's roof[35]—that heroic trunk is nonetheless incomplete, infirm, and its monstrous strength is also weakness. Without the flower of sensuality and passion—without the free, wild, rebellious seed that detaches itself from the tree and flies afield to sprout elsewhere,[36] it could not survive.

The vegetable metaphor, which is so natural to many authors, serves as the foundation for an organic allegory of man. But to restrict oneself to such a simplification, which is the essence of a certain narrowly defined type of poetry, could only impoverish a writer's psychological material. The harvest of images that the writer culled from his dreams and fantasies provided him with the raw material for psychic amalgams and molds. Proceeding by intuitive touch, Hawthorne allowed his critical intelligence to doze while the eyes of his imagination dilated in the half-darkness. It is in the workshop of the dark, from materials melted in a crucible of shadow, that the artist models the beings into which he then breathes life. Not content with caressing the form he animates, he places himself in the center of the consciousness he creates. The creator admires himself in his creation. More, he casts a spell upon it from within, inhabits it, and grows within it as it grows in him. To create is to love the being that one is creating with one's own hands. It is at the same time to wrestle with it—the struggle with the Angel, which does not necessarily take on human form, and indeed increasingly rejects it in modern art, including the art of the novel. But the gestures of creation remain the same, even though the attitude of the mind directs them toward different ends. Where Robbe-Grillet would create the descriptive geometry of an objectified anguish, Hawthorne, at the very heart of Hester's consciousness in the pillory, lives the tribulations of his heroine subjectively, climbs with her up onto the scaffold, accompanies her in her solitude, and commits adultery with her in imagination. And at the same time he also struggles with her in order to obtain from her the most total possible image of one woman's destiny. And to the same end he also makes his the images that come into being within the tortured soul of the minister. He identifies himself with that consciousness as it forms itself, disintegrates itself, reforms itself, and writhes in agony, inextricably mingled with his own consciousness. The act of creation, an act of the heart, must—even at the risk of a change in its nature—rely also on the will. At the frontier of creation the intellect comes into play. The dialectic of sympathy and intelligence confers upon its creations the inseparable liberty of a primal ambiguity, but the balance between the creative imagination and the systematic intellect is often imperiled by the latter. Hawthorne's psychological creation was perpetually being impeded by his allegorical tendency. It was a danger difficult to avoid for a type of creation too exclusively autonomous in nature, since the novelist was constantly seeking on every side for reflections of his own multifaceted and narcissistic self, rather than attempting to enrich his multiple individuality by contact with others. Working in depth, thanks to an acute sense of man's inward reality, Hawthorne succeeded in creating living beings to exactly that degree in which he permitted them to add to his own self, to transform it, to enable it to be reborn to itself—the miracle accomplished by Hester—and to detach themselves from it without insisting upon their remaining mere moral and dramatic commodities. The causes of creative failure, as with the causes of creative success, are inherent in the psychological make-up of the artist. We must also agree that Hawthorne found himself presented with recalcitrant, reluctant human material—that provided for him by the descendants of the Puritan tradition.

IV. THE PURITAN COMPLEXES

In Hawthorne's tales and romances, we are often dealing with beings whose development and inclinations have been forcibly repressed, whose generous vitality is obliged to conceal itself beneath a mask of neutrality,[1] and whose natures, tormented by a need to communicate, have been reduced to following the counsels of distrust. Hawthorne is frequently examining minds that Calvinism has rendered hyperconscious of their own leaning toward introspection, or even self-inquisition, and that the existence of this same leaning in others disturbs and paralyzes. The gossip of old women—of witches[2]—and clerical censure, not to mention the penetrating scrutiny of the doctor or the mesmerist, place the individual in Hawthorne's works in the center of a sort of spy ring. They are enmeshed, in other words, by the Puritan complexes of repression and reticence. In order to elude the effects of gossip, of censure, of the law, there is but one alternative: hypocrisy or playing possum. But the fact remains that no external pressure can prevent the consciousness from living its own life, even if that inner life obeys a dynamic of constraint.

Most of Hawthorne's characters are victims of Puritan repression, social repression, and—above all—the moral repression that the individual, influenced by his environment, exercises upon himself. Girls betrothed, then abandoned,[3] wives of the dead[4]—forbidden by an emotional fashion and a Draconian moral code to seek consolation or attempt to start life again—recluses, creatures imprisoned in ill-fated houses,[5] the guilty, the convicted, the afflicted, they all make their way through life bowed down, sometimes deformed[6] by the weight of a grief or a crime, all clothed in mourning or shame,[7] except when their pride and their power weighs them down further with armor[8] or rich, burdensome cloaks.[9] Any office, like misfortune, becomes a mantle of lead. Crushed by the weight of their responsibilities, their honors, or their infamy, they are burdens upon one another as well as upon the earth that bears them and summons them to their rest in it. There is no doubt that their existence has weight, but it is threatened in its vital dynamic: so many of these consciousnesses live only at the most sluggish rhythm—joy, suffering, desires, all reduced to minute and inward modifications. And upon first soundings we find an equal parsimony in the emotional secretions produced, whether in a hardened heart like the Judge's, in that of a melancholy Othello like Roderick Elliston,[10] or in the mourning heart of a Hepzibah, which is likened to a rusty lock:[11] a standard psychological image for the reticent heart.

These consciousnesses frustrated in the flowering of their inclinations, threatened from without by a repressive society, are obliged to turn back into themselves in order to find compensations, consolation, refuge.[12] Having renounced all outward expression, they are all the more open to the fertilizing influence of their own meditations upon an inward reality, which is always concerned with remorse and memories. They provide a rich field of observation, not in their outward demonstrations, but in their hidden recesses. Psychology in depth also means, ipso facto, psychology of solitude—and in Hawthorne's case, an introspective psychology of individual consciousnesses turning in an inner maze. Hepzibah's mind is unable to leave the House, which has become the mold into which it has poured itself. To such effect that no change of environment could ever, it seems, restore its fluidity. Her brain is carried off by the train, but her mind remains immobile in the center of the House: a typical example of the consciousness that feeds upon one single image. This "mental image"[13] is a primary image, an archetype with which the entire psyche has become interfused. Other characters live simply upon one idée fixe: the Judge, and all the searchers after an inheritance, or an elixir, or an absolute. In that case we are dealing with consciousnesses that have become mechanical. More interesting are those that are tormented by a sense of abandonment and depravity. Their anguish and their scruples drive them into the realm of fine psychological subtleties and shadings. Wakefield's ingenious and roundabout methods of simultaneously seeking and avoiding happiness,[14] and Reuben Bourne's of avoiding the curse whose fulfilment he in fact voluntarily precipitates,[15] show that we are in the presence of consciousnesses constructed like labyrinths, victims of an excessive concentration of the psychic fluid that generates obsessional patterns. These beings, unable to find release either in suffering or action, create their own partners in order to play out their inward dramas: they are like Roderick, at once Othello and Iago[16]—all the characters needed contained in a single individual. This splitting up of the personality is not in their cases accompanied by a fragmentation of the self but by a multiplication of its aspects. We have only to consider the complexity, the luxuriance revealed in Dimmesdale's soul by his constant caprices, retreats, and contradictory impulses, whether he is on the point of abandoning himself once more to his flesh, of corrupting his parishioners, or of confessing his crime.[17] The ecstasies of sainthood are in no way less potent than the delights of guilt and remorse, than the pleasure to be derived from infamy and from sinning in order to chastise oneself afterwards. In this circle of crime and punishment, the minister is seeking satisfactions that he knows he can no longer find elsewhere. Which paves the way to certain perversions: Dimmesdale, as he scourges himself, imagines he is at Hester's feet,[18] and when Hester makes her sufferings into an excuse for absolving her passion[19] is she not also trying to transmute her affliction into a new form of love-pleasure?

These beings enmeshed in a web of contradictions, constraints and thwarted caprices—some of whom are so skilled at converting frustration and pain into pleasure, while others seem irreparably extinguished by them—are sometimes, unknown to themselves, concealing unknown resources. The lymphatic and trembling Hepzibah suddenly rears up like a dragon to face the Judge.[20] Clifford, who has been plunged by his long seclusion into a state of intellectual torpor but in whom a miracle of "second growth"[21] occurs, finds the most untoward energy and intelligence at his command in circumstances that should have rendered him helpless. Though his reaction is nonetheless faithful to the deepest level of his artistic temperament: the drama of the situation automatically galvanizes his entire psyche.[22] Hepzibah on the other hand, being insensitive to the beauty of the drama and impressed only by the sadness of the spectacle, remains paralyzed. But when her brother's nervous excitement has exhausted the current that fed it, she becomes once more the elder, protective sister.[23] Dimmesdale, exhausted by the tortures he inflicts upon himself, is still capable of fits of anger.[24] Hester, condemned by society, threatened in her rights as a mother, turns at bay like a hunted animal, prepared to sacrifice the man she is still able to love for the sake of her child.[25] They all have consciousnesses that are still fluid and alive, filled with irrepressible desires whose unexpected resurgences may be characterized by an extreme violence. Dimmesdale's strange temptations on the way back from the forest constitute a whole series of unrealized acts— the rapes he would like to commit, now that passion has once more erupted in his flesh. The cause of Wakefield's flight is also probably sexual in nature. And W. Ludlow's murderous frenzy is in all likelihood simply the brutal awakening of a latent sadism exasperated into action by his wife's spiritual sentimentality.[26] Hawthorne's works abound in eruptions of repressed instincts and acts of psychic release: Hester ripping the emblem of adultery from her breast,[27] Clifford softened into feelings of tenderness[28] or gripped by vertigo[29] when faced with an open window, then finally deciding upon his flight with Hepzibah.[30] The oppressed consciousness feels an imperative need to burst its bonds occasionally in order to restore its equilibrium. Miriam avoids madness only by yielding to hysteria and by agreeing to her persecutor's murder.[31] And Young Goodman Brown, whose demented cries and laughs betray the morbid state of his mind, would also perhaps have become a murderer but for that nocturnal debauch. Confession, of course, is the supreme psychological remedy. The more unspeakable our desires and crimes seem the more necessary it is to confess them: such is the law one might deduce from a superficial interpretation of Hawthorne's thought.[32] But those that confess most freely are those that have nothing to confess: Hilda merely relieves herself of the burden of someone else's crime;[33] hardness of heart weighs scarcely at all upon a "pure" conscience. Those that feel personally guilty, the Narcissuses of sin who ought to be tempted by sensational confession, content themselves on the other hand with pretenses of it[34] or with living their moments of truth in dreams.[35] And even if they do go as far as the "revelation,"[36] they make sure that it remains ambiguous. It is not so much the light of truth they fear as the curtailment of the self it would involve, the abolition of their inward depths. To confess one's crimes, one's perversions, one's heresies, is to render them common property, a thing to which the individual proud of his uniqueness cannot consent. All communication tends to exorcise not only the sense of guilt but also the sense of singularity. To be alone is to be sick. And there is only one remedy according to Hawthorne: to bathe oneself in the stream of humanity.[37] Opposed to the spheres of isolation, to the dungeons, to the prisons, there stand the spheres of reunion, of reconciliation.[38] Love, which elsewhere is sorcery, also has a power of exorcism which at least provides the outcast individual with a twin. And the woman's role is often that of a psychoanalytic catalyst enabling the lost hero to find his way back to the fold of normality. Elinor removes Roderick's obsessions,[39] and one senses that Wakefield too is about to find the calming influence he needs in his home life.[40] But to adapt, to become like other people, is also, for a being truly set apart, to renounce the self.

The Puritan, who is, in the last analysis and despite the aberrations of his intolerance, a savage individualist—his God, after all, is a personal God—recoils from the enrichment of his soul through passion, that total rape of the being. The love whose remedial virtues Hawthorne extols is an extremely desexualized love: wishfully, he sees it as a path to serene maturity that will avoid those intermediate storms, those extravagances on nature's part, that society attempts to repress. But how much less interesting the study of man would be without passion—that irreplaceable psychological experience and source of dramatic power. Is it not precisely the contagious fever of passion that recharges the minister's failing psychic energies when the total and dazzling revelation of woman's being is unleashed upon him in Hester's person?[41] The scene in the forest is a veritable psychodrama in which two beings find themselves involved to the very depths of their beings and delve down to discover their true psychological essences, each at last embodying his or her true role—Dimmesdale that of lover and son, Hester that of the mother-beloved. Without this decisive experience, would Dimmesdale have gone as far as the pillory? Would he have found sufficient strength or sufficient fear in himself to drive him on? Is this awakening of the entire being from "sleepy innocence"[42] brought about by passion not—like the fatal knowledge of sin—a progress of the soul? Without the "madness" of love[43] the forces lying dormant in Donatello would never have produced the moral precipitate of conscience. And this change, which is also a psychic enlargement, has as its corollary a metamorphosis, an expansion of the area this new soul is able to contemplate:[44] the ways of the world and the world itself become strange; everything seems to recede in order to make room for the reinvented being; or is it in order to keep him apart? Through passion the heart also learns excess, and that way lies damnation.

Passion is necessary: yes. But a source of happiness: no. The "mad" bliss of lovers cannot last: no Puritan soul could ever conceive that. Happiness lulls the soul to sleep, and therefore it must always undergo a fresh ordeal: the death of love, death through love—we are back once more with the fatality of Dionysiac tragedy. Lovers in Hawthorne's universe, each bewitched by the other, are irremediably separated. The couples that stay together do not experience passion.[45] For passion is the essence of emotional suffering—shattering when it awakens in Hester's heart only to be doomed to immediate death—heart-rending in the sad and gentle voice of Miriam as she cradles the murderer who can never again be a child[46]—so all-devouring in Zenobia that it leads her to suicide:[47] invariably it bears the mark of misfortune. Puritan passion draws from the constraint in which it exists an explosively destructive power, whether in the form of forbidden love or in that of the love-hatred we find in Strindberg's heroes,[48] who loathe paying tribute to human affection and refuse to accept it except when disguised as its opposite. The Puritan passion most easily borne—apart from that for power[49]—is undoubtedly that of hate, the passion that believes itself pure because it rends instead of caressing, but which is in fact, just as much as lust, a desire for possession, and just as much a slave of its captive as love is of its object—to such an extent that it cannot live without it.[50] Hate, however, is free to explode in the light of day. Love is obliged to shut itself away, to hide itself; whereupon it turns sour, and becomes just as much a poison in the soul of the lover as in that of the jealous man.[51] The "hideous" secret of the human heart often turns out to be such a thwarted, tortured, denatured passion. We are on the threshold of the realm of "cold passions" and "quick eyes,"[52] of the spying serpent, of intellectualized passions dissecting their own nerves. The Puritan societies are precisely those that were to give birth to the psychologists of the hidden consciousness, and that were to provide them with their richest field of observation. Like all true writers, Hawthorne was by instinct a psychoanalyst: he knew what he was doing on the occasions when he turned impromptu doctor of souls,[53] but where others were to attempt to illustrate a priori theories,[54] Hawthorne—in an age when men's minds were still oriented to moral analysis, and though his own avowed aims were those of a moralist—brought about the psychological revolution of American literature, a revolution that in no way prefigured the introduction into the average American's everyday life of a psychoanalysis imbued with a superstitious regard for the social norm, but, on the contrary, that upheld both the rights of the outstanding individual and the rights of the poet.

Part Three

THE KEYS OF THE WORLD

ALLEGORY

· I ·

Intellectual Creation

I. FREEDOM AND CREATION

Ambiguous, erotic, disturbing mother images, father figures inspiring fear, admiration, repulsion—all so many resurrections effected by the writer: Hawthorne held himself alone responsible for his dead. Based upon memory, introspection, and the quest for a unified being, his works appear as another form of remorse—a reparation. But in running counter to the pious "monuments" of the conformists they did not take long to become a scandal, for the remorse was no more than a dynamic hypothesis giving rise to an autonomous creation that went beyond its data and respected no other will than its own—when the artist dared to give his creative powers full rein at least—which presupposes a liberty, the perquisite of poets, that Hawthorne, encumbered as he was by Puritan scruples and inhibitions, was sometimes reluctant to exercise. The problem of freedom poses itself at the highest degree at the level of the artist's self and his freedom from other tasks, and in the second degree at the level of the gestures required to realize the work, which is the creation of a new world from the starting point of the world as it exists. Can the art that wishes to regulate everything within its domain produce free beings? Can it work with living elements? True and sincere art does not merely seek to establish its absolute sovereignty but rather to base its own reality upon the contradictions of a fertile mind making use of the ambiguous and fluid life that it assimilates, then transmutes without destroying, to nourish the

239

seeds growing within it. The search for the keys of the world relies upon a double alchemy, on a dialectic of the domination and liberation of the elements of creation, while the artist's mind, in a reciprocal alternation, is at one moment liberating itself in its moving and multiple work, at another fixing itself in its hardened material. As in the field of psychology, the alchemy of the experimenting, authoritarian, allegory-making mind is both allied and opposed to the alchemy of the heart with its love for poetic and seductive reality.

This dialectic of fluidity and hardening could not be better illustrated than by the example of the spring—the spring, the artesian well of the soul,[1] as it flows and congeals. The pool in the "Hollow of the Three Hills" is the heroine's already dead conscience.[2] The fountain of the visions, and Maule's well,[3] in which images appear and melt away, contain the whole dialectic of creation hesitating between movement and immobility, between research and the immutable form. The spectator who attempts to master these reflections wishes to petrify them, to freeze them—he will obtain nothing but a collection of inert objects, of curiosities, and he himself will be turned into a statue.[4] He who wishes to muse upon those forms in depth, to be present at the mystery of their birth and their death, of their renascence, will take good care not to make any disturbing gesture, or to utter any fatal formula. These two attitudes are complementary in Hawthorne. In "Alice Doane," the petrifaction of the world by the frost is followed by a scene of resurrection,[5] which, though phantasmagoric, is nonetheless indicative of the author's intention. In the same way, the Great Stone Face comes to life and hardens again by turn, at once flesh and rock.[6] And Ethan Brand's heart is endowed both with the hardness of marble and with the mobility of the fire devouring it.[7]

Reality in Hawthorne, as with the consciousness, is always being either alternately or simultaneously caught in moments of immobility and/or photographed while in motion. Through the gallery of portraits and statues there wends the procession of ancestors or of visitors[8]—unless it is the pictures and statues themselves that become the procession.[9] Hawthorne systematically set up contrasts between inert objects and vehicles,[10] between sedentary characters and nomads: the sluggish minister anchored to his habits and Oberon with his far-flying fantasy; embittered recluses and carefree wanderers; resigned wives and husbands out in search of nocturnal adventures;[11] Hepzibah's "vegetable" nature and Clifford's "winged" nature.[12] On the one hand he gives us the weighty structures embodying the past, the law, and institutions, on the other he evokes—as though in irony or criticism— the free, natural life,[13] and lovers who ignore all prohibitions. Such repeated contrasts engender monotony and would become purely mechanical if there were not a deep and underlying poetry breathing secret life into the allegory. The best proof of the existence of such a current is to be found in the mysterious life of the weightiest, most massive elements of Hawthorne's allegorical creation—the life of the closed, stagnant, subterranean worlds: the spellbound world of the Letter, the hermetic House, the valley with no way out, all of them crucibles in which life is oppressed, fermented and disintegrated but in which the vital and creative energy is reborn and transforms itself in order to set off in new directions. That these metamorphoses are carefully watched, willed to occur, is undeniable. But there is a difference in kind between the intellectual and moral control that is exercised from without and the instinctive guiding force that points the way along the great, primal dream avenues and enables man to follow the essential paths that his secret self is searching for in a world specifically proportioned to his inclinations and imagination, which is to say as much created by him as analyzed by him. A mind whose activity relies upon perpetual antagonisms, divided between psychological experimentation and intuition as Hawthorne's was, has several sorts of keys at its disposal in order to make its inventory of reality and open the doors of its secret domain. The traditional keys lock those doors rather than opening them, for they imply a will to moral domination that will impose its a priori molds upon a hardened, set reality. The forbidden keys attempt to force open all the doors—which leads to intellectual rebellion and to the oneirism of frustration, the two combining in an effort to explode all the given structures of the world. The keys of the imagination open everything from inside: the oneirism of the fusion that takes place in the living elements, combined with that of the metamorphoses and the disintegration brought about in appearances, leads finally to poetic creation.

II. SYMBOLIC ABSOLUTISM

The will toward moral domination tends to reduce the world and the beings in it to abstract images, to reflections of the ideas that the mind forms of them. In which case the universe is entirely composed of symbolic superstructures imposed upon realities that reject or destroy them: the schematic universe of the Puritan theologians,[1] of the scholastic allegorists, in which everything is codified, hierarchized, explained, and foreseen, in which the irruption of any fantasy or surprise must necessarily imply the existence of a subversive and therefore evil mind that is seeking to disturb the harmony of the world. The allegorist, adept in white magic, regulates all the movements of his universe, or halts them, in such a manner as to make manifest the existence of an order in which he occupies a privileged position, embodying as he does, in his person and in his works, a symbolic absolutism, the poetic justification for all other forms of absolutism.

Hawthorne could not help but be struck as a child by the absolute, authoritarian character of the Puritans' laws, symbols, and principles. The New England of the Mathers, in which he lived in imagination, was simply a "vast allegory,"[2] and the "singular unity" both of the Puritan mind[3] and of its interpretation of the world was certainly of a kind to impress itself upon his lively moral and esthetic sensibility. And lastly, the influence of the great allegorists upon his mind and his art left an ineradicable stamp upon them both. But we must be careful not to confuse thought with moral imagination. Hawthorne had two allegorists inside him: the allegorist of private realities and the allegorist of surfaces. His use of allegory was sometimes an authentic mode of writing, sometimes a mannerism. But it is certainly true that allegorical forms have a repressive effect upon the imagination, one that becomes even more fatal if the artist's whole cultural education encourages the use of allegorical methods. His eye then becomes Medusalike. Woe to the poet afflicted with this fatal gift if he has not been granted others to compensate for it. A new Midas, he will merely turn everything he touches into stone. And Hawthorne's imagination did sometimes tend to become a Puritan Medusa in this way.

All the varieties of allegory—classical, cabalistic, Gothic, Biblical—bear in him the impress of Puritanism, which is able on the one hand to confer upon them an impressive severity but which, on the other, is also liable to make even the most fertile of fables barren. Thus the figure of the wizard, of the alchemist, takes on an intense dramatic relief from its contact with the Puritan figure of the father. And the anodyne metaphor of dawn is very happily superseded in *The House of the Seven Gables* by the luminous image of Phoebe, even though, despite its Bunyanesque inspiration,[4] it does verge on the sentimental. Just as the political, democratic allegory is a by-product of classical allegory—the eagle of the Custom House,[5] and the demagogue moon in *The House of the Seven Gables*[6]—so Greek mythology found itself more or less taken over by the Puritan brand. The Jupiter we meet in *The Wonder Book* could also very well be a New England governor,[7] Ulysses an Endicott,[8] and Mercury a Prospero whose caduceus has been transformed into a magic staff.[9] The heroes of the mythological tales, like the early American settlers, are clearers of forests: Cadmus, who plows the land and sows his dragon's teeth.[10] Or they are extirpators of heresy, destroyers of myths and monsters: Hercules overcoming the Old Man of the Sea[11] and Antaeus;[12] Theseus slaying the Minotaur;[13] Cadmus, the Dragon;[14] Jason, the Serpent.[15] Whereas the imagination naturally breeds chimaeras and harpies and hydras, it is the aim of moral censure to prevent the mind from dreaming, to destroy the images it decides are unwanted and to replace them with images that are useful, decorous, but useless as objects of oneiric power. The amoralism of the Greek myths, like nudity in statues, paralyzed Hawthorne's esthetic sense; so much so that he becomes dishonest in his dealings with them, particularly in the way he strips them of all their sexual character, in order, he says, to remain faithful to the true spirit of the legends, whereas he is in fact perverting their true nature by forcing them into an a priori moral mold—that of the innocence of the Golden Age, understood in its most Victorian sense.[16] And while he was about it, animated by such moral sentiments, Hawthorne even set about making the Bible more palatable: the story of the "New Adam," which could have been an idyll full of freshness and delicate sensuality, tends to become a conventional sampler of the moral life: the young couple, chaperoned by an invisible mentor, being its edifying exemplars. Thus the spirit of traditional allegory cleared away the glades of living images in order to sow its own rigid, ritual images that were powerless to breed and repeople the consciousness.

When this happens, art can no longer engender anything but inert objects that will merely pile up in the allegorical museum: art's tomb.[17] This museum, which was Hawthorne's storehouse, was also his refuge, whether he was using its forms as a shelter because he was afraid of going to the heart of his material's physical or psychological substance, or whether he was allowing himself to be seduced by formulas that freed him from the necessity for all research, all boldness. This cow-

ardice of the imagination is particularly perceptible in the occasional
pieces, such as "Time's Portrait,"[18] which are quite as artificial as certain articles in the "Magazine," in which an account of Mexican customs gives rise to banalities on the subject of human sacrifices[19] or in
which the French soldier is used as an allegory for an entire nation.[20]
For the allegorical method, like caricature, is convenient for fixing
objects and beings in a simplified form that is expected by a given
public, accessible to every member of it, and acceptable to all. Hawthorne did not deprive himself of the use of it, especially in his tales
for children, the pretext for which was essentially moral: the laziness
of Little Daffydowndilly,[21] the goodness of Little Annie,[22] the benefits
of temperance, made available by the Town Pump.[23] Virtues and vices
all neatly codified, illustrations for the use of pedagogues and sermon writers.[24]

The "gothick" was the fashionable compromise of the day between
art and authoritarian morality. Based upon insincerity, it seems to have
been a means of accommodating the brutal realities of life, love, and
death to Victorian taste, and the intention was to provide disguises in
the form of spiritual emotions for thrills whose sado-masochistic nature
can frequently not even be termed equivocal, even in Hawthorne,
whether the fantasies involved are of the macabre kind—"Graves and
Goblins," "The White Old Maid," "The Wedding Knell"[25]—ethereal
—"Sylph Etherege"[26]—or pseudohistorical—"The Antique Ring"[27]—
all the lifeless bric-a-brac and so-called penetration into the mysteries
of the beyond merely serving to distract both the creator's energy and
the reader's attention from their true object, with the result that the
imagination merely exhausts itself in a chase after artificial phantoms.

Moreover Hawthorne was prone to confuse poetry and superficial
brilliance,[28] poetry and bland etherealism—defects he never ceased to
condemn, but which he himself was the first to fall into whenever he
tried to be a poet himself. For he willed himself to be one too consciously, and in doing so turned the poetic wish into a game—a game
of allegorical clouds,[29] of changing colors that becomes merely an immaterial ballet for the eye,[30] a moral divertissement of statues and conventional characters forming processions, symbols of the past and the
future—the Oldest Inhabitant, Monsieur On-Dit, the story writer, the
quack, the Master Genius of the Age[31]—all of which we are obliged to
watch without being given any sense of futurity or of the existence of
any real memory. The formal allegory cannot but disappoint both

heart and esthetic sense. Only a mind imbued with the most rigid principles can take delight in the mechanical illustration of ready-made truths about the meaning of life, the vanity of human efforts, or the emptiness of earthly happiness. Was it simply in order to display these broad platitudes that Hawthorne took the trouble to write "The Procession of Life," "The Ambitious Guest," and "The Canterbury Pilgrims"? There seems to be no doubt that he took pleasure in playing the puppeteer in a marionette theater whose flesh or rag puppets limited themselves to demonstrations of the danger of sin and passion, to acting out Puritan "morality" plays. For allegory can automatically create its own spectacle, its own drama, since it is also governed by a law of contrasts. An allegory always comes into being in opposition to another allegory: it is born into a Manichean universe in which every human action involves God and the Devil,[32] the Puritan simplification of all moral problems.[33] Allegory in Hawthorne's work feeds on schematic antagonisms: good and evil, purity and defilement, communication and solitude. It is possible to construe the dramas of most of Hawthorne's principal characters in this restricted sense, standing as they all do between the sign of the Angel and the sign of the Beast; while even the forms, if not the forces, of nature itself are depicted as being mobilized to the same end, stylized in such a way as to illustrate the moral conflict—herbs of grace,[34] perfumed flowers, and rosebuds against unsightly plants culled in graveyards,[35] weeds,[36] poisonous plants,[37] the black forest.[38] The decor of the stories is often reduced to a level of mere mechanical exhibition, the human drama to a series of encounters and coincidences that smack of the deus ex machina, and the realities of the consciousness to figures that have a distressing way of evoking the examples used in the proving of theorems. Clifford's demented gesture is too evidently an illustration, too much commented upon as such, so that it remains a mere illustration instead of being a psychological fact.

Abuse of such a method could lead to the employment of a veritable abstract code constantly requiring copious explanations—a form to which Hawthorne was to come, despite himself, in his last novels, though without being able to elevate it into a technique. In the remainder of his work, though he is not attempting to make the given tale or novel into a rational demonstration, it is his intention to provide us with moral keys. We find characters who *are* Vice, Evil, unscrupulous Ambition (the Judge), Pride (Lady Eleanore), Egoism (Roderick

Elliston), Joy, Light (Phoebe), Angel (Hilda). But in this respect Hawthorne was simply falling in with the paraliterary tendencies of his age. Thus we find *The House of the Seven Gables* being interpreted as a detailed social allegory,[39] the Judge being Power, the Maules the dispossessed Laboring Class, Hepzibah Aristocracy, and Uncle Venner Poverty. And we also find the Concord Transcendentalists allotting theological roles to the main characters of *The Marble Faun*:[40] thus, Miriam was the Soul, Hilda Conscience, Kenyon Reason, Donatello Nature, and the Model Temptation. That Hawthorne himself should have approved of this is perhaps not surprising.[41] A large number of his principal characters are human victims of allegory: Chillingworth and Phoebe, one identified with the Demon and the other with the Angel, are both crushed beneath theological burdens disproportionate to their strengths and to the degree of humanity with which they have also been endowed. Whereas this is not the case for the Model or Hilda, both of whom, on the contrary, are able to bear the same symbolic weight with ease because they are abstract beings. These beings imprisoned within a definition—for it is a characteristic of traditional allegory that it is to be construed in only one sense—are reduced to a surface appearance upon which they are judged, and once having named them, their creator forgets to give them substance. Hawthorne, who was more mistrustful of characters created out of "thin air" than anyone, reacted by attempting to root his art in concrete forms. This is why he materialized to the maximum degree all the external emblems and objects with which his characters are identified: the Letter, the serpent, the red flower, the statue. But in doing so he aggravated even further the rigid character of his works, which seem to be no more than a priori meanings imposed on the living material. This concretization of exterior forms—the Judge's smile, Westervelt's false teeth—can lead to caricature, to the imposition of stylized masks that conceal a complex reality, do it a disservice—the Judge's character is much richer than his allegory—and even prevent it from developing.

When these tendencies are taken to the extreme, life in the allegorist's hands becomes no more than a shadow of itself and bears the marks of mortification. Whereas great allegory, on the contrary, is an animation of death: the *Danse Macabre,* the nightmare of essential fear walking hand in hand with that of the plague, of living sin. But the writer who tries to allegorize the everyday without integrating it into an apocalypse has only dead images at his disposal in order to describe it. Yet it is with those images that the author who will not allow himself access to living images is condemned to work. Which is why he is continually twisting his worn-out symbols this way and that in an attempt to give them a new lease on life. And why, to help him in this process, he summons to his aid the method of multiple interpretation or alternative possibilities,[42] which enables him to leave the choice to the reader: does Dimmesdale really have a mark on his breast? Does Donatello really have faun's ears? This is a mechanical trick, not an organic form of writing as with Robert Penn Warren;[43] it is too often merely a way of disguising the writer's own poverty and should not be confused with the technique of ambiguity, since it is usually unable to create anything more than an aura of mystery strongly tinged with "gothick" horror. The hypothesis revised by a hundred differing echoes vanishes in smoke. The mysterious object is always presented in a distorting gallery full of sliding, wheeling mirrors that create innumerable differing reflections and disintegrate every image as soon as it is formed. The allegorist has no sooner materialized his idea than he deprives it of all reality by taking refuge in conjuring tricks. It is hardly surprising, therefore, that Poe—who did not, it is true, read any of the novels—after reading the *Mosses* advised Hawthorne to get himself "a bottle of visible ink,"[44] and that James so deplored his abuse of allegorical figures.[45] Though it should be added that Hawthorne himself was the first to express a wish to be rid of them.[46] Even though he was not at all sure how to do without them—his posthumous works are the sad proof of that—he nevertheless sensed that when he yielded to his allegorical inclination and habits he was impoverishing his universe by the use of an antipoetic and antihuman method. And this awareness made him turn to the use of means that his conscience told him were illicit in order to provide himself with a living reality; for he could not remain content with his warehouse full of traditional allegorical properties.

III. THE WOULD-BE FAUST

In addition to the allegorist, there was another Hawthorne, one who, unlike his companion, was not satisfied with the apparent order of the world. His intuition told him that reality was not as others would have him see it, and that men were not what society expects them to be but mysterious beings refractory to superficial analysis. Should he dare to bring everything tumbling down, reduce the world to a tabula rasa, build everything up anew with fresh material—insist on his right to know everything, to establish new laws, a new morality, and, like another Blake, insist on his right to rebellion, to freedom of interpretation, freedom to live, freedom to create? Would he dare at last to be a prophet or a poet?

Happiness, liberty, knowledge, these are things that man must steal. And man in Hawthorne's work, owing his moral existence to Puritan law and his social existence to the principle of authority, rarely has the courage to do so. He cannot infringe that law or flout that authority without incurring remorse and anguish: "The law we broke," such are the last words of the dying Dimmesdale,[1] unable to forgive himself for having once, for a moment, taken the side of undisciplined nature against the established order and attempted to follow forbidden paths.

Hawthorne's women, however, have fewer scruples, for a woman's disobedience is disobedience against man, against the father, against the husband, and thus, according to the new ideas, becomes a just revolt against a usurping tyrant. Whereas man's revolt, whether directed against his superiors, the state, or the law, is always a revolt against God. However violently Hawthorne reacted against feminism openly, he was nevertheless much more deeply influenced by it than he cared to admit to himself, for his inclinations, like Coverdale's, led him to dream of "kneeling before a woman ruler."[2] Consequently, we sometimes find him on the verge of arriving at the strange paradox that woman is able to rebel with impunity, or at least without thereby entering into league with the devil—even, perhaps, in order to prepare the ways of Providence. Whereupon his masculine Puritanism immediately awoke and demanded that the guilty woman should receive a social punishment—though not a theological condemnation. Hester, the sanctified woman of sin, is saved, and even Zenobia, the suicide, dies in "the attitude of prayer,"[3] whereas Ethan Brand, the masculine rebel, is doomed to hell, or at least, like Dimmesdale, dies in doubt. By demanding his right to the harshest of punishments, man—rebellious and timorous—recovers his sense of his own responsibility and moral superiority. He makes it his whole pride to load himself down with a crushing burden in order to conserve that privilege: conscience, for Hawthorne as for D. H. Lawrence, was a masculine virtue. Though the anima, using the strength it derives from the inadequacy of the animus, is always seeking to appropriate this virtue in order to turn it to its own ends—in order to become the woman-destroyer or the woman-redeemer, which are the same, in the event, as that dominating female being whose triumph explains the conditioning of the entire American psyche by the power of the womb. The masculine quest for the totality of the self, which includes the search for the superfeminine in which the desire to be enslaved always has its part, ends by extrapolating the conquering Amazon who absorbs the masculine being into hers. Even Whitman was unable to arrive at his exaltation of the total self except through a use of the archetypal mother enlarged to the dimensions of all America. Hawthorne seems to be desperately seeking to free the animus, which he can sense already sliding toward the oblivious womb from which Edward Albee—*Who's Afraid of Virginia Woolf?*—is still furiously attempting to rip it free. Yet it was from the victorious anima that he was in fact expecting man's—the son's—regeneration, by the route he both desired and feared, so that he could then at last require it to assume, over and above its superfemininity, a virile strength. American man, like Hawthorne's minister, was taken literally.

The need to take pleasure in life, to seize all her opportunities at last, and also the desire for absolute motherhood, is doubtless the reason why modern woman allows herself to be tempted by the role that man is abandoning to her. The anima grows greater by just so much as the animus is abased: the very principle of tyranny lies there. When beings help one another to grow, then true democracy will be possible, and happiness will no longer be a crime. The right to happiness written into the American Declaration of Independence would seem to be concerned first and foremost with woman. There is a natural hedonism in Hester that her lover cannot comprehend: happiness in Dimmesdale's eyes cannot be anything other than temptation.[4] For the minister, God is duty—for the sinning woman, God is desire. Hollingsworth's plans for reform do not really matter to Zenobia: love is all that counts. Having been deceived in her expectations she kills herself, and her suicide is a way of demanding from death what life would not give her. Miriam, on the other hand, finds a fullness of being in her passion that gives her "an ecstatic sense of freedom"[5]—both happiness and freedom are temporary, but their existence is enough to create a new world, a world on the margin of the world ordinarily subjected to the law and to the inevitability of misfortune. Having dared to believe in herself and in love, as Hester Prynne did, and as Margaret Fuller said that woman should,[6] Miriam sees the possibility of a new morality rising before her,[7] or at any rate discovers the existence of a "special law"[8] that has been created specifically for her and for her lover, but which could also apply to all those who love, thereby revolutionizing the whole of social ethics. Simone de Beauvoir's *The Second Sex* was later to make clear those ideas that enable man to see in woman his "future."

It was through his heroines as intermediaries that Hawthorne called the social and moral orders of his day into question. It was the feminine side of his nature that rose in rebellion, while the masculine side provided a counterweight in favor of the status quo. Does this argue a feminine titanism? The problem will perhaps appear in its true light if we examine it from the point of view of the scission in the alchemist-personality.[9] Beatrice, Rappacini's "earthly child,"[10] is recreated by him in the image of the poisonous plants that she, the anima, tends with affection, while her father never approaches them without fear:[11] she becomes the woman alchemist. Apparently the masculine genius, terrified by its own boldness, wishes to discharge its illicit activities upon its feminine double. Rappacini wants a daughter as "terrible" as she is beautiful, capable of doing evil instead of being limited to suffering it.[12] In this he is akin to the Puritan Dimmesdale, who requires of Hester that she should be "strong" for him, to carry his burden for him.[13] Both abdicate, and their eagerness to press weapons into the hands of their animas makes clear their secret desire to be subjugated by them.

But the woman is given this share of power only to be ultimately disappointed,[14] for the man who was never able—and now refuses—to follow her to the end in love, also refuses, whether from impotence or resentment, to do so in the sphere of intellectual speculation. Beatrice, seeing that Giovanni disapproves of the genius in her, renounces her gifts—which for her comes to the same thing as suicide. We do not yet find in Hawthorne the type of woman who sacrifices love for a career. But those of his heroines whose hearts remain unemployed do venture forth alone, without guides, into the paths of forbidden thought.[15] It is as though Marguerite, reacting aginst her fate, has become the Faust.[16] Was Hawthorne trying in *The Scarlet Letter*—perhaps even as early as "Rappacini"—to create the outline of a modern, feminine Faust as a counterpart to the great masculine Faust of the Renaissance and Goethe?[17] Certainly the minds of his rebellious heroines were capable of much more spectacular leaps than those of the witches clambering up the Brocken during Goethe's *Walpurgisnacht*.[18] But since they lacked a framework they were no less given to divagations.

Hawthorne's feminine Faust, like Strindberg's, either shamelessly plunders the masculine mind[19] or calls it to her aid in secret, as Miriam does when she implores the statue of Marcus Aurelius for help.[20] Man's resignation leaves woman, even when she is a genius, in a maze. But the inverse is equally true: there is no stronger sex.

Given the bankruptcy of the female genius, will the male genius attempt to shine again? Dimmesdale and Coverdale both content themselves with learning lessons from their women, the first that of courage, the second that of seemliness.[21] Kenyon too receives a lesson in moral and intellectual boldness from Miriam.[22] Though alarmed, he is delighted at being able to appropriate her discovery for himself and then goes on to shock the ultraconservative Hilda—a thing only too easily done—by expounding the idea of the Fortunate Fall.[23] It is a pitiful farce: the timorous man of talent trapped between the intellectual sphinx and the conventional angel! Ethan Brand, the only male rebel Hawthorne depicted, is merely a negative figure whose development is ultimately paralyzed by his Puritan ambitions and the temptation of the superfeminine. Roderick, the man with the serpent,[24] who after his cure stands up in the face of Him who had created him unhappy as a reproach, does not in fact carry anything more than the seed of a rebellion against heaven within him. As for Holgrave, whose mind is not without a certain vigor, he is only too eager to imprison his ironic demon within the limits of the very strictest conventions in order to please the Victorian Phoebe,[25] something that Hawthorne himself was probably obliged to do, up to a certain point, in order to maintain his domestic peace. Hawthorne's Faust was sacrificed in advance upon both the matrimonial altar and that of his secret psychological tendencies, not to mention that of Puritan morality. Trapped between Puritanism and feminism, Hawthorne was no more capable than Strindberg was of reconciling the ideal of the superior woman with that of the exceptional and gifted man. They would have liked to choose but were unable to, since they both felt a need for both, their geniuses being, like all authentic genius, androgynous. For the masculine element and the feminine element cannot be truly reconciled except when they are fused in a single being or in the love of two such exceptional beings as Robert Browning and Elizabeth Barrett.[26]

The thirst for knowledge and the will to create would have been in great danger of making do with counterfeits in Hawthorne's case had he not also contained within him an ironist who refused to be duped by appearances and an artist able to employ even those inner tendencies most contrary to his art. It was they, however, and his knowledge of the eighteenth-century and Renaissance periods that suggested to him the archaic expedient of alchemy as a means of interpreting the world even in its most modern aspects. By this choice of a method once condemned as illicit by religion he was seeking to put himself in the wrong from the moral and theological point of view quite as much as to avoid the attacks of the conformists. Though there was one side of his nature that was spontaneously inclined to psychological and poetic researches, there was also another that refused to engage in them without the guarantee of tradition and without insisting upon being in some way to blame. The pretext of alchemy could serve as a mask for the psychologist's secret intentions—and it could also serve to ensure their condemnation. The evil genius of Hawthorne's Faust was not Mephistopheles but the Puritan censor who sees the devil everywhere outside the beaten path. The seeker—the alchemist—is in league with the witch,[27] and therefore with Satan. What better proof could there be of the "philosopher's" diabolism than his moral sadism,[28] which is only to be equalled by the malignity of scolds and fortunetellers?[29] Fearing his own demon as he did, in arraigning the man of false learning for whom science is a means of inquisition and oppression, Hawthorne also condemned the true scientist, the man who works, like Galileo, for man's liberation.[30] The study that is a pretext for evading the true problems of mankind is bound to pursue mean or sinister ends. Only the science that makes possible the enlargement of the consciousness possesses the keys of the future. These diverse aspects of learning were at war in Hawthorne's mind, and he was afraid of not being able to keep a tight enough rein upon those tendencies that paralyzed both his imagination and his sympathy at the same time.

He was now forced into a new compromise: he was to apply to reality—interior as well as exterior—an analytic method, at once intellectual and imaginative, that would lead, depending on which of the two poles his mind chose as its location, either to sterility or to creation. Intellectual authoritarianism was in constant cohabitation with his poetic imagination, and also represented a constant threat to his art. The angel of moral prudence was always attempting to dissuade the man from touching life, whether in order to create or in order to kill. Since creation was a divine privilege—the Father's privilege—any act that tended to pierce its mystery or to counterfeit it was a sacrilege, whether of a sexual, scientific, psychological, or poetic order. And the consequences of such an act were unforeseeable. Uncontrollable forces were unleased that took possession of both man and nature. Alchemic or poetic marriages gave birth to unsanctified spirits, just as all unions not blessed by heaven gave rise to a monster child or a witch-child.[31] If the child is not happy, good, healthy, normal, must it not be on account of the culpable liberties taken by a man and a woman with the organs that transmit life and with the mind that transmits thought? Crimes committed from motives of self-interest or vengeance are ultimately paid for less dearly than liberties taken with sex, with knowledge, with creation. Lovers, seekers, and creators are unhappy, are tormented, are unable to enjoy either their love or their gifts, and are prevented by their bad consciences from living and acting freely, which means, in consequence, from arriving at the passionate disinterestedness that is required by love, by science, and by art.

The alchemist, living in fear, labors pettily. The field of his activity is restricted and mean. Physically and morally he is truncated, deformed:[32] the artist in Hawthorne, discontented with himself, took this stunted creature as a caricature of his self, a scapegoat to be burdened with all those tendencies in the artist himself that were evil or considered to be so. The ambitions of this debased alter ego were therefore necessarily limited, lacking in stature, egotistical. Sometimes he is aiming at the gratuitous violation of another's soul with no other aim but that of satisfying his own thirst for vengeance or will to power,[33] sometimes he engages upon a frenzied quest for an elixir that will permit the privileged individual to escape incurable diseases,[34] to regain his youth,[35] to live forever,[36] and to hold a monopoly of earthly wealth.[37] Hawthorne disapproved of such egotism both from the democratic and from the religious points of view. And he used that disapproval as a pretext for labeling as perverse and damnable the observations and meditations undertaken by Septimius Felton upon plants, minerals, and the whole of nature in his attempt to make it yield up the keys to life[38]—a quest that leaves him, as it did Hawthorne himself, perplexed and unsatisfied,[39] eventually undermining his health and leading him to ruin more surely than any vice. Such is the end result of the esoteric art practised by an egocentric and pusillanimous Faust who risks nothing—neither his life nor his soul—yet ultimately loses everything, not because he has staked it, but because he did not dare to.

Just as he used the "rhymester" to rid himself of the doggerel versifier that lurks in every writer, so Hawthorne made use of the alchemist to exorcise his artistic defeatism. The alchemist does not believe in his work, and if he works in perpetual constraint for fear of engendering monsters that is because he lives in fear of impotence. But he prefers to believe that he is enjoined by moral imperatives to punish himself by condemning himself to sterility. Thus the work of the artist, like the fruit of an illicit love, is condemned in advance. If we read Hawthorne in his alchemic sense, then the child is the symbol of the "great work."[40] A creation of flesh as much as a creation of the mind, the offspring of alchemy is rarely enduring. Beatrice, created by Rappacini's art, is killed by the art of another alchemist,[41] just as Georgiana is killed by that of Aylmer.[42] Such symbolic sacrifices betray the writer's fear when faced with the responsibility he incurs in giving life to human creatures. But the witch-child, on the other hand, demonstrates the existence of forces that are able to triumph gloriously over the intellectual, sterilizing tendencies. Pearl, who is as much the spiritual daughter of Chillingworth as she is the natural child of the minister, is the most ironic product not only of the esoteric art but also of the novelist's art. She bears witness to the life that inhabits Hawthorne's creation—often despite its author. She flouts all the alchemists, the doctors, the censors, and the theologians, and poses her own insoluble enigma—human, poetic, multiple—to her creator. She embodies the only rebellion that can lead to victory, that of irresponsible, irresistible nature, the third force between the blocs of good and evil. The child appears in her as the most bewildering and disturbing of beings—the new being that can bring with it both the worst and the best. The fear its arrival was able to inspire caused both art and love to retreat in its creator. Was it to be a new creator or the destroyer of life and of the beautiful?[43] Corresponding to the monster child there is the monstrous work, the work that hurts, or, like *The Scarlet Letter*—viewed with astonishment and alarm once completed—is perhaps capable even of destroying its author if he is no longer strong enough to measure up to it. The timorous mind that searches for reasons to avoid giving "substance" to the "shadows" that flit within it[44] is not of the necessary caliber for art. For art needs a sturdy mind that will ignore all prohibitions and for which the good, even if it will not admit as much, is one with the work. And the intelligence, instead of remaining analytical, must become synthetic, not by enslaving itself to any system, but by marrying itself with the processes of the creative thought, by aiding the imagination with a subtle maieutic technique. It must not, whatever happens, substitute itself for the imagination, but rather draw up to the light the mind's deepest images, and give them their full psychological, moral, social, and esthetic value without stripping them of their oneiric value, which is the value that makes the distinction between superficial, frozen allegory and great allegory.

· 2 ·
Poetic
Creation

I. AMBIGUITY

Over and above the superstructures erected by the spirit of intolerance and oppression, the reassuring appearances, the theories that satisfy the intelligence with a bounded outlook, and the beliefs that simplify or suppress man's problems, there remain the real universe and the moving consciousness that perceives it, imagines it, and struggles to comprehend it and to comprehend itself without reducing things to diagrams, without denying the existence of the inexplicable, or the horrible, or everything that can drive one to despair, but by seeking tirelessly to enlarge its frontiers by means of science and art. The artist's soul is ballasted with a great weight of anguish, the anguish of a whole torn universe and of the self as they seek to organize themselves around that painful nucleus, that agonizing point where the conscience awakens, and which, for Hawthorne, is a consciousness of evil, a symbolic and burning letter, a secret crime that clamors for the light of truth. What the Puritan wishes to repress the artist must use: it is by means of creation that he struggles against evil—against his evil, his sickness —which presupposes an imaginative power capable of restoring to the world and to the self their fundamental duality and ambiguity, the echo of the torn universe reverberating in man—himself tormented—like the call of destiny.[1] Reality, with its myriad facets, impossible to grasp, at once good and bad, kind and terrible, joyous and tragic, Manichean and Dionysian, torments the allegorist but fascinates the poet. Just as Thoreau had a sense of tragedy in nature,[2] Hawthorne had the sense of tragedy in the human sphere. Holgrave, waiting to see the denouement of the Pyncheon drama, is not a sadist but an artist appreciative of beauty and sadness.[3] It is not perhaps beside the point here to recall that Hawthorne liked to associate beauty with melancholy:[4] the whole of Hester's fate is, after all, to be beautiful but unhappy. And is the beauty of sin[5] not made of the triumphant sadness of the "black flower"? Greatness of stature on the human level rests, from the tragic point of view, upon the gravity of the offenses committed by nature and man against man. The hero is a great criminal or an exemplary victim, often both together; and his greatest misfortune is the greatest beauty of his life. This means that capital punishment, as Baudelaire claimed,[6] is an esthetic necessity, and it becomes understandable how the spectacular punishments employed by the Puritans should, over the distance of the years, have influenced Hawthorne's conception of the tragic. The obsessive image of the scaffold, far from being merely a symbol of repression, also makes us thrill—even when cloaked beneath Puritan appearances—to the great Dionysian current, the source of lyric frenzy as well as of terror and pity, now found flowing again, even though drained of its joyous vein, in an artist haunted by a sense of sin that plunges him all the more deeply into the horror of life and forces him to live that horror in all its intensity:[7] Hawthorne reveals and exploits the ambiguity of Christianity and the cult of Dionysos, sometimes with trepidation, as in *The Marble Faun*, sometimes with great power, as in *The Scarlet Letter*, and without knowing it achieves a reconciliation between Christ and Dionysos—a Dionysos in the image of Oberon. Sacred horror and panic terror reign together in Hawthorne's forest. Nor does he recoil from facing its monsters. For the artist, witchcraft, all crimes, and all perversions exist. Nor is their existence a matter of superstition or vice; it is a necessity, since art needs to use all the obscure forces that contribute both to the disturbing ambiguity of reality and to the birth of tragedy. If the writer has his fetishes, they are there to protect his creative revery: he must have images that will be the esthetic equivalent of hypnotic human beings, prepared to undergo all the "transformations" required, as vile and petty as you like, and yet "admirable" and "Divine" (as with Hester and her hieroglyph). Art exists only in the dialogue between man and myths.

The "metamorphosis of the gods" could never take place without the existence of human ambiguity. The more the universe is impregnated with it, the more it demands to be translated into terms of art.

Ambiguity is a sign of division: a Dionysian division between joy and suffering, a Christian division between good and evil. A double ambiguity in which the mind becomes lost, and which lets unreality in at every step. The play of mirrors, of surfaces, of mocking, grimacing, agonized masks that diverted the spectator of the world's comedy, and which the puppeteer was wont to stress overmuch, was unable to satisfy Hawthorne's inward clamor for truth, which required a tragedy in which the whole being was committed: "Be true!"[8]—take all your humanity upon yourself— such is the deep meaning of his exhortation to the man who contents himself with playing a subtle and cruel game with his contradictions, instead of pushing them to their limits in order to transform his conflict into a destiny and the source of his being's contradictory plenitude. Any drama played without conviction, any feigned reality produces a feeling of unease, for the ambiguity they contain can only be that of the illusion that masks a void.[9] The whole of art in that case is reduced to covering the void with seductive surfaces or to contenting oneself with an exhibition of puppets, simply for the bitter satisfaction of showing that they are made of nothing but tinsel and thin air: a form of creation that doubts both life and itself, and which is merely amusing itself by embroidering on a nonexistent fabric.

Hawthorne also embroiders upon the stuff of reality, however, and it is then that he truly merits the name of artist. The external iridescence becomes emblematic of the ambiguity of an interior, moving, shifting, but living substance, like Clifford's alternately happy and wretched consciousness.[10] The brilliant exteriors can also be an irony. The flamboyant motifs created by Hester with "the nicest art of needlework" of her prototype are a pathetic fantasy born of despair.[11] Unprepossessing appearances may also be deceptive. Hepzibah's frown, far from betraying any hardness of heart, is the involuntary tic that condemns her heart to silence.[12] This is why it is an error to claim that the outward apparel and physical aspects of Hawthorne's characters correspond with their secret selves. It would be even more erroneous to attempt to transfer those physical exteriors onto the characters' moral and psychological interiors. The apparel, the outward color is there only as an invitation to the mind to enter. They do not attain their true significance until afterwards, considered as functions of the substance from which they emanate or which they conceal. The purpose of the black veil, for example, is to attract the eye with its haunting darkness and so incite the gaze to pierce the secret it is hiding. It is not an abstract symbol but the emanation of a consciousness living the words of David's psalm in all their original intensity,[13] evoking the web of shadows in which God conceals himself and in which the soul gripped by the terror of doubt is fated to struggle. Those words are not written upon the veil—and we are not meant to read them there, but to relive them in the Reverend Hooper's soul: the light of the world is uncertain, and man, whether saint or sinner, is alone. Saint and sinner, moreover, are in reality one, bound together within a single being occupying a place of derisory prominence, an object of suspicion, respect, pity, and terrified admiration. Singularity in man, whether manifest or hidden, if it bears witness to the intense inner life of his consciousness creates a magic sphere, a magic circle of isolation[14] in which there forms the halo of ambiguity inherent in good and evil, in sin and affliction,[15] in love and hate, which inspires the artist to depict the soul from contradictory viewpoints, caught at that crucial moment when the knot of its anguish is forming. Thus, beneath a uniform veil, there lurk the conflicting possibilities contained within a single consciousness. And here we recognize one of the fundamental tendencies of Hawthorne's mind: the use of structures fitting one inside another, the creation of interlocking organisms, the development of reciprocally enveloping themes. All reality was for him a storehouse of hidden forms and substances. Every being had its share of several different natures: the angel or the demon? human child or elfin child? the woman, the plant, or the serpent?[16] This kind of ambiguity has nothing in common with the intellectual and mechanical game of "possible alternatives":[17] it is an organic ambiguity, an ambiguity residing in the very substance of the world, of living beings, and of man's moral and psychological make-up.

This ambiguity, perceptible to the imagination and a reflection of its duality, is eminently dialectic; it is a contributory factor in keeping the imagination on the alert, as well as endowing it with the magic touch that causes "new intellectual and moral forms"[18] to spring up in the mind. Without the dialectic of ambiguity, the imagination would be powerless to restore their "image-strength"[19] to moral symbols drained of their dynamics by the spirit of authority, as well as to extract examples, signs, from the natural and human spheres. These signs correspond with the inmost concerns of the consciousness, as with the Letter and the meteor: both interpreted differently by various people.[20] Hester's tormented soul is merely following its natural inclination, its profound vocation for unhappiness, when it yields to Pearl's insistent mime and resumes the emblem of its shame.[21] The moral imagination enters even upon the path of duty with a poetic gait. It is when it intellectualizes itself that it experiences the need to codify the images it creates in order to transform them into imperatives and precepts. Donatello's spiritual collapse after his crime, his incapacity to enjoy the pleasures of love, are images that convey his fall so adequately that they preclude the necessity for adding any formal condemnation.[22] Hawthorne was aware of the value that could reside in an ambiguous—and therefore natural—morality, one that neither condemns nor redeems, but points out to the imagination the paths that the soul can take in order to exercise its dialectical powers of good and evil. Any poetic morality is a morality of the heart, and those acts to which man commits himself truly, inspired by love, find their own consecration in themselves.[23] It is also a relativist and dynamic morality. The imagination, according to its needs, can invert such a morality's signs or values if needs be: since good and evil, high and low, past and present, love and hate all contain one another reciprocally they are all of them always prepared to be transformed into their contraries. Without imagination, evil cannot produce good, or a fall an ascension —love cannot come out of hate,[24] the past cannot live again in the present. For imagination, with its ambiguities that embrace all contraries, with its power to use time and space as it will, is a faculty of the heart, the great universal converter and the great creator. And how, without imagination, behind the old masks, the faded brocades and lace[25] or the dazzling embroideries, beneath the shifting waters of the well, could life lie in ambush, ironic, murderous, pathetic, or heart-rending, or passion lurk in a statue, or beneath the garments of a self-ordained nun,[26] or beneath those of a condemned woman? Such lightning flashes could only proceed from a consciousness haunted by fertile myths.

II. HUMAN ALLEGORY.

The allegory that clothes abstractions in human guise is no more than a rigid counterpart of the shimmering spectacle whose shadows the puppeteer seems to experience a malign pleasure in persuading us to take for substance.[1] It is no more than a conjuring trick, and cannot claim to be of any use as a foundation of true poetry. The true allegory in Hawthorne's work, however, is seeking to express the very substance of the consciousness: it is human allegory, whether the human element is taking on new significance by clothing itself in symbols or assuming a resemblance to objects, or whether the symbols and objects are humanized. It is always man who is illumined by this stylization. The guilty lovers illustrate sin as much as sin is illustrating itself and taking on specific form in them. On the one hand a great fresco of symbolic figures takes shape, on the other we perceive a deepening and a multiplication of the human elements that draw their power from allegory.

Everything in Hawthorne's created world passes through man and refers back to him. The very objects and substances in it, whether they are the seeds of the work or mere accessories, are drawn forth living from the most inward regions of the consciousness and invariably bear the stamp of hidden passions. They are the external arabesques of an inner fire,[2] or else the sluggish upwellings of the soul's secret blackness, which we see rolling, dense and substantial, in the dusky air[3]—or else they are the nightmares of grief and shame, the weather-stained wood of the pillory,[4] oozing wretchedness and remorse, like the beams and timbers of the House of the Seven Gables.[5] These objects are all monsters, in the same way as the Gorgon, the Phorkiades, the Minotaur, or the Stymphalides,[6] but they are part of Hawthorne's personal mythology, and instead of being merely picturesque are endowed with a disturbing and ambiguous life. But is it really life that resides in them, or is it an active form of death, avid for destruction, that endows the pillory with aggressive reflexes, with a faculty for prehension, with a strangling power,[7] that endows the scaffold with the magnetism with which it attracts the guilty man and freezes him to the spot,[8] that makes the prison into a stone and iron organ animated with the will to grasp and enclose? And by what mimetic process would all these monsters tend so toward the human if they were not in fact made of human substance either only half formed or else thwarted in its development? The monster is always an unfinished or deformed man clamoring for his rightful form and his soul: the cry of Caliban. The pillory, a tragic scarecrow, would like to walk, to seek out its own victims, to pronounce its own sentences, and to identify itself with those condemned.

Inversely, Circe's victims, trapped by the enchantress in the skins of animals,[9] try desperately to retain their human shape. The guilty and the criminal, all those who are obsessed nevertheless experience the temptation to identify with the object that symbolizes their fate: Dimmesdale with the pillory, Hester with the Letter,[10] to such an extent that she comes to believe she has given birth to a living hieroglyph:[11] Pearl, the allegory-child, the monster-child, the daughter of the Letter, not of the woman. By means of this ironic complicity between the elf and the infernal and "mystic"[12] sign, the human incvitabilily of a literal transformation of her sin into an ineradicable image is forced upon the martyrized mother, whose torture constantly springs up afresh beneath the gaze of her child,[13] the Letter made flesh.

Images from the world, images from dreams, they all contribute to Hawthorne's statues and portraits of man: statues of stone, of wood, of snow,[14] portraits painted or reflected, all aspiring to conscious individuality, but often expressing the inadequacy, the infirmity, or the wretchedness of mankind. In the reflection from the suit of armor the soul of valor imprisoned in the rigid corselet swims up to the surface, while the gigantically magnified image of the Letter stands out in glaring proportions:[15] animus and anima struggling for possession of the fetish. The wonderful butterfly is yet another soul lighting up only to be extinguished again: the ephemeral work. But these reflections, these undertows, these lightning flashes all spring from inexhaustible fountains and fires: the fire and the shadows of the cave—shadows and gleams of the depths, storehouses of images and works both delicate and durable. Allegory in Hawthorne is allegory of the soul, sometimes somber, sometimes brilliant. Man is the link of flesh that quivers and hesitates between the statue of darkness or mud and the statue of marble or light.[16] The poet, spectator of his own dream, is continually bringing new forms into being, caressing them and using them to people his universe. Thus the allegorical procession of life finds the number of its pilgrims continually increasing, while the great figures that reappear at regular intervals and eventually give the long fresco of tales and romances its style steadily grow in substance and clarity of outline. Between the luminous gate of the lost Eden, object of a perpetual quest, and the river of death, there pass again and again the figures of the archetypal mother and father, the orphans, the guilty and the victims, the successive incarnations of the fascinating and fearsome Beatrice. And among them, under cover of ironic and sinister masquerades, we find the emissaries of evil insinuating themselves in the form of disturbing strangers or monsters sprung from the hell of conscience, awakening men's most secret obsessions or fears, and the madness that sends those already lost rushing even further into the darkest depths of the forest. Sin—blood and fire, crime and sex—is unleashed at the sabbath, around the bonfire, in the maze of that nocturnal Babylon defiled by crimes as old as its stones, and takes up its stand at high noon in the market place wearing the masks of beauty, or saintliness, or love. The world serves as an avenue, as an arena and an inevitable circle for this procession of living sin, rotting and tortured beneath all its fine raiment in the agonies of a mortal disease: the disease that Lady Eleanore carries beneath her mantle of pride, and Roderick in his breast like a serpent, that gnaws at Hester and Dimmesdale like the red death and knots lovers together in the coils of crime, a new image of Laocoön.[17] And is the child of sin not the child of the plague in popular legends?[18] All human activities and passions are manifestations of the plague of life: sex, cruelty, ambition, all those appetites of which one must be purged[19] before becoming worthy of one's eternal inheritance. Is it surprising then if, besides the hysterics, the convulsives,[20] the deformed creatures from a beggars' meeting,[21] the visionaries, the frenzied slaves of passion, we also find fanatical penitents, flagellants, and black-hooded figures from an auto-da-fé among the crowd of pilgrims? And who are those disquieting maskers there, if not emissaries from the powers of hell or fate? The archetypal figure of the father often appears as the representative of a jealous fate,[22] summoning a victim to death or annihilation as well as to sin and punishment. This idea of annihilation, which Melville symbolized in his white whale, Hawthorne embodies in his Black Man, as Goya did in the masks of his *Caprichos*. Thus the work born of the passion to create contains the shadow that threatens it with annihilation, and echoes with the snicker that negates it. Hawthorne instinctively rediscovered the apocalyptic tradition embodied in Dante, the theme of the danse macabre that dominated an entire age of medieval art, and to which Strindberg, Brecht, Kafka, Ingmar Bergman, Camus, Faulkner, and Pasternak[23] have all added infinite variations. This was the great, genuinely Gothic allegory that was handed on to Hawthorne through Renaissance English poetry, through the austere symbols of the Puritan theologians, and set the irreplaceable mark of a style upon the visions that haunted him.

But mingling with the figures of the dance of death, with the medieval Gothic horror, there are also the joyful and pathetic accents of the reel of life and the echoes of Dionysiac savagery. The dance around the maypole is no more than a prelude to the dance of the condemned man around the whipping post,[24] to the pacing of the prisoner in his cell, to the tortuous progress through the maze of anguish. Among the carefree crowds, whether made up of New England tavern haunters, dancers of the international saraband,[25] or lovers in quest of their Eden, there slip in, under cover of the general euphoria and the ambiguous lighting, the killjoys: Puritans, specters, demons, the devil himself,[26] and his ally Death, hell's contracted purveyor of souls. And nature in its winter garb, the Puritan law in all its rigor, together with Death, the implacable ironist, deliver their stinging challenge to the joy of life. Before long, the human procession has ceased to wheel around the symbol of its joy in order to trudge around the symbol of its pain and grief. The pillory is a masochistic symbol of delight in misfortune; it is also a deformed cross,[27] hideously seeking to embody human suffering; and it is lastly the mutilated, tortured phallus, image of the vision-haunted minister's sexual crime as he stands before that ambiguous image of Calvary and castration—a monster endowed with a universal power of fascination that can draw to it the guilty and the innocent, tortured souls and maypole dancers,[28] dignitaries and hucksters,[29] for it recalls forbidden joys as well as representing renunciation and mortification—so that it transforms all the pilgrims, vagabonds and penitents alike, into condemned men, into prisoners of pain, and into creatures haunted by sex and sin.

The world as it is created by the tradition of misfortune and the obsession of guilt is hell for those creatures of the Golden Age who believe in earthly happiness, whose fate is linked to that of the inquisitors and men of hate, and who are crushed to the earth by this confrontation with the destructive forces of the elements and the repressive forces of society. Only those who possess both inner tenderness and inner hardness can embrace the full and whole life, and—according to the circumstances and their temperament—defy or embody authority: be an Endicott or a Hester. Hester is a force of nature, nature itself shackled by the law and tearing itself free. The impetuous gusts of life breathe through Hawthorne's world with the same force that animates the music and the cinema of the Nordic races: Hester's sexual resurrection, a revival of the sap and the senses, is a thawing of the ice-bound flesh after the long Puritan winter.

That this breath of spring should be perceptible—physically perceptible—as we read a work is the sign of great art. It is as though the shock had been created by the author's own psychic energy, transmitted to his creations, and then hurled in a solid mass against our receptive consciousnesses. Hawthorne was not content with simply giving us, and himself, a diverting spectacle: his whole being is within what he created, he made himself one with the material of his work, so that it became the place where his consciousness lived, his labyrinth as well as his abode. To create, for him, meant to attempt to mold himself from within to all the sinuosities of the moral and psychological sensibility, which meant to make man his house, so that he could fill out his great symbolic figures with living matter. And inversely, he endowed all the places he frequented with a human consciousness.

The house is not merely the historic house—the museum—the utilitarian house, the roof over the head, but the memory house, the dream house.[30] The edifice constructed by the carpenter Maule was no more than an artificial excrescence on the ground as long as it had not been adopted by nature[31] and created internally by the misfortune and melancholy of its recluses, then by the songs of its little housewife,[32] so that in the end even its very walls and furnishings assume human attitudes and habits.[33] Nothing could make it easier to gauge the difference between dead and living allegory than to find the man-house and the house-made-human confronting one another in the same book. The man-house, whether Clifford or the Judge, or even poor Hepzibah,[34] is a ponderous, rigid, and risible monster. Imagine a character compartmentalized from top to toe into rooms of varying lightness or obscurity—chambers into which an inferior strain of humorous fancy has even introduced gaslighting.[35] A house rigged out with a "brow,"[36] with eyes and ears, in short endowed with a complete and detailed face, would be equally intolerable, reminiscent of the very worst kind of movie cartoons. Hawthorne is not always able to check his tendency toward such things in time. But it is by means of a quite different and truly poetic method that he humanizes objects, and particularly the house: by reliving his own organs and consciousness in every domestic interior he imagines.

Any man who has identified himself with the house of his childhood is creating a natural allegory from it by yielding to his individual oneiric inclinations. Hawthorne's childhood house was a vast mansion with a multitude of rooms: a house oneirically complete, the house to which he irresistibly returned in his creative reveries, which still contained that favorite corner[37] to which he had retired as a child to indulge in his esoteric imaginative child's games. It had become an extension of his self. Just like a living being, the House of the Seven Gables breathes, and absorbs the light and the images of the outside world:[38] the beings that approach it become assimilable matter, nourishment;[39] one has the feeling that it is digesting the world, that it is casting its gaze at all the life around it in order to appropriate it to itself, or else looking out upon things with a bitter pride[40] or a sense of frustration.[41] The intimate resemblance between man and object then becomes an emotional resemblance. Hepzibah, Clifford, or Peter Goldthwaite, conceived in the mind of their creator together with the houses that give them shelter,[42] are themselves desolate and deserted dwellings, visited solely by remorse, by mourning, by bad dreams. They are the very heart of abandonment, of solitude, and that heart becomes a house,[43] a complex vertical maze. The compartmentalization is such that the upper stories do not know, or do not wish to know, what is happening in the lower stories, in the cellar.[44] The heart and the head are more often than not separated from one another and cut off from the world. Closed doors, bolts, unwilling locks, and rusty keys[45] all convey the extent to which the soul is its own prison.[46] And internal communications are no more easily effected than exchanges with the outside world. Peter Goldthwaite, living in a house reverberating with the echoes of his secret thoughts,[47] relentlessly pursues his laborious exploration, demolishing walls and floors, burning its beams like a Bernard Palissy of the conscience. The house's internal vertical dimension is that of moral psychology, just as its horizontal aspect is reserved for conveying the dimension of the labyrinth, which is psychologically on the level of the basement. Peter Goldthwaite first climbs up into the loft: he consults his reason first. Then he gradually descends, following the logic of his instinct, despite all obstacles and warning signs.[48] We are not permitted to be present at the discovery of the treasure: the chest has already been brought up to the ground floor by the time we are allowed to investigate its contents with our own eyes. Poe would have insisted on a subterranean search. Hawthorne, on the other hand, takes less pleasure in lingering in the cellar: he is more inclined to evoke the dungeon and the tomb indirectly than actually to spend time in them. His natural underground is the forest: the house built of *wood* is merely a denser kind of forest. It was not until his mind was in decline that it felt any wish to enclose itself inside an abode of stone, a walled dungeon.[49] While in its prime, his mind preferred the dry and aromatic half-light of the loft to dank darkness.

Hawthorne's "final" house, a symmetrical counterpart to the childhood house,[50] existed for him in fact as well as in imagination. He had had his—though it brought him nothing but disappointment and he refused in the end to die in it—just as the principal characters of *The House of the Seven Gables* have theirs, one that bears a strange resemblance to the house of misfortune they have left, and upon which the curse attached to ill-gotten wealth still weighs, since it previously belonged to the Judge.[51] Is it necessary then, in order to escape from both the protection and the oppression of the ancestral house, to destroy it?[52] It would only spring up again from its ashes in the incendiary's soul: for the house is his soul. It is also that soul's tomb, if the inhabitant allows the too ponderous structure to weigh down and crush him, instead of himself devouring it from within as Peter Goldthwaite does. The house is the emblem of the ancestral heritage that alone can feed the individual flame, when it does not choke it. As for the one-night-stand house, it is that of the individual without a past, a house that one casts aside as one does a piece of clothing, a house like the train that one boards at one station only to leave it at the next,[53] so that one can go through the whole of one's life without ever having felt that one has any roots in time. The nomad's tent[54] is perhaps the ideal form of habitation, for it permits him to be free, in communion with nature, body and soul, while retaining all the prestige of a Biblical simplicity. A dwelling for every individual, a cottage like Hester's,[55] and for the duration of only a single lifetime, how could that idea have held any satisfaction for Hawthorne, he who with his art intended to raise a lasting monument? For the house must remain: it must be inhabited or haunted; it must bear witness to the passing of a living being; it must share with him and after him in the life of the world.

For the house in Hawthorne is the suffering being magnified, the solitary heart enlarged to the dimensions of a world, the tormented consciousness projecting its image to the four corners of the horizon: the House of the Seven Gables comes to life wherever Hepzibah moves inside it,[56] and its roots intertwine with those of the tree it resembles, proud as a vast elm standing alone in the midst of the forest,[57] with its complicated roof like folded branches. In the world of dynamic allegory, the house, like the human being, is vegetable. Hut or palace, the house in Hawthorne is also a cosmic dwelling place, and like the dwelling of the Valkyrie it partakes both of the life of the earth and that of the air. It may be besieged, assailed by those same elements, like a ship, like a human soul, as Peter Goldthwaite's house is in the winter night.[58] It may, like the tower, be the trunk that unites the underground world with the world of light. In *The Marble Faun*, that microcosm of towers and belvederes,[59] Donatello's tower and Hilda's tower have foundations that meet in the catacombs and also confront one another like tall trees in the sky. The structures of house, tree, and tower, are always for the imagination those of man's body and consciousness, which participate in the universe by taking their substance from it and then by flowing back into its veins.

III. SUBSTANCES AND STRUCTURES

The universe seen from within is a body in which man recognizes himself, is extended, and magnifies himself to infinity. The substances and elements of that universe did not interest Hawthorne for their own sake, however, but only as raw materials and possible images of the developed human consciousness. He makes use of substances in order to give body to the intangible, in other words to the consciousness, a thing woven of light and shadow whose fabric he tries to make tangible for us in the form of an embroidered letter or a black veil.[1] Instead of distant suns, instead of the alien night, he chooses to show us human flames and shadows that he has magnified to cosmic dimensions while still preserving their earthly colors and weight.

Hawthorne is very prone to associate his creations, always in an allegorical manner, with selected natural elements and substances. Apart from the wooden, stone, metal, or snow statues, there are characters placed under the sign of fire (Ethan Brand, Hester, Miriam), of air (Pearl, Hilda, Phoebe), of earth (Hollingsworth, Aminadab), of bronze (Endicott), and of gold (the Judge).[2] Some partake of several elements at once:[3] air and fire (Pearl), fire and earth (Chillingworth). Dimmesdale is akin to fire through his passion, to the air through his aspirations, to the earth through the burden that overwhelms him;

Zenobia, a creature of fire, becomes a creature of water for and by her death. And similarly, the creative consciousness is able to change from substance to substance or element to element with an amazing versatility, always returning eventually to the element of its predilection. We have just seen once more the importance of fire as a common denominator in the majority of the main characters in these stories—stories that are themselves occasionally forged in the "fire of Hell" as Hawthorne himself had it, aware as he was of the element in which he lived. But does this mean that we must view him definitively as a creator of the fiery sphere? For he is a creature of air as well: Oberon, the Ariel of the night, dreams of light, of materials, of objects that shed all heaviness, that turn to vapor. He rejects the heaviness of earth, which seems to him oppressive, degrading. Yet in the airy element, in the thin air, both irreality and ideality leave him unsatisfied. Hate it though he may, Hawthorne is an earthly being who sometimes denies that status and sometimes fails to achieve its embodiment. Either reality repels him, or else it loses substance as he touches it,[4] yet without his being able for all that to extirpate its heaviness from his own being. It is essential for him that the matter he feels to be so gross and burdensome should irrupt across the threshold of his moral repugnancies, conquer his nervous debility, and solicit his imagination without shocking his sensibility. And to this end it frequently presents itself in more refined forms. But under cover of this apparent spiritualization, the fleshly weight of earth, feminine, but also the irreplaceable source of all desires, all impulses, is able to invade Hawthorne's created world with all its Dionysiac train. The heavy, remorse and sensuality laden air, the concentrated, dense compacted light of the Carbuncle,[5] are weighed down with terrestrial gravity; the fire that flames upward, the scarlet letter flowering from the soul's coal-black pyre, the fire that boils like dense lava in the lime kiln,[6] is the central furnace of the human, earthly heart; the slow, melancholy water flowing heavy as blood[7] in the dark night of the forest fire[8] and the suicide, or teeming with creatures that moment born,[9] flows on into the tree with its knotty trunk, into the power-filled roots that build up an earthly sphere in the air.[10]

If Hawthorne makes himself into a creature of air, he does so in order to embrace his familiar world below more widely. When Oberon flies, it is not up into the ether but through an atmosphere filled with the scents of field and wood, with the stench of human smoke and pestilence. He must always know that his feet are really on the ground. Though Phoebe[11] and Hilda (and of course Sophia) are sylphs depicted in conformity with the Romantic and Victorian myth of the young lady, Hester's feet (once she has been turned to stone in the pillory), the luxuriant Zenobia's, and the stamping Miriam's, are all incumbent on the earth. And it is not the soaring flight of a Shelley but the winged walk of a Beethoven, the earth-shaking dance of Dionysos that is mirrored in Pearl and Donatello[12]—just as we find the frenzied leaps of Goodman Brown providing an earthly equivalent for Satan's dusky flight[13] when Hawthorne is depicting demoniac intoxication. And lastly, when the euphoria fades, the fall back into reality is less vertiginous than drear—a dismal descent that ends in the labored trudge of the lonely and the guilty, or the subterranean slither back into the maze. Chillingworth's furtive gait, bent toward the earth,[14] and that of the Model emerging from the Catacombs[15] evoke the same image in two inverse aspects: the first is preparing to crawl back into the serpent's skin, while the other is emerging from it after a long and sinuous progress. It is significant that Hawthorne was able to depict the identification of man with the most terrestrial of animals embodying evil with such intensity, whereas his angelic transfigurations are insipidity itself. He needed matter in order to evoke the immaterial, just as El Greco needed color in order to paint eternity and Turner in order to paint light. Even music, the supremely spiritual art, borrows the rhythms, the joyful or heartrending accents, of the flesh. Hawthorne wrote for the human voice, and gave it a substance whose quality stirs us and awakens the deepest terrestrial harmonies within us, making perceptible not merely the beating of the heart but also the vibrations of the soul. Hepzibah's voice when she is moved to the depths by her brother's return has the "rich depth and moisture"[16] of a freshly welling spring; Dimmesdale's during his sermon is at times impregnated with an emotional liquidity,[17] at others with the enveloping sadness of an autumn wind[18]—yet it could also have the compactness, the impactive force of a projectile[19]—and Miriam's voice in the dusk acts like water and fire at once: it softens the heart and makes it melt.[20] Just so does the mind stir matter into motion before molding it to its ends.

These were Hawthorne's methods as he sought, by poetic intuition, through and beyond the substance of flesh and earthly elements, to grasp man in both his secret and his cosmic beings. Though he refused to limit himself to being merely a pastoral poet, he was nonetheless aware of the forces in nature that can also, through the agency of science and above all of the creative imagination existing in all myths, become human forces. He participated intensely in the landscapes he mused over, particularly if they were hilly scenes. When he followed rivers upstream, it was as though he was working his way back toward his own heart, mingled with that of the universe. The mountains supported vast invisible arches with their age-old strength. The myth that sprang spontaneously into Hawthorne's mind when he saw them was that of the giant, expressed in terms of Bunyanesque allegory and the classical fables of Hercules, Atlas, and Antaeus[21]—the sign of a very terrestrial mental bias. Even the clouds[22] in a typical Hawthorne sky become wrestlers struggling to free themselves from a dense, clayey mold, just as monsters struggle to become human, just as men writhe in the grip of their evil. Caliban would have liked to become Ariel; but he could not forgo his native earth.

The terrestrial element is the only one that Hawthorne really explored imaginatively in depth. It is the one that invites us to secret, nocturnal expeditions. At night, the consciousness becomes earthy. And it was from this embodied consciousness that Hawthorne dug up his materials, his seeds, his precious stones[23] and the painful roots of his work.[24] It was upon this fundamental element that all the spheres his mind and his creation inhabited were built, and not in the air, floating like clouds as he himself liked to think.[25] Those spheres have umbilical roots, even their lightest elements are ballasted with a weight of flesh, and vast though they may be they are always inward, always womb-like. For Hawthorne, the whole wide world was still a room. And inversely, rooms were worlds. The poetic intelligence alone is able to posit the absolute equality of the infinitely small and the infinitely great.

In each work, corresponding to the room occupied by the haunted mind, there is a more or less closed, more or less vast sphere in which the images move into orbit around a nucleus—the procession, the fairground of the world[26] around the pillory or the house, and then, inside the house itself, the specters, materialized by innumerable physical noises, around the dead man[27]—for the nucleus is often a mother-nucleus: the house contains its inhabitants like so many seeds, and the Letter contains the pillory, which itself recurs separately in all the characters it forces to identify with it. Thus attraction, the cosmic form of sympathy, draws all the elements of the work into an even more compact agglomeration. The terrestrial solidity of objects and beings is the law of all human creation, even when that creation attempts to escape into ideality; moreover, though the artist breaks down reality, it is only so that he can go on to reassemble the fragments into new groupings, making use of the essential heaviness that causes them to settle downwards and enables them to be decanted—which is what Hawthorne does in the eye of his magic lantern, or the mirror, or the armor[28]—the inward and ever-present eye of the creator. This sedimentation, which goes on secretly and unceasingly in the artist's mind, building up a rich loam of materials, takes place more rapidly in the process of creation: sometimes the material is precipitated out suddenly as though in a test tube, the snow or the clay from which a statue is then made—or else it is sometimes the crucibles themselves that provide it as they ooze or crumble, their hollows filling gradually with the vessel's own barren matter.[29] But the shadows that mass around the fire, far from choking it, protect it. All this nocturnal humus is necessary in order for the light, the fantastic silhouettes of Ethan Brand and his companions, and even their voices, their cries, their laughter, to emerge from the incandescent furnace.[30] Similarly, Rappacini's garden is a hothouse[31] whose confined, heady, tropical atmosphere engenders the luxuriantly flowering plants it contains, as well as the woman who feeds upon their scent: the cycle of life is accelerated by the heat. And the black veil is not merely a central object but the envelope of a whole moral universe. Beneath it there is hatched an entire destiny, an entire drama, in an atmosphere propitious for the "black flower" that was later to scatter its seeds in the wind of witchcraft, that dark wind laden with echoes of the past, of suffering, and of passion.[32] In this way the protected seed is able to reproduce itself and search for other spheres to fertilize: it is a matter not of flight, of sublimation, but of an organic separation followed by transplantation, or a form of colonization specifically characteristic of artistic creation. Instead of the seed being blown in search of new terrain, it is the terrain that develops spontaneously around the seed, as much created from the substance of the seed itself as called into being by it. The darkness is as much brought into being by the furnace as the fire is born of the darkness. And the spectators who cluster in the daylight around the showman's box, the diurnal equivalent of the hearth, can have emerged from it as well as seeking to return into it. When the

Letter is reflected in the armor it is not the armor that is inviting the reflection: it is the Letter that needs the mirror, that needs panoplies, heraldic symbols, all the pomp of wealth and power, in order to allow its literal meaning to blaze forth. It is the Letter that causes the Governor's house and the Governor himself to exist. And it is Pearl, the Letter's daughter, who calls the entire natural microcosm of the forest into being around her in order to reveal her ironic meaning: the roots of sin beneath the appearance of penitence—just as it is the meteor that creates the setting for the nocturnal pillory scene in order to reveal its prophetic significance.

The place where this fecundation occurs, the point of departure of the work as a whole, is always the homologous sphere of the creative consciousness, that of the created consciousness, in which a symbol of guilt, of solitude, or of suffering, plays the determining role. This individual sphere is situated at the point where all the others meet. It is sometimes narrowed down to the self, to the lonely room, sometimes greatly enlarged as the self itself enlarges and becomes fused with the microcosm of the valley,[33] the town,[34] or the public square.[35] Its function is that of a heart circulating the necessary fluids to an entire network of organs. It also functions as a revolving stage: the square and pillory platform which three times assembles all the main characters and twice disperses them—one returning to his cell, one to his laboratory, and one to her cottage—until the final meeting, which is an ultimate separation: Dimmesdale's death is also the last beat of the book's central organ. The various currents directed by life toward the House are then redistributed by it. In its final spasms, this sclerosed organ brings about the death of the Judge, but liberates the other characters and also, acting as the revolving stage of time, directs them into their future.

The central sphere of Hawthorne's novels is often a composite organ. In *The Scarlet Letter*, the laboratory, the oratory and the scaffold form a network of elements arranged in a triangle: the circuit around which the red spark travels. The interconnecting rooms of the House, on the other hand, are the elements of a benumbed organ brewing a thickened fluid in its recesses: instead of electrical alchemy, a digestive alchemy. The main characters of *The House of the Seven Gables* undergo the gradual metamorphosis of Jonah before emerging as new beings, an analogy of which Hawthorne was probably aware, since Melville was at that time working on the myth of the whale. The farm common room, the assembly room, and Coverdale's observatory in *The Blithedale Romance*, being less solidly welded together, form a less powerful central organ, and the "veil" that binds them together is extremely loosely woven. The organic inevitability created by the valley is much less powerful than that engendered by the pillory and the house. Even though the sluggish pulse of the river summons Zenobia to her suicide, the assembly and dispersion of the Blithedale "dreamers" lacks tragic inevitability. At the center of *The Marble Faun*, instead of a single allegory of the human heart we find a fragmented allegory: shreds of morbid consciousness and tatters of esthetic awareness intertwining in a number of rooms, caves, niches, compartments. And this division, mirroring the fragmentation of the principal organ, deprives the work of its vital force. Finally, in the posthumous novels the motor organ is totally absent: we never once feel its pulse, and there could be no greater sign of the state of exhaustion Hawthorne had by then reached. It nevertheless remains true that the typical Hawthorne work takes the form of a group of strongly interconnected organs visibly gorged with images of the world and the self. According to the degree of allegory they contain, these images constitute either horizontal or vertical chains that make up the living body of a universe. The horizontal chains are those of the earthly microcosm, that of Cervantes and Bunyan, of the hills and valleys traversed by carefree or ambitious vagabonds and by pilgrims inwardly gnawed by disquiet and remorse—and of the cities peopled by the sedentary, by recluses locked in the prisons of their own obsessions and passions. The vertical chains are those of the allegorical cosmos that runs from heaven down to hell and passes through the earth on its way, that of the medieval mysteries and Dante. And these two series of chains intersect at the center of the consciousness, in man's heart. Thus Hawthorne's work is a series of interconnected vessels, and its form, should one wish to represent it graphically, may be said to resemble certain illustrations in the old alchemists' secret books: the Cloverleaf, the Rose,[36] the symbol of the Great Work.

In the stories, the number of spheres is generally limited, and the horizontal chains are preponderant. But the principal spheres of the vertical chain usually coincide with the spheres of the microcosm. In "The Hollow of the Three Hills," we have only one sphere, nocturnal and terrestrial, but it extends downward through the water of the mere and upward through the air charged with maleficent incantations.[37]

The spheres of nature and of Puritan society in "The Gentle Boy" cannot do without either heaven or hell. The same two spheres in "Young Goodman Brown" extend only in the one direction, down to the subterranean world, the realm of Satan. And those of day and night in "Ethan Brand" open out into two inverse infinities at either end of a vertical axis. Hawthorne was seeking from the very outset to combine the two chains, but we have to wait for the novels before the vertical chain reaches its full development, and it is the first of them that achieves the most perfect balance between all the various organs, doubtless because it constitutes a summing up, an arrival. *The Scarlet Letter* presents us with a plan in the form of a double hourglass: facing one another horizontally, nature and the town, and in the very heart of the latter the square in which the crowd assembles and from which all roads diverge before ramifying into tracks and paths; then, on the vertical axis of Letter and pillory, the vault in which the meteor glows and below it the underground of the forest. The soul, like the work itself, yields more readily to the geotropism that roots it to the earth than to the phototropism that is unable to uproot it, and which, moreover, produces more poisonous flowers than it does lilies. In *The Blithedale Romance*, in which we again find the town and nature forming the horizontal axis, the vertical chain is crushed together: we scarcely ever go any higher than the top branches of Coverdale's tree, and although the river bed leads on down into an underground labyrinth, it does not have the same complexity here as in *The Marble Faun*, where the roots of the universe ramify downward in a monstrous fashion: crypts, charnel houses, dungeons, secret hiding places[38]— Hawthorne's Rome is one immense warren: all the monuments, from the Colosseum to the Trevi Fountain seem to be conjured up in the Catacombs.[39] In this novel, Hawthorne creates a myriad of smaller niches within the work's primary, compact spheres. In the air, he sets up his towers, but it is principally in its downward extension that the weight of the vertical chain falls. And the horizontal chain too becomes more complex: nature is subdivided into pagan nature and Christianized nature; the city is at the same time the city of the past, the city of art, the modern city, and the city of the soul.[40]

The House of the Seven Gables is a striking exception to the golden rule of the four symmetrical spheres. Its plan is that of the simple vertical hourglass—the same formula as for "Peter Goldthwaite" and "Rappacini."[41] Here, the horizontal chain remains embryonic. It comprises only a single element: the sphere of the outside world in opposition to the vertical self. Nature, which is absent from "Peter Goldthwaite" altogether, has been integrated in both "Rappacini" and *The House of the Seven Gables* into the central sphere: both garden and well emerge from the shadows only to sink back into them again immediately. The House, the tree, and the well have a common origin: the dense deposit with its wealth of reserves that lies upon the floor of the consciousness like nourishing earth. It is this silent organ of nutrition that first engenders the cycle of life subsequently accelerated by the central heart. From the depths of Maule's well rises the sap that nourishes the Pyncheon elm and infuses the House with its secret life. From the deep strata of the past, of human joy and pain, comes the fluid that floods the hearts of the guilty lovers, seeps its way even into the fibers of the pillory, and is drawn up in vapor from the ground in order to form the meteor and the sunbeam that dances in the forest.[42] A circulation of heavier elements takes place horizontally around the focal pillory,[43] whose malignant and magnetic attraction reduces murmuring crowds and solemn processions alike to a single cortege of Sisyphuses always returning to the same point in time and space. Such is the iron law that forbids all hope.[44] In *The House of the Seven Gables*, on the other hand, the tree trunk and the tall structure of the House draw up from below the slow movement of "the ascending spiral," which also originates in the well—the past here being, in the strictest sense of the term, the depths of the ages—capturing the vehicles in its motion as it goes—those of the past (cart and omnibus)[45] and those of the present and future (the railroad), and converting their horizontal and rectilinear motion into a function of its own circular and ascending course. It is as though the heavenly bodies themselves obey this attraction, rising and falling along the spiral as they wheel about the House.[46] And rising imperceptibly with the spiral from the well there is also the upward movement of the microcosm and its human inhabitants, as though on the very back of the dragon, of the Serpent turned instrument of Providence—an embodied, terrestrial Providence, since the Serpent is the endless chain of life: such is the poetic vision that becomes perceptible, running through *The House of the Seven Gables* like a watermark as we read it.

Thus, though it may be heavily weighted down at the outset, life is always struggling toward a final victory in Hawthorne's created world, and comes very near to liberating itself by drawing fresh strength from the earth, from its roots. But for Hawthorne, it so happens that the roots of life are also the roots of evil, and that is why, in the last resort, they prove traitorous to life. The beings and things created by a mighty uprush of sap soon weaken and fail: the guilty man drags himself along beneath his burden, the house rots, the plant dies. The sap no longer flows up into them, or becomes a poison. They must perforce return in the end to the humus from which they sprang, in order perhaps—who can tell?—to achieve a definitive liberation. The "marriage" of heaven and hell takes place in Hawthorne's work on earth—in the case of *The Scarlet Letter* one might even say beneath the earth[47]—or in the depths of the muddy waters in which Zenobia makes the gesture that may restore her to life.[48] Coverdale, a new Oberon infatuated with the glamor of ambiguity and unreality, has more physical existence than probably suits him, if he is to play the role that so attracts him—that of the disembodied thief of nature's and other men's secrets.[49] The very "veil" of the mystic marriage to which he would like to be the invisible witness remains terrestrial and fleshly. The "veiled lady," the imponderable Priscilla, appears for the first time in thick, coarse clothing,[50] thus setting off Zenobia's rich and sensual attire. The mist of unreality covering the happy valley finally condenses, and fuses, like Zenobia's body, with the river of death— which is, for Hawthorne, a very earthly river, endowed with a wholly countrified sluggishness. The inward cycle of each of Hawthorne's tales and novels, like the cycle of his work as a whole, corresponds with his own bodily rhythm: the sap rises, the tree sprouts, the flower unfurls, then everything sinks back earthward again: image of the inevitable life cycle in a man deeply rooted in the earth, a man unable to perform his chosen labors unless he has first stored up within him- self a fund of psychic energy equivalent to the energy latent in his native soil.

With his intensely physical imagination, his inborn feeling for living material, Hawthorne could have been, as Whitman would have wished, and a century before Robert Frost, the poet of New England, the earthly poet of a precarious paradise. And this same material imagina- tion could also have made him into the first American realist novel writer, if allegory, upon which he had staked his whole career, had not directed his talents toward the prose romance.

ART

· I ·
Fancy

I. THE PSEUDOPROBLEM OF REALISM

His invincible tendency to resort to allegory was without doubt an obstacle that hindered Hawthorne from developing all his themes and from achieving a total expression of his self.[1] And yet, except upon the level of the American Faust, this tendency also proved to the artist's advantage, since it forced him to express himself in an indirect fashion, to renounce the use of immediate realism, and thereby to fight his way through to another reality, fuller and intenser than the other— a poetic reality. Though an esthetic necessity, this tendency can also be explained as the result of a moral determination that was never able to engender a work, but that never ceased to do battle within the mind of Hawthorne the Puritan heir. He could not believe in gratuitous art, in art for art's sake. But could he believe in utilitarian, edifying art either? If beauty must be of use—of use to man in elevating his soul and providing him with a better consolation than nature left to herself,[2] it should not perform that function in the brutal manner of certain reformers and preachers, but with grace, leaving those it visits in full possession of their freedom. Beauty is neither utilitarian nor gratuitous, simply disinterested. When Hawthorne speaks as an artist, moreover, we find him showing no remorse in contradicting his inclinations as a moralist obsessed by the Adamic myth of purity: art becomes in his eyes the supreme value and the supreme instrument of salvation, even though it cannot expunge the primal stain, and despite the fact that it bears, even in its religious manifestations, the mark of the tempter. As, for example, Guido Reni's painting of St. Michael.[3] Art, the conquest of "overcome" man, is nonetheless a form of ethics. Moral consciousness and esthetic consciousness in the artist, whether Hawthorne or Baudelaire, are closely interwoven. The moral imagination's magic lantern and the screen of the poet's haunted mind both function in the same way, representing their images in the same light and in the same ambiguous atmosphere. The moral imagination, which is not the same as the narrower moral sense, proceeds in accordance with the esthetic method, while the esthetic imagination seeks for a moral basis. Thus allegory is wedded to poetry, the first being freed of its characteristic rigidity and the second renouncing its gratuitousness: the ethical element becomes an artistic element, at least in the works that count. The converse does not happen except in the minor works or the failures, when Hawthorne uses allegory as a refuge instead of as a means of expression. *The Marble Faun,* of all his novels the one in which there is most talk of art, is also the one that most lacks esthetic unity: the foreign elements take on a disproportionate importance that threatens to stifle the work. This is because Hawthorne was on the point of forgetting that in the artist's universe it is beauty that is moral, not the converse. It is enough that the image should be true, full of meaning, and human.

Art, for Hawthorne, had an ethical and an esthetic definition at the same time, an attitude that followed logically enough from the particular roots of his work, which were ancestral as well as literary, colonial as well as modern. However great his desire to equal "the proudest productions of the scribbling sons of John Bull"[4] it was his intention to be a truly American writer. He was not seeking to provide a substitute for the European tradition of allegory and narrative fiction, but he was, on the other hand, seeking to incorporate into it new, home-grown, specifically autochthonous elements. These elements were provided in his case, not by the very recent "frontier" tradition, but by the history of the colonial period. And though literary nationalism was never a major preoccupation with him, Hawthorne was concerned, even in the early stages of his career, with attempting to lead the writers of his own country along the right path.[5] And indeed, what simpler means could he have found of establishing his originality in relation to his predecessors and English contemporaries than that of "being American enough"?[6] He attempted from the very outset to escape from European exoticism, and set the action of *Fanshawe* very close to his own native haunts: Harley College is Bowdoin, the topography is that of the mountains, rivers, and forests of Maine. Hawthorne was giving his art roots. He also stamped it with a mark of origin by making use of the primitive arts of Puritan days, arts that were more utilitarian than decorative in intent. Antique knickknacks, curious and rustic pieces of furniture, old houses with carved ornaments, allegorical weathervanes and figureheads,[7] were all, for him, wooden fetishes representing America. He often used them as symbols representing the work of art in preference to the monuments, statues, and paintings provided by the civilization of Europe. The paintings he presents us with are usually executed by provincial miniaturists, or by painters of primitive subjects like Benjamin West or Washington Allston. It was manifestly in Hawthorne's mind to create a prototype for the American Pygmalion. And this Pygmalion is the sculptor Shem Drowne, the primitive artist who receives the homage of Copley, the master adept in all the "continental" techniques,[8] and who falls in love with the figurehead that he discovers rather than carves in the trunk of an American tree. Hawthorne, like Robert Frost in this century,[9] was rediscovering the myth of the hamadryad. Using very ancient materials and images, he was in search of a new art less in the "nothing is nameable" strain of Samuel Beckett than in the "everything from the beginning again" vein. Hawthorne was trying to regenerate the traditional esthetic of his day with an injection of unfamiliar primitive forms, and to enrich it at the same time with a stylization of metallic structures and machines that looks forward to the trends of modern art: Owen Warland's butterfly may well be considered a prefiguration of Calder's mobiles.

This determination to be American and modern forced him more than once into self-contradiction. The plebeian artist he would have liked to be—a figure modeled in his mind on Burns, whom he admired so much, resembling Whitman, of whom he had never heard, and caricatured in the blacksmith Danforth[10]—was in perpetual conflict with the aristocratic and solitary artist he was in reality. It is not Holgrave, the ingenious artisan and opportunist who abandons brush and pen for the daguerreotype, who represents the true Hawthorne, but a combination of Drowne and Owen Warland. If the latter had been offering his contemporaries a new mechanical invention he would have been immediately understood; but his invention is a new form of art.

The American so eager to recognize Benjamin Franklin, Edison, the Wright brothers, and Henry Ford as its sons was more reluctant when it came to Poe, Hawthorne, or Conrad Aiken. The "black mixture" offered by the author of "Ulalume" in his poems, and the timeless mixture of archaism and modernity achieved by that of *The Scarlet Letter*, still both remain less accessible and more mysterious to the general public than the "barbaric"[11] but epic and aggressively American voice of Whitman. Hawthorne goes too far and penetrates too deeply not to encounter secret veins of reticence even in his most enthusiastic readers.[12] He is one of those artists one discovers gradually and late.

The material reality upon which Hawthorne drew was thus particular and local. But far from the influence of these materials being such that the form of the work, the idea that gave birth to it, and the detail of its execution are all exclusively dependent upon it,[13] we find that it is the material itself which is obliged to conform to the artist's purpose and subject itself to his style. Any intrinsically dramatic reality is a temptation to the artist to allow himself to be taken over by it, to rely upon it to guarantee him an immediate but superficial success, and to allow it to compose his work for him instead of taking on that responsibility himself. The artist is not a chronicler: the work should never upon any pretext be obscured by its anecdotal content. Suffering as he did from his lack of popularity, Hawthorne was dissatisfied with what he felt was his excessive skill in transforming reality into a work of art, withdrawing it as it were from circulation. He deplored this fatal gift, this alarming faculty that led him to lay an even greater emphasis upon life's particularity of meaning and mystery, instead of extracting from it the kind of banal significance that would be valid for everyone. He would have liked to be the *American Author* the *American Public* was expecting, or else the realist novelist exemplified by Trollope and Dickens.[14] But that would have meant renouncing what he in fact was. And he perceived from the very outset of his career that one can never really do anything at all before one has first found oneself.

He had scarcely left college before he made his first attempt at the novel. But that was a false start. For his concentrated imagination the novel was too loosely knit a form. He needed a tighter sheath in order to test his strength, even though he was later to explode it. "The

Gentle Boy" is already a novella. Later, with "Rappacini" and "The Artist of the Beautiful," the need to break the bounds of the short tale became much stronger. And finally, "Ethan Brand," that "chapter from an abortive romance,"[15] is a prelude to the series of works that were to "possess substance enough to stand alone" and to warrant a volume all to themselves.[16] Nevertheless, whether he wrote enough material to make up twenty chapters or only one, Hawthorne was never to produce anything but novellas of varying lengths, never any true novels. In the shortest, he isolates a theme and treats it as a separate entity, in the way that a poet will devote a single poem to a particular image. Every theme has its own tale: "The Gentle Boy," "The Grey Champion," "My Kinsman, Major Molineux," and "Young Goodman Brown" all have common roots, but Hawthorne treats the orphan theme, the guilty conscience theme, and the great feats of the past theme all separately. He lops the branches off the trunk once he has allowed them to grow. But the trunk is still there: the simultaneously single and multiple consciousness searching for itself while at the same time seeking to remain secret. This quest is at times sporadic, at others concentrated.[17] In his youthful period he seems to have concentrated strongly upon the orphan theme, even though it is dealt with in a number of different works and not in a single large one.[18] In the 1828–29 tales the main theme was that of the labyrinth,[19] in the 1831–33 works[20] that of the "quest," and in those composed between 1834 and 1835 the solitary self.[21] Later, the tendency to sporadic use of themes grows more marked. From 1834 onward, there is an admixture of "gothick" elements, of historical sketches, and poetic myths[22] mingled with the great, austere themes. It may well be that it was only the lack of one seed more powerful than the others, and of the circumstances able to make the organization of his material around that seed a matter of urgency, that prevented the house of the haunted mind from becoming a more tragic forerunner of the House of the Seven Gables—or Wakefield's maze from becoming that of the adulterous minister. For the same reasons, Endicott could well have made way, as early as 1837, for Hester, and the hideous fascination of the pillory have drawn into a cluster around it the houses of Peter Goldthwaite, Dr. Heidegger, and Sylph Etherege,[23] as well as the bloody pilgrims of the forest carrying their bell[24] and the Adam and Eve of the night.[25] The direction was already given, but it was only one possibility among several. The same phenomenon of divergence preceded the grouping together of the themes that were to give birth to *The Scarlet Letter*: "Main Street" is an incursion into the realm of the provincial past, "The Snow Image" into that of childhood, and "Ethan Brand" into that of illicit acts and thoughts.[26] These scattered elements were soon to be gathered together into a single tight and powerful sheaf that was to produce the density of a great work when bound with the necessary tragic and noble strands. So that, without knowing it, Hawthorne was putting into practice both in his psychic life and his work the principle laid down by Baudelaire: "the vaporization and centralization of the Self: it all comes down to that."[27] After the numerous explorations made by the alchemist-psychologist and the poet in every direction, *The Scarlet Letter* became the point of convergence of many forces whose conjunction had been long delayed, and which now made themselves manifest with an intensity all the greater for that delay. And this book, the key to Hawthorne's work as a whole, was later to serve as a sort of switchboard redistributing the currents that had first found their confluence in it. The vast, spreading tree was pruned back, the sturdy sheaf was thinned out, and the sap flowed less and less abundantly. In *The House of the Seven Gables*, the major themes were absorbed by the minor ones: the theme of the past by that of the present, the theme of hell and conscience by that of a rather insipid Eden. In *The Blithedale Romance*, the theme of the past has disappeared altogether, and the themes of alchemy and the violation of another's consciousness are perilously close to becoming merely those of scientism and mesmerism. Lastly, in *The Marble Faun*, we are presented with a veritable dissociation of the work's elements in both time and space.

In its allegorical conception, its predominantly supernatural atmosphere, and lastly in its dimensions, *The Scarlet Letter* remains a tale.[28] Which is a token of the quality and purity of the writer's art. The works that followed, each coming increasingly nearer to the novel, often appear to be merely a sequence of tales or novellas artificially linked together. Each of them, moreover, contains at least one tale introduced on some dramatic or picturesque pretext in the very midst of the main plot,[29] which proves clearly enough that Hawthorne was incapable of giving up his nonrealist esthetic for the sake of the realist esthetic of the modern novel. Realism, about which he worried a great

deal, albeit late in life, was never to be more than a complementary
element in his work. With him, it was nothing more than a whim
born of a desire to compete with more fortunate rivals, never a genuine
inclination or even a natural aptitude.[30] Yet he did genuinely imagine
that his lack of ability forced him to let slip by the opportunity of
writing the great book based on real life, on life as it is lived, the
book that would have at last been the masterwork he dreamed of.[31]
It was an illusion, for the realist too starts from a reality that is
relative in the first place to himself, and must therefore organize his
material with reference to imaginative values. Instead of the central
myth attracting the stylized objects and beings to it, it is the objects
and the beings that conjure up the hidden myth by their very presence.
And the images of the consciousness are also realities, realities that
the poet has the ability to render tangible. What would the poet be
if he were not the creator of what, without him, would not exist, or
remain an object of contempt—the unconscious, the irrational—if he
were not the artist who unveils for the imagination, or restores to it,
the virgin face and particular aspects of the universe that are masked
by utilitarian appearances and conventional façades, if he were not,
therefore, the artist who in the end has the most acute sense of
reality of all? There is an internal realism and an external realism, the
expressions of two interpenetrating realities. The squabble about realism and nonrealism is therefore a futile one. As one would have
thought Bergson had made quite clear once and for all.[32] There are
simply those works that are founded upon a reality, whatever it may
be, causing it to emerge from the shadows and yield up its significance,
and those that merely deal with appearances. Yet Hawthorne, dissatisfied as he was with his materials and his art, wanted to replace
those materials with "solid" materials, and compress them into "re-
sistant blocks." He allowed himself, he of all people, to be taken in
by appearances and to confuse the false reality with the true, thereby
running the risk, when he was unable to control this tendency, as in
The Blithedale Romance and The Marble Faun, of allowing his
"shadows" and "chimaeras" to stray among the objects of everyday
reality, without either giving the latter their true density or using them
to give a greater relief to his phantoms, which tend to become mere
paltry theatrical props, like Westervelt and the Model. The scene of
the search at night for Zenobia's body is "padded" with an odd clumsiness of details, which is made even worse by the far too explicit moral

intention.[33] Instead of being enriched, the substance is weighed down and rendered inert. As for the vast descriptive panels imported with such artifice and pains into the story of the faun, they simply help to transform the work into an imposing machine in which it is no longer possible to recognize the hand of the Artist of the Beautiful. One critic has seen fit to classify Hawthorne as a prenovelist,[34] probably in order to spare him the purgatory of the "nonrealist" writers and the hell of the "poets." But it is in fact when he attempts to approach the ideal of the novel that he sinks into mediocrity, and it is only when he makes no attempt to do so that he is truly a writer. Moreover the novel, despite the vogue it presently enjoys, is a very treacherous genre, and what is more, inadequate as a form of art. The best proof of this—a point forcibly made by André Breton as long ago as his 1924 "Manifesto of Surrealism"—is that the first failure who comes along can turn himself into a novelist. And he also quoted the remark made by Valéry that Claude Mauriac decided to turn into a book for a bet![35] Hawthorne, however, chose a form of art that does not tolerate mediocrity. Those of his works that have "dated" are precisely the ones in which he tried to make a show of modernism. The authentic avant-garde in art does not follow the fashion. It is made up, on the contrary, of those who are making their ways, along secret paths, sometimes without any publicity at all, toward unsuspected truths.

And this implies the rejection of appearances, which are of two sorts: the appearances of reality, based upon superficial observation and the current fashion—and the appearances of the imaginative sphere, based upon sentimental and esthetic conventions. Though Hawthorne lacked a sense of immediate reality, he did possess in a very acute form that of hidden reality, together with the gift of changing brute objects into symbolic objects. But this metamorphosis of objects does not always coincide with his individual imaginative quests. The imaginative quest in *The Marble Faun* is pursued through piles of monuments and cumbersome ruins: the tourist guide has difficulty finding time for the tribulations of the soul. An even more total failure occurred in the case of the "English novel," for the notes taken from life utterly refused to combine with the inert bric-a-brac that forms the substance of all the posthumous works. Hawthorne was obliged to give up the novel in order to devote himself to a series of petrified fantasies, simply because he was unable to grasp simultaneously, in all their complexity and diversity, both of the realities which, had he been able to fuse them into one, would have constituted an unprecedented literary monument that would have had no rival until the works of Faulkner. Faulkner's imagination is a river that tears up the whole of reality by the roots and carries it along in its stream, apparently in a raging chaos, but in reality arranged along irresistible lines of force. Hawthorne's imagination was a whirlwind, sometimes circling slowly, sometimes swiftly, and only giving up its images gradually, after the necessary settling process had taken place. Hawthorne and Faulkner, the same obsession, but two opposite tendencies of artistic creation: totality and rarity—which are not, moreover, mutually exclusive. There is the rarity of Whitman's or Wolfe's sensorial chaos—there is the totality of the world that moves in orbit around the pillory, of the besieged, catalytic consciousness triggering the precipitate of shadows—the colors, the scents, and the sounds that have still not ceased their exhalations from Baudelaire's "Correspondences." There is always a new poetic will, a new poetic intuition presiding over the work that lasts. The so-called *nouveau roman* is merely exploiting, after a certain lapse of time, the methods of writing and expression invented by modern poetry, the avant-garde cinema, and abstract art, so as to be freer to desert to the side of objects and cast away outworn psychology.

This objectivism, which is only one aspect of total creation—and let us not forget what Hawthorne was able to do with a block of wood, a scrap of material—made possible the eye-shattering images of Bunuel's *Un Chien Andalou* on the movie screen, as well as the revelations that Fellini in *La Dolce Vita* was able to wrest from the Roman architecture that had been Hawthorne's Waterloo—in painting, the constantly increasing starkness of Cézanne's interpretations of the Mont Ste. Victoire—in poetry, the shattering nudity achieved by Reverdy, or the abrupt resurrection of primitive myth in *Carnac.* Guillevic's[36] and Frost's stones,[37] like Hawthorne's wood, are a substance immanent in the hand that touches them. But Robbe-Grillet's surfaces remain surfaces, the object whose ricochets should reconstruct the consciousness perceiving it schematize it instead: the novel has become no more than a scenario.[38] Technique cannot precede art without killing it. Every artist must first discover in his inmost being the law that is going to govern his work and that contains all his creative processes in germinal form: in Hawthorne's case, the formation of his interconnecting spheres and the perception of light in darkness—a law that he could verify in a poem, in a metaphysical essay, just as well as in the short story and the novel. For there is no precise, absolute partitioning of the different forms of literary creation. In total creation they even tend to disappear altogether: Kierkegaard's meditations and Sartre's *La Nausée* both verge at times on poetry and at others on satire; Claudel's poetry verges on drama and theology. And one might say that ever since the *Iliad* and the *Odyssey*, poem, drama, and novel have always been fused together whenever there has been a man possessed simultaneously by the lyric daemon, the dramatic daemon, and the passion to tell stories. It is to such happy conjunctures that we owe Homer, Cervantes, Shakespeare, and— nearer to our own time—the works of Knut Hamsun and Hermann Broch,[39] Neruda's *Canto General*, and Aragon's *Le Roman Inachevé*. Though the novel decorated with poetic posies is a facile genre, the poem whose robust and flexible structure will accommodate both the purest oneirism and novelistic material demands a Hugo, a Kafka, or a Melville. But if Melville was able to conceive the myth of Moby Dick, was it not perhaps because Hawthorne had shown him the way? Melville, like Hawthorne, was a poet in the sense that he always saw the world as a function of his inward vision. And the paradoxical law is, that even when opting for the world as it is supposed to be, the realist obeys the law of the world of consciousness, and that if, con- versely, the latter is subjected to the influence of the former, that influence can be exercised only with the permission of the previously prepared mind, which organizes the given material around a selective idea that is progressively clarified and modified as it draws material into its field of force. Every image perceived is formed, taken apart, and re-formed in the mind, a simultaneously withdrawn and projected space that is the ground of all the worlds "supplementary to this one."

Mere borrowing pure and simple from the external world can never suffice to make a work of art. The creative idea is a net that draws the usable materials it needs from the dark depths of the consciousness or the teeming opacity of reality. The assembly of these materials takes place in accordance with a thematic dominant more or less imperiously imposed upon them: the light in the darkness, the vision, in spring- time, of the earthly paradise. Crane proceeded no differently in *The Red Badge of Courage*, when he concretized the war that rages in men's minds in his image of the battlefield. The techniques vary according to the materials and the individual viewpoint, but the creative process is always reducible to some given combination of two essential methods. The artist starts from an inward and distant music and goes in search of the densest or most secret material reality, a journey that ends in the poem—or he starts from the most diverse or particular reality and then attempts to seek out the music, a journey that leads to the work of narrative fiction. Nothing could be more mistaken than to define the novel in terms of reality and poetry in terms of its opposite. The paths that lead from one to the other, divergent though they may be, eventually converge, and the pursuit of reality, like that of imaginative reality, is never other than relative to the man who undertakes it. Like Peter Goldthwaite opening the window after his exhausting labors, Hawthorne used to cast a glance outside—a reference to be made, a piece of advice to be sought, the need for relaxation —then return to his work. His instinct told him that it is sometimes good to get out of oneself, but it also warned him that the greatest possible error would be obstinately struggling to transcribe the spectacle of the world without referring it to his dreams. In the historical sketches, as in the sketches taken from nature, he soon encountered his limitations—and the limits of the genre. There is no doubt that he had good reason to avoid that sort of realism, which, if one is not extremely careful, soon begins to dilute the elements of the real world instead of concentrating its substance to a greater density. One must be a very great painter indeed if one is not to be trapped into facility once the necessary expertise to achieve resemblance has been acquired. And what an inferior kind of skill is that of the sculptor who, like Kenyon, turns himself into a couturier making sure that his statues are all dressed in the latest fashion. "Ethan Brand" may originally have been an unfortunate attempt to produce a "likeness" of reality. The story of Esther,[40] whose name was to reappear later, was perhaps no more than a novel of manners, a portrait of contemporary society without any artistic unity, which the author later reduced to its correct proportions—which is to say, merely a discreet echo—in order to make room for a study in depth of one human consciousness. Here again we see how much reality depends upon imaginative reality—and also how much the latter depends upon the interiorization of outward reality. The pursuit of the one ends in a conjunction with the other, though in an adapted form favorable to the fusion from which that living organism we term a work of art may then emerge. The form in which Hawthorne was able to assimilate reality had of necessity to prefigure what was already haunting him but had still not attained particular form.[41] The imaginary, seeking to concretize itself, went out to meet the symbolic object offered to it, shaped itself upon it and attempted to resemble it, as Hester identifies herself with the Letter and the minister with the pillory. Seen from this point of view, art seems at last to reveal its true nature and aim, which is to confer a value upon reality in the world of the imaginary, and to set upon the imaginary the stamp of reality.

II. THE PROBLEM OF FORM

The true writer cannot content himself with literary fantasies. There is no standard of comparison between Hawthorne's translation of reality, even in the most anodyne of his sketches, and that provided by his friend Bridge in his travel stories.[1] Not to limit oneself to following the intellectual or artistic current of the day is another principle of which there was certainly no need to remind the man who avoided even a physical proximity with the Transcendentalists, and who refused to let himself be influenced by even the most eminent of them, despite the fact that he recognized him as "a great and original thinker."[2] From which there follows the absolute rule: first and foremost, draw your material from your own personal store, rather than wasting your pains finding different ways of expressing someone else's opinions or reworking accepted platitudes. The important thing is not to know "*how* to say things, but *what* to say."[3] Form is a function of the work's substance, it "springs from an inner chaos crying for order."[4] Which is why it is not enough simply to write at the dictation of one's imagination either: another rule that Oberon might well have formulated for his own guidance, given as he was to making use of his own obsessions and dreams. No image destined for integration into a work can be admitted to the esthetic sphere until it has first been detached, not only from its everyday, traditional, and moral roots, but even from its psychological roots as well. Only then can it eventually be restored to its original context—of which it has by then ceased to be an exclusive property. All creation assumes, in effect, a character of autonomy.[5] It always tends, to a greater or lesser degree, to be creation in the absolute, or if it does not, then it is in danger of never rising to the dignity of true art. Hawthorne, choosing the cavern as his allegory for the heart,[6] sets to work as a moralist-psychologist and finds his way to an idealist—in the dynamic sense—concept of creation. Beyond the words that offer yet another reflection of neo-Platonism, the real signification appears: it is through darkness that one finally attains the light—the very light of the darkness itself—it is through the dream, that inward reflection, transformed by the soul, not passively accepted, that beauty is achieved—it is by means of night and torment that birth is given to the work that is to last and prove the counterpoise to night, to nothingness. The battle the artist wages must not remain merely the battle of his creative will against the external influences it has admitted inside it in order to make use of them. It must also become the battle between beauty and tragedy, the battle between Apollo and Dionysos—a battle which, in Hawthorne's case soon swings in favor of Dionysos, in favor of his daemon Oberon. The Apollonian artist, the Artist of the Beautiful, does certainly exist in him, but more for others, for those minds sensitized to the Emersonian esthetic doctrine who composed his circle—and especially Sophia, who saw her husband even more as the god incarnate of transcendent harmony than as the musician god with his Orphic lyre.[7] Though Hawthorne's most characteristic themes are Dionysian and stem from his Oberon self, they must nevertheless mingle with the Apollonian stream in him in order to receive the consecration of form and to enrich themselves with fresh human implications.

Creation begins as a sensorial or imaginative experience provoking deep and distant stirrings that subsequently well up to meet the new impressions destined to enrich them. Lyric, dramatic, and tragic echoes are awakened. And the mind's conscious labor forces the images to take on greater precision, to modify themselves, to form themselves into esthetic schemes. At the heart of the imaginative ebullition, of the fevered boiling in the mind, there takes shape, or is preserved, the pure line of the thoroughbred work, the "iron rod"[8] that underpins the complex interweavings of the fabric. The growth of the work thus often occurs along the line of a trunk (the ancestral tree, the tall House with its gables), of a straight path ("The Canterbury Pilgrims"), or of a sinuous path (that of Goodman Brown in the forest). Though the magic wand may bend, it nevertheless still attains its end, which is to clear away everything that is not essential to the work. For it is much more important to "prune" away superfluous elements than to "fill up vacant spaces,"[9] as in *The Marble Faun*, and even *The House of the Seven Gables* and *The Blithedale Romance*, with dissertations. There are none of these vacant spaces filled in after the event in "Young Goodman Brown," "The Maypole of Merry Mount," or "Wakefield." And if there were at one time in "Ethan Brand," the author eliminated them by tightening up his material. When it came to increasing the dimensions of *The Scarlet Letter*, instead of expanding the substance of the book itself—for example by inserting descriptive chapters dealing with the history and manners of the period in which his story was set—Hawthorne wrote an introduction that can without disadvantage be separated from the tale itself. It is to this deliberate choice, as well as to the artist's refusal to adulterate it, that the work owes its purity of line, not only from the dramatic point of view, but also ethically, pictorially, and musically. It was also by a skilled combination of the two processes, pruning and filling in by turns or simultaneously, that he achieved the fully rounded form of the perfect sphere: that of the Letter, that of the House, the microcosm of the valley that sprang to life and peopled itself beneath its creator's gaze.

In his search for form, the artist borrows from all the arts. The statue has achieved a certain recognition as the preferred symbol for the work of art—it being the Platonic symbol par excellence—but the technique of sculpture and its full, hard forms, have very little application to a creative act based on ambiguity; they are also too specific—the technique for designating the line of the narrative or poem, the forms for evoking their nuances. Only abstract sculpture, seen in dim or changing lighting, could do so: Michelangelo's statue of Lorenzo de' Medici has precisely this quality of mystery, its shadows being used to conceal the work's structure while revealing its inner substance.[10] But the literary work has its architecture too, and many of Hawthorne's tales have a strong resemblance to monuments, the central image imposing itself upon the mind in such a way that the narrative takes on the form of the house in which the characters live, leading us from room to room—of the square where the Puritan leader is drilling his soldiers, of the walled garden where the new Adam and Eve live in their new Eden, of the bridge over which the procession of vehicles rumbles. The romance of the faun is attempting to be a vast cathedral built in the image of St. Peter's: "The World's Cathedral,"[11] only rather more Gothic-seeming with its niches and asymmetrical towers. Unfortunately, however, having created a masterpiece with his country church serving the eighteenth-century community of Boston, clustered in tight-knit unity around its austere and primitive symbols, Hawthorne failed when he attempted to make a whole from the disparate stones of the universal basilica.

We shall be obliged to return later to the interior decoration of Hawthorne's monuments, which in fact goes much further than mere ornamentation and cannot be reduced to just a series of paintings hung from the walls. A painting can also turn out to be the work itself: a "Night Sketch,"[12] a "Sketch of Transitory Life,"[13] a miniature of birds and buds,[14] a "Picture of the Past,"[15] or a vast historical fresco. The naturalist precision of Audubon, the chiaroscuro technique of Ryder, the sense of composition of Allston were at his command, yet Hawthorne could not refrain from wasting his gifts, because he delighted so much in deploying all the resources of the genre painter, a type of artist who, like the architect, tends to lose his grip as soon as he leaves his own territory and attempts, like Thomas Cole, to produce panoramas of antiquity or vistas of the world of fantasy. One might well draw a parallel between those ambitious canvases entitled "The Course of Empire" and the great descriptive passages in *The Marble Faun*.[16] If one thinks of them in terms of the fabled cities that have risen to the sound of music,[17] the city dreamed up by Cole and the city that Hawthorne conjured up out of the limbo of paganism did not wait for the deepest notes of the soul to sound before they reared themselves up before their creators, as cold and artificial as the miracles of modern magic. Whereas the village among the hills and the Colonial house sprout up quite naturally, as though to the sound of rustic instruments playing ancient, simple tunes. As long as he continued to use those melodies, those that one hears in one's native air, and even those, "sweeter still," that one does not hear, Hawthorne was always revealed as a true musician in his work. The tale of "The Canterbury Pilgrims" is constructed like a sonata: as the two processions file past, one ascending, one descending,[18] the development of these two melodic lines, creating an ever increasing tension between them, is reminiscent of Beethoven's "Moonlight" sonata[19] or Alain Resnais' *Hiroshima mon amour*. The "Night Sketches" hover in the air like the luminous notes of a Chopin nocturne, notes that we hear again in "The Wives of the Dead," a short étude played pianissimo to the accompaniment of raindrops splashing into puddles by lantern light.[20] "Young Goodman

Brown," like "The Hollow of the Three Hills," offers a richer orchestration more akin to Moussorgsky's *Night on Bald Mountain* or the
last movement of Berlioz' *Symphonie Fantastique.* There are the works
that shriek themselves at us, and those that simply tell themselves—the
works that are songs and those that are murmurs. The inner tone is
always there to be found by the receptive reader whose mind is willing
to improvise the right accompaniment. Though there are other works
that are above all visual in their forms and colors. Hawthorne's art,
like all complete art, addresses itself to all the senses: it is, on the literary level, a particular synthesis of all the means of expression and all
the forms of artistic interpretation that the various elements of reality
it contains demand and are able to accommodate—a synthesis that in
its combination of fantasy and humor and its use of symbols and
tragedy is clearly recognizable as specific to Hawthorne's work.

III. THE TALE OF ROMANCE

Spenser had introduced the romance into poetry. Hawthorne seized
upon this precedent and made the tale or short story into a form that
was as much poem as romance, one in which the fantastic, the dramatic,
the psychological, and the tragic all overlap, combine, and complement
one another. Moreover, Poe[1] and others of his contemporaries perceived this quite clearly. Beneath the variety of their forms, all Hawthorne's tales are akin to the poem. And first of all on account of their
Biblical and popular inspiration. The subtitles he applied to his works
—parable, morality, mystery, miracle[2]—all have a somewhat medieval
savor, though it is the religious and moral half of the tradition they
continue rather than the humorous and bawdy side. We find no equivalent of the fabliau in his work, except perhaps in "Feathertop" and
"Mrs. Bullfrog."[3] But we do find "fairy legends" and "fantasies"[4] that
spring from a tradition quite as old as that of the Bible—the tradition
of ancient legend. This tradition, whether of Nordic or Mediterranean
origin, has always managed to transplant itself successfully in any favorable new soil, where it then impregnates itself with the spirit of its
new site. This process of acclimatization is particularly visible in Washington Irving. But in Hawthorne's case, the Catskills of "Sleepy Hollow" and "Rip van Winkle" have been transported into a Bunyanesque
realm, which signifies a withdrawal of several steps back into the imag

inary world. We find ourselves on the borders of the region of primitive romance, of the supernatural, of dreams. We are entering a land of chimeras where everything is possible, where everything is capable of metamorphosis: houses transformed into vegetables, human trees, wooden figureheads with faces of flesh—we stand once again in the province of magic—in which objects and beings are simultaneously themselves and other than themselves, change their faces, their forms, their colors, appear and disappear (the roots of ambiguity are also to be found in the dream)—a country in which animals speak, or behave, as the spectators expect the showman's dog to behave,[5] like a human clown—the country in which things become animate, in which living beings suddenly become statues, in which the dead move, in which man is on the same scale as nature and of the same caliber as his past. Any novel that limits its ambitions to reducing the actions and deeds of human beings to the dimensions of everyday life is merely stripping them of their significance, damping all their reverberations. The characters of the "Comédie Humaine" and the trials and tribulations undergone in Paris by Rastignac, Rubempré, and Vautrin, are quite as fabulous for the imagination of a true Balzac addict as certain hobgoblins, monsters or giants born of our age-old fears and desires. That which is fabulous is *more* than real. Hawthorne was perfectly aware of this, and so we find him offering us the werewolf in the guise of his Black Man, a Giant Despair beneath the unexceptionable exterior of the Judge,[6] the ogre from "Mother Goose" appearing at the window of the haunted house,[7] and Bluebeard in his seventh room lurking in the recesses and cellars of the castle. Bartók's opera on the same theme, perhaps the only truly psychological opera so far written,[8] is charged with the selfsame poetic intensity that we find in the tales that Hawthorne was able to imbue with the "charm of romance"—the charm that had begun to elude him even in *The House of the Seven Gables.*[9]

As so often happens with storytellers, and even with poets, Hawthorne's oneirism could always be destroyed by the intervention of the critical intellect if it decided to override intuition and attempt, for fear of ridicule, to give a rational explanation of the irrational. The graceful idyll of "The Vision of the Fountain" is spoiled by all the precautions and details intended to make us believe in its probability.[10] And who really cares what Miriam's origins actually were, or whether Donatello does really have long ears or not![11] Hawthorne was allowing himself to be trapped here into futilities, and contenting himself with

a game of "gothick" ambiguities. Perhaps, however, we ought to excuse him on the grounds of humor? In his early works, being under
the influence of Shakespeare, he had attempted to achieve comic contrasts in his writing, particularly by the introduction of preposterous incidents such as we find in Fielding: Dr. Melmoth loses his way and ends
up in a tavern in much the same way as Parson Adams ends up in Dame
Slipslop's bedroom.[12] Later on, the comic element, becoming the complement of the tragic, was to be based on moral grotesquerie: Dimmesdale, taken at his word by the demon inhabiting the pillory where
he had intended to make a simulated confession of his crime, standing
paralyzed with rheumatism on the scaffold while his parishioners cluster
round still rubbing the sleep out of their eyes;[13] the Judge, in a gallant
mood, kissing the thin air instead of the little salesgirl who is the object
of his lascivious intent.[14] Hawthorne the ironist cannot be separated
from Hawthorne the allegorist and portrait painter of the conscience:
his comedy is not only sparse but also imbued with the selfsame sadness
that so struck Musset in Molière, when he touches upon the essential
aspects of human psychology. The grotesque pillory after the tragic
pillory would make us laugh, if we could only isolate the situation, with
all its possibilities of social ridicule and gossip, from the content of the
individual consciousness quivering with the pain of being violated by
others' eyes. On the other hand, the parody-image of the Governor's
head resting on its ruff like St. John the Baptist's on its charger has no
reference to any deeper context.[15] The humor that is the comic author's
surest ally, and perhaps the source of a certain kind of poetry because
of the play of ambiguity it makes possible, is one of the poet's worst
enemies. Apprehensive as he was of being taxed with extravagance,
Hawthorne was one of those who are prepared to negate some of their
most precious inspirations. Why did he fail to pursue the image of the
child emerging from the mirror, liquid by definition,[16] except from lack
of courage? And elsewhere he goes to inordinate trouble to prove to
us that the mirage in the fountain is a flesh and blood person instead
of making us feel the reality of his vision. Similarly, at Niagara, he rejected his poetic dream of the falls.[17] And was it not a sin against his
own dreamworld to bring Adam and Eve back to life in a town?[18] In
"Peter Goldthwaite" he destroys the myth of the cloud-house in the
bud.[19] Why should a house not fly away some stormy night? Which of
us has not at some time dreamed of a house in the air? And for the same
reasons, reinforced by his moral prejudices, Hawthorne also destroys

the vital principle of belief—even in its lesser form of "suspension of disbelief"—when he retells the Greek myths.[20] He makes Cadmus into one of those loathsomely clever little creatures in modern movie cartoons[21] instead of making us relive the hero's digestive metamorphosis within the dragon's belly. One forgives him a little for having sacrificed the myth of Hercules to his pygmies because of the wealth of invention he deploys in the process. But no artist can sap the myth of the giant with impunity, for the giant is the image of the creator himself. Though it may not be enough to see big in order to create a great work, it is certain that one must have a giant's hands to hold a Lilliput. Though Hawthorne's Lilliput did not appear in its true light except in the microcosm of provincial America, and even then, as we shall see, the light was slanted in a very particular way.

If the dream world is destroyed by humor—which is more often than is supposed the accomplice of prosaic reason—the supernatural is debased by the "gothick" and by that inferior brand of fantasy whose dated paraphernalia is to be found in many of Hawthorne's minor tales[22] and even in certain of the major works, including *The House of the Seven Gables*, whose author was only too aware himself that he was "careering on the verge of a precipitous absurdity"[23] when he made a purely gratuitous use of elements that he was perfectly capable of employing elsewhere for artistic and psychological ends. In "The Wedding Knell," as in "The Christmas Banquet," we find the macabre being employed for purely sensational ends: shrouds, sepulchral urns, death's heads, funeral torches.[24] In *The House of the Seven Gables*, and to an even greater extent in *Grimshawe*, there is a multiplicity of secret staircases, secret doors, trick pictures, hidden drawers, old books and parchments, all features of an artificial plot whose function is to create a factitious interest and to maintain the action in motion until the final chapter, when the secret of the puzzle is at last revealed.[25] The story of the Pyncheons is used as a pretext for one set of variations in the sentimental-idyllic mode[26] and another in the fantastic mode, with the latter sometimes descending to the level of the merely sensational or even of the "whodunit."[27] Though Dostoevski may have been able to combine a detective story plot with the most overwhelming psychological revelations, all Hawthorne could manage with his was to swathe it in an atmosphere of "gothick" romance.

If it were not for the other aspect of his use of romance, the poetic and tragic aspect—the secret of which he possessed more fully than

any of his contemporaries, including Poe—his work would long since
have ceased to possess any revelatory powers, and would by now have
been relegated to the ranks of literary curiosities. But Hawthorne did
not merely content himself with embroidering upon macabre and fantastic backgrounds, as Charles Brockden Brown and Mrs. Radcliffe
did, or upon historical events as Sir Walter Scott did, in order to delight the reader with their picturesque compositions. It was more from
Spenser and Bunyan than he learned how to construct a scene and
make it at once epic and symbolic: Endicott in his armor defying England, Hester in the pillory. Instead of limiting himself to mere adventures, to the picaresque, he elevated his themes to the level of an ideal
quest that in works like "The Great Carbuncle" has more in common
with that of Don Quixote than that of Gil Blas. Far from limiting himself to sentimental idylls, he leads us with him, sometimes to Arcadia,
as in *The Marble Faun*, at other times, and more gladly, toward Eden,
at times bathed in light, at times beneath a pall. Finally, in an age when
Emersonian optimism was at its triumphant peak, no one had a
greater feeling than Hawthorne for tragic inevitability. The "dark necessity"[28] that presides over the unfurling of the plot in *The Scarlet
Letter*, or "Young Goodman Brown," or "The Minister's Black Veil,"
is an organic, Dionysiac necessity. And it is here that we are able to put
our finger on the all-important difference between the work born of the
heart's experience and the work born of the mind's will. *The House of
the Seven Gables* is based upon a moral and sociological idea[29] and
upon the melodramatic search for a material inheritance, not upon the
imaginative re-creation of time past. Psychology and art, life and form
do not always obey the hand that attempts to assemble the materials of
a book as an intellectual wager, rather than as an object guided by an
esthetic intuition and the imperious desire to create. And later on, this
divorce between art and thought, between moral interpretation and
organic development, continually increased. *The Scarlet Letter*, for instance, which is based upon an innate knowledge, as it were, and upon
an experience slowly ripened in accordance with the logic of themes
by then in the forefront of the artist's preoccupations and demanding
urgent utterance—*The Scarlet Letter* found its natural formulation, the
form that the subject was crying out for. Moreover it is the work that
marks the richest moment of Hawthorne's consciousness, the moment
at which it attained its maximum of psychological, moral, and esthetic
depth and scope. And the scope is here a function of the depths: the

confined setting of pillory and market place extends much further into the imaginary sphere than his later and disproportionately vast décor of ancient monuments and the Roman campagna, or than all of James's "transatlantic" background. The denser a work's substance is wrought, the greater its power of explosion. It is the sign that the workman began his task at the very heart of life. Hawthorne's works are embroidery in depth.

IV. OBERON'S ARABESQUES

The storyteller, in the beginning, took over a given, traditional theme upon which he then improvised—embroidered—as his fancy dictated. Hawthorne was not content merely to invent new episodes and incidents: he wove his fabric inwardly and upon multiple levels. This fundamental fabric for his work would begin to form into twisted threads as soon as the germs and themes started to develop. "Tendrils"[1] would reach out, tentative extensions that far from remaining divergent would meet each other, join, and intertwine as they alternately moved away from the central germ, then back to it again. The arabesque thus formed was inscribed in the very genes of the work, in the convolutions of the consciousness itself. And later, as the thematic motifs met the decorative motifs, the arabesque became more complex and highly developed still. Each work being a sphere, this interwoven fabric found itself enclosed by an inward facing mirror in which it was constantly being reflected back into itself. In "The Hollow of the Three Hills," the concave rock walls send the echoes and images whose interweaving fills the hollow perpetually ricocheting back into the center of it; in "Young Goodman Brown," the black arras of the forest is moving in a circle around the central character just as much as he is exploring his own inner labyrinth through the forest's sinuosities; and in "Main Street," it is the images that circle around the inside of the showman's box as well as time.

In the novels, the dramatic threads intersect: the fates of Hester, Dimmesdale, and Chillingworth are indissociable, and the images that evoke each of their lives all move in orbit around the pillory. The same phenomenon occurs on a flattened or merely curved screen in the works that tend to stand apart from the main Hawthorne canon, particularly in The Marble Faun. The arabesque defines the broad lines and the movement of the work; it holds all its elements together in a more or less tightly knit web. The story of young Goodman Brown develops psychologically in accordance with a blueprint based on the nocturnal growth of trees and the intersecting toils of forest paths—esthetically, in accordance with the theme of the embroidery created by the branches overhead. Hester's story unfolds into a rose window from the tragic, central starkness of the pillory—the tree, the deformed human being, which is about to explode into red, eruptive, insinuating flower. Hawthorne, in his art as well as his personal inclinations, was torn between stark severity and luxuriance. By concealing her hair—her "light and graceful foliage"[2]—Hester identifies herself with the shape of the pillory, which signifies the mortification of the flesh; by loosing it, she identifies herself with the Letter as she herself has embroidered it, the emblem of her generous and sensual nature.[3] On the one hand she oscillates between ascetic petrifaction and the flowering of her flesh, on the other she hesitates between statuesque beauty and the exuberance of the forest's virgin foliage.[4] This is certainly the image suggested to the mind by the lovely Georgiana, the "Gothic" Scheherazade against the background of tapestries and hangings that have transformed the laboratory into a harem, and by the radiant Beatrice among her tropical flowers. Hester, a statue of beauty and scarlet sin, is not, any more than her sisters, a statue of Apollonian inspiration, naked beneath the devouring light that insists upon absolute and abstract perfection of line. She stands in a vast "Gothic" and Dionysian tapestry like Botticelli's Venus in the center of the bow for which she is the arrow. Phoebe, who moves like a bird of paradise among the somber leaves and dismal objects around her, and Hilda, with her halo of doves in flight, both share, though on another level, in the movement of this arabesque, which also bears among its leaves and flowers and fruits the red buds of the liana of sin and poisonous berries, and which orders the variousness of life and its moral contrasts in obedience to the esthetic line of its growth. The foliage that Endicott holds to be superfluous, Hawthorne, on the other hand, takes to be necessary: it is useful to him in creating this arabesque that is at the foundation of his art, and which, far from merely being a method of ornamenting and framing his allegorical characters in a vast decorative composition, insinuates its innumerable ramifications deep inside them in order to twine itself into the complex fabric of the consciousness from which it drew its sap. The Letter that covers Hester with its fiery flowers certainly serves in the office of a mask or veil: it is the finest of finery as well as a sign of degradation, a shimmering mantle of poverty and pride. It is its wearer's social and metaphysical double, angel and demon, which exteriorizes itself and is reflected in every mirror.[5] But is it no more than a reflection—a psychological and moral illusionist's trick? The metamorphosis occurs in both directions: the woman becomes the Letter just as much as the Letter becomes the woman. The threads of the Letter and the fibers of Hester's consciousness are inextricably mingled, to such an extent that they quiver with pain in unison, for the outward embroidery, far from being no more than an ornament, is the substance of the living being beneath revealed in all its living ambiguity and complexity.[6]

In opposition to the vegetable arabesque we also find the geometrical arabesque. The abstract line first sketched in the streets through which Wakefield and Robin both wander[7] is continued in the stylized contours of the monuments that serve as Endicott's constant background as well as in those of Peter Goldthwaite's house, then reappears in the simplified features of the Great Stone Face before reaching its highest peak of elaboration in the House of the Seven Gables, where it is nevertheless complemented by the vegetable curves of the tree. We find, moreover, that the serpentine vegetable forms, the snaky sinuosities and coiling lianas in Hawthorne's work actively provoke the antagonism of the straight line, the acute, aggressive angle.[8] The dragon calls out for the lance and the lance for the dragon. The hydra of the Letter challenges the pillory and the Puritan sword; the bellicose gables of the Pyncheon house challenge the feminine womb of the elm; the "blithe dale" opposes the ugly and dismal buildings of the town; just as the capricious line of the faun's saraband and the convolutions of his final pilgrimage are measured and marked out by rigid milestones in the form of immobile churches, palaces, and towers.

Sinuous, broken, or combining vegetable tracery with geometric precision, the arabesque surrounds and invades all the elements of the work, and the broadness of its conception in no way mars the minuteness of its details. The picturesque elements, the local color, instead of being a mere surface layer are integrated into the ancestral theme: the miniatures and historic cameos have their proper places in the epic of the past; the pointed gables of the houses, the pointed Puritan hats, the stiff furniture, and the suits of armor are all there not so much in order to reconstitute an epoch to which many Americans looked back with nostalgia as to evoke, in contradictory terms of protection and oppression, throughout the whole length of a vast symbolic tapestry, the figure of the father. The "Dutch minuteness"[9] that is to be found in the descriptive passages of *The House of the Seven Gables* is closely related to the architecture of the whole and to the fundamental themes. The ornaments of angular and pointed iron bring out the aggressive, masculine, paternal character of the House, the wooden globes its feminine and maternal nature.[10] And the old furniture, the portrait of the ancestor, the pictured tiles, the worn carpet, the map of the old Pyncheon estate,[11] far from having an air of stagey bric-a-brac, seem quite at home in the half light of the parlor, which is like a recess, a hidden fold of the past. Even the culinary details are perceptible emanations of a past age relived in all its joys, its customs, and its beliefs: the fabulous fish, the abundant game of the new Eden, like Hepzibah's meticulous preparation of Clifford's food, are the materials of succulent still lives, more worthy of delighting the noses and palates of pagan gods than of weighing down the tables of dignitaries and ministers for whom all food was a gift of Providence.[12] Though admittedly the haphazard collection of cabinetwork, statuettes, and coins that occurs in the story of Alice is less happily used, its only real function being to provide an excuse for the introduction of a moral conceit:[13] it shows Hawthorne already yielding to the unfortunate tendency toward clutter and allegorical heavy-handedness that was to destroy his art. The market place in *The Scarlet Letter*, on the other hand, presents us with a perfect example of his ability to integrate a great variety of elements. Around the central symbol of the woman-hieroglyph, there is the tightly clustered provincial microcosm that comprises both a picture of ethnic evolution and a retrospective evocation of Europe, not for the sake of its monuments, but representing the image of a distant childhood that can never be recalled:[14] measuring the distance between Hester and modern America, we are able to embrace at a glance the changing condition of woman in time, without any useless dissertations. The unity is achieved by stylization, by nice subordination to the inward theme, and by dint of poetic and dramatic short cuts.

Certain objects are outlined with particular care by the curling fronds of the arabesque and set apart in the same way that the characters sometimes are. In this way they are wrought and lit within the work as a whole as they have been once already in the mind of the allegorist. The blacksmith Danforth's hand would be inadequate for this task: it needs that of an Owen Warland to provide the final finish. Similarly, Holgrave's dark room, though suitable for honest artisan work, could never have brought forth such striking images had its occupant not been to some small degree a wizard. As for Kenyon's statues, they would be no more, in fact, than "nameless machines in human shape,"[15] if he too did not possess the secret he makes use of, in his studio, and even more in his mind, of playing with specters. The objects thus isolated and brought into prominence by means of delicate manipulations that already begin to cast light and shade in a cinematographic role, become objects of art, or at any rate, fetish objects that are struggling to achieve poetic existence. The pagan, almost druidic, altar in its circle of fire[16] is at the same time a nightmare object and a poem object, as is the lime kiln that actually contains the fire within itself, and rages redly in its sheath of night.[17] The tree-gibbet, stark as a lance in the cold,[18] becomes that other, mutilated tree—outlined with tragic shadow like Grünewald's *Crucifixion*, or with glaring light like certain of Goya's dwarfs—the pillory, that magnetic central point of the dismal human orbit. The pillory was without doubt the most extraordinary of the surrealist objects that Hawthorne discovered and employed, long before the strange agglomerations created by André Breton. No other fetish in his work, except the black veil, achieves the same intensity of suggestive power—not the wooden figurehead, or the snow image, or the metal butterfly, or the Great Stone Face. And lastly the House, the most common of objects, yet naturally a reservoir of dreams, succeeds, thanks to an elaborate process of stylization, in imposing itself as a massive poem object, many-visaged, encased in greenery, lit by the sun and the moon, and moated round by the currents of humanity and time. The pictures, too, are set in relief by the curls of the arabesque, folds of darkness or half-darkness from which we see emerging the faces of the ancestors[19] or the pastel tints of a young man or woman's portrait, that of Clifford or Phoebe.[20] The Rembrandt-like portrait Hawthorne paints for us of Hepzibah is framed in doorways[21] or dark corridors against a background of pitch, or lit by a slanting light beneath the low and beamed ceiling of the parlor, against a background of tapestry like an illuminated manuscript: the picture becomes a miniature comparable to a certain portrait of Ann Pollard by an unknown artist,[22] stiff and clumsily limned, but, like the figure of Lady Pepperell all in dark browns and black,[23] bearing the unmistakable stamp of a style: the Puritan style, and also, in a sense, by contagion with the "gothick," Pre-Raphaelite as well, the style we see most fully realized in the complex depiction of Hester —a style whose secret Hawthorne was to hand on to Henry James, another portraitist of "ladies,"[24] who owed a great deal to Oberon's use of the arabesque.

Moreover, even the flora and the fauna have their role to play in Hawthorne's arabesques, functioning, as in medieval illuminations and primitive paintings as ornaments and symbols. The picture book and the fairy tale have always made an inseparable pair. Peter Goldthwaite's house is decorated inside with naive allegories,[25] and the Reverend Mr. Dimmesdale's apartment is hung with a tapestry whose Biblical subject,[26] that of David and Bathsheba, evokes the adultery of a "saint." The House of the Seven Gables has its pictured tiles,[27] its toys and its gingerbread figures,[28] its cookery book illustrated with engravings,[29] and above all the map with its pictures of wild beasts and Indians, and the tea service decorated with its grotesque figures of birds and beasts.[30] Similarly, in one corner of the forest landscape we find a tame wolf,[31] in the autumnal Eden of *The Marble Faun* a lizard with two tails to startle the guilty Adam,[32] and close by the fountain, the plant with its fiery flowers[33] like an orange tree painted by Hieronymus Bosch.

Oberon's arabesques have a double substance: they are composed both of luminous color and living shadow, interglazed. There is the somber background of forest vegetation and Puritan austerity, and then, standing out from it, the proud façades of the aristocratic houses,[34] the dazzle of armor, the bright, vivid colors of the flower garlands that underline the grace of the tiny witch,[35] the moving lines of the great decorative and dramatic curves that draw the characters of the poetic allegory out into a vast procession, following a ritual path that is Spenserian in origin but totally original in its oneiric and esthetic themes, even down to the palette and the musical invention employed. Color[36] has an emotional and allegorical value as well as a pictorial value in any literary work. Hawthorne is the painter of vivid clashes rather than subtle shadings. The fresh green of youth and the new shoot—and even the Letter has its green season[37]—the gold of summer, of wealth, of corn and hair,[38] and above all the dazzling explosion of red, we find them all slashed over grounds of dark green—which to the mind's eye is black: the melancholy trees, the moss on the tombs[39]—over the brown of bare earth,[40] the grey of old age, poverty and dreary frost,[41] and the white of the beautiful but cruel winter, which is that of lilies and those who die too young.[42] Though this does not prevent colors and seasons from commingling in the poet's eye.[43] The intensity of the color is closely dependent upon its psychological associations: the scarlet of the Letter is a visual obsession. Which is why it is also possible—and Hawthorne excels at this—to create color simply by conjuring up objects—trees, cabins, desolate fields[44]—or even acts and thoughts: what could be greyer than his evocations of Hester's and Hepzibah's daily lives? Elsewhere, things are stripped of their specific colors in order that they may lend them to some interior landscape:[45] it is inside the minister's soul that the "grey twilight" of the forest falls;[46] it is inside Ethan Brand's that the fire rages; it is inside Peter Goldthwaite's imagination that the gold shines. Though Hawthorne, like a "Sunday" painter, employs simple and vivid colors, those of Homer and the Song of Roland, though he does not hesitate to reproduce the rainbows of primitive art,[47] it is always against a somber background—black velvet sky, pitch-black night—that he sets them blazing. It is still the New England Indian summer flaming in the thickets of the arabesque, but transformed into a nocturnal firework display: the blackness makes the red and the green and the yellow sing, as in a poem by Apollinaire.[48] But to set against this hellish and tragic blackness, it is not cerulean blue that Hawthorne chooses, but red again, the red of blood—the color and the substance that of all others are the most propitious for the most various of combinations. What painter is not also an alchemist? Color is only apparently fixed: portraits live, for in each likeness he paints the painter rouses a Dorian Gray. The painting is a ground of perpetual metamorphoses under cover of dim shadows. The nocturnal shapes that glow around a central ember, instead of standing out against a pale background melt into a twilit, flickering environment. We perceive the "black flower" by its psychic aura rather than by its color. And the silhouettes of Hepzibah, of Dimmesdale, of Chillingworth, and Goodman Brown all form an integral part of this nocturnal arabesque. They are shadow bodies that draw their substance from the shadows. And in the same way, those with bodies of fire are incorporated into the arabesques of flame, the forest fire, the aurora borealis, which also needs the dark if it is to exist. The forest lights up: the eyes of the beast—Blake's Tyger; incandescent silhouettes appear —Milton's Lucifer, whom we are perhaps seeing in the shape of flaming pines, or the meteor. These are the scarlet flowers of the great black tree, the lianas of fire winding around the charcoal tree, the negative of the tree of life, whose sap seeks in the underground dark for employment. The symbol of the Letter appears once more in its many-faceted richness: the red flower, the flower of evil, is also, like Baudelaire's flowers, the flower of life: the fibers of the arabesque intertwine at every level, all the elements are woven each into the others—good and evil, life and death—all united in a single intricate web. Even the voices become mingled with the visual images: the cries in the forest split its blackness like lightning flashes;[49] Pearl's scream is a sudden rent in the austere Puritan tapestry.[50] This art, composed in contrasts, is akin to the esthetic of Beethoven. *The Scarlet Letter* is a vast concerto in red and black: a formula that Hawthorne has in fact more claim to than Stendhal if one is thinking in terms of color alone. Moreover the soloist's role and the orchestral contribution are interchangeable: the central theme is taken up at times by the red element (Hester in the pillory),[51] sometimes by the black (Hester at her sewing)[52]—both of them possessing the same psychological and esthetic ambivalence. But as a symphonist, despite his mastery of his art, Hawthorne failed in the same way as he failed as a fresco painter. The faun's symphony, imperfectly constructed as it is, can hardly sustain the comparison with Beethoven that might have suggested itself if the author's ambition alone were what counted. In fact, however, the work is no more than an abortive masterpiece consisting, as it were, of a few fragments of the "Pastoral" that have somehow been put together with some larger chunks from the "Choral."[53] Oberon's arabesques could not survive being unfurled; they had to remain coiled in upon themselves: they represent an involutive dream-process as much as a decorative and esthetic method.

Hawthorne's work is essentially circuitous: a circuitousness dictated by art as well as by modesty, by caprice as well as by allegorical ritual. His treatment of all his principal themes is based upon the arabesque, which is the very image both of the storyteller's profound contradictions and of his brilliant gift of fancy. The House is enveloped in its spiral; the embroidery of the Letter ramifies out even into the forest and the meteor, thus achieving cosmic proportions. Its tendrils encircle all the secondary spheres of the work, and their interweaving is apparent even in its smallest details: the sinuous path traced by Reverend Wilson's lantern, or by the stream, or by the serpent, or by Pearl in her capricious flights—the entire labyrinth of a universe created in the image of the red and gold threads winding over the breast of an adulterous woman, in the image of the human heart's inward labyrinth. What circuitous routes to state the facts, but also what a wealth of meaning, what complexity those facts acquire in the process—so that they cease in the end to be facts and become the stuff of life. It is a further proof of this circuitousness that Hawthorne, instead of simply illustrating the perdition of a man's soul, makes him wander through every possibility in human nature from crime to saintliness, including hypocrisy on the way. And it is also by dint of the same circuitousness that this Puritan book, dealing with adultery after its consummation, succeeds in conveying the violence of sexuality with such overwhelming intensity. It took the conversion of the terrible Puritan inhibition against the flesh into an equally terrible indiscretion at once spurred on and checked by remorse, to produce this incredible fabric of prudish evasions, tortured scruples, and reluctant but also at times explosive revelations. An art that requires such virtuosity of its author is at the mercy of the slightest weakening of the creative faculty. And Hawthorne, as soon as he felt himself slipping, began to overload, to generalize, to become sententious; so that his allegory became a mask for poverty. The theme was lost, his work was buried beneath the overabundance of details, of implications that were referring to nothing central, or essential, or vital. Why do we believe so little in the myth of the faun yet so strongly in that of the tiny witch-girl, if not for these reasons? He almost succeeds in convincing us—the tiny noises among the leaves, the abrupt appearance of the lizard—but no, the Orphic charm remains inoperative, and the author has not dared to make his hero a real faun, whereas Pearl is without doubt, in every accepted meaning of the term, a real witch.[54] Once such a physical presence has been created, the superabundance of the details becomes a matter of invention and fancy.[55] In "Alice Doane," "The Artist of the Beautiful," and "Rappacini's Daughter" every touch is infinitely precious, whether it be a ray of moonlight, a studio, or a garden.[56] Excelling as he did in poetic renderings of the invisible and of the soul's secrets, Hawthorne reveals himself as a master of indirect evocation. The tragedy of Walter Ludlow and his wife Elinor is told to us through their portraits —that is to say, in the person of their doubles,—and Reverend Hooper comes to understand what he is through the intermediary of a mirror.[57] In like manner, Hawthorne, instead of showing us the Great Carbuncle unveils its light: for it refers to a truth that is not meant to be gazed upon by the observer's eye, but by the inward eye.[58] The truth contained in the Letter, the pillory, and the House is of the same order. The supreme circuitousness of Hawthorne's art lies without doubt in the fact that he was able to take the beliefs and superstitions of the past and to couple them with his personal obsessions in order to give birth to miraculous monsters: Pearl, the little witch-girl and her fairy train of legend, Hester, the adulteress who, through her passion, and because she is presented to us in a wholly unprecedented light, achieves the beauty and the truth of a myth restored to youth, a myth made modern.

· 2 ·

The Diorama

I. LIGHT AND SHADE

Hawthorne was revealed to himself by Bunyan and Spenser. He borrowed from them what already belonged to him, in advance and by right. Far from contenting himself with employing Spenser's own form of the arabesque, he elaborated it in depth and, through his particular use of lighting effects, worked his way toward an entirely new form of the romance. His own use of the arabesque permitted the emergence of a cinematic use of pictorial depth and images.

Every reality is calling out for its poet. But the poet must nevertheless have a means at his disposal of capturing that reality, and generally speaking this means is revealed to him by his very vision of the world. If Hawthorne continued after his illness was over to shut himself away in order to look at things in the dark,[1] if he displayed an interest in magic lantern shows and fairground dioramas,[2] he did so in no dilettante spirit but with deliberate intent. It was upon a foundation of shadow that he built up his technique of indirect lighting. Light came for him, as it did for Van Gogh, through darkness. The light of the world after the Fall, the "pensive shade" in which man developed after the first sin was to his eyes richer in significance and artistic possibilities than the "brighter sunshine."[3] It was against this "strange and somber background of superstition and mystery" that he admitted to depicting the human soul. So that his filtering vision was provided, on the esthetic level, with good justification, since it naturally facilitated both the interplay of shadows and the perception of abysmal vistas. Hawthorne saw and touched the consciousness rather than heard its murmur, and he unveiled its secrets in visual terms.[4] The chiaroscuro of his own consciousness, which was that of the attic room, not that of the cellar, encouraged interior "shots." Though the light may at first seem to be devoured by the shadows, it is none the less capable of giving brilliance to the black tones—the armor, Hester's hair—and though it does not manifest itself except through shadow, it is by its means that the shadow achieves its form and brilliance.

Hawthorne's images had, from the very outset, a cinematic value. His reveries, full of reflections and phantasmagoria, seized first of all upon schematic forms, black cutouts that he sometimes left imprinted upon a wall or a floor—his characters' specters[5] or doubles.[6] The spark was produced by friction, and the puppet of wood or cloth, the black cutout profile became a rough draft of the figurehead, of Hester, of Hepzibah. From a female form long caressed in the mind there was to emanate the light that also lit up its satellites by reflection. The Scarlet Letter lights up all the spectators, the square, the prison, the church, the notables' Areopagus. It is the center around which the circle is described, from which the sphere grows. The light's rays, instead of being divergent, are convergent; they are reflected back by peripheral mirrors onto the central object: the pillory, the House, revolve in the beams of klieg lights. Their aspects become various, their significance is enriched. In the same way, the stiff and naked puppets clothe themselves in light and shadow, begin to live; shadow and light become flesh, or at the very least, movement. The beams projected through the tracery of the arabesque glimmer in changing forms, like the dappled sunlight of an arbor.[7] The Letter on Hester's breast shines, projects its contradictory signals, writhes, twists out of shape, and becomes, in its turn, as it were a magic lantern beaming its own magnified and wavering form up onto the screen of the sky.[8] Hawthorne's beings and things often seem to have been draped in this way with the poet's mantle through which the carbuncle glows.[9] It is also by the relations of dark and light, by the use of different light values, that he suggests the presence of a particular object or character, as Michelangelo made use of shadows and hollows to create mystery and drama in the realm of sculpture.[10] The furious onrush of the Puritans intent on cutting down the Merry Mount maypole is materialized as an irruption of shadows,[11] and the town beadle emerging from the prison is simply a black mass advancing into the light.[12] Hawthorne even goes further than this when his psychological and moral vision of blackness within blackness leads him to invent a technique of shadow overlaying shadow, or shadow inlaid in shadow. Goodman Brown, the witch of "The Hollow of the Three Hills," Chillingworth, Dimmesdale, and Hepzibah all appear to us in a cinematic dream shot in black and black, black against a dark background, like Ryder's[13] Siegfried and Macbeth, molded out of the dense substance of human grief itself.

Conversely, he also has a technique of light within light. The radiance of the carbuncle blazes out into an atmosphere already luminous in itself,[14] the dazzle of the Letter becomes even more feverish in the sparkle of noon, and the child in the wood is another Little Red Riding-Hood who glows even brighter in her ray of sunlight.[15] Hester's metamorphosis is the consecration of woman by light: the hair, a fetish to Baudelaire, here mingled with the arabesques of the foliage, becomes bright and shining, yet also retains a lustrous, shadowy density.[16] It is at the same moment an image of love and of death, of the flesh and the soul, and the face emerges from these shimmering, multiple contrasts like a spring of youth. The whole of nature shares in this renewal: the leaves flame, the stream laughs its luminous laugh back at the sun, and the leaden heart of the shadowy forest turns to gold as the woman is transformed into the queen of the fairies.[17] This process of sublimation, which is also an esthetic "developer," is a method usually restricted to the use of the halo, which enables us to view a scene as though in a lighted aquarium, a face in the glowing circle of a lamp, at the fireside,[18] or, in Phoebe's case, lit by its own inner radiance.[19] The story of "The Wives of the Dead" is told to us wholly through images formed in a succession of such haloes. The lamp moves from one room to another, awakening the ghosts that lie asleep in the old furniture,[20] then glows around the figure of a woman at the window, while below, in a glowing circle of redness, the innkeeper appears.[21] Then, after the lantern of the messenger as he moves away has offered us fragmentary glimpses of a world by night,[22] we return to the chiaroscuro of the room above in time to see a second figure appearing at the window, a twin of the first, a figurehead in front of whom the young sailor stands dripping and shining beneath the moon.[23] And the tale ends with the vision of a woman asleep in the circle of a lamp,[24] a vision worthy of La Tour in its delicate sensuality. In *The Scarlet*

Letter it is an entire galaxy that glitters into life during the night of
the minister's vigil: the lamp of the Governor, and that of the witch,
and Reverend Wilson's lantern. This short passage is the equivalent
of Van Gogh's *Starry Night*. Then, when all these minor luminaries
have been absorbed by the pillory's dark night, suddenly the great
rout of the darkness occurs: the black sky is invaded by the flaming
redness of the Letter, dilating like a luminous eye upon a screen.

Any attempt to reduce the visual technique Hawthorne conceived
and employed to its "gothick" or Romantic elements is merely a refusal to see. We do not look at Van Gogh's paintings in order to see Rembrandt in them. Hawthorne invented the visual technique of the cinema
on a literary level before the movie camera even existed, whereas
Dos Passos simply transposed cinematic techniques into the novel
after they had been established. This visual technique is based upon
chiaroscuro, which gives his objects that "charm of romance" to which
admirers of fashionable literature were at that time peculiarly sensitive.
In Hawthorne, however, this surface charm is only one very deceptive
aspect of his methods of creating atmosphere and pictorial or dramatic
effects. Far from merely contenting himself with a softening of his
light and forms in order to obtain pleasant and anodyne illusions, his
intention was to create a total ambiguity that would enable him to
achieve the freest possible interplay of substances, identities, and
physical, moral, and psychological realities. What a difference between
the simply mystery of the "Veiled Lady"[25] and that of Reverend
Hooper. When the black veil moves as he speaks,[26] it is not only the
man's breathing that we perceive but also his soul. In the same way,
Hawthorne's half-hidden portraits allow us to sense their secret life.
The sickly-pale faces of the nervous, imaginative, tormented beings
that Hawthorne was so prone to select as his protagonists are best
suited by a livid or filtered light, one that adds a play of ambiguity to
the play of emotions in their facial expressions. The Puritan crowd
with its austere costumes and expressions provides a setting for Chillingworth's features exactly equivalent to the half-darkness they must
have in order to reveal the hate beneath them and set off their serpentine writhings.[27] Dimmesdale's, which give such intense expression to
his contradictory feelings,[28] avoid direct light.[29] Hepzibah's face as she
sits back from the window receives a reflection of the evening light
that emphasizes her pallor and reveals, not merely the expression of
the face, but the quality of the hidden emotion.[30] The Judge's bloodless

face cries out for the cold light of the moon, which suggests the coldness of death, ultimate image of inhuman coldheartedness.[31] Donatello, Miriam, and the Model, demand the uncolored lighting that falls upon the wan plaster casts in painters' and sculptors' studios at that bleak hour when masks can assume such suddenly disquieting expressions.[32] The dark, demoniac faces call rather for the reflections from a fire, etching them into deep, tragic lines, like Ethan Brand's, or Chillingworth's, which popular imagination has even covered in a layer of soot.[33] A single hurried smudge of the thumb, and art could become mere artifice.

As the arabesque slows down a work's movement with its circuitousness, so this use of light and shade is a source of indecisiveness, of hesitation. All art, whether allegorical or cinematic, contains an element of ceremony that is not mere mannerism but a deliberately selected method directed toward a particular goal. We often find Hawthorne's principal characters appearing in a neutral atmosphere, in a "grey medium,"[34] or a brown one: Wakefield, Hepzibah, Dimmesdale —whose very name conjures up the grey of fading light. What Hawthorne was experimenting with here, in the literary field, was the "soft focus," a method that Griffith was to rediscover later for the movies.[35] This process not only renders the faces indistinct, evasive, but also means that we do not see them until after they have passed across the screen: it filters out the details, the features, and then allows them to settle gradually into their final forms. Hepzibah's features are as vague as her own nearsighted image of the world.[36] There is an identification of the character with her vision of things—of the character and the world as that character's mind conceives it: black in Reverend Hooper's case,[37] red and black in Hester's and Dimmesdale's. The chiaroscuro that surrounds these characters and reigns in their minds is a direct emanation from the consciousness of their creator. In the shortest of his works ("The Hollow of the Three Hills," "The Wives of the Dead") the purely atmospheric images, freed from having to compete with plot images and explanatory visual additions, preserve all their power; so that their suggestive values are sometimes able to take the mind much further than even the longest novel. In *The House of the Seven Gables*, the fleeting pastoral evocation in the half-light of the parlor[38] only makes one regret all the more sharply the presence of certain other, nugatory pages.

Sound is an enormously important element in the creation of atmos-

phere. It can associate itself with light to the point of acquiring a value
of luminosity itself. The richness of the sound track in Hawthorne's
work often goes hand in hand with the visual intensity of light and
shade. Sound and light combine, echo one another, or create a counterpoint. While the flotsam of the wreck burns in the hearth, the voice of
the ocean moans outside.[39] As dusk descends, the witch's incantation
rises.[40] Answering the blows on the door below, the lamp lights up the
window.[41] As young Goodman Brown shrieks with demented laughter,
the flames of the forest fire flicker in reply.[42] Or the shouts in the
darkened town suddenly become flaming torches.[43] Elsewhere, sounds
and light, or sounds and darkness, are fused. Hepzibah's skilfully re-
tarded entrance is preceded by evocative sounds of footsteps and
stiff, rustling silks in the half-darkness.[44] Indirectly, without insisting,
Hawthorne is making us think of ghosts. When he does in fact insist,
then the effects are more elaborate, less surely brought off, and certainly less poetic. Phoebe, about to fall asleep, hears heavy steps and
"a strange, vague murmur": we are already on the path to "gothick"
horror.[45] The ray of light that plays across the Judge's face is also
attempting to lead us a little too deliberately into the world of phantasmagoric fantasy. But the noises, the creaks, the bellowings, the
sighings, and sobs for which the House serves as a resonating box[46]—
the House can be a demoniac organ—are orchestrated with a master's
hand, and not only in such a way as to awaken disquiet, to alert
sensation seekers, even though the furtive apparition of the "grimalkin"
does introduce a somewhat cabalistic note.[47] The same cannot be said,
however, of Westervelt's appearance in the dusky light of the wood,
reverberating with distant Spenserian and Shakespearian echoes as the
traitor's false teeth glimmer in the gloom.[48] Or of the exhibition of
the monk's corpse that starts to bleed to the accompaniment of almost
spell-like chantings.[49] How much more subtle, more striking, and more
beautiful the associative inspirations used to create atmosphere are
in the works that precede *The House of the Seven Gables.* The steps
that tell Sylph Etherege of her beloved's approach,[50] falling as they do
into the void of her expectation, attain a wholly different and greater
degree of value than those of Clifford in Phoebe's ears. And the murmur of lowered voices "whispering many comfortable passages of the
Scriptures" in the half-light of a house in mourning has strange and
infinite reverberations.[51] When material objects have been dematerial-
ized by the play of light and shadows, then it is the immaterial that

materializes in its turn, and sounds first and foremost. The minister's voice itself turns to metal as it gives the hollow armor a soul.[52] The silhouettes of the two mourning sisters become blurred into the background of the darkened room, while the laments of the one and the silence of the other fill the stage like two beings of flesh and blood.[53] "The confused and doubtful sound of voices" passing overhead in the night is sufficient to indicate the flight of the witches without it even being necessary to name them.[54] Dimmesdale's cry, a flash of fire through the night, becomes a hard and solid object with which evil spirits play at ball:[55] one is reminded of Rip van Winkle. But the implications of the fantasy here go much further: it is an entire universe of beliefs, of superstitions, and of suffering, that is being evoked.

The "soundtrack" in Hawthorne's work, though it is for the most part discreet and fades to a pianissimo when accompanying scenes bathed in a veiled or diffused light, can also well up, as it does during Goodman Brown's journey through the night, into a succession of wave-like crescendoes. Everything begins with an inward murmur: Goodman Brown talking to himself.[56] The laugh of the stranger[57] and the old woman's cry[58] are a prelude to the uproar that is to follow. The horsemen appear: the horses' hoofs are a warning drum.[59] They pass by, and the first wave of hellish murmurs fills the sky.[60] Goodman Brown begins to shriek like a man possessed. A second wave of cries unfurls around him.[61] Now he is wholly maddened, and the forest in its frenzy submerges him beneath a third wave of panic-struck cries that hurls him panting onto the fringe of the clearing.[62] At that point he seems to become deaf, as though no longer able to perceive anything but the play being acted out by the shadows. Then the chanting begins again, sad, funereal, only to be swept aside by yet another wave of wild cries. Then comes the thunder of the voice announcing the hellish baptism.[63] Goodman Brown is all eyes during the ceremony, up until the moment when we find him again, utterly drained, in the extinguished forest flooded with the calm of returning dawn.[64] Silences can be no less intense than cries. That which expresses the fixity of the gazes concentered on Hester's breast, gazes heavy with mortifying fascination and spellbound with sexuality[65]—that which expresses the effort of the mental rapist to penetrate his victim's mind, or his satanic ecstasy when he has done so.[66] At those moments, everything is concentrated in the eye. At others, it is all in the ear. Though the cry also has a visual value. It is a fiery point, an explosion of pain, like the shriek of childbirth that Hester restrains in the pillory.[67] That cry is, in fact, recorded. From the psychological and esthetic point of view it counts: we are pierced by it, just as Hester is torn apart by it inwardly in the process of giving birth—before the eyes of all—to the letter *A*, and its inward reverberation adds even further to the cruelty of the flaming noon. Pearl's screech,[68] a cry of warning and arousal, is uttered among all the gathered dignitaries and is a dagger in the heart of the father who dares not acknowledge the witch-child, the child of the Letter, as his own. The highest point of auditory intensity is attained during the night scene on the pillory: it is the cries that create the light. Dimmesdale's, an indirect reference to that earlier illicit and agonizing birth, lights the townspeople's lamps, while Pearl's repeated laughter summons the meteor.[69] The final cry of the book is Dimmesdale's confession, a stifled, pathetic cry upon which everything dissolves and falls apart.[70] By punctuating his works in this way with auditory explosions that tear through the arabesque in those places where it becomes densest, Hawthorne gives proof of genuine mastery over the technique of montage on multiple levels. By dint of delving into man's consciousness and seeking for the means of rendering it palpable, of revealing its torments, its complexity, and its hidden beauty, he discovered a new art. It was the mind's eye that was to provide him with the literary equivalents of the movie screen and camera.

II. SCREEN AND CAMERA

The mirror, the painting, the wall—all ancestors of the movie screen. The mirror has an esthetic as well as a psychological function. It receives images, stores them up, then gives them back to us again at certain privileged moments[1] by means of its blurry magic and its chiaroscuro spell. It is in the mirror that the "visions" besieging the mind become intensified.[2] The mirror is in reality an inward thing: it is upon the screens of their imaginations that Hawthorne's characters see themselves and discover what they are—as Reverend Hooper, Roderick Elliston, and Hester Prynne all do. What passes across that screen is more real than reality. It is in the mirror that the true scene of the elixir of youth's false miracle takes place:[3] with Swiftian savagery Hawthorne displays beneath the brutal rivalry of two young men in love the soured jealousy, the bitter lees of conscience, that lies rankling in the minds of men when they are old. It is not on the shoulders of some beautiful creature whose charming features may be lying that the true face of love is to be found, but in the waters of the spring,[4] from which the face of terror can also look out.[5] It is in the water of the Trevi Fountain that the trinity of crime come, even before their crime, to drown their heavy shadows like stones, like damned souls weighted with sin.[6] For Hawthorne there is no real image but the most inward image of all, whether it be utterly hideous or utterly beautiful. This is why his characters need their inner reflections: they need both to know the truth about themselves and also to provide us with an image of themselves capable of taking shape with equal intensity in the recesses of our consciousness, and of finding out its own resemblance there. Paintings, portraits, mirror: all screens for the soul to project itself upon. The old portrait of Colonel Pyncheon is still able to throw as much light on the character of the Judge as the freshly printed daguerreotype can.[7] The delicate miniature so piously preserved by Hepzibah is, for all time, the real Clifford. It is the only happy image that still lives on, safe in the cranny it has always occupied, within the dimmed imagination of an old woman whose true emotional face is the one revealed to us by her inward mirrors[8] in one of those enigmatic perspectives so dear to Quentin Metzys and Memling. We also see Hester and Pearl reflected in this way, figures in a Dutch interior, as well as the allegorical figures of Fancy, Memory, and Conscience through the faceted Madeira glass.[9] In *The Marble Faun*, the art gallery extends away into infinity, and every character has his or her pictorial double supplied by a subtle interplay of symmetry and mirrors. Miriam only reveals the true tenderness and violence of her soul in the presence of her "sister," her ideal being, Beatrice Cenci.[10] For the screen also functions in a temporal dimension. David and Bathsheba, represented in the tapestry, are already the adulterous couple in Boston,[11] and Donatello is not truly himself except in the presence of Praxiteles' Faun. The Model's features are borrowed from Guido Reni's devil, just as Hilda's are taken from the St. Michael who turns his eyes away from the devil in disgust.[12] As well as his halo technique, Hawthorne also had a cameo technique for telling a story. "Sylph Etherege" is a succession of cameos projected into the reader's mind by Fancy's magic lantern. Framed in a window, the drapery of the curtain and the folds of her dress outlining her delicate form with an arabesque of whiteness,[13] the young girl holds in one hand a miniature, the idealized image of the one she loves, whose features are a counterpart of hers.[14] The Sylph's animus and anima become one in the superimposition of these two pastels.[15] But the focus suddenly blurs, the features change, the pastel miniature becomes a charcoal drawing executed with harsh, aggressive strokes: the beloved's secret face.[16] This disillusion kills the Sylph, who dies in order to find the image that she loves elsewhere: the eye of the camera stares out into infinity.[17]

Though he had nothing to show him the way other than the diorama, the magic lantern, and the daguerreotype, Hawthorne's rightful place is nevertheless among the great modern magicians of shadow and light: Griffith, Eisenstein, Ingmar Bergman, Jean Renoir. The shadow of Gervayse at the Christmas banquet,[18] that of Dimmesdale, betrayed by the sun, wavering on the floor as the minister hides his face in vain in the folds of the curtain,[19] that of Hepzibah above all, grotesque and disproportionate, thrown by the firelight onto the wall or by the sunshine onto the parlor floor,[20] make one think of the astonishing profile of Ivan the Terrible.[21] Conversely, is it not possible to see the black inner labyrinth of young Goodman Brown in the black faces so violently hurled against the screen by King Vidor[22] and in the chase through the woods in *Birth of a Nation*,[23] or the flickering torch of his madness in the burning at the stake in *The Seventh Seal*.[24] And the fire of Blithedale still burns in the castle of *Les Visiteurs du Soir*,[25] just as that which lights up the "Vision" and the mermaid still flickers in the potion scene of *L'Eternel Retour*.[26] Hawthorne knew how to compose a figure in close-up, how to place it like the great moviemakers in the center of a picture that is to become the basis of a sequence. Hester's face eventually fills the whole of the imaginary screen in the market square sequence, and one thinks of the face of Lillian Gish—who did in fact play the role in Seastrom's movie[27]—as she appeared in Griffith's *Enoch Arden*. And just as Griffith filled the whole screen with Lillian Gish's eyes, so Hawthorne fills our whole inner field of vision with the eyes of Pearl as they reflect Hester and the Letter. It is as though Hawthorne had nothing more to learn about the art of presenting and using a pictorial or cinematic image, as though he had already invented everything for himself, a half century before Griffith, as though, one is tempted to add, he had in fact produced, in *The Scarlet Letter*, before cameras and projectors were even invented, the first great work of the American cinema, as Dostoevski undoubtedly created the first great Russian movie with *The Brothers Karamazov*, and Stendhal the first great French one in *Le Rouge et le Noir*. But of the three books, Hawthorne's is undoubtedly the most cinematic. He experiments in it with images, with "shots," as he had never done before. There are shots that spread wider and wider, like an opening door, beginning from a single dark point,[28] or like a face flowering into a smile, a luminous iris in the shadowy undergrowth;[29] shots that shrink in upon themselves under the pressure of the surrounding shadows,[30] or become distorted in obedience to some capricious law of magic;[31] simultaneous[32] or reciprocating shots of twin or mutually fascinated beings;[33] superimposed shots in which different periods of the same life overlap;[34] maelstroms of shots in a conscience convulsed by remorse, which gradually settle to form ectoplasmic female figures —the mother, the mistress,[35] the tiny witch-child;[36] shots that well up out of eyes or objects;[37] shots that ebb away like the sea receding from its sands. The shot of Dimmesdale dying is already that of Tristan stretched out on the upturned boat at the end of *L'Eternel Retour*. The imagination is drawn into a perspective that recedes into infinity: as the long-drawn, breaker-like murmur of the crowd rolls heavily in the background, so Dimmesdale's soul withdraws, leaving his body lying like a still pool on the strand.[38] But there is one photographic invention of Hawthorne's that still remains without any equivalent on the movie screen to this day: the black image on the black background,[39] the total negative of the scene at the pillory by night, in which only Pearl's laugh, for the first few seconds, introduces its tiny and momentary cascade of light. Then silence, without even the vaguest movement from the three silhouettes holding one another by the hand up on the scaffold. Their presence is perceptible only by touch. This tactile image requires that we close our eyes the better to sense—the better to *see*, for darkness is a "good conductor"—by the light of an inward spark, the reality of the love as strong as death that is uniting these beings in the heart of darkness. Darkness makes all communications possible. "Darkness is immanence," Wladimir Jankelevitch wrote.[40] It is also the deep, the watery spring from which light emerges. The mind's eye, the poet's eye, and the eye of the camera are all born of those waters, which are as much mingled with man's being as he is steeped in them. Hawthorne drew upon them abundantly: light and darkness were always, for him, the substance of man, as the screen was always that of his consciousness.

The screen cannot be separated from the camera, and in literary creation they constitute but a single instrument, though one adaptable to different functions. If the screen is an eye that receives the image, the camera is the eye that seeks it out. It is always the eye of the consciousness that is in operation, without having to work, as in filming, through the intermediary of a machine. This eye, capable of changing its imaginative position in space,[41] of functioning either as a receiver of vision or a creator of vision, alternately or simultaneously, can be, as we have seen, the most sensitive and magical of mirrors; it can with equal facility become the most easily handled and the most selective of all visual recording instruments, one additionally endowed with the power of creating images, then modifying them, then inserting them into a dramatic and esthetic series. It begins by projecting into imaginary space a sphere symmetrical to its own and specifically intended to receive the light its operator desires, which is not the pure and simple light of the sun,[42] nor the white light of innocence,[43] but a strange, unfamiliar light: lunar, tinged with blue,[44] red and glowing,[45] or iridescent like that from stained glass windows.[46] The interplay of lighting and mirror then causes a scene to appear, to a greater or lesser degree animated, shimmering, or mysterious, and the camera begins to travel through the enclosed space as though on wings, sometimes slowly, sometimes swiftly, taking long shots as it does so of the square with Endicott as its central point, or the crowd around the scaffold; then it halts, focuses on a shadowy mouth that vomits forth two human forms, one of which suddenly bursts into flame in the light.[47] The eye of the camera follows this figure, then holds on it again as it takes up its stand in the pillory. In the forest undergrowth, it scrutinizes the alternating patches of brightness and gloom, while the running child is held in its sunny follow-spot.[48] The "traveling" shot is one of Hawthorne's favorite tricks, and goes hand in hand with the theme of the procession. The camera may also remain motionless in a window and allow vehicles and characters to file past it.[49] The steep downward shot is used with equal felicity to convey both the closed nature of walled-in worlds and the vastness of deep vistas. Rappaccini's garden is photographed from Giovanni's window, but from a considerable distance inside the room, as with the view from the Gothic arched window in *The House of the Seven Gables,* and the graveyard scene in which Chillingworth and the minister spy upon Hester and Pearl as though through a loophole.[50] The scene is "swallowed" by the camera, as a landscape is by the all-devouring onrush of the train.[51] This theme-technique of the open window is also a common one in painting, much used by both Van Gogh and Matisse. But it can work in both directions: Hawthorne also likes to film his interiors through windows. It is by means of the window that we gain access to Phoebe's room.[52] It is from her own window that Hepzibah keeps watch on another window framing the face of a dressmaker: from a distance, she feeds upon the spectacle of a solitude that is the counterpart of her own.[53] Similarly, it is through the glazed door that the curious attempt to pierce the House's secret with their gaze.[54] Hawthorne knows how to choose his angles. Sometimes he places the camera in a doorway and allows the image of the provost or of Hepzibah to move toward it.[55] Sometimes he takes it traveling along corridors, along the underground tunnels of the labyrinth: it seems almost to become tentacular itself. Or else he sets it up in the middle of a room or a consciousness and revolves it, as in the parlor of the House, or inside Hepzibah's or Dimmesdale's mind. He turns it from the portrait to the armor, from the armor to the Letter, or else uses it to catch and fix all the fleeting images that pass through the minister's mind during his vigil.[56]

In the exteriors, the camera generally remains above the ordinary level of vision: borne aloft by Oberon's oneiric flight, it hovers above the crowd, at the level of the pillory, rises to the height of the balcony in order to view the scene from the angle of Judgment, or else plunges downward in a sort of kneeling movement, coming to rest at the feet of the deified woman below as if before an icon.[57] Here, the image is taking possession of the cameraman as much as the cameraman is taking possession of the image—so that he can then concretize it with the passion of his own mind, whose dimensions become as it were materialized by the intensity of its concentration upon the dream of a physical presence. The "exteriors" are in fact the result of an internal scission of the mind, which is dreaming itself in its exploration of the world. The "interiors," on the other hand, are the dream of the camera as it penetrates the impalpable, as it enters a blurred and moving environment in which the objects its filtered vision accepts reveal, by the transformations they undergo and by the way in which they are distributed or displaced in space, the currents, the eddies, and the reefs of a consciousness. And it is these currents and eddies that it sets itself to follow, refusing to be satisfied with merely being borne along by them. The camera is the consciousness itself in the process of self-discovery, returning once more to the status of mirror, of screen, when it has harvested the images it needs. The characters that file past in Dimmesdale's mind have no sooner entered into the camera's field of vision than we see "insets" appearing on the screen, reminding one in a less rudimentary form of one of the cinema's first attempts at psychological trick photography. These images are refilmed by the camera, which at the same moment turns itself into a projector, then into a screen to receive them, only to re-receive them in the way that the eye of the movie viewer would, then to project them and to take them back yet again. This cycle can continue, without any of the takes having to be scrapped, until the required perfection has been achieved; it is still going on even in the mind of the reader. This flexibility, this polyvalence on the part of the apparatus, together with the multiplicity of the various shots filmed and projected, make every kind of superimposition possible. Often, having first established the setting with a variety of moving shots, the camera will halt in order to allow an object, or a figure, to move into its field. After an interior traveling shot in the parlor, it freezes and allows Hepzibah to enter the Rembrandt-like background it has provided for her. Or else we have a shot like that of young David Swan[58] asleep swimming up through the procession of human figures and vehicles. And the image of Hester standing like a statue in the pillory is always there behind the eddying images emerging from her memory. Conversely, we also find static images in close-up superimposed upon an action sequence, or providing us with a frozen allegorical equivalent of it, as in the case of the drawings on the walls of Peter Goldthwaite's house[59] or the prophetic pictures, which are reminiscent of the Biblical frescoes employed by Sjöberg and Bergman.[60] The significance of the parallel between Peter's descent toward the cellar and the content of the drawings is somewhat simplistic; but we must remember that superimposed upon it there are the sequences of feverish searchings through the labyrinth of the inner self. So that allegory becomes a means enabling Hawthorne to reach a deeper awareness of the mind's own cinematic techniques.

III. MOVEMENT AND MONTAGE

Hawthorne's art, as opposed to that of rigid moral allegory, is founded upon movement—a movement essentially cinematic in nature. We have seen with what fluidity Oberon deployed his camera in space. But we also find that his images frequently accelerate or decelerate their tempo across the screen. And the use of slow-motion and speeded up motion is a cinematic method of increasing the flexibility of time and space. In the neutral, intermediate zone that encircles the House,[1] it is as though the various vehicles slow down, and the procession, passing in front of the window, provides us with close-ups of faces frozen with their own weary self-importance.[2] The train, on the other hand, accelerates as it carries the two "owls" away from their former haunts. Its speed liberates the landscape, things, beings, even the House itself,[3] from all their customary moorings. All the images of the world float out into the stream, disencumbered, free to form fresh combinations, new agglomerations. But everything is eventually restored to the ineluctable ancestral order: things, colors, and images all settle and fade in the rain, in the grey tones of the tiny, deserted station. The image of the House resumes its awful immobility. Clifford and Hepzibah's impulsive energy leaves them, so that their minds, drained of all power, slowly collapse in upon themselves as the light fades. Though movement and light are not automatically associated. The most rapid sequences of all take place in fact in the dark: the flight of the witches, or that of Goodman Brown through the forest, as well as that of the demon, the black chariot, swifter than the sun. Pearl's irregular course takes her from shadow into light and back again, a broken tracer line, quick-footed, lighting up will-o'-the-wisps in the dusky air, and highlighting the hieratic stance of the woman-hieroglyph. On the other hand, the most dazzling of all the scenes in Hawthorne's work, that of the pillory, is a static image. Though the inside of Hester's consciousness, as revealed to us by the camera, is a raging maelstrom. In the exteriors, Hawthorne's preferred tempo is undoubtedly that of the procession (it may also occur in interiors), which enables him to have a whole epoch pass in review before us, and also, above all, to introduce meditative pauses: thanks to the slow movement of the procession, the camera is able to take time out for one more shot of Dimmesdale.[4] It is also the mode of motion that best enables him to wait, to suggest, to create an atmosphere, to prepare his *coups de théâtre,* his sudden onslaughts of light or darkness—the speed, in short, that gives him most time for establishing a relationship between the characters and the background. In Hawthorne's scenes and tableaux there is a relation between foreground figures and background objects for which no equivalent exists in Scott or Irving. In their cases, the background always remains a canvas backdrop. In Hawthorne, exchanges occur: Endicott, in his armor, is himself a reflection of the scene that is centered around him, a pictorial device, but also one employed by the avant-garde surrealist moviemakers. The figure of Hester is built up by a system of ricochets, of reflected and re-reflected beams, radiations, and echoes. Though conceived in a less tumultuous mode than King Vidor's sermon scene in *Hallelujah!*, there is nevertheless a battle taking place in the square, a battle waged with sunlight, looks, and voices.

Hawthorne's art, however circuitous in some ways, is nevertheless immediately striking to the imagination: his work is above all a dramatic spectacle.[5] Even his circuitousness is that of light and the moving camera. When it becomes overprolix, as happens even in *The House of the Seven Gables,* and even more so in the later works, not only do the spirals of the arabesque lose their tension, but the cinematic quality is lost. The visual shortcut (concision is also an inherent element of all true cinema) reinforces this quality even further: instead of the narrated, explicated scene that draws itself out and chatters on, the scene that is seen makes its mark and therefore stays in the mind. The spectacle may be reduced, as in "Fancy's Show Box" or "Main Street," to a suggestive pantomine. But such puppets may also be merely the foreshadowers of a more complex spectacle for which they are merely giving a preview. The diagrammatic, daytime diorama has its nocturnal counterpart in the play of shadows filmed from such a variety of angles around the lime kiln.[6] Hot on the heels of the puppet exhibition in the market square, and superimposed upon it, we have the human drama, highlighted by that of flickering shadows that deepen and enlarge our whole perspective. But when the Italian barrel organist's tiny figures[7] mime the actions of the characters in *The House of the Seven Gables,* they are merely demonstrating the vanity of man's feverish activity, whereas if the artist had used the painful pathos that attaches to all incomplete beings to make us think of our own lacks, they could also have been used to make us more aware of life's intensity. Hawthorne had reached the stage where he was trying to "think" his work too much, instead of remaining "merely" the artist who knew so well how to let the great shadows take possession of the cardboard figures aping life for the greater amusement of the ironist, and instill in them the dramatic, esthetic, and human ambiguity without which no masterpiece can exist.

The structure of Hawthorne's work as a whole is that of the movie rather than that of the novel, the play, or the painted fresco. There are no interminable chapters of exposition as in the average Victorian novel. The story generally begins quite abruptly: a path leading into the forest, an indistinct figure walking along it: we are about to live through Young Goodman Brown's adventure with him. A prison door opens, the woman with the Letter appears, the tragedy is under way. A track through the snow, shadows moving slowly toward a distant light —then the camera cuts swiftly to the warm atmosphere of the house— everything begins beneath the signs of fire and ice: knocks on the door, unfamiliar visitors covered in snow—the tale of the future Eden is really a winter's tale. Now Rome, the statue of the faun, then, close beside it, its double in flesh and blood: we leave the museum for Arcadia. Though the outlines grow heavy later on,[8] the first scene is away like an arrow. Hawthorne had learned how to get straight to the point by writing short stories. The introduction to *The House of the Seven Gables,* a work already trying to be more of a novel than *The Scarlet Letter,* is rather overweighted. The story does not begin till Hepzibah's first appearance, and even that is an exercise in pure cinema. The camera gropes in the half-darkness, moves here, moves there, refusing to see anything with precision. We move past closed doors. We listen at them. It is already the "Invisible Man": the character whose presence one is aware of only from the objects he moves about.[9] The flight is excellent, but neither the technique nor the style were able to maintain that degree of purity. The same observation can be applied to *The Blithedale Romance* and *The Marble Faun.* On the other hand, as long as he remained master of his chosen methods, Hawthorne is to be classed among the ranks of the great artists, not merely among those of the precursors. Chapter division was always to remain an arbitrary matter for him: his chapters, when they do in fact have a true organic function, link together to form sequences.[10] Most of the early tales consist of a single sequence only: "Young Goodman Brown" is a unilateral nightmare sequence in which scenes and shots are all linked by the play of light and shade alone, with the aid of the soundtrack. The same single unwinding strand occurs in "My Kinsman Major Molineux," though more involuted, with a curve back toward its starting point: the image of the father's house requiring a daylight scene set between the two dark ones.[11] "Endicott" is a daylight sequence divided into two scenes, beginning with a close-up, moving into a traveling sequence, then returning to the central character. In "The Haunted Mind," a rapid succession of superimposed shots suggests the associative process of revery,[12] and "The Wives of the Dead" offers us a remarkable series of cross-cuts: from one room to the other, from house to street, and vice versa. Once more one is forcibly reminded of Griffith.[13]

In the longer and more complex works, the linking and interweaving of greater numbers of scenes and sequences brings the problem of unity into greater prominence. It would have been easy enough to make Ilbrahim's story into a three-volume novelette; whereas Hawthorne condenses his material into three short episodes: the child's rescue, his martyrdom, and his death. Everything is built around these three moments, all the shots buttress those three fixed images: the child abandoned at the foot of the pine, the child bleeding beneath his tormentors' blows, the child working the miracle of love as he dies. Beatrice's story unfolds on two levels: that of the alchemy of love, which provides us with four beautiful scenes, and that of scientism, in whose name we are subjected to three tedious interludes.[14] Moreover the entire work is organized around a feminine image that seems to have been drawn from an erotic dream. Owen Warland's story is a long sequence made up of scenes and shots that move forward in jerks: abrupt halts, psychological collapses on the part of the artist, setbacks in his work, sudden onsets of energy. It is clearly apparent that each part is constructed around the image of the work that is struggling to take root, shimmering, fading, glowing to life again, until the final catastrophe.[15]

In the novels, the number of shots being necessarily much larger, it is the linking of the various parts that leaves most to be desired from the technical point of view. Though one might well claim that in *The Scarlet Letter* Hawthorne did in fact foresee the cross-fade, which is now a part of cinematic rhetoric. Though he does sometimes make use of clumsy and artificial literary transitions,[16] there are also other, brilliantly successful ones suggested to him by the very nature of the images filing past in the half-dark of his mind. The image of Hester fading away in the corridor returns in close-up in the prison.[17] That of Dimmesdale leaving his house in the dark of night vanishes for a moment only to reappear close to the pillory.[18] That of Chillingworth recedes, vanishes, then fades back into the picture and resumes its distinctness again: it is the same face that returns to haunt us after having pretended to leave us.[19] We also find sudden substitutions taking place, as they do in dreams: the shot of the minister writing the sermon is suddenly replaced by that of Hester.[20] A deliberate coincidence: the further the minister thinks he is from temptation, the nearer temptation is.

The Scarlet Letter is the only one of Hawthorne's works in which all the chapters have an organic function within the sequences that constitute the individual moments of the tragedy.[21] The first begins with a clash of dark against the sunlight and then unfurls in progressively slower motion until we reach the immobility of the pillory, upon which the light culminates in an intolerable silence. Then comes Hester's return into the prison, like a dragon slithering back into its cave leaving a trail of fire behind it.[22] The next scene ends with the doctor's ambiguous words: "Not thy soul . . . no, not thine!"[23] The second sequence begins by relaxing the dramatic tension briefly with a peaceful picture of Hester at her needlework: the slow tempo is one of torpor and boredom. But with Pearl's awakening, torment and disquiet spring to life again. The movement speeds up, the play of light becomes more intense: the glittering shards on the walls of the house reflect the bubbling capriciousness of the hieroglyph-child. After the interview with the Governor, a dramatic, emotional, and auditory paroxysm, we hear the whispered hisses of the witch through an equivocal gloom.[24] The third sequence is a descent into the realms of consciousness: all kliegs dimmed, the camera makes its solitary way for three chapters from sphere to sphere through communicating corridors, until the moment when it begins to follow Dimmesdale on his nocturnal expedition; then it comes to rest at the height of the pillory, above which there is unleashed a sort of magnetic and psychological storm that forms the dramatic and geometric center of the book. The fourth sequence brings a second period of calm, a second relaxation of tempo: light, voices, colors, all are muted. The Letter itself, when it reappears, is not red but green—the green of jealousy—and its substance has grown softer: instead of bright hard flame, the viscous weeds, the whole scene bathed in a grey-green underwater light.[25] The fifth sequence is an explosive awakening: the kliegs all flash on and start to probe into the shadows once again, then Hester's gesture unleashes a fairy tale pageant of music and light—universe and human creature both achieve their total and simultaneous flowering in a blaze of rising sap and sensuality, then almost immediately begin to wither again: the light fades, the human butterfly crawls back into its chrysalis, the universe retracts into itself: Paradise has been lost again. In the sixth sequence, the camera follows Dimmesdale, the Adam driven forth from Eden, the wizard on his way back out of the forest. The unfamiliar appearance of the most everyday objects underlines the moral bewilderment that has made havoc of the minister's whole vision of the world,[26] and the rhythm of the shots conveys the growing panic that now has him in its grip, until the moment when he rushes up to his cell in order to avoid being tempted any further. The seventh sequence begins with a Dionysiac commotion into which a sad and pathetic note gradually insinuates itself; finally it takes over entirely; the triumphal procession becomes an ascent to Calvary, and the work itself a tragedy. Then, as if they are fading back into the box of the diorama, all the characters disappear: Dimmesdale into his grave, Chillingworth into the dungeon of his own heart, Hester and Pearl into the oblivion of solitude—which is to say, into our solitude, into us. Such is the shape of this admirable book, Hawthorne's masterpiece, in which everything is linked together in obedience to an esthetic and tragic necessity, in which the hidden inward movements are rendered visible through the agency of a new art form that is nevertheless also potentially present in the material itself[27] and wonderfully well adapted to the subject—a book heavy and pregnant with strange shimmerings, in which the inward life attains its paroxysm in the light of despair.[28] It is in this sense that it gapes onto the same abysses as those depicted by Milton and Dante, onto the black night of Michelangelo and Van Gogh, of Marlowe and *Macbeth*. *The Scarlet Letter* is, perhaps, Hawthorne's "Macbeth," in that it makes him, after Shakespeare and before Dostoevski, one of the inventors of the cinematic consciousness.

IV. THE CINEMATIC CONSCIOUSNESS

Hawthorne's drama exists wholly in the images. It is in them that we must seek for both the human and the esthetic qualities of his work. The cinema of the past, when it takes on its true significance, is not simply a matter of picturesque details; it is a projection onto a screen of the consciousness attempting to rediscover itself in the past. Hawthorne attempted to make his all the images that haunted the region in which, perhaps at the behest of some predestination, he had been given birth. He conjured them to him, and drew them together into the inward microcosm of his mind: the first settlers, Endicott, Mrs. Hutchinson, the Hathornes, the Quakers, Hester Prynne—the Puritan community of Massachusetts, the nation that was soon to grow around it—the American consciousness that was expanding like America itself, moving away from its vital center—that center to which Hawthorne stubbornly insisted upon returning. He was one of those who retrace the steps of former pilgrims in order to salvage deserving images from oblivion. And once he had withdrawn them from the world of actuality he was able to claim them as his alone. Hawthorne, the historical moviemaker, composed his shots in the studio, not from life. He needed the sense of internal germination, and preferred in consequence to recreate shattered images from their remains, just as he liked to reconstruct men's lives from their footprints,[1] from the odor or the echo still lingering in spots consecrated by heroic deeds, by passion, or by suffering. The principal character is often absent from the scene, but the objects that remain, impregnated with his presence, can furnish the house,[2] the images he has meditated upon and that reflect his destiny are still there in the diorama,[3] and the companions in the tavern still remember. Who will the spectators of this ghost play be? Other ghosts? Yes, if it were merely a matter of an "evocation" that might brush the surface of the mind without awakening it. But these unrealities are the substance itself from which is created a new being, one made of freshly minted images dreamed by a poetic consciousness, images that will only take on their true significance when viewed from a distance. The spectators of Hawthorne's "ghost sonata" are spectators of the future. And the heroes invented with that audience in mind, instead of being "established" once and for all, as a novelist's characters are often expected to be—an unhappy confusion with caricature and satire that Hawthorne himself was guilty of in his portrait of the Judge[4]—reveal themselves to us progressively: they become what they are to be within us, drawing nourishment from our consciousness even as they enrich it. They themselves are consciousnesses rather than characters. Which is why one imagines them more than one sees them—for they are beings inside us, rather than actors we are watching.

And that, perhaps, is Hawthorne's great secret—that of all true writers: he leads his readers, solely with the aid of a book's inner atmosphere, to create an entire pageant, incidents, characters, tragedy, for themselves. His memories of childhood and youth evoke Clifford's inner tragedy[5] better than all the "gothick" paraphernalia with which the character is surrounded. The poetry of memory is not—any more than any other kind of poetry—created solely out of sunny hours recalled, but those hours take on all their emotional and esthetic value when set in opposition to the somber hours, to the throbbing pangs of remorse, to the searing pangs of regrets and old shames whose cruel, insistent, ruthless images are projected by Fancy's Show Box,[6] which is also able to console us with the spectacle of illusions and desires come true. In the haunted mind, nightmare and revery touch: it contains the entire cinema of consciousness, with its methods, its technique, its screen, its camera. Hawthorne was simply consciously exploiting the cinematic resources of the soul. He was one of the first to discover, and to demonstrate in dazzling fashion, that the cinema had always existed potentially in our imagination, and that it is part of our mental activity—the corollary being that the real movies, when they came, were obliged to raise themselves to the level of psychological signification, and, like the other arts, struggle, through things, to reveal the imaginary world. As for Hawthorne, it is certainly the *other* reality that he intends to reveal, through evident reality and in place of it— the other reality that appears in the "alien" lighting of the mind.[7] In his own way, like Rimbaud, Hawthorne is saying that "we are not in the world"—the only world truly existing being that of memory, of desire, of dreams: the created world. The work of art exists to the degree in which it recreates and replaces the evident world.

Though total reality is necessary to any great poetic or dramatic work, little of its raw material is in fact borrowed directly. What is true for Racine is also true for Hawthorne. Hawthorne's dramatic action is already concisely present in its first image, which, far from "representing," is a reference to a style: a man in the maze of a town or forest,[8] a child at the foot of a tree that has served as a gibbet,[9] a woman in the pillory with a child in her arms,[10] an old aristocrat whom necessity, or some bad spell, has obliged to turn shopkeeper.[11] Affinities and antagonisms then weave a complex web around this image, not in accordance with the law that controls human relations in social life, but in accordance with the laws of dream and tragedy—and therefore of the imagination. Around Ilbrahim there forms the tight fabric of an individual and collective hatred against which all compassion is powerless and whose implacable progress is evoked in images of the most eloquent sobriety. The hostility of the crowd, the malevolent cunning of the doctor, the hypocritical silence of the minister as they enwrap Hester in their inextricable toils are forced into our minds by a series of close-ups: the spiteful matrons, the closed Puritan faces, that of the husband, writhing with jealousy, and the lover, hand convulsed over his heart. Priscilla's first entrance crystallizes the situation in *The Blithedale Romance* from the very start: Zenobia stiffens, but Coverdale's sympathy is obvious.[12] This Ophelia of the snow is another cinematic anticipation: she is already the "starry" image of "the world's sweetheart" who magnetizes both masculine and feminine eyes in opposite ways—looks of love and looks of hate clash above the humbly triumphant head of the little beggar girl who feels herself becoming a star. And where is the Hollywood fantasy of compensation not already surpassed in advance by the forest scene of *The Scarlet Letter*?

The conflicts in Hawthorne's works are essentially conflicts produced by sexual passion. But blow-by-blow accounts of the passions are omitted, with rare exceptions. Why did the storyteller, when evoking the lovers of Monte Beni, betray his own esthetic by not placing the crime at the beginning, or even before the beginning of the work? Coming in the center of the plot as it does, it requires a relief that the allegorist of ambiguity refuses to give it, without compensating by affording it the depth of a dream. The awful savagery of Raskolnikov or Dmitri Karamazov reduces Donatello's vague gesture to zero; but it cannot efface the scene on the pillory. Yet the minister's clandestine acts of love are not described, any more than Ethan Brand's crime. It is only by such restraint that Hawthorne can hope to lead us as far as Dostoevski with his supremely powerful realistic imagination. Moreover the conflicts of interest, the dramas and tragedies of money that take up so much of Balzac's foregrounds, are reduced to even more of a minimum: Moodie's bankruptcy and the struggle between the Maules and the Pyncheons for the possession of a piece of land were of little more than incidental interest to Hawthorne. He was not attempting to depict men as they appear from their behavior, their acts, or their social acquisitiveness; he was trying to reveal his characters' souls rather than their outward characteristics, and to do so he needed to catch an attitude, an equivocal gesture made in the half-darkness, as though inside the dreamer's own mind. The pathetic irony of Hepzibah's fate—that of a being endowed with a loving nature whose efforts to please only irritate the person she wishes to enwrap in her affection[13]— is expressed in the simple gesture with which she takes up a miniature to fix it with her melancholy gaze, as is Miriam's despair in the furtive attitude she assumes in the midst of the crowd.[14]

It is passion's private life that Hawthorne recounts for us in his ambiguous images. He is offering us a seat in the passionate, guilty, or haunted character's private projection room. It is upon the tragedy of solitude that he raises his curtain (a fact that is not without its irony, for even the most absolute solitude then becomes an observed, a shared solitude), and the consciousness revealed, so proud of its self-sufficiency, is compelled, whether it wishes to or no, to communicate, to acknowledge that it is no longer one of a kind. Goodman Brown discovers that all his fellow citizens have the same secret inclinations as himself. Dimmesdale laments at being a creature apart, impenetrable, and at having neither friend nor enemy to know him for what he is, when all the time he has as his intimate a man who never ceases to spy on him[15]—a revelation that fells him utterly, that annihilates him. The true drama of solitude is the drama of the individual who, like Hawthorne, pretends to reject it, to loathe it, but in reality loves it above everything, just as the Kierkegaardian self clutches his anguish to him even as he attempts to escape it. Goodman Brown's bitterness is that of an individual deprived of his originality, no longer free to lead the double life he requires, or enjoy his nocturnal holidays in peace, because his night now also belongs to others. The oneiric wealth of the consciousness is at the same time the most common of properties and yet the most personal: in fact, the solitudes of individuals do not interpenetrate—they must be violated. And to violate solitude is to kill it. Even at the very height of the nocturnal sabbath, at the very heart of his dream, Goodman Brown is still a spectator: he does not participate, because only the social self can ever participate. The deep, truly inner self never gives itself up to another—must not give itself up, even in sleep, even in love. Which is why Dimmesdale chooses to die: to preserve his individuality, to be alone with *his* God. And who is that God, if not himself, the ultimate image of his self? Neither the man who hates him nor the woman who loves him shall come between him and his supreme being.[16] And like Dimmesdale, even in spite of their "return," Wakefield and Roderick also recognize solitude as the very substance of their being. For Clifford, the sensitive soul whom the wind of the outside world must not visit too rudely, solitude is essentially protective and womb-like.[17] For Miriam and Donatello it is a psychological and metaphysical distancing, a gap between them and the rest of the world, and lastly, a fated separation of ill-starred lovers.[18] For Hawthorne, as for Aeschylus and Racine, human beauty and dignity stand upon the foundation of a tragic destiny. Thus the irony turns in the end against destiny itself, against the "Dieu qui s'amuse" evoked by Gide in *Les Faux Monnayeurs*; for the catastrophe, instead of destroying the hero, creates him; the crime, instead of disintegrating the soul, calls it into existence. That is the profound Dionysian meaning of Hawthorne's work, a meaning paradoxically drawn from the wellsprings of Puritan pessimism in order to enrich the drama and aggravate the torment of man's consciousness. From this strange but inevitable alliance in the mind of a man who was fundamentally, however much he may have struggled against it, a poet, and one stamped moreover with the seal of Protestant anguish, there was born the duel of the great shadows. And man emerges from the combat enlarged—enlarged by what kills him, as by the void created around him by misfortune, fatality, and his own singularity. The shadows of Endicott, Hester, or Ethan Brand, projected larger than life by Hawthorne's tragic and fateful lantern, remain and bear witness.

If one wishes to seek for a philosophic tendency in Hawthorne's work,[19] then it is not toward Transcendentalism that one must look. Hawthorne's position is decidedly existential—not out of any intellectual conviction, but instinctively, as is clearly apparent from the deep inward sense he had of the individual's radical solitude, an ineradicable sense of apartness that he is able to communicate to us all the more easily today because it is the deepest obsession of the modern soul—so deep that modern man is terrified of it, rejects it, and seeks for refuge in violent collective activity. Existential solitude, yearning for a lost Eden that perhaps never existed and that can therefore never be recovered, images of irremediable evil, suffering, and death, such is the substance of which Hawthorne's work is really made, below and beyond all the superficial, reassuring, consoling myths of an America on the road to prosperity and discount happiness. But neither America nor the world as a whole has ever thanked anyone for dismissing its myths of the easy life and preferring the kind of tragic myths that involve man in a wholly different way, thus forcing him to look at himself, not as he appears from his conventional gestures or in retouched and idealized photographs, but upon the screen of his own consciousness. Hawthorne refused to follow fashion. He chose to create a period of his own—a solitude in time where man could at last be what he is and ought to be, an existing being in search of himself. As Faulkner invented "penitential time,"[20] in which one imprisons oneself in order to find one's own gestures, one's own deeds, one's own face at last, so Hawthorne discovered the time of solitude, in which man is equal to himself, to the universe, and to his God. Are we to reproach him, as Valéry did Rilke, with this "abuse of intimacy with silence"?[21]

· 3 ·
The Style

I. NARRATIVE

An author's future style is there from the very outset in his themes, if the themes he uses are personal to him and not merely borrowed. The meeting of this store of material with its form takes place—aided by confrontations with models that very early in his career open up silent vistas to the young artist—during the course of long interior monologues, of esoteric experiments with images and words. So that, little by little, images and words are drawn together by a mutual attraction in order to become the written poetic reality. This is the battle that the writer must wage against himself, against his chimeras, his monsters, his fantasies, his accomplished or projected actions. From the continual stirring of these realities, this way and that, there may one day emerge a style: a way of telling things, a way of making us see, making us hear, making us feel, in which we shall recognize the artist's choice at every step. The personal style for the personal reality.

It is not without an effort, nor without often finding himself off the right path in dead ends, that a writer succeeds in finding himself. Hawthorne found himself in his very earliest stories: his meeting with the themes of his future works had been long prepared by the forced seclusion of his childhood—a seclusion that he never ceased to cultivate,[1] even at college, to the point of neglecting the prescribed academic exercises in order to attend his own private classes in writing. There was but one style possible for him: the allegorical style, the Puritan

334

style—that of Spenser and Jonathan Edwards. Though he was to be led astray from his path later—usually with unfortunate results—by his distress at finding himself always the same, at having, like most of the masters, only *one* style, his own. He became tormented by a desire to change himself, to be someone else, to find relaxation in mere literary games, or to prove that he too had a claim to be counted among the creators of the dawning realist era's "new novel," yet remained perpetually disappointed at having to admit his inability both to change his own esthetic and to juggle with the superficies of a style or counterfeit the gestures of creation. It is to these vagaries, these feelings of self-distaste, these fancies, that we owe his least characteristic works, those that do not truly belong in the Hawthorne canon. For example, the sketches with Transcendentalist leanings, such as the introduction to the *Mosses*[2] and the story, "The New Adam and Eve"[3] —or those with humorous and familiar intentions, after the manner of the English essayists, such as the lengthy introduction that makes us wait so long for *The Scarlet Letter,* or the nugatory pages in *The House of the Seven Gables* that so exasperated André Gide[4]—or, lastly, those with an objectivist tendency, which acquire that unfortunate inventory-like quality, wholly lacking in evocative power, that is the hallmark of the mediocre realist school. Though it is true that Hawthorne scarcely ever essayed this genre outside his notebooks.[5] All these tentative departures from himself, all these infidelities merely succeeded in driving his natural qualities away for a while, before they flooded back with added brilliance. It was to the bare and severe but intense style of the Oberon-inspired arabesque, crammed with shadows yet shimmering with animation, that he owed his great successes, until the day when the steel lost its temper, and the arabesque became heavy and drooping, like a climbing plant whose host has collapsed beneath it.

The narrative that follows the sinuosities of the mature arabesque carries the mark of Hawthorne's true style, the style that we have seen asserting itself on the various levels of his work, and whose ritual atmosphere is not always exempt from a certain pompousness. His long procession of characters derives from history, as well as from the legend and the epic, a majesty that becomes the gravity of certain themes, but that can also become overweighty. Miriam and Donatello in the fleeting intoxication of their love[6] walk like two allegorical automata. The esthetic distance[7] required by the tragic, historical, or epic label, maintained upon all the levels of a narrative by means of a stiff and weighty style, can deprive certain scenes of all grace, all freshness. The stiffness of the Shakers, their mortified sensibility, is very moving.[8] But when Holgrave the homespun philosopher gives Phoebe one of his pedantic lectures,[9] he seems merely clumsy and pretentious. Far from creating a legendary distance, this laboriously mannered idyll takes on a distressingly artificial tone. When Hawthorne treats the Adamic theme on the contemporary level, the ritual of love tends to be reduced, as in "The New Adam," to heavy and cloying Victorian prudishness.[10] This lack of grace often goes hand in hand with a lack of boldness. The long, strictly applied allegories in which Hawthorne lacks the courage to follow his intuitions to their ruthless conclusions lose their impetus in vain meanderings. The utopia in the happy valley—a valley which is always an improbable "elsewhere"— ought to have been a miraculous and tragic mirage of the heart, instead of shrinking to the dimensions of an illusion destroyed by the mind. This diminution of theme means that Coverdale's purification by illness[11] and even Zenobia's suicide, lose a great deal of their emotional value and their meaning. Obsessed by the worm in the fruit of his new Eden, Hawthorne made his heroes into pitiable mummers who do not seem to believe any more than their author in their great quest for joy. Miriam and Donatello believe in theirs, to the point of despair and the commission of irreparable acts. But then, having become concerned with writing as a man of "experience," Hawthorne lacks the courage to follow up this brilliant beginning: the all-devouring and despairing quest drags on and on through an increasingly tedious maze. Yet it is this same ceremonial approach that governs the forest scene in *The Scarlet Letter*: another masque played out in a gloomy labyrinth. But instead of mere decorative or moral rhetoric there is drama, pain, human beauty— spellbinding incantation.

The logic of Hawthorne's narratives is a poetic logic. As soon as that logic fails, or gives way to a mixture of everyday pseudo reality— as perceived by a mind anxious to respect the bounds of convention —with fantasies wholly lacking oneiric foundations, chimaeras of which even the storyteller himself makes sport, then we are left with nothing but empty artifice. The structure of Hawthorne's best works is that of the movie and that of the poem. The links are associative rather than narrative. Certain sketches are true prose poems. "Footprints in the Sand" is simply a succession of cinematic discoveries: the scattered objects and images, all bathed in the same atmosphere, are combined into a whole simply by the artist's dreaming yet selective fancy, the same fancy that we recognize in the evocation of Pearl playing on the seashore.[12] The "Night Sketches," whose musical quality we have already noted, are organized in obedience to a structure provided by the revery of lights shining in darkness. "Buds and Bird Voices," despite the scholarly artifices of the composition, is a rediscovery of the freshness of spring and the profound cycle of nature's vital sap.[13] In "The Old Apple Dealer," the realism of the detail is an illusionist's trick, a bait for the imagination, which is soon drawn, unawares, into the avenues of the past: what has every appearance of being a sketch from life turns out to be a retrospective vista through time.[14] Hawthorne was a narrator-poet as Frost was a poet-narrator. The same intensity, the same concision, the same restraint that are so striking in the best stories of the one are also present in the best poems of the other. The story of young Goodman Brown winds its way to its conclusion in obedience to the logic of the night and that of a dreaming man's delirium, just as the central episode in the poem "A Servant to Servants" moves in obedience to the logic of the cries uttered by a madman in a cage.[15] We are back once more in the realms of Faulkner and Shakespeare. The story of the "Mermaid" and that of the "Vision," like Frost's idyll "Paul's Wife," owe their existence to the logic of the miraculous apparition.[16] Others follow the logic of fairy tales or dreams, never—at least in the works that count—that of a structure based purely upon the incidents in a plot, or that of literary mechanisms or mannerisms, as in the novelette, the "gothick" novel, or the vast edifices of the George Eliot school. It is the poetic and psychological obsession alone that constitutes the thematic and dramatic thread. Everything that is generally referred to as the "technique" of the novel, the method of constructing it or of avoiding arbitrary construction altogether, must flow originally from a central theme and a well-defined form. It is the theme itself, and the form it has itself chosen to pour itself into—the form that suits it best, since it has molded it from its own substance—that must invent its own technique. And that form in this case is the cinematic arabesque that recounts the romance of Oberon's consciousness.

In *The House of the Seven Gables*, this technique assumes a much greater importance than in *The Scarlet Letter*: when the processes of art become apparent, then that art is in peril of death. It is clear that Hawthorne, having attained the summit of his creation and achieved a total expression of his self, became more permeable to the influence of his age. But it is always in vain, and to its own greater shame, that the mind, whether scientific or poetic, prostrates itself before know-how and technique: neither of them can do anything to advance either science or art unless they are wielded by a true artist or a true scientist. Already, a hundred years ago, the utilitarians would have been glad to refuse art the keys to the city. The same imaginations that took such delight in the "gothick" novel, that by-product of scientism and Puritanism, also claimed that Poe lacked genius and attempted to pass over Hawthorne's work in silence. Lovers of fairground sensations, whose minds turn to vapor when made to spin fast enough, are always clamoring for new machines to give them a thrill and to kill them quickly. But there are forms of speed that do not stimulate the intelligence, and that sterilize the imagination. The fear and the trembling that poets speak of, whatever its origin, is not "sensational"; it can do without machines; it can even do without precise objects,—as anyone who has read Frost's "The Fear" or James's *The Turn of the Screw* will know.[17] There is simply fear in its pure state, all the possibilities it contains, the vistas it opens up, the images it lets loose. The object of fear, like the culprit's crime in Hawthorne's works, remains an object, a crime, a "dagger of the mind." The narrative, like the poem, is a movement of images—swell, whirlpool, procession, plunge, or flight of images that can be used by the poet and the storyteller, each in his own way. These waves of images form sequences, some more clearly dramatic, others purely poetic. The artist selects according to his genius. But they could never achieve true existence, necessary precision, without language.

II. THE LANGUAGE: THE WORDS

Language is the vehicle of rhythms and images that have become conscious. It is the net in which the mind attempts to capture dream and reality; it is also, for the writer, the given element in which he must leave his mark. Hawthorne chose to imitate the inimitable, to renew what had acquired an absolute value. But this temerity did not prevent his prose being recognized in his own lifetime as "the best written on either side of the Atlantic."[1] He chose hardly any models later than the eighteenth century. And the influence of Spenser and

Bunyan, as well as that of the Puritan theologians and preachers, was to be infinitely greater on his language than that of Scott or Irving. The tone in which he speaks of sin or witchcraft is decidedly not that of a writer of society novels or a wit. We have already pointed out numerous traces of elements taken from Bunyan, Spenser, and Milton[2] in the "amalgam" that Hawthorne's language fundamentally is—though an amalgam so particular to him as to be personal from the very outset. Living in the past as he wrote, Hawthorne did not forbid himself the use of archaisms—indeed, he cultivated them with a kind of coquettish discretion. The very subject of *The Scarlet Letter* entails the use of a certain number of them, particularly in the mouths of historical characters such as Bellingham and the Reverend Wilson, grotesque creations such as Mrs. Hibbins the witch, or minor roles intended to provide historical color, such as the chorus of Puritan women.[3] Without going as far as mannerism or affectation, his choice of vocabulary tends to the abstract: he had an affection for certain words of Latin origin that were current in the language of the eighteenth century, as well as in that of preachers and doctors.[4] The novelties of language held little interest for him. The characteristic speech of New England must have been in the process of crystallization during the nineteenth century, yet he makes hardly any use of it. The English of Consul Hawthorne must have differed very little from that of Leigh Hunt and Browning. We find scarcely any "Yankee," popular, or vulgar expressions outside of the Notebooks[5] and the *Grimshawe* drafts,[6] except for the few timid examples provided in *The House of the Seven Gables* by the sagacious Dixey and his companion, whose talk can certainly not be accused of excessive vigor or bluntness. The peak of crudity in Hawthorne's dialogue is certainly attained by women: the matrons around the pillory, and Mrs. Gubbins,[8] though even their coarseness is anodyne enough. Like Racine and Gide, however, Hawthorne proves elsewhere that he knew the secret of depicting the starkest realities in the chastest of terms without any loss of force.[9] Similarly, it is with the aid of the most generalized vocabulary that he depicts the particular. His characters only very rarely speak the language of a particular environment, sect,[10] or trade.[11] Endicott hardly uses any military terms at all.[12] Apart from the doctor, the minister, and the artist—all of whom employ the language of their professions on the metaphorical rather than the realistic level, the painter's colors, the apothecary's mixtures, and the minister's sermons all being used as means of expressing the unconscious—his characters all speak the same, as it were generic language, impregnated with an Old Testament tone, and used as a vehicle for both their temperaments and their individual passions. Uncle Venner's homely remarks,[13] the vociferations of the wizard and the lime-burner,[14] and Dimmesdale's preaching all bear the stamp of a single style. James justly congratulated Hawthorne upon his refusal to fall in with the prevalent fashion of slang and dialect.[15] Though he did indulge in the "gothick" mode of writing: the "spectral" music of the harp,[16] the "ethereal" texture of a veil.[17] These are terms that relate to spiritism and mesmerism, but which, as we have seen, also permit a perpetual, almost imperceptible progression from the supernatural into the psychological.[18] Science and technological progress also provided him with some modern additions in the realm of electricity[19] and the machine, particularly in the case of the railroad.[20] Where furnishings are concerned, he eschews all novelty.[21] Similarly, the houses he describes are all of the purest Colonial style.[22] But he was obliged to take contemporary fashions into account when describing the Judge's sartorial equipment, since he could not otherwise have contrasted it with the clothes of the ancestor.[23] He also depicts Zenobia's various toilettes in some detail, again in order to contrast them with Priscilla's rather poverty-stricken attire, and in the "Night Sketches" pays homage to the feet of a young girl wearing "rubbers":[24] the desirable figure of the modern woman is thus already to be seen emerging in his pages.

But the Hawthorne in complete possession of his style hammered out his own personal language in a region beyond all fashion. Even though the vocabulary he employs often appears to be that of the "gothick" novel, this is merely a matter, as with the themes, of coincidence. The words "shadow," "vault," "veil," "secret," "mystery," "dungeon," and "phantom" did not have the same value for Hawthorne as they had for Charles Brockden Brown or even for Poe. The labyrinth into which they lead the mind is not the fairground house of horrors whose sole purpose is to thrill, but the maze through which man seeks his inward self.

A writer's favorite words are not simply words; they are forms, substances, beings. For Hawthorne, the word "sphere"[25] is spherical, it is a described space, inhabited and pregnant. The word "circle" is a magic or material circular line,[26] like Brecht's chalk circle.[27] The word "house" is endowed with an enormous emotional coefficient: it materializes as soon as it is used, takes on body, color, and weight, blocks the light, projects its shadow, and is also, for Hawthorne, synonymous with a well-defined style. The word "solitude" is man, desolated consciousness, cold heart. The words "sun," "bird," "flower," "fruit," "stream" are Eden, unless the water, the air, or the plant is poisoned. And in order to express the fevers and furies of the soul being gnawed at by evil, by passion, by madness, he is obliged, as Perry Miller puts it, to force words to conjure up hell.[28] The "anguish" and the "pangs" of the moral pillory[29]—the "tortures" of remorse[30]—pain, solitude, and grief —all achieve a physical intensity in his language. Hawthorne experienced words with his senses: they are touched, felt, plucked, tasted; they are sensorial fetishes and allegories. These word-substances, these word-images, summon up other word-substances or produce further word-images. The word "heart" is for Hawthorne the supreme mirror-word, the word enclosing all others: it is sphere, house, temple, prison, cave, grave, lake, fountain, and furnace.[31] The word "head," its antithetical homologue, is, in comparison, lackluster, indigent, barren. And both the attic and the aerie, images of the observing and sovereign consciousness, refer us back yet again to the central organ that symbolizes better than any other all man's hidden inclinations. For Hawthorne, consciousness was not a brain but a heart, sometimes a womb. And poetic language is not a language of the brain but of the heart.

Even the proper names that Hawthorne employs bear the stamp of his mind's particular mold. Hardy did not hesitate to call one of his heroes Angel,[32] and James was fond of names with intellectual echoes: Archer, Ambient, Aspern;[33] but Hawthorne, even though we find an Aylmer in his work, a man for whom nothing matters but the mind,[34] as well as a sylph,[35] a mermaid,[36] a beaming Phoebe,[37] and even a "Saint Hilda,"[38] nevertheless tends to put a more personal stamp upon his creations by choosing names for them that evoke the penumbra of the bruised and guilty heart: Dimmesdale (the valley—the heart—in which the light is growing dusky, as in "The Hollow of the Three Hills," the "Valley of the Shadow of Death"), Coverdale[39] (who covers or is covered with a veil), Holgrave (the searcher of graves, the unearther of secrets). Or else it is the hell of ice: Chillingworth—or that of fire: Ethan Brand.

The adjectives similarly possess a strong emotional coefficient. What accumulated horror and repulsion there is in the word "dark" applied to the dying minister still hidden behind his black veil.[40] And the description of the tree in "Gentle Boy" as "unhappy"[41] endows it with a disquieting prominence and color: the word confers a psychological attitude upon it. And how many sad-sounding epithets have attached themselves to the picturesque and pitiable name of Hepzibah,[42] helping to create the creation's physical outline. The same adjectives elsewhere express astonished grief: "the wretched minister,"[43] or reprobation: "this man's miserable soul."[44] These are the epithets of the preacher, which may sometimes extend as far as sarcasm, not to mention anathema: the Judge is depicted, by implication, as "bold, imperious, relentless, crafty; laying his purposes deep, and following them out with an inveteracy of pursuit that knew neither rest nor conscience."[45] Hawthorne does not often resort to such accumulations, except in allegorical passages—the House, in a metaphor that also involves the seasons and human emotions, is honored with five consecutive adjectives[46]—in deliberately humorous contexts,[47] or when the author is giving vent to his spleen: indignation against hypocrisy, rancor against the excessive burden of the past.[48] In such places we hear the man's own temperament speaking. It is this same unstable temperament, capable of unleashing fits of passion, anger, or enthusiasm as well as of depression in an individual who elsewhere gives proof of such patience, that we recognize in the arrow-like flight of certain verbs expressing cries, impulses, flight, or aggression,[49] and in the overwhelmed and burdened quality of certain others expressing slowness, solemnity, or torpor.[50] The esthetic rendering of rapid movement, of the hurling gesture, takes on an explosive intensity. The projectile—cry or beam—springs out of a psychic paroxysm: it is an arrow or dagger of the mind. Conversely, the expression of weight and repose by means of verbs acquires a static value so absolute in certain contexts that the verb itself ceases to express a state and becomes a thing.[51] This happens in the pillory scene with the verb "to stand" and with others used to evoke immobility, crushing weight, and petrification.[52] In the House, Hepzibah's stiff, awkward, painful movements as she searches for the absconding marbles on her knees impose themselves upon the reader's mind by way of the sentence's cruelly precise adjectives and substantives, which absorb the motion of that most banal of verbs "to go," are welded together by it, and make it into the mainspring of an ancient, rusty, creaking mechanism.[53] The rhythms of the sentence bring out also the particular value that words can assume in Hawthorne's writ-

ing, and the organic, sometimes even fleshly quality—when it is revealed in its full purity—of this least rhetorical of styles.

III. THE LANGUAGE: THE SENTENCE

The mold into which Hawthorne's sentence most naturally flowed was
the period, a product of classical literature and Puritan sermon-writing
which the psychologist and the artist, avoiding its more obvious effects,
endowed with a new, inward flexibility and ramified to suit the patterns
of his arabesque. A writer may possess several styles within his main
style—he may also have styles that exist outside his style proper, or
even as a substitute for one—styles that will be of a familiar, descriptive, satirical, realistic, or poetic character according to circumstances.
This phenomenon may be observed especially in the facile kind of
writer who is able to turn his elegant hand to everything, but without
ever really creating anything. Hawthorne too was able to use a surface
style, one not truly his own, but that has nevertheless taken people in
and is largely responsible for a false reputation the writer has acquired.
Hawthorne did, in fact, suffer from a very strong temptation to indulge in oratory, and his introverted temperament, his shyness at expressing himself in public, led him to delight in his own eloquence
privately, as though in a secret vice. He loved speeches, harangues,
and imaginary sermons. Even in his letters, his private notebooks, and
his sketches we find him becoming caught up in this oratorical current,
which carries the words away, almost despite themselves, into avenues
of commonplaces, some magniloquent, some familiar—supposedly
literary—and which, far from liberating his thought, merely imprison
it. This is undoubtedly why certain of Hawthorne's pages, ones that
ought to have been among his freshest,[1] are in fact spoiled by his use
of the Victorian style, which is a crystallization of all the most unfortunate tendencies of those that preceded it, and the most antipoetic
that ever existed. Though it does seem to flower more naturally in the
satirical passages, in which the bureaucratic and political rhetoric[2] is
more at home. When carried away by indignation, Hawthorne tended
to allow his oratorical tendency free rein; it is at such moments that we
are obliged to listen to Holgrave's long diatribe,[3] or to the ironic
eulogy of the Colonel, or to that of the Judge, in which the eloquence

of the political platform, and that of official banquets, not to mention that of the bar or the pulpit, combine to form wholes of varying success.[4] If we add to these the Judge's own harangues, speeches, and fulminations—the paternal or sly tone of his remarks according to whether he is addressing Phoebe or Hepzibah,[5] the solemnity of his threats[6]—then we already have a great deal of Hawthorne's most declamatory work, *The House of the Seven Gables*, which deceived even its author about his own creation. For it is true, alas, that we always take the good orator for a great man, and skill in juggling with words for genius. The surface style that is a cover for vast, sonorous voids is based either upon formal rhetoric or else upon antirhetoric, an offshoot of our new literary snobbism. Hawthorne kept to traditional rhetoric: repetition—once the oratorical machine has been set in motion, the word "dead" is repeated ten times in the course of one page[7] —negations, exclamations, rhetorical questions, multiplication of grammatical links: "too . . . nor does . . . so far as . . . so also as"[8]— pure and simple accumulation of juxtaposed propositions, piled up in even layers, cemented together as though with the "inasmuches" of a court sentence, until we reach the peroration that serves as the edifice's foundation.[9]

Perhaps, despite his shyness, with the help of faith, Hawthorne would have made a great preacher in the days of Jonathan Edwards. Certainly there is a great deal of the savage eloquence of the Puritan ministers and politicians in Endicott's forceful harangue.[10] Goodman Brown, when he cries: "Come, devil: for to thee is this world given," is merely inverting the words of a preacher pronouncing the anathema.[11] The vehemence is the same. And the almost Marlovian fury of the lime-burner exists on the same theological plane as *Dr. Faustus*.[12] Even in the most homely circumstances, Hawthorne finds a Biblical tone and dignity quite natural.[13] And the debt of the moralist to the solemn cadences of Scripture is even more evident in his exhortations and warnings to a sinful world: the vanity of the entire earth's holocaust as long as the hidden "sphere" of the human heart still remains impure[14] —the vanity of the "splendid rubbish" covering over the sewer of conscience.[15] We meet echoes of Ecclesiastes, of the Apocalypse, of Bunyan at every step. But above all these voices, it is for the eloquence of the heart that we must listen in the savage and passionate laments of Hester,[16] in the heart-rending accents of Dimmesdale, the guilty minister, whose appeals penetrate our hearts by paths unknown to ordinary eloquence, those of the most subtle sympathy and poetry, which render us sensitive to even the most equivocal discourse, to even the strangest reverberations of that disturbing litany of evil and the knowledge of evil intoned by the satanic one officiating in the forest.[17]

Hawthorne's sentence, like his work as a whole, is a movement of the consciousness. If the mind goes directly to its goal, then the sentence is a dart, an arrow: command, insult, attack, violent start of the whole being.[18] More often, the thought progresses by way of circumvolution or in a circle, and the discourse evolves in accordance with a circular or sinuous plan. The slow, spiralling movement of Dimmesdale's voice during the sermon unwinds into a long musical period, not an oratorical one.[19] Hawthorne's sentence is a labyrinth-sentence, an anticipation of Faulkner's. Delays, folds, detours, and doublings back are the rule. There is the way that we find the words circling, for example, around the figures conjured up by Hester's memory in the pillory: the old father, the anxious mother, the young girl, the pale scholar—then the stream begins to follow the labyrinth of the city streets as seen in her dream, at which an abrupt reversal brings us back into the market place.[20] Hepzibah, searching for Clifford, leads us through a maze of sentences that is homologous with the labyrinth of the House itself, and packed, like it, with memories.[21] The torment of the heart agitated by inward convulsions expresses itself in a series of serpentine sentences, slow reptiles that writhe in a melancholy and melodious hissing progress: "punishment"—"salvation"—"sin"—"suffering"; "silence"— "tenderness"—"shame"—"sin"; "secret"—"silence"—"hypocrisy"— "sin"; words that recur again and again, litany, disguised confession, obsession, contradiction—a prayer crying out for both punishment and secrecy, the drizzling downfall of a crushed and conquered soul already beginning to inflict its secret punishment upon itself.[22] The serpent-sentence delicately modulates the melancholy of the labyrinthine soul, the tendril-sentence probes and spirals down into the sick consciousness. The torture inflicted upon his victim by Chillingworth thus takes on the cruelty of a "turn of the screw": by means of a series of interrogations he stirs up unease, then pain, and each of his remarks renews the grip of dread around the minister's heart.[23] Or else it is the slow descent into the darkness in search of the secret: the sentence follows all the movements of the man of hate as he gropes his way nearer, almost reaches his goal, and at the least alert retires.[24] The direction of the Hawthorne sentence tends to be a downward one: the weight of the

words causes it to descend: "gold"—"tomb"—"evil"—"rotting flesh."
Emotionally and morally speaking evil and flesh are heavier than gold:
the sentence has a weightier and weightier burden to bear as it progresses, and the rhythm slows down as the descent continues.[25]
Dimmesdale, in the course of his ascetic practices, makes a descent into
his inner self. During the vigil, the progressive intensification of the
light indicates his progress inward: the sentence rises, but the minister's
soul is too heavy to climb up after it.[26] Then the maelstrom begins
again, the mill wheel, the hell-sent dance of visions—angels, demons,
the mother, the mistress—sometimes vague, sometimes intense:[27] the
sentence follows the movement of the return to the surface, which ends
with a slow drifting followed by a silent sedimentation. Pearl's raised
finger works like a spell; words heavy with penitential symbolism fall
to the bottom of the consciousness, cemented together by muffled,
cavernous sonorities.[28] The movement may also be emphasized by
caesuras comparable to those in verse. In one passage from "The Wives
of the Dead," for example, we find six rhythmic elements each ballasted with a heavy, accented word—in some cases two—which produces a series of "feet," two of them spondees.[29] Another sentence, in
this case in *The House of the Seven Gables*, contains anapaests.[30] These
metrical methods help in the first example to make us imagine an indefinitely prolonged descent as the ripples it causes die away on the
surface. Similarly, the voices and words that rise from the depths of the
well help us to make our way down into it. Like Hemingway in *A Farewell to Arms*, Hawthorne makes use of both rhyming refrains and
hammered rhythms.[31] They both have a tendency to draw upon the
resources of prosody to provide superficial ornaments, and not always
to aid in the birth of an image.

In such skilled—too skilled—hands there is always a danger that
poetry may remain mere "literature." No technique should ever
cease to be the servant of art. And although Hawthorne does not insist overmuch on these obvious methods, the rhythm of his sentences,
once it escapes from the underground labyrinth, does depend more or
less upon their conscious or unconscious use. His descriptive sentences
in particular, the bounding, dancing sentences that are used to evoke
Pearl's games or the faun's caperings,[32] need to be sustained by metrical artifices. Moreover, and this is the danger, though true poetry has
very little time for regularly hammered syllables, the same cannot be
said of oratory. The same is true of music: the metronome is all very

well for giving the beat in a ballet, but not for conducting a symphony. And Hawthorne's true music, like that of Beethoven or Brahms, must be looked for in his profound, complex, sinuous movements, with their imperceptible crescendoes and their interminable decrescendoes. In Beethoven, the wave form predominates: in Brahms the spiral. Though there may not exist any equivalences from one art to another, there are "correspondences"[33] that enable us to discern Brahmsian echoes in Hawthorne in the same way that it is possible to hear echoes of Verlaine in Debussy. The accents with which Hawthorne endowed English prose, like those that Brahms bestowed on music, are accents characterized by sinuous modulations, by siren songs interrupted with brief Dionysiac dances and sudden dazzling explosions. The poetic breath that runs through the work symphonizes the themes. Hester's resurrection is not without its "forest murmurs," and the tragedy based upon a primitive oneirism vibrates with the music of the passions. That music and those movements, to use Bachelard's term, "deposit" forms, images of the consciousness they haunt and that first gave them birth.

IV. THE IMAGE

Every true work of art has a foundation of psychological oneirism running parallel to another of poetic oneirism—a foundation of images, that is, which must then receive the consecration of art and style. The primary images that Hawthorne made use of originated in the Puritan storehouse of his consciousness. They bear the stamp of the ancestral imagination, which was strong and intensely material rather than spiritual[1]—an imagination that by a sort of psychological alchemy gave life and substance to both the most fantastic fables and beliefs[2] and also to the most profound obsessions. Evil is a stain, a thing that can be seen and touched, like the Letter. The devil is a being, a man, not an entity: for Hawthorne, he was even more Dionysos than he was Satan,[3] the demon of creation—for though he returned to these ancestral beliefs, the journey was made through his own obsessions as an artist, so that they become, not unequivocally, the sign of those obsessions as well as that of a certain moral order. Under cover of this confusion there sprang up a remorse for having dared to create. And it is then that we find intruding, between the writer and his personal images, those sterilized symbols and literary metaphors that second-rate authors are never able to transcend, so that their images are never more than added ornaments. And we do certainly find examples of the pedantic and nugatory mythological allusion[4] in Hawthorne, as well as traces of bad taste.[5] His moral conceits can sometimes have a Spenserian grace[6] or a Biblical charm: the American settler's wife always made him think of a "verse of household poetry."[7] But what are we to say of those long drawn out metaphors that are the scourge of all literature,[8] to say nothing of the occasional incursions of flowery keepsake sentimentality?[9] The humorous style, like the ornamented style, is prone to metaphor.[10] And that in *The House of the Seven Gables* presents us with some regrettable examples: the metaphor of the gridiron,[11] and also that of the gas![12] And the allegorical caricature for which those "feathered riddles,"[13] Hepzibah's hens, are used as a pretext is far too heavy-handed. The explicit metaphor betrays even its author's best intentions: the dim mist and the rainbow that play about Hepzibah's face remain stubbornly meteorological and allegorical.[14] The less obvious a metaphor is the more valuable it becomes: it retains its poetic ambiguity and thus ceases to be a metaphor. What does it matter that an image is not listed in the official catalogue of rhetoric! To speak of the "solemn symphony that rolled its undertones through Hepzibah's and her brother's life"[15] is easy; actually to write that symphony is much less so. The "littérateur" contents himself with the surface appearance of images; he scatters the "flowers" of rhetoric with an easy profusion. The poet goes to the substance, and his style is certainly not just a matter of "images" in that sense. Hawthorne, like so many others, sometimes spoils his best inspirations with self-conscious show: the simile of Hepzibah's voice as "a black silken thread, on which the crystal beads of speech are strung," is a manufactured and intolerable stylistic contortion.[16] It is also an example of how false poetry and false literature, if unchecked, will always find a way to take precedence over their genuine counterparts. Following fashion does not, any more than "purifying" one's style in the name of some abstract ideal, constitute a true artistic labor. It constitutes a betrayal of both one's poetic dream and reality. It means that one has become an accomplice to a futile game that falsifies one's values and is a soporific to the unconscious.

To find a true image is to awaken oneself to one's self. To dare to use it is an act of courage. When Hawthorne makes clouds into sculptures,[17] he is straying from his particular genius. When he makes them into an open tent letting the sunlight in, then he is true to it.[18] As he is when he makes an echo into the voice of a reflection,[19] or when he sees his own eyes on the ground staring up at him:[20] at such moments, though he never dares to raise his voice above a whisper, he is speaking with the voice of surrealism—the eye was beginning to exist for him, as it did for André Breton, "as a wild thing"—the eye of the consciousness outside itself, set free from its shackles, turning upon its owner either to drown him in images or to tear him to pieces. The strange, unfamiliar, or terrifying image is the sign of a hidden reality. Hawthorne too often tried to soften that reality, to make it "acceptable." He was ashamed, he was afraid to believe in his dreams. And when he finally lost his right of entry into the world of strange dreams, he was obliged to resort to gratuitous absurdity.[21] Already, in *The House of the Seven Gables*, his humorous fancy is beginning to take precedence over the genuine dream images. To describe the earth as a brain animated by electricity,[22] to personify the east wind as a "grim and disconsolate" old woman[23] is not enough. These images must be connected to an archetype, and that central organ is the House, the static symbol of the heart and the ancestral tree as well as the vehicle of the dream. Similarly, the metaphor of the money in Peter Goldthwaite's chest[24] is poverty-stricken in the extreme if one goes no further than its literal meaning, whereas it takes on a much fuller significance as soon as it is taken as an image of the incommunicable. The real wealth, the only true wealth, is that which resides in the mind. It is our dreams that decide the value of gold. But the true gold, like that of the mystic alchemists who are the direct ancestors of poets like Rimbaud and Milosz, is that of the dreamer.[25]

All alchemy takes place in the imagination, and it is also in the imagination that style is born: it is not simply a polishing process after the work is finished, but the struggle of an artist's personal images into their definitive form. The existence of a style presupposes the existence of a whole world behind it, nourishing it and supporting it. The dimensions of style are those of the imagination, which is why any purely technical approach can never do more than imitate its surfaces, thereby merely creating a confusion between the genuine writer and the sham one. Racine's worst line of all, so outrageous in its alliteration, has become his most famous! Yet what would Racine be if he were not first and foremost a cruel, insistent, compassionate consciousness fascinated by all our human passions? What would Hawthorne be if he were not, beyond the words and the sentences, that gradual and implacable invasion of the consciousness, that inward growth of the plant unfurling symmetrically with the world-tree in which the whole moral, psychic, and esthetic cycle is contained? This explains the twin growth of the pillory, the prison, the rose, the Letter, and the elf. Love, terror, the cruel law, all have a common trunk, while sensuality, repression, pleasure, guilt, punishment, redemption, like branches and roots, all intermingle and exchange their essences. Hawthorne's whole forest is but a single tree. Light and darkness are the most powerful agents of its growth, and we are the spectators, as in the vegetable kingdom of the external world, of veritable esthetic and psychological phototropisms and geotropisms. The spellbound plants sprout up, sometimes in the night—flaming trees, blazing explosions from a lime kiln, the black flower—sometimes beneath an artificial, ultratropical sun—the tree in a poisoned Eden, the suffering pillory-tree. The plant is always human, and poetic logic is that of the inward growth of the consciousness. Which is why any great poetic book must be a source of life. Hawthorne has enabled us to touch it for ourselves, as it were, this ill-defined reality, this unfrontiered province that we are so prone to isolate from reality, either in order to grant it an immaterial existence apart, or in order to deny its existence altogether. Indeed, Hawthorne does better: he makes it into an organ, a thing of flesh whose substance may be tenuous but which can also become extremely dense and weigh down with a great weight in the physical world. But in order to fathom it, to exploit its riches and render it present to the senses, only one method will serve—the method that a poet alone instinctively discovers. Hawthorne himself, when he resorted to pseudoscientific artifices, lost his way. The only valid method consists in identifying oneself with the substance of the images and with the currents of the consciousness, which is to say, with the imagined world. The introspective gaze must always be inherent in the reality gazed at, as light rays shining through water are incorporated into it, so that they, the rays, become oozing light, and the water a liquid reflection: the shadowy consciousness and the inward eye then combine to form a whole that is humid light,[26] as they can also be shadowy light, opaque light, shadow-light—consciousness awake and consciousness asleep —consciousness questing or fleeing, following its own arabesques, mingling with itself, fighting against itself without cease. The seeking mind must be a net stretched across the threshold upon which images alight, like the foliage of the pear tree in *The House of the Seven Gables* catching the fleeting voices as they pass,[27] or the branches of the summerhouse filtering the moonlight and the breeze[28]—the drops of water from the depths, the sounds, the muffled calls, the flickering reflections must all be soaked in by osmosis at the orifice of the spring, of the artesian well.[29] The spheres, images of the heart and head, exchange their fluids, their blood, and fuse together like those two drops symbolizing the passionate loves and hates of the faun and his nymph.[30] Such a fusion does not exclude individuality. The mixing of the elements in Hawthorne is always followed by a process of settling and sedimentation, and the Hawthorne hero always returns into himself "pure," like good and evil lying unmixed in the peaceful conscience, both as solitary as the first being on earth. The work, created in the image of its author, is apart. It belongs to the individual time of its creator, that of an age chosen and created by him, not accepted and submitted to.[31] Instead of conforming to the changing caprices of fashion, it follows an austere curve, it clothes itself in that narrow sheath that Gide held to be so necessary. The Hawthorne arabesque, though it loses its tension in the later works and becomes a thing of fluttering tatters, nevertheless created in *The Scarlet Letter* a harmoniously and powerfully coiled Laocoön. This "convulsive" beauty later insisted upon by Lautréamont has always been characteristic of works charged with human significance.

Conclusion

Whenever the problem of creation is posed for any man, everything ultimately is reduced to the conflict between the inward and the outward, between the self that wishes to perpetuate itself in the work and the world that attracts the work to itself and destroys it, between art and the appearance of art. Hawthorne, torn between the extremes of archaism and modernism, whenever he was fully himself listened exclusively to his artist's instinct, which told him to make use of his ancestral and personal stores of material in order to create his work. His cultural background was European in origin, but his materials, which were colonial in origin, belonged to him alone. His art, which was to some extent that of the alchemist and wizard, characters quite as suspect in the New World as in the Old, came to him from the depths of the ages as though from a deep and secret revery—that of the haunted mind—which, even for James, contained reverberations that were too disturbing for conformist minds.[1] Yet it was for precisely this reason that he was, as James himself wrote, "the last specimen of the more primitive type of men of letters,"[2] just as he was the first of the explorers into the modern American consciousness, a consciousness that would have liked to be wholly new in its new-found, virgin world of solitude, yet was also secretly tempted, like Hester's,[3] by the idea of a return—a consciousness less rooted in the New World than still rocked by the fluctuations of the ocean so recently crossed. And the voice of that ocean, which still sang its lullaby to the inhabitants of the House of the Seven Gables,[4] held promise not only of the ancestral pre-colonial world but also of the world still to be built, that of the pioneers. If Hawthorne was, more than any other writer of his age, "American"—if he recreated the Puritan pilgrimage in the esthetic realm,[5] it was because he was seeking to give that still ocean-rocked American soul the roots that were a first condition of the growth to come. His vision preceded and went beyond any objective intention of creating a national literary tradition. Where others went to such pains to solicit the intervention of disembodied spirits bearing messages, he sought for a physical, bodily contact with the ancestors. He searched them out in their graves in order to ask them to lend him their strong virtues and their no less strong passions, so that he could make his own dreams live, so that he could infuse blood into his tragic images, so that he could give bodies to the tormented souls, the demons, and the monsters struggling within him, so that they could at last, through the strength of his art, become beautiful—even the pillory—like the Minotaur in Gide's *Thésée* and provide the American consciousness with striking and disturbing images that would satisfy its desperate quest for mirrors.

Masterpieces are neither "pleasant" nor flattering; they invariably exercise, like *Phèdre* and the Mona Lisa, a shadowy fascination. In great poetry, in great painting, in great music, black predominates—the black from which the artificially feminized "white psyche," always seeking to "play the angel," dreams of purging out the male "demon" of revolt and creation which, without distinction of sex, inhabits Emily Brontë and Virginia Woolf just as much as Thomas Hardy and James Joyce. The *noir mélange* of the consciousness is the earth, the rich humus in which the complex, polyvalent, multiple work can germinate. In Hawthorne's work, the psychological Oberon-themes, the arabesque, and the cinematic play of those shimmering figures that tantalize and intimidate their dreamer, all flow from the ambiguity of darkness and light that exists in it on every plane. To create means to give life in the imaginary sphere, or to restore life to those greater than oneself. The artist does not become himself except in his creations, and it is by giving a style to his obsessions that he imposes them upon the world. Hawthorne's universe, born of a sense of man's irremediable solitude and his guilt, as well as from that most secret, most absorbing, most revealing of colors—at once moral, pictorial, and cinematic— black, is the legendary universe that finally succeeded in replacing a historical period, in order to endow a certain form of consciousness with a more intensely personal quality and with more broadly human dimensions. Man is multiplied and enlarged in his work, freed both from the fatality of time and instinct and from that of unhappiness. Religions attempt to neutralize despair, to make it change its sign and its sense; poetic creation transmutes it into psychic energy. There can be no creation that is not in secret harmony with those vital forces that are alone able to give birth to a being, to a work. Even science—whose techniques are always attempting to usurp absolute power—would be deprived of its roots without the aid of imagination, and be forced to build in a void. *The Scarlet Letter* has strong roots—though *Uncle Tom's Cabin* is not without them too. Yet one is a sturdy tree and the other a mere shoot—which once more illumines the misunderstanding about art: Mrs. Stowe put her trust wholly in the document, in its journalistic value. Hawthorne made his into brand new material. His *Twice Told Tales*, of which perhaps only the *Contes Cruels* of Villiers de l'Isle-Adam offers, in French literature, the equivalent in quality, color, and tone, each forms a whole, a closed system, an esthetic individuality, thus proving in advance that Bergson's theories of "creative evolution" are also valid for art,[6] whose essential tendencies, in the realm of imagination, are the same as those of living matter. The creative faculty in Hawthorne, as in any artist worthy of the name, is nothing else but the poetic faculty directed toward the imaginative depiction of reality, psychology, and the profound images or musical translation of the inward universe—directions that may all converge to create a work of genius when a psychic spark has been flung into an intense and vibrating oneiric-realistic complex of sufficient potency to make the atom of human thought unleash its power—as with the sudden inward blaze of the Letter, from which there emerged the book that so profoundly disturbed its author's own consciousness. It is to this book that so harrowed his soul, and to a number of "profound"[7] stories, that Hawthorne owes his continuing position as the poet of New England, the poet whose Dionysiac and ancestral feeling for the land of his birth was so strong that it becomes substantial shadow, light, and the voice of the earth itself in the pages of his work. Though his writing may have been an attempt to fill an agonizing void, there is no doubt that he did fill a space in the world, a space where there had previously been nothing, with a reality, with a music,[8] with images that are all irreplaceable. His work, a lived and expressed world-image, is one of the great poems of the New World and the human consciousness—one of those great upwellings of the being that true creation must always be.

Notes

REFERENCES

Unless otherwise noted, references to Hawthorne's own works cite volume and page numbers as given in the Riverside Edition of *The Works of Nathaniel Hawthorne*, 12 volumes (Boston and New York: Houghton Mifflin Co., 1883). *Dr. Grimshawe's Secret* (abbreviated "Grim.") was added to the Riverside Edition later as Volume XIII; reference is made to this version, edited by Julian Hawthorne, as well as to E. H. Davidson's version, *Hawthorne's Dr. Grimshawe's Secret* (Cambridge, Mass., 1954). Notes on Hawthorne's various notebooks will refer either to the Riverside Edition or to certain notebooks as edited by Randall Stewart.

These notes have been corrected, insofar as was possible, in the light of the corrected bibliography.

ABBREVIATIONS

A.Doane	"Alice Doane's Appeal"
A.G.	"The Ambitious Guest"
Am.Nbks.	*American Notebooks*
A.o.B.	"The Artist of the Beautiful"
Birth.	"The Birthmark"
Bl.R.	*The Blithedale Romance*
Cel.Rlrd.	"The Celestial Railroad"
D.in Mss.	"The Devil in Manuscript"

Dr.H's Exp.	"Dr. Heidegger's Experiment"
D's W.Im.	"Drowne's Wooden Image"
E.R.'s P.	"Ed. Randolph's Portrait"
E.B.	"Ethan Brand"
Eng.Nbks.	*English Notebooks*
F's Sh.B.	"Fancy's Show Box"
G.B.	"The Gentle Boy"
G.C.	"The Great Carbuncle"
Gd.F's Ch.	*Grandfather's Chair*
Grim.	*Dr. Grimshawe's Secret*
H.	Hawthorne
H.of3H.	"The Hollow of the Three Hills"
It.Nbks.	*Italian Notebooks*
Lady E.	"Lady Eleanore's Mantle"
M.F.	*The Marble Faun*
M.M.M.	"The Maypole of Merry Mount"
Mosses	*Mosses from an Old Manse*
M's B.V.	"The Minister's Black Veil"
My Kinsman	"My Kinsman, Major Molineux"
N.A.&E.	"The New Adam and Eve"
O.O.H.	*Our Old Home*
N.H.	Nathaniel Hawthorne
P.Gold.	"Peter Goldthwaite's Treasure"
Rapp.	"Rappacini's Daughter"
R.M.'s B.	"Roger Malvin's Burial"
7G.	*The House of the Seven Gables*
7Vag.	"The Seven Vagabonds"
S.L.	*The Scarlet Letter*
Sn.Im.	*The Snow Image*
Tangle.	*Tanglewood Tales*
T.T.T.	*Twice-Told Tales*
W.Bk.	*A Wonder Book*
Wives	"The Wives of the Dead"
Wks.	*The Works of Nathaniel Hawthorne* (Riverside Edition)
Y.G.B.	"Young Goodman Brown"

Miscellaneous abbreviations:

G.P.L., Life	"Biographical Sketch" in Volume XII of Wks.

J.H.,H.&W	Hawthorne, Julian, *Nathaniel Hawthorne and his wife* (Boston, 1885).
R.S.	Randall Stewart
R.S., Biog.	Randall Stewart. *Nathaniel Hawthorne: A Biography* (New Haven, 1948).
Recoll.	Hawthorne, E. "Recollections of Nathaniel Hawthorne by his sister Elizabeth." Edited by Randall Stewart. *AL*, XVI, January 1945.

INTRODUCTION

(1) For all general supplementary information, readers are referred to the analytical bibliography at the end of this book. Notes will be given only on the particular references made in the course of this introduction.

(2) Letter to Una Hawthorne, June 15, 1876 (Pearson, "Elizabeth Peabody on H.," EIHC, XCIV, 1958).

(3) Julian Hawthorne, *H. and his Wife*, I (notably the story of the duel: cf. Pearson, "H's Duel," EIHC, XCIV, 1958).

(4) This character is the man seen from the outside, the social persona. Which is why some writers have sought to dissociate the writer from the man (e.g. Julian Hawthorne, Th. Parker, Alcott, Loring; cf. Austin Warren, *Rage for Order*, 1948, p. 85).

(5) See Bibliography, IV, D, 2.

(6) McKiernan, *The psychology of N.H.*, 1957.

(7) Hoeltje, *Inward Sky: the Mind and Heart of N.H.* (Durham, N.C., 1962) bases his interpretation on the close correlation between life and work.

(8) The main works in *England* have been:
Japp (pseud., Page), *Memories of H.*, London, 1872.
Stephen, *Hours in a Library*, N.Y., 1875, and *N.H.*, London, 1877.
Symons, "N.H.," in *Studies in Prose and Verse*, London, 1904.
Read, "H.," *Hound & Horn*, III, 1945 (complex of British superiority).
In *Germany*:
Schönbach, "Beitrage zur Charakteristik NHs." *Eng. St.*, 1884
Böhmer, *Brook Farm und Bl. R.*, Berlin, 1936.
Veen, *Die Erzählungstechnik in dem Kurzerzählungen Hs.* Münster, 1938.
Reti, *Hs. Verhältnis zur Neu England Tradition*. Rüstringen, 1955.
In *Scandinavia*:
Johansson, *Det Speglade Livet*. Stockholm, 1924.
Lilijegren, *Some Notes on H.* Upsala, 1949.
Lundblad, *H. & European Lit. Tradition*. Harvard and Upsala, 1947.
In *Italy*:
McKenzie, *Conferenze sulla Litteratura Americana* (H. and Poe). Bari, 1922.
Prezzolini, "Gli H. a Roma." *Nueva Antologia*, LXXXV, 1951.
Guidi, "Le Ambiguita di H." *St. Am.* I, 1955.
Izzo, "Un Metafisico della narrazione, N.H." *St. Am.* I. 1955.
Marenco, "H. e il Bl. R." *JA*, VI, 1960.
In *Japan*:
Hamada Masajiro, "S.L., a Tale of 3 Prisoners." *Bungaku-kai Ronshu*, Konan University, 1960.

(9) Voight, "N.H., Author for Preachers," *Lutheran Ch. Q.*, XXI, 1943, and, on

the other hand, an anonymous Protestant article (N & Q., Apr. 1943) against the defenders (including Read) of H., that morbid and conscience-less author.

(10) This is, however, the explanation given by numbers of American scholars, among them Levin, Davidson and Pearson.

(11) Pearce, "H. and the Twilight of Romance," *YR*, XXXVII; Lundblad, note (8).

(12) Carpenter, "Scarlet A Minus." *CE*, V, 1944.

(13) Kirk, "Moral Conservation of H." *Contemp R*, 182, Dec. 1952. This is also the personal opinion of Professor Lynn of Harvard.

(14) F. O. Matthiessen. *American Renaissance*. N.Y., 1941.

(15) Montégut, "Un Romancier Socialiste en Amérique." *Rev. des Deux Mondes*, 1852.

(16) Arvin, *H.* (Boston, 1929): "If the T.T.T. . . . are not great literature it is because of the factitious fatalism that pervades them" (which is unjust).

(17) Montégut, "Un Romancier Pessimiste en Amérique," *Rev. des Deux Mondes*, 1860.

PART ONE: OBERON

CHAPTER 1
I

(1) Cantwell, *N.H.: The American Years*, 1948, Ch. I.

(2) Hawthorne Boulevard. There is also a Hawthorne Hotel at the intersection of this boulevard and Union St. Similarly, there is a Hawthorne St., in Cambridge and a Hawthorne Lane in Concord, opposite "Wayside."

(3) Salem, contraction of Jerusalem, Psalm LXXVI, 2: "In Salem also is his tabernacle, and his dwelling place in Zion"; founded by John Endicott in 1628. Had 5,000 inhabitants in 1767, with an annual traffic of 350 ships. By the time of H.'s birth, the town had a population of 12,000 (that of Boston at that time was less than 20,000), and 100 ships in its port. By 1805 there were only 66. In 1808 came the embargo. In 1812, the harbor was blocked by an English ship *Shannon*. Salem never recovered, and its traffic was absorbed by Boston, the suburbs of which stretch out today as far as Lynn.

(4) John Hope Franklin, *From Slavery to Freedom*, p. 100. The *Desire*, a ship from Salem, docked at Boston in 1638 and unloaded "a cargo of salt, tobacco, cotton, and Negroes."

(5) Great shipowning families of Salem. The Crowninshields even had a wharf named after them (Cantwell).

(6) Eng.Nbks., ed. R.S., pp. 40 and 383 (July 13, 1856): research undertaken in the archives by H. abandoned on account of fatigue.

(7) The "w" was added by H. himself, "not long after receiving his University degree," R. S. says (Biog., 1), i.e. about 1825. H.'s sisters, Elizabeth and Louisa, were to follow his example; Mrs. Hathorne herself was to call herself "Mrs. Hawthorne," perhaps in order to associate herself more closely with her son's fame. Many authors, Van Wyck Brooks particularly (*Flowering of New England*, 291), accept that H. was merely following the Transcendentalist fashion of euphonic transformation of proper names: thus Emerson called his wife Lydian instead of Lydia; Alcott was originally named Alcox; and Thoreau inverted the order of his first names, calling himself Henry David, rather than David Henry as Dr. Ripley had wished. But if we remember that there was hardly any talk of Transcendentalism before 1835 (Emerson published *Nature* in 1836), we see that there can be no question of its influence here. The "w" was rather one of H.'s typical quirks of fancy, and one in which the poetic association with the hawthorn

bush doubtless played some part. Moreover he seemed to enjoy using the French pseudonym "De l'Aubépine" when signing letters to his fiancée; he also used it in the introduction to Rapp. (Mosses, 107). But to conclude from this the existence of French ancestry, as Julian H. does (*H. and His Wife*, I, 8), is pushing things rather far.

(8) J. Winthrop (1588–1649), first governor of Massachusetts. Cf. S.L., Wks., V, 183.

(9) This document is reproduced as an appendix to Dhaleine's thesis (*N.H.*, 1905), together with the note in H's writing appearing on the back of it: "Copy of a letter supposedly written by Major W. Hathorne of Massachusetts, defending the colony against the accusations of Charles II's Commissioners and excusing the Court General for its refusal to send Governor Bellingham and himself to England in conformity with the King's orders."

(10) Perry Miller (*From Colony to Province*), without excusing these excesses, sheds light on the true intentions of the Puritan leaders, who often had their hands forced by circumstances and the superstitions of their day.

(11) S.L., Wks., V, 24, "The Custom House."

(12) R.S., Biog., p. 32: Bold Daniel, "the sternest man that ever walked a deck." He was one of Massachusetts' 626 privateers during the War of Independence. Cf. Lathrop, in Wks., XII, 488, and Cantwell, p. 7.

(13) Elizabeth was born in 1802; Nathaniel, on July 4, 1804; Louisa, in 1808.

(14) R.S., Biog., p. 3.

(15) G.P.L., Life, Wks., XII, 454.

(16) Mark Van Doren, *N.H.*, 1949, Ch. I.

(17) Recoll.

(18) J.H., H.&W, I, 177.

(19) Recoll.

(20) Ibid.

(21) Ibid.

(22) Quoted in J.H., H.&W, I, 99.

(23) Rimbaud, *Poésies*: "Les Poètes de Sept Ans."

(24) J.H., H.&W, I, 36.

(25) Ibid.

(26) Autobiographical letter to his friend Stoddard, intended as material for an article in the *National Review*, 1835: "a grievous disinclination to go to school" (quoted in J.H., H.&W, I, 95–98).

(27) Details given by Cantwell, *N.H.: The American Years*. Foster: a name used by H. later in Bl.R., Wks., V (Silas Foster, the farmer).

(28) Browne's Folly: *Tales and Sketches*, Wks., XII.

(29) Julien Green, *Un Puritain Homme de Lettres*, 1928, p. 10.

II

(1) Recoll.

(2) R.S., Biog., p. 4.

(3) "Recollections."

(4) Ibid.

(5) Ibid.

(6) G.P.L., Life, Wks. XII, 442–3: "gambrel roof," and also the immense loft. A reconstruction of this house now stands near the House of the Seven Gables.

(7) Dr. Peabody, father of Sophia, later H's. wife, attended the young H. during his illness.

(8) S.L., Wks., V, 69: "It might be that . . . an undutiful child . . . was to be corrected at the whipping-post."

(9) Recoll.

(10) Ibid.

(11) Ibid.

(12) Perhaps a legend started by Elizabeth Peabody (who had certain literary pretentions) around the origins of a writer who had become famous? Possibly. Most of H.'s contemporaries and his more recent biographers seem to accept that this was what happened. But discounting certain exaggerations, Mrs. H.'s attitude, if we are to believe Elizabeth Peabody herself, was not particularly strange: "It was considered, at that time, a mark of piety and good taste for a widow to withdraw herself from the world" (quoted by J.H., H.&W, I, 177).

(13) E. Peabody, quoted in J.H., H.&W, I, 181–2 (see next note).

(14) Ibid. "Mrs. H. always looked as if she had walked out of an old picture, with her antique costume, and a face of lovely sensibility and great brightness,—for she did not *seem* at all a victim of morbid sensibility, notwithstanding her all but Hindoo self-devotion to the manes of her husband . . ."

(15) Letter to his mother, March 7, 1820.

(16) Am.Nbks, R.S., July 1849.

(17) S.L., V, 177.

(18) G.P.L., Life, Wks., XII, 449.

(19) Recoll.

(20) No precedents are to be found, particularly on the Hathorne side, for Hawthorne's talent. The only writing his father left behind him was a logbook of his voyages; and his grandfather the privateer was content to borrow from Sidney's *Arcadia* when he needed the help of poetry to declare his love for Mary Rondel (J.H., H.&W, I, 34–35).

(21) See Claude-Edmonde Magny, *Rimbaud*, Poètes d'Aujourd'hui, Seghers, No. 12.

(22) Rimbaud, *Les Illuminations*, "Mémoire":
> Madame se tient trop debout dans la prairie
> prochaine où neigent les fils du travail; l'ombrelle
> aux doigts; foulant l'ombrelle; trop fière pour elle
> des enfants lisant dans la verdure fleurie . . .
> *Poésies*, "Les Poètes de Sept Ans":
> ". . . Elle avait le bleu regard,—qui ment!"

(23) Recoll.

(24) Robert Calef, *More Wonders of the Invisible World*. Sarah Good, who appeared before the Salem court on June 30, 1692, answered as follows to the magistrate Noyes, Judge Hathorne's assistant: "You are a liar,—I am no more a witch than you are a wizard, and if you take away my life, God will give you blood to drink!" Cf, 7G., Wks., III, 21: "God will give him blood to drink!"; 35: "He has Maule's blood to drink!"; 152: "God would give them blood to drink"; 248: "so, you have old Maule's blood to drink!" Calef's book, H.H. Hoeltje says (*Inward Sky, the Mind and Heart of N.H.*, Durham, N.C., 1962) "was . . . burned in Harvard Yard during the Mather dynasty" (p. 11).

(25) G.B., Wks., I.

(26) S.L., "Custom House," Wks., V, 25.

(27) "Alice Doane," Wks., XII; "Roger Malvin's Burial," Wks., II.

(28) The theme of the Bloody Footstep in the posthumous novels: *The Ancestral Footstep*, Wks., XI, and Grim., Wks., XIII.

III

(1) Rev. L. Fick (*The Light Beyond*, 1955); F. P. Stearns (*The Life and Genius of N.H.*, 1906); F. O. Matthiessen (*American Renaissance*, 1941); and H. B. Schneider (*The Puritan Mind*) all agree on this point. However, the anonymous author of an article in Emmerton, "Clippings about H. and his Salem from Salem and Boston newspapers," in the Essex Institute, advances one religious reason among those he gives for H.'s remaining isolated from Salem society: H. was not a Unitarian.

(2) Pickard, *H.'s First Diary*: "a minute observer of religious festivals, fasts, and Sabbath days."

(3) Recoll.
(4) R. H. Lathrop, *Memories of H.*
(5) Worcester, a distinguished legicographer, gave his pupil a copy of his dictionary.
(6) Recoll.: "As soon as he was old enough to buy books for himself he purchased Spenser's *Fairy Queen*."
(7) R.S., Biog., p. 5.
(8) *Richard III*, I, 2, 1. 38.
(9) Recoll.
(10) Ibid.
(11) G. P. Lathrop, *A Study of H.*, III, 67–69.
(12) "Monsieur du Miroir," II, 182.
(13) Stearns, *Life and Genius of N.H.*, 1906. "*It is presumable that* N.H. also became a Unitarian, so far as he can be considered a sectarian at all."
(14) Cotton and Increase Mather, famous theologians and administrators, exercized considerable influence in the colony of Massachusetts during the 17th century. Cotton, son of Increase, author of hundreds of small literary works, also wrote *Magnalia Christi Americana* (1702). H. devoted Chapters IV and V of Gd.F's Ch., Part 2, to him (Wks., IV).
(15) Jonathan Edwards (1703–58) used to terrorize his hearers with his descriptions of hell's torments (*Sinners in the Hands of an Angry God*, 1741). Perry Miller has devoted a remarkable study to him (*Jonathan Edwards*, 1949) in which he presents him as an unjustly neglected writer of the first rank. We find H. using the Biblical expression "tongue of fire" later in S.L., Wks., V, 173, without any reference to Edwards. The reference is to a verse from Isaiah (XXX, 27: "his tongue as a devouring fire").
(16) Emerson's childhood, though perhaps more austere than H's., nevertheless contained no equivalent prolonged confinement, nor was it haunted by any noticeable sense of guilt. Emerson never viewed H.'s obsessions as anything but a moral infirmity. He defined sin as "the soul's mumps and measles."
(17) Sören Kierkegaard (1813–55), a writer of whom H. had never heard, and misunderstood like H. in his own country, was to publish under a pseudonym, in 1849 (one year before *The Scarlet Letter*) his *Sickness Unto Death*.
(18) The Giant Despair is a figure in Bunyan's *Pilgrim's Progress*.
(19) "No man can escape his anguish," he wrote, "because he loves it; or love it truly either, because he is trying to escape it."
(20) H. does not use the word anguish in the philosophical sense but in the moral sense, and even more often in the purely physical sense. Cf. S.L., Wks., V, 76, 172 (prick and anguish); 173 (crime or anguish); 174 (agony with which . . . veneration tortured him); 180 (agony of . . . guilt); 299 (miserable agony); 300 (doubt and anxiety); 301 (full of anguish); 303, 304.
(21) Cestre, *La Littérature américaine*, 1929–30. "He felt himself an artist, and contrary to the Puritan tradition he had resolved to make art his profession. He was to use the Puritan way of life as the background to his pictures, the Puritan conscience as a source of moral action, Puritan superstition as his insubstantial settings, the Puritan conflict between religious obsession and natural desires as a dramatic fulcrum."

IV
(1) Recoll.
(2) Ibid.: Elizabeth is probably quoting her brother's own words.
(3) Woodberry, *N.H.* 1902, p. 7.
(4) The Rev. J. Eliot (1604–90), founder of the Praying Indian colonies, is introduced into *S.L.* as a friend of the Rev. Dimmesdale (Wks., V, 264). H. also devoted a chapter of Gd.F'sCh. to him: "The Indian Bible" (Wks., IV). The Apostle's work was destroyed by King Philip's war (1675).

(5) Woodberry, *N.H.*, 1902, pp. 7-8.

(6) This notebook, an exercise-book in fact ("blank-book" Lathrop calls it, while other authors term it an "album" or "scrapbook"), a present from his uncle Richard, is a source of much dispute (Cf. Bibliography), but certain descriptive and anecdotal passages are probably by H.

(7) Recoll.: Elizabeth confirms that there were bears in the Sebago district at that time.

(8) G.P.L., Life, Wks., XII., 457.

(9) Recoll.

(10) Letter to J. T. Fields, 1863: "I lived in Maine like a bird of the air, so perfect was the freedom I enjoyed. But it was there I first got my cursed habit of solitude."

(11) Cantwell, *N.H.: The American Years*, p. 54.

(12) Dr. Heidegger (Dr. H.'s Exp., Wks., I); Aylmer (Birth., Wks., II); Rappacini (Rapp., Wks., II); Chillingworth (S.L., Wks, V); Dr. Grimshawe (Grim., Wks., XIII); Septimius Felton (*Septimius Felton*, Wks., XI); Dr. Dolliver (*The Dolliver Romance*, Wks., XI). Cantwell sees the name of H.'s tutor as a possible origin of this last name: B. Lynde Oliver: Dolliver.

(13) Letter to his mother, October 1820.

(14) See Bibliography.

(15) Eliz. Chandler Lathrop, *A Study of the Sources of the Tales . . . by N.H.*, 1926, indicates "the Pin Society" as being contemporaneous with the "Spectator" (1820).

(16) Ibid.: "By an unanimous vote of the Society, Nat. Hawthorne, Esq. was appointed advocate to plead in all the disputes which may affect the Pin Society, with the title of Honorable, and Marie Louise Hawthorne was appointed Second Pin Counter, with the title of Accurate" (Spectator).

(17) R.S., Biog., p. 37: when playing cards with some friends after his time at college, H. distributed the titles of Chancellor, Cardinal, etc. among them, finally bestowing upon himself that of Emperor!

(18) Cantwell even claims that he wrote to his mother and sisters with invisible ink in order to hide his opinions from the Mannings.

(19) Letter of June 21, 1821.

(20) Like many affluent people at that time, the Mannings had built a "folly" at Raymond that was in no way extravagant or aristocratic, unlike Browne's Folly or General Knox's place.

(21) A letter to Sophia Peabody written on Nov. 30, 1839 is signed "Deodatus."

(22) Letter of March 7, 1820: "Shall you want me to be a Minister, Doctor, or Lawyer? A minister I will not be."

(23) Letter of March 13, 1821: "I have not yet concluded what profession I shall have. The being a minister is of course out of the question. I could not think that even you could desire me to choose so dull a way of life. Oh no, mother, I was not born to vegetate forever in one place, and live and die as calm and tranquil as—a puddle of water . . . Oh that I was rich enough to live without a profession! What do you think of my becoming an author, and relying for support on my pen? . . . How proud you would feel to see my works praised by the reviewers, as equal to the proudest productions of the scribbling sons of John Bull."

(24) Same letter as preceding note. Woodberry, N.H., 1902, pp. 15-16.

CHAPTER 2

I

(1) The charter was granted in 1794. The college was not in fact opened until 1802 ("The Commemoration of the Opening of the College," 1852).

(2) *Sn.Im.*, Preface, Wks., III, 386–87: ". . . watching the great logs, as they tumbled along the current of the Androscoggin . . ."

(3) R. S., Biog., p. 14: out of 114 students in 1821 84 were from Maine, 19 from New Hampshire, 9 from Massachusetts.

(4) H. Bridge, *Personal Recollections of N.H.*, 1893.

(5) W. B. Mitchell, "A Remarkable Bowdoin Decade (1820–1830)".

(6) Penalties were laid down for neglecting one's studies, failing in religious observances, and insubordination. For the more serious offences (frequenting taverns—such as Woodworth's, which was to become that of Hugh Crombie in *Fanshawe*, Wks., XI—letting out cattle, gambling for money) the penalty was rustication. Details may be found in Mitchell.

(7) R. S., Biog., p. 22: the name was a humorous deformation of the word potato. There seems little doubt that the invention bears the stamp of H.'s sense of humor.

(8) Bridge, *Personal Recollections.*

(9) R. S., Biog., p. 22: the Puritan Sunday, still observed in Brunswick, began on Saturday evening.

(10) Letter to his sister Elizabeth quoted in R. S., Biog., p. 22: "I have a great mind to commence playing again, merely to show him that I scorn to be seduced by another into anything wrong."

(11) Letter quoted by Julian H. in H.&W, I, 123.

(12) 5 feet 11 inches, according to his son Julian ("N.H.'s Blue Coat," *Bookman*, LXXV, 1932).

(13) G.P.L., Life, Wks., XII, states that H. did not have dark eyes ("Dark, brilliant, and most expressive," is Bridge's description in *Personal Recollections*, however).

(14) J.H., H.&W, I: H. used to sculpt wooden toys for his children.

(15) Bridge, *Personal Recollections.*

(16) Ibid.

(17) Competitive sports already existed in New England, but outside the colleges, and they sometimes led to dangerous excesses. Sophia Peabody's brother George, for example, having competed in a race between Boston and Roxbury, was to pay for his painfully won victory with a long period of illness and finally his death (J.H., H.&W, I: extracts from Sophia's Diary).

(18) G.P.L., Life, Wks., XII, 555.

(19) H's. nickname at college, one of his pseudonyms during the earliest part of his literary career, and the name of the hero of "The Devil in Massachusetts" (Sn. Im., Wks. III) and of "Fragments of a Relinquished Work" (Wks. XII).

(20) "He is a lion, a bear, a tiger." And, in affectionate protest, "The man's a satyr: there's no tiring him out."

(21) "An essentially feminine cast of mind."

(22) Millicent Bell, *H's. View of the Artist*, New York, 1962 gives her Ch. 6. the title: "Oberon, the Mask of N.H." and refuses the "temptation" of seeing anything in the name beyond a literary disguise.

(23) Thomson's *Castle of Indolence*: one of the young H's. bedside books.

(24) H. was probably to read Balzac's philosophical novella *Louis Lambert* later (Lundblad, *H. and European Literary Tradition*, 1947). But it is very likely that Deane was the real-life prototype of Fanshawe (Cantwell, *N.H.: The American Years*, 100).

(25) "Autobiographical Essay," J.H., H.&W, I, 95–98: "I was an idle student . . . rather choosing to nurse my own fancies than to dig into Greek roots and be numbered among the learned Thebans."

(26) N. H. Pearson, "The College Years of N.H." (Unpubl. monograph): "We know but . . . the shell of his Bowdoin life . . . the Sturm und Drang of his emotional life remains an empty page."

(27) Whittier: "He never seemed to be doing anything, yet did not like to be disturbed at it."

(28) Bridge, *Personal Recollections.*

(29) Lloyd Morris, *The Rebellious Puritan,* 1927, insists on the impression H. made at college on his fellow students. Other critics are evidently afraid of emphasizing the inherent ambiguity of his personality in case they should make him appear homosexual, and eagerly pass on to describe the masculine brutalities of which he was sometimes capable (Cantwell, p. 85).

(30) Letter to his mother, March, 1821.

(31) When addressing the graduating students on the subject of "Our Native Writers" in September 1825, Longfellow exclaimed: "Yes!—palms are to be won by our native writers!—by those that have been nursed and brought up with us in the civil and religious freedom of our country" (Quoted by R. S., Biog., p. 25).

(32) This is the opinion of Elizabeth Chandler Lathrop (*A Study of the Sources*), of Elizabeth Hawthorne (Recoll.), and of H. H. Hoeltje ("H. as a senior at Bowdoin," *EIHC*, 1958): "7 Tales of my Native Land" (of which only 3 have survived) and *Fanshawe* were all, if not written, at least sketched at Bowdoin.

(33) Sn.Im., Preface, Wks., III, 386–87: "If anybody is responsible for my being . . . an author, it is yourself" . . . "it was your prognostic of your friend's destiny, that he was to be a writer of fiction."

(34) Eighteenth out of a class of 38 students (R.S., Biog., p. 18).

(35) Hoeltje, "H. as a senior at Bowdoin," *EIHC*, 1958: Apthorp, author of "Confessions of a Country Schoolmaster."

II

(1) Letter to his sister Louisa, August 11, 1824, J. H., *H.&W*, I, 114.

(2) Salem was beginning to become a minor center of provincial culture. Hoeltje, *Inward Sky, the Mind and Heart of N.H.*, Durham, N.C. 1962, p. 9: Salem "had become self-conscious and introspective . . ."

(3) "Alice Doane's Appeal," Wks., XII.

(4) Quoted by G.P.L., Life, Wks., XII, 470: "We do not even live at our house."

(5) Ibid., Introd., IX, 12: "In this dismal chamber FAME was won" (Salem, Union Street, August 31, 1836).

(6) Wks., IX, 222: "Salem, Oct. 4th, Union Street (Family Mansion)." According to Lathrop this is a lapse of memory and we should read "Herbert Street."

(7) Cantwell, *N.H.: The American Years,* p. 117: one of H.'s abandoned projects.

(8) Wks., II, 459: ". . . they can anticipate nothing but evil of a young man who neither studies physic, law, nor gospel, nor opens a store, nor takes to farming . . ."

(9) Recoll.

(10) "Autobiographical Essay," J.H., H.&W, I, 95–98: "seldom going out except at twilight . . ."; and a letter to Longfellow, June 3, 1837: "like the owl, I seldom venture abroad till after dark."

(11) "Y.G.B.," Wks., II.

(12) "Autobiographical Essay": "I scarcely held human intercourse outside my own family . . ."

(13) Wks., II, 459: "public opinion . . . ranked me with tavern haunters and town paupers" (*Relinquished Work*).

(14) H.&W, I, 85–87.

(15) During the summer of 1833. In the fall of the same year he wrote "The Mermaid" (*Village Uncle*, Wks., I).

(16) Cantwell, *N.H.: The American Years,* 150.

(17) G. B. Cheever, a Congregationalist minister convicted of having slandered a farmer with a private still (cf. Recoll., 328, Note 29).

(18) Recoll.: "Conscious of being utterly unlike every one else . . . he began to withdraw into himself . . ."
(19) Eng.Nbks., Wks., VII, 550.
(20) Eng.Nbks., ed. R.S., 96: "still that same dream of life hopelessly a failure!" (a passage omitted by Mrs. Hawthorne).
(21) Ibid., Wks., VII, 549.
(22) Letters to Sophia, Oct. 4, 1840, Wks., IX, 223.
(23) "An Old Woman's Tale," XII (the moonlight).
(24) Am.Nbks., ed. R.S., 26: "Old Susy Ingersoll, proud of being proud" (possibly a model for Hepzibah Pyncheon, 7G., Wks., III).
(25) "Night Sketches," I, 477.
(26) "Autobiographical Essay," J.H., H.&W, I, 95–98.
(27) Cantwell, N.H.: The American Years, p. 139.
(28) "The Toll-Gatherer's Day." Wks., I, 234.
(29) Recoll.
(30) Ibid.

III

(1) "Fragments from the Journal of a Solitary Man." Wks., XII, 16.
(2) "Autobiographical Essay" in J.H., H.&W, I, 95–98.
(3) Between Albany and Schenectady (Mohawk and Hudson Railroad). The Boston-Albany section was not finished until 1841.
(4) Am. Nbks., Wks., IX, 13: "Salem, June 15, 1835." Any possible entries before this date do not appear to have been preserved.
(5) The fragments that have been preserved figure in the Riverside Edition under the titles: Sketches from Memory (1st Series, Mosses, Wks., II—2nd Series, Wks., XII), Passages from a Relinquished Work (Wks., II), "Fragments from the Journal of a Solitary Man" (Wks., II) and "My Visit to Niagara" (Wks., XII).
(6) Title of a collection suggested to Goodrich in 1834 but never published.
(7) "Night Scene," XII, 21: "The steamboat in which I was passenger for Detroit." Cf. R.S., Biog., p. 42 (Detroit and Montreal: it seems that H. decided not to cross the frontier on account of a cholera epidemic). See also: "An Ontario Steam Boat," sketch for the Am. Mag., 1836 (Arlin Turner, H. as Editor, 1941).
(8) R. S. places the stay at C. N. in 1832, advancing as irrefutable proof a letter from H. to his mother dated September that year.
(9) Possible Chronology of H's. summer trips:
    1825, '26, or '27: first long expedition (Niagara?).
    1828: journey through Connecticut.
    1829: same.
    1830: second long trip (Canada? Niagara? Detroit?).
    1831: visit to Canterbury Shakers.
    1832: Crawford Notch, Lake Champlain, perhaps Niagara or Montreal.
    1833: Swampscott.
    1834: Niagara? Great Lakes as far as Detroit? (R.S., Biog., p. 42).
    1835: Martha's Vineyard (Cf. sketch for the Am.Mag., Turner, H. as Editor)
(10) "Rochester," Wks., XII, 17: "one who had not yet seen Niagara"; "The Haunted Quack" (unpub., quoted by Cantwell, N.H.: The American Years, 162: "In the summer of 18—, I made an excursion to Niagara").
(11) R.S., Biog., 30: Goodrich offered him 35 dollars for "The Gentle Boy."
(12) 7Vag., Wks., I, published in The Token (1833), may have been first drafted in 1830 (cf. Eliz. Chandler Lathrop) after the trips through Connecticut.
(13) The comparison between Burlington and Montreal ("Inland Port," Wks., XII, 15) leads us to believe that H. visited the frontier region more than once. So do the two passages referring to Niagara ("Solitary Man," Wks., XII; "My Visits," ibid.).
(14) "David Swan," Wks., I.

(15) "Canterbury Pilgrims," Wks., III, 518.
(16) "A Fellow-Traveller," *Relinquished Work.*, Wks., II, 464.
(17) 7Vag., Wks., I, 392.
(18) "Canterbury Pilgrims," Wks., III, 530: "The lovers drank at the Shaker spring."
(19) "Fellow Traveller," Wks., II, 464–65.
(20) "The Notch," Wks., II, 476: "loitering toward the heart of the White Mountains."
(21) Ibid., 477: "all the secrets of the mountain's inmost heart."
(22) "Great Carbuncle," Wks., I.
(23) Those of the first Presidents of the United States, Washington, and Adams, and that of La Fayette.
(24) Profile Mountain, above Profile Lake (cf. "The Great Stone Face," Wks., III).
(25) Quoted in R.S., Biog., 41.
(26) "Ambitious Guest," Wks., I (the avalanche).
(27) "The Notch," Wks., II, and A.G., Wks., I, (cf. sources: Cameron, "Genesis of A.G.," *Historiographer of the Episcopal Diocese of Connecticut, 1955:* H. made use of a newspaper item, the catastrophe of 1826; various newspapers, including the Salem *Essex Register* of Sept. 7, 1826, mention an avalanche.)
(28) "Inland Port," XII, 13.
(29) "The Old French War," "Old News," II, Wks., III.
(30) "Old Ticonderoga," Wks., XII, 18–19.
(31) "Rochester," Wks., XII, 18–19.
(32) Phineas Taylor Barnum was about to begin his rise to notoriety by exhibiting an aged negress said to be Washington's nurse.
(33) See: 7Vag., Wks., I, Journal of North Adams, ed. R.S., and E.B., Wks., III, 477.
(34) From Albany to Buffalo: "I embarked . . . 30 miles below Utica" ("Canal Boat," Wks., II).
(35) "Canal Boat," Wks., II, 488.
(36) Ibid., 487.
(37) "Solitary Man," Wks., XII.
(38) "My Visit," Wks., XII.
(39) We find him mocking the "Byronism" flowering into sonnets in the snows of Mt. Washington (Wks., II, 278). H. the letter writer may sometimes indulge in romantic exaggeration (Letter to his mother, Sept. 1832, R.S., Biog., 42), but the author of the *Notebooks* never permits himself such lapses.
(40) "My Visit," Wks., XII, 47: "before my departure for the Far West . . ."

IV

(1) 7Vag., Wks., I, 412–13.
(2) *Relinquished Work*, Wks., II, 457–59: a symbolic image of his uncles, probably.
(3) H's. own reflection upon receiving a check from Hillard (thank-you letter, Jan. 30, 1850).
(4) Blake on Milton: ". . . he was a true poet and of the Devil's party, without knowing it."
(5) "Intelligence Office," Wks., I, 328–42.
(6) My Kinsman, Wks., III, 616.
(7) *Legends of the Province House*, Wks., I, 328–42.
(8) Letter to his sister Louisa, summer of 1836, quoted by R.S., Biog., 33.
(9) *Peter Parley's Universal History*, for the use of children.
(10) Letter to Louisa, quoted in R.S., Biog., 33.
(11) Goodrich, in *Recollections of a Literary Life*, N.Y. gives a rather unsympathetic portrait of H.: "brow thick, mouth sarcastic, complexion stony, aspect cold, moody, distrustful . . ."

(12) Eliz. Peabody, quoted in Julian H., *H. and His Wife*, I, 178.
(13) "Village Uncle," Wks., I, 357: ". . . the Daughter of the Sea was mine."
Cantwell, *N.H.: The American Years*, 168, concludes from this that the "mermaid" did actually become Hawthorne's mistress.
(14) A. Doane, Wks., XII, 279, and "Solitary Man," Wks., XII, 33–34.
(15) "Sights," Wks., I, 221.
(16) 7Vag., Wks., I, 400 and "Village Uncle," Wks., I.
(17) Am.Nbks., ed. R.S., 22.
(18) Ibid.
(19) Ibid.
(20) "Solitary Man," Wks., XII, 26: "Even a young man's bliss has not been mine."
(21) "Sights," Wks., I, 223: "I, enacting on a steeple top, the part of Paris."
(22) "Alice Doane's Appeal," Wks., XII, 294: "the well-spring of their tears."
(23) "Solitary Man," Wks., XII, 26: "I have never truly loved and perhaps shall be doomed to loneliness throughout the eternal future, because, here on earth, my soul has never married itself to the soul of woman."
(24) His sister Elizabeth seems delighted to report this fact (Recoll.).
(25) A tendency expressed in Lady E., Wks., I, 312 (Gervayse offering himself as a doormat) and in M.F., Wks., VI, 60–61: the Miriam sketches (Jael and Siser, Judith with Holofernes' head, Herodias accepting that of John the Baptist), 65: Miriam compared to "Judith . . . when she vanquished Holofernes . . ." As for the Model who persecutes her, is he not in reality seeking to be similarly vanquished?
(26) The authenticity of this anecdote seems to have been definitively established by N. H. Pearson ("H's Duel," *EIHC*, XCIV, 1958). Mary Silsbee was the daughter of the mayor of Salem, who later took his revenge.
(27) J.H., H.&W, I, 167–74, gives a ludicrously jumbled account of the affair.
(28) The incident with Mary, as the origin of the tale published in 1838, may have been written late in 1837 or early in 1838 (E. C. Lathrop).
(29) Preface, Sn.Im. Wks., III, 378.
(30) Letter to Sophia, Oct. 4, 1840, *Portable H.*, Viking Press, 611–13.
(31) Preface, Sn.Im. Wks., III, 387.
(32) Letter to Longfellow, June 4, 1837, *Portable H.*, 607–610.
(33) Ibid.
(34) Quoted, G.P.L., Life, Wks., XII, 467.
(35) Letter to Sophia, Oct. 4, 1840, *Portable H.*, 611–13.
(36) Preface, T.T.T., Wks., I, 13.
(37) Letter from Bridge, Oct. 22, 1836 (J.H., H.&W, I, 142).
(38) *Relinquished Work*, Wks., II, 459: ". . . my readers must have heard of me in the wild way of life which I adopted."
(39) "Devil in Mss.," Wks., III, 574.
(40) "Solitary Man," Wks., XII, 23.

CHAPTER 3

I

(1) I Kings, 29 : 12: "and after the fire a still small voice . . . Elijah heard it."
(2) Letter to Sophia, Oct. 4, 1840, Wks., IX, 222–23.
(3) Am.Nbks., ed. R.S., July 1837: "My circumstances at least cannot continue as they are and have been."
(4) Letter to Longfellow, June 4, 1837, letters to Sophia, preface to T.T.T., etc.
(5) Mark Van Doren, *N.H.*, 1949: "The world had become absolute for him, a fairyland of fact . . . he was somehow self-prevented from exploring."
(6) Am.Nbks. ed. R.S., 17 (Mr. Schaeffer).
(7) Ibid., 12.
(8) Ibid., 18.

(9) Ibid., 19.
(10) Ibid., 14.
(11) Ibid., 8.
(12) R.S., Biog., 43 (the idyll on Martha's Vineyard).
(13) My Kinsman, Wks., III, 525–26: the girl with the scarlet petticoat ("her bright eyes possessed a sly freedom, which triumphed over those of Robin").
(14) M.F., Wks., VI, 149 (Cleopatra's statue).
(15) *Love Letters of N.H. (1839–1851)*. Privately printed, Society of Dofobs, Chicago, 1907, p. 87: letter dated April 5, 1842: "my queen and liege-lady."
(16) According to Mark Van Doren. Though R.S. places the meeting in the fall, "The Threefold Destiny" (pub. March 1838, *Am. Mth. Mag.*) seems to justify M.V.D.'s view, especially since it concerns a young man who finds the girl he has searched for vainly everywhere in his own village (Wks., I).
(17) Elizabeth Peabody, quoted in J.H., H.&W, I, 179.
(18) J.H., H.&W, I, 49: "grey, soft, and full of gentle light."
(19) Letter to Sophia, Oct. 4, 1840, Wks., IX, 222–23.
(20) "Circe's Palace," Wks., IV, 306.
(21) "Hall of Fantasy," Wks., II.
(22) Letter to Sophia, Feb. 27, 1842, quoted by H. G. Fairbanks, "H. and the Vanishing Venus," *UTSE*, XXXVI, 1957: "there seems to be a tacit law, that our deepest heart-concernments are not to be spoken of."
(23) Ibid.
(24) Letter to Sophia, Sept. 14, 1841, quoted by Rev. Leonard Fick, *The Light Beyond*, 1955: "the crime and the punishment are neither of them the most serious things in the world."
(25) N. H. Pearson, "H's. Duel," *EIHC*, XCIV, 1958.
(26) No form of treatment, including the stay in Cuba and later on the sessions of mesmerism, was able to rid her of her chronic headaches. It was only after the marriage that these attacks finally disappeared.
(27) 7G., Wks., III: the esthetic and moral conflict between the two heroines may perhaps have sprung from the contrast between the two Peabody sisters.
(28) Am.Nbks., Wks., IX, 122: entry made between July 10 and 13, before H. left Salem. The North Adams diary makes no mention of Sophia at all.
(29) Letter from Sophia to her sister Elizabeth, quoted in J.H., H.&W, I, 192.
(30) Feb. 24, 1838, in a duel. In the obituary (Wks., XII, 264–75) H. reverses certain unfavorable judgments on his friend (Wks., IX, 75–77). According to his sister Elizabeth, Cilley's death affected him a great deal.
(31) As a consequence of a disastrous flooding of the Kennebec.
(32) Am.Nbks., Wks., IX, 134.
(33) Ibid., 147–48 (Hudson's Falls).
(34) Ibid., 195–6.
(35) Ibid., 179–80.
(36) Ibid., 139.
(37) Ibid., 144–45.
(38) Am.Nbks., R.S., 43. L. Marx, *The Steam Fiend, the Development of a Symbol*, failed to use this passage.
(39) Ibid., 97.
(40) G.P.L., Life, Wks., XII, 484.
(41) "Solitary Man," Wks., XII, 25: "The truly wise after all their speculations, will be led into the common path . . . will gather gold, and till the earth, and set out trees, and build a house."
(42) G.P.L., Life, Wks., XII, 484.
(43) Such as G. Bancroft, later a bitter enemy of H., who referred to him by the Spenserian nickname of "The Blatant Beast" (R.S., Biog., 76).

(44) Letter to Sophia, July 3, 1839, Wks., IX, 213.
(45) Ibid., 213.
(46) Birth., Wks., II.
(47) Letter to Sophia, July 15, 1839, J.H., H.&W, I, 206.
(48) Ibid.
(49) Letter to Sophia, May 29, 1839, J.H., H.&W, I, 205.
(50) Cantwell, *N.H.: The American Years*, p. 253, concludes from this that H. was not really very deeply in love.
(51) *Love Letters*: May 26, 1839 (already referred to), April 22, 1840, J.H., H.&W, p. 216: the virile man seeking the "protection" of a "frail and tender invalid"; March 15, 1840, ibid., I, 214-215: "Most absolute little Sophie!" "They are not great letters," according to N. H. Pearson, when compared to those of Melville and Dickinson (during a private conversation, Yale, Dec. 1962).
(52) Letter to Sophia, April 14, 1841, Wks., IX, 225-26.
(53) Ibid., May 29, 1840, 220.
(54) Ibid., April 19, 1840, 217.
(55) Ibid., March 13, 1840, 215.
(56) Margaret Fuller launched the *Dial* in 1840.
(57) Quoted by R.S., Biog., 58.
(58) He invested $1,500 in it, almost his entire capital, and lost the greater part of it (Metzdorf, H's. Suit against Ripley and Dana," *AL*, XII, 1940).
(59) The community was called: "The Brook Farm Institute of Education and Agriculture." Nothing remains of it. Cf. Helen H. Clarke, *H.'s Country*, 1913, Introd., which remarks that a "charitable institution" was set up in the place where Hollingsworth (Bl.R., Wks., V) dreamed of founding a philanthropic establishment.
(60) Cantwell, *N.H.: The American Years*, p. 319.
(61) Letter to Sophia, April 13, 1841, Wks., IX, 227.
(62) Ibid., April 14, 228.
(63) Ibid., April 16, 229.
(64) Ibid., April 13 and 16, 227 and 229.
(65) Cantwell, *N.H.: The American Years*, p. 316 (many possible models for Westervelt, Wks., V).
(66) Am.Nbks., Sept. 28, 1841, Wks., IX, 252.
(67) Ibid., 252.
(68) Bl.R. (Wks., V).
(69) Letter to Sophia, April 16, 1841, Wks., IX, 229-30.
(70) Ibid., August 12, 1841, Wks., IX, 235.
(71) Ibid., Jan. 1842, R.S., Biog., 60-61. Even spoken words had been insufficient for a long time. Yet the "more adequate" language of hand pressures and kisses was still not "precise" enough.
(72) Am.Nbks., ed. R.S., 280.
(73) Letter to Sophia, Oct. 4, 1840, Wks., IX, 222-23.
(74) Ibid., Nov. 27, 1840, J.H., H&W, I, 225.
(75) Ibid., Jan. 25, 1840, quoted by R. R. Male, *H's. Tragic Vision*, 10.
(76) Ibid., undated, quoted R.S., Biog., 62.
(77) Cf. *Fanshawe;* H.of3H. (Wks., I); 7G. (Wks., III: Alice's bewitchment); Bl.R. (Wks., V: the psychic rape of Priscilla); M.F., (Wks., VI: Miriam and the Model); and also the posthumous novels.
(78) "The Old Manse," Wks., II, 22.
(79) Ibid., 22.
(80) "The New Adam and Eve," Wks., II, written after H's. marriage. See letter, April 21, 1840, J.H., H.&W, I, 215 (Nathaniel and Sophia: the Adam and Eve of a virgin earth).
(81) S.L., Wks., V, 234.
(82) Letter to S., quoted in R.S., Biog., 56 (wondering what will happen to earthly joys in the heavenly Paradise).

(83) Am.Nbks., R.S., 154.
(84) Ibid., 187 (Sunday, July 9, 1843).
(85) Sophia's diary, quoted in R.S., Biog., 63: "I am the spring with all its birds, its streams, its buds, singing, flowing, impetuous . . ."
(86) Am.Nbks., R.S., 187: H. describes life as swelling beneath him like an ocean.
(87) Ibid., 187.
(88) "Cantique du Rhône."
(89) H. was about to become a father. After an initial disappointment (Am.Nbks., R.S., early in July 1843), their first child, given the Spenserian first name Una, was to be born on March 3, 1844.
(90) Am.Nbks., R.S., 155.
(91) Ibid., 175.
(92) Ibid., 160.
(93) Ibid., 159.
(94) Ibid., 104.
(95) Ibid., 104.
(96) Ibid., 169 (like a sabbath seems this place).
(97) Ibid., 159: "[I] love the Sabbath, though . . . [I have] no set way of observing it."
(98) "The Old Manse," Wks., II, 35: H. is in agreement here with Wordsworth and Thoreau.
(99) Am.Nbks., R.S., 155.
(100) M.M.M., Wks., I.
(101) "The Old Manse," Wks., II, 31-36.
(102) Am.Nbks., R.S., 112-15, July 9, 1843 (Martha Hunt, a 19-year-old schoolteacher).
(103) October 1845. Samuel Ripley, the owner, decided to live in the Old Manse himself.

II

(1) Am.Nbks., Wks., IX, 335.
(2) S.L., Wks., V, "Custom House," 35.
(3) Letter from Sophia to her mother, J.H., H&W, I, 313, Sept. 10, 1847.
(4) Am.Nbks., R.S., 205.
(5) Ibid., 210.
(6) J.H., H.&W, I, 324: "The mother sees goodness and divinity shining through everywhere; the father's attitude is deductive and moralizing."
(7) Letter to S., quoted in R.S., Biog., 84 (accusing himself of no longer being able to keep her as a "lady" should be).
(8) Though in a letter to her mother she claims that she would rather live in a barrel than be separated from her husband (J.H., H.&W, I, 308).
(9) Letter to Sophia, quoted in R.S., Biog., 83.
(10) By virtue of the "spoils system."
(11) Sumner's description, quoted by R.S., Biog., 89.
(12) Letter to Longfellow, June 5, 1849, quoted by A. A. Kern, "H's. Feathertop and R.L.R.," PMLA, LII, 1937.
(13) S.L., Wks., V.
(14) Letter to Longfellow, June 5, 1849.
(15) Am.Nbks., R.S., 209-10.
(16) Letter from Sophia to her mother, R.S., Biog., 98.
(17) Letter to Hillard (who, together with Longfellow, took up a collection for H.'s benefit) quoted by Woodberry, N.H., 1902, p. 177.
(18) S.L., "Custom House," Wks., V, 23: "it would be quite as reasonable to form a sentimental attachment to a disarranged checker-board." Cf. letter to S., Nov. 27, 1840, in J.H., H.&W, I, 224-25: "methinks, all enormous sinners should be sent . . . to Salem, and compelled to spend a length of time there, proportioned to the enormity of their offences."

(19) Letter to Bridge, April 13, 1850, quoted in R.S., Biog., p. 98.

(20) S.L., "Custom House," Wks., V, 63.

(21) A. C. Coxe, *Church Review,* 1850, quoted in R.S., Biog., 97.

(22) 7G., Wks., III, 135 (said of Clifford). Cf. Am.Nbks., R.S., 118: "Some men have no right to perform great deeds or think high thoughts."

(23) H. had already visited the Berkshires during his excursion in 1838.

(24) Am.Nbks., R.S., July 28, 1851: "The Red Shanty." Cf. Jay Leyda, *The Melville Log,* N.Y., 1951, I, 393: engraving.

(25) Letter from Sophia to her mother. June 23, 1850, J.H., H.&W, I, 366–72.

(26) Even before his marriage, H. was fascinated by children at play (Am. Nbks., Wks., IX, 280–81, June 1, 1842: "the navy of Lilliput").

(27) Am.Nbks., R.S., 223: Twenty Days: "a remarkable echo."

(28) Cf. the titles of several of the mythological tales written at this period: "The Chimaera," "The Dragon's Teeth," "The Gorgon's Head" (W.Bk., Wks., IV) "The Minotaur," "The Pygmies" (in which we find Hercules) (Tangle.).

(29) Ehninger, a realist painter of American life. Hester coming out of prison is one of the compositions to which Sophia alludes (J.H., H.&W, I, 374).

(30) According to J. T. Fields, quoted by R.S., Biog., 107.

(31) Melville was 32, Hawthorne 47. Melville talks of the feeling of "security" H. inspired in him (quoted by J. J. Mayoux, *Melville,* 1960, 98).

(32) In 1837. Despite all their efforts, Bridge and Pierce failed to obtain the post of historiographer of the South Seas Expedition for him (letter from Bridge, Pierce and Reynolds, J.H., H.&W, I, 152–57).

(33) Sophia (letter quoted in J.H., H.&W, I, 377) called him by the title of one of his novels: *Omoo* (1947). Mayoux talks with reason of a social "comedy" (p. 99).

(34) Sophia, quoted in R.S., Biog., 108–9.

(35) Am.Nbks., R.S. ("Twenty Days"). Cf. letter from Melville to H., June 30, 1851, Mayoux, *Melville,* p. 69 ("bottle of brandy . . . heroic drink").

(36) Ibid.: "Twenty Days with Julian and little Bunny."

(37) Cantwell, *N.H.: The American Years,* p. 371. Cf. "Henpecked Immortals: H. censured by his wife" in *Nation,* Dec. 1932 (Lady Burton, Mary Clemm and Sophia H.) also Am.Nbks., R.S., Intro., deploring the retouching and mutilations inflicted upon H's. MSS.

(38) Hawthorne to Duyckinck, in R.S., Biog., 107.

(39) Melville to H., Pittsfield, Nov. 1851, *Portable Melville,* Viking Press, 452.

(40) Ibid.

(41) Ibid.

(42) Eng.Nbks., R.S., 113–14: "Poor reverend devil, drunkard, whoremaster," he says to himself.

(43) Since H's letters to Melville have disappeared, we are reduced to conjecture. When Julian H. visited the aging Melville in New York, in 1883, the latter confessed to having destroyed them long before ("When H. Melville was Mr. Omoo," *Lit. Dig. Internat. Bk. Rev.,* August 1926).

(44) Eng.Nbks., R.S., 432, Nov. 20, 1856: "I do not wonder that he found it necessary to take an airing through the world, after so many years of toilsome penlabor *and domestic life* . . ." (Italics not in orig. text.)

(45) "Solitary Man," Wks., XII ("My Home Return").

(46) April 1853.

(47) September 1852: once again he felt himself the king of an island microcosm and filled his Notebook with jottings: inscriptions on gravestones, parish register entries, Am.Nbks., R.S., 276–80 (Gosport), traditions, legends, reported events (as the occurrence of an enormous wave that flooded one of the island's valleys). Ibid., 264.

(48) Letter to Sophia, Philadelphia, April 1853, quoted by R.S. in Biog., 144.

(49) Liverpool, Nov. 1856. London, March 1857.

(50) Eng.Nbks., R.S., 432.
(51) Mayoux, *Melville*, p. 99, certainly feels that H. was the great unhappy love of Melville's life.
(52) Eng.Nbks., R.S., 432.
(53) Melville, "H. and his Mosses," *Lit Wld.*, August 17 and 24, 1850.
(54) Cf. "Agatha Letters" (See Part 2).
(55) Letter to Hillard, Jan. 30, 1850, quoted by Woodberry in *N.H.*, 1902, p. 187: "There was much that was sweet—and something too, that was very bitter—mingled with that same moistness."
(56) To Duyckinck, quoted in R.S., Biog., 112: "What a book Melville has written!" he exclaims, not without envy.
(57) Una, then Julian, and lastly Rose (May 20, 1851).

III

(1) Am.Nbks., R.S. (Twenty Days).
(2) Letter to Pike, R.S. Biog., 118: "I am not so vigorous as I was . . ."
(3) Judge Pyncheon (7G., Wks., II) the model for whom was probably Upham, a minister of the First (Unitarian) Church of Salem, author of a work in two volumes, *Salem Witchcraft* (1887), and an active member of the Whig party. We should point out that Judge P. is also presented as an unscrupulous politician who aspires to "the honors of the republic" (7G., Wks., III) and as hypocritically pious (7G., Wks., III, 157: "reverently lifting his eyes").
(4) Bl.R., Wks., V (1852).
(5) See Part Two, II, Ch. 3, III ("Psychological Creation").
(6) Bl.R., Intr., Wks., V, 332.
(7) Letter to Duyckinck, quoted in R.S., Biog., 123–24: Alcott had called his house "Hillside." It is in fact at the foot of the hill and on one side of the road.
(8) Letter to Longfellow, June 4, 1837, *Portable H*, Viking Press, 611–13.
(9) Letter of June 9, 1852, quoted in L. S. Hall, *H., Critic of Society*, 1944, p. 46.
(10) Letter to Ticknor, quoted by L. S. Hall, op. cit., 46: novel not identified; moreover H had not yet received the documents on "Agatha."
(11) Letter to Bridge, Oct. 13, 1852, quoted by L. S. Hall, op. cit., 47.
(12) Ibid.: "I seek nothing from him."
(13) "Young America" was an activist movement of the day.
(14) H. expressed his disappointment to him personally (letter of July 1, 1854, quoted by L. S. Hall, op. cit., 101).
(15) Am. Nbks., R.S., 48: "more of an abolitionist in feeling than in principle."
(16) Cf. *Le Spleen de Paris* and *Mon Coeur mis à nu*.
(17) The spontaneity of some of the Notebook entries is in contrast with the detachment, even the coldness, that emanates from *O.O.H.* (Wks., VII).
(18) Eng.Nbks., R.S., 321: ". . . the very Jew of Jews . . . I rejoiced exceedingly in this Shylock, this Iscariot; for the sight of him justifies me in the repugnance I have always felt towards this race."
(19) Ibid.: he also compares her to Rebecca (she being the daughter of the old Jew just described: Miriam and her Model in M.F., Wks., VI).
(20) Cf. J-P. Sartre: *Réflexions sur la Question Juive*, 1954.
(21) This is brought out by L. S. Hall, *H., Critic of Society*, 25.
(22) Eng.Nbks., R.S., 112 (men shanghaied in ports); 51 (blows, wounds, burns); 266–67 (murders: death of a sailor in hospital as a result of ill-treatment).
(23) Letter to Eliz. Peabody, Liverpool, 1855, quoted by Woodberry: "I have done no good—none whatever. Vengeance and beneficence are things that God claims for Himself. His instruments have no consciousness of His purpose . . ."
(24) Ibid.

(25) Which is why he abdicated in favor of Providence (*Life of Pierce*, Wks., XII, 417).

(26) Cf. Part Two, Ch. 3, II ("Sympathy and the Violation of the Consciousness") and Part Three, Ch. 1, III.

(27) Pierce did not forget his biographer once he had become President. H. received his appointment as consul on March 26, 1853.

(28) Letter to Ticknor, March 4, 1858 (Caroline Ticknor, *H. and his Publisher*, 220): ". . . to write for my own occupation and amusement."

(29) M. P. Schlefer, "The Magic Circle: the Art of N.H.," Harvard Honors Thesis, 1942, 39–40 (the old world was for H. the future, the ideal).

(30) Eng.Nbks., R.S., 328.

(31) He never saw either Dickens or Thackeray and refused to meet George Eliot. Apart from Leigh Hunt, he was to content himself with the mediocre and irritating Martin Tupper, the self-loving author of *The Proverbial Philosophy*, an obscure poetess ("gifted creature") encountered at a civic banquet. (Eng.Nbks., R.S., 314–16) and Douglas Jerrold, the splenetic critic (at the same banquet).

(32) Letter to Ticknor, Jan. 1855 (Caroline Ticknor: *H. and his Publisher*, 141): "a damned lot of scribbling women."

(33) Delia Bacon, over from America with the intention of forcing the secret from Shakespeare's tomb, published *The Philosophy of the Plays of Shakespeare Unfolded* at her consul's expense (1857).

(34) Eng.Nbks., R.S., 368–87: he was nevertheless agreeably surprised to find that she was younger than he had thought.

(35) Ibid.: "unquestionably, she is a monomaniac."

(36) In his introduction to D. B's. book he defends the young woman against an English author who was claiming her theory for himself.

(37) Eng.Nbks., R.S., 184: H. expresses the view that it is impossible to enjoy traveling if one has children.

(38) Letter to Fields, April 13, 1854, L. S. Hall, *H. Critic of Society*, p. 65: "I am a good deal changed . . . And . . . my past self is not very much to my taste."

(39) Eng.Nbks., Wks., VIII, 585: certain enormous hairy spiders, for instance.

(40) Ibid., VII, 560. Cf. R.S. edition, 17: "Drama of low life."

(41) Eng.Nbks., R.S., 43 and O.O.H., "Glimpses of English Poverty," Wks., VII, 341–42 (the intolerable gaze of the man who was nothing but a Herculean trunk).

(42) Ibid., R.S., 43: "One feels a curious and reprehensible sympathy for these poor nymphs." An example of the kind of detail that S. made it her duty to expunge.

(43) Ibid., R.S., 276–77: "Did God make that child?" This anguished question does not occur in O.O.H. "Glimpses," Wks., VII, 352–56.

(44) Story written after a visit to Smithell's Hall (Eng.Nbks., R.S., 193–94 and 196) which anticipates *Dr. Grimshawe's Secret*.

(45) It.Nbks., Wks., X, 12.

(46) Comp. "The Old Manse," Wks., II, and It.Nbks., X, 270–73.

(47) It.Nbks., Wks., X, 172–73 and 182 (cut). Cf. Mayoux, *Melville*, 1960, pp. 119–20.

(48) Ibid., 272: "one of the brightest and most uncareful interludes of my life . . ."

(49) Letter to Fields, quoted in Woodberry, *N.H.*, 1902, 266–68, and It.Nbks, Wks., X, 377–81.

(50) He was already complaining of this in England: Eng.Nbks., Wks., VIII, 543: "My nerves recently have not been in an exactly quiet and normal state."

(51) R.S., Biog., 204: in Feb. 1859 (simply a fever, or a first heart attack?).

(52) He compared Rome to a worm-eaten cadaver during his first winter there

(It.Nbks., passage restored by R.S., Biog., 188). Cf. It.Nbks. at time of his return, Wks., X, 484: "life pressed down by a weight of death."

(53) It.Nbks., Wks., X, 453: "their religion has so many admirable points." But, in X, 452: "a mere fossil shell." H. was never, as Cavigan would have it ("H. in Rome," *Cath.World*, Sept. 1932) "an unconscious Catholic."

(54) Ibid., expurgated passage, restored and quoted in R.S., Biog., 198: "it seems as if God must have ordained it."

(55) Am.Nbks., R.S., 165: "we certainly do need a new revelation."

(56) Am.Nbks., R.S., 159 (already quoted. Ch. 3, I, Note 97). H. did not believe in churches, though this did not prevent his having a religious turn of mind.

(57) *S.L.*, Wks., V, 167 ("between the sufferer and his God").

(58) The death of his mother (Am.Nbks., R.S., 209–10: "What a mockery . . . if there were nothing beyond; for then it would have been a fiend that created us . . ."); the accidental death of his sister Louisa in the *Henry Clay* fire (R.S., Biog., 128, extract from Sophia's diary: H. shut himself up in his room and refused all consolation).

(59) H. to Pierce, quoted by R.S. in Biog., 205.

(60) It.Nbks., Wks., X, 221: painting by Carlo Dolce in Florence (the All-Powerless).

(61) Eng.Nbks., Wks., VII, 444–45 (not feeling "at home" in England), and R.S., 424.

(62) Ibid., R.S., 184.

(63) Ibid., R.S., 96: "I hate a naturalized citizen."

(64) Statement made to Motley, quoted by R.S. in Biog., 212.

(65) Letter to Bridge, March 1854, quoted by Woodberry: "If compelled to choose, I go for the North."

(66) Letter to Bridge, March 1854, quoted by Woodberry, 281: "New England is quite as large a lump of earth as my heart can really take in."

(67) In memory of Montauto, probably. This tower still exists.

(68) Letter to Bridge, quoted by G.P.L., Life, Wks., XII, 542–43 (May 26, 1861).

(69) Letter to an English friend, quoted by E. Mather, *N.H.*, 1940, 316–17: "whether killed by a bullet or not, one must still die."

(70) Same letter: ". . . it [the war] invigorates every man's whole being . . . the whole world, on this side of the Atlantic appears . . . more natural and sensible, and walks more erect . . ."

(71) It. Nbks., Wks., X, 327: "an innate antipathy to constables."

(72) As war correspondent for the *Atlantic*. See "War Matters," Wks., XII, 336–37: "It could not be called a vessel . . . it was a machine . . . it looked like a gigantic rat-trap . . ." He also refers to it as "devilish" and a "war-fiend."

(73) O.O.H., Wks., VII. Cf. letter to Fields, spring of 1863, quoted in R.S. Biog., 232: ". . . it would be a piece of poltroonery in me to withdraw either the dedication or the dedicatory letter."

(74) Daguerreotype reproduced in the Club des Libraires de France edition of S.L.

(75) On Hawthorne Boulevard, past the Essex St. intersection as one goes down to the harbor.

(76) Rose Hawthorne, Lathrop, *Memories of H.*, pp. 422–23: he forbade Una to write.

(77) E. H. Davidson, *H.'s Dr. Grimshawe's Secret*, 1954.

(78) Sophia, quoted in R.S., Biog., 235.

(79) M. Van Doren, *N.H.*, Ch. 7: "The Wayside in Wartime."

(80) Sophia to Annie Fields, quoted in R.S., Biog., 236.

(81) Information received from Miss Lathrop, last of H.'s indirect descendants, present occupier of "Wayside" and author of *The Wayside*, 1940.

(82) Hepzibah and Clifford, 7G., Wks., III, Ch. 17, "The Flight of Two Owls."

(83) Pierce, letter to Bridge, May 21, 1864 (Bridge *Personal Recollections,* 196–200) thought that the disease was one of the spinal column or brain.

(84) Letter from Sophia to Annie Fields, May 20, 1864 (Fairbanks, "H. and the Vanishing Venus," *UTSE,* XXXVI, 1957): "such an unviolated sanctuary was his nature, I his inmost wife never conceived or knew."

CONCLUSION

(1) The emphasis was nevertheless on his shyness: "painfully shy" (Camillia T. Crosland: *My Exp. of Spiritualism, Landmarks of a Literary Life,* 1893). "Painful shyness," "morbid delicacy" (Anna Maria Hall: *Retrospect of a long Life*; Am.Nbks., R.S., Notes). "Very bashful in manners" (Allingham) and "the heaviest and most awkward person," writes Ch. Mackay, *Forty Years' Recollections* (quoted in Am.Nbks., R.S., Appendix).

(2) W. D. Howells, in "The Personality of H.," *N. Am. Rev.,* XXXIV, 1903, 872–82, saw him as a good, kind father and a man of good sense. H.'s "personality" escaped him entirely! Emerson, when all is said and done, was even more perspicacious in his view of the old Oberon: "H. rides well his horse of the night," quoted by Julian H., *H. and his Circle.*

(3) Arnavon, *Histoire Littéraire des Etats-Unis,* 162.

(4) Am.Nbks., Wks., IX, 335 (Salem, March 1843): "a cloudy veil stretches over the abyss of my nature."

(5) Am.Nbks., Wks., IX, 223: "here my mind and character were formed."

(6) Brownell, *American Prose Masters,* 1910, p. 126, on the other hand, attributes to H. a perpetually phlegmatic temperament, equally incapable of enthusiasm and discouragement. He allowed himself to be misled by H.'s mask of insensitivity, by the neutral tone of his prefaces, by his classical discretion as a writer.

(7) A.o.B., Wks., II.

(8) Am.Nbks., R.S., 181.

(9) Ibid. Cf. also Woodberry, 153: "dullness of temperament."

(10) Kierkegaard, *Journal,* June 1847.

(11) Dr. Jean Delay: "La Jeunesse d'André Gide," 1957.

(12) André Gide, *Journal,* 1916, p. 554 (Pléiade edition, N.R.F.).

(13) Sophia, quoted by G.P.L., Life, Wks., XII, 464–65: "his low, almost irresolute voice." G. W. Curtis, ibid., 562–63, evokes the expressive quality of his silences: "his silence was most social. Everything seemed to have been said."

(14) Eng.Nbks., R.S., 315–16: he uses the word "acrid" to describe the criticisms that Jerrold might make of Thoreau.

(15) Zangwill, "A Case of Paramnesia in N.H., *Char. & Pers.,* XIII, 1945.

(16) It will be remembered that he loathed "declamation" and oratorical exercises. Cf. Woodberry, *N.H.,* 1902, p. 21: "nervously shy about declaiming" (his classmates in Salem made fun of him).

(17) S.L., Wks., V, 159: "This man . . . hath inherited a strong animal nature from his father or his mother," Chillingworth says to himself.

(18) Dr. Loring: "tempestuous and irresistible," quoted by Woodberry, *N.H.,* 1902, p. 167. Sophia: "the lion was roused in him," quoted by Woodberry, 175 (at the time of his troubles with the Customs). Woodberry, p. 167, also recalls an incident at the Boston Customs (Cf. Letters, Wks., IX, 224) when he lost his temper with a ship's captain.

(19) The theme of the double is to be found everywhere in his work: "Monsieur du Miroir," Wks., II, "Wakefield," Wks., I, Y.G.B., Wks., II, and in most of the novels, not to mention Am.Nbks., Wks., IX, 42 ("half of the visage . . . one mood, and the other half another"), 107 (". . . a wicked life in one place . . . a virtuous and religious one in another").

(20) Cf. Part Two, I, Ch. 3, II ("The Creative Will") and Notes 23 and 24.
(21) F's Sh.B., Wks., I.

PART TWO: THE SPHERES

CREATION

CHAPTER 1

I

(1) Marion Kesselring, "Books Read by N.H., *EIHC*, LXVIII, 1932.
(2) R.S., Biog., 18-19 (quotation). The library of the Athenians Club also contained contemporary works (Irving, Cooper, Paulding).
(3) T. C. Upham, professor of philosophy and patriotic poet.
(4) R.S., Biog., 16-17.
(5) Natural science was then called natural philosophy.
(6) Bridges, *Personal Recollections of N.H.*, London, 1893.
(7) Neo-scholastic philosophy, though already outmoded at that time, still made its influence felt, and H., in his study of theological works and books on witchcraft (*Magnalia; Wonders of the Invisible World*) was affected by its backwash. A typical example of these weighty works is the *Technologia sive Technometria Ars Encyclopaidia* . . . (1714), by Dr. S. Johnson of King's College, Yale, in which art (summum genus) is divided into species and genera, these being subdivided into archetypes and types, these in turn into entypes and ectypes, and finally into rules, methods, and species. Cf. Woodberry, *N.H., How to Know Him*, Ch. 5, and Schneider, *The Puritan Mind*, 160.
(8) At 15, he had read Scott and Godwin (letter to Louisa, 1820, R.S., Biog., 8), not to mention Smollett, Fielding, and Rousseau.
(9) Brownell, *American Prose Masters*, 107, maintains that H. did more brooding than reading.
(10) Letter to his mother, March 7, 1820, quoted G. P. L., Wks., XII, 461.
(11) Recoll.
(12) Kesselring, "Books Read by N.H.," *EIHC*, LXVIII, 1932, records that Rousseau's works were taken out five times, Voltaire's six, Racine's three, and Swift's fourteen.
(13) Ex: *Faerie Queene* (letter to Sophia, quoted by R.S., "H. and The *Faerie Queene*, *PQ*, XII, 1933; Rose H. Lathrop, *Memories of H.*, 1897, p. 54; and J.H., H.&W, II, 9). Also Milton, Shakespeare, Scott (Julian H., "Books of Memory," *Bookman*, LXI, 1925). H. was always to excel at reading aloud: "He was a living Wonder Book," his son wrote ("N.H.'s Blue Cloak," *Bookman*, LXXV, 1932).
(14) J. T. Fields, *Yesterdays With Authors*, London, 1881, p. 54.
(15) Lundblad, *H. and European Literary Tradition*, 171-72, even draws a parallel.
(16) Am.Nbks., Wks., IX, 327.
(17) Julian H., "Books of Memory," *Bookman*, LXI, 1925.
(18) Letter to Sophia, J.H., H.&W, I, 210 (Jan. 1st, 1840), referring to a library with room for 200 volumes: "We will have to collect it in small lots." For the family library, see Julian H., "Books of Memory."
(19) Am.Nbks., IX, 333-39: allusion to Tieck. He had also read J-P. Richter.
(20) O.O.H., Wks., VII, 121.
(21) Eng.Nbks., pp. R.S., 132-33 and O.O.H., Wks., VII, 127.
(22) Ibid., 131, 133.
(23) Ibid., 293. Also 107 (the penholder) and 148-49 (the statue).
(24) Ibid., 151-2.
(25) *Biographical Stories* (1842), Wks., XII, 167.

(26) S.L., Wks., V, 298–304.
(27) O.O.H., Wks., VII, 167. He wrote an article on the same subject for the 1857 *Keepsake* before returning to it in his book on England.
(28) O.O.H., Wks., VII, 253.
(29) Ibid., 250–51.
(30) Eng.Nbks., R.S., 457–77; "Virtuoso," Wks., II.
(31) It.Nbks., Wks., X, 260.
(32) P. M. Ryan, "Young H., at the Salem Theater," *EIHC*, XCIV, 58, instances Kotzebue's *Lovers' Vows*, the Rev. J. Home's "gothick" drama *Douglas or the Noble Shepherd*, and *The Weathercock*, a farce.
(33) Uncollected articles for the "Salem Advertiser," R.S., *A.L.*, V, 1934, 337–41.
(34) Am.Nbks., R.S., 551–52.
(35) P. M. Ryan, "Young H. at the Salem Theater."
(36) Letter from H., Feb. 18, 1830, quoted in Ryan.
(37) Louise Tharp, *The Peabody Sisters of Salem*, 1950, Ch. 1.
(38) It.Nbks., Wks., X, 300.
(39) *Biographical Stories*, Wks., XII, 144–55. We know that H. visited the art gallery of the Athenaeum during his time with the Boston Customs (Wks., IX, 221.)
(40) Whistler, born in Lowell, Mass., in 1834, was lucky enough to travel in England and Russia before returning to the U.S.
(41) *Bowdoin College*, text by Rev. F. H. Allen, 1886. There are portraits by Stewart (of Jefferson and Madison) and reproductions of Rembrandt, Poussin, Claude Lorrain, Titian (Woman and Child), as well as the Corregio Madonna.
(42) Goodspeed, "N.H. and the Museum of the Salem East India Marine Society," *Am. Neptune*, V, 1945.
(43) The dictionary was a gift from the lexicographer J. E. Worcester.
(44) In his own "Spectator" (Eliz. Chandler Lathrop, "H's 'Spectator,' " *NEQ.*, IV, 1931) and in the "Magazine." Among the books H. read in 1835–36 were: Turner's *Sacred History* (cf. "Preservation of the Dead"), Hamilton's *Progress of Society; Encyclopedia; Museum of Literature and Science;* Babbage's *Economy and Machinery; Guide to the Observation of Nature; Description of Trades.* In 1837: Scott's *Natural Magic, Demonology & Witchcraft.* Compare some of the titles in the "Magazine": "Mexican Customs"; "Soldiers"; "Preservation of the Dead"; "Warriors Ancient and Modern" (uniforms, insignia, armor); "Noses"; "Snakes"; "Bells"; "Relics of Witchcraft"; "Witch Ointment": a veritable curiosity shop of items. Cf. Kesselring (*H's. Reading*) and A. Turner (*H. as Editor*, 1941).
(45) Barnum Museum, Bridgeport, Conn.
(46) C. G. Jung, *Psychologie und Alchemie*, Zurich, 1944: numerous illustrations of astrological and alchemical symbols: the red and white rose of alchemy (Rappacini's Flower, Wks., II, the rose in S.L., Wks., V, 68, and the Letter itself), the Tree of Life (Pyncheon Elm, 7G., Wks., II), the Disciples' Mount and the Temple (M.M.M., Wks., I, and "Lily's Quest," Wks., II), the Stone ("The Great Carbuncle," Wks., I), the Retort (Birth., Wks., II and *Septimius Felton*, Wks., XI).
(47) It.Nbks., Wks., X, 300: "pictorial art"; "magic," 312; "old Dutch wizards."
(48) "Prophetic Pictures," Wks., I; "E.R.'s P." ibid.
(49) Kesselring, "H.'s Reading, 1828–1850," *BYNPL*, 1949: Dunlap's *History of the Arts of Design, Encyclopedia of Architecture, Modern Painters, The Artists of America* (1846).
(50) Letter from Sophia to her mother, June 20, 1850, J.H., H.&W, I, 366–72: more than 20 engravings and various works of art can be established, among them "the divine Madonna del Pesce," Apollo (a bust), Endymion (a copy by Sophia), "two aspects of Psyche," "Michelangelo's frescoes of the Prophets and Sybils," and "one of Raphael's Angels."

(51) S.L., Wks., V, 77: ". . . the image of Divine Maternity."
(52) Am.Nbks., R.S., Intro, and Eng.Nbks., R.S., 137: "Gothic architecture . . . as deep and rich as human nature . . ."; 138: "Grecian edifices . . . uninteresting to me, being so cold and crystalline." But he admired the Roman remains.
(53) Eng.Nbks., R.S., 359.
(54) Ibid., 201 and 349.
(55) Ibid., Wks., VIII, 207.
(56) Ibid., R.S., 392.
(57) Ibid., 253 (National Gallery, London).
(58) Ibid., 550 (painted gingerbread).
(59) It.Nbks., X, 245–46: Cimabue, Piero della Francesca.
(60) Ibid., 137.
(61) Eng.Nbks., R.S., 348: touching "relics."
(62) It.Nbks., Wks., X, 312: Gerard Dow, Van Mieris.
(63) H. posed for Osgood in 1840 (a somewhat idealized portrait, reproduced in Van Doren's N.H.); for Thomson in 1850 (cover of Viking Ed.; description by G.P.L., Wks., XII, 557–58); for Leutze in 1863. There was also the bust executed by Sophia and the generally disappointing daguerrotypes. The most "Oberon-like" of the portraits is certainly that by G. P. E. Healey.
(64) It.Nbks., X, 120–21.
(65) Ibid., 91.
(66) Ibid., 108.
(67) Ibid., 112–13.
(68) Ibid., 199 and Eng.Nbks., R.S., 393.
(69) Ibid., 169.
(70) Ibid., 285.
(71) Ibid., 132.
(72) Ibid., 121.
(73) Ibid., 216.
(74) Ibid., 290–93.
(75) Ibid., 39.
(76) Ibid., 330–31.
(77) Ibid., 399.
(78) Where the Knickerbocker group was then flourishing.
(79) He nevertheless took the risk of writing to him. S. T. Williams, Literary History of the United States, 1953, Ch. 27, mentions a letter of homage from H. to Irving.
(80) Faust, H.'s Contemporaneous Reputation; Chorley (Athenaeum, 1835): "the most pleasing writer of fanciful prose, except Irving; Hoffman (Am. Mag., 1838), comparison with Lamb and Irving; Dutton (New Englander, Jan. 1847): "quiet equal to Irving."
(81) They did, however, condescend to praise Emerson (Cantwell, N.H.: The American Years, 1948, pp. 262–63).
(82) "The Old Manse," II, 41.
(83) Ibid., 41.
(84) Ibid., 42.
(85) Am.Nbks., IX, 234.
(86) Eng.Nbks., R.S., 273 (Mrs. Grosland's conversazione); 232 (Mrs. Steven's).
(87) Letter to Monckton Milnes, Nov. 13, 1854 (R.S., Am.Nbks., notes), M. M. had asked Ticknor for a list of typically American books and manifested a desire to be acquainted with Leaves of Grass. H. spoke of L. Mansfield, Julia Ward Howe, and Anna Cora Mowat, without alluding at all to Whitman, whose name does not occur at any point in his writings.
(88) Eng.Nbks., R.S., 553.
(89) Ibid., 255.
(90) It.Nbks., X, 292–97 (Florence, 1858).

(91) See the articles written for the "Salem Advertizer" (R.S., *AL*, V, 1934) on Simms, Longfellow and Melville ("Melville's *Typee*," March 25, 1846: "voluptuously colored . . ."

II

(1) The cultured public was demanding a national literature. But it wanted it to be the equivalent of contemporary English literature. Rufus Choate (H. and Literary Nationalism, quoted, Doubleday, *N & Q*, Apr. 1941) wanted the history of New England celebrated in novels of the "Waverley" variety (lecture in Salem, 1833).

(2) "The Bosom Serpent," II, 303: reminiscence of Don Roderigo the Goth (Southey).

(3) "Dr.H's Exp., I. Compare Pope, *The Dunciad*, Bk. I, 1.290.

(4) "Wakefield," I.

(5) Heroine of Bl.R., V; Priscilla, Spenser, *Faerie Queen*, VI, parts 2 and 3.

(6) Heroine of Rapp., II, Matthews. "H.'s Knowledge of Dante," *UTSE*, July 1940, points out various allusions. E.g., Rapp., II, 109 (the immortal agonies of his Inferno); Bl.R., V, 437 (Dante's ghostly forest). For M.F., the comparison goes too far.

(7) Hero of M.F., VI, Cf. Brodtknob, "Art Allegory in M.F.," *PMLA*, LXXVII, 1962.

(8) Phoebe (7G., III), Zenobia (Bl.R. V).

(9) Rev. J. H. Allen, "The Bible in the Works of N.H.," *Zion's Herald*, June 29, 1904, pp. 811–12, points out the importance of the Bible in H.'s work. He uses many names of Biblical origin, e.g.: *Hephzibah* (2 Kings, 21 : 1): "Manasseh . . . his mother's name was Hephzibah."); *Aminadab* in the "Birthmark," I, (Matt, 1 : 4). Cf. Thompson, "Aminadab," *MLN*, LXX, 1936, and Heilman, "The Birthmark: Science and Religion," *AQ*, XLVIII, 1949 (the Levite of the Bible becomes the priest of utilitarianism); *Reuben* in "Roger Malvin's Burial," I (1 Chron., 5 : 1: "Reuben . . . he defiled his father's bed."). Cf. Thompson, "Biblical Sources of Roger Malvin's Burial," *PMLA*, LXXVI, 1962. Lastly, Hester before the Governor (S.L., V, 136–40) is comparable with Esther before Ahasuerus. As for Rich. Digby ("Man of A.," III, 565) his name is associated with that of Elijah ("Elijah's cave at Horeb") and Abraham ("Abraham's sepulchral cave at Machpelah").

Various other borrowings: Rapp.: *Memoirs of Benvenuto Cellini* (Rafaello Lappacini; cf. R. R. Male, "Dual Aspects of Rapp., *PMLA*, March 1954); Aminadab, "Ethan Brand": *Annals of Salem*. Borrowings from *Magnalia Christi Americana*: Deacon Gookin (Y.G.B.). See Turner, "H.'s Literary Borrowings," *PMLA*, LVII, 1936. We should also note that W. P. Pyncheon was the founder of the Colony of Springfield, Mass., in about 1649. One of his descendants accused H. of defamation in 7G. Cf. letter from H. to Fields, Aug. 18, 1851 (N.Y. Public Library, Berg Coll.).

(10) Recoll.

(11) Cf. Prof. J. P. Fruit, "H.'s 'Immitigable,'" *PMLA*, XXIX, 1910: "To Bunyan is due his bent to allegory, when issued his prose form of literary art, the Romance."

(12) Bl.R., Wks., V, 557: "Shepherds of Arcadia, and allegoric figures from the Faerie Queene." Compare Am.Nbks., Wks., IX, 252.

(13) Milton, *Areopagitica*: "Our serious Poet Spenser." Cf. Leibowitcz, "H. and Spenser: Two Sources," *AL*, XXX, 1959. We should also add the names of the other allegorists: Bunyan, Thomson (*Castle of Indolence*), Dante, Tasso.

(14) *Faerie Queene*: I, Part 2: Archimago deceives Red-Cross by means of dreams; Part 3: takes on form of R. C. to deceive Una; II, Part 3: betrays Guyon with lies. Another magician: Busiranus, III, part 1 and 12, and, of

course, Milton's Comus (M.M.M., Wks., I, 72: "the crew of Comus," and Bl.R., Wks., V, 557: "Comus and his crew").

(15) Ibid., II, Part 4: Furor and the sorceress Occasion; III, Part 10: Malbecco, allegory of jealousy (cf. S.L.: Chillingworth; R.S., "H. and *The Faerie Queene, PQ,* XII, 1933).

(16) Lundblad, *H. and the Tradition of the Gothic Romance.*

(17) *Faerie Queene,* I, Parts 4 and 5: Lucifera (cf. "Lady Eleanore"; R.S., "H. and *The Faerie Queene*"); I, Parts 4, 7, and 8: Duessa; II, Part 12: Acrasie.

(18) Ibid., III, Parts 1, 5, 7, 8: Florimelle, to preserve her chastity, finally throws herself into the sea in the arms of Proteus; III, Part 4 and IV, Parts 11 and 12: Marinel, son of a nereid, hearing F.'s laments, falls in love with her and persuades Neptune to release her. Zenobia and Priscilla are also reminiscent of the true and the false Florimelle.

(19) Ibid., I, 6, stanzas 22–23: ascendance of Satyranus. Comp. M.F., Wks., VI, 269–70.

(20) Ibid., II, 12: the grove of delights on Acrasia's island. Cf. Rapp., the garden.

(21) "Golden Fleece," Tangl., Wks., IV.

(22) Rapp., Wks., II.

(23) *Faerie Queen,* I, 1, stanza 13. Cf. S.L., Ch. 16. Cf. R.S. "H. and *The Faerie Queen,*" 203.

(24) *FQ,* I, 9, stanzas 33–34. Cf. R.S., "H. and *The Faerie Queene,*" 204–05.

(25) Y.G.B., Wks., II, 100. Chillingworth, Ethan Brand, Westervelt all belong to the same type.

(26) *Paradise Lost,* I, 666–69. Compare Chillingworth, S.L., Wks., V, 169; Miriam, M.F., Wks., VI, 186; "Howe's Masquerade," I, 288 (the last specter); Eng.Nbks., Wks., VIII, 76 (Bloody Footstep); *The Ancestral Footstep,* Wks., XI, 444.

(27) *Pilgrim's Progress,* Collins, 36.

(28) *P.P.,* 37. Cf. "Prophetic Pictures," I. Other sources: *Hist. of . . . the Arts of Design,* Dunlap (Turner, "H.'s Lit. Borrowings," *PMLA,* LI, 1936).

(29) *P.P.,* 38. Compare "Select Party," Wks., II, 79.

(30) *P.P.,* 37–38. Cf. 7G., III, 103–04.

(31) *P.P.,* 20. Cf. Cel. Rlrd., Wks., II.

(32) *P.P.,* 70. Cf. Cel. Rlrd.

(33) *P.P.,* 79. Cf. Cel. Rlrd. and Job 10: 21–22.

(34) *P.P.,* 188. Cf. S.L.: "The Interior of a Heart."

(35) *P.P.,* 166. Cf. "David Swan," I and 7G., III, 119.

(36) *P.P.,* 145. Cf. M.F., Wks., VI, Ch. 27: "Myths."

(37) *P.P.,* 148. Cf. Cel. Rlrd., II, 231 (Miller, "H. and Melville: The Unpardonable Sin," *PMLA,* LXX, 1955).

(38) Cel. Rlrd., Wks., II.

(39) "The Great Carbuncle," Wks., I.

(40) *Melmoth the Wanderer* by Maturin. H. was also acquainted with Mrs. Radcliffe, Godwin, Charles Brockden Brown and Lewis (cf. letters to his sister Louisa, 1819 and 1820, quoted by R.S., Biog., 8).

(41) H. was not to read Bürger's "Lenore" until later (Am.Nbks., IX, 332). But in any case he did know Coleridge's *Rime of the Ancient Mariner* and Burn's *Tam o' Shanter* (quoted, Bl.R., V, 557).

(42) *Newgate Calendar, English State Trials, God's Revenge against the . . . Sin of Murther* (trans. from the Italian) were compilations of accounts of horrible crimes and even more horrible executions (Julian H., "Books of Memory," *Bookman,* LXI, 1925).

(43) "The Duston Family," Old Manse Ed., Vol. 17. H. had read *The Wars with the Indians* and drew the subject of the tale from the *Magnalia Christi.*

(44) A classification of this bric-à-brac has been made by Jane Lundblad, *H. and the Tradition of the Gothic Romance.*

(45) *Pilgrim's Progress,* 43.
(46) *P.P.,* 138–39. Cf. 7G., III, 299.
(47) *P.P.,* 113 (Vanity Fair).
(48) *P.P.,* 47. Cf. "Cel. Rlrd.," II, 217 and letter to Sophia, Wks., IX, 220.
(49) Cotton Mather, *Magnalia Christi Americana,* London, 1702, Book VII, Appendix (Remarkable Occurrences . . .). See Gallup, "On H.'s Authorship of 'The Battle Omen,' " *NEQ,* IX, 1936.
(50) E.g. that given by Bacon, quoted in Turner, "H. as Editor," 253 ("Witch Ointment") as also "Relicts of Witchcraft," 252.
(51) Such as *Wonders of the Invisible World,* by Robert Calef (or Calfe), an enemy of Cotton Mather (cf. Boas, *Cotton Mather, Keeper of the Puritan Conscience,* 1928).
(52) Montégut, "Un Romancier Socialiste en Amérique," *Rev. des Deux Mondes,* Dec. 1852.
(53) Montaigne, *Essais,* a title included in Kesselring's list of H's reading in 1829, '31 and '37.
(54) Lundblad, *H. and European Literary Tradition,* pp. 68–69.
(55) *Nouvelle Héloïse* and *Confessions* (Kesselring and R.S., Biog., 8.).
(56) Wordsworth, Southey, Coleridge.
(57) R.S., Biog., 246.
(58) Am.Nbks., Wks., IX. 14. Elsewhere, p. 395: "a bitter satirist."
(59) *G's Travels,* Zephyr, 285. Cf. "New Adam & Eve," II.
(60) Ibid., 191 (Academy of Lagado). Cf. "The Hall of Fantasy," II. Similarly, the fable of the Struldbrugs may perhaps be recognized in "Dr. Heidegger's Experiment" (Alice Cooke, "H.'s Indebtedness to Swift," *UTSE,* July 1938.
(61) Letter to Delia Bacon, June 21, 1856, quoted in Lundblad, *H. and European Literary Tradition.* H. took Montaigne, Shakespeare and Bacon as his examples and implicitly associated himself with them.
(62) Letter to his sister Eliz., March 22, 1836, Turner, *H. as Editor,* p. 5. A tendency attributed by Lundblad (*H. and European Literary Tradition,* 77) to his desire to be purely American.
(63) "H.'s Spectator," E. C. Lathrop, *NEQ,* IV, 1931 (No. 1.: "On Solitude"; No. 5: "On Hope"; "Address to the Sun"; "to the Moon," etc. . . .)
(64) The five missing stories from *Seven Tales* perhaps.
(65) *Fanshawe,* Wks., XI, 187–88. We are a long way from the poetry of Wives, I.
(66) In H.of3H. and "Alice Doane's Appeal."
(67) *Fanshawe,* Wks., XI, 208 (precipice) and 194 (cavern), not to mention the psychological and moral "spheres" (heart and mind).
(68) C. Bode, "*Fanshawe,* the Promising of Greatness," *NEQ,* XXIII, 1950. Cf. R. E. Gross, "H.'s First Novel: The Future of a Style," *PMLA,* LXXVII, 1963.

CHAPTER 2

I
(1) Am.Nbks., R.S., 155: "I could be as happy as a squash, and much in the same mode."
(2) Letter to Louisa, March 20, 1820, quoted by Ryan, "Young H. at the Salem Theater," *EIHC,* July, 1958: "a concert . . . Handel, Haydn and other celebrated composers."
(3) Cantwell, *N.H.: The American Years,* 319: H. tried to keep out of the intellectual and artistic activities of Brook Farm.
(4) Am.Nbks., Wks., IX, 333: "Thoreau's musical box."
(5) Eng.Nbks., R.S., 375.
(6) Ibid., 376.

(7) Ibid., Wks., VII, 162. Cf. It.Nbks., X, 452.
(8) *Faerie Queene*, I, part 1.
(9) *Winter's Tale*. Cf. A. Fields, N.H., p. 67.
(10) Unpublished poem, quoted in J.H., H.&W, I, 102.
(11) Letter to Sophia, Oct. 4, 1840, Wks., IX, 222–23, in which he evokes the loneliness of his youthful years and the change brought about in him by love.
(12) Am.Nbks., R.S., 98: "Wits and poets at a police court."
(13) "The Great Carbuncle," Wks., I, 175–76.
(14) Bl.R., Preface, Wks., V, 323.
(15) "Great Stone Face," Wks., III, 413.
(16) "P's Corresp.," Wks., II, 422: "Great poets should have iron sinews" (referring to Keats).
(17) Letter to Ticknor, Aug. 7, 1855 (Caroline Ticknor, *H. and His Publisher*, referring to Allingham).
(18) T.T.T., Introduction, Wks., I, 16.
(19) "A.o.B.," Wks., II, 510.
(20) Including those of Sterne (Kesselring, "H.'s Reading 1828–1850," *BNYPL*, 1949).
(21) "P's Corresp.," Wks., II, 408–12 and 419–20.

II

(1) Am.Nbks., R.S., 104.
(2) Ibid., Wks., IX, 98: "a general vacancy in the field of vision," James said, in *H.*, 1879, deploring H.'s lack of active observation.
(3) Eng.Nbks., R.S., 182: "I am slow to feel . . ."
(4) Ibid. 529: "my sluggish powers of perception."
(5) Am. Nbks., R.S., 79. James (*H.*, p. 133) can only echo H.'s own words.
(6) Ibid., 170: "the reflexion is indeed the reality."
(7) Letter to Sophia, Wks., IX, 237: "The real Me" (Sept. 3, 1841).
(8) Ibid., IX, 235: "free to think and feel" (Aug. 12, 1841).
(9) Samuel Longfellow, *Life of H. W. Longfellow*, 1891, III, 357: "H. . . . would go behind the window curtain and remain in silent revery the whole evening."
(10) Bl.R., Wks., V: "Coverdale's Hermitage."
(11) "Sights," Wks., I, 220: "A spiritualized Paul Pry."
(12) 7G., Wks., III: "The Arched Window," 199–200.
(13) Ibid., 115–16. Cf. Gaylord Clark, *Knickerbocker*, 1842, who compares H.'s mind to "the plates of a daguerreotype."
(14) Am.Nbks., R.S., 98: "at the entrance there is sunshine and flowers growing . . ."
(15) Ibid., 110.
(16) Ibid., 181: "If I had wings I would gladly fly, yet would prefer to be wafted by the breeze . . ."
(17) Ibid., 254–55: "Were I a solitary prisoner." Cf. Wks., IX, 36: "a recluse like myself."
(18) Eng.Nbks., R.S., 483: "modified and mollified."
(19) Brownell, *American Prose Masters*, 1910, p. 83: "H. coquetted and sported with (reality)."
(20) Am.Nbks., R.S., 241: "to catch Nature at unawares." Cf. It.Nbks., Wks., X, 88: "not . . . when gazed at of a set purpose."
(21) It.Nbks., Wks., X, 88: "a peep-hole" (textual restoration by R.S. Mrs. H. had preferred the word "vista."
(22) Waggoner, *H.: A Critical Study*, Introd.: "Janus-faced."
(23) Particularly Beatrice Rappacini (Rapp., Wks., II).
(24) Letter to Longfellow, June 4, 1837, quoted in *Portable H.*, 609.
(25) Letter to Fields, Feb. 11, 1860 (*Portable H.*, 628).

(26) For which James (*H.*, 1879, p. 45) and Brownell (*American Prose Masters*, 107–08) critize him.

III

(1) And therefore quite the opposite of Sophia's diary (extracts in J.H., H.&W, I, 75–81, 192, 288).

(2) Pickard, *H.'s First Diary*. 1897.

(3) Mosses, Wks., II, *Tales & Sketches*, Wks., XII.

(4) Eng.Nbks., R.S., 456: "a matter of conscience."

(5) Thomson (*The Seasons*), Izaak Walton (according to Foster, "H.'s Literary Theory," *PMLA*, XVII, 1942).

(6) Am.Nbks., R.S., 75–76.

(7) Ibid., 41 (arch), 45, 50 (portal of some infernal . . . structure), 56, 60 (archway of an enchanted palace).

(8) Ibid., Wks., IX, 251 (the goddess Diana).

(9) Ibid., R.S., referring to Una (elfish or angelic).

(10) Ibid., 79. Other examples: Ibid., 40. Ibid., 103. Also the Judge's nose in 7G. (Wks., III, 334). Ibid., 117, Cf. 7G., the monkey taking the collection (Wks., III, 197–98). Other examples: the bird (spiritual visitor, p. 171), the ants (phalanstery, p. 104).

(11) Ibid., 155.

(12) Ibid., 151 ("individual characters . . ."; "harsh and crabbed"; "churlish . . . illiberal").

(13) It.Nbks., Wks., X, 435.

(14) Am.Nbks, R.S., 43 (machine), It.Nbks., Wks., X, 75.

(15) S.L., Wks., V, "The Governor's Hall."

(16) Am.Nbks., R.S., 39.

(17) Ibid., 43.

(18) Ibid., 52.

(19) "Tollgatherer's Day," Wks., I.

(20) Am.Nbks., R.S., 77.

(21) Ibid., 59. Compare E.B., Wks., III.

(22) Ibid., 45 and 58.

(23) It.Nbks., Wks., X, 243.

(24) Ibid., 232, 33, 34.

(25) Ibid., 270. Cf. Bunyan, *Pilgrim's Progress,* Collins, 188–89.

(26) Am.Nbks., R.S., 41.

(27) Ibid., 31.

(28) R.S., Introd., Am.Nbks. and Eng.Nbks. (Mrs. H.'s modifications).

(29) "The Birthmark," Wks., II.

(30) Am.Nbks., R.S., 16.

(31) Ibid., Wks., IX, 147 and 184.

(32) Ibid., 147 (the marks of eddies . . . in the solid marble).

(33) Cf. the story of Quattlebum related by J.H., H.&W, II, 44–47.

(34) "Old Manse," Wks., II, 22.

(35) Am.Nbks., R.S., 182: "on a small scale, the process of the deluge."

(36) Ibid., 105, (observations on an ant colony).

(37) Ibid., 16.

(38) Ibid., 46.

(39) Ibid., 6.

(40) Ibid., 16.

(41) Ibid., 60–61 (Shelburne Falls) and 68: "descending pavement."

(42) Ibid., 16.

(43) Pickard, *H.'s First Diary*. He even wrote a poem on the death of the Tarboxes, according to Hildegarde, *H., Romantic Rebel*, 45–46.

(44) Am.Nbks., R.S., 69: the transhumance of an uncontrollable herd of pigs.

(45) Ibid., Wks., IX, 99.
(46) Ibid., R.S., 223.
(47) Ibid., 156–57: referring to a friend of Emerson ("a sturdy fact . . . something to be felt and touched").
(48) Ibid., 27–28 (accumulation of material details and physical traits). Cf. Eng.Nbks., R.S., 426 (inventory) and 546–47 (vehicles).
(49) Ibid., 119–20 ("Browne's Folly").
(50) Ibid., 4 and 46.
(51) A.o.B., Wks., II, 507: "the character of Owen's mind was microscopic . . ."
(52) Am.Nbks., R.S., 276–80 and 267 (the lighthouse island).
(53) Letter to Louisa, quoted by R.S., Biog., 41.
(54) Ibid.
(55) Am.Nbks., R.S., 156–57.
(56) Ibid., Wks., IX, 186–87.
(57) Ibid., R.S., 43 (negro's laugh); 48 (a drunken negro supported by two negresses); 54 (an Indian halfcaste).
(58) Ibid., Wks., IX, 113–14.
(59) Engl.Nbks., Wks., VIII, 188 (Mersey Iron Foundry).
(60) *War Matters*, Wks., XII, 328–29.

CHAPTER 3

I

(1) J.H., H.&W, I, 396–97. R.S., Biog., 102 (H.'s manual dexterity).
(2) Ibid., "N.H.'s Blue Coat," *Bookman*, LXXV, 1932: "He was a living Wonder Book."
(3) G.P.L., Life, Wks., XII, 464: "If only I could make tables."
(4) J.H., H.&W, I, 121: "large and muscular."
(5) Example: Drowne (D.'s W. Im., II), Kenyon (M.F., VI) and even Owen Warland (A.o.B., II).
(6) Letter to Sophia, Jan. 3, 1840, J.H., H.&W, I, 211: "I have often felt that I could be a painter."
(7) C. G. Jung, *L'Energétique Psychique*, Fr. trans. by Y. Lel Lay, 1956, pp. 22–24: Jung believes that the lack of data makes it impossible to examine the problem of the relationship between the physical and the psychic. The transmission of energy we refer to is certainly not direct and immediate, as N. de Grot (quoted by Jung) would have it, but may perhaps operate via the memory's recording apparatus.
(8) Eng.Nbks., R.S., 182: "I am slow to think—slow, I suppose, to comprehend," and, Am.Nbks., R.S., 99: "The advantage of a longer life . . ."
(9) Such as Rousseau, Marivaux. Cf. G. Poulet, *Etude sur le Temps Humain*, 1952, II, Ch. 1.
(10) Davidson, *H.'s last Phase*, 1949, p. 144: "He . . . spent days and months in apparently idle speculation . . ."
(11) Sophia Peabody, quoted in *H. and His Wife*, I, 491: "the furor scribendi has seized Mr. Hawthorne, we shall not see him for days . . ."
(12) G.P.L., Life, Wks., XII, 215: H. meditating alone in a sunken lane.
(13) Letters to Sophia, Wks., IX, 215 ("This unblest Custom House"; "grievous thraldom"); 217 (darksome dungeon); 235 ("Of all hateful places this (Brook Farm) is the worst."). And to Ticknor, referring to the consulate, in 1854 (quoted in Lloyd Morris, *Rebellious Puritan*, 1928): "sick and weary of this office."
(14) A.o.B., Wks., II, 513.
(15) Ibid., 525.
(16) Ibid., 508: "he cared no more for the measurement of time than if it had been merged into eternity."
(17) Ibid., 526: "a vital faith in our invulnerability to the shaft of death."

(18) Warm climates like that of Florence, even though they may have stimulated his imagination (letter to Fields, Sept. 3, 1858: "a plethora of ideas") were not favorable to the intense labor of composition (same letter). He needed Northern or Oceanic climates in order to be himself ("the fogs of Old England or the east wind of Mass . . . ," Ibid.). Cf. letter to Bridge, quoted in *Personal Recollections*, 1893, pp. 123–26: "winter is the season when my brain-work is chiefly accomplished" (Feb. 4, 1850).

(19) Letter of Oct. 1, 1850, J. T. Fields, *Yesterdays with Authors*, p. 64. E. C. Lathrop's study does in fact show that H.'s main period of production fell between Oct. and May (*A Study of the Sources*).

(20) James, *H.*, 1879, pp. 101–02, claims the contrary: "When he was lightest at heart he was most creative." He is nevertheless wrong to generalize.

(21) Letter to Fields, A. Fields, *H.*, p. 93: "In the process of writing, the political . . . turmoil has subsided within me."

(22) A.o.B., Wks., II. 509.

(23) Ibid., 517–18.

(24) Ibid., 523: "through the medium of successful love . . . driven . . . back . . . with concentrated energy upon his (art) . . ."

(25) Am.Nbks., Wks., IX, 25.

(26) A.o.B., Wks., II, 534–35.

(27) Coughlan, *The Private World of William Faulkner*, New York, 1954, 54–55.

(28) A.o.B., Wks., II, 506: "to depend on main strength . . . takes nonsense out of a man."

(29) On account of the accident during adolescence that doomed him to sexual impotence.

(30) See Part One, Conclusion: "The Contradictory Personality."

(31) Brownell, *American Prose Masters*, p. 126, could discern no enthusiasm in him and portrayed him as living and creating in a state of passivity.

(32) A.o.B., Wks., II, 526–27: "When we desire life for the attainment of an object, we recognize the fragility of its texture." "The poet leaves his song half sung . . . the painter . . . leaves half his conception on the canvas."

(33) Letter to Bridge, quoted in H. Gorman, *H.: A Study in Solitude*, p. 41.

(34) It is not the disappointment over not being loved that makes O. Warland drink but the destruction of his work by the women he loves. (A.o.B., II, 518–19)—his despair stems not from love but from his work (525).

(35) A.o.B., Wks., II, 515.

(36) Ibid., 517.

(37) J. T. Fields, *Yesterdays with Authors*, p. 54, classes H. among the nervous geniuses who sleep lightly.

(38) For he himself states that he had not often gazed upon the "ceremony" of dawn. (It.Nbks., Wks., X, 467).

(39) Letter quoted by Van Doren, *H.*, Ch. 7: "I hope there will be a break. A couple of thousand years or so of sleep . . ." (written at the time of the Civil War). Cf. "Old Manse," Wks., II, 40: "the great want . . . of mankind . . . is sleep." See also "Nature of Sleep" (Turner, *H. as Editor*.)

(40) Between 1828 and 1838 at least. Between 1830 and '38 forty or so stories out of about fifty were written in the fall and winter (Cf. E. C. Lathrop) which gives a series of regular waves:

Fall 1830–Winter 1931: 7Vag. and Wives (possibly others destroyed).

Fall 1831–Winter 1832: three or four pieces, including "Canterbury Pilgrims."

Fall 1832–Winter 1833: three, including A.G.

Fall 1833–Winter 1834: twelve, including "Haunted Mind," "Wakefield," M's B.V.

Fall 1834–Winter 1835: failure of *Story–Teller*.

Fall 1835–Winter 1836: six, including "Prophetic Pictures," F's Sh.B.

Fall 1836–Winter 1837: seven, including "Night Sketches," "Endicott."

Fall 1837–Winter 1838: six, including "Footprints" and "H.'s Masquerade."

(41) Approximate tabulation of lean periods: (1) fall 1834–winter 1835 (failure of *Story–Teller*); (2) 1839–40 (Boston Custom House); (3) 1841 (Brook Farm); (4) 1846 (Salem Custom House) and 1847 (Custom House and successive houses movings); (5) 1849 (Custom House and dismissal); (6) 1853–57 (political and consular activities).

II

(1) Jung, *L'Energétique Psychique*, 1956, p. 44: "Mental development cannot take place by intention and will alone, it must also have the magnetic symbol whose quantum of importance exceeds that of the causa."

(2) Am.Nbks., Wks., IX, 28: Four Precepts "to do nothing against one's genius."

(3) Ibid., 28: "to break off customs" (1st precept).

(4) Ibid., 28: "to shake off spirits ill-disposed" (2nd precept).

(5) Ibid., 28: "to meditate on youth (3rd precept).

(6) Gide, *Journal*, (N.R.F.), 48–49. Cf. in particular H.'s third precept and the following "training methods": "Idea of imminent death. Emulation; precise feelings about one's wife . . . Artificial awareness of one's age; emulation by comparing the biographies of great men."

(7) Rose H. Lathrop, *Memories of H.*, 1872, Ch. 15, "The Artist at Work": "He wrote principally in the morning." Cf. "H.'s Diary for 1859," *Nation*, 1912: during the composition of M.F. he sometimes wrote from 10 A.M. to 3 P.M.

(8) Recoll., p. 325.

(9) Ibid.

(10) Eng.Nbks., Wks., VIII, 101: evocation of Sir Walter Raleigh in his prison.

(11) Am.Nbks., R.S., 185: "I hate all labor, but less that of the hands than of the head."

(12) Ibid., 181: ". . . a good deal troubled with the sense of imbecility . . . the consciousness of a blunted pen, benumbed fingers and a mind no longer capable of a vigorous grasp. My torpidity of intellect makes me irritable."

(13) "Custom House," Wks., V, 54.

(14) Whether concerned with his children (Am.Nbks. R.S., 200, 205, 210), a young suicide (ibid., 112–15), old books (ibid., 158, "Old Manse"), machines (ibid., 43), or animals (ibid., "Twenty Days," the rabbit).

(15) E.g.: *Sketches from Memory*, I and II, "Sights," "Snow Flakes," "Footprints" (Cf. Nbks., Wks., IX, 13, 16, 102–05) "Night Sketches" (Nbks., IX, 84, and R.S., 24: "Sparkles of seafire glittering through the gloom"), "Buds and Bird Voices" (Nbks., R.S., 182–84) "Old Apple Dealer" (Am. Nbks., R.S., 90).

(16) Am.Nbks., passage quoted by J.H., H.&W, I, 498–505: nature from individual plants and their leaves right up to the very largest ensembles. The composition is that of an essay, not mere notes. Also, Nbks., IX, 102–5 (admirably composed seascape); 100–102 (picture of autumn).

(17) There are few documents dealing with the composition of the stories. In the case of the novels, however, there are numerous letters containing such information.

(18) R.S., Biog., 93.

(19) G.P.L., Life, Wks., XIII, 497–98.

(20) Letter to C. W. Webber, Dec. 1848, quoted in R.S., Biog., 95.

(21) "Custom House," Wks., V, 56–57.

(22) Letter to Fields, Aug. 1850, quoted in R.S., Biog., 112–13.

(23) Letter from Sophia to her mother, quoted in A. Fields, *H.*, 1899, p. 93.

(24) Letter to Fields, Oct. 1, 1850, J. T. Fields, *Yesterdays with Authors.*

(25) Ibid., Nov. 1850: "requires more care than *S.L.*"

(26) Ibid., Dec. 9, 1850.

(27) It. Nbks., Wks., X, pp. 107 and 172–73 (Apr. 18, 1858).

(28) *The Ancestral Footstep*, Wks., XI.
(29) Letter to Fields, 1858, J. T. Fields, *Yesterdays with Authors,* and It.Nbks., Wks., X, 275.
(30) "H.'s Diary for 1859," *Nation,* May 1912 (unpublished extracts from his Redcar and Leamington diary): Work resumed on Ms. of M.F. on July 24, 1859: "many idle pauses . . . no good result"; "Slow and poor progress"; or else: "middling success"; "a little more satisfactory than heretofore"; and then again: "could write out nothing; discouraged and depressed."
(31) Julian H., *H. and His Circle,* 1903, p. 53, affirms that his father composed in his head and also that no trace of "rough drafts" had been found. Cf. R. H. Lathrop, *Memories of H.,* Ch. 15.
(32) H.&W, I, 368 (letter from Sophia to her mother).
(33) R. H. Lathrop, *Memories of H.,* Ch. 15: ". . . fearless blot of the finger."
(34) Complete title: "E.B., a chapter from an abortive romance" (Wks., III).
(35) Letter to C. W. Webber, Dec. 1848, quoted in R.S., Biog., 93.
(36) Levin, *The Power of Blackness,* 1958, p. 58, supposes that only the final chapter was involved.
(37) J. T. Fields, *Yesterdays with Authors,* pp. 49–50.
(38) Letter to Fields, 27 Feb. 1851.
(39) It.Nbks., Wks., X, 391.
(40) Letter to J. T. Fields, *Yesterdays with Authors.*
(41) E.g.: *Sketches,* 7G., (Lady Pepperell and Hepzibah), Bl.R. (the drowning) and the descriptive passages in M.F.
(42) Whitman, *Leaves of Grass,* "Song of Myself."

III

(1) Am.Nbks., Wks., IX, 1835 (pp. 19–28); 1836 (30–44); 1837 (86–87, 89, 97–98, 105–110); 1838 (113, 124–25, 205–08); 1839 (208–210); 1840 (210–212); 1842 (272–275, 282–83).
(2) E. H. Davidson, *H.'s Last Phase,* 1949, p. 144.
(3) Am.Nbks., Wks., IX, 21: "much might be wrought out of this"; 282: "this to be wrought out (moral & physical disease); 123: "interesting points"; Indian story, 212: "This might be thought out at great length" (selfishness inspiring love); 106: "might be made emblematical"; 206; "could be symbolical of something."
(4) Ibid., IX, 275: "people with false hair and other artifices."
(5) Such as his old aunt Ingersoll, or his own mother.
(6) Am.Nbks., Wks., IX, 87. Cf. "Footprints," Wks., I, 515.
(7) Ibid., 26. Unconscious association with Dante and Milton perhaps, but above all haunting memory of Gallows Hill. Cf. "A. Doane," XII, 280.
(8) H.&W, I, 326–27 (Letter to Sophia, June 1848).
(9) Eng.Nbks., R.S., 98.
(10) H.&W, I, 205–6 (letter to Sophia, May 1839). See psychoanalytical interp. by Morris, *Rebellious Puritan*: incomplete since it remains whole on the sexuality (libido)–purity level.
(11) "Earth's Holocaust" and "N.A.&E.," Wks., II, latter dating from 1842, former from 1843 (cf. E. C. Lathrop).
(12) Am.Nbks., R.S., 98: "To write a dream which will resemble the real course of a dream."
(13) Ibid., 100: "Pearl, the English of Margaret, a pretty name for a girl in a story."
(14) Ibid., Wks., IX, 205–6.
(15) Ibid., 41.
(16) See reference to the duel incident in Part One.
(17) Augusta (1837) and North Adams (1838) diaries.
(18) Am.Nbks., Wks., IX, 43.
(19) Ibid., 274.
(20) Ibid., 100 (ruins of Browne's Folly), 206 (old house and tower in ruins), 87–88 (Essex Hist. Society).

(21) Ibid., 25: "Two lovers . . . utmost solitude" (1835).
(22) Ibid., 37: "Two lovers . . . pleasure house" (1836). Cf. "Lily's Quest," Wks., II.
(23) Ibid., 41.
(24) Ibid., 107.
(25) Ibid., 205–6.
(26) Ibid., 110, 133, 207, 208, 209–10, 273 (1838 to 1842).
(27) Ibid., 395: "The print of blood of a naked foot . . ."
(28) "Endicott," Wks., I, 487: . . . a young woman, with no mean share of beauty, whose doom it was to wear the letter A . . ." (which might date back to reading done before 1837, the date of the story's publication).
(29) Am.Nbks., R.S., 107.
(30) E.g.: M.'s B.V., Wks., I; "Monsieur du Miroir," Wks., II; "Antique Ring," Wks., XII.
(31) "Christmas Banquet," Wks., II.
(32) "A Rill from the Town Pump," Wks., I.
(33) A.o.B., Wks., II; "Canterbury Pilgrims," Wks., III.
(34) Many hieroglyphs particularly: inscriptions on gravestones (Martha's Vineyard, Isles of Shoals, Am.Nbks., R.S., 276–80), letters filled with moss (green letters, Eng.Nbks., R.S., 571–72, which H. tried to make use of in O.O.H., Wks., VII, 74: "raised, letters of living green"), Gothic letters ("Black letter": Eng.Nbks., R.S., 29, 123–24, 142), old books and documents ("legal document, ibid., 95–96). H., haunted by the memory of the *Letter*, was searching for a symbol around which to construct his "English" novel.
(35) A.o.B., Wks., II, 507: "microscopic," "the minute."
(36) Woodberry, N.H., 1905, p. 44: "the nucleus . . .is the physical object that he seizes upon." Waggoner, H.: A Critical Study, 1955, pp. 60–62, tries to find an organic interpretation of the development of H.'s themes, but sees no connection between the Notes and the stories.
(37) "The Birthmark," Wks., II.
(38) S.L., Wks., V, 312: "On a Field sable, the Letter A, Gules."
(39) E.g.: the veil (Nbks., IX, 35, 1836: "M.s B.V." composed 1834, pub. 1836); the stone heart (ibid., 273: "monstrous crime . . . without sense of guilt," 1842: "Man of Adamant, 1835, pub. 1837), not to mention the "germs" from 1850, many of which dealt with possible "articles" (Nbks., IX, 393–97) at a time when H. was to write no more stories or sketches.
(40) E.g., narcissism (Nbks., IX, 125, 1838, whereas "Monsieur du Miroir" dates from 1836), and the quest for the father (ibid., 209, 1839, ten years after R.M.'s B. and My Kinsman).
(41) Gide, for example, whose Journal teems with unused ideas. As H. grew older so the barren seeds multiplied: Eng.Nbks., R.S., 59–60 (coffin filled with locks of hair); 199 (phantom: became the "Ghost of Dr. Harris," *Nineteenth Century,* XLVII, Jan. 1900); 106 (Bloody Footstep); 201 (Sam Patch); 437 (Indian Story); 36 ("Letter to a dead man gone to Hell").
(42) S.L., Wks., V, 214 (the letter A— . . . freshly green). Cf. Hoffman, *Form and Fable in American Fiction,* 1961, p. 11: H. (97–118), Ch. 5: "The Scarlet Letter and the Green" (two forms of Providence according to Hoffman).
(43) Am.Nbks., IX, 210 ("little boats . . . a magnet in one and steel in the other").
(44) Ibid., 210 (ice in one's blood); 206 ("to kindle . . . household fire").
(45) Ibid., 210 (the semblance of a human face).
(46) Ibid., 43 (the good deeds of an evil life).
(47) E. H. Davidson, H.'s Last Phase, 1949, p. 144: "In the germination of a romance, H.'s mind seized two things . . . a moral law . . . and a romantic image or episode."

(48) Nbks., IX, 107 (Sorrow), 396 (Century, Death), 107 personification of the winds).

(49) Plays on words: Nbks., IX, 26 (A scold and a blockhead—trimstone and wood); 273 (A tri-weekly paper . . . the Tertian Ague); 397 (The North Pole for a fishing-pole).

(50) Nbks., IX, 407: "The best of us being unfit to die . . ."; 107 (great toil . . . for . . . wealth); 394 (Generosity is the flower of justice); and 118, R.S.: "Our most intimate friend is not he whom we show the worst, but the best, of our nature."

(51) Which refutes the postulate according to which H.'s first concern was to find a moral design that he could then illustrate. Davidson, *H.'s Last Phase,* 144, does speak of the two necessary elements "meeting" (abstract moral . . . visualized object) but keeping their identities distinct, which dooms them to sterility.

(52) The maxim quoted in Note 50 was reworked in more complex form in the theme of sincerity and hypocrisy in S.L. ("The Interior of a Heart"); it becomes an exhortation in the conclusion (Wks., V, 307: "Be true!").

(53) *H.'s Last Phase,* 145: "a symbol . . . I shall define as the fusing of the image and the moral." But he aggravates the error we mentioned (51) by adding: "The Symbol was the fixing of the moral idea in concrete terms"; thus, for Davidson, the esthetic dynamic is not contained within the germ. He extends to all H.'s creations what applies particularly to the posthumous works.

(54) Am.Nbks., R.S., 98.

(55) "Bosom Serpent," Wks., II.

(56) Nbks., IX, 38 and 37.

(57) Ibid., 38.

(58) Ibid., 27 (life by instalments).

(59) Levin, *The Power of Blackness,* 1958, p. 47.

(60) Nbks., Wks., IX, 38.

(61) Am.Nbks., R.S., 98.

(62) Nbks., Wks., IX, 109.

(63) Am.Nbks., R.S., 132.

(64) R. M.'s B., Wks., I.

(65) Am.Nbks., R.S., 36.

(66) My Kinsman, Wks., III.

(67) "David Swan," Wks., I.

(68) G.B., Wks., I.

(69) *H.'s Last Phase,* 147 (central event, central scene).

(70) S.L., Wks., V, Chs. 2, 12, 23; Bl.R., Wks., V, Chs. 6, 12, 17, 18 (the room); 7G., Wks., III, Chs. 2, 3, 4, 11, etc. (most of the scenes are interiors) and Chs. 1, 13, 18 (ancestral chair).

(71) "M.'s B.V.; G.C.; H.of3H. (Wks., I); Y.G.B. (Wks., II).

(72) "Lily's Quest," Wks., II.

(73) "Procession of Life," Wks., II.

(74) Nbks., Wks., IX, 38 (1st germ: 1836), 87 (note, 1837), 102 (portrait, 1838).

(75) Ibid., 204 (all the dead . . . drowned in a certain lake to arise). Similarly, R.S., 93 (Satan in Pandemonium).

(76) "Endicott," Wks., I, 486–87. Cf. humorous treatment: "reflexions in the Pillory" (Goodrich, ed. of *Tales of Humor,* 1840), 119 (wooden cravat), 122 (Pinnacle sublime).

(77) This is even more evident in the novels, which absorbed a greater quantity of experience than the stories.

(78) Am.Nbks., R.S., 130: "a darkened room where a dead man sits in solitude."

(79) 7G., Wks., III, Ch. 18.

(80) Letter to Fields, Jan. 27, 1851 (J. T. Fields, *Yesterdays with Authors*: "I likewise prefer it to S.L. . . . ."

(81) Suicide of Martha Hunt, also drowning of Margaret Fuller (July 1850)

(82) His sister Louisa's death by drowning in the Hudson (July 27, 1852) occurred only a few days after publication of Bl.R. (July 14, 1852).

IV

(1) The wandering storyteller: *Passages,* "The Village Theatre," Wks., II, 470.

(2) A.o.B., Wks., II, 527: "let all this be imagined."

(3) Preface III, Wks., I, 16: "the sketches are not . . . profound."

(4) Letter to Sophia, May 1840, Wks., IX, 219: "not that I have any love of mystery, but because I abhor it . . ." Cf. another letter, IX, 335 (no love of secrecy).

(5) *Relinquished Work,* Wks., II; "Solitary Man," Wks., XII; D in Mss.; Wks., III; "Custom House," V, etc.

(6) Preface III, Wks. I, 16–17: "in the style of a man of society."

(7) H. scarcely ever talked shop, even with Melville. The example of "Agatha" is the best proof of how totally impossible collaboration was for him.

(8) Letter to Lewis Mansfield, Feb. 20, 1850, quoted in Blodgett, "H. as Poetry Critic," AL, XII, 1940: "interfering with the process of creation."

(9) Letter to Fields about M.F., Sept. 1858, quoted A. Fields, *H.,* 1899, (plethora of ideas).

(10) 7G., Wks., III, 139 (sluggish); 171 (intellectual decay).

(11) S.L., Wks., V: The Interior of a Heart, The Minister's Vigil. The M. in a Maze.

(12) Waggoner, *H.: A Critical Study,* p. 9: "what thoughts come to the mind half way between sleep and waking" (apropos of "The Haunted Mind").

(13) Cantwell, *N.H.: The American Years,* p. 103, maintains that H. rose late, worked during the afternoon, and often composed at night, which is perhaps true in the case of the *Seven Tales,* which were probably written at Bowdoin outside of study hours, and, generally speaking, when the inspiration was insistent (S.L., V, 268: composition of the sermon: "thus the night fled away."

(14) "Custom House," V, 49–50 and S.L. (Hester at her Needle).

(15) A.o.B., Wks., II.

(16) It.Nbks., Wks., X, 397–98: "as if the artist had bestirred himself to catch the first glimpse of an image . . . forecasting thought, skill and prophetic design."

(17) See facsimile, Wks., XII, 501 (Letter to Fields, Feb. 27, 1851) and S.L. edition published by Club des Libraires, trans. Cestre, p. 364. R. H. Lathrop, *Memories of H.,* Ch. 15, speaks of "small rounded, but irregular letters . . . formed obscurely, though . . . fascinatingly."

(18) "Am.Nbks., R.S., 348 (Manchester art gallery: the pictures) and, of course, "Custom House," V, the Letter, pp. 49–50.

(19) G.P.L., *A Study of H.,* 1876, p. 295.

(20) "P's Corresp.," Wks., II, 413 (more substantial).

(21) D. in Mss., Wks., III, 519.

(22) S.L., Wks., V, 185–86 (an electric chain).

(23) Am.Nbks., R.S., 97: "the light of the mind . . . on obscure objects.

(24) James, *H.,* 1879: "his cat-like faculty of seeing in the dark," p. 99.

(25) R. Michaud, *Le Roman Américain d'Aujourd'hui,* 1928, defined H. as "the detective of the Puritan conscience."

(26) D. in Mss., Wks., III, 597 (to dig); S.L., V, 151 (scrutinized); 152 (to go deep, delving, prying into, probing, investigator); 156 (to burrow); 159 (to dig); 167 (lay open . . . the wound); 169 (thrust aside the vestment); 234 (violated).

(27) "Prophetic Pictures," Wks., I, 207: "O glorious art! . . . the innumerable forms, that wander in nothingness, start into being at thy beck . . . ." Cf. critical article on Simms, May 2, 1846, "Salem Advertiser," ed. R.S., *AL,* Jan. 1934: "The *magic touch* that should cause new intellectual and moral shapes to spring up . . ."

(28) Am.Nbks., R.S., 153: watching the plants growing in the garden of the Old Manse: "we love to see something born into the world"; and 137, the sprouting of the new grass: "a green blush."
(29) "Buds and Bird Voices," Wks., II.
(30) A.o.B., and "D.'s W. I.," Wks., II.
(31) A.o.B. Wks., II, 529–30.
(32) "Earth's Holocaust," Wks., II; Rapp., ibid.; Sn.Im., Wks., III.
(33) Bergson, L'Evolution créatrice, Ch. 2.
(34) Eng.Nbks., R.S., 182: "like the anaconda, I need to lubricate any object a great deal before I can swallow it . . . ."
(35) M.F., Wks., VI, (Hilda).
(36) Am.Nbks., R.S., 250: decorations, flowers, children, etc. We know H.'s opinion on women writers: "I cannot enough than God that . . . thou hast never . . . prostituted thyself to the public, as that woman [Grace Greenwood] has . . ." (Letter to Sophia, quoted in Fairbanks, "H. and the Vanishing Venus," UTSE, XXXVI, 1957).
(37) Cantwell, N.H.: The American Years, 372–73, considers Sophia to have been a frustrated artist.
(38) "Custom House," Wks., V, 53 (a tarnished mirror).
(39) Woodberry, N.H., 1902, Ch. 4: "faintness of life"; "low vital tone."
(40) Cf. Prefaces. Arlin Turner, N.H., an Introduction and Interpretation 1961, Ch. 6, "Reality in the Romance," pp. 66–67, talks of H.'s "belief in self-criticism," in particular in the Preface to T.T.T. (1851). He does not perceive that the passage referred to is self-defense rather than genuine self-criticism. Cf. A. Turner, "H. as Self-Critic," SAQ, XXXVII, 1938, who emphasizes H.'s tendency to give way to disappointment. He quotes an undated letter: "How little have I told! and of that little . . . almost nothing is . . . tinctured with any quality that makes it exclusively my own."
(41) D in Mss., Wks., III, 597.
(42) Ibid., 597.
(43) "G.C.," Wks., I.
(44) Letter to Webber, R.S., Biog., 93, referring to E.Br.: "like a tooth ill-drawn."
(45) "Dragon's Teeth," Wks., IV.
(46) "D. in Mss.," Wks., III, 597.
(47) E. R.'s P., Wks., I (Alice Vane); "D's W.Im.," Wks., II (Drowne); A.o.B., ibid. (R. Danforth); S.L., V (Hester); A.o.B., II (O. Warland); Birth., II (Aylmer).
(48) A.o.B., Wks., II, 512: "It is requisite for the ideal artist to possess a force of character that seems hardly compatible with its delicacy."
(49) In the ms. of Grim.
(50) In which it differs from the scientific discovery, which is spectacular in its applications but not an inner spectacle in itself.
(51) "Solitary Man," Wks., XII, 27: "the secret of my powers."
(52) Letter to Fields, quoted in R.S., Biog., 113: "having written so fiercely."
(53) S.L., V, 268–69: the sermon (a vast, immeasurable tract of written space).
(54) Gide, Journal, N.R.F., 541: "The work of art is always the result of anxious perseverance."
(55) S.L., V, 268–69: brief but striking evocation: "he wrote with such an impulsive flow of thought and emotion that he fancied himself inspired . . . he drove his task onward with earnest haste and ecstasy."

V

(1) Hildegard H., Romantic Rebel, 1932, p. 121: skating: "no better start to a day of work" (H.'s own words repeated by Sophia).
(2) Letter quoted in J.H., H.&W, I, 205 (the dusky glow of firelight); "Custom House," Wks., V, 55–56 (smouldering glow).
(3) "Custom House," Wks., V, 54–55 (a streak of this magic moonshine).
(4) Letter to Sophia, H.&W, I, 203 (I invite your spirit to be with me).

(5) Ibid., 213 (I gaze at them by all sorts of lights, daylight, twilight . . . candle-light . . . firelight).

(6) It.Nbks., Wks., X, 269 (reflexion . . . from a copper kettle).

(7) Am.Nbks., R.S., 56, 170 (space surrounded by trees; cf. S.L., scene in forest); 130, 209–210 (the house; cf. P.Gold., Wks., I, 7G., Wks., III); 102 (Sleepy Hollow); 133 (a glen); 45, 58 (villages in valleys); 54 (cloud, scenery); 63 (cloud world).

(8) Engl.Nbks., R.S., 167; "transfusion of sky-light through the gloom."

(9) Letters to Sophia, Wks., IX, 213 (dream of having wings); 217–18 ("to fling myself on the gentle wind, and be blown away"); 346 (flying with gulls in the imagination: "you go up among the clouds, and lay hold of these soaring gulls, and repose with them . . .").

(10) *Portable H.*, 611-12, Oct. 4, 1840: "a light deep downward and upward in my soul. . . ."

(11) Flight of Goodman Brown, Y.G.B., Wks., II, and Dimmesdale's projected flight, S.L., Wks., V (A Flood of Sunshine).

(12) E.g.: *Relinquished Works*, "Niagara," etc. Wks., XII.

(13) Am.Nbks., R.S., 98: "a region that seems, in some sort, to reproduce the flowers and sunny beauty of the entrance. . . ." Cf. Turner, *H. as Editor*, p. 158: "a picture of what the exterior world would be."

(14) Nbks., Wks., IX, 110, 113 (a man in the midst of a crowd . . . completely in the power of another). Cf. S.L., V (The Leech and His Patient).

(15) Which G. Poulet has proved in Balzac's case (*Etudes sur le Temps Humain*, II, "La Distance Intérieure"). Nevertheless, the exterior space annexed by the mind is only an imagined space, not real space.

(16) Bachelard, *Poétique de l'Espace*, P.U.F., p. 197.

(17) "Solitary Man," Wks., XII, 29–30.

(18) J-J. Rousseau: *Rêveries* and "Lettres à Malesherbes."

(19) A. Doane, "Old W's Tale," Wks., XII, 291 (indistinguishable cloud); 111-13 (mistiness).

(20) Y.G.B., Wks., II, 98 (black mass of cloud); 100 (dark wall); 102 (glowing arch).

(21) "Man of Adamant," Wks., II.

(22) P.Gold, Wks., I; 7G., Wks., III.

(23) A.Doane, Wks., XII, 288 (a frigid glory).

(24) Letters to Sophia (particularly, Oct. 4, 1840, *op. cit.*, note (10) and S.L., Wks., V, forest scene: expansion of universe beginning from inner self.

(25) Am.Nbks., R.S., 102: "In moods of heavy despondency . . . to sink down in some quiet spot, and lie forever, letting the soil accumulate . . ."

(26) It.Nbks., Wks., X, 275 (six months of uninterrupted monotony), 311 (I need . . . monotony . . . before I can live in the world within). Cf. letter, 1857, C. Ticknor, *H. and His Publisher*: "If I could be perfectly quiet for a few months."

(27) *Approximate time of composition for the novels*: 1) S.L.: Sept. 27 1849–Jan. 15, 1850, then on till Feb. 3: i.e. five full working months, to which we should add two or three for the getting under way. 2) 7G.: Aug. 1850–Nov. 1850, then Nov. 1850 to Jan. 25, 1851: i.e. only three full working months and another three for getting started. 3) Bl.R.: Sept. 1851–Apr. 30, 1852, i. e. eight months in all. 4) M.F.: July–Sept. 1858 (Florence); Nov. 1858–Jan. 30, 1859 (Rome); July 26, 1850–Nov. 8, 1859 (Redcar and Leamington), i.e. four months for the final draft and three months each for the preliminary drafts (dates, cf., R.S., Biog., 1949).

(28) With individual exceptions: an occasional piece like "Sisters Years" (Wks., I) requiring a shorter time, whereas a story possibly intended to become a novel ("Ethan Brand") required several months.

(29) R.S., Biog., 98: "He writes immensely," Sophia wrote.

(30) Y.G.B., Wks., II.

(31) M.M.M., Wks., II.

(32) M.F., Wks., VI.
(33) Ibid., Ch. 17: Colosseum scene.
(34) S.L., Wks., V, Chs. 2 and 3.
(35) Y.G.B., Wks., II, and S.L., Ch. 18 ("A Flood of Sunshine"); Ch. 20 (the return through the woods).
(36) A.o.B., Wks., II, 512–13 (the clock in the church steeple); 508 (O. Warland indifferent to mathematical time).
(37) S.L., Wks., V, 268–69: "the night fled away . . . morning came . . ." (the coming of morning marks the end of the mind's fever).
(38) Ibid., 184–85: Dimmesdale while in the pillory in the dead of night imagines his shame displayed in broad daylight.
(39) Ibid., 304: Dimmesdale's farewell.
(40) 7G., Wks., III, 332–33: "the watch has ceased to tick" (arrest of inner time, whereas external time goes on: "the night is well-nigh passed") and, 329: "one of the city clocks."
(41) Though lacking astronomy, H. had documented himself on astrology (cf. witchcraft).
(42) S.L., Wks., V, 187–88.
(43) Letters, Wks., IX, 219: "Lights and shadows are continually flitting across my inward sky. . . ."
(44) Nbks., Wks., IX, 106: "Chasing Echo to her hiding-place. . . ." Cf. the cries in Y.G.B., Wks., II; S.L., Wks., V, 133 (Pearl: "eldritch scream"); 180 (Dimmesdale: "shrieked aloud")—and the laughs: Y.G.B., Wks., II, 99–100; E.B., Wks., III, 482: "slow, heavy laugh"; "the madman's laugh"; "the wild screaming laugh."
(45) Bergson, L'Evolution créatrice, P.U.F., p. 221.
(46) "Monsieur du Miroir," Wks., II; "Dr.H's Exp.," Wks., I, 268–69; "Endicott," Wks., I, 486; S.L., V, 132; 7G., Wks., III, 332.
(47) "Sights," Wks., I (the light); "A Flight in the Fog," Passages (fog); "Night Sketches," Wks., I.
(48) Y.G.B., Wks., II; S.L., V,: Dimmesdale.
(49) Letter, Oct. 4, 1840, Portable H., 611–12 (". . . upward . . . downward . . .").
(50) S.L., Wks., V, 148–49.
(51) Grim., ed. Davidson, 1954, pp. 197–201.
(52) Duyckinck, Dem.Rev, Apr. 1845: "H. combines qualities masculine and feminine." Longfellow (Nth. Am. Rev., Apr. 1842) accords him both depth and tenderness. One is also reminded of V. Woolf's androgynous Orlando.
(53) "Prophetic Pictures," Wks., I, 207: "O glorious art. Thou are the image of the Creator's own."
(54) G. Poulet, Essais sur le Temps Humain, I, Introd., 17–18: continuous creation.
(55) "Procession of Life," Wks., II, 251–52: "Onward, onward . . . And whither! We know not; and Death . . . our leader, deserts us by the wayside . . ."; also, Dimmesdale's reticence on his deathbed (S.L., V, 303–4).

CHAPTER 4

I
(1) "Custom House," Wks., V, 50: "I experienced a sensation . . . as of burning heat." The painter Leutze even claimed later on, in a letter published in Art Union Bulletin, that he had seen the original of the Letter.
(2) Eng.Nbks., R.S., 225, and Wks., VIII, 119–20.
(3) Ibid., 225: "my eyes would fill and my voice quiver."
(4) Letter to Lewis Mansfield, Dec. 26, 1849 (Blodgett, "H. as Poetry Critic," AL, XII, 1940; "Manuscript is as delusive as moonshine, Print is like common daylight.")

(5) In 1829: R.S., Biog., 30. A first attempt had already failed in Salem with the printer Caleb Foote (Cantwell, *N.H.: The American Years*, 130).

(6) R.S., Biog., 31–32.

(7) A. Turner, "A Note on H's Revisions," *MLN*, Nov. 1936: 7Vag. (suppression of an allusion to the heroine's ankles), "Monsieur du Miroir": passage concerning disreputable haunts and drunkenness. On the other hand, G.B. (edit. 1832) added passages justifying the Puritans in their attitude towards the Quakers (Orians, "Sources and Themes of H.'s 'The Gentle Boy,'" *NEQ*, XIV, 1941).

(8) Y.G.B. and R.M.'sB., for example, had to wait for the publication of Mosses, and "Canterbury Pilgrims"; Wives, and My Kinsman, that of Sn.Im.

(9) *Peter Purley's Universal History* and *American Magazine of Useful & Entertaining Knowledge*, edited in 1836 on Goodrich's behalf (cf. A. Turner, *H. as Editor*, 1941).

(10) Am.Nbks., Wks., IX, 24 (two notes concerning "Man of Adamant") 24 (the bells); 26 (alchemy): all dating from 1835.

(11) A. Turner, *H. as Editor*, 88–89 (Preservation of the Dead); 185 (Bells).

(12) "Canterbury Pilgrims," fall of 1831 according to E. C. Lathrop (cf. "Ancient Pilgrims," *H. as Editor*, 110); "G.C.," fall of 1832 or winter 1833 (cf. "Rainbows," *H. as Editor*, 188: the quest for the ideal).

(13) "Fire Worshippers" (*H. as Editor*, 255); cf. "Fire Worship," Nov. 1843, Wks., II.

(14) Goodrich was never to pay him what he owed him. Moreover, H. himself stated that 300 dollars per annum was the maximum he expected to earn by his pen (letter to Bridge, quoted R.S., Biog., 32).

(15) Recoll., p. 328: "The Seven Tales . . . which he ought not to have burnt. . . ." Letter to Sophia, Oct. 4, 1840: "Here I have written many tales—many tales that have been burned to ashes . . ." Preface to T.T.T., Wks., I, 14: "the Author burned them without mercy or remorse." And, Am. Nbks., IX, 445: "I burned great heaps of . . . letters and . . . papers."

(16) "Earth's Holocaust," Wks., II, 455: after the destruction of all man's works the human heart remains unchanged: it therefore remains tormented with the need to create.

(17) D. in Mss., Wks., III.

(18) A.o.B., Wks., II, 516: "re-creating the one idea to which all his intellectual activity referred itself."

(19) E. A. Poe, *Graham's*, Apr. 1842. One is reminded of the lost story referred to by Julian H., in H.&W, I, 24 ("Susan Grey").

(20) He recurs in A. Doane, Wks., XII (the storyteller and his feminine audience); "Antique Ring," XII (storyteller, Ed. Caryl, in a society setting); Rapp., II (storyteller as presenter and critic); "Christmas Banquet," II (Roderick and Rosina, main characters of "Bosom Serpent," one of the *Allegories of the Heart*, which were to form a whole); and above all, in *Legends of the Province House*, Wks., II, (the tavern storyteller, Bela Tiffany); Gd.F's Ch., W. B. and Tangle., Wks., IV (storyteller surrounded by children); without mentioning the "tales" inserted in the novels: 7G., III, Ch. 13: Alice Pyncheon (Holgrave as storyteller, Phoebe as audience); Bl.R., V, Ch. 13: Zenobia's legend ("The Silvery Veil"), the storyteller being the "woman of genius" surrounded by her admirers: M.F., VI., Ch. 27: "Myths" (storyteller being Donatello, his narrative in the nature of a confession).

(21) *Passages*, Wks., II, 461: "Frames perhaps more valuable than the pictures themselves . . . embossed with groups of characteristic figures, amid the lake & mountain scenery, the villages and fertile fields of our native land." And he adds: "I write the book for the sale of its moral. . . ."

(22) *Sketches from Memory*, I (Wks., II) and II (Wks., XII). See Part One: "The Vagabond."

(23) H.'s own title was *The Itinerant Story-Teller* (letter to Ticknor, June 1855, C. Ticknor, *H. and His Publisher*, 126–27). According to G.P.L. (Wks., I, intro. 9), the storyteller was to illustrate the sermons of his companion, a young preacher, each story being accompanied by a brief account of the circumstances in which it was told (Wks., II, 61), and from which it would thus have been equally possible for it to spring (e.g., "A.G."), R.S., *Biog.*, 32, identifies at least four of the tales that were to figure in it: "Mr. H.'s Catastrophe," "Grey Champion," "A.G.," Y.G.B. There could scarcely have been more than twelve to fifteen of them if we remember that the first edition of T.T.T. only contained eighteen (R.S., Biog., 33), and also the importance that H. seems to have accorded to the frame (cf. Note 21). Of the frame, there remain only the *Passages* and *Sketches* reprinted in accordance with the fragments published by P. Benjamin, *N. Eng. Mag.*, 1835. Twenty years later, H. gave Ticknor carte blanche (letter, June 1855) which means that we probably now have all that could be recovered. With the help of the itinerary, incomplete though it is, we can provide a sketched reconstruction of fragments of the work:

1. *Passages* (Wks., II): escape of ambitious young man and meeting with his other self. First tale: "Mr. H.'s Catastrophe" ("Village Th.," Wks., II, 473), to which some sketches of village life may have been appended ("Little Annie," "Town Pump," perhaps "Village Uncle,") not to mention the witch stories (A. Doane, H.of3H., Y.G.B.). 2. "The Notch" (Wks., II; mountain stories and legends—"A.G.," "G.C."). 3. Canal Boat" (Wks., II): possible session on board river steamer. 4. "Inland Port" (Wks., XII): proximity of Canadian border possibly used to introduce historical sketches ("Old Ticonderoga") and patriotic tales ("Grey Champion"). 5. "Rochester" (Wks., XII): further stage in journey. 6. "Night Scene" (Wks., XII): transition (another stage in journey, Detroit (Wks., XII, 21: "I was a passenger for Detroit"). 7. "Solitary Man," (Wks., XII); the return via Niagara (Wks., XII). It is impossible to tell at what moment, or for what reasons, the storyteller renounced his art and his wanderings. However, "Solitary Man" does seem to have been intended to close the storyteller cycle, since it includes (XII, 26) a reminiscence of a former "wanderlust" (II, 467: "round the globe."). Moreover, the moralizing intent of the book (II, 361) is confirmed by Oberon's edifying end ("Home Return," XII). Thus, the storyteller, whether in conformity with the initial plan or after revisions after the failure of the work, would have become Oberon.

(24) "Gentle Boy, a Thrice-Told Tale," with an original illustration (by Sophia Peabody), 1839 (N. C. Browne, *Bibliography of N.H.*).

(25) Brownson, *B.'s Rev.*, July 1850: "Genius perverted or employed in perverting others."

(26) Ann. W. Abbott, *Nth.Am.Rev.*, July 1850, attacked Hester in particular as being a proud and sensual creature.

(27) Rev. Coxe. *Church Rev.*, Jan, 1851, wondered: "Is the French era actually begun in our literature?" And the Rev. A. P. Peabody in *Nth.Am.Rev.* Jan. 1853, referring to Bl.R. and S.L., wrote: "H . . . has defamed the fathers of New England . . . violated one of the most sacred canons of literary creation."

(28) Rev. Coxe, *Church Rev.*, Jan. 1851.

(29) D. H. Lawrence, *Studies in Classic American Literature*, discusses the American obsession with purity (The White Psyche).

(30) Letter to Bridge, Feb. 4, 1850, *Personal Recollections*, pp. 123–26: "a hell-fired story, into which I found it impossible to throw any cheering light."

(31) Melville, "H. and His Mosses," Duyckinck's *Lit. Wld.*, Aug. 1851, (article published anonymously): "this great power of blackness in him . . ."

(32) Poe, "Marginalia," *Dem.Rev.*, Dec. 1844: "Noted merely to be damned by faint praise."

(33) Preface, T.T.T., Wks., I, 13: "no incitement to literary effort," 14: "Dearth of nutriment." Pref. Sn.Im., III, 387: "my forgotten or never-noticed stories."

(34) Letter to Longfellow, June 5, 1849, quoted R.S., Am.Nbks., 292: "one little drop of venom"; and further on: "they (his enemies) should be taught what it (imagination) can do in the way of producing nettles, skunk-cabbage, deadly night-shade, wolf's bane, dog-wood."

(35) A. A. Kern, "H.'s Feathertop and 'R.L.R.' " PMLA, LII, 1937.

(36) Letter to J. T. Fields, Yesterdays with Authors, near the end of his life: "I am glad that my labor with the abominable little tool is drawing to an end." And, in a letter to Ticknor, referring to M.F., (R.S., Biog., 210), he considers that it is not "wholesome" to hold a pen.

(37) Cf. E. H. Davidson, H.'s Last Phase, and the text of Grim. as reconstructed by the same author, 1954.

(38) Grim., Davidson, 105 (Follow the clue stubbornly, stubbornly), and 107 (keep hold of this idea stubbornly).

(39) Ibid., 47 (if we modify the negation: "his energies . . . for lack of that spring . . . could (had) no longer (never) be(en) put into action). Cf. letter to Fields, 1865 (Van Doren, H., 1949): "my mind has lost its temper and fine edge."

(40) Ibid., 190 (constantly tortured, until torture becomes the necessity of his life).

(41) Ibid., 104 (What? I can't make it out:—'twon't do—How? Nothing of this—'twon't do, 'twon't do—What? What? What? How! How! How!); 146 (unimaginable nonsense); 164 (I never was in such a predicament before).

(42) Ibid., 54 (a good man or an enormous villain?); 150 (What? What? What? A worshipper of the sun? a cannibal? a ghoul? a vampire?); 104 (The art of making gold? a peculiar kind of poison?); 150 (A man with a mortal disease? a leprosy? a eunuch? a corkleg? a golden touch? a dead hand? a false nose? a black eye?).

(43) Ibid., 122 (the poison of his great spider); 123, 150 (the great spider); 123 (a snarled skein truly); 207 (cobweb); 209 (the Doctor in the spider's web is H. himself); 164 (spider's web). H. Levin, The Power of Blackness, London, 1958, p. 82, sees the symbol of the web, the tangle, even in the title—"shaw" being an archaic term for "thicket" and thus evoking the tangle of the thornbush.

(44) Ibid., 164 (one chain attached . . . about his neck).

(45) "Man of Adamant," Wks., II.

(46) Grim., Davidson, 120 (this clue he spends his life in seeking till he gets to be insane). Cf. Louise Tharp, The Peabody Sisters, 1950, who claims that H., when old and sick at the end of his life, was afraid of going mad.

(47) Rose H. Lathrop, Memories of H., 422–23: "I forbid you to write them!"

(48) Letter, shortly before his death, quoted in Van Doren, H., "I hope there will be a break. A couple of thousand years or so of sleep." Cf. "Old Manse," II, 40.

II

(1) Letter to Fields, Jan. 27, 1851, Yesterdays with Authors, referring to 7G. (the cold fit . . . of a fever), Eng.Nbks., Wks., VIII, 199: "I was in a very nervous state then" (after S.L.). Letter to Ticknor, quoted R.S., Biog., 210: "worn down" (after M.F.).

(2) He applauded his own "merit" in having written 7G. (letter to his sister Elizabeth, R.S., Biog., 112) and in having persevered to the end of his draft of M.F. (more than 500 pages) which cost him the greatest pains (letter to Ticknor, Nov. 17, 1859, R.S., 210).

(3) Woodberry in his N.H., 1905, nevertheless speaks of intellectual immaturity ("a touch of nonage," p. 132) as well as artistic immaturity ("studies" . . . "prentice work," (124–25)). This is untrue.

(4) Cf. "Niagara," Wks., XII, "Monsieur du Miroir," Wks., II.
(5) E.g., R.M.'sB., G.B., My Kinsman, all three dating from 1828 or 1829 (E. C. Lathrop), preceded by A.Doane, and H.of3H.
(6) *Fanshawe*, Wks., XI, in particular. Cantwell, *N.H.: The American Years*, 100 and 119, emphasizes the romantic character of the hero. Another example: "Solitary Man," Wks., XII.
(7) Several of the "Old Manse" stories are topical in content: Cel.Rlrd., "Hall of Fantasy," "Select Party," etc.
(8) D. H. Lawrence, *Studies in Classic American Literature*.
(9) Less "natural" at least, coming from his pen, than the following work (letter to Bridge, March 15, 1851, *Personal Recollections*, 138–39).
(10) Letter to Fields, A. Fields, *H.*, 1899, pp. 86–87: "The same dark idea . . . will weary very many people. . . ." Cf. letter to Bridge, Feb. 4, 1850, *Personal Recollections*, 123–26.
(11) As was proved by the anonymous article (*N & Q.*, April 1943) in which H. was labeled a "bête noir."
(12) Whipple, *Atl.Mth.*, May 1860: "He cannot use his genius, . . . his genius uses him."
(13) M.F., Wks., VI, 167–68: the demon painted by Guido Reni (the painter looses the demon that haunts him into reality, H. says).
(14) Letter to Fields, Nov. 1850: "careering on the utmost verge of a precipitous absurdity . . ."
(15) Letter to Bridge, Oct. 18, 1852, *Personal Recollections*, 145: "a new romance—which if possible I mean to make more genial than the last (Bl.R.). Cf. letter to Fields, *Yesterdays*, after M.F. (April 1860): "I will try to write a more genial book."
(16) Letter to Fields, *Yesterdays*, 75 (April 13, 1854): "my past self is not very much to my taste."
(17) Letter to Bridge, R.S., Biog., 122: "to put an extra touch of the devil into it."
(18) Rev. A. P. Peabody, *Nth. Am. Rev.*, Jan. 1853: "H . . . has defamed the fathers of New England."
(19) Letter from Fields to Miss Mitford, Oct. 13, 1853, R.S., Biog., 134: "From all I can gather from this silent genius, it will be in the *Scarlet Letter* vein." Cf. letter from Melville to H., Aug. 13, 1852 (Jay Layda, *Melville Log*, 1951): "this thing lies very much in a vein with which you are particularly familiar." Harrison Hayford, "Significance of Melville's Agatha Letters," *ELH*, XIII, 1946, taking H.'s own declarations after S.L., at face value, assumes that he failed to find the subject gay enough.
(20) The "cheering" light that was precisely what was missing from S.L. (letter of Feb. 4, 1850 to Bridge).
(21) Letter to Bridge, March 15, 1851: "more proper and natural for me to write."
(22) J-J. Rousseau, third letter to Malesherbes.
(23) 7G., Wks., III, 306: "He (Clifford) had a winged nature."
(24) Eng.Nbks., R.S., 553: "a madman," then adds: "indeed an Englishman of genius . . . is great abnormally . . ." And earlier: "Morbid painfulness."
(25) Ibid., 255–56.
(26) It.Nbks., Wks., X, 297.
(27) E.g., the painter in "Prophetic Pictures" (Wks., I); Westervelt (Bl.R. Wks., V); Ethan Brand (Wks., III); Chillingworth (S.L., Wks., V).
(28) Cf. "Prophetic Pictures" (Wks. I), S.L. (Wks., V), M.F. (Wks., VI: Miriam and the Model).
(29) S.L., Wks., V: Hester, though married to Chillingworth, has no child by him.
(30) It.Nbks., X, 317.
(31) Recoll.: "he never liked to have his writings spoken of."
(32) Letter to L. Mansfield (Blodgett, "H. as Poetry Critic," *AL*, XII, 1940):

"I have no business, nor mean to have any, but my pen" (March 19, 1850).
(33) "Custom House," Wks., V, 65: "I am a citizen of somewhere else . . . there has never been, for me, the genial atmosphere which a literary man requires."
(34) Letter of Oct. 4, 1840, *Portable H.*, 611: "the world found me out in my lonely chamber, and called me forth . . . with a still small voice."
(35) Letter to Ticknor, July 17, 1857, C. Ticknor, *H. and His Publisher,* 204: "I wish I were . . . richer; and I doubt whether you would ever advertize another book by the author of *The Scarlet Letter.*"
(36) We should remember the letter quoted by N. Arvin, "H. as Self-Critic," *S.A.Q.*, XXXVII, Apr. 1938: "How little have I told!"

III

(1) Witness the dream he had at the age of 50 (Eng.Nbks., R.S., 98).
(2) It.Nbks. Wks., X, 513–14.
(3) Letter to Fields, *Yesterdays with Authors,* p. 51: "If *The Scarlet Letter* is to be the title, would it not be well to print it on the title-page in red ink?"
(4) For 7G., he first suggested: "The House of the Seven Gables," the "The 7 Gabled House" or "The 7 Gables" (letter to Fields, Oct. 1, 1850, *Yesterdays with Authors,* 54). Then, in November, "The Old Pyncheon House"; "The Old P. Family, or the H. of the 7 G, a Romance"; For M.F. we find, among others: "Monte-Beni, or, the Faun, a Romance"; "The Romance of Monte-Beni"; "The Romance of a Faun"; "The Faun of Monte-Beni"; "Monte-Beni, a Romance"; "Miriam, a Romance"; "Hilda, a Romance"; "Donatello, a Romance"; "Marble & Man, a Romance" (letter of Oct. 10, 1858, Fields, *Yesterdays with Authors*).
(5) A tendency that H. attributed, in a debased form, to Clifford (7G., Wks., III, 169): "mortal existence should have been tempered to his qualities . . ."—his nature being nourished, H. wrote, exclusively by Beauty.
(6) It.Nbks., X, 77.
(7) "Prophetic Pictures," Wks., I, 195: "untutored beholders."
(8) Letter to Longfellow, June 4, 1837. *Portable H.*, 609: "If my writings had made any decided impression. . . ." Preface T.T.T., Wks., I, 17: "to begin an intercourse with the world." "P's Corresp.," Wks., II, 424: "the universe is ready to respond . . ."
(9) Like Pierce at the moment of his election to the presidency of the U.S. (letter from H. to Bridge, *Personal Recollections,* 145, Oct. 18, 1852: "in the intensest blaze of celebrity"), whereas all he himself ever knew was a phantom of fame (letter to Bridge, ibid., 138–39), March 15, 1851: "the bubble of reputation . . ."). And his last wish (to Fields, Feb. 25, 1864, *Portable H.,* 631): "ending a life of much smoulder . . . in a blaze of glory. . . ."
(10) Poe, "The New York Literati," *Godey's,* 1841: "H. is a poor man and . . . he is not an ubiquitous quack."
(11) It.Nbks., Wks., X, 107 (necessity for the state of grace, for giving of oneself).
(12) Pref. T.T.T., Wks., I, 15: "The author . . . was merely writing to his known or unknown friends"; Pref. Sn.Im., Wks., III, 385: "I have been addressing a very limited circle of friendly readers . . ."; Pref. M.F., Wks., VI, 13: the public thought of not as a group of individuals but as a single "congenial friend," more intimate and better than a brother.
(13) Letter to Mansfield, March 19, 1850, Blodgett, "H. as Poetry Critic," *AL,* XII, 1940.
(14) A.o.B., Wks., II, 332.
(15) N. C. Browne, *Bibliography of N.H.,* p. 5: Oberon, Ashley Allen Royce (or Rev. A. A. Royce), Aubépine (Intr., Rapp., Wks., II) Jo Nicholson ("The Haunted Quack," Old Manse ed., Vol. 16, Appendix). Or else he would sign with just his initials or designate himself simply as "The Author" of

various previous tales ("Gentle Boy," "Sights," "Grey Champion"). Many pieces were simply signed "The Author of the G.B.": "Man of Adamant" (*Token*, 1837); "Grey Champion" (*N.E.Mag.*, Jan. 1835); "Little A." (*Youth's Keepsake*, 1835); M.M.M. (*Token*, 1836); 7Vag. (*Token*, 1837); "Sunday at Home" (ibid.). Even after T.T.T., H still published "Night Sky," "Endicott," etc., anonymously (Faust, *H.'s Contemporaneous Reputation*).

(16) Preface, T.T.T., Wks., I, 13.

(17) Duyckinck, *Arcuturus*, Jan. 1841, of T.T.T.: "what lay sermons full of hope and tranquillity and beauty." The same critic said of 7G. (*Lit. Wld.*, Apr. 1851): "of all laymen he will preach you the closest sermons." Reactions to S.L.: F. D. Mayo (*Universalist*, July 1851): "the chief value of the novel is religious." Duyckinck (*Lit. Wld.*, Feb. 1850: "a sounder piece of Puritan divinity than we have been of late accustomed to hear." And Whipple (*Graham's*, 1850): "H. . . . mastered the whole philosophy of guilt." More recently, Voight, "N.H., Author for preachers," *Lutheran Ch. Q.*, XXI, 1943, sees H.'s tales as ready-made parables. And Fick, *The Light Beyond, a Study of H.'s Theology*, attempts to find an expression of religious convictions in H.'s work.

(18) Gaylord Clark, *Knickerbocker*, Nov. 1837.

(19) Pierpont, author of *Wanderers of the Deep*.

(20) A fate shared by many other great writers. Cf. Gide, *Journal*.

(21) Longfellow, Rev. T.T.T. (Faust, *H.'s Contemporaneous Reputation*) went into ecstasies over "Town Pump." The Rev. Peabody (*Christ. Examiner*, April, 1839) preferred "Little Annie," and Rufus Griswold (*Prose Writers of America*, 1847) also kept most of his praise for "Town Pump" and Cel.Rlrd.

(22) Letter from Emerson to Thoreau (*Thoreau's Familiar Letters*, F. B. Sanborn, 1894).

(23) Pref. T.T.T., Wks., I, 18: "a mild, shy, gentle . . . and not very forcible man."

(24) Letter to Ticknor, Jan. 12, 1885 (Eng.Nbks., R.S., Appendix).

(25) Hoffman (*Am.Mth.Mag.*, March 1838): ". . . many Apollos but Jove has not yet assumed his thunder." He then places H. in the topmost echelon of genteel literature. Similarly, C. Winterfield (C. W. Webber), *Am.Rev.*, Sept. 1846, states that many native writers surpass H.

(26) "Select Party," Wks., II, 79.

(27) See Part Two, Ch. 4, I, Notes 25, 26, and 27.

(28) Melville, letter to H., April 16, 1851. Jay Leyda, *Melville's Log*, 1951, in which he congratulates him on making things *visible* (as opposed to *usable*, which is what almost all authors try to do. Cf. N. H. Pearson, "H.'s Usable Truth," 1949), and upon knowing how to say "NO, in thunder." Whipple (*Graham's*, June 1851); Chorley (*Athenaeum*, London, May 1851: "rich in humours and characters"); not to mention Duyckinck, (Note 17).

(29) Cheever referred to him as a "mahomedan" (Manning Hawthorne, "H. and the Man of God," *Colophon*, II, Vol. 2).

(30) Emerson, *Journals*, IV, 476: "no inside to it" (referring to "Footprints"). Moreover he considered H.'s moderate success as "a mere tribute to the man." And after his death: "I thought him a greater man than any of his wks. betray (*Journals*, X, 39).

(31) *Life of Pierce*, Wks., XII, appeared at the same time as Bl.R., or almost (Bl.R., July 14, 1842; *Life of Pierce*, early Sept.: "Mr. H.'s latest romance," the Whigs ironically termed it, R.S., Biog., 132.

(32) Whitman, *Brooklyn Eagle*, June 1846. See Zunder, "Walt Whitman and H.", *MLN*, XLIII, 1932.

(33) Faust, *H.'s Contemporaneous Reputation*, p. 144: "In his later years he elected Whipple as his literary mentor" (after the latter's review of S.L. in *Graham's*, 1850: "a true artist's certainty of touch"); approbation particu-

larly from the moral point of view (cf. Note 17) and reservations as to the uniformity of the artistic treatment (which doubtless contributed to making H. change his manner).

(34) Eng.Nbks., R.S., 219.

(35) Preface to T.T.T., Wks., I, 16 (an effect of tameness).

(36) It.Nbks., Wks., X, 122 (only the greatest artists deserve to remain); 357 (burn, respectfully, those works that are not irreplaceable). Cf. M.F., VI, 389: "For the rest, let them be piled in garrets, just as the tolerable poets are shelved, when their little day is over."

(37) Ibid., 149.

(38) Ibid., 180 (the glory of a picture fades like that of a flower); 342–43 (poor faded relics . . . as if the Devil had been rubbing and scrubbing them . . .— my heart sinks and my stomach sickens").

(39) Duyckinck, *Arcturus*, Jan. 1842: "not essential to his [H.'s] success."

(40) Letter to his sister Elizabeth, R.S. Biog., 34, after the article by Chorley, who renewed his praises in 1850 (*Athenaeum*, London, 1850).

(41) Poe, *Graham's*, April 1842: "His originality both of incident and reflection is very remarkable." And further on: "Mr. H. is a man of truest genius."

(42) Melville, "H. and His Mosses," *Lit.Wld.*, August 17 and 24, 1859. Mrs. Rawlins, a relation of the Peabodys, protested: "No man of common sense . . . would seriously name Mr. H. in the same day with S." (letter to Mrs. Peabody, in J.H., H.&W, I, 384).

(43) Poe, "Tale-Writing," *Godey's*, April 1847: "peculiar but not original." Then he attacks the allegory: "Let him mend his pen, get a bottle of visible ink."

(44) "Hall of Fantasy," Wks., II, 204.

II

THE THEMES

Chapter 1

I

(1) Paganism seemed less far away in time than Christianity, since the latter goes back to the very origins of the soul (It.Nbks., Wks., X, 160).

(2) J-P. Sartre, *Situations*, I, "La Temporalité chez Faulkner."

(3) E.B., Wks., III, 490.

(4) 7G., Wks., II, 116–17.

(5) "Howe's Masquerade," Wks., I and 7G., Wks., III.

(6) Cel.Rlrd., Wks., II.

(7) M.F., Wks., VI, Ch. 49: "A Frolic of the Carnival."

(8) Am.Nbks., Wks., IX, 251–52. Cf. Bl.R., Wks., V, Ch. 24: "The Masqueraders."

(9) 7G., Wks., III, 147–48 (transformation of the ancestor who becomes the Judge).

(10) Ibid., 199 (the arched window).

(11) "Hall of Fantasy"; cf. "Select Party" (Wks., I).

(12) 7G., Wks., III, 304: "a village had grown up . . . ; a few breaths more, and it had vanished, as if swallowed by an earthquake."

(13) "Main Street," Wks., III, 440 and 445; cf. 7G., III, 308: "the past is but a coarse and sensuous prophecy of the present and the future."

(14) "Prophetic Pictures," I, 207: "there is no Past . . . all that is great becomes for ever present . . ."

(15) Typical example: Cel.Rlrd., Wks., II.

(16) Cf. "Custom House," Wks., V, 23: his hometown lost all its magic in his eyes (a disarranged checker-board).

(17) The very one of which he speaks in the preface to 7G., Wks., III, 14.

(18) 7G., Wks., III, 219: "Shall we never, never get rid of this Past? . . . It lies upon the present like a giant's dead body!" Cf. Eng.Nbks., Wks., VIII, 207: "the present is burdened too much with the past."

(19) "Sister Years," Wks., I, 378 (progress: "onward and upward") and 380.

(20) "Bosom Serpent," Wks., II, 321: "The past . . . shall fling no gloom upon the future . . . we must think of it as an anecdote in our Eternity." Cf. Cel.Rlrd., II, 233 (crossing the river of Death) and "Procession of Life," II, 252.

(21) 7G., Wks., III, 308: "an ascending spiral curve . . . ."

(22) "Prophetic Pictures," I, 207: "The faintly revealed Past . . . the shrouded Future to meet." Cf. M.F., Wks., VI, 466–67: "encountering tides."

(23) Ibid., 207: "that narrow strip of sunlight which we call Now." Cf. M.F., Wks., VI, 467: "this narrow foothold of the present . . ."

(24) Pilgrim's Progress, Collins, 199: "Then I saw that there was a way to hell, even from the gates of heaven . . ."

(25) M.F., VI, 520: Kenyon (guide me home!).

(26) Cf. Part Two, I, Ch. 4, "The Devil's Manuscript."

(27) The theme of the Italian murderer, psychological in M.F., becomes "gothick" in Grim. (Lord Braithwaite, the poisoner, has Italian blood).

(28) Cf. Fanshawe (Wks., XI); Grim. (Wks., XIII); Sn.Im., E.B. (Wks., III); S.L. (V, 149 and 181), 7G, (III: "Flight of Two Owls"), M.F., (VI, Ch. 32: "Scenes by the Way").

II

(1) 7G., III, 221: "I dwell in it (house) . . . that I may know the better how to hate it (the Past, i.e. the Pyncheons).

(2) Ibid., 315.

(3) Ibid., 32: the Waldo county that H. talks about is the estate his ancestors once owned in Maine ("Maine Sources in 7G.," Griffiths, "Maine Sources in 7G.," maintains that it was not a county but the entire state of Maine, and that the House is Knox Mansion in Thomaston; same author, "Montpelier and 7G., Knox's Estate and H.'s novel," NEQ, Sept. 1943). J.H., H.&W, I, 26: "These possessions . . . were more extensive than many a dukedom . . . on European soil."

(4) "Dr. Bullivant," Wks., XII, 83: "recognized no distinction between private ill conduct and crimes that endangered the community."

(5) 7G., III, 281: "The butcher, the baker, the fish-monger . . . and many a prying old woman, have told me several of the secrets of your interior."

(6) "Main Street," Wks., III, 119.

(7) Cf. 7G., Wks., III; A.o.B., Wks., II; and Bl.R., Wks., V.

(8) 7G., Wks., III, Ch. 21: The Daguerreotypist, 211: "schoolmaster, salesman, editor, pedlar . . . dentist . . ."; 212: "supernumerary official . . . public lecturer . . ."

(9) Bl.R., Wks., V.

(10) 7G., III, 375–76: Uncle Venner was to be provided with a cottage in a sort of New Eden or mythical land of milk and honey.

(11) Old Moodie on the other hand is abandoned by everyone (Bl.R., Wks., V, Ch. 1: "Old Moodie"; Ch. 10: "A Visitor from Town"; Ch. 12: "Fauntleroy."

(12) Emerson, Nature, 1836.

(13) Thoreau, Walden, 1854.

(14) 7G., Wks., III, "Flight of Two Owls."

(15) Ibid. (the railroad); 313–14 (the telegraph).

(16) Male, "H. and the Concept of Sympathy," PMLA, LXVIII, 1953.

(17) 7G., Wks., III: H. contrasts the rough magic of Maule (242–50) with the scientific mesmerist (Holgrave); 212: public lecture on mesmerism) we find embodied by Westervelt (Bl.R., Wks., V).

(18) Allusion in Fanshawe, Wks., XI, 144. Sophia Peabody in her pre-marriage diary (J.H., H.&W, I, 79) declares her faith in this then fashionable science.

(19) Bergson, *L'Evolution créatrice.*
(20) Coleridge was already using such organic concepts.
(21) Bl.R., Wks., V., 382–84.
(22) "Hall of Fantasy," Wks., II, 205: "men whose faith had embodied itself in the form of a potato . . . others whose beards had a deep spiritual significance. Here was the abolitionist, brandishing his one idea like an iron flail." Cf. Am.Nbks., Wks., IX, 20–21: "a modern reformer" (the narrator presents him as an escapee from a lunatic asylum).
(23) "Sister Years," Wks., I, 321.
(24) Notably in Grim., (ed. Davidson, 1954) in which H. desperately attempts to bridge the gap between pioneering America and a still aristocratic England. Faulkner found it much easier to bridge the gap between pre-Civil War and post-Civil War America.
(25) Lewis, *The American Adam,* 1955, pp. 110–26: "The Return into Time," shows this very well, but makes too close a connection between the return into time and the return to society; this very American viewpoint leads him to neglect the metaphysical aspect. R. R. Male, *H.'s Tragic Vision,* p. 25, considers the House as "the womb of Time" (cf. 7G.).
(26) Though Grim. and *Absalom* may not be strictly comparable, there are nevertheless points in common between H. and Faulkner, and even, as O'Connor points out, a similarity of temperament ("H. and Faulkner, Some Common Ground," *Q. Rev.,* XXXIII, 1957).
(27) 7G., Wks., III, Ch. 21: "The Departure," 372 (country-house).
(28) M.F., Wks., VI, 207–8.
(29) Oneida: utopian colony founded by J. H. Noyes in 1848. Noyes dreamed of establishing the kingdom of heaven in America.
(30) Fruitlands, founded by Alcott, near Harvard (1842–43).
(31) "Hall of Fantasy," Wks., II, 204–5.
(32) The cant expression of the day in frequent use by expansionists was "manifest destiny" (our manifest destiny to spread over this whole continent). It may have been originated by J. O'Sullivan, a friend of H.'s and founder of *The U.S. Mag and Democratic Review* in 1845, at the time of the annexation of Texas.
(33) D. H. Lawrence, *Studies in Classic American Literature.*
(34) 7G., Wks., III, 149, 150, 272, 273.
(35) A.o.B., N.A.&E., Wks., II.
(36) "Hall of Fantasy," Wks., II, 202 (perpetual motion); "Procession of Life," Wks., II, 245 (the demon of machinery); Nbks., IX, 106 (absurd inventions).
(37) "Select Party," Wks., II, 86 (paradise of Fools).
(38) Hall, *H. Critic of Society,* 1944, pp. 45, 122, makes this very clear. In fact, H. was so little a Yankee that he felt he had quarrelled with his country just before the Civil War.
(39) Eng.Nbks., R.S., 92: H. even goes so far as to wish England aid from the U.S. He even envisages a new colonialism in the reverse direction.
(40) Thoreau, *Walden,* Portable Libr., p. 488, the Ponds.
(41) H. Miller, *Big Sur and the Oranges of Hieronymus Bosch,* London, 1958.
(42) N.A.&E., Wks., II: in which H. preaches a return to nature (p. 280); "Procession of Life," II, 245 (the prison, the insane asylum . . . the almshouse, the manufactory . . . the cotton field . . .": all calamities of the modern world.
(43) R. R. Male, *H.'s Tragic Vision,* 142, sees the snow in Blithedale as an allegory of virgin America.
(44) W. Rathenau, quoted by André Gide in his *Dostoievski,* Plon, p. 197.
(45) M.M.M., Wks., I, 79.

III

(1) Francis Parkman (1823–93), author of a vast historical fresco: *France and England in North America.*

(2) Kesselring, "H.'s Reading 1828-1850," *BNYPL,* 1949, e.g.: *History of Massachusetts Bay* (Hutchinson, 1746); *History of Boston* (Caleb Hopkins Snow, 1825); *History of New England, History of the District of Maine* (Sullivan, 1795); *Annals of Salem* (Felt); *Ancient Charters, Journal of 1644* (Winthrop); *American Biographical & Historical Dictionary* (W. Allen, President of Bowdoin College).

(3) Only Whitman's inspiration was to prove strong enough to evoke the vastness of America in a satisfactorily lyrical manner without at the same time sliding into the historico-patriotic genre. Lanier's "Psalm of the West" (1876) is an example of other unfruitful attempts.

(4) Allusions: Nbks., Wks., VIII, 537 and Gd.F's Ch., Wks., IV, Ch. 2, 434.

(5) Larkin, *Art and Life in America,* 1949, p. 12 (in New Amsterdam).

(6) Ibid., p. 12 (at Naumkeag, i.e. Salem). See Gd.F's Ch., Wks., IV, 437-38 (wretched hovels and huts).

(7) At the Old Manse (Concord Mass.) one is still shown the beam used to reinforce the door in case of Indian raids.

(8) "Mrs. Hutchinson," *Biographical Sketches,* Wks., XII, 225-26.

(9) Gd.F's Ch., Wks., IV.

(10) *Les Natchez* and *Hiawatha,* not to mention the Cooper novels.

(11) "Endicott," Wks., I, 488: "A few stately savages, in all the pomp and dignity of the primeval Indian . . ."; "Main Street," Wks., III, 440; S.L., Wks., V, 69: "an idle and vagrant Indian, whom the white man's fire had made riotous . . ."

(12) Gd.F's Ch., Wks., IV, 267 (an Indian's life . . . less precious . . . than that of a white man) and 469 (an inferior race of beings).

(13) *Sketches from Memory,* Wks., II, 488: "I do abhor an Indian story." Cf. Gd.F's Ch., IV, 476: "who wants to hear about tomahawks and scalping-knives?" Thoreau felt differently on this point ("Old Manse," II, 19-20: "Thoreau who has a strange faculty of finding what the Indians left behind them . . .").

(14) "The Duston Family," Wks., Old Manse ed., Vol. 17.

(15) Gd.F's Ch., Wks., IV.

(16) Ibid., 516: "How glorious it would have been . . . if our forefathers could have kept the country unspotted with blood."

(17) "Dr. Bullivant," Wks., XII, and Gd.F's Ch., Wks., IV, 480.

(18) "E. R.'s P.," Wks., I, 297: "the arch-enemy of New England."

(19) Gd.F's Ch., Wks., VI, 563.

(20) Ibid., 590-92.

(21) Ibid., 560. Cf. "Howe's Masquerade," Wks., I.

(22) Ibid., 563. H. saluting Bradstreet as the "last of the Puritans," 481.

(23) "Grey Champion," Wks., I.

(24) Gd.F's Ch., Wks., IV, 440.

(25) Ibid., 440.

(26) "Endicott," Wks., I: H. precedes E.'s protestation ("civil rights . . . liberty to worship God . . . ," p. 491) with a picture of Puritan persecutions. In Gd.F's.Ch., ("The Red Cross," IV, 445), since he is writing for children he avoids irony.

(27) In the Body of Liberties (1641) slavery was condemned but provision was made for permitting individuals to sell themselves as slaves of their own free will (i.e. when they had been reduced to utter extremities).

(28) Gd.F's.Ch., Wks., IV, 512: "Was not the witchcraft delusion partly caused by Cotton Mather? . . . He was the chief agent in the mischief."

(29) Ibid., 471: "The Indian Bible."

(30) Ibid., 580-81 ("The Hutchinson Mob").

(31) Hall, *H.: Critic of Society,* 1944, p. 74, states categorically that H. was opposed to the Puritan theocratic society, as well as to the feudal system and its survivals. In fact, it was only in England, motivated by a sudden patriotic reaction, that H. was to become at all violently opposed to aristocracy.

(32) Gd.F's Ch., Wks., IV, 579: "The Hutchinson Mob."
(33) S.L., Wks., V.
(34) Ibid., 70–71 and 7G., III, 103: Phoebe, the young daughter of New England and her "lady-like attributes." In England, H. was utterly shocked by the plainness of the women and made many disobliging comparisons with American women: (Eng.Nbks., R.S., 18: "not a pretty girl . . . all coarse and vulgar"; 28: "more atrociously ugly than any other human beings"; "Ladies look like cooks and housemaids . . . You think of them as composed of sirloins . . ." Contrasted: the young and pretty American girls passing through the consulate (229). Similarly, the American "gentleman" seemed to him much superior to any English nobleman (Grim. ed. Davidson, 85): "more aristocratic than a thousand Englishmen of good birth."
(35) Am.Nbks., R.S., 59: a young peasant of Herculean strength: "this giant was not ill-looking, but of rather intelligent aspect . . ."
(36) Gd. F's Ch., Wks., IV, 602: "there was quite as much of these qualities (integrity and honor) on one side as on the other."
(37) Ibid., 592–93: "The Boston Massacre."
(38) Ibid., 620–21: "I love New England well. Heaven bless her and bring her again under the rule of our gracious king."
(39) "Old News," "The Old Tory," Wks., III.
(40) "Old Esther Dudley," Wks., I.
(41) Gd.F's Ch., Wks., IV, 590 et seq.
(42) Ibid., 547 et seq: "The Acadian Exiles."
(43) Ibid., 611, 612, 613.
(44) Biographical Stories, Wks., XII.
(45) "Endicott," Wks., I and Gd.F's Ch., IV: "The Red Cross," 455 et seq.
(46) Gd.F's Ch., IV, 555, 556, 557.
(47) Ibid., "Liberty Tree," 581–82: oath not to enforce the Stamp Act.

IV

(1) Legends of the Province House. Wks., I, 272 et seq. and S.L., Wks., V.
(2) Ibid., 273–74: the tavern set up actually inside the former Province House. Ryscamp, "New England Sources of S.L.," AL, Nov. 1959, gives a plan of Boston in 1645 showing the Governor's House, the Prison, and the market place.
(3) Larkin, Art and Life in America, 1949, pp. 12–13.
(4) J.H., H.&W, I, 8–9, letter from Eliz. H. to Una in which the family crest is mentioned, it being the same, according to Eliz., as the one that occurs in "The White Old Maid" (Wks., I, 422: "Azure, a lion's head erased, between three flower-de-luces"). We should also remember the heraldic emblem at the end of S.L. (Wks., V, 312: "On a field, sable, the letter A, gules").
(5) E.g. "Old News," Wks., III; "Old Ticonderoga" and "A Bell's Biography," Wks., III.
(6) "Endicott," Wks., I; "An Old Woman's Tale," Wks., XII.
(7) "Howe's Masquerade," Wks., I and S.L., Wks., V.
(8) "Main Street," Wks., III.
(9) S.L., V, 188: "The belief was a favorite one with our forefathers, as betokening that their infant commonwealth was under a celestial guardianship of peculiar intimacy and strictness." Cf. "Dr. Bullivant," XII, 81: "men who looked heavenward without a wandering glance on earth."
(10) Gallup, "On H.'s Authorship of 'The Battle Omen'," NEQ, IX, 1936 (sketch attributed to H.).
(11) S.L., V, 192: "a great red letter in the sky . . . for . . . Governor Winthrop was made an angel this past night . . ."
(12) Orians, "The Angel of Hadley in Fiction," AL, Nov. 1932, in which the Grey Champion is compared to Scott's Peveril of the Peak.

(13) "E.R.'s P.," Wks., I, 295: Abercrombie's defeat heralded by the change in the portrait's expression.
(14) S.L., V, 188: "It was . . . a majestic idea, that the destiny of nations should be revealed, in awful hieroglyphics, on the cope of heaven."
(15) Ibid., 181 and 184 (Mrs. Hibbins' "night ride"); Y.G.B., II. Cf. Orians, "New England Witchcraft Fiction," AL, II, 1930 (sources of Y.G.B.).
(16) H.of3H., Wks., I, 230–33; Fanshawe, Wks., XI, 201–22.
(17) 7G., III (Maule); Bl.R., V (Westervelt).
(18) 7G., III, 21.
(19) Y.G.B., II, 100: comparison with a church service maintained throughout the scene (. . . an altar or a pulpit . . . candles . . . evening meeting . . . congregation). H. borrows skilfully from the vocabulary of religion; ibid., p. 102: "Another verse of the hymn . . . ," and the exclamation: "Bring forth the converts!"
(20) S.L., V, 143 (Pearl); Y.G.B., II, 100 (the demoniac).
(21) M.M.M., Wks., I (idolatry); H.of3H., Wks., I (ritual crime); Y.G.B., Wks., II (satanism); E.B., Wks., III, (satanism).
(22) S.L., Wks., V, (Mrs. Hibbins). Cf. R. & L. Boas, Cotton Mather, Keeper of the Puritan Conscience, 1928, 95–96; Y.G.B., II, 103 (Goody Cloyse (or Clouse) and Martha Cerrier, "who had received the Devil's promise to be queen of Hell. A rampant hag was she"). H. is using Mather's very words: "a rampant hag . . . promised by the Devil that she should be Queen of Hell" (Boas, 122).
(23) S.L., V, 147, 148, 149 (Chill.); Rapp., II; Birth., ibid. (Aylmer).
(24) G.B. Cf. Orians, "Sources and Themes of H.'s G.B.," NEQ, XIV, 1941, ed. Token, 1832: "To destroy the unity of religion, might have been to subvert the government."
(25) M.M.M. Wks., I: Morton and the colony of Mount Wollaston (cf. Orians, "H. and M.M.M.," MLN, LIII, 1938).
(26) "Main Street," Wks., III, 463–64: "Anne Coleman—naked from the waist upward, and bound to the tail of a cart . . . while the constable follows with a whip of knotted cords."
(27) "Mrs. Hutchinson," XII; Gd.F's Ch., IV, 466 (Mary Dyer and two other Quakeresses).
(28) Arthur Miller, The Crucible, 1949. Cf. Dhaleine, N.H. sa Vie et son oeuvre, Appendix: Giles Corey of the Salem Farms (Longfellow, New England Tragedies), which introduces Judge Hathorne, Mather, Mary Walcot, Tituba, etc. (cf. Miller).
(29) 7G., III, 21 and The Crucible (Miller).
(30) Gd. F's Ch., Wks., IV, 501–2 (executions of the innocent).
(31) "Custom House," V, 24–25: "I, the present writer . . . hereby take shame upon myself for their sakes . . ."
(32) Letter to his sister Louisa, Nov. 4, 1831, in J.H., H.&W, I, 126–27.
(33) Boas (Cotton Mather), Miller (Crucible), Longfellow (Giles Corey of the Salem Farms).
(34) Orians, "H. and Puritan Punishments," CE, XIII, 1952.
(35) In particular, "Endicott," I, 486, 487, 488: "The head of an Episcopalian . . . grotesquely incased in the former machine (pillory) . . ."; and on 487: "The woman wore a cleft stick on her tongue . . ."; and further on: "Ears cropped, like those of puppy dogs . . ."
(36) Kept principally for blasphemers and forgers (Orians, "H. and Puritan Punishments." Cf. S.L., V; "Endicott," I, 486; "Old News," III, 534; "Dr. Bullivant," XII, 81.
(37) Used for drunkards, idlers, and undisciplined soldiers (Orians). Cf. "Endicott," I, 486: "a fellow-criminal, who had boisterously quaffed a health to the king . . ."
(38) Used for scolds and blasphemers (Orians).

(39) For theft, burglary, drunkenness, vagabondage, fornication, defamation of magistrates, disobedient children, Antinomians, heretics (Orians). Cf. "Endicott," I, 436; S.L., V, 69 ("a sluggish bond-servant or an undutiful child . . . to be corrected at the whipping-post . . . an Antinomian, a Quaker, or other heterodox religionist was to be scourged out of town"). Also M.M.M., I, 81; "Bullivant," XII, 81.

(40) "Old News," Wks., III, 534 (the pillory, the whipping-post, the prison and the gallows); "Endicott," I, 486–88.

(41) "Endicott," I, 487.

(42) Ibid., 487.

(43) Ibid., 437.

(44) Ibid., 437.

(45) Ibid., 487.

(46) Orians, "H. and Puritan Punishments," CE, XIII, 1952.

(47) "Dr. Bullivant," XII, 83.

(48) Bl.R., V, 503.

(49) SL., V, 70: "a penalty, which in our days, would infer a degree of infamy and ridicule, might then be invested with almost as stern a dignity as the punishment of death itself."

(50) Mills, "H. and Puritanism," NEQ, XXI, 1948, observes that H. contradicted himself on the subject of Mather. In A. Doane, XII, 249 ("Cotton Mather . . . the one blood-thirsty man in whom were concentred those vices of spirit and errors of opinion that sufficed to madden the whole surrounding multitude"), he draws a sinister portrait of him, whereas in Gd.F's Ch. he makes him a sympathetic figure. Doubtless he would have liked to retain this children's picture-book version of the man, but his intution made that impossible.

(51) "Dr. Bullivant," XII, 78. Cf. S.L., V.

CHAPTER 2

I

(1) Lewis, The American Adam, 124, sees the problem from an exclusively sociological viewpoint.

(2) G.B., Wks., I, 88, 89, 90 (execution of Ilbrahim's father: a Quaker).

(3) Ibid., 104 and 113 (the mother); 119 (the old Quaker who lets his daughter die in obedience to the voice of God). Cf. H.of3H., I, 233 (the criminal mother: "the mother who had sinned against natural affection and left her child to die").

(4) Ibid., 110–11.

(5) Dostoyevsky, Brothers Karamazov, Book X.

(6) G.B., I, 120 (the boy hath done his work); 125–26 (redemption of the mother by the son).

(7) Ibid., 109–11: the deformed child may be considered as an orphan, since he tries to find a home outside his own family.

(8) Ibid., 111 (shrewdness above his years).

(9) Ibid. (moral obliquity). Cf. E.B., Wks., III.

(10) In most cases the parents are dead or else scarcely mentioned. We may also add Robin in My Kinsman, III, 632 (excluded from his home).

(11) S.L., Wks., V, 177.

(12) Ibid., 79.

(13) 7G., Wks., III, 316.

(14) S.L., V, 186.

(15) Bl.R., V.

(16) 7G., III, 96 (Phoebe no longer has a father, and her mother has remarried); 211 (Holgrave has been left to himself since childhood).

(17) M.F., VI, 32 (Is Miriam the daughter of a Jewish banker, a Southern plantation owner, or a German princess?); 73 (Hilda: "an orphan"; cf. James: the expatriates).
(18) "J. Inglefield"; H.of3H., Wks., I (the guilty daughter).
(19) "Wakefield," Wks., I.
(20) "Intelligence Office," II, 364–65 ("I want my place! my own place! my true place in the world!")
(21) E.B., III, 485: "The sin of an intellect that triumphed over the sense of brotherhood with man and reverence for God . . ."
(22) 7G., Wks., III, and Bl.R., Wks., V.
(23) 7G., 219.
(24) Bl.R., V, particularly Ch. 14: "Eliot's Pulpit."
(25) M.F., VI, 186: "Miriam's Trouble."
(26) Y.G.B., II; E.B., III.
(27) SL., V: "The Interior of a Heart."
(28) M.F., VI, Ch. 28, 241: "Do not come nearer, Miriam!" Which does not prevent her from demanding moral support from the woman she refuses from then on to consider as a friend (245–46).
(29) My Kinsman, III, 634.
(30) Passages, Wks., II, 458: Parson Thumpcushion.
(31) "G.B.," I (Tobias Pearson), and especially "Mr. Higginsbotham," Wks., I.
(32) Endicott in M.M.M., Wks., I.
(33) "Great Stone Face," Wks., III.
(34) The Governor's house, a symbol of paternal as much as political authority (S.L., V, Ch. 7: The Governor's Hall) and the House of the Seven Gables, an ancestral symbol (7G., III).
(35) Passages, Wks., II.
(36) My Kinsman, Wks., III.
(37) Fanshawe, Wks., XI, Ch. 9.
(38) S.L., Wks., V, "The Market Place."
(39) Bl.R., V, 337–38.
(40) M.F., VI, Ch. 6: "The Virgin's Shrine."
(41) N.A. & E., II, 285: "a Great Face looking down upon us."
(42) O'Neill, conversely, was to invoke "God the Mother" through the mouth of Nina Leeds in Strange Interlude.
(43) Bl.R., V, 594: Blithedale Pasture (Hollingsworth and Priscilla); M.F., VI, 520 (Kenyon and Hilda).
(44) My Kinsman, III, 625–26.
(45) M.F., VI, 115: "The iron chain . . . which, perhaps, bound the pair together by a bond equally torturing to each," and 117: allusion to an unnatural bond (equal horror). Miriam is perhaps the daughter of the Model, her incestuous father.
(46) Brothers Karamazov: Dmitri Karamazov.
(47) O'Connor, "H. & Faulkner," VQR, Winter 1957, quotes Absalom and The Sound and the Fury to very good effect, and alludes, with reference to M.F., to the consanguine marriages prevalent in Renaissance Italy: he sees Miriam and her Model as descendants of the Cenci. Cf. Haselmayer, "H. and the Cenci," Neophil., XVII, 1941 (incest theme; cf. pictures: Fornarina (Raphael), Beatrice Cenci (Guido) in It.Nbks., X).
(48) A. Doane, XII.
(49) R.M.'s B., II.
(50) S.L., V: the doctor (Alchemist) and the demoniac priest (Minister in a Maze).
(51) Y.G.B., II, 99 (pink Ribbon). Cf. R. R. Male, H.'s Tragic Vision, p. 77.
(52) Rapp., II.
(53) H.of3H., I.
(54) "J. Inglefield's Thanksgiving," III.

(55) At Brook Farm (cf. Part One), then at Concord, driven to desperation by Margaret Fuller's lack of reticence, H. refused to take in two Transcendentalist "angels" as "paying guests" at the Old Manse (letter of Aug. 28, 1841, J.H., H.&W, I, 252).

(56) S.L., V, 139–40.

(57) Bertha Aalund, the heroine of *Comrades,* is, like Miriam, a painter, and conducts a merciless war against men.

(58) Bl.R., V, Ch. 25: Hollingsworth, seeing Zenobia ruined, turns from her.

(59) R.M.'s B., Wks., II.

(60) M.M.M., Wks., I.

(61) E.R.'s P., Wks., I.

(62) Bl.R., V: just as Old Goriot asks Rastignac to tell him about the daughters who refuse to see him, so Moodie asks Coverdale for news of Z. and P. (416–18) and hides so as to be able to see them without their knowing (419–20).

(63) D. H. Lawrence, *Studies in Classic American Literature.*

(64) Bl.R., V, 458-59: Zenobia, though she gives way eventually before her rival, is not taken in by her: " 'Poor child!' exclaimed Z. contemptuously. 'She is the type of womanhood such as man has spent centuries in making it.' "

(65) S.L., V, 91: "Wondrous strength and generosity of a woman's heart!" Cf. Miriam, M.F., VI, 123–24 (faced with the Model's corpse).

(66) D. H. Lawrence, *Studies in Classic American Literature,* 114, uses the term with reference to Hester. But H. himself was the first to see Hollingsworth's abasement as a sort of punishment: Zenobia was to be "avenged" by her sister (Bl.R., V, 568) who is later shown to us "happy" at her companion's weakness (594).

(67) Certainly the first in America. Irving was too much the man of letters to approach such a problem, and Poe was too much involved in the sadomasochism of his passions for little girls and in necrophilia.

(68) "Lily's Quest," Wks., I.

(69) M.M.M., Wks., I.

(70) Y.G.B., II, 102: The young man thinks he recognizes "his own dead father" in the venerable figure officiating at the sabbath.

(71) My Kinsman, III, 629. Connors, "My Kinsman; A. Reading," *MLN,* LXXIV, 1959, sees it as representing the "false colors" of hypocrisy.

(72) Ibid., 629.

(73) Ibid., 628 (shrewd); and 641 ("you are a shrewd youth").

(74) Rapp., II; cf. R. R. Male, "Dual Aspects of Evil in Rapp.," *PMLA,* March 1954.

(75) Bl.R., V, 557 (Comus and his crew: the phrase Coverdale uses to describe the masquerade in the wood where he meets Westervelt (Ch. 11: "The Woodpath").

(76) M.F., Wks., VI.

(77) Y.G.B., II and S.L., V. Ch. 4 ("The Interview"—for Hester and Pearl, the black man is Chillingworth (p. 100).

(78) Since he has attached himself to Miriam, D. cannot avoid meeting the Model (M.F., V).

(79) My Kinsman, III, 461: "without the help of your kinsman . . ."

(80) M.F., VI: Donatello.

II

(1) S.L., V, 180–81 (he shrieked aloud).

(2) M.F., VI, 186: "the beautiful Miriam began to gesticulate extravagantly, gnashing her teeth, flinging her arms wildly abroad, stamping with her foot."

(3) 7G., III, Ch. 1 and M.F., VI, Ch. 18 and 19.

(4) Except for the murder of the uncle (7G., III, 37) in which (as in "Mr. H.'s Catastrophe," Wks., I) there is a reference, albeit no direct allusion, to the

murder of the businessman White (cf. Cantwell, *N.H.: The American Years*), and for the murder of the Model, for which (according to his son Julian in H.&W, II, 236) H. made use of his memories of the Praslin Choiseul affair. On August 13, 1847, the Duc de Praslin had murdered his wife, who was of Italian origin (her name alone—Altarice Rosalba Fanny Sebastiani—must have struck the novelist's imagination) and then poisoned himself. The governess, Henriette Deluzy, was accused, then acquitted. Later, in New York, she married the son of the Rev. D. D. Field, and Nathalie Wright ("H. and the Praslin murder," *N&Q*, 1942) even goes so far as to suppose that H. could have met her. Extremely beautiful, possessed of a great gift for drawing, she might have served as a model for Miriam (M.F., VI, 486, the name of Miriam "in connection with a mysterious and terrible event").

(5) 7G., III: Clifford's imprisonment.
(6) E.R.'sP., I, 305: "choking with the blood of the Boston massacre." Cf. 7G., III, 29 (death of the Colonel) and 310 (the Judge, dead, and his neckcloth stained with blood).
(7) Strindberg's *There are Crimes and Crimes.*
(8) F's Sh. B., Wks., I.
(9) Ibid., I, 250: "What is Guilt? A stain upon the soul." Cf. 7G., III, 359 (black stain).
(10) "Lady E.," Wks., I.
(11) Régis Michaud, in *le Roman Américain d'Aujourd'hui*, 1928, studies H. in his role as initiator of the psychological novel in the U.S., and as a precursor of Freud. Vladimir Astrov, in "H. and Dostoievsky as Explorers of the Human Conscience," *NEQ*, XV, 1942, is of the same opinion, and points out that Dostoievsky had read H., whose works were translated into Russian very early (7G. in 1852, S.L. in 1856, and M.F. in 1861).
(12) Y.G.B., II, 90–91.
(13) S.L., V, 189.
(14) M's B.V., Wks., I. Walsh, "Mr. Hooper's Affable Weakness," *MLN*, LXXIV, 1959: inability to share another's point of view.
(15) "Bosom Serpent," II, 311–12.
(16) S.L., V, 110–11: "the scarlet letter had endowed her with a new sense."
(17) Camus, *Caligula.*
(18) Camus, *The Fall*, Gallimard, pp. 127-28, 132 and 164: "to be able to permit oneself everything, merely at the price of proclaiming one's own indignity."
(19) "Wakefield," Wks., I.
(20) 7G., III, 171: "the wretch beneath mankind, the wretch aside from it or the wretch above it."
(21) A. o. B., Wks., II, 518.
(22) 7G., III, 37.
(23) Like Clifford, Hepzibah, Wakefield and Dimmesdale.
(24) Camus, *The Fall.*
(25) "Man of Adamant," III.
(26) M's B.V., I.
(27) S.L., V, 175: "The godly youth! . . . The saint on earth!"; 174 (mouthpiece of Heaven's message).
(28) Ibid.: "The Interior of a Heart."
(29) 7G., III, 146 ("The Pyncheon of To-Day"); 273 (Behold therefore, a palace . . .).
(30) Ibid., 24 (the glittering plaster, composed of lime, pebbles and bits of glass, with which the woodwork of the walls was overspread). Cf. S.L. V, 128–29 (The Governor's Hall: "stucco, in which fragments of glass were plentifully intermixed . . . glittered and sparkled.").
(31) S.L., V, 307.
(32) Ibid., 307.

(33) Ibid., 176: "a bloody scourge"; "to fast . . . until his knees trembled beneath him"; "in utter darkness . . . [where] with a glimmering lamp . . ."
(34) "Man of Adamant," Wks., III.
(35) E.B., Wks., III.
(36) We constantly find this opposition in H. between heart and head, between Richard Rigby and Mary Goffe ("Man of Adamant"); between Aylmer and Georgiana (Birth.); between Holgrave and Phoebe (7G.). Cf. F. O. Mathiessen, *American Renaissance,* 1942, Bk. Two, VIII, 2: "H.'s Psychology: the Acceptance of Good and Evil." Mathiessen sees this conflict as the source of all Hawthorne tragedy. D. A. Ringe, "H.'s Psychology of the Heart and Head," *PMLA,* LXV, 1950, sees the opposition between them as the key to the whole of H.'s work.
(37) S.L., V, 198–99.
(38) Ibid., 229: The Pastor and his Parishioner: "Were I a wretch with coarse and brutal instincts . . .": words by which he implicitly condemns himself, since that "wretch" exists only too clearly inside him.
(39) M's B.V., Wks., I.
(40) "Man of Adamant," Wks., III.
(41) Lady E., I. Cf. Am.Nbks., IX, 106 (definition of the unpardonable sin).
(42) "Bosom Serpent," II: the serpent is that of jealousy.
(43) E. B., III, 489: "Esther . . . the girl . . . Ethen Brand had made the subject of a psychological experiment . . ."
(44) Cf. Kierkegaard.
(45) E.B., III, Cf. Levy, "E.B. and the Unpardonable Sin," *BUSE,* V, 1961.
(46) "Christmas Banquet," II, 345: Gervayse Hastings: "Mine—mine is the wretchedness! This cold heart—this unreal life!" Cf. Malcolm Cowley, *Portable H.,* Introd., p. 11: "Ice not fire was the torment H. suffered in his private hell."
(47) F. O. Mathiessen, *American Renaissance,* p. 154, justifies H. and D. against Chill.
(48) S.L., V, 234.
(49) Dr. H's Exp., Wks., I; *Septimius Felton,* XI and *Dolliver Romance,* XI (Colonel Dabney).
(50) Matthew, 10, 39.
(51) N.A.&E., II, 288: "Man has never attempted to cure sin by LOVE."
(52) F's Sh. B., I, 257.
(53) 7G., III, 250 (Alice Pyncheon).
(54) Ibid., 51 (her heart never frowned).
(55) Ibid., 210 (less girlish, but more of a woman).
(56) M.F., VI, 241 (repellent gesture).
(57) S.L., V, 303–04.
(58) "Procession of Life," Wks., II.
(59) M.F., VI, 247.
(60) S.L., V, 304: "Hush, Hester . . . The law we broke! . . . I fear. I fear!"
(61) "Egotism," Wks., II.
(62) Parable of the Gadarene swine, Luke 8: 32–37, used by Dostoievsky in *The Possessed.* Cf. "Circe's Palace," IV and "Bosom Serpent," II.
(63) 7G., III, 200 (Clifford: "had I taken that plunge . . . it would have made me another man."
(64) M.F., VI, 491 (Adam's sin: "the destined means by which . . . we are to attain a higher, brighter, and profounder happiness . . ."). Cf. ibid., 519 and Am.Nbks., R.S., 186 (use of weeds and tares) and Rev. L. Fick, *The Light Beyond, a study of H.'s Theology,* 1955, Part III: Sin (fortunate Fall).
(65) Letter, April 7, 1840, Nbks., IX, 217.
(66) M.F., VI, 243: "You need a sin to soften you."
(67) Gide, *Dostoievski,* Plon, 105–06.
(68) S.L., V, 187.

(69) Ibid., 301–04. Cf. Manning: "H. and Dostoievski," *Slavonic Rev.*, XIV, 1936: false comparison (the confessions of Raskolnikov and Stavrogin are made in a wholly different spirit. Dimmesdale is as free from exhibitionism in his humility as in his pride.).

(70) G.B., I (Ilbrahim) and *Gd. F's Ch.*, IV, 465–66 (referring to the Quakers).

(71) J. C. Gerber, "Form and Content in S.L.," *NEQ*, March 1944, sees D.'s destiny as an ascending curve (gravitation heavenward), whereas Hester's orbit remains terrestrial.

III

(1) Am.Nbks., R.S., 209–10.

(2) 7G., III: "The Arched Window."

(3) M.F., VI, 452: "When the lamp goes out do not despair."

(4) S.L., V: "The Meteor (The Minister's Vigil)."

(5) Ibid., 520: "Let the black flower blossom as it may."

(6) E.g., "Canterbury Pilgrims," I; "Lily's Quest," II; "Pr. of L."; Ibid. (cf. S.L., V: "The Procession").

(7) G.C., Wks., I.

(8) "Golden Fleece," Wks., IV.

(9) S.L., V, 68.

(10) Bl.R., V, 337 (a single flower . . . exotic, of rare beauty).

(11) 7G., III, Ch. 20: "The Flower of Eden."

(12) Bachelard, *Psychanalyse du Feu*, 86, referring to Novalis.

(13) 7G., III, 308.

(14) Rapp., II (Beatrice and the plant); "Golden Fleece," IV (Medea, the tree, and the dragon).

(15) "Buds and Bird Voices," II, 172: "There are some objections to the willow; it is not a dry, clean tree, and impresses the beholder with an association of sliminess."

(16) O'Neill, *Desire under the Elms* (stage directions: "Two enormous elms . . . a sinister maternity in their aspect, a crushing, jealous absorption.").

(17) "Buds and Bird Voices," II, 172: "No trees, I think, are perfectly agreeable as companions unless they have glossy leaves, dry bark, and a firm, hard texture of trunk and branches." The Pyncheon Elm (7G., III, 43) is both masculine and feminine (masculine: "Strong and broad maturity . . . ," feminine: "pendent foliage." Similarly, Cloverdale's tree (Bl.R., V, 431–32): the tree has a virile strength but, being entirely covered with a Virginia creeper, becomes a womblike symbol.

(18) My Kinsman, III, 632; M.F., VI, 93 (D. embraces the trunk of a tree: the paternal tree). Cf. Am.Nbks., R.S., 75–76.

(19) 7G., III, 93.

(20) Rapp., II: this is one of the tale's multiple meanings (poisonous thing, 143). Male, *H.'s Tragic Vision*, 63 (Beatrice's ambiguity).

(21) My Kinsman, III, 625–26 and 623 (runs away to escape temptation).

(22) "Hall of Fantasy," II, 209–20.

(23) "Bosom Serpent," II, and Rapp., ibid.

(24) 7G., III, (Alice Pyncheon possessed by the wizard, Ch. 13, 249–50).

(25) Ibid., 352–53: allegory of Eden (the garden) abandoned by the Angel (Phoebe) in which Evil triumphs (weeds, and the overflowing of Maule's well) and in which the Evil One (the black cat: "a strange Grimalkin") has chosen to reside, only to remove himself again when the messenger of Grace returns.

(26) S.L., V: they live under the same roof (The Leech and his Patient).

(27) A. Doane, XII; "Lily's Quest," II; Y.G.B., II; Rapp., II; M.M.M., I; S.L., V; Bl.R., V; M.F., VI.

(28) 7G., III, Ch. 20: the Judge's death is an exorcism—feelings can at last be expressed, desires realized (p. 362).

(29) Ibid., 147: the Judge compared to the serpent, "which as a preliminary to fascination, is said to fill the air with his peculiar odor."

(30) Birth., II, 48–50: the mark, in the shape of a hand, reddens sometimes to the point of rendering Georgiana's beautiful face loathsome: the blush of shame, of sin, of sex. Cf. Rapp., II, 133 (the imprint of Beatrice's hand).

(31) Rapp., Wks., II.

(32) S.L., V, 209: "Do as thou wilt! There is no good for him—no good for me—no good for thee! There is no good for little Pearl!"

(33) Particularly in his tales for children and in "Old Manse," II.

(34) Am.Nbks., R.S., 149: from the divine watchdog to the celestial house is but a step.

(35) *Dolliver Romance*, XI: Dr. D. and little Pansie.

(36) Am.Nbks., R.S.. 39–40.

(37) 7G., III, 69–70: he means to get his money's worth, and would be quite glad not to pay Hepzibah at all.

(38) She is the Pearl of the Gospel ("one pearl of great price," Matt. 13 : 46. Cf. S.L., V, 138), who has apparently strayed and lost herself in the fire of passion and sin (Cf. "Intelligence Office," II, 370–71: "having once let it escape . . . you have no . . . claim to it . . .") and even changed her nature.

(39) D. H. Lawrence, *Studies in Classic American Literature* (the little devil of a modern child already bearing the modern woman within it).

(40) S.L., V, 127 (Crimson velvet tunic).

(41) Ibid., 221.

(42) Ibid., 222: In the forest, Pearl never ceases to question her mother about the Black Man, one of the father images that haunt her.

(43) Ibid., 138 (her Heavenly Father): Pearl is still haunted by the idea of her unknown father and tells the Rev. Wilson she was never "created" at all, thus defining herself as a gratuitous being. Cf. 124 ("I have no Heavenly Father").

(44) Strindberg: *There are Crimes and Crimes, Advent, Easter* (the simple mind being in this case an equivalent of the child).

(45) G.B., Wks., I.

(46) S.L., V, 77 (the image of Divine Maternity). It is significant that this "Virgin" is carrying a female child in her arms (S.L., V, 311: "The angel . . . of the coming revelation must be a *woman* . . ."); Bl.R., V, 458: "Heaven grant that the ministry of souls be left in charge of women . . . God . . . has endowed her with the religious sentiment . . . refined from that gross, intellectual alloy with which every masculine theologian—*save only One who merely veiled himself in mortal and masculine shape, but was in truth divine*" (H. does not dare to add "and feminine," but he thinks it, even though he refuses to go as far as O'Neill). This obsession may have been strengthened in H.'s mind by the fact that there were a great many women preachers among the Quakers persecuted by his ancestors (Ann Hutchinson, Cassandra Southwick. "Main Street," III, 642). Moreover, the Shakers openly believed in the reincarnation of Christ as a woman. J. Wardley, the founder of the sect, even claimed that his own wife was the reincarnated Christ.

(47) Mary Silsbee (see Part One).

(48) Everything conspired toward the creation of the type represented by Hester (S.L., V, 73–74); Zenobia (Bl.R., V, 337–38); and Miriam (M.F., VI, 231).

(49) S.L., V, 236–37 (Up and away!); 238 (Thou shalt not go alone!)

(50) N. A. & E., II, 279: "The Day of Doom has . . . swept away the whole race of men."

(51) S.L., V, 234: "What we did had consecration of its own."

(52) Marlowe, *Dr. Faustus*, final soliloquy.

(53) Cf. Baudelaire.

(54) E.B., III, 489.
(55) S.L., V, 199–201.
(56) Bl.R., V, 456 (Zenobia's harangue).
(57) M.F., VI, 71–72.
(58) *Septimius Felton*, XI.
(59) Rapp., II, 112 (the Eden of the present world). Cf. XI, 490 (the Adam and Eve of the new epoch). Cf. Lewis, *American Adam*, Stanton, "The Trial of Nature: an Analysis of Bl.R.," *PMLA*, LXXVI, 1961, emphasizes the Adamic intent of Hawthorne's Arcadia.
(60) In *East of Eden* and *Big Sur*.
(61) "The Old Manse," Wks., II.
(62) Rapp., II. Cf. R. R. Male, *H.'s Tragic Vision*, 1957: The Ambiguity of Beatrice. M.M.M.; G.C.; "Ancestral Footstep."
(63) 7G., III: Clifford, the "thunder-smitten Adam" (p. 182), dreams nevertheless of the paradise he has lost (190: "I want my happiness").
(64) M.F., VI: by loving Donatello.
(65) Dr. H's Exp., I, and Rapp., II.

CHAPTER 3

I

(1) M.F., VI: this is the whole meaning of D.'s "transformation." Rev. L. Fick, in *The Light Beyond* (1955), p. 1, defines H. as "an anatomist of Sin." Reid, "The Role of Transformation in H.'s Tragic Vision," *Furms*, V, 1958, reduces this metamorphosis to its negative elements (disillusion).
(2) M. Le Breton, *The Student's Anthology of American Literature*, 167: "not Calvinist determinism, but a problem of psychology."
(3) Melville, "Rev. of Mosses," *Lit.Wld.*, Aug. 17 and 24, 1850: "Black conceit"; "blackness."
(4) Ibid.: "this great power of blackness in him derives its force from its appeal to that Calvinist sense of Innate Depravity and Original Sin . . ."
(5) 7G., III, 136: Clifford ("his face darkened, as if the shadow of a cavern or a dungeon had come over it"); 174 ("Had this veil been over him from his birth?"); 25: "thoughtful gloom" that shrouded the House's inhabitants.
(6) Audiberti talks of the "secret blackness of milk" in one of his sonnets. It is such a blackness that H. makes visible in M.'s B. V.
(7) James, *H.*, 1879, p. 99.
(8) Am.Nbks., R.S., 98: "The human heart to be allegorized as a cavern . . . You step within but a short distance, and begin to find yourself surrounded with a terrible gloom, and monsters of divers kind; it seems like Hell itself. You are bewildered and wander without hope. At last a light strikes upon you . . ."
(9) 7G., III and P. Gold., I.
(10) Am.Nbks., R.S. 98 (terrible Gloom). See Note 8.
(11) Kierkegaard, *Treatise on Despair*, 1849: the man of immediate reality, dress, appearances. Cf. Swift's *Tale of a Tub*.
(12) "Feathertop," II.
(13) 7G., III, 273, 274, 275 (the Judge).
(14) Ibid., 210: "She was not so constantly gay . . . Her eyes looked larger, and darker, and deeper . . . She was . . . more of a woman."
(15) Ibid., 131 ("a flickering taper-gleam in his eye-balls") and ("intellectual lamps"); 177 ("lambent flame") then ("the glow left him . . .").
(16) S.L., V, 221: the beam of light that follows Pearl and recedes before Hester. Cf. Am.Nbks., R.S. 205 (Una).
(17) Ibid., 176: Dimmesdale's vigils.
(18) Novalis, quoted by Bachelard in *Psychanalyse du Feu*, 84.

(19) "Pomegranate Seeds," IV, 351 (somber brilliance of precious stones in the darkness).

(20) Y.G.B., II, 101.

(21) My Kinsman, III, 639.

(22) S.L., V: "The Minister's Vigil."

(23) Ch. Nodier, quoted by Bachelard in *Psychanalyse du Feu*: "any descent into hell has the structure of a dream."

(24) S.L., V, 268-69.

(25) Blake: "Cruelty has a human heart / And jealousy a human face; / Terror the human form divine, / And secrecy the human dress."

(26) Y.G.B., II; "Wakefield," I; My Kinsman, III; S.L., V (The Minister in a Maze); 7G., III (Clifford in the House's dark passages).

(27) My Kinsman, III, 629 (the deformity and enormity of the two-faced demon suggest an allegory of Pride).

(28) Ibid., 625-26 (scarlet woman).

(29) Y.G.B., II, 99 (pink ribbon); My Kinsman, III, 626 (scarlet petticoat); Rapp., II, 111 (purple blossoms); 128 (adultery of various vegetable species); S.L., V, 127 (velvet tunic) and, of course, the Letter.

(30) Y.G.B., II.

(31) "Bosom Serpent," II.

(32) S.L., V, 169 (Chillingworth's discovery: the letter on the minister's breast); 302-3 (the revealing of it).

(33) The gentle light that emanates from Phoebe (7G., III, 94: the transformation of the shadowy room, and 130: "He saw Phoebe . . . and caught an illumination from her youthful and pleasant aspect . . . like the circle of reflected brilliancy around the glass vase . . .). The firelight (7G., III, 131: "the heart's household fire."

(34) 7G., III, 130: Clifford compared to a damped fire.

(35) Cf. the Ogress (Part One); M.F., VI, 504 (Titaness).

(36) IV, 420.

(37) "Circe's Palace," IV. Cf. Miriam and Donatello in the coils of the serpent (M.F., VI, 205).

(38) S.L., V: A Flood of Sunshine.

(39) Pearl is at once a blessing and a curse to Hester. Cf. Isaiah, 45 : 7: "From the light I create darkness: I make peace and create evil: I the Lord do all these things."

(40) Marlowe, *Faustus*, final soliloquy.

(41) S.L., V: Dimmesdale, 304.

(42) D. H. Lawrence, *Studies in Classic American Literature*, understood this, though he does not place the problem in its alchemical context.

(43) H. uses the word "psychology" very little, but when he does so he gives it its full meaning: Pref. Sn.Im., III, 386 (psychological romance); E.B., III, 389 (psychological experiment); 7G., III, 252 (psychological conditions); Bl.R., V, 547 (psychological Phenomena); 458 (psychological experiments). He used the word "alchemy" a great deal however, as well as "sorcery" and "mesmerism," in order to denote psychic phenomena.

II

(1) S.L., V, 262.

(2) M.F., VI (Miriam and the Model).

(3) "Man of Adamant," III.

(4) S.L., V, 186 (magnetic chain); 7G., III, 71 (sympathetic chain); 167 (electric sparkle of ill-humor); M.F., VI, 483 (electric shock); E.B., III, 495 (electric chain). Cf. Male, "H. and the Concept of Sympathy," *PMLA*, LXVIII, 1953.

(5) D. H. Lawrence, *Studies in Classic American Literature*, referring to Poe: love-knowledge.

(6) Zola, *Le Roman Expérimental*, and in U.S., Dreiser. H. himself alludes to

psychological experiments in Bl.R. in terms of chemistry (V, 547: chemical discovery) but in order to express disapprobation.

(7) 7G., III, 144 (fleshy effulgence).

(8) Letter to Sophia, quoted R.S., Biog., 60–61 (Jan. 1842).

(9) Bl.R., V, Ch. 3: "A Knot of Dreamers."

(10) S.L., V, 186.

(11) Ibid., 158: Chill. ("a light . . . blue and ominous"); 165 (wary eye); 166 ("an eye bright with intense and concentrated intelligence"). And this cold hatred is answered by Dimm. with a passionate hatred, 167 ("his eyes full and bright, and with a kind of fierceness"). M.F., VI, 176: Donatello ("tiger-like fury gleaming from his . . . eyes").

(12) M.F., VI, 56 and 187: Donatello's sad and supplicating gaze when in love.

(13) Ibid., 203–4: "I did what your eyes bad me do, when I asked them with mine."

(14) S.L., V, 242–43: "There played around her mouth, and beamed out of her eyes, a radiant and tender smile, that seemed to be gushing from the very heart of womanhood."

(15) Bl.R., VI, 339–40: "One felt an influence breathing out of her, such as we might suppose to come from Eve, when she was just made . . ."

(16) S.L., V, 159: "Dimmesdale . . . would become vaguely aware that something inimical to this peace had thrust itself into relation with him"; 171: "evil influence watching over him" (Chill. is hateful to him without his knowing why).

(17) Am.Nbks., pages quoted in *Portable H.*, 569: "In the eyes of a child . . . the image of . . . an angel . . . ; in those of a vicious person, a devil." Cf. S.L., V, 122: Pearl's gaze: "a face fiend-like."

(18) 7G., III, 169: "he grew youthful while she sat by him."

(19) Ibid., 210: Phoebe's eyes so described.

(20) M's B.V., I, 62: The Rev. Hooper escapes from his fiancée behind the black veil.

(21) O'Neill: *Desire under the Elms* (Abbie's sexual witchcraft).

(22) 7G., III, 249–50 (Alice P. was forced by Maule to go out and degrade herself at night).

(23) Ibid., 115: "For you are a Pyncheon?" Holgrave asks Phoebe.

(24) Ibid., 252–53 (an influence . . . as dangerous . . . as disastrous, as that which the carpenter . . . exercised over the ill-fated Alice).

(25) Bl.R., V, 549–50: Priscilla, psychically violated by Westervelt, calls Hollingsworth to her aid.

(26) Woodberry, *H.*, 1902, p. 147: "It is noticeable that the clergyman, the physician and the artist are the only specific types that attracted Hawthorne."

(27) The nameless painter of the "Prophetic Pictures," Wks., I.

(28) A.o.B., Wks., II.

(29) D's W.Im., II, and M.F., VI.

(30) Bl.R., V.

(31) Birth., II; Rapp., ibid.; and S.L., V.

(32) 7G., III and Bl.R., V.

(33) M's Bk. V., I and S.L., V.

(34) S.L., V, 153 (Dimm. and Chill, live under the same roof); 154 (they each occupy a wing of the house, D. living on the sunny side, Ch. on the shady side); 155 (they often visit one another "passing from one apartment to the other").

(35) James, *H.*, 1879.

(36) S.L., V, 166.

(37) Ibid., 303: Old Roger Ch. knelt down beside him, with a blank, dull countenance.

(38) 7G., III, 280 (". . . one of the bad impulses of our fallen nature . . .").

(39) Ibid., 360 ("had he any object to get by putting Clifford to the rack . . .").

(40) S.L., V, 152 (the kind and friendly physician) and further on (to bring his mind into such affinity with his patient's that this last shall unawares have spoken, what he imagines himself only to have thought).

(41) "Haunted Mind," I, 345: the imagination of the waking dreamer "imparting vividness to all ideas, without the power of selecting or controlling them."

(42) 7G., III, 247: Maule's method when he hypnotizes Alice P.

(43) S.L., V, 150 (putting his hand to his heart, with a flush of pain flitting over his brow); 82: Chill. in the square ("A writhing horror twisted itself across his features like a snake gliding swiftly over them").

(44) Ibid., 167 ("Not to thee! cried Mr. Dimmesdale passionately . . . With a frantic gesture he rushed out of the room").

(45) 7G., III 117-18 (allusion to Clifford's crime, and this particularly hurtful remark: "As to his character, we need not discuss its points; they have already been settled by a competent tribunal . . .").

(46) M.F., VI: the Model drives Miriam to the end of her tether at the risk of becoming her victim: 47 (in the Catacombs); 112-13 (at the Porta del Popolo); 175-77 (at the Fontana Trevi); 186-87 (in the Colosseum: M's attack of hysteria); and lastly, 202 (the Tarpeian rock: seventh and fatal encounter).

(47) Lady E., I.

(48) D. H. Lawrence, *Studies in Classical American Literature.*

(49) 7G., III, 214 (It is holy ground where the shadow falls).

(50) Ibid., 116-17 (the daguerreotype of the Judge). Cf. Ibsen, *Peer Gynt* (the devil makes "negatives" of the human soul).

(51) "Prophetic Pictures," I.

(52) M.F., VI, 140.

(53) Ibid., 141. Cf. D's W.Im. (the human shape contained in advance in the block of wood), II, 353.

(54) Ibid., 152-53.

III

(1) Am.Nbks., IX, 125.

(2) Hart, "S.L., One Hundred Years After," *NEQ,* XXIII, 1950: Hester saved by her creative faculty.

(3) S.L., V, 120: Pearl (ever-creative spirit).

(4) Fogle, "Simplicity & Complexity in M.F., *TSE,* II, 1950, nevertheless discerns in her the symbol of art as the imitator of the ideal. James, *H.,* 1879, p. 167, enthused over the symbol of purity: "an admirable invention—one of the things that make a man of genius." Perhaps he saw Hilda as prefiguring his own heroine Isabel Archer.

(5) 7G., III, 214.

(6) Apart from the historical characters, the following may be noted: *Catharine,* Ilbrahim's mother (G.B., I), visibly a counterpart of Mrs. Hutchinson; *Susan* ("Village Uncle," I) the girl in Swampscott; the *Rev. Hooper* (M's B.V., V), in whose case H. judged it expedient to mention the Rev. J. Moody as an influence in a note (I, 52); *Lady Eleanore,* who is more or less Mary Silsbee; *Mr. Wiggleworth* ("Chippings," I) the monumental mason, one of the artisans H. met at Martha's Vineyard (Turner, *H. as Editor,* 117: the graveyard); the *Shakers* ("Shaker Burial," I: Father Ephraim, Brother Adam, Sister Martha); *the old apple dealer* (Wks., II. Cf. Am.Nbks., R.S., 90); *Drowne* (D's W. Im., and *Legends of Province House,* I, 272: the Indian on the weathervane carved by "Deacon Drowne," the famous wood-carver); *Hester Prynne* (S.L., V) is both H.'s mother and the beauty of Martha's Vineyard (also to be found perhaps in "Chippings," I, 462: "a comely woman") and an adulteress sentenced to the pillory in 1642. Cf. Murphy, "Hester in History," *AL,* March 1960. She is above all Hester Prynne; *Pearl* (S.L., V) is Una (Am.Nbks.,

R.S., 200, 201: "her beauty . . . flitting . . . ; 205: possessed by an "earthly monster"; 209: imagination; 210: "elfish") plus the author's own imagination; *Hepzibah* is his mother (when old), his sister (as an old maid), and Eliz. Peabody; *Phoebe* is Sophia (H. uses the same metaphors for both: Am.Nbks., R.S., 182: she [S.] is birdlike in many ways—7G., III, 168 (a bird); 167 (lightsome); *Zenobia* (Bl.R., V) is Margaret Fuller, with beauty added; *Hollingsworth* (ibid.) is perhaps Elihu Burritt, "the learned blacksmith" (a friend of Emerson's), and may derive his sturdy physique from Hodge, the blacksmith of North Adams (Nbks., IX, 141, 142: "no man . . . seems more like a man, more indescribably human than this sturdy blacksmith"); *Miriam* (M.F., VI) has the features of the beautiful Jewess in London and the talent of the Praslin-Choiseuls' governess.

(7) My Kinsman, III (Robin); Lady E., I (Gervayse); "Christmas Banquet," II, (G.Hastings); "Wakefield," I (Wakefield); "Endicott," I (Endicott); A.G., I (the ambitious young man).

(8) It is not merely a matter of an artificial and "chivalrous" reversal (R. R. Male, *H.'s Tragic Vision*, pp. 67–69) of the roles of Adam and Eve in the original temptation.

(9) E.g.: S.L., Ch. 4 (Hester and Chill.); Ch. 6 (H. and Pearl); Ch. 7 (H. and the Governor); Ch. 10 (Dimm. and Chill.); Ch. 12 (Dimm., H. and Pearl at the pillory); Ch. 14 (H. and the Physician); Ch. 15 (H. and Pearl); Ch. 17 (The Pastor and his Parishioner): a procedure that eventually becomes mechanical.

(10) R. Michaud, *Le Roman Américain d'Aujourd'hui*, 23–24, praises the intuition H. possessed of the female heart, particularly that of the young girl. In fact, the problem of feminine psychology presented itself to H. quite differently, and on another level.

(11) James, *H.*, 1879, p. 167, remarks on this in fact when referring to the schematic nature of H.'s characters: "they are all figures rather than characters . . . pictures rather than persons."

(12) The terminology used here is that of Jung (*Die Psychologie der Uebertragung*, Zurich, 1946).

(13) Bachelard, *Poétique de la Rêverie*, P.U.F., 64 and 69: "the 'double' is the double of a double being."

(14) Jung, *Psychologie und Alchemie*, Zurich, 1954, p. 384: Der Artifex und seiner "Soror mystica" (Fig.) Cf. Birth.," II (Aylmer and Georgiana); Rapp. (doctor and daughter).

(15) James, *H.*, 1879, pp. 163–64.

(16) S.L., V, 122–23: Hester sees her own image in Pearl's eyes take on the shape of a devilish goblin. And, 118: "Her only . . . comfort was when the child lay in the placidity of sleep . . . until . . . little Pearl awoke": the glimmer she sees dancing in P's eyes is the Letter.

(17) Ibid., 132 (the letter magnified by the distorting mirror); 250: the image of P. imperiously pointing at Hester's breast is reflected in the stream, and H. uses this three times as a symbol of necessity. (p. 242); before this, the stream had already refused to carry the fatal emblem away.

(18) Ibid., 176–77.

(19) Ibid., 177.

(20) "The Vision of the Fountain," I.

(21) 7G., III, 186. Cf. Nbks., 1846, quoted by Cowley, *Portable H.*, 569 (a pool . . . paved . . . with mosaic-work—images and various figures . . .).

(22) M.F., VI, 283.

(23) Bachelard, *Poétique de la Rêverie*, 98.

(24) Am.Nbks., R.S., 210: "there is something that almost frightens me about the child—I know not whether elfic or angelic, but at all events supernatural . . . I cannot believe her to be my own child, but a spirit strangely mingled with good and evil, haunting the house where I dwell." A description repeated almost word for word in S.L., V, Ch. 6: Pearl.

(25) M's B.V., I. Cf. H.'s note, p. 52.

(26) 7G., III, 293–94.

(27) Ibid., 129 (a child's first journey across the floor); 130 (a wayward infant); 180 (childish delight); 293 (childish aspect). H. seems to take pleasure in insisting upon this point.

(28) "Custom House," V, 55 and 7G., III, 104: Phoebe (a ray of firelight that dances on the wall).

(29) G.B., I (Ilbrahim and the tragic pine); M.M.M., I (the May couple); "Mr. H's C.," I (Mr. Higginbotham and the pear tree); Rapp., II (Beatrice and the plant); S.L., V (Pearl and the rosebush); 7G., III (the Pyncheons and their elm); Bl.R., V (Zenobia and the rose; Coverdale and his leafy nest); M.F., VI (Donatello transformed into a tree-dweller).

(30) R.M.'sB., II (Reuben Bourne); Y.G.B., II (Goodman Brown); S.L., V (Hester and Dimm.).

(31) 7G., III, 190.

(32) S.L., V: "A Flood of Sunshine."

(33) Am.Nbks., R.S., 280: H. says of caresses that they are "necessary to the life of affections, as leaves to the life of a tree. If they are wholly restrained, love will die at the roots."

(34) M.M.M., I, 83.

(35) 7G., III, 44 and Ch. 19 ("Alice's Posies").

(36) S.L., V (Pearl).

IV

(1) S.L., V, 197–98: Hester (All the light and graceful foliage of her character had been withered up . . . leaving a bare and harsh outline . . ."

(2) Ibid., 144 (Mrs. Hibbins tries to make Hester confess her rebellion); 245–46 (another scene of provocation: this time Dimm. is the object of the witch's mockery); 287–88 (the witch appears in the crowd like a personification of slander as the town dignitaries, and the minister in particular, pass by). Cf. 7G., III, 281 (many a prying old woman), and *Dolliver Romance*, XI, 32 (the old Doctor, the "wizard," feels that all his movements are observed.)

(3) "Ed.Fane," I (Rose Grafton, a victim of the social prejudices of the privileged class) and "Sylph Etherege," III.

(4) Wives, III.

(5) 7G., III (Clifford). Cf. P. Gold., I.

(6) S.L., V, Chillingworth, 156 (something ugly and evil); 211 (deformed old figure).

(7) "M's B. V.," I, and S.L., V.

(8) "Endicott," I (Endicott); S.L., V, 131 (Bellingham).

(9) "Lady E.," I.

(10) "Bosom Serpent," II.

(11) 7G., III, 91 (the rusty key . . . in the reluctant lock).

(12) S.L., V, 79–80 (she takes refuge in her past).

(13) 7G., III, 306 (Hep's *mental images*: H. is here using a term of modern psychology).

(14) "Wakefield," I.

(15) R.M.'sB., II (Reuben Bourne returns to the spot where he had left his "father" to die (cf. Bible, I Chron., 5 : 6: "Reuben . . . he defiled his father's bed", and where he is accidentally to kill his son, born from his union with Roger Malvin's daughter.

(16) Am.Nbks., IX, 45.

(17) S.L., V, The Minister in a maze, and, on the other hand, the disguised confessions in the pulpit (p. 175) and the pretence on the scaffold.

(18) Why should Dimm. torture himself as he does unless he derives a bitter pleasure from his pain? Even though H. does not employ words that underline the algolagnic ambivalence (Michaux's interpretation in *Le Roman*

Américain d'Aujourd'hui, 24–25, of the term "exquisite" is inaccurate) and emphasizes the absence of respites in the minister's sufferings (S.L., V, 176: "without . . . momentary relief"), it is clear that we are being confronted with a case of masochism. D. strikes himself in order to punish himself in his flesh and at the same time to take pleasure in his suffering (we must remember that Hester's image materializes before him during his vigils and scourging sessions [S.L., V, 177]).

(19) S.L., V, 103: the reasons for the morbid attachment Hester conceives for the places where she has suffered her shame.

(20) 7G., III, 155–56 (dragon).

(21) Ibid., 208.

(22) Ibid., 297 (tone of brief decision); 298 (the *will* [italics mine] which Clifford expressed . . .); and further on: "C., ordinarily so destitute of this faculty . . ."

(23) Ibid., 316 ("You must take the lead now, Hepzibah!")

(24) S.L., V, 167 (anger at Chill.); 232 (upon discovering the truth about Chill. he is filled with a violent surge of hate: "the minister looked at her . . . with all that violence of passion . . . Never was there a blacker or fiercer frown . . . it was a dark transfiguration.") Also the enormous expenditure of nervous energy represented by the sermon. But D.'s reserves are quickly exhausted and his strength soon betrays him. He collapses to the ground in the forest, (p. 233) and later on he dies after the effort of the final revelation.

(25) S.L., V, 139–40.

(26) "Prophetic Picture," I.

(27) S.L., V, 242.

(28) 7G., III, 136 (An open window!).

(29) Ibid., 200 ("The Arched Window").

(30) Ibid., ("The Flight of Two Owls").

(31) M.F., VI, 186 and 203–04.

(32) S.L., V, 307: "show freely to the world . . . some trait whereby the worst may be inferred."

(33) M.F., VI, 406–12 ("The World's Cathedral").

(34) S.L., V, 153 (a strange reserve).

(35) Ibid., (night scene at the pillory). Gerber, in "Form and Content in S.L.," *NEQ*, March 1944, gives an interpretation that hardly stands up to serious examination: D., awakened by his own cry (S.L., V, 180: shrieked aloud), finds three opportunities for confessing his crime. But the Governor, the witch, and the Rev. Wilson make a strange trio of confessors. In fact, the whole scene takes place in an ambiguous atmosphere, D.'s consciousness being throughout in a sort of trancelike state.

(36) S.L., V, Ch. 23: "The Revelation of the Scarlet Letter."

(37) 7G., III, 201.

(38) Ibid., 171.

(39) "Bosom Serpent," II, 319–20: Roderick only has to forget himself in love for another (jealousy is also narcissism).

(40) "Wakefield," I, 163–64: "a good night's rest to W!" But perhaps he will set out on yet another escapade tomorrow.

(41) S.L., V, 242: "Do I feel joy again? . . ." Brownell, *American Prose Masters,* 93, sees no trace of passion in S.L., for his part, only "the postlude of passion." Sanders, "S.L., as a Love-Story," *PMLA*, LXXVII, 1962, restores the book to its status as a study of passion.

(42) M.F., VI, 206–7.

(43) Ibid., (a bliss, or an insanity).

(44) Ibid., 206.

(45) The contrast between the lovers (S.L. and M.F.) and the "loving couple" (7G.) is easily made.

(46) M.F., VI, 206–7.

(47) Bl.R., V, Ch. 27: "Midnight."
(48) Strindberg's *Dance of Death*: "It is called love-hatred, and it hails from the pit."
(49) O'Neill, *Desire under the Elms* (Ephraim Cabot identifies himself with God).
(50) S.L., V, 303: Chill. "knelt down . . . with a blank, dull countenance, out of which the life seemed to have departed."
(51) Ibid., 233: Dimm. comes to hate Hester in this way. Cf. Note 24.
(52) Nbks., IX, 110: Men of cold passions have quick eyes.
(53) As witness the confidential letters he received (and destroyed) after the publication of *S.L.* (J.H.,H.&W, I, 358): ("letters . . . from spiritual invalids . . .").
(54) Dreiser and biochemistry. O'Neill and psychoanalysis.

PART THREE: THE KEYS OF THE WORLD

I: ALLEGORY

CHAPTER 1

I

(1) 7G., III, 210 (artesian wells).
(2) H.of3H., I.
(3) "Vision of the Fountain," I, and 7G., III, 186.
(4) "Man of Adamant," III.
(5) A. Doane, XII, 288 (the frozen world); 290 (graveyard scene).
(6) "Great Stone Face," III.
(7) E. B., III.
(8) 7G., III, 330–31 (the ghosts moving past the portrait of the ancestor); "Prophetic Pictures," I (the living moving among the paintings); M.F., VI (the human drama in the museum).
(9) "Howe's Masquerade," I.
(10) P. Gold., I, 444–45 (the house and the sleighs); 7G., III (the House and the bustling world around it); 193: "a cab, an omnibus . . . that vast rolling vehicle, the world . . ."; 194: "the railroad . . . a glimpse of the trains, of cars flashing, a brief transit across the extremity of the street," and further on: ". . . jolting carts . . . the butcher's cart . . . the fish-cart . . . the country-man's cart . . . the baker's cart . . ."; 195: the knife-grinder; 196–97: the puppeteer; 199: the procession.
(11) "Wakefield," I and Y.G.B., II.
(12) 7G., III, 306: "He had a winged nature; she was rather of the vegetable kind."
(13) "The Old Manse," II; "Hall of Fantasy," ibid., 209; and M.F., VI.

II

(1) Herbert Schneider, *The Puritan Mind*, 1930: a schematic universe that re-pelled H. ("He professed to hate his Puritan heritage, but he never scorned it," p. 257) but of which he made use. Cf. Boas, *Cotton Mather*, 1928.
(2) Yvor Winters, "Maule's Curse, H. and the Problem of Allegory," *Amer. Rev.*, LX, 1937.
(3) Herbert Schneider, *The Puritan Mind*.
(4) 7G., III, 94 (See: Part Two, I, Ch. 1, "The Library").
(5) "The Custom House," V, 19–20 (satiric allegory). Cf. "The Bald Eagle," *Tales of Humor*, 1840, pp. 27–41.
(6) 7G., III, 254 ("the moon . . . like an ambitious demagogue").
(7) "The Miraculous Pitcher," W.Bk., IV.
(8) "Circe's Palace," Tangle., IV.

(9) "Miraculous Pitcher."
(10) "Dragon's Teeth," Tangle., **IV.**
(11) "The Three Golden Apples," W. Bk.: the Old Man is a gothick and Spenserian monster who certainly has nothing Greek about him.
(12) "Pygmies," Tangle., **IV.**
(13) "Minotaur," ibid.
(14) "Dragon's Teeth," ibid.
(15) "Golden Fleece," ibid.
(16) Letter to J. T. Fields, May 23, 1851, *Yesterdays with Authors*: "Of course I shall pump out all the old heathen wickedness and put in a moral wherever practicable."
(17) "Virtuoso's Collection," II.
(18) "Time's Portrait," XIII. Cf. Nbks., IX, 396 ("Personify the Century"), also ("Death as a Cook").
(19) "American Magazine," A. Turner, *H. as Editor,* 74–75.
(20) Ibid., 82.
(21) "Little Daffydowndilly," III.
(22) "Little Annie," I.
(23) "A Rill from the Town Pump," I.
(24) Woodberry, *H.,* 1902, Ch. 4, "The Old Manse": They [the tales] pleased the reader . . . because they were a faithful reproduction of the commonplace, played upon by sentiment and slightly moralized . . ."; 129: "H. was to the village what Thoreau was to the wildwood."
(25) "Graves and Goblins," XII; "White Old Maid" (original title: "The Old Maid in the Winding-Sheet," cf. E. C. Lathrop, *A Study of the Sources*); and "Wedding Knell," I.
(26) "Sylph Etherege," III.
(27) "Antique Ring," Wks., XII.
(28) "Select Party," II, 70 (palace of clouds, gilding, reflections); 82–83 (moonlight). Cf. 7G., III, (the silvery beams . . . embellished . . . the old house); II, 84 (curtains made of the many-colored clouds of sunrise . . . virgin light . . . rainbows); 82 (misty poet!).
(29) Cf. preceding note and Am.Nbks., R.S., 139 (the face and bust of a beautiful woman gazing at me from a cloud); 149 (gigantic figure of a hound crouching down, with head erect). Cf. "Old Manse," II, 36, Nbks., R.S., 42–43, 45, 54 and 63 (more descriptions of clouds, less allegorical).
(30) "Old Manse," II, 32 (reflection in stream) and "Select Party" (cf. Note 28).
(31) "Select Party," II.
(32) Herbert Schneider, *The Puritan Mind.*
(33) Yvor Winters, "Maule's Curse, H. and the Problem of Allegory," *Amer. Rev.,* LX, 1937.
(34) Letter to Longfellow, quoted R.S., Am.Nbks., 292 (see Note 34, Ch. 4, I: "herbs of grace").
(35) Cf. same letter. Compare S.L., V, 68 (rose-bush); 122 (wild flowers: thrown by Pearl at her mother); 120 (weeds: which P. treats as enemies to be trampled upon); 147 (native herbs and roots: used by apothecaries and wizards); 160 (unsightly plants: gathered by Chill. in the graveyard); 164 (pricky burr: thrown by P. at Dimm.); 210 (black flower); 211 (poisonous shrubs); 211 (deadly nightshade, dogwood, henbane: associated with Chill.); 249–50 (adornment of flowers and wild foliage: the witch-child's pagan finery). The graceful, brightly colored flowers only occur at the beginning and the end, associated with P.
(36) See preceding note.
(37) Ibid.
(38) Y.G.B., II and S.L., V.
(39) *Taits Edinburgh Magazine,* Jan. 1855.
(40) Gale, "M.F.: An Allegory with a Key to its Interpretation," *New Eng.* Oct. 1861.

(41) B. Faust, *H.'s Contemporaneous Reputation*, 1939, Part 3.
(42) E. H. Davidson, *H.'s Last Phase*, (The Keen Edge and the Blunt) and Winters, "Maule's Curse," *op. cit.* (the possible alternatives).
(43) R. P. Warren, *The Cave*, 1959.
(44) E. A. Poe, "Tale-Writing," *Godey's*, Nov. 1847: "Let him mend his pen, get a bottle of visible ink . . . hang (if possible) the editor of the "Dial" [i.e., Margaret Fuller] . . ."
(45) James, *H.*, 1879, p. 63: "H. in his metaphysical moods is nothing if not allegorical, and allegory, to my sense, is quite one of the lighter exercises of the imagination." He is much more willing to allow H. "fancy" in Coleridge's sense. Cf. p. 27 (shadowy fancies and conceits). Similarly Poe, "Tale-Writing": "the strain of allegory." But Poe also considered *Pilgrim's Progress* "a ludicrously over-rated book." Other comments: Woodberry, *II.*, p. 43 (he had the allegorizing temperament) and Brownell, *American Prose Masters*, 1910, p. 80 (He was allegory-mad. Allegory was his obsession).
(46) Letter to J. T. Fields, April 13, 1854, *Yesterdays with Authors*, p. 75 (those blasted allegories). Cf. Rapp., intro., II, 107: "an inverterate love of allegory."

III

(1) S.L., V, 304: "The law we broke! . . . I fear! I fear!"
(2) Bl.R., V, 457–58.
(3) Ibid., 586.
(4) S.L., V, 265: "Tempted by a dream of happiness, he had yielded himself with deliberate choice, as he had never done before, to what he knew was deadly sin."
(5) M.F., VI, 207.
(6) M. Fuller, *Woman in the XIXth century*, 1893, p. 337: "Woman is born for love and it is impossible to turn her from seeking it." Cf. Cronin, "H. on Romantic Love and the Status of Women," *PMLA*, LXIX, 1954.
(7) Carpenter, "Scarlet A Minus," *Coll.Eng.*, V, Jan. 1944.
(8) M.F., VI, 207: "a special law had been created for them alone."
(9) Rapp., II: not only the splitting of the archetypal father (where Honig, *Dark Conceit, the Making of an Allegory*, 1959, sees only a conflict between orthodoxy and heresy, p. 137), but the splitting of the alchemist into animus and anima.
(10) Ibid., 142 (earthly child). But has she not just said: "at the hour when I first drew breath, this plant sprung from the soil, the offspring of his science . . ." and further on: "I grew up and blossomed with the plant and was nourished with its breath."
(11) Ibid., 112–13 (Rapp.'s mistrust and precautions: thick gloves).
(12) Ibid., 147 ("as terrible as thou art beautiful") instead of being "a weak woman exposed to all evil and capable of none."
(13) S.L., V, 235: "Think for me, Hester! Thou are strong. Resolve for me."
(14) Ibid., 200.
(15) Ibid.: Had Hester been as lacking in the maternal instinct as Catharine (G.B., I) she would not have limited herself to intellectual speculation but gone on to subversive activity.
(16) Ibid., 202: Hester takes the same path as Chill.
(17) Had H. read Goethe? There is no indication to the contrary. He had certainly read Tieck and J-P. Richter. There are no allusions to G. in the Nbks., however. On the other hand his name is mentioned in "Hall of Fantasy" (II, 188), published Feb. 1843, which permits us to suppose that he had read certain articles printed at that time in the *Dial* ("German Literature," by T. Parker, and "Goethe" by M. Fuller). These could scarcely have been his first revelation of G.'s existence (for in 1835 he had read Schiller [Kesselring, "H.'s Reading, 1828–1850," *BNYPL*, 1949]), and

"Faust" had penetrated into America in about 1820 (Stein, *H.'s Faust*, 1953), but they may well have awakened a certain interest in him as an author made fashionable by the Transcendentalists (Stein, p. 87, lists five "Fausts" in H.'s work at this period: Birth., Rapp., A.o.B., D's W.Im., E.B.—precursors of S.L., the "New England Faust," Ch. 8). It is not until the It.Nbks. (X,71) that we find H. mentioning Goethe's name again, when referring to W. Story's statue of Marguerite. H. nowhere mentions any intention on his part of using the Faust theme. It nevertheless exists in his work, and it is difficult to believe, in the case of so conscious a writer, that we are merely dealing with unconscious reminiscences beyond his control. Deliberate concealment seems more likely. For it is a theme, in his hands, that touches very closely upon the burning question of feminism. He therefore kept it more or less a secret. Higginson for his part ("H.'s Last Bequest," *Scrib. Mth.*, V, Nov. 1872) does not hesitate to compare *Septimius Felton* to *Faust*. Stein, *H.'s Faust, a Study of the Devil Archetype*, 1953, makes this theme the subject of an entire book. He also emphasizes the feminine aspect (p. 113).

(18) Goethe, *Faust, Part Two*.
(19) Strindberg, *Comrades*.
(20) M.F., VI, 196–97.
(21) S.L., V (scene in forest and the very ironic exhortation of the sinning woman by the minister, pp. 89–90) and Bl.R., V, 500–1 (the curtain pulled to shut out the curious gaze).
(22) M.F., VI, 491.
(23) Ibid., 519.
(24) "Christmas Banquet," II, 323: again we see how carefully H. disguises the theme of rebellion against heaven and that of satanism. Roderick (Oberon, Hawthorne) takes shelter behind the old man in the tale and behind G. Hastings in order to blaspheme.
(25) 7G., III, 262–63 ("to conform myself to laws and the peaceful practice of society").
(26) H. had of course known the B.'s intimately both in London and Florence. He makes a delicate allusion in M.F. (VI, 146) to this union of two such rare beings ("Harriet Hosmer's clasped hands of Browning and his wife, symbolizing the individuality and heroic union of two high, poetic lives").
(27) Though Chill. does not converse with her, as Hester and Dimm. do, one senses the existence of a close bond between him and Mrs. Hibbins. Is Chill. not perhaps the Black Man that the witch is so familiar with, and that Hester herself says she met once ("Once in my life I met the Black Man . . . This Scarlet Letter is his mark," p. 223)?
(28) Am.Nbks., R.S., 92 (the injection of crime and sin). Cf. E.B., III.
(29) Nbks., IX, 395.
(30) B. Brecht, *Galileo Galilei*. H. did in fact become interested in Galileo while in Italy. He compares him to Newton (It.Nbks., V, 401).
(31) Of which Pearl is obviously a typical example, S.L., V, 118 ("a born outcast of the infantile world . . . no rights among Christened infants"). The Puritans would certainly have seen her as the perfect illustration of their theories on illegitimate children.
(32) Chill. (S.L., V, 156, 205, 211). Rapp., though not deformed, is "emaciated, sallow . . . sickly-looking" (II, 112). S. Felton (XI, 264) is presented as being a man of mixed blood, a half-breed, and more or less repulsive.
(33) Chill. (S.L., V, 158: "dug into the . . . clergyman's heart . . . ,"; 234: "He has violated in cold blood the sanctity of a human heart". E.B. (III, 489: "psychological experiment . . . annihilated her soul in the process").
(34) Turner, *H. as Editor*, 211 (incurable diseases).
(35) Dr.H.'s Exp., I; *Septimius Felton*, XI: *Dolliver Romance*, ibid. And the wine of Monte Beni (M.F., VI, Ch. 25) has a strange resemblance to the wine of the alchemists.

(36) *Septimius Felton,* XI; *Dolliver Romance,* ibid. (3rd fragment: Colonel Dabney episode).

(37) Ibid., 335 (visions of wealth).

(38) Ibid., 232: "brooding, brooding, his eyes fixed on some chip, some stone, some common plant, any commonest thing, as if it were the clew and index to some mystery . . ." The best proof of his creator's condemnation of *Septimius Felton* is the fact that continuing his researches involves being shut out from love (p. 353: love forbidden; 398: the alchemist should be "sufficient to himself"; 380: but his life will be an "eternity of abortive misery"; 382: moreover he will become a "traitor to humanity."

(39) Ibid., 232: "a kind of perplexity, a dissatisfied, foiled look . . ."

(40) There are many other alchemical symbols running through H.'s work like watermarks. The *Letter* bears a strange resemblance to certain astrological figures, to the eight-stemmed Rose, to Dante's celestial Rose, to the red and white Rose of Alchemy (the red letter embroidered with gold, S.L., V, 73). The *Sphere,* the retort (Chill.'s in S.L., Aylmer's in Birth.), evokes the transmutation of elements. Also to be noted in S.L., is the communication between laboratory and oratory, as in the engravings in books of alchemy (cf. Jung, *Psy. and Alch.,* 396). The *Serpent* ("Bosom Serpent," II, S.L., and Bl.R., V: the stream, the river, and 7G., III, 308: the spiral) evokes the cycle of the elements, of life. One may even find echoes of the Uroboros in the circular movements that stubbornly curve back upon themselves. The *Tree* (7G., III, the Pyncheon elm; Rapp., II: the plant; My Kinsman, III, 632: "the great old tree which has been spared for its huge twisted trunk . . .") is the Tree of Life. The *Mount* of the Disciples is to be found, in one sense, in Merry Mount, and also in "Hall of Fantasy" and "Select Party" topped by the Temple. We also, of course, find the *Stone* (G.C., I) and the *Secret Book* (D. in Mss., III). The Symbol of Anthropos is of course to be found passim, but the image of human nature allied to bestial nature appears most particularly in M.M.M., I, 71–72 (the bear and the maypole dancers) and in M.F., VI (Donatello), though it never actually goes as far as the Tetramorph of alchemy. It is quite possible that H. had seen such illustrated works as *Ancient Pagan and Modern Christian Symbolism* by T. Inman or *History of the Devil* by P. Carus. And it is certainly established that he could have consulted Scott's *Demonology and Witchcraft* (Kesselring, "H's Reading 1828–1850," *BYNPL,* 1949).

(41) Rapp., II (Dr. Baglioni).

(42) Birth., II.

(43) A.o.B., II.

(44) Letter to S., Nbks., IX, 219: "Light and shadows are continually flitting across my inward sky . . . It is dangerous to look . . . into such phenomena. It is apt to create a substance where there was a mere shadow."

CHAPTER 2

I

(1) Nietzsche, *Birth of Tragedy,* makes precisely this point: that lyricism is a product of the self charged with Dionysiac intoxication, not of the egotist self.

(2) Thoreau, *Walden*: Spring ("I love to see that Nature is so rife with life that myriads can be afforded to be sacrificed . . .") could convert nature's very cruelty into material for an optimism worthy of Zarathustra, whereas H., on the other hand, was saddened by it (Nbks., IX, 89): "the excruciating agonies which Nature inflicts upon men . . . to be represented as the work of tormentors."

(3) 7G., III, 258: "It is my impulse . . . to look on . . . and to comprehend the drama which for almost two hundred years has been dragging its slow length . . . ," and 260: "Destiny is arranging its fifth act for a catastrophe." Cf. Bl.R., V, 499: "I began to long for a catastrophe."

(4) Am.Nbks., R.S., 8.

(5) It.Nbks., unpublished passages (complete edition prepared by N. H., Pearson): "Sin, art, morality of sin; beauty; beauty of sin, and sin again" (H. was thinking of M.F. at the time, particularly the character of Miriam).

(6) Baudelaire, *Mon Coeur mis à Nu*, XXI: "The death penalty is the result of a mystic idea totally uncomprehended today. The aim of the death penalty is not to *save* society, at least not materially. Its aim is to *save* (spiritually) both society and culprit. For the sacrifice to be complete, there must be a joyful assent on the part of the victim." But torture "springs from the infamous part of man's heart . . ."

(7) Something Melville perceived clearly (letter to H. after 7G., April 16, 1851, quoted in J. Leyda, *Melville's Log*, 1951): "A certain tragic phase of humanity . . . was never more powerfully embodied than by H. We mean the tragedies of human thought in its own unbiassed, native, and profounder workings . . ." H. Schneider (*History of Am. Philosophy*) criticizes H. however for his inability to think philosophically. He is concerned with H.'s thought, however, not with the "existential," emotional and esthetic sense that H. had of tragedy. The artist need not necessarily have a head for philosophy (cf. Part Three, II, Ch. 2, IV, end). P. E. More for his part (*Shelburne Essays,* 1st series, "The Solitude of H."), acclaims H. as an American Aeschylus.

(8) S.L., V, 307.

(9) "Feathertop," II.

(10) 7G., III, 163–66 (Hep.'s company makes him sad and sullen, whereas Phoebe's restores his good humor and vivacity of mind).

(11) S.L., V, 74 (Her attire . . . seemed to express . . . the desperate recklessness of her mood . . .). Cf. "Endicott," I, 487 ("Sporting with her infamy, the lost and desperate creature had embroidered the fatal token in scarlet cloth, with golden thread and the nicest art of needlework . . .").

(12) 7G., III, 50 ("this forbidding scowl was the innocent result of her near-sightedness"). Cf. 132 ("that wretched scowl . . . her near-sightedness").

(13) 2 Samuel, 22 : 12: "And he made darkness pavilions round about him, dark waters and thick clouds of the skies."

(14) S.L., V, 74 (the halo of . . . misfortune and ignominy); 118 (inviolable circle); 279 (Magic circle); 293 (magic circle of ignominy), M.F., VI, 208 (strange lonesome paradise).

(15) M's B. V., I, 165 (ambiguity of sin and sorrow). Cf. Fogle ("An Ambiguity of Sin and Sorrow," *NEQ*, XXI, 1948), who attempts, in conformity with the theory of multiple choice, to formulate various hypotheses (obsession, pride, crime, perverse fancy) as though they were verifiable.

(16) S.L., V, 147 (Dimm.: "heaven-ordained apostle," but, 332: "the portion of him . . . the Devil claimed"); Rapp., II, 142 (the plant, Beatrice's twin sister, is also akin to those that writhe, "serpent-like," on the ground).

(17) Y. Winters, "Maule's Curse," *Amer. Rev.,* LX, 1937.

(18) N.H., critical article by Simms in *Salem Adv.,* May 2, 1846, quoted by R.S. in *Am.Lit.,* Jan. 1954.

(19) Bachelard, *Poétique de l'Espace,* 58: "to the new image, a new world."

(20) "Endicott," I, 487 ("Admirable . . . rather than Adulteress"), S.L., V, 77 ("Had there been a Papist . . ."); 195–96 ("Many people refused to interpret the scarlet A by its original signification. They said it meant Able . . ."); 292 ("Indians . . . conceiving the wearer . . . must needs be a personage of high dignity"). And the meteor, S.L. 189 ("an immense letter—the letter A . . . another's guilt might have seen another symbol in it"); 192 ("the letter A, which we interpret to stand for Angel").

(21) S.L., V, 252–53.
(22) M.F., VI, Ch. 22. Precisely for this reason this chapter is one of the book's best: D.'s grief is sufficiently heavy with its own signification.
(23) S.L., V, 284 ("What we did had a consecration of its own").
(24) 7G., III (Holgrave loves Phoebe while hating the Pyncheons).
(25) "Old Esther Dudley," I, 337 (the aged woman in the most gorgeous of her mildewed velvets and brocades); Hepzibah, 7G., 48 (a tall figure clad in black silk); 164–65 (her ridiculous dress, her turban).
(26) S.L., 195: "She was self-ordained a Sister of Mercy."

II

(1) 7G., III, 145 (the Judge prided himself . . . on never mistaking a shadow for a substance).
(2) S.L., V, 80: While Hester takes refuge in her memories, the crowd gazes at the letter "fantastically embroidered with gold thread on her bosom."
(3) M's B. V., I, 59: "a cloud seemed to have rolled duskily from beneath the black crape" and 65: "from beneath the black veil there rolled a cloud into the sunshine."
(4) S.L., V, 76–77 (ugly engine); 199 (black and weather-stained), 298 (weather-darkened scaffold).
(5) 7G., III, 42–43 ("so much had been suffered . . . that the very timbers were oozy, as with the moisture of a heart").
(6) The Gorgon ("Gorgon's Head," W. B., IV); the Phorkiades (ibid., IV, 33–35) whom H. refers to as the "Three Grey Women"; they are recognizable from the single eye and tooth they use in turn. In Part Two of *Faust*, Goethe had made admirable use of Mephistopheles' metamorphosis into such a Fate (Act II, tragedy of Helen); the Minotaur ("Minotaur," Tangle., IV); the Stymphalides ("Golden Fleece," Tangle., IV, 402) referred to by H. as birds with steel feathers.
(7) S.L., V, 77 ("that gripe about the neck . . . the proneness to which was the most devilish characteristic of this ugly engine").
(8) Ibid., 183: during Dimm.'s nighttime visit to the pillory "he felt his limbs growing stiff . . . and doubted whether he should be able to descend the steps of the scaffold); 184–85 ("the Rev. A. Dimmesdale . . . half frozen to death, overwhelmed with shame . . ."
(9) "Circe's Palace," Tangle., IV.
(10) Cf. Note 8. As for the identification with the Letter, that is the very subject of the book. It is flagrant in the mirror (armor) scene (p. 132): "the scarlet letter was represented in exaggerated and gigantic proportions, so as to be greatly the most prominent feature of her appearance."
(11) S.L., V, 127 (the scarlet letter endowed with life).
(12) Ibid., 292 ("the *repugnance* which the *mystic* symbol inspired"—the italicized words being those that express the moral and theological ambiguity).
(13) Ibid., 121–22 (Pearl's complicity with the Letter: "old expression . . . evil spirit . . . peeped forth in mockery").
(14) "Great Stone Face," III; "D's W.Im."; Sn.Im., III.
(15) S.L., V, 132 (cf. Note 10).
(16) "Old Manse," II, 16; "the *earthliest* human soul has an infinite *spiritual* capacity and may contain the better world . . ." The italics (not H.'s) emphasizing the opposition elsewhere underlined by the juxtaposition of "mud" and "flower" (p. 15) or "mud" and "marble" (7G., III, 59) in which one senses Sophia's influence.
(17) M.F., VI, 205: "the deed knots us together, for time and eternity like the coils of a serpent"; and: "Their deed . . . had wreathed itself . . . like a serpent, in inextricable links about both their souls, and drew them into one, by its terrible contractile power."
(18) S.L., V, 128.

(19) 7G., III, 149: "Judge Pyncheon could endure a century or two more of such refinement as well as most other men."

(20) Gervayse Helwyse, who allows Lady Eleanore to use him as a doormat, is a masochistic mystic ("Lady E.," I, 312); Miriam is an hysteric (M.F., VI, 186) and the Model (ibid., 185–86) performs a penance in the Colosseum worthy of a Medieval fanatic.

(21) Chill. (S.L., V), and the Model (M.F., VI, 45: his costume lending him the aspect of a hairy satyr and 176: his hands—"brown, bony talons").

(22) "Lily's Quest," II (the old man); M.F., VI (the Model).

(23) Strindberg (*Dance of Death*); Brecht (*Kaukasische Kreidekreis* and *Furcht und Elend des Dritten Reiches*); Kafka (*The Castle* is an allegory of Fate and Death); Ingmar Bergman (*The Seventh Seal*); Camus (*La Peste, Le Malentendu, Caligula*); Faulkner (*As I Lay Dying* and *Absalom*: Wash. Jones, allegory of Death armed with his scythe); Pasternak (*Dr. Zhivago*, not to mention the poems, in which the breath of death is felt constantly).

(24) M.M.M., I, 81: "give each of these bestial pagans one other dance around their idol. It would have served rarely for a whipping-post."

(25) M.F., VI, 109.

(26) M.M.M., I (irruption of the Puritans among the maypole dancers); M.F., VI, 100 (the Model appearing at the dance in the wood); Bl.R., V, 557 (grim Puritans among the maskers); 558 ("Silas Foster . . . in his customary blue frock . . . disenchanted the scene with his look of shrewd, acrid, Yankee observation . . .") and Coverdale is usually playing the role of intruder, spy, or critical observer.

(27) Honig, *Dark Conceit, the Making of Allegory*, 1959, pp. 124–25, states that H., like Kafka, could not represent the Crucifixion other than "obliquely," ironically: is not the pillory in S.L., a mutation of The Cross?

(28) S.L., V, 277: the sailors—"rough-looking desperadoes," who would be more likely to side with Morton than Endicott. Cf. Orians, "H. and M.M.M.", *MLN*, LIII, 1938: Mt. Wollaston.

(29) Ibid., 276 ("on the platform of the pillory . . . two masters of defence were commencing an exhibition . . .").

(30) Bachelard, *La Terre et les Rêveries du Repos*, 98.

(31) 7G., III, 24–25 (a house that had yet to make its place among men's daily interests) as opposed to 43–44 ("green moss . . . flower-shrubs [Alice's Posies]), and further on: "observe how Nature adopted to herself this desolate . . . house."

(32) Ibid., III, 94–95: "a chamber of very great and varied experience, as a scene of human life": love, birth, death, then solitude, desertion, awaiting its exorcism (p. 95) by light and joy.

(33) Ibid., III, 49: the oak chair is a symbol of the ancestor ("*high* back, carved *elaborately* in oak . . . *roomy depths* . . ."): Italicized words being those that evoke pride, richness, solidity, hardness, and lastly protectiveness; 93: "the tall stiff chairs, one of which stood close by her bed-side . . . as if some old-fashioned personage . . ."

(34) 7G., III, 130–31: Clifford (from the image of the hearth ["embers"] we pass on to that of the mansion in ruins ["intellectual lamps in the dark and ruinous mansion . . .]); 273–74 (the Judge: "Behold therefore a palace!"). There is even a comic analogy between the house with its flower-decorated roof and Hepzibah thinking of trimming her turban with colored ribbons (p. 165). Similarly, Hep.'s frowning aspect is also found on the house's face (p. 34: "meditative look").

(35) Ibid., 87 ("the chambers of her brain . . . lighted up with gas.")

(36) Ibid., 44 (brow). H. doesn't specify the other attributes, but we find "visage" several times (76: rusty-visaged; 104: battered visage) as well as animistic adjectives (25: thoughtful gloom; 43: meditative look; 228: cheery expression).

(37) Bachelard, *Poétique de l'Espace*, 132.

(38) 7G., III, 24–25: "a whole sisterhood of edifices *breathing* through the spiracles of one great chimney"; 49: the house visited by the sunlight; 92–93: "The morning light . . . stole into the aperture . . . betwixt those faded curtains."; Ch. 11 ("The Arched Window"): the house attracts objects magnetically.

(39) Ibid., 90: Phoebe is first "absorbed" by the shadowiness of the house before being "assimilated" to it in the form of light. Similarly, 144: the Judge in the grey atmosphere of the shop takes on the color of the place like a chameleon: at the same time, the darkness of the past begins to take a hold upon him.

(40) Ibid., 24 (pride).

(41) Ibid., 110 (looked sideways with a dark solemnity).

(42) Ibid., and P.Gold., I.

(43) 7G., III, 91: Hep., when she thinks of the reluctant lock is merely evoking the image of her own heart. And 94: Hep's deprived heart has become the deserted house ("not a guest for many years gone by, had entered the heart or the chamber").

(44) Ibid., 274: "beneath the show of a marble palace, that pool of stagnant water . . . that secret abomination . . .".

(45) Ibid., 91: "the door ought to be shoved back, and the rusty key be turned in the reluctant lock."

(46) Ibid., 204: "what other dungeon is so dark as one's own heart! What jailer so inexorable as one's self" (Cf. Milton, *Comus*: "himself in his own dungeon.")

(47) P. Gold., I, 434.

(48) Ibid., 442 (the drawing on the wall: the devil and the treasure-seeker).

(49) Grim. XIII: contrast with the *wooden* house ("P.Gold., I; S.L., 7G."). In 7G., III, 309, H. inveighs against "these heaps of bricks and stones consolidated with mortar."

(50) Bachelard, *Poétique de l'Espace*, 69. It is noteworthy that the "final house" of Cliff. and Hep. is also made of wood (p. 372).

(51) 7G., III, 372.

(52) Ibid., 221: "the house ought to be purified with fire . . ."

(53) Ibid., "The Flight of Two Owls."

(54) Ibid., 307–08: the "nomadic phase" of civilization as evoked by C. must imply the nomad's tent, now brought back into esteem by the vogue for camping.

(55) S.L., V, 104: This Colonial period cottage (little, lonesome dwelling) was situated somewhere on the shore of Back Bay, a site now occupied by a Boston residential neighborhood. Cf. Murphey, "Hester in History," *AL*, March 1960.

(56) 7G., III, 306: "This one old house was everywhere! It transported its great, lumbering bulk with more than railroad speed, and set itself phlegmatically down on whatever spot she glanced at."

(57) Ibid., 337: "as if this human dwelling, being of such old date, had established its prescriptive title among primeval oaks . . ."

(58) P.Gold., I, 449 and 451.

(59) M.F., VI, 55 (Miriam's studio at the top of an old Roman palace); 68 (Hilda's tower: "medieval . . . square, lofty . . . battlemented and machicolated at the summit"); Ch. 18 ("The Tarpeian Rock"); Ch. 24 (the Tower among the Apennines); Ch. 28 ("The Tower"); Ch. 29 ("On the Battlements"); Ch. 36 ("Hilda's Tower"), which H. makes use of again in Ch. 44: "The Deserted Shrine" and Ch. 45: "The Flight of Hilda's Doves."

III

(1) S.L., V, and M's B. V., I, 64–65 ("horror . . . interwoven in the threads).

(2) *Ethan Brand* hurls himself into the lime kiln like Empedocles into Etna (III, 496: "Come deadly element of Fire—henceforth my familiar friend!

Embrace me, as I do thee!"); *Hester* identifies herself with the red Letter (the fire of evil, sex, passion); *Miriam*, through the love she inspires and her temperament is also a creature of fire, as is *Beatrice* (Rapp., II); *Pearl* (S.L., V, 291: "Mistress Hibbins says my father is the Prince of the Air!"— who is also the Prince of Hell); *Hilda* (M.F., VI: tower and doves); *Phoebe* (7G., III, 90: "airy little jump"; 39: "like a bird in a shadowy tree . . ."; 103: "as graceful as a bird . . ."); *Hollingworth* (Bl.R., V, 352: "his features seemed to have been hammered out of iron"—his physique is that of the Titan, or the genius of the Great Stone Face). Lower in the scale of earthly spirits we find *Silas Foster*, the farmer (Bl.R., VI, 354: "Grim Silas Foster . . . perpetrating terrible enormities with the butter plate . . ." H. compares him to an ogre); and *Aminadab*, Aylmer's servant (Birth., II, 68–69, the demon of matter: "ah clod! ah, earthly mass" mocks the mind that fails in its quest for the absolute: "Thus does the gross fatality of earth exult . . ."); *Endicott* (the armored man, the man of iron); *Judge Pyncheon* (7G., III, 337: "a . . . branch . . . transmuted to bright gold": symbol of hope, but also of the lust for gold that causes the Judge's death). Cf. Havens, "The Golden Branch as a Symbol in 7G.," *MLN,* LXXIV, 1959.

(3) Pearl, dressed in red, the color of fire. Chill. (S.L., V, 156: the *fire* of his laboratory had been brought from the *lower* regions). Similarly, E.B. gives himself to the fire, but his heart remains marble (III, 498). Clifford, 7G., III, 130: "a flame which we see twinkling among half extinguished embers" (fire and earth); 133: coarser expression; 134: animal being (fresh terrestrial element); but 306: "He had a winged nature". The Judge (7G., III, 144: fleshy effulgence; 156: hot fellness of purpose—fire and earth combine in him); Phoebe, because of her liquid voice (7G., III, 99 and 168) is also a creature of water as well as air.

(4) 7G., III, 129: the objects Clifford touches seem to vanish beneath his touch ("He took hold of the knob . . . then loosened his grasp": as if the object had ceased to exist).

(5) G. C., I, 186–87: H. does not show us the stone itself but the *earthly* light that emanates from it.

(6) E.B., III, cf. P. Gold., I, 438–39: fire considered as structure, as architecture.

(7) S.L., V, 225: the melancholy stream (mournful, repining).

(8) Y.G.B., II, 104: "Did it contain water reddened by the lurid light? was it blood, or perchance a liquid flame?" (cf. H.of3H., I, 228: "green, sluggish water").

(9) 7G., III, 186 ("faces looked upward to him . . . beautiful faces, arrayed in bewitching smiles . . ."; and then in contrast: "The dark face . . ."). Cf. "Vision in F.," I, 243.

(10) 7G., III (the Elm); Bl.R., V (Coverdale's tree).

(11) Ibid., 90 (airy little jump).

(12) S.L., V, 127: Pearl (elfin dance, will o' the wisp); 128 (the witch-child's stamping); 129 ("caper and dance": the young girl-faun); M.F., VI, 29: Donatello (the very step of the Dancing Faun); 55 (the light foot of D.); 108 (dancing with frisky step).

(13) Milton, *Paradise Lost,* Bk. II, 629 *et seq.* and 927: "At last his sail-broad vans / He spreads for flight, and, in the surging smoke / Uplifted, spurns the ground . . ."

(14) S.L., V, 211.

(15) M.F., VI.

(16) 7G., III, 120 ("In Hepzibah's tone . . . there was a certain rich depth and moisture, as if the words . . . had been steeped in the warmth of her heart").

(17) S.L., V, 288–89 ("Murmur and flow . . . gushed . . .").

(18) Ibid., 289 ("the low undertone, as of the wind sinking down . . . then its volume seemed to envelop her").

(19) Ibid., 289 (burst its way through the solid walls).

(20) M.F., VI, 287 and 310.

(21) "The Pygmies," Tangle., IV. In "The Minotaur" (ibid.) we meet Talus, the robot giant. Elsewhere, the myth of the giant is fused with the paternal archetype ("Great Stone Face," III, and 7G., III, 219: the past, the house itself can be considered as a giant, and the Judge, by his death, becomes fused with the ancestor and becomes the Ogre or the Giant Despair [III, 299]).

(22) Though they do not always take the shape of Titans, they are made of the same material as terrestrial giants (Am.Nbks., R.S., 63: "a heavy, sombre . . . mass or "ledge" of clouds—looking almost as solid as rock": thus the clouds become mountains. And mountains are in any case giants, just as Atlas and Antaeus ("Pygmies," IV) are mountains.

(23) G.C., I.

(24) Letter to Weeber about E.B. ("like a tooth ill-drawn"), quoted by R.S. in Biog., 93.

(25) Prefaces: T.T.T., I, 18: his tales are akin to dreams ("Dreamland of . . . youth"), not reality. Rapp., II, 107: "The aspect and scenery of people in the clouds"; 7G., III, 16: "a Romance having a great deal more to do with the clouds overhead . . .". And Bl.R., V, 322: "Faery Land."

(26) 7G., III, S.L., V, and P.Gold., I.

(27) 7G., III, 327–28.

(28) The mirror, the inner eye, only gives back the images left in it from time to time: when the magic lantern man turns on his machine (E.B., "Main Street," III) when the Haunted Mind awakens (7G., III, 35: "a large, dim looking-glass . . . fabled to contain within its depths all the shapes that had ever been reflected there." H. had already made use of this mirror in order to give us "Howe's Masquerade," and the procession of Pyncheons and Maules (25–26) to which he was to return (pp. 330–31). Maclean, "H.'s S.L.: The Dark Problem of this Life," AL, XXVII, 1955, emphasizes the revelatory, prophetic role of mirrors in it: he characterizes the novel itself as a mirror from whose depths the characters emerge.

(29) "Man of Adamant," II.

(30) E.B., III, 480: E.B. is revealed in silhouette when Bartram opens the furnace door; he appears in person lit by the glow of the fire (479) and, once E.B. himself has stirred up the fire (484) it is by its light through the gaping furnace doors that the other characters are seen.

(31) Rapp., II: everything contributes to producing a sensation of heat—the walled garden, the tropical plants, the scents, Beatrice's "oriental" beauty (127: "the Oriental sunshine of her beauty").

(32) S.L., V, 210 (black flower); the Black Veil (M's B. V., I) exists in all H.'s serious tales.

(33) Bl.R., V, and H.of3H., I.

(34) S.L., V (Boston); M.F., VI (Rome); 7G., III (Salem).

(35) S.L., V, ("The Market Place").

(36) See illustrations to Jung's Psychologie und Alchemie. The double hour-glass shape may also be thought of as a mandala.

(37) H.of3H., I.

(38) M.F., VI, Ch. 3 (the Catacombs); 182–84 (the Colosseum whose arches serve as niches and hiding-places, cf. Miriam, 186); 225–26 (the charnel-house); 310 (M.'s voice emerging from the secret chamber below); 473 (Hilda's disappearance: "prisoner in one of those religious establish-ments"); 479 (discovery of the Venus in a "cellar-like cavity").

(39) Ibid., 182 (Colosseum); 173 (Fontana di Trevi): both depicted at night, by moonlight.

(40) It.Nbks., X, 219: expression taken from Byron (Childe Harold).

(41) P. Gold., I: the house (the loft window looks out on the sky, but if one digs in the cellar one goes toward hell); Rapp., II (Giovanni's observatory and the garden); Birth., II (the laboratory with its metaphysical dimensions: Aylmer's mind attempting to raise itself through alchemy—sublimation; the "ideal" setting in which Georgiana lives, 55–56: "a pavilion among the clouds"—but matter refuses to follow his ascent; the laboratory is in contrast with the "boudoir"; 63, and Aminadab's laugh plunges us into the depths of the abyss.

(42) "Buds and Bird Voices," II, 175: "there is no decay."

(43) S.L., V, 290: "the whole *orb* of life . . . was connected with this *spot*"; this image of the circle and its center is valid for all the main characters in the book.

(44) Woodberry, *H.*, 1902, Ch. 5: "This romance is the record of a prison-cell unvisited by any ray of light", which lead hims, on p. 203, to this conclusion: "in the highest sense, it is a false book."

(45) 7G., III, 193–94.

(46) Ibid., 48–49: the sun never "forgets" the House; 92, H. again notes the Sun's punctual visitation of the House; 189: the westering sun (when the seven gables cease to be sunlit, 190, life withdraws for Clifford). Similarly the moon (254) sheds its light expressly upon the old house in order to give it a new luster.

(47) S.L., V: if one considers the forest as being underground.

(48) Bl.R., V, 586.

(49) Coverdale's name is moreover symbolic: it evokes once again the veil. H. probably found it in a biographical dictionary (English preacher of 15th cent., translator of the Bible). F. K. Davidson, "Toward a Re-evaluation of Bl.R.," *NEQ*, XXV, 1952, lays great stress on the symbol of the veil.

(50) Bl.R., V, 350–51.

II: ART

CHAPTER 1

I

(1) Lewisohn, *Expression in America*, 1932, pp. 172–73, quotes T. Mann to support his thesis: the "normal" artist is seeking to justify his self.

(2) M.F., VI, 388.

(3) Ibid., 167–68.

(4) Letter quoted in R.S., Biog., 11.

(5) "Solitary Man," XII, 40.

(6) Corresponding to the Solitary Man's "let me remind him that he is an American," we have James's phrase "just by being American enough," from his *H.*, 1879.

(7) D's W.I., II, and 7G., III. Cf. Helen D. Schubert, "H. as Puritan Artist." Master's Thesis, Cornell, 1939. Among Drowne's famous works were: Indian Archer weathercock, Old Province House (cf. *Legends of Province House*, II, 272: "gilded Indian") and Grasshopper weathervane, Faneuil Hall.

(8) Ibid., II, 355 and 361.

(9) Frost, "Paul's Wife" (*Poems*, Modern Library, p. 211).

(10) A.o.B., II, Cf. Fogle, *H.'s Fiction: The Light & the Dark*, 83, who limits himself to the obvious symbolism.

(11) "Song of Myself," 52: "my barbaric yawp over the roofs of the world."

(12) Woodberry, *N.H., How to Know Him*, decided that it was then still too early to say whether or not H. was a classic, defining him as a provincial

author (Ch. 6) and claiming that S.L. owed much of its success to anti-
puritan feeling at the time and the Transcendentalist movement (Ch. 5).

(13) D's W. Im., II, 353.

(14) H. admired Trollope for his "substance" (Eng.Nbks., quoted by R.S.,
Biog., 219) and Dickens for his vitality (ibid., R.S., 36). Cf. Roper,
"The Originality of H.'s S.L.," *DR*, XXX, 1950: "H. wrote the kind of
fiction he had to write, not the kind he admired."

(15) E.B., II, 477.

(16) "Old Manse," II, 13: "a novel that . . . should possess substance enough
to stand alone."

(17) If we follow the chronological order established by E. C. Lathrop (*A Study
of the Sources*) this phenomenon will appear clearly enough from a comparison of the works' principal themes. Typical examples will be found
in the next few notes.

(18) A.Doane (the orphans, sexual guilt); H.of3H. (the witch, the guilty
daughter); R.M.'sB. (the guilty son); My Kinsman (orphan, labyrinth).

(19) R.M.'sB. (forest); My Kinsman (the city); Y.G.B. (the forest, the night).

(20) 7Vag. (the joyful cortege); "Canterbury Pilgrims" (the melancholy procession); *Sketches from Memory* (journey); A.G. (quest for fame);
G.C. (quest for the ideal).

(21) M's B.V. (guilty conscience); "Sunday at H." (the room); "Prophetic
Pictures" (secret consciousness); F.'s Sh.B. (remorse); "Man of Adamant"
(egocentric self); "Monsieur du Miroir" (Narcissus).

(22) "Gothick" pieces: "Graves and Goblins"; "White Old Maid". Various
sketches: "Little Annie"; "Town Pump"; "Old News". Poetic fantasies:
"Vision of the Fountain." These works are close neighbors to "Haunted
Mind," "Wakefield," and D. in Mss.

(23) P. Gold., Dr. H.'s Exp., and "Sylph Etherege": all three tales written
1836–37.

(24) "A Bell's Biography," III, 503.

(25) "Night Sketches," II.

(26) We ought also to add Rapp., II, despite its much earlier date (1844).

(27) Baudelaire, *Mon Coeur mis à nu*, I, Ed. de Cluny, p. 129.

(28) Fields, *Yesterdays with Authors,* states that he urged H. to "elaborate"
his story, to add sufficient material to make it into a "romance." H. originally intended the *Letter* to take up only 200 pages, the rest of the volume
to be taken up with shorter works (*Old-Time Legends together with
Sketches Experimental and Ideal*). In any case, the *Letter* as it appears in
the definitive edition does not even make up 250 pages, including the conclusion. In order to make it up to the 300-page mark we have to include
the 60 pages of the introductory "Custom House."

(29) 7G., III ("Alice Pyncheon"); Bl.R., V ("The Silvery Veil"); M.F., VI
("Myths").

(30) "Custom House," V, 56–57: he confesses his inability to reproduce the
"picturesque" language of his colleagues directly.

(31) Ibid. 57: "a better book than I shall ever write was there . . ."

(32) Bergson, *Le Rire*, Ch. 3, 1947.

(33) Bl.R., V, Ch. 27 ("Midnight"); A. Turner, "Autobiographical Elements in
Bl.R.," *UTSE*, XV, 1935, admires!

(34) Philip Rahv, "Dark Lady of Salem," *Image and Ideas*, 1947.

(35) André Breton, "Premier Manifeste du Surréalisme," 1924 (*Les manifestes
du Surréalism*, 1946, pp. 18–19).

(36) Guillevic, *Carnac*, 1961.

(37) Frost, *Poems*, Modern Library, 1946, p. 35 ("Mending Wall").

(38) A. Robbe-Grillet, *La Jalousie*, 1957.

(39) Hamsun, in particular *Hunger,* and Broch, *La Mort de Virgile, Le Ten-
tateur.*

(40) E. B., III, 489.

(41) Am.Nbks., IX, 219: "Lights and shadows . . . flitting across my inward sky."

II

(1) Horatio Bridge, *Journal of an African Cruiser,* Introduction by N.H.
(2) Mosses., II, 41.
(3) Introduction by G. P. Lathrop, V, 13.
(4) A. Miller, *Collected Plays,* Introduction, 38.
(5) Bachelard, *Poétique de l'Espace,* P.U.F., 12–13.
(6) Am.Nbks., R.S., 98.
(7) J.H., H.&W, I, 265: letter from Mrs. Peabody to Sophia (it is clear that the expression "native Apollo" denotes H., while "Plato" is Emerson). S. herself (letter of Dec. 27, 1843) refers to her husband as Apollo (273).
(8) Letter quoted by N. H. Pearson, Introd., *Complete Novels & Selected Tales by N.H.,* XIV, "In all my stories . . . one idea . . . like an iron rod."
(9) Letter of March 14, 1858, quoted by C. Ticknor, *H. and His Publisher,* 1913: ". . . I had written a Romance [M.F.]. It still required a good deal of revisions, trimming of exuberances and filling up of vacant spaces."
(10) It.Nbks., X, 333–34.
(11) M.F., VI, Ch. 39.
(12) "Night Sketches," II; *Sketches from Memory,* II, Wks. XII (Night Scene).
(13) "Toll-Gatherer's Day, a Sketch of Transistory Life," III.
(14) "Buds & Bird Voices," II.
(15) "Old Ticonderoga, a Picture of the Past," III.
(16) T. Cole, "The Course of Empire," New-York Historical Society. See Larkin, *Art and Life in America,* 203. Cole provided an example of the most unfortunate kind of artistic development when he abandoned his poetic meditations on the American landscape (E.g.: *The Oxbow*) for the frozen dream in bogus marble.
(17) Am.Nbks., IX, 209.
(18) Sonata No. 14 in C sharp minor, Opus 27, No. 2.
(19) Waggoner, *H.: A Critical Study,* 1955, "Canterbury Pilgrims" (Theme & Structure), pp. 66–68, the themes of water and moon.
(20) Wives, III, 601.

III

(1) Poe, "H.'s T.T.T.," Fordham, VI, 115–16 (the tale as made famous by H. is akin to the poem). And G. W. Curtis, letter, 1845, quoted in C. Ticknor, *H. and His Publisher,* 1913, 47–48, considers H. as a poet ("the wide Emerson, the poetic H."). W. S. Lawton, *New England Poets,* 1898, places H. beside Longfellow, Whittier, Lowell and Holmes, though this does not prevent him delivering himself of some strange opinions about "J. Inglefield" (unpleasant melodrama) and R.M.'sB. (excessive tragic atonement), while at the same time recognizing the role of the morbid in poetry. Leavis, "H. as a Poet," *SR,* LIX, 1951, (poet of contrasts).
(2) M's Bk. V., a *parable;* "Man of Adamant," an *apologue;* "The Lily's Quest," an *apologue;* "F's Show Box," a *morality;* "The Gt. Carbuncle," a *mystery* of the White Mountains; "The Snow Image," a childish *miracle;* "Feathertop," a *moralized legend.* (All these tales appear in the Riverside Edition with these descriptions as subtitles.) There is also the parable of "The Celestial Railroad," that of "The New Adam.," etc. "The Village Uncle" was originally entitled "The Mermaid: *a Reverie*" (*Token,* 1835). According to Woodberry, *H.,* 1902, p. 119, S.L., is "a *parable* of the soul's life in sin."
(3) "Mrs. Bullfrog," II, Cf. Abel, Le Sage's *Limping Devil* and "Mrs. Bullfrog," *NEQ,* April 1953 (theme of disguise—cf. Goya).
(4) "Threefold Destiny," a *fairy legend,* I; "David Swan," a *fantasy,* I.
(5) E. B., III, 492.
(6) 7G., III, 299.

(7) Ibid., 350 (some giant or ogre).

(8) Bela Bartok: *Bluebeard's Castle*. Cf. M.F., VI, 255 ("Blue Beard's Castle").

(9) 7G., III, 254 (a charm of romance). Cf. letter from Griswold to Fields, Jan. 24, 1850, quoted Marsh, "H. and Griswold," *MLN*, Feb. 1948: "The greatest literary man in this country . . . the *greatest in romance,* now writing in the English language."

(10) "Vision of the Fountain," I.

(11) M.F., VI, pp. 26, 27, 527.

(12) *Fanshawe,* XI, Ch. 5. Cf. Fielding, *Joseph Andrews.*

(13) S.L., V, 179 and 184 ("Minister's Vigil").

(14) 7G., III, 145.

(15) S.L., V, 134. Cf. "Mrs. Bullfrog," II. H. himself was severe in his judgment of this farcical tale, one of the very few he wrote (others: "The Bald Eagle" and "Reflexions in the Pillory," Goodrich, *Tales of Humor,* 1840: "As to Mrs. Bullfrog, I give her to the severest reprehension. The story was written as a mere experiment in that style; it did not come from any depths within me" (letter quoted by E. C. Lathrop, *A Study of the Sources*).

(16) N.A. & E., II, 290.

(17) "My Visit," XII, 45.

(18) N.A.&E., II.

(19) P. Gold., I, 448.

(20) This is very much the opinion of G. Bachelard, who does not seem to have read anything else by H. apart from his mythological tales. Cf. in particular: J. Corti, *L'Air et les Songes,* 1943, pp. 238–39 ("Miraculous Pitcher") and *La Terre et les Rêveries du Repos,* 1948, p. 158–59 ("Dragon's Teeth").

(21) "Dragon's Teeth," IV, 297–98.

(22) *Fanshawe,* "White Old Maid," "Wedding Knell," etc. The elements of this gothick paraphernalia have been more or less exhaustively catalogued by Jane Lundblad in *H. and the Tradition of the Gothic Romance,* 1946.

(23) Letter, Nov. 1850, quoted by J. T. Fields, *Yesterdays with Authors*: "in writing a romance a man is always, or ought to be, careering on the verge of a precipitous absurdity . . ."

(24) "Christmas Banquet," II, 324 and 332.

(25) That of the lost parchment and the mysterious crime in 7G., of the "veiled lady" in Bl.R., and of Miriam's origins in M.F.

(26) 7G., III (Holgrave and Phoebe).

(27) Marks, "Who Killed Judge Pyncheon?," *PMLA,* LIII, 1956.

(28) S.L., V, 210.

(29) 7G., III, Preface.

IV

(1) Woodberry, *H.,* 1902, Ch. 4: "his genius seemingly put forth many tendrils, seeking directions and support and growth, and gradually in these hundred tales he found himself and his art."

(2) S.L., V, 197: "All the light and graceful foliage of her character had been withered up,"; 198: "a sad transformation . . . her rich and luxuriant hair . . . cut off."

(3) Ibid., 242–43: "her hair . . . fell upon her shoulders, dark and rich."

(4) These contradictory tendencies scarcely seem to have been perceived by the critics. Cf. C. C. Walcutt, "S.L. and its modern Critics," *NCF,* 1953, and Abel, "H.'s Hester," *CE,* who emphasizes the Puritan asceticism (withered foliage), whereas J. Erskine, *CHAL,* II, 26–27, says that H. "lets the sin elaborate itself (in Hester) into nothing but beauty."

(5) J-J. Mayoux, "Vivants Piliers," *Lettres Nouvelles,* 1960, No. 6, expresses this aspect of Hawthorne's ethical and esthetic doubleness very well. Maclean, "H.'s S.L., the Dark Problem of this Life," *AL,* XXVII, 1955, emphasizes the role of the moral mirror.

(6) S.L., V, 74: "Her attire . . . seemed to express . . . the desperate reckless-

ness of her mood"; 109 (the Letter has the sensitivity of raw flesh); Ch. 6 (the torture of Pearl's gaze).
(7) "Wakefield," I; My Kinsman, III.
(8) L. Schubert, *H., The Artist, Fine Arts Devices in Fiction,* 1944, Ch. 3: Design, and H. H. Waggoner, *H., a Critical Study,* 1955, pp. 154–55, have both examined this aspect of H.'s art, but without moving outside the sphere of moral allegory (the second in particular) and above all without connecting the various elements to a central theme.
(9) Letter, Nov. 1850, quoted in J. T. Fields, *Yesterdays with Authors,* London, 1881.
(10) 7G., III, 25.
(11) Ibid., 48–50 (pictured tiles, carpet; chairs; map of the Pyncheon territory; the portrait of old Colonel Pyncheon).
(12) Ibid., 126 ("The vapor of the broiled fish arose like incense from the shrine of a barbarian idol . . ."). Cf. 24 (game and fish).
(13) Ibid., 231 (carpet; marble woman; pictures; cabinet of ebony; "the room was an emblem of a mind industriously stored with foreign ideas, and elaborated into artificial refinement . . .").
(14) S.L., V, 70 and 79–80.
(15) M.F., VI, 141.
(16) Y.G.B., II, 100.
(17) E.B., III.
(18) G.B., I, 88.
(19) "Prophetic Pictures," I; Howe's Masquerade," ibid.; 7G., III.
(20) 7G., III, 48 ("a miniature . . . in Malbone's most perfect style"), Phoebe, 103–4, more pretty than beautiful, is a better subject for a miniature than Alice, who was too proud and imposing (p. 240: "a lady born").
(21) 7G., III, 48 ("Forth she steps into the dusky, time-darkened passage, a tall figure, clad in black silk") and 158 ("Hepzibah spread out her gaunt figure across the door").
(22) Portrait of Ann Pollard by an "unknown limner," Massachusetts Historical Society, Boston (Reproduced in Larkin, *Art and Life in America,* 1950, p. 21.
(23) Am.Nbks., IX, 277.
(24) James: the heroine of the novella "The Beldonald Holbein"; Mrs. Ambient, in the Pre-Raphaelite style ("Tha Author of Beltraffio"); Mme. de Vionnet (*The Ambassadors*); Mme de Mauves, etc.
(25) P. Gold., I, 442, (charcoal sketches).
(26) S.L., V, 154 (tapestry . . . from the Gobelin looms . . . representing the Scriptural story of David and Bathsheba . . .).
(27) 7G., III, 49.
(28) Ibid., 52–53 (Jim Crow . . . in gingerbread . . . leaden dragoons).
(29) Ibid., 123 (cookery book . . . illustrated with engravings).
(30) Ibid., 49–50 (a map . . . grotesquely illuminated with pictures of Indians and wild beasts . . .).
(31) S.L., V, 245 (wolf) and earlier "a fox," "a squirrel."
(32) M.F., VI, 230–31 (A brown lizard with two tails . . . made him start).
(33) Rapp., II, 111.
(34) My Kinsman, III, 633 (wooden house with balcony and Gothic window); "Great Stone Face," III, 418 (Mr. Gathergold's house with pillared portico and tall windows); "Bosom Serpent," II, 317 (a large, somber edifice of wood, with pilasters and a balcony); S.L., V, 128–29 (the Governor's house glittering with shards of glass); 7G., III, 24 (glittering plaster). Cf. Gannon "Houses in which H. lived, thought and wrote."
(35) S.L., V, 246 (nymph-child . . . infant dryad); 249 (adornment of flowers and wreathed foliage). Cf. M.F., VI, 104 (M. and D. wreathe themselves in garlands) and M.M.M., I, 73 (the youths wearing roses, the priest wearing vine leaves).

(36) Cf. L. Schubert, *H., the Artist*, 1944, Ch. 5, notes the predominance of *red, black*, and *white*, followed by green and yellow, with blue and brown last. Waggoner, *H., a Critical Study*, 1955, 125 and 130–31, makes a particular study of the color in S.L., but without going beyond the level of moral symbolism, and in order to produce this strange conclusion: ". . . the largest generalization we may draw from a study of the approximately 425 light and color images is that H. conceived, but did not strongly feel, the possibility of escape from evil and the past" (p. 131)! Blair, "Color, Light & Shadow in H.'s Fiction," *NEQ*, XV, 1942, emphasizes the color contrasts.

(37) "Buds and Bird Voices," II, 171–72 (green blades of grass . . . verdant tracts . . . verdure). S.L., V, 214: Pearl in her green weeds ("the letter A,—but freshly *green*, instead of scarlet"). Pink, the complementary color of green, from the pictorial and psychological point of view, is also present in Pearl (126: bright complexion).

(38) "Old Manse," II, 31 (golden light); 35 (golden thought). M.F.: Schneider emphasizes the golden atmosphere (*H., the Artist*, Ch. 5) VI, 249 (glowing color . . . honey); 250 (yellow moss); 251 (yellow wash); 272 (golden wine); 296 (sunny smile). But in the expression "the purple air of Italy" the obsession with red returns, reborn from the contact with Catholicism (scarlet superstition, 473) and its stained glass windows (flame of scarlet, 417). As to richness, the following may be noted: "gilded staff" (M.M.M., I, 72); "golden corn"; "dish covers of gold"; "silver gilt"; "pure gold"; "woven gold"; "pillar of gold" (P.Gold., I, 435–36); "gold-headed cane"; "solid realities, such as gold"; "cornices . . . gilded." (7G., III, 148 and 273); branch . . . transmuted to bright gold" (7G., III, 337).

(39) M.M.M., I, 72 (melancholy forest . . . black wilderness); M's B. V., I, 69: the mosses in the graveyard (though L. Schubert, in *H., the Artist*, Ch. 5, sees them as a splash of green) do not escape the black contagion. Moreover H. does not mention their color. But in S.L., V, 160, he definitely writes "*black* weeds."

(40) "Buds and Bird Voices," II, 172.

(41) G.B., I, 87: "grey frieze cloak" characterizing the moral and physical atmosphere.

(42) "Lily's Quest," I, 501 (whiteness of marble—the pallor of the beloved about to die).

(43) M.M.M., I, 76–77: the spring is *green*, but the summer and fall are *red* ("roses of the deepest blush" then "red and yellow gorgeousness"). Cf. Nbks., IX, 268, Oct. 1841 (motley picture . . . shades of color . . . Autumn in her cloak of russet-brown). And winter, like a ray of frozen sunlight, is also gilded.

(44) "G.B.," 187–88 ("low, straw-thatched houses"—the thatch turned grey by the harsh weather—and "autumn wind . . . leaves . . . fir-trees . . . hillock of fresh-turned and half-frozen earth").

(45) S.L., V, 223–24: the "Darksome shade" of the forest transferred to the human tragedy—the "events of somber hue."

(46) Ibid., 227 (grey twilight . . . cloudy sky . . . heavy foliage).

(47) M.M.M., I, 70 (banner colored like the rainbow); 7 Vag., I, 399 ("her gay attire, combining the rainbow hues of crimson, green, and deep orange . . .").

(48) S.L., V, 242–43: "the sunshine pouring a very flood into the *obscure* forest, gladdening each *green* leaf, transmuting the *yellow* fallen ones into gold . . .". And we must remember that the *red* letter has just been thrown down among these latter.

(49) Y.G.B., II, 98: " 'Faith!' shouted Goodman Brown, in a voice of agony . . . cry of grief, rage and terror . . . piercing the night"; 99: "a scream drowned . . . in a louder murmur of voices . . ."; and even Goodman B.'s

laughter (p. 100): "blasphemy . . . shouting . . . laughter . . . echoes . . . a hymn rolling solemnly . . . many voices." Lastly, the chorus "of all the sounds of the benighted wilderness pealing in awful harmony together," which recalls the last movement of the *Symphonie Fantastique*. Though Schubert's allusion to Beethoven's Ninth Symphony (*H., the Artist*, Ch. 5) is really going a little too far.

(50) S.L., V, 133.

(51) Ibid., 74: "that Scarlet Letter, so fantastically embroidered," 73: "red cloth" with its complementary color in the "gold thread"; 132: the mirror —"the scarlet letter . . . in exaggerated and gigantic proportions." Schubert (*H., the Artist*, Ch. 7). tells us that the Letter is named 90 times.

(52) Ibid., 107: "Her . . . dress was of . . . the most *somber hue*"—the Letter against a black background.

(53) In his Ninth Symphony, Beethoven apparently intended to express his entire poetic and musical conception of the universe, starting from chaos and the birth of the world, going on to evoke the struggle between Dionysian paganism and Christianity, suggested by overlapping themes, and finally depicting man's irresistible ascent toward the light. M.F. could scarcely be claimed to provide an equivalent for anything more than the central section.

(54) We have only to compare the scenes in which Pearl exercises her magic power (or black spells) over plants, animals, and human beings, with that in which Donatello attempts to tame the denizens of the forest (M.F., VI, 287).

(55) Rapp., II, 207, Introd.: "not altogether destitute of fancy or originality."

(56) A.Doane, XII, 288 (moonlight, aurora borealis and hoarfrost); A.o.B., II, 505 (the forge); Rapp., II, 111 (the garden).

(57) "M'sB.V.," I, 59: "catching a glimpse of his figure in the looking-glass, the black veil involved his own spirit in the horror with which it overwhelmed all others."

(58) G.C., I, 186–87. Moffitt Cecil, "H.'s Optical Device," *Am. Quart.*, XV, 1963, emphasizes H.'s indirect vision.

CHAPTER 2

I

(1) Dion-Levesque, "N.H., un 'Puritain' au Pays de la Liberté," *La Patrie du Dimanche*, Montreal, Oct. 30, 1960: "Like Poe, who influenced him, . . . H. only lived at night."

(2) "F's Sh.B.," I, Am.Nbks., IX, 179–80 ("a German . . . with this diorama in a wagon"). Cf. E.B., III, and "Main Street," ibid., and 7 Vag., I, 400.

(3) M.F., VI, 318–19: "Adam saw it [Eden] in a brighter sunshine, but never knew the shade of pensive beauty which Eden won from his expulsion." Cf. Lewis, *The American Adam*, 1955, p. 126.

(4) L. Schubert, *H., the Artist*, 1944, Ch. 5: "H. has a graphic mind, he thinks in pictures." But Schubert is thinking only in terms of paintings, he ignores the cinematic aspect.

(5) Christmas Banq.," II, 345 (Gervayse Hastings).

(6) 7G., III, 127 (Hepzibah).

(7) Ibid., 177–79: "ruinous arbor, or summer-house . . . green play-place of flickering light," and 254–55 (the same arbor by moonlight).

(8) S.L., V, 187–88 (the meteor).

(9) G.C., I, 180.

(10) It.Nbks., X, 333–34.

(11) M.M.M., I, 79 ("some of the black shadows have rushed forth in human shape.")

(12) S.L., V, 72: "like a black shadow emerging into sunshine."

(13) Albert Pinkham Ryder, contemporary of Whistler, considered by some to be the American Van Gogh.
(14) G.C., I, 186–87.
(15) S.L., V, 220–21.
(16) Ibid., 243: "dark and rich, with at once a shadow and a light."
(17) Ibid., 243: "transmuting . . . to gold."
(18) "The Vision of the Fountain," I, 248.
(19) 7G., III, 130: "Phoebe . . . threw a cheerfulness about the parlor, like the circle of reflected brilliancy around the glass vase of flowers."
(20) Wives, III, 600 (passing of the lamp and movements of the furniture).
(21) Ibid., 601.
(22) Ibid., 602.
(23) Ibid., 604.
(24) Ibid., 605.
(25) "Wedding Knell," I and Bl.R., V, Ch. 13 ("The Silvery Veil").
(26) "M'sB.V.," I, 54: "It shook with his . . . breath, as he gave out the psalm."
(27) S.L., V, 82: "A writhing horror . . . like a snake."
(28) Ibid., 140: "pale . . . emaciated . . . large, dark eyes . . . melancholy depth."
(29) Ibid., 142.
(30) 7G., III, 120.
(31) Ibid., 326–27: "swarthy whiteness."
(32) M.F., VI, Ch. 13 (Miriam in Kenyon's "dreary" studio); Ch. 30, p. 314 (K. working on the bust of D. accidentally rediscovers the ferocious expression his friend wore on the night of the crime).
(33) S.L., V, 156: "his visage was getting sooty with the smoke."
(34) 7G., III, 144.
(35) "Soft focus" was first used in an American movie by Griffith in *Broken Blossoms* in 1919.
(36) 7G., III, 50 (her near-sightedness); 50–51 (she looks at herself in a "dim looking-glass"); 132–33 (her features, when she is in the grip of emotion, disappear behind the "warm and misty glow").
(37) An essential element in the *unity* of the tale (Stiblitz, "Unity in H.'s M's B. V.," *AL*, XXXIV, 1962).
(38) 7G., III, 126: "butter . . . smelling of clover-blossoms and diffusing the charm of pastoral scenery through the dark-panelled parlor."
(39) "Village Uncle," I, 149.
(40) H.of3H., I, 229–30.
(41) Wives, III, 601 and 604.
(42) Y.G.B., II.
(43) My Kinsman, III.
(44) 7G., III, 47: "a rustling of stiff silks; a tread of backward and forward footsteps."
(45) Ibid., 122: "footsteps mounting the stairs . . . strange, vague murmur."
(46) Ibid., 327–28: "That puff of the breeze was *louder* . . . a tone . . . dreary and sullen . . . *bemoaned* itself . . . It now comes *boisterously* . . . The old house *creaks* . . . vociferous . . . *bellowing* . . . A *rumbling* kind of a bluster *roars* . . . A door has *slammed* . . . what wonderful *wind-instruments* are these old timber mansions . . . which *sing,* and *sigh,* and *sob,* and *shriek* . . ."
(47) Ibid., 332.
(48) Bl.R., V, 423: "This is your forest of Arden," Westervelt says to Coverdale.
(49) M.F., VI, 221: "blood had begun to ooze from the dead monk's nostrils."
(50) "Sylph Etherege," III, 514–15.
(51) Wives, III, 598.
(52) S.L., V, 140: "a voice sweet, tremulous, but powerful, insomuch that the hall reechoed, and the hollow armour rang with it . . ."
(53) Wives, III, 599.
(54) Y.G.B., II, 98: "Aloft in the air . . . a confused and doubtful sound of

voices." Cf. S.L., V, 181: "the noise of witches, whose voices, at that period, were often heard to pass over the settlements or lonely cottages, as they rode with Satan through the air."

(55) S.L., V, 180–81: "an outcry that went pealing through the night, and was beaten back . . . and reverberated from the hills . . . as if a company of devils . . . had made a plaything of the sound, and were bandying it to and fro." Cf. M.M.M., I, 78: "when a psalm was pealing from their place of worship, the echo which the forest sent them back seemed often like the chorus of a jolly catch, closing with a roar of laughter."

(56) Y.G.B., II, 90.
(57) Ibid., 92.
(58) Ibid., 94.
(59) Ibid., 96.
(60) Ibid., 97.
(61) Ibid., 98.
(62) Ibid., 100.
(63) Ibid., 102.
(64) Ibid., 105.
(65) S.L., V, 78: "the heavy weight of a thousand unrelenting eyes."
(66) Ibid., 166: "an eye bright with intense and concentrated intelligence," and 169: "a wild look of wonder, joy and horror."
(67) Ibid., 78: "she felt . . . as if she must needs shriek out."
(68) Ibid., 133: Similarly, Miriam's exclamation in the church, which seems to topple the statues of the popes and endow them with the power of speech (M.F., VI, 404).
(69) S.L., V, Ch. 12 ("The Minister's Vigil").
(70) Ibid., 229–304.

II

(1) 7G., III, 35: "a large, dim looking-glass . . . was fabled to contain within its depths all the shapes that had ever been reflected there." These images, either by magic or mesmerism, are able to reappear.
(2) S.L., V, 177.
(3) Dr. H's Exp., I, 269–70.
(4) "Vision of the Fountain," I.
(5) 7G., III, 186: "The dark face gazes at me!"
(6) M.F., VI, 175: "Three shadows . . . all so black and heavy that they sink in the water! There they lie at the bottom, as if all three were drowned together."
(7) 7G., III, 116–17.
(8) Ibid., Ch. 2: We do not see Hep. in person but only her reflection in the glass (p. 47: "in the oval, dingy-framed toilet-glass"; 50–51: "gazing at herself in the dim looking-glass").
(9) F's Sh. B., I, 251: "through the brilliant medium of his glass of Madeira, he beheld three figures." L. Schubert (H. the Artist, Ch. 2) makes comparisons with Chagall and Kandinsky.
(10) M.F., VI, 85: "her expression had become almost exactly that of the portrait"; 86–87: she identifies with Beatrice and laments for her: "Poor sister Beatrice!"
(11) S.L., V, 154. Maclean ("H.'s S.L., the Dark Problem of This Life," AL, XXVII, 1955), who sees mirrors even in the trees and rocks, does not think of this rather obvious example.
(12) M.F., VI, 167: "the demon . . . scowls vindictively at the Archangel, who turns his eyes away in painful disgust," and 168: "this strong, writhing, squirming dragon . . . is Miriam's Model!"
(13) "Sylph Etherege," III, 508–9.
(14) Ibid., 510.
(15) Ibid., 512.

(16) Ibid., 513.
(17) Ibid., 517.
(18) "Christmas Banq.," II, 345.
(19) S.L., V, 142–43.
(20) 7G., III, 127.
(21) Eisenstein: *Ivan the Terrible.*
(22) King Vidor: *Hallelujah!*
(23) Griffith: *The Birth of a Nation.*
(24) Ingmar Bergman: *The Seventh Seal.*
(25) Marcel Carné: *Les Visiteurs du Soir.* Cf. Bl.R., V, 334 and 346–48.
(26) Cocteau: *L'Eternel Retour.* Cf. "Vision," I, 248, and "Village Uncle," I, 350.
(27) Seastrom: *The Scarlet Letter* (1927). Lillian Gish played Hester and Lars Hanson, Dimmesdale.
(28) S.L., V, 72–73: "the door of the jail being flung open . . ."
(29) Ibid., 243: "a radiant and tender smile . . ."
(30) Ibid., 77–78: the sombre gathering of notables around the pillory; 253: by taking back the sign of her shame and hiding her hair again, Hester withers herself, shrinks, blows herself out.
(31) Ibid., 132: the mirror and the armor.
(32) Ibid., 85–86: Hester in the pillory and Dimmesdale on the balcony; 154–55: laboratory and oratory.
(33) Ibid., 122: mother and daughter (the reflection in Pearl's eyes); 242–43: mutual transformation of Hester and Dimm. rediscovering their love.
(34) Ibid., 79–80: Hester in the pillory recalling her memories.
(35) Ibid., 77: "through the chamber . . . glided Hester Prynne."
(36) Ibid., 79–80: "reminiscences . . . came swarming back upon her . . . an instinctive device of her spirit to relieve itself."
(37) Ibid., 222 (Hester in Pearl's eyes); 132 (the letter in the armor).
(38) Ibid., 304: "murmur that rolled so heavily after the departed spirit."
(39) Ibid., 185–86.
(40) Wladimir Jankelevitch, "Le Romantisme allemand," No. spécial *Cahiers du Sud,* May–June, 1937, p. 77: "Darkness is a good conductor; in the dark, all sorts of communications are made between souls . . . the night is immanence."
(41) This eye may be a character into whom the author projects himself. As with Coverdale in Bl.R., Cf. Hoffman, *Form and Fable in American Fiction,* p. 216.
(42) 7G., III, 117 (the light of day—i.e., the "truth").
(43) M.F., VI, 417: "give me—to live and die in—the pure, white light of heaven!" It is the moralist speaking, not the artist.
(44) "Old W's Tale," XII, 111–12; "Custom House," V, 54–55; 7G., III, 254.
(45) Am.Nbks., IX, 112–13: "red light . . . people . . . look warm and kindled with mild fire. A love-scene should be laid on such an evening." Cf. the firelight in "Village Uncle," I; E.B., III; and the reflection of the Letter.
(46) M.F., VI, 417.
(47) S.L., V, 72–73.
(48) Ibid., 220–21.
(49) 7G., III, 193–94 ("The Arched Window"). Fogle, *H.'s Fiction: The Light and the Dark,* p. 138: "the window is the eye of the house."
(50) Rapp., II, 110 (Giovanni . . . looked down into the garden); 7G., III ("Arched Window"); S.L., V, 163–64 (looking from the open window).
(51) 7G., III, 304 (as if swallowed by an earthquake).
(52) Ibid., 92–93.
(53) Ibid., 286.
(54) Ibid., 345.
(55) Ibid., 48.
(56) S.L., V ("The Interior of a Heart," "The Minister's Vigil").

(57) Ibid., 77 (as Hester climbs up to the pillory—her pedestal—the camera swings down into the crowd and creates a meditative, religious pause).

(58) "David Swan," I.

(59) "P.Gold., I, 442.

(60) Sjöberg, *The Road to Heaven*; Bergman, *The Seventh Seal*.

III

(1) 7G., III, 144 (the shadow of the elm that invites the passer-by to halt beneath it); 17: "for the sake of passing through the shadow of these two antiquities"; 207: the Judge's menacing pause.

(2) Ibid., 199: "each man's visage, with the perspiration and weary self-importance on it . . .).

(3) Ibid., 304 (the world racing past); 306 (This one old house was everywhere! It transported its great, lumbering bulk with more than railroad speed . . .).

(4) S.L., V, 297 ("How feeble and pale he looked").

(5) Waggoner, *H.*, 65, refers to "Canterbury Pilgrims" as a pageant.

(6) E.B., III.

(7) 7G., III, 196–98. Though not exact homologues of the characters in the book, these little figures do symbolize certain of their physical or moral aspects: "the lady with her fan" (Alice); "the milkmaid" (Phoebe); "a miser" (the Judge). Holgrave is partly represented by both the man with the book and the lover. Only Hepzibah is not caricatured in this puppet-gallery.

(8) Howe, "H. and American Fiction," *Am.Merc.*, LXVIII, 1949, also feels that there is a "change of tone" in the second part of Bl.R., in which allegorical rigidity gains predominance.

(9) 7G., III, 47 (drawers pulled in and out, chairs moved, etc. . . .).

(10) We shall examine the grouping of the chapters of S.L. into movie sequences later. This grouping is achieved less and less satisfactorily in the later books. Among the attempts made to divide H.'s novels into more or less equal sections, we would call the attention of the reader to the following:

——— S.L.: Gerber, "Form and Content in SL," NEQ, March 1944 (four equal parts, six chapters each, based on the fragile idea of the dramatic predominance of one or other of the characters. As though each protagonist were given the whole stage in turn). Schubert, *H., The Artist*, Ch. 7 (play in three acts: eight scenes in the first, seven in the second, nine in the third—with the great scene in "two": "Minister's Vigil"—which may seem convincing at first glance. But can one have both the minister's inner torments and Hester's daily life in the same "act"? One can in a film sequence, of course.) Ryscamp, "New England Sources of S.L." *AL*, Nov. 1959: four acts, each being one of four moments in the seven years (S.L., V, 194: "seven years old") of Hester's penance (I: June 1642, the Pillory; II: summer 1645, visit to Governor; III: a May night of 1649, the pillory at night; IV: end of May or early June 1649); the chronology being established from the starting-point of Winthrop's death (May 26, 1649) and the probable date of his successor's election sermon (S.L., V, 182: "Minister's Vigil," and Ch. 22: "Procession").

——— 7G.: Schubert (*H. the Artist*, Ch. 2) bases his division on the number seven (seven gables, seven characters, including Ned H.: but one could also include Dixie and his companion, Mrs. Gubbins, etc. . . . and seven ghosts: in fact they are legion, and lastly, three times seven chapters —which is conceivable—the first "act" ending with the arrival of the guest and the second with Phoebe's departure—but not seven times three (since Ch. 12 would then be separated from the following two, with which it forms a whole: story of Holgrave, story of Alice, and Phoebe's departure).

—————— Bl.R.: Schubert sees the possibility of a division into two sections: before and after Holl. and Coverdale's quarrel (Ch. 15) which provides only a very loose structure, but then the book is in fact very loosely constructed.

—————— M.F.: Merle E. Brown, "Structure of M.F.," *Am.Lit.*, Nov. 1956, sees a symbolic parallelism in the successive "transformations" of the four protagonists. It is hard to see, though, why each should need a quarter of the book to itself. Or, above all, what transformation the frigid Hilda and Kenyon are supposed to undergo.

(11) My Kinsman, III: Schubert divides it into two parts, the second being "like a scene in the centre of an involved spiral."

(12) "Haunted Mind," I, 347–48.

(13) The technique of "cross-cutting" or "inter-cutting" was first experimented with by Griffith in "The Lonely Villa" in 1903. He brought it to its highest degree of perfection in *Intolerance*.

(14) Rapp., II, comprises seven sections in effect: four "male" sections and three "female" sections," to employ Schubert's terminology—doubtless inspired by the Beethovian comparisons he makes. Rosenberg, "H.'s Allegory of Science," *AL*, XXXII, 1960, sees it as a linearly developed scientific allegory.

(15) Schubert also splits A.o.B. into two sections: "four major separated by three minor."

(16) Such as the opening phrase of Ch. 6 (V, 113: "we have as yet hardly spoken of the infant") or that on p. 145 ("Under the appellation of Roger Chillingworth . . . the reader will remember") and also Ch. 11, p. 170 ("After the incident last described").

(17) *The Scarlet Letter*, V, Ch. 3–Ch. 4.

(18) Ibid., Ch. 11–Ch. 12.

(19) Ibid., Ch. 14–Ch. 15.

(20) Ibid., Ch. 20–Ch. 21.

(21) The first three sequences are of equal length and each take up four chapters. The fourth takes up three (13, 14, and 15). Ch. 20 is a toss-up, since it is not an integral part either of the metamorphosis sequence or that of the procession.

In *The House of the Seven Gables,* the sequences are already less well defined and connected:

Seq. 1: Ch. 1 (Introduction).
Seq. 2: Chs. 2, 3, 4 (Hepzibah: Rembrandtesque shots).
Seq. 3: Chs. 5, 6, 7 (Phoebe, Hep., Cliff.: intimate interiors).
Seq. 4: Ch. 8 (the Judge).
Seq. 5: Chs. 9, 10, 11 (Clifford).
Seq. 6: Chs. 12, 13, 14 (Holgrave and Phoebe).
Seq. 7: Chs. 15, 16 (conflict between Judge and Hepzibah).
Seq. 8: Ch. 17 (Flight of Two Owls).
Seq. 9: Ch. 18 (Governor Pyncheon).
Seq. 10: Chs. 19, 20, 21 (Paradise regained).

In Bl.R. it is much easier to assign each chapter an organic function, since the work is a strictly worked out allegory:

Ch. 1 (Introduction); Ch. 2, 3, 4, 5 (the story of Blithedale is introduced beneath the signs of fire and ice); Chs. 6, 7, 8, 9 (Coverdale's illness: a sort of purification on the threshold of the New Eden); Chs. 10, 11, 12, 13 (the alien, the intruder: the New Eden is not impervious to evil); Chs. 14, 15, 16 (break between C. and Holl.: where evil has entered harmony no longer reigns); Chs. 17, 18, 19, 20, 21, 22, 23 (town sequence: the lair of evil); Chs. 24, 25, 26 (Interlude: the masque—and the tragedy: Zenobia's disillusion); Ch. 27 (the suicide: the happy valley becomes the valley of death); Chs. 28 and 29 (Z.'s funeral oration—Holl. the defeated giant: the dream of the happy valley has caused a great deal of suffering for nothing).

In M.F., the grouping of chapters is more difficult: the material, especially after Ch. 19 ("The Faun's Transformation"), is drawn out to excessive lengths, the story is kept going without sufficient dramatic motivation, until Ch. 50, after the event that should, according to the law of tragedy, have been the catastrophe.

(22) S.L., V, 91: "a lurid gleam."

(23) Ibid., 100.

(24) Ibid., 144 ("Hist! hist!").

(25) Ibid., 213-14: "snail-shells . . . jelly-fish . . . sea-foam . . . grey bird . . .seaweed . . . eel-grass."

(26) Ibid., 258: "an impression of change; 259: "his own church . . . so very strange"; 260: "total change of dynasty and moral code."

(27) Many critics have not noticed this: Woodberry, *H.*, 1902, Ch. 5, accuses H. of "deforming" reality and slandering the Puritans. In his second book, *N.H., How to Know Him* (1918) he renews his attacks, describes S.L. as an artificial work, and seems more struck with its "arbitrary" symbolism than with its art (p. 143 *et seq.*); Gates, *Studies and Appreciations,* 1910, finds the meteor symbol artificial; Roper, "Originality of H.'s S.L.," *DR,* XXX, 1950, criticizes the characters, the allegory and the technique as being the "stock material of sub-literary fiction"; Maclean's clumsy praise in H.'s "SL., the Dark Problem of This Life," *AL,* XXVII, 1955 (he discovers a "triple heroic quest" in the book that does not include Hester!) does nothing to redress the balance. N. H. Pearson, however, in "H.'s Usable Truth," 1949, writes that: "as for significance . . . S.L., is like . . . *Paradise Lost*" (p. 14).

(28) Woodberry blames H. precisely for having written a despairing book: "in the highest sense, it is a false book. It is a chapter in the literature of moral despair." (*N.H.,* 1902, p. 203).

IV

(1) "Footprints," I, 507: "retrace our steps . . . our tracks. Thus, by tracking our footprints in the sand, we track our own nature in its wayward course": and at each step he reconstructs the deeds accomplished according to the traces left upon the shore.

(2) 7G., III, 49-50 (the chairs, the ancestor's chair, the map, the portrait).

(3) E.B., III, 490-93: Ethan Brand sees the enormous hand of Fate in the diorama. Then his laugh disperses the curious onlookers, who go back into the darkness—the box—from which they have been taken.

(4) 7G., III, particularly Ch. 8 ("The Pyncheon of To-Day") and Ch. 18 ("Governor Pyncheon").

(5) Ibid., 136 (memory of the garden as he saw it when a child): "An open window! . . . Those flowers . . ." mingled with the possible memory of a lost sweetheart recognized in Phoebe: "That young girl's face . . ."; 194-95 (the various carts that remind him of his childhood).

(6) "F's Sh. B., I, 253: "Conscience . . . strikes a dagger to the heart," and 254, 255, ibid.

(7) H.of3H., I, in which the lighting is a source of images. Also "Haunted Mind," ibid.

(8) Y.G.B., II and My Kinsman, III.

(9) G.B., I.

(10) "Endicott," I and S.L., V.

(11) 7G., III.

(12) Bl.R., V, 351-52: "I never thoroughly forgave Zenobia for her conduct on this occasion."

(13) 7G., III, 163: "How patiently did she endeavour to wrap Clifford up in her great warm love"; 165 (all her efforts are in vain): "she was a grief to

Clifford"; 167 (C.'s ill humor): "electric sparkle of ill-humor whenever Hepzibah endeavoured to arouse him."

(14) M.F., VI, 60 (Jael and Sisera, Judith and Holofernes, Herodias); 131: "Miriam knelt down on the steps of the fountain" (a disguised gesture of supplication).

(15) S.L., V, 230: "Had I one friend—or were it my worst enemy!"

(16) Ibid., 167: "who art thou . . . that dares thrust himself between the sufferer and his God?" Cf. M.'s B.V., I, 62: "even you, Elizabeth, can never come behind it" ("it" being his veil).

(17) 7G., III, 170–71: the solitude that suits C. is that enjoyed by the only child in its family life. He needs a home (p. 171) to be the center of.

(18) M.F., VI, 206 (the world for M. and D. is left behind). But, 233–34, their own separation is nonetheless inevitable, since they cannot see one another without at the same time seeing the murdered Model's face.

(19) Cf. Note 1, Part Two, Section I, Ch. 2, I.

(20) J-J. Mayoux, "Vivants Piliers," *Lettres Nouvelles,* 1960, No. 6. Cf. Woodberry, *N.H.,* 1902, Ch. 5, referring to S.L.: "this romance is the record of a prison-cell."

(21) Rainer-Maria Rilke, *Poésies,* translated by Betz, published by Emile-Paul, Introduction, p. 39.

CHAPTER 3

I

(1) J-J. Mayoux, "Vivants Piliers," *Lettres Nouvelles,* 1960, No. 6, remarks very justly that H. "cultivated" his illness, probably for esthetic ends.

(2) "Old Manse," II.

(3) N.A.&E., ibid.

(4) Gide, *Journal,* 1939–49, N.R.F., p. 24.

(5) Eng.Nbks., R.S., 546–47: "I beguiled my idle time for half an hour by setting down the vehicles that went past . . ." (there then follows a list that Sophia termed "trivial"). And especially the many descriptions of monuments (Conway Castle, seven pages, 79–85; Smithell's Hall, p. 106; Bebington Church, 118–19; Bond's Hospital, 139–40; Lichfield Cathedral, 149; Furness Abbey, 157; Westminster 312–13, etc.: the tedious homework of a conscientious tourist.

(6) M.F., VI, 207: "They trod through the streets of Rome, as if they . . . were among the majestic and guilty shadows . . . turned aside for the sake of treading loftily past the old site of Pompey's Forum."

(7) O'Connor, "H. and Faulkner," *Virginia Q. Rev.,* Winter 1957, links the two authors by saying that they were both "respectful of the principle of aesthetic distance."

(8) "Shaker Bridal," I.

(9) 7G., III, 219 ("Shall we never, never, get rid of this Past . . .") and 220–22 (in which he expounds his theories as though giving a lecture or sermon); 225 ("I never watched the coming of so beautiful an eve . . ."): conventional and sentimental.

(10) N.A.&E., II, 283–84 (his first concern is to provide the inhabitants of the New Eden with decorous apparel); 291 (narrow conception of the woman's role expressed in almost ludicrous terms: embroidery and a broom!)

(11) Coverdale's illness (Bl.R., V, Chs. 6 and 7) precedes his entry into the "Modern Arcadia" as though to purify him and make him worthy of it.

(12) "Footprints," I, and S.L., V, Ch. 15.

(13) "Buds & Bird Voices," II.

(14) "Old Apple Dealer," ibid.

(15) Y.G.B., II. Cf. Frost: "A Servant to Servants" (*Poems,* Modern Library, 1946, p. 74); Faulkner: *The Sound and the Fury;* and *Macbeth.*

(16) "Village Uncle," I, 351 (apparition of the "mermaid"); "Vision," I, (the water sprite). Cf. Frost, *Poems,* 211 ("Paul's Wife").

(17) Frost, *Poems,* 107.

II

(1) Remark attributed to W. C. Bryant. Moreover, as early as 1836 Park Benjamin was acclaiming the young author of G.B. as "the most pleasing writer of fanciful prose . . . in the country" (quoted R.S., Biog., p. 34). Griswold, *The Prose Writers of America,* 1856, p. 471, praised H.'s style in the following terms: "great simplicity, purity, tranquility . . . most poetic imagery . . . calm, chaste, flowing and transparent . . ." And shortly after his death, the London *Spectator,* Sept. 1864, in a review of the fragment entitled "Pansie" (cf. *Dolliver Romance*) was to place him "nearer the classical standard of English authors than any Englishman who could produce."

(2) Cf. Part Two, I, Ch. 1: "The Library."

(3) S.L., V, 71: "Marry" (Shakespearian oath); "I trow not" (archaic verb); 82: "you must needs be a stranger"; 129: "yea forsooth: bondservant." From Rev. Wilson the following examples: 85: "Hearken unto me, Hester Prynne"; 156: "Prithee young one . . . Dost know thy catechism?" And from Gov. Bellingham, 135: "I was wont to . . . how gat such a guest into my hall?" Lastly, from the witch, 264: "yonder potentate you wot of." Hester herself, when talking to Chil., employs certain archaisms, as though the presence of her husband were taking her back through time: 95: "ere thou beholdest me quaff it."

(4) E.g.: "chamber" (Am.Nbks., IX, 222: 7G., III, 94: "chamber . . .", "bed-chamber"); "egotism" ("Egotism or the Bosom Serpent," II); "adamant" ("The Man of Adamant," II; "Old Adamant Dealer," II, 503; "everlasting adamant"; "pastor" (S.L., V, "The Pastor and His Parishioner"); "minister" (ibid. and also M's B.V.); "herb" (S.L., V, 211). And also, 267–68: "drugs"; "administered"; "physician"; "medicine"; "remedies"; and 209: "Thou hadst great *elements* [term from alchemy]. Cf. E.B., III, 496: "familiar friend" [familiar demon].

(5) Am.Nbks., R.S., 14: "scientific swing" (of a man scything); 19: "a little she-brat"; 50 "unpolished bumpkins"; 248 "elderly ragamuffin" (then less respectable than now). Eng. Nbks., R.S., 322 "whipsyllabub and flummery" which has a picturesque accuracy to be set beside the pedantic lunacy of "transmogrification" (p. 157); 194 ("it is all humbug" referring to the legend of the bloody footprint), cf. Grim., ed Davidson, p. 183 (Bubble and Squeak); Eng.Nbks., R.S., 114: "Poor, Reverend devil! Drunkard, Whoremaster!" But on p. 232 we have "poor nymphs," not "whores." Similarly, H. often employs "lady" for "woman" and almost always "bosom" for "breast" (S.L., V, 174: "white bosoms"; 262 "tender bosom"); exceptions: Am.Nbks., R.S., 19 and 251–52 "the whole breast, and the apex"—a crowd scene at the Boston Theater. In Eng.Nbks., R.S., 89, we also find this piece of anatomical precision unusual for H.: "thick steaks on their immense rears." H. also employs "autumn" not "fall" (M.M.M., I, 76 "autumnal garlands . . . Autumn . . . Autumn . . ."; G.B., I, 87: "autumn wind"; Am.Nbks., IX, 218 (autumn). Lastly, in 7G., III, 320, we find the word "quidnunc" to set beside "transmogrification."

(6) See Part Two, I, Ch. 4, I, Notes 41 and 42. Also, Note 5 above.

(7) 7G., III, 65–67 (two laboring men. The expression "poor business" recurs on p. 334).

(8) Mrs. Gubbins's vulgarity, 7G., III, 341 (repetition of "Old Maid Pyncheon") is somewhat reminiscent of the market square viragos in S.L. (V, 71): "the naughty baggage"; 74 "the brazen huzzy."

(9) Howe, "H. and American Fiction," *Am. Merc.,* LXVIII, 1949, contrasts the "virile" prose of the early novels with the edulcorated style of the later ones.

(10) E.g.: the Quakers; cf. G.B., I, in which the word "friend" recurs periodical-

ly, as well as such Quaker phrases as (p. 118): "I have been moved to go forth"; (121): "Rejoice, friends!". It is permissible to wonder whether Chill.'s interlocutor in the square is not also, in H.'s mind, a member of this sect (S.L., V, 82: "You must needs be a stranger in this region, friend"; and 83: "Truly, friend"; 84: "Of a truth, friend").

(11) Danforth, A.o.B., II, employs the vocabulary of the smithy; Peter Hoverden (ibid.), that of the clockmaker; Bartham, E.B. (III), that of a lime-burner; Hepzibah and Phoebe (7G., III: "A Day Behind the Counter") that of trade; Holgrave (ibid.), that of photography; and Kenyon (M.F., VI), that of sculpture.

(12) "Endicott," I, 491-92: "Fellow-soldiers" is about the only military term.

(13) 7G., III, 83-85 (particularly in his poetic evocation of Hep.'s childhood).

(14) Y.G.B., II and E.B., III.

(15) James, H., 1879, p. 4, and, referring to 7G., p. 6: "His characters do not express themselves in the dialect of the Biglow Papers."

(16) 7G., III, 95 (dead music); 108 (sadly . . . spiritual touch); 164 (dirges . . . spiritual fingers); 378 (strain of music . . . touch of a spirit's joy).

(17) Bl.R., V, 451 (slight ethereal texture).

(18) See Part Two, II, Ch. 2, 55—Notes 4 and 7.

(19) Ibid. and Part Three, Ch. 1, I.

(20) Cel.Rlrd., II, 213 (station-house); 214 (ticket-office); 216 (brakeman, car, engine); 210 (tunnel); 221 (track); 233 (steam ferry-boat). 7G., III, 303 ("train of cars" instead of just "train," and locomotive); 304 (tickets); 306 (railroad speed). Though H. certainly does not exhaust the railroad vocabularly available. He preferred to evoke the train allegorically as a demon or magic vehicle. The passages in the Nbks. he used are scarcely any more precise (Am.Nbks., IX, 369-70). Cf. Marx, The Steam Fiend, Master's Thesis Harvard, 1949.

(21) See Part Three, II, Ch. 1, I, and Note 7.

(22) Ibid., IV, and Note 34.

(23) 7G., III, 148 (velvet doublet, sable cloak, richly worked band, steel-hilted broadsword) vs. (white collar and cravat, coat, vest . . . pantaloons, gold-headed cane).

(24) Bl.R., V, 337 (especially her hair, the flower stuck in it like a great diamond); 496 (fashionable morning-dress). Contrast with Priscilla; 350 (poor but decent gown). Leavis, "H. as a Poet", SR, LIX, 1951, sees Zenobia and Priscilla as the "two Americas" of Dos Passos—"Night sketches", Wks., I, 482: "she wears rubber overshoes."

(25) Dhaleine, H., sa Vie et son Oeuvre, 1905, p. 409, criticises H. for making excessive use of the term, thus echoing James, H., 1879, pp. 119-20.

(26) H.of3H., I, (the hollow, the lake); S.L., V, 279 (wherever Hester stood . . . a sort of magic circle—had formed itself about her).

(27) Brecht's Caucasian Chalk Circle. And "die Warheit ist konkret."

(28) Perry Miller, Jonathan Edwards, American Men of Letters, 1949, pp. 160-61.

(29) S.L., V, 76, 172, 173, 174, 180, 303.

(30) Ibid., 304.

(31) Schroeder, "That Inward Sphere [an expression taken from H.'s story "Earth's Holocaust," II, 455], Notes on H.'s Heart Imagery," PMLA, LXV, 1950, gives numerous detailed examples.

(32) Angel Clare in Tess of the d'Urbervilles.

(33) Isabel Archer (Portrait of a Lady); Mark Ambient (Author of Beltraffio); Jeffery Aspern (The Aspern Papers).

(34) Birth., II.

(35) "Sylph Etherege," I.

(36) "Village Uncle" (originally called "The Mermaid, a Reverie"), I.

(37) 7G., III (Phoebe: Greek etymology—and association with Bunyan: "the shining one").

(38) M.F., VI, 71: "I should not wonder if the Catholics were to make a saint of you like your namesake of old." Miriam's name, on the other hand, evokes her double nature (R. R. Male, *H.'s Tragic Vision*, 169, sees it as an association of Mary and "rebel"). As for Pearl, her name comes directly from the Bible (Matt. 13 : 16: "one pearl of great price"); cf. S.L., V, 138.

(39) Name probably discovered by H. in the Dictionary of National Biography. The important thing is not its origin but its symbolic value.

(40) M's B.V., I, 68 (Dark old man!).

(41) G.B., I, 83 (unhappy tree).

(42) 7G., III, 50 ("poor Hepzibah's brow"); 54 ("poor old Hepzibah"); 58 ("our miserable old Hepzibah"); 88 ("poor Hepzibah"); 162 ("our poor, gaunt Hepzibah").

(43) S.L., V, 180: ("Poor miserable man!") 265 ("The wretched minister!").

(44) 7G., III, 274.

(45) 7G., III, 117.

(46) 7G., III, 44 (this desolate, decaying, gusty, rusty old house).

(47) Ibid., 183 ("sufficiently old, withered, and experienced": of a hen). It is also to be noted that H.'s humorous style tends to include the use of pedantic and polysyllabic words: 182 (gallinacious); 183 (progenitors, antiquated, equilibrium, unscrupulousness); 184 (obstreperous); 185 (gratulation).

(48) Ibid., 215 ("the moss-grown, rotten Past"); 310 ("a rusty, crazy, creaky, dryrotted, damp-rotted, dingy, dark and miserable old dungeon").

(49) S.L., V, 180–81 (Dimm.'s cry, like a projectile into the darkness "pealing through the night . . . beaten back . . . bandied to and fro . . ."); 137 (Pearl's impulsive escape from the old man who wants to tame her: "The child . . . escaped through the open window and stood on the upper step . . . ready to take *flight*); and 299 ("The child *flew* to him" [sensing him to be her father]); ibid. ("old Roger Chillingworth . . . *thrust* himself through the crowd . . . to *snatch back* his victim . . . *rushed* forward . . . *caught* the minister . . .").

(50) 7G., III, 128–29 (Clifford's approach: "The approaching guest . . . appeared to *pause* . . . he *paused* . . . in the descent; he *paused* again . . . he made a *long pause*" [the verb becomes a noun, a thing]. Then, "took hold of" and "loosened his grasp."

(51) See previous note.

(52) S.L., V, 76 ("her sentence bore, that she should *stand* a certain time . . ."); 78 ("The unhappy culprit . . . *sustained* herself . . . under the heavy weight . . . eyes all *fastened* upon her, and *concentrated* at her bosom).

(53) 7G., III, 54 ("with so tremulous a touch that it *tumbles* upon the floor . . . she has *upset* a tumbler of marbles . . . her rigid and rusty frame *goes down* upon its hands and knees . . .")

III

(1) "Buds and Bird Voices," II, 73–74: the comparison between trees and men is already sufficiently banal without also introducing the notion of respectability into it: "still they [the apple trees] are respectable." Similarly, 176: "the gulls are far more respectable."

(2) "Custom House," V, 28–29: the official style, the style of reunion banquet speeches, solemn phrases, banal and grandiloquent metaphors (the whirlpool of political solicitudes; the pedestal of gallant services; life's tempestuous blast).

(3) 7G., III, 219 (Shall we never, never get rid of this Past?)

(4) Ibid., 149–50 ("old Colonel Pyncheon's funeral discourse" presented in parallel with the eulogy that is bound to be made of the Judge) and 272–73 ("The Judge . . . was a man of eminent respectability").

(5) Ibid., 145 ("my own little kinswoman"); 153 ("my little cousin"); 154 ("my dear"); and 156 ("Hepzibah, my beloved cousin . . .").

(6) Ibid., 153 ("What is the matter with you, young woman"); 158 ("Wom-

an!") and particularly 281–82: the deliberate and calculated weightiness of his speech ("From all this testimony, I am led to apprehend . . . that . . . he cannot safely remain at large. The alternative . . . will depend . . ."; "the alternative is his confinement . . . in a public asylum").

(7) Ibid., 219 ("dead man . . . much longer dead . . . dead man . . . dead men's books . . . dead men's jokes . . . dead men's pathos . . . dead men's diseases . . . dead men's forms and creeds . . . a dead man's icy hand . . . we must be dead ourselves . . .").

(8) Ibid., 149–50.

(9) Ibid., 275 ("The purity of his judicial character . . . —What room could possibly be found for darker traits in a portrait made up of lineaments like these": in all, thirty-one lines and fourteen subdivisions, the third comprising three parts, the sixth two, the eighth being dragged out to suggest the reluctance of the pardon granted, the ninth having two parts, the twelfth six, and the thirteenth four different actions).

(10) "Endicott," I, 491: "Fellow-soldiers—fellow-exiles! . . .").

(11) Y.G.B., II, 99.

(12) E.B., III, 496 ("O Mother Earth . . . who art no more my Mother . . . O mankind whose brotherhood I have cast off . . . O stars of heaven, that shone on me of old . . . [Cf. Marlowe, *Faustus,* final soliloquy: "Ye stars that reigned at my nativity"] farewell all, and forever. Come deadly element of Fire—henceforth my familiar friend! Embrace me as I do thee!").

(13) 7G., III, 83–85: Uncle Venner evoking Hep.'s childhood.

(14) "Earth's Holocaust," II, 455.

(15) 7G., III, 274.

(16) S.L., V, 139–40 ("God gave me the child! . . . She is my happiness—she is my torture . . . Ye shall not take her! I will die first!").

(17) Y.G.B., II, 103–04 ("Welcome, my children . . . to the communion of your race . . . Evil must be the nature of mankind. Evil must be your only happiness.").

(18) Endicott's harangue, Goodman Brown's imprecations, the Judge's fulminations, and Dimmesdale's defensive reaction: S.L., V, 167: "No—not to thee . . . But who art thou that meddlest in this matter?—that dares thrust himself between the sufferer and his God?").

(19) S.L., V, 288–89 (enveloping, insinuating voice). Cf. Miriam's voice: M.F., VI, 310.

(20) Ibid., 78–80.

(21) 7G., III, Ch. 16 (Clifford's Chamber). The concentric circles formed by the current of life around the house are conjured up by an image, p. 344 (. . . current . . . eddy . . .) while the sentence also curls around upon itself.

(22) S.L., V, 89.

(23) Ibid., Ch. 10 ("The Leech and his Patient"); 160, "some hideous secrets"; "the powers of nature call . . . for the confession of sin"; 161: "why not reveal them here?"; 162: "Yet some men bury their secrets . . ."; "These men deceive themselves"; 165–66 (Ch. asks for details about his patient's illness, in reality in order to distress him, so that he can deliver the final blow); 167: "first lay open to him the wound . . . in your soul."

(24) Ibid., 159.

(25) Ibid., 158: "He now dug into the . . . clergyman's heart . . ."

(26) Ibid., 176: "He kept vigils . . . glimmering lamp . . . most powerful light . . ."

(27) Ibid., 177: "seen doubtfully . . . by a faint light of their own . . . or more vividly . . . within the looking-glass."

(28) Ibid., 177: "pointing her forefinger, first at the *scarlet letter* on her *bosom* and then at the clergyman's own *breast.*"

(29) Wives, III, 601: ". . . as if her *heart* / like a *deep lake* /, had *grown calm* / because its *dead* / had *sunk* down / so *far* within."

(30) 7G., III, 120: ". . . as if the words / commonplace as they were / had been *steeped* / in the *warmth* / of her *heart.*"

(31) "Edward Fane," I, 517:
> . . . so age-worn and woeful are they,
> seem never to have been young and gay.

Ibid., 512: "his world /, his home /, his tomb—at once / a dwelling / and a burial-place . . ." Cf. Hemingway, *A Farewell to Arms,* Zephyr ed., 115: rhyming dialogue: "rain—rain"; "tell me—make me"; 175 (song: ". . . it wasn't the small rain but the big rain down that rained . . .").

(32) S.L., V, 126: ". . . and frisked onward / before Hester / on the gras / sy path, / with many / a harm / less trip / and tumble."

Ibid., 163: "She now skipped / irreverently / from one grave / to another . . ." H. did not consider it worthwhile to point the rhythm of this dance on the graves any further!

MF., VI, 107:
> Donatello / snapped his fingers / above his head,
> As fauns / and satyrs / taught us / first to do.
> And seemed / to radiate / jollity
> Out of / his whole / nimble / person.

(33) These "correspondances," and the question of poetic rhythm, have been examined in greater detail by S. Lanier in an essay on the poetry.

IV

(1) Gallup, "H.'s Authorship of 'The Battle Omen,' " *NEQ,* IX, 1936: "strong but not . . . elevated imagination."

(2) 7G., III, 152: "ancient superstitions, after being steeped in human hearts and embodied in human breath . . . become imbued with an effect of homely truth."

(3) Stein, *H.'s Faust, a Study of the Devil Archetype,* 1953, p. 8: "For our sardonic romancer, the Devil is a myth" (a myth in the strong sense of the term).

(4) 7G., III, 53: "her breast was a very cave of Aeolus"; 145 (Ixion embracing a cloud); Nbks., IX, 106 (chasing Echo to her hiding-place).

(5) 7G., III, 157 (smile . . . sunshine . . . vinegar); 156 (smile . . . trellis of grapes); 160 (water-carts . . . dust . . . sunshine).

(6) M.F., VI, 104: "as if a melancholy maiden and a glad one were both bound within the girdle about her waist." Also, the metaphor on p. 425: "the amaranthine flower."

(7) G.B., I, 104: Dorothy, wife of T. Pearson ("her mild and saddened features . . . were like a verse of fireside poetry") and 7G., III, 172: Phoebe ("he listened to her as if she were a verse of household poetry").

(8) 7G., III, 172, referring to Phoebe: vegetable metaphor (ripeness . . . budding . . . blossoms . . . fruit-tree). And the nautical metaphor concerning Clifford (voyage . . . islands . . . bark . . . tempestuous seas . . . mountain-wave . . . shipwreck . . . harbor . . . strand).

(9) Ibid., 377: "love's web of sorcery."

(10) "Custom House," V, 23: "the besom of reform"; 28–29: (examples have been quoted in Note 2 of Part Three, II, Ch. 3, II; also 64 "political guillotine."

(11) 7G., III, 125: "her own heart . . . on the gridiron."

(12) Ibid., 87: "the . . . melancholy chambers of her brain, as if that inner world were . . . lighted up with gas."

(13) Ibid., 148.

(14) Ibid., 127.

(15) Ibid., 168–69.

(16) Ibid., 164.

(17) Am.Nbks., R.S., 42–43; 54; 63 (the Notch); 139 (cloud picture—or rather sculpture).

(18) Ibid., 228.

(19) Ibid., IX, 106.

(20) Ibid., R.S., 107.
(21) Grim., Davidson, p. 123 (the spider); 149–50 (quest for the fantastic and monstrous); 194 (H. could apparently no longer base his work on anything but gratuitous absurdity: "at whatever expense of absurdity . . .").
(22) 7G., III, 313: "round globe . . . instinct with intelligence."
(23) Ibid., 266.
(24) P. Gold., I, 452–53 (the chest full of devalued notes and coins).
(25) Ibid., 435–36 (the house transformed into gold).
(26) Wives, III, 601, 604.
(27) 7G., III, 168: "through the foliage of the pear-tree." Cf. 190: "his . . . thoughts . . . glistened . . . through the arbour, and made their escape among the interstices of the foliage."
(28) Ibid., 254.
(29) Ibid., 210: "her eyes . . . like Artesian wells."
(30) M.F., VI, 112: "two drops of water or of blood do not more naturally flow into each other than did her hatred into his."
(31) 7G., III, 127 (writers of society).

CONCLUSION

(1) James, H., 1879, p. 102: "if it meant anything it would mean too much."
(2) Ibid., 162.
(3) S.L., V, 79: "she saw again her native village, in Old England . . ." and 236: "the broad pathway, of the ocean . . . it will bear thee *back* again."
(4) 7G., III, 254: "A hundred mysterious years . . . whispering . . . whenever the . . . *sea breeze* found its way thither . . ."
(5) Fogle, *H.'s Fiction: The Light and the Dark*, 70, defines A.o.B. as "an aesthetic Pilgrim's Progress." One is tempted to apply the formula to H.'s work and artistic experiment as a whole. They then assume a stature that Montégut seems implicitly to deny them when he speaks of "those little literary urns (the tales) in which are contained the dust and ashes of Puritanism" (*Revue des Deux Mondes*, Dec. 1, 1852: "Un Romancier pessimiste, N.H.").
(6) Bergson, *l'Evolution créatrice*, P.U.F., pp. 14–15.
(7) Poe, "Tale-Writing," *Godey's*, Nov. 1847, was one of the first to perceive what he called "a *very* profound under-current" beneath the deceptive surface of the easy, classical style and the allegory.
(8) "His wild witch-voice," Melville wrote in "H. and his Mosses," quoted by L. Mumford, "The Writing of *Moby Dick*," *Am.Merc.*, Dec. 1928.

Bibliography

An exhaustive bibliography of Hawthorne and his work would exceed the limits of the present work. We therefore refer the reader, for precise descriptions of the manuscripts, unpublished works and various documents, as well as for the complete list of the various editions of works published separately (except the principal ones), to the specialized bibliographies, as well as to the appropriate libraries (the Widener in Harvard, the New York Public and Morgan Libraries of New York, and the Essex Institute in Salem). For literary comparisons and works of psychology we refer the reader to the Notes and the Index. We shall do no more here than attempt a sketch for an analytic bibliography.

As far as possible, this bibliography from the original French edition has been corrected for this English-language edition.

I. WORKS OF REFERENCE

BIBLIOGRAPHIES

Browne, N. C. *A Bibliography of Nathaniel Hawthorne.* Boston, 1905.
Chandler, E. L. *A Study of the Sources of the Tales and Romances written by Nathaniel Hawthorne before 1853.* Northampton, Mass., 1926.
Dhaleine, L. N. "Nathaniel Hawthorne, sa Vie et son Oeuvre." Thesis, Paris, 1905.
Faust, B. *Hawthorne's Contemporaneous Reputation: A Study of Literary Opinion in America and England (1828–1854).* Philadelphia, 1939.
Stovall, F. *Eight American Authors.* New York, 1960.
Tashjian, N. and Eckermann, D. *Nathaniel Hawthorne: An Annotated Bibliography.* New York, 1948.

451

LITERARY HISTORIES

Arnavon, C. *Histoire Littéraire des Etats-Unis.* Paris, 1945.
Brodin, P. *Les Maitres de la Littérature Américaine.* Paris, 1948.
Cestre, C. *La Littérature Américaine.* 1945.
Erskine, J. *Cambridge History of American Literature.* II, 16–31, 1918.
Le Breton, M. *The Student's Anthology of American Literature.* Paris, 1948.
Lewison, L. *The Story of American Literature.* New York, 1937.
Michaud, R. *Panorama de la Littérature Americaine Contemporaine.* Kra, 1946.
Quinn, A. H. *American Fiction.* New York, 1936.
Spiller. *Literary History of the United States.* 1953.
Winters, Y. *Aspects of American Literature.*

II. HAWTHORNE'S WORKS

COMPLETE EDITIONS

The Centenary Edition of the Works of Nathaniel Hawthorne. Edited by Char-
    vat; R. H. Pearce; and C. M. Simpson. Columbus, O., 1962–.
The Complete Works of Nathaniel Hawthorne, with introductions and notes by
    G. P. Lathrop. 13 vols. New York, 1909.
Hawthorne's Writings. 22 vols. Boston, 1904.
The Riverside Edition of Hawthorne's Works. 12 vols. Boston, 1883.

SELECTIONS

The Best Known Works of Nathaniel Hawthorne: Including The Scarlet Letter,
    The House of the Seven Gables, and the Best of the Twice-Told Tales. New
    York, 1941.
Complete Novels and Selected Tales. New York, 1937.
Hawthorne. Edited by Bliss Perry. Garden City, N.Y., 1922.
Hawthorne. Translated by C. Cestre. Aubier, 1934.
Hawthorne's Short Stories. Edited by N. Arvin. New York, 1946.
Portable Hawthorne. Edited by M. Cowley. New York, 1948.
Representative Selections. Edited by A. Warren. New York, 1934.
Selections. Houghton Mifflin, Boston, 1882.
Selections from Twice-Told Tales. New York, 1901.
Seven Stories. Edited by C. Van Doren. New York, 1920.

SEPARATE WORKS

Fanshawe: A Tale. Boston, 1828.
Twice-Told Tales. Boston, 1837; Vol. 2, 1842; second ed., 1851, with preface.
Grandfather's Chair. Boston, 1841.
Famous Old People: Being the 2nd Epoch of Grandfather's Chair. Boston, 1841.
Biographical Stories for Children. Boston, 1842.
Mosses from an Old Manse. New York, 1846; revised ed., Boston, 1854.
The Scarlet Letter: A Romance. Boston, 1850.
True Stories from History and Biography. Boston, 1851.
The House of the Seven Gables. Boston, 1851.
A Wonder Book for Girls and Boys. Boston, 1852.
The Snow Image and Other Twice-Told Tales. Boston, 1852.
The Blithedale Romance. Boston, 1852.
Life of Franklin Pierce. Boston, 1852.
Tanglewood Tales. Boston, 1853.
The Marble Faun: first published in England as *Transformation,* February,
    1860; first American ed., Boston, March, 1860.
Our Old Home. Boston, 1863.
Pansie: A Fragment. London, 1864.

THE NOTEBOOKS

The notebooks remained for a long while in a scattered manuscript state. Only some fragments, often retouched by Mrs. Hawthorne, were published:

Our Old Home and English Notebooks. Boston, 1883.

Passages from the American Notebooks. Boston, 1868.

Passages from the English Notebooks. Boston, 1870.

Passages from the French & Italian Notebooks. Boston, 1872.

Passages from the Note Books of Nathaniel Hawthorne. London, 1869.

The definitive texts of the American and English Notebooks have been established by Randall Stewart:

The American Note Books. Edited by Randall Stewart. New Haven, 1932.

The English Note Books. Edited by Randall Stewart. New York, 1941.

Stewart, R. *"Editing Hawthorne's Notebooks."* More Books, XX, September, 1945.

————. "Hawthorne in England: the Patriotic Motive in the Note Books." *NEQ,* VIII, 1935.

The Heart of H's Journals. Edited by N. Arvin. Boston, 1929.

"H's Diary for 1859." *Nation,* May 1912.

Pearson, N. H. "The Italian Note Books." Unpublished doctoral dissertation. New Haven: Yale University, 1942.

CORRESPONDENCE

The originals of Hawthorne's letters are extremely scattered; they are to be found in the Lockwood Memorial Library, Buffalo University; the Grolier Club, New York; the Morgan Library, New York; the New York Public Library; the Berg Collection, New York; the Bowdoin College Library; the Harvard University Library; the Boston Public Library; the Amherst College Library; the H. E. Huntington Library, San Francisco; the Essex Institute, Salem.

Bridge. *Personal Recollections of Nathaniel Hawthorne.* New York, 1893.

Blodgett, H. "Hawthorne as Poetry Critic," *AL,* XII, 1940.

Dhaleine, L. N. "Nathaniel Hawthorne, sa Vie et son Ouevre," 1905.

Eagle, N. L. "An Unpublished Hawthorne Letter." *AL,* XXLLL, 1951.

Longfellow, S. *Life of Henry Wadsworth Longfellow.* Boston, 1857.

Hawthorne, J. *Hawthorne and His Wife.* Boston, 1885.

Hayford, H. "The Significance of Melville's Agatha Letters." *ELH,* 1946.

Malcolm, C. *Portable Hawthorne.* New York, 1948.

Manning, H. "Nathaniel Hawthorne Prepares for College." *NEQ,* XI, 1938.

————. "Hawthorne's Early Years." *EIHC,* LXXXVIII.

————. "Hawthorne and Utopian Socialism." *NEQ,* XII, 1929.

————. "Nathaniel and Elizabeth Hawthorne, Editors." *Colophon,* No. 3, 1929.

Morrison, S. E. "Melville's Agatha Letters to Hawthorne." *NEQ,* 1929.

Stewart, R. "Hawthorne and Politics: Unpublished letters to W. B. Pike." *NEQ,* V, 1932.

————. "The Hawthornes at the Wayside, 1860–64." *More Books,* XLX, 1944.

————. "Hawthorne's Last Illness and Death." *More Books,* XIX, 1944.

————. *Nathaniel Hawthorne: A Biography.* New Haven, 1948.

Ticknor, C. *Hawthorne and His Publishers.* Boston, 1913.

Love Letters of Nathaniel Hawthorne, 1839–41 and 1841–63. 2 Vols. Chicago, 1907.

Letters of Nathaniel Hawthorne to W. J. Ticknor (1851–1864). 2 Vols. Newark, 1910.

"The Hawthornes in Lenox, Told in Letters." *Century,* November 1894.

POSTHUMOUS AND APOCRYPHAL FRAGMENTS AND MISCELLANEA

1. The Boyish Note Book (Raymond):

Pickard, S. T. *Hawthorne's First Diary, with an Account of Its Discovery.* Boston, 1897.

2. The "Spectator":

Chandler, E. L., ed. "Hawthorne's 'Spectator.' " *NEQ*, IV, 1931.
   3. The works of compilation:
Turner, A., ed. *Hawthorne as Editor: Selections from his Writings in the American Magazine of Useful and Entertaining Knowledge.* Baton Rouge, 1941.
   4. The "Story-Teller" and Miscellaneous Projects:
Nelson, F. "The Early Projected Works of Nathaniel Hawthorne." *Papers of the Biblio Society,* XXXIX, 1945.
   5. Articles and reviews:
Stewart, R. "Hawthorne's Contributions to The Salem Advertiser." *AL*, V, 1934.
————. "Two Uncollected Reviews by Hawthorne." *NEQ,* IX, 1936.
   6. Sketches not included in the Riverside Edition:
Gallup, D. C., ed. "On Hawthorne's Authorship of 'The Battle Omen.' " *NEQ,* IX, 1936.
   7. Introductions:
Bacon, D. *The Philosophy of Shakespeare's Plays Unfolded.* Preface by Nathaniel Hawthorne. London, 1857.
Bridge, H. *Journal of an African Cruiser.* Edited by Nathaniel Hawthorne, New York, 1853.
Browne, B. F. *The Yarn of a Yankee Privateer.* Edited by Nathaniel Hawthorne, New York, 1926.
   8. The unfinished novels:
Published under Julian Hawthorne's supervision: *Septimius Felton* (1871–72); *The Dolliver Romance* (1874–76); *Dr. Grimshawe's Secret* (1883); *The Ancestral Footstep* (1882–83). Julian Hawthorne wrote profusely about the posthumous works:
————. "Hawthorne's Elixir of Life—How Hawthorne Worked." *Lippincott's,* XIV, 1890.
————. "A Look into Hawthorne's Workshop—Being Notes for a Posthumous Romance." *Century,* XXV, January 1883.
————. "Scenes of Hawthorne's Romances." *Century,* XXVIII, July 1884.
The most important work on *Doctor Grimshawe's Secret* is:
Davidson, E. H. *Hawthorne's Last Phase.* New Haven, 1949, together with his edition of the entire text: *Hawthorne's "Doctor Grimshawe's Secret."* Cambridge, Mass., 1954.
Stein, W. B. "A Possible Source of Hawthorne's English Romance." *MLN,* LXVII, January 1952.

TRANSLATIONS AND ADAPTATIONS
Astrov, V. "Hawthorne and Dostoievski as Explorers of the Human Consciousness. *NEQ,* June 1942.
Ferguson, J. D. "The Earliest Translations of Hawthorne." *Nation,* January 1915.
French Translations
   1. Tales:
Boulanger, L. *Contes du Far-West.*
Borjane, H. *Les Contes Prodigieux.*
Cestre, C. *Hawthorne, Contes.* Paris, 1934.
Loge, M. *Contes de Hawthorne,* 1927.
Rabillon. *Le Livre des Merveilles.*
Spoll, E. A. *Contes Etranges imités d'Hawthorne.* 1866.
   2. Novels:
The Scarlet Letter:
Carnavaggia, M. *La Lettre Ecarlate.* Preface by J. Green, 1946.
Cestres, C. *La Lettre Ecarlate.* Les Belles Lettres, Illustrations and extracts from
Leyris, P. *La Lettre Ecarlate.*
   the study by P. Brodin (Les Maitres de la Litterature Americaine) 1955.
The House of the Seven Gables:
Carnavaggia, M. *La Maison aux Sept Pignons.* 1945.

Fagnes, E. *La Maison aux Sept Pignons.* Monaco, 1947.
The Blithedale Romance:
Carnavaggia, M. *Valjoie.* Preface by A. Maurois. Paris, 1952.
The Marble Faun:
Villaret, F. Introduction by R. Lalou. 1949.
   3. Miscellaneous:
Life of Pierce:
Le *Général F. Pierce, Président des Etats-Unis.* Reprint from *Revue Britannique,*
   CVIII, 1853.
American Note Books:
"Feuillets du Journal d'Amérique." Translated by Marcelle Cibon. *La Table
   Ronde,* No. 67, July 1953.
Adaptations
   1. Tales:
"The Maypole of Merry Mount":
   Dramatic poem for music (3 acts), Rich Stokes, 1932;
   Opera by same author (4 acts), 1933.
"The Snow Image": "La Petite Fille de Neige." Adaptation by J. de Kerlecq,
   1951.
   2. *The Scarlet Letter:*
Scarlet Letter: Broadcast, 1950 (Westinghouse Studio One, New York).
Scarlet Letter: Film directed by Seastrom, 1927.

III. THE MAN

FAMILY; CHILDHOOD; COLLEGE
   1. The Hawthornes and Salem:
Emmerton and Waters. "Gleanings from English Records about New England
   Families." *EIHC,* XVII, January, 1880.
Hungerford, E. B. "Hawthorne Gossips about Salem." *NEQ,* VI, 1938.
Hunt. "Visitor's Guide to Salem." *EIHC,* 1927.
Loggins, V. *The Hawthornes: The Story of Seven Generations of an American
   Family.* New York, 1951.
Tharp, L. *The Peabody Sisters of Salem.* Boston, 1950.
   2. Childhood:
Manning, E. "The Boyhood of Hawthorne." *Wide Awake,* 1891.
Manning, H. "Hawthorne's Early Years." *EIHC,* LXXV, 1938.
————. "Parental and Family Influences on Hawthorne." *EIHC,* LXXVI, 1940.
Stewart, R. "Recollections of Hawthorne by his Sister Elizabeth." *AL,* Janu-
   ary 1945.
   3. Bowdoin:
Burnham, P. E. "Hawthorne's *Fanshawe* and Bowdoin College." *EIHC,* LXXX,
   1944.
"Hawthorne's Pot-8-O' Club at Bowdoin College." *EIHC,* LXVII, 1931.
Hoeltje, H. H. "Hawthorne as Senior at Bowdoin." *EIHC,* XCIV, 1958.
Manning, H. "Nathaniel Hawthorne Prepares for College." *NEQ,* XI, 1938.
————. "Nathaniel Hawthorne at Bowdoin." *NEQ,* XIII, 1940.
Mitchell. "A Remarkable Bowdoin Decade (1820–1830)." Bowdoin, 1952.
Pearson, N. H. "The College Years of Nathaniel Hawthorne." Unpublished
   monograph.

SOLITUDE; CONCORD; THE CUSTOM HOUSE
   1. Solitude: the "intermediate" years (1823–38).
Cowley, M. "Hawthorne in Solitude." *New Republic,* CXIX, August 1948.

Gorman, H. S. *Hawthorne, a Study in Solitude.* New York, 1927.
Miller, H. P. "Hawthorne Surveys his Contemporaries." *AL*, XII, May 1940.
   2. Engagement and marriage:
Adams, R. P. "Hawthorne: The Old Manse Period." *TSE*, VIII, 1958.
Cowley, M. "The Hawthornes in Paradise." *AH*, X, December 1958.
Jepson, G. E. "Hawthorne and the Boston Custom House." *Bookman*, XIX, 1904.
Lagermann, J. K. "Husband to the Month of May." *Christian Science Monitor*, XXXVIII, July 1946.
Pearson, N. H. "Hawthorne's Duel." *EIHC*, XCIV, 1958.
————. "Elizabeth Peabody on Hawthorne." *EIHC*, XCIV, 1958.
Prochnov. "Housekeeper to Genius." *Coronet*, 1949.
   3. The Custom House; Politics:
Nevins, W. S. "Hawthorne's Removal from the Salem Custom House." *EIHC*, LIII, 1917.
Stewart, R. "Hawthorne and Politics: Unpublished Letters to Wilbur B. Pike." *NEQ*, April 1932.
————. "Hawthorne's Speeches at Civic Banquets." *AL*, VII, 1936.
————. "Hawthorne and the Civil War." *SP*, XXXIV, January 1937.
Streeter, R. E. "Hawthorne's Misfit Politician and Edward Everett." *AL*, XVI, March 1944.

TRANSCENDENTALISM; BROOK FARM; LITERARY ASSOCIATIONS

   1. Brook Farm:
Bohmer, L. *Brook Farm and Hawthorne's "Blithedale Romance."* Jena, U. Buchdruck, 1936.
Brooks, V. W. "Retreat from Utopia." *SRL*, XIII, February 1936.
Emerson, R. W. "Historic Notes of Life and Letters in New England." *Portable Emerson*, p. 513. New York.
Hawthorne, M. "Hawthorne and Utopian Socialism." *NEQ*, IX, 1936.
Metzdorf, R. H. "Hawthorne's Suit Against Ripley and Dana." *AL*, XII, 1940.
   2. Intellectual and Social Atmosphere:
Brooks, V. W. *The Flowering of New England, 1815 to 1865.* New York, 1936.
Matthiessen, F. O. *American Renaissance: Art and Expression in the Age of Emerson and Whitman.* Oxford University Press, 1941.
Parrington, V. L. *American Dreams: A Study of American Utopias.* Providence, 1947.
Stewart, R. "The Concord Group." *SR*, XLIV, 1936.
   3. Literary Associations:
Cantwell, R. "Hawthorne and Delia Bacon." *AQ*, I, 1949.
Cargill, O. "Nemesis and Nathaniel Hawthorne." *PMLA*, LII, 1937.
Hawthorne, J. *Hawthorne and his Circle.* New York, 1903.
Kimball, L. E. "Miss Delia Bacon Advances Learning." *Colophon*, II, 1937.
Manning, H. "The Friendship Between Hawthorne and Longfellow." *Eng. Leaflet*, XXXIX, 1940.
Mayoux, J. J. *Melville.* 1958.
Randel, W. P. "Hawthorne, Channing and Margaret Fuller." *AL*, X, January 1939.
Sanborn, F. B. *Hawthorne and his Friends: Reminiscence and Tribute.* Cedar Rapids, Iowa, 1908.
Simon, J. "Herman Melville: Marin, Metaphysicien et Poete." Thesis, 1937.
Stewart, R. "Melville and Hawthorne." *SAQ*, LI, 1952.
Thorner, H. E. "Hawthorne, Poe and a Literary Ghost." *NEQ*, VII, 1934.
Warren, A. "Hawthorne, Margaret Fuller and Nemesis." *PMLA*, LIV, 1939.
Zunder, T. A. "Walt Whitman and Hawthorne." *MLN*, XLVII, 1932.

TRAVELS; EUROPE; SOCIETY

Cavignan. "Hawthorne in Rome." *CathW*, September 1932.
Fairbanks, H. G. "Hawthorne and the Machine Age." *AL*, May 1956.

——— "Citizen Hawthorne and the Perennial Problem of American Society." *RUO,* January–March 1959.
Hall, L. S. *Hawthorne: Critic of Society.* New Haven, 1944.
Hewit, A. F. "Hawthorne's Attitude towards Catholicism." *CathW,* XLII, 1866.
Hibler, von. "Hawthorne and Victorian England." Paper read at the international conference of Anglo-American literature, Paris, 1953.
———. "Hawthorne in England." *Die Neueren Eprachen,* September 1955 (?)
Osborne. "Nathaniel Hawthorne as American Consul." *Bookman,* XVI, 1903.
Prezzolini, G. "Gli Hawthorne a Roma." *Nuova Antologia,* LXXXV, September 1950.
Sedan. "The Two Bostons." *Coming Events in Britain,* October 1953.
Turner, A. "Hawthorne and Reform." *NEQ,* December 1942.

THE BIOGRAPHIES

1. Memoirs, Recollections, and Fragments:
Bridge, H. *Personal Recollections of Nathaniel Hawthorne.* New York, 1893.
Curtis, G. W. *Homes of American Authors.* New York, 1853.
Fields, A. *Hawthorne.* Boston, 1899.
Fields, J. T. *Yesterdays with Authors.* Boston, 1871.
Goodrich, S. D. *Recollections of a Lifetime.* New York, 1856.
Hawthorne, E. "Recollections of Nathaniel Hawthorne by His Sister Elizabeth." *AL,* XVI, January 1945.
Hawthorne, J. "Nathaniel Hawthorne's Blue Cloak." *Bookman,* LXXV, September 1932.
Japp, A. [H. A. Page]. *Memories of Hawthorne.* London, 1872.
Lathrop, R. *Memories of Hawthorne.* Boston, 1897.
Pearson, N. H. "Hawthorne and the Mannings." *EIHC,* XCIV, 1958.
Perry, B. "Hawthorne at North Adams." *Atlantic Monthly,* May 1893.
Ryan, P. M., Jr. "Young Hawthorne at Salem Theatre." *EIHC,* July 1958.
Ticknor, C. *Hawthorne and His Publisher.* Boston, 1913.
Ticknor, H. M. "Hawthorne as seen by His Publisher." *The Critic,* XLV, July 1904.
Turner, A. "Hawthorne and Martha's Vineyard." *NEQ,* XI, 1938.
2. Biographical Studies:
Arvin, N. *Hawthorne.* Boston, 1929.
Bewley, M. *The Complex Fate.* London, 1952.
Cantwell, R. *Nathaniel Hawthorne: The American Years.* New York, 1948.
Conway, M. D. *Life of Nathaniel Hawthorne.* London, 1890.
Gorman, H. S. *Hawthorne: A Study in Solitude.* New York, 1927.
Hawthorne, H. *Romantic Rebel: The Story of Nathaniel Hawthorne.* New York, 1932.
Hawthorne, J. *Nathaniel Hawthorne and his Wife.* 2 vols. Boston, 1885.
Lathrop, G. P. *A Study of Hawthorne.* Boston, 1876.
Mather, E. J. *Nathaniel Hawthorne: A Modest Man.* New York, 1940.
Morris, L. *The Rebellious Puritan: Portrait of Mr. Hawthorne.* New York, 1927.
Stearns, F. P. *The Life and Genius of Nathaniel Hawthorne.* Philadelphia, 1906.
Stewart, R. *Nathaniel Hawthorne: A Biography.* New Haven, 1948.
Van Doren, M. *Nathaniel Hawthorne: A Critical Biography.* New York, 1949.
Wagenknecht, E. C. *Nathaniel Hawthorne: Man and Writer.* New York, 1961.
3. The Personality:
Alcott, A. B. *Concord Days.* Boston, 1872.
———. *Sonnets and Canzonets.* Boston, 1882.
Curtis, G. W. "The Works of Nathaniel Hawthorne." *N. Am. Rev.,* XCIX, 1864.
Fairbanks, H. G. "Hawthorne and the Vanishing Venus." *UTSE,* XXXVI, 1957.
Hoeltje, H. H. *Inward Sky: The Mind and Heart of Nathaniel Hawthorne.* Durham, N. C., 1962.
Howells, W. D. "The Personality of Hawthorne." *N. Am. Rev.,* XXXIV, 1903.
Symons, A. *Studies in Prose and Verse* (pp. 52–62). London, 1904.

Zangwill, O. L. "A Case of Paramnesia in Nathaniel Hawthorne." *Char. & Pers.,* XIII, 1945.

HOUSES; MUSEUMS; ILLUSTRATIONS

"Catalogue of Portraits in the Essex Institute." *EIHC,* LXXI, April 1935.
Clarke, H. A. *Hawthorne's Country.* New York, 1910.
Gannon. "Hawthorne and the Houses of the Seven Gables." Salem, 1955.
———. "Houses in Which Hawthorne Lived, Thought and Wrote." Calem, 1955.
Goodspeed, C. E. "Nathaniel Hawthorne and the Museum of the East India Marine Society." *American Neptune,* V, October 1945.
DeLeuw. *Hawthorne House.* Macmillan, 1950.
Lothrop, M. *The Wayside.* New York, 1940.
Stewart, R. "The Hawthornes at the Wayside, 1860–1864." *More Books,* XIX, September 1944.

IV. CRITICAL WORKS ON THE WORKS AS A WHOLE

INFLUENCES AND COMPARISONS

Allen, J. E. "The Bible in the Works of Nathaniel Hawthorne." *Zion's Herald,* June 1904.
Astrov, V. "Hawthorne and Dostoievski, as Explorers of the Human Conscience." *NEQ,* XV, 1942.
Baldensperger, F. "A propos de Nathaniel Hawthorne en France." *MLN,* LVI, May 1941.
Baxter. "Independence vs. Isolation: Hawthorne and James on the Problem of the Artist." *NCF,* X, December 1953.
Bell, M. "Melville and Hawthorne at the Grave of St. John (A Debt to Pierre Bayle)." *MLN,* 1952.
"Books Read by Hawthorne (1828–50)." *EIHC,* LXVIII, January 1932.
Brant, R. L. "Hawthorne and Marvell." *AL,* XXX, November 1958.
Cooke, A. L. "Hawthorne's Indebtedness to Swift." *Tex. St. Eng.,* July 1938.
Davidson, F. "Hawthorne's Hive of Honey." *MLN,* LXI, 1946.
———. "Thoreau's Contribution to Hawthorne's Mosses." *NEQ,* XX, December 1947.
———. "Hawthorne's Use of a Pattern from the 'Rambler.' " *MLN,* LXIII, 1948.
———. "Voltaire and Hawthorne's 'The Christmas Banquet.' " *BLPQ,* III, July 1951.
Fruit, J. P. "Hawthorne's 'Immitigable.' " *PMLA,* App., XXIX, 1910.
Hawthorne, J. "Books of Memory." *Bookman,* LXI, July 1925.
Hayford, H. "Hawthorne, Melville and the Sea." *NEQ,* XIX, 1946.
Hearn, L. *A History of English Literature.* Tokyo, 1958.
Johnson, W. S. "Hawthorne and 'The Pilgrim's Progress.' " *JEGP,* L, 1951.
Kesselring, M. "*Hawthorne's Reading 1828–1850.*" BNYPL, 1949.
Leibowitz, H. A. "Hawthorne and Spenser: Two Sources." *AL,* XXX, 1959.
Lundblad, J. *Hawthorne and European Literary Tradition.* Cambridge, Mass., 1947.
———. *Hawthorne and the Tradition of the Gothic Romance.* Cambridge, Mass., 1946.
Lunden. "The Melville-Hawthorne Relationship in *Pierre* and *The Blithedale Romance.*" *WHR,* Fall 1956.
Lynch, J. J. "The Devil in the Writings of Irving, Hawthorne and Poe." *NYFQ,* Summer 1952.
Manning, C. A. "Hawthorne and Dostoievsky." *Slavonic Review,* XIV, January 1936.
Matthews, J. C. "Hawthorne's Knowledge of Dante." *U. of Texas S. E.,* 1940.

More, P. E. "The Origins of Hawthorne and Poe." *Shelburne Essays,* 1st Series, 1904.

Moyer, P. "Time and the Artist in Kafka and Hawthorne." *MFS,* IV, 1958–59.

Mumford, L. "Influence of Hawthorne on Melville." *American Mercury,* XV, December 1928.

Niess, R. J. "Hawthorne and Zola—An Influence?" *RLC,* XXVII, 1953.

O'Connor, W. V. "Hawthorne and a Literary Ghost." *NEQ,* VII, 1934.

Pritchard, J. P. *Return to the Fountains: Some Classical Sources of American Criticism.* Durham, N. C., 1942.

Scudder, H. H. "Hawthorne's Use of *Typee.*" *N&Q,* October 1944.

Sherman, P. "Hawthorne's Debt to Ahab." *N&Q,* CXCVI, June 1951.

Stanton, R. "Hawthorne, Bunyan, and the American Romances." *PMLA,* LXXI, 1956.

Stewart, R. "Hawthorne and The Faerie Queene." *PQ,* XII, 1933.

———. "Hawthorne and Faulkner." *CE,* XVII, February 1956.

Thorner, H. E. "Hawthorne, Poe and a Literary Ghost." *NEQ,* VII, 1934.

Turner, H. A. "Hawthorne's Literary Borrowings." *PMLA,* LI, 1936.

Warren, A. "Hawthorne's Reading." *NEQ,* VIII, 1935.

Warren, R. P. "Hawthorne, Anderson and Frost." *New Republic,* LIV, May 1928.

Woodbridge. "Le Surnaturel dans l'oeuvre de Hawthorne et Poe." Brussels, 1928.

Wright, N. "*Mosses from an Old Manse* and *Moby Dick*: the Shock of Discovery," *MLN,* LXVII, 1952.

Yates, N. "An Instance of Parallel Imagery in Hawthorne, Melville and Frost." *PQ,* XXXVI, April 1957.

HAWTHORNE: ROMANTIC OR CLASSIC? TRANSCENDENTALIST? REALIST OR UNREALIST?

Arvin, N. "The Relevance of Hawthorne." *New Students,* VII, 1928.

Bier, J. "Hawthorne on the Romance: His Prefaces Related and Examined." *MP,* August 1955.

Cronin, M. "Hawthorne on Romantic Love and the Status of Women." *PMLA,* LXIX, March 1954.

Curl, V. "Pasteboard Marks: Fact as Spiritual Symbol in the Novels of Hawthorne and Melville." Cambridge, Mass., 1931.

Dony, F. "Romantisme et Puritanisme chez Hawthorne a propos de *La Lettre Pourpre.*" *Etudes Anglaises,* IV, 1940.

Foster, C. H. "Hawthorne's Literary Theory." *PMLA,* LVII, 1942.

Hawthorne, H. *Romantic Rebel.* New York, 1932.

Just. *Die Romantische Bewegung in der American Literature.* Munster, 1930.

Lang, A. "America's Classic Author: Hawthorne." *Critic,* 1890.

Lawrence, D. H. *Studies in Classic American Literature.* New York, 1923.

Lawton, *The New England Poets.* New York, 1898.

Leavis, Q. P. "Hawthorne as a Poet." *SR,* LIX, 1951.

Liljegren. "Some Notes on Hawthorne and Hawthorne Research." Upsala, 1949.

More, P. E. "The Solitude of Hawthorne." *Shelburne Essays,* 1st Series. New York, 1904.

Parrington. *The Romantic Revolution in America.* New York, 1927.

———. *Main Currents in American Thought.* New York, 1927.

Russell, A. I. "Hawthorne and the Romantic Indian." *Educ.,* XLVIII, February 1928.

Stephen, L. *Nathaniel Hawthorne.* London, 1877.

Wagenknecht, E. C. *Cavalcade of the American Novel.* New York, 1952.

HAWTHORNE IN THE LIGHT OF THE PURITAN PAST AND PURITAN ETHICS

Abel, D. "Modes of Ethical Sensibility in Hawthorne." *MLN,* LXVIII, February 1953.

Arvin, N. "Puritan Romancer." *London TL Supp.,* No. 2495, November 1949.

Chretien, L. E. *La Pensee Morale de Hawthorne, Symboliste Neo-Puritain: Esquisse d'une Interpretation.* Paris, 1932.

Dion-Levesque, R. "Nathaniel Hawthorne, un 'puritain' au pays de la liberté." *La Patrie du Dimanche,* Montreal, October 30, 1960.

Eisinger, C. E. "Pearl and the Puritan Heritage." *CE,* XII, March 1951.

Fairbanks, H. G. "Sin, Free Will and Pessimism in Hawthorne." *PMLA,* LXXI, 1956.

Faverie, S. de la. *Les Premiers Interpretes de la Pensee Americaine: Essai d'Histoire de la Litterature sur l'Evolution du Puritanisme aux E.-U.* 1909.

Fick, L. *The Light Beyond: A Study of Hawthorne's Theology,* Westminster, Md., 1955.

Green, J. *Un Puritain Homme de Lettres.* Toulouse, 1928.

Griswold, M. J. "American Quaker History in the Works of Whittier, Hawthorne and Longfellow." *Americana,* XXXIV, 1940.

Kirk, R. "The Moral Conservatism in Hawthorne." *Contemp. R.,* December 1952.

Killing, C. "Hawthorne's View of Sin." *Personalist,* XIII, April 1932.

Levin, H. *The Power of Blackness.* New York, 1958.

Male, R. R. *Hawthorne's Tragic Vision.* Austin, Texas, 1957.

Maurois, A. "Un Puritain." *NL,* No. 1311, October 1952.

McDowell, T. "Nathaniel Hawthorne and the Witches of Colonial Salem." *NEQ,* March 1934.

McPherson, H. "Hawthorne's Mythology: A Mirror for Puritans." *UTQ,* XXVIII, 1959.

Merill, L. J. "The Puritan Policeman." *Am. Soc. Rev.,* X, December 1945.

Miller, P. *The American Puritans, Their Prose and Poetry.* New York, 1956.

———. *Jonathan Edwards.* New York, 1949.

Mills, B. "Hawthorne and Puritanism." *NEQ,* XXI, 1948.

Montegut, E. "Un Romanier Socialiste en Amerique." *RDM,* 1852.

———. "Un Romancier Pessimiste en Amerique." *RDM,* 1852.

More, P. E. "Hawthorne Looking Before and After." *Shelburne Essays,* 2nd series, Boston, 1905.

Murdock, K. B. *The Puritan Tradition: The Reinterpretation of American Literature.* 1928.

Myers, G. "Hawthorne and the Myths about Puritans." *American Sptcator,* II, April 1934.

Orians, G. H. "Hawthorne and Puritan Punishments." *CE,* XIII, 1952.

Pattee, F. L. *Development of the American Short Story.* New York, 1923.

Pearson, N. H. "Hawthorne's Usable Truth." New York, 1949.

Reti, E. *Hawthorne's Verhaltnis zur Neu England Tradition.* Rustringen, 1955.

Schneider, H. W. *The Puritan Mind.* New York, 1930.

———. "Hawthorne's Democratic Conscience as an Expression of New England Puritanism." (lecture delivered at Bowdoin, April 17, 1952).

Sherman, S. P. "Hawthorne, a Puritan Critic of Puritanism." *Americans,* New York, 1922.

Van Doren, C. *The American Novel.* New York, 1921.

Voight, G. P. "Nathaniel Hawthorne, Author for Preachers." *Lutheran Ch. Q.,* XXI, January 1943.

Warren, A. *Rage for Order.* Chicago, 1948.

HAWTHORNE IN THE LIGHT OF THE DEVELOPMENT OF AMERICA, OF SCIENCE, AND OF PSYCHOLOGY

1. Americanism; Modernity:

Doubleday, N. F. "Hawthorne and Literary Nationalism." *AL,* XII, April 1941.

Fairbanks, H. G. "Hawthorne and the Atomic Age." *RUO,* XXXI, 1961.

———. "Hawthorne and the Machine Age." *AL,* XXVIII, 1956.

Hosmer, E. "Science and Pseudo-Science in the Works of Nathaniel Hawthorne." *AL*, March 1930.

Marx, L. *Hawthorne and Emerson: Studies in the Impact of the Machine Technology upon the American Writer.* Cambridge, Mass., 1950.

———. *The Steam Fiend, the Development of a Symbol.* Cambridge, Mass., 1949.

———. "The Machine in the Garden." *NEQ*, XXIX, March 1956.

Matthiessen, F. O. *American Renaissance: Art and Expression in the Age of Emerson and Whitman.* New York, 1941.

Stein, W. *Hawthorne's Faust: A Study of the Devil Archetype.* Gainesville, Fla., 1953.

Wegelin, C. "Europe in Hawthorne's Fiction." *ELH*, 1947.

2. Attempts at Psychological Analysis:

Askew, M. W. "Hawthorne, the Fall and the Psychology of Maturity." *AL*, XXXIV, November 1962.

Atkins. "Psychological Symbolism of Guilt and Isolation in Hawthorne." *AI*, XI, 1954.

Bewley, M. *The Complex Fate.* London, 1952.

———. "Hawthorne and the Deeper Psychology." *Mandrake*, II, Autumn–Winter 1956.

Cowley, M. "Hawthorne in the Looking-Glass." *SR*, LVI, 1948.

———. Introduction to *The Portable Hawthorne.* New York, 1948.

Laser, M. "Heat, Heart and Will in Hawthorne's Psychology." *NCF*, X, 1955.

Male, R. R. "Hawthorne and the Concept of Sympathy." *PMLA*, LXVIII, 1953.

Mayoux, J. J. "Vivants Piliers." *LetN*, 1961, No. 6.

McKiernan, J. J. "The Psychology of Nathaniel Hawthorne." Unpublished doctoral dissertation, State College, Pa.: Penn. State Univ., 1957.

Michaud, R. *Le Roman American d'Aujourd'hui.* Boston, 1928.

Morris, L. *The Rebellious Puritan: A Portrait of Mr. Hawthorne.* New York, 1927.

Ringe, D. A. "Hawthorne's Psychology of the Head and Heart." *PMLA*, LXV, 1950.

Schroeder, J. W. "That Inward Sphere: Notes on Hawthorne's Heart Imagery and Symbolism." *PMLA*, LXV, 1950.

Waples, D. "Suggestions for Interpreting *The Marble Faun.*" *AL*, XIII, 1941.

HAWTHORNE AND HIS ART

Abel, D. "The Theme of Isolation in Hawthorne." *Personalist*, XXII, 1951.

Abele, R. von. *The Death of the Artist: A Study of Hawthorne's Disintegration.* The Hague, 1955.

Anderson, O. K. "Hawthorne's Crowds." *NCF*, VII, 1952.

Bell, M. *Hawthorne's View of the Artist.* New York, 1962.

Beers, H. A. *Four Americans.* New Haven, 1919.

Birdsall, J. O. "Hawthorne's Fair-Haired Maidens: The Fading Light." *PMLA*, LXXV, June 1960.

Blair, W. "Color, Light & Shadow in Hawthorne's Fiction." *NEQ*, XV, 1942.

Brickell, H. "What Happened to the Short Story." *Atlantic Monthly*, CLXXVIII, September 1951.

Brownell, W. C. *American Prose Masters.* Edited by H. M. Jones. Cambridge, Mass., 1963.

Carlisle, K. "Wit and Humor in Nathaniel Hawthorne." *Bard. Rev.*, III, 1949.

Carpenter, F. I. "Puritans Preferred Blondes: the Heroines of Melville and Hawthorne." *NEQ*, IX, 1936.

Cohen, B. B. "A New Critical Approach to the Works of Nathaniel Hawthorne." *WE Remb.*, IV, 1950.

Coleridge, M. E. "The Questionable Shapes of Nathaniel Hawthorne." *Living Age*, Ser. 7, vol. 24, 1904.

Doubleday, N. F. "Hawthorne's Satirical Allegory." *CE,* III, 1942.
————. "Hawthorne's Use of Three Gothic Patterns." *CE,* VII, 1946.
Erskine, J. *Leading American Novelists.* New York, 1910.
Everett, L. B. "How the Great Ones Did It." *Overland,* LXXXVIII, March 1930.
Fogle, R. H. "The World of the Artist: A Study of 'The Artist of the Beautiful!' "
Tulane, I, 1949.
————. "*Hawthorne's Fiction: the Light and the Dark.* Norman, Okla., 1952.
Forgues, E. D. "Nathaniel Hawthorne." *RDM,* 1852.
Foster. "Hawthorne's Literary Theory." *PMLA,* LVIII, 1942.
Gates, L. E. *Studies and Appreciations.* New York, 1900.
Geyer. "Hawthorne, Allegorist and Artist." Lexington, Ky., 1960.
Hart, J. E. "Hawthorne and the Short Story." Berkeley, Calif., 1900.
Hoffman, D. G. *Form and Fable in American Fiction.* New York, 1961.
Holmes, O. W. "Nathaniel Hawthorne." *Atlantic Monthly,* XIV, July 1864.
Howe, I. "Hawthorne and American Fiction." *American Mercury,* LXVIII,
March 1949.
Kimbrough, R. "The Actual and the Imaginary: Hawthorne's Concept of Art in
Theory and Practice." *TWA,* L, 1960.
Kingley. "Outline Study of *Twice-Told Tales.*" *Educ.,* February, 1921.
Lathrop, R. H. "My Father's Library Methods." *Ladies Home Journal,* March
1894.
Lewis. *The American Adam.* Chicago, 1955.
Marsh, P. "Hawthorne and Griswold." *MLN,* February 1948.
Matherly, E. P. "Poe and Hawthorne as Writers of Short Story." *Educ.,* XL,
January 1920.
Matthiessen, F. O. *American Renaissance.* New York, 1941.
Pearce, R. H. "Hawthorne and the Twilight of Romance." *YR,* XXXVII, 1948.
Read, H. "Hawthorne." *Hound and Horn,* III, 1945.
Reid, A. S. "The Role of Transformation in Hawthorne's Tragic Vision." *FurmS,*
VI, 1958.
Robinson, H. M. "Materials of Romance." *Commonweal,* X, October 1929.
Schlefer. "The Magic Circle: The Art of Nathaniel Hawthorne." Unpublished
Master's Thesis. Cambridge, Mass., Harvard University, 1942.
Schonbach, A. E. "Beitrage zur Charakteristik Nathaniel Hawthornes." *Eng.
Studien,* VII, 1884.
Schubert, L. *Hawthorne the Artist: Fine Arts Devices in Fiction.* Chapel Hill,
N. C., 1944.
————. "Hawthorne Used the Melodic Rhythm of Repetition." *Ch. Sc. M.,* 1945.
Selby, T. G. *The Theology of Modern Fiction.* London, 1896.
Trollope, A. "The Genius of Nathaniel Hawthorne." *Nth. Amer. Rev.,* CXXIX,
1879.
Turner, A. "Hawthorne as Self-Critic." *SAQ,* XXXVII, 1938.
————. "A Note on Hawthorne's Revisions." *MLN,* November 1936.
————. *Nathaniel Hawthorne: An Introduction and Interpretation.* New York,
1961.
Tuttiet, M. G. "Hawthorne the Mystic." *XIXth Cent.,* LXXXVII, January 1920.
Van Doren, M. *Nathaniel Hawthorne: A Critical Biography.* New York, 1949.
Waffle, A. E. "The Wizard of the New World." *Cosmopolitan,* I, March 1886.
Waggoner, H. H. *Hawthorne: A Critical Study.* Cambridge, Mass., 1955.
Veen, W. *Die Erzahlungstechnik in dem Kurzerahlungen Nathaniel Hawthornes.*
Munster, 1938.
Whipple, E. P. *Character and Characteristic Men.* Boston, 1886.
Winters, Y. "Maule's Curse, or Hawthorne and the Problem of Allegory." *Amer.
Rev.,* LX, 1937.
Woodberry, G. E. *Nathaniel Hawthorne.* Boston, 1902.
————. *Nathaniel Hawthorne, How to Know Him.* Indianapolis, 1918.

V. CRITICAL OPINIONS OF INDIVIDUAL WORKS

CONTEMPORARY CRITICS AND ARTICLES DEALING WITH GROUPS OF WORKS
1. Principal "reviews" published in Hawthorne's lifetime (taken from Bertha Faust's *Hawthorne's Contemporaneous Reputation.* Philadelphia, 1939.
Twice-Told Tales:
Belden, H. M. "Poe's Critique of Hawthorne." *PMLA*, Append. II, LXVII, 1899.
Hoffman, C. F. Review. *American Magazine*, March 1838.
Longfellow, H. W. "Hawthorne's *Twice-Told Tales*." *Salem Gazette*, March 1837.
Poe, E. A. Review. *Graham's*, April 1842.
————. Review. *Graham's*, May 1842.
————. "Marginalia." *Dem. Rev.*, December 1844.
————. "Author's Introduction" to *The Literati of New York. Godey's*, May 1846.
Mosses from an Old Manse:
Chorley, H. F. Review. *Athenaeum*, London, August 1846.
Melville, H. "Hawthorne and His *Mosses*." *Literary World*, 1850.
The Scarlet Letter:
Chorley, H. F. Review. *Athenaeum*, London, June 1850.
Duyckinck, E. A. Review. *Literary World*, March 1850.
Loring, G. B. "Hawthorne's *Scarlet Letter*." *Mass. Q.*, III, September 1850.
Ripley, G. Review. *N. Y. Tribune*, April 1850.
Whipple, E. P. Review. *Graham's*, May 1850.
The House of the Seven Gables:
Chorley, H. F. Review. *Athenaeum*, London, May 1851.
Clark, L. G. "Notice of *The House of the Seven Gables*." *Knickerbocker*, May 1851.
Duyckinck, E. A. Review. *Literary World*, April 1851.
Whipple, E. P. Review, *Graham's*, June 1851.
The Snow Image and Other Twice-Told Tales:
Whipple, E. P. Review. *Graham's*, September 1852.
The Blithedale Romance:
Brownson. *Brownson's Q. R.*, VI, October 1852.
Montégut, E. "Un Romancier Socialiste en Amerique." *RDM*, December 1852.
Whipple, E. P. Review. *Graham's*, September 1852.
The Marble Faun:
Chorley, H. F. Review. *Athenaeum*, London, March 1860.
Gale, M. T. "*The Marble Faun*: An Allegory with a Key to Its Interpretation." *New Eng.*, October 1861.
Lowell, J. R. Review. *Atlantic Monthly*, March 1860.
2. Criticisms of Groups of Works:
Adams, R. P. "Hawthorne's Provincial Tales." *NEQ*, XXX, 1957.
Arvin, N. Introduction to *Hawthorne's Short Stories*. New York, 1946.
Brumbaugh, T. B. "Concerning Nathaniel Hawthorne and Art as Magic." *AI*, XI, 1954.
Cohen, B. B. "Hawthorne and Legends." *Hoosier Folklore*, VII, September 1948.
Howe, M. A. de W. "The Tale of Tanglewood." *YR*, XXXII, 1942.
Marks, A. H. "German Romantic Irony in Hawthorne's Tales." *Symp.*, VII, November 1953.
McPherson, H. "Hawthorne's Major Source of His Mythological Tales." *AL*, November 1958.
Reed, A. L. "Self-Portraiture in the Works of Nathaniel Hawthorne." *SP*, XXIII, 1926.

Shabo. "Hawthorne's Holgrave and Hollingsworth." *NEQ*, December 1960.
Warren, A. Introduction to *Representative Selections of Nathaniel Hawthorne.* New York, 1934.
Yates, N. "Ritual and Reality: Mask and Dance Motifs in Hawthorne's Fiction." *PQ*, XXXIV, 1955.

INDIVIDUAL WORKS (chronological order established by E. C. Lathrop: *A Study of the Sources* [Northampton, Mass., 1929]).
"Alice Doane's Appeal":
Gross, S. L. "Hawthorne's 'Alice Doane's Appeal.'" *NCF*, X, December 1955.
Waggoner, H. H. "Alice Doane's Appeal." *UKCR*, XVI, 1950.
"The Hollow of the Three Hills" (*Salem Gazette*, November 1830):
Burhans, C. S. "Hawthorne's Mind and Art in 'The Hollow of the Three Hills.'" *JEGP*, LX, 1961.
Poe, E. A. "Tale-Writing." *Godey's*, November 1847.
Fanshawe (Boston, 1828):
Bode, C. "Hawthorne's *Fanshawe*: the Promising of Greatness." *NEQ*, XXIII, 1950.
Burnham. "Hawthorne's *Fanshawe* and Bowdoin College." *EIHC*, LXXX, 1944.
Carlton, W. N. C. "Hawthorne's First Book: *Fanshawe, a Tale.*" *Am. Coll.*, IV, June 1927.
Goldstein, J. S. "The Literary Source of Hawthorne's *Fanshawe.*" *MLN*, LX, 1945.
Gross, R. E. "Hawthorne's First Novel: The Future of a Style." *PMLA*, LXXVII, 1963.
Little, G. T. "Hawthorne's *Fanshawe* and Bowdoin's Past." *Bowdoin Quill*, 1904.
Orians, G. H. "Scott and Hawthorne's *Fanshawe.*" *NEQ*, XI, June 1938.
"Roger Malvin's Burial" (*Token*, 1832):
Birdsall, V. O. "Hawthorne's Oak Tree Image." *NCF*, XV, April 1960.
Orians, G. H. "The Sources of 'Roger Malvin's Burial.'" *AL*, X, 1938.
Thompson, W. R. "The Biblical Sources of Hawthorne's 'Roger Malvin's Burial.'" *PMLA*, LXXXVII, 1962.
"The Gentle Boy" (*Token*, 1832):
Dauner, L. "The 'Case' of Tobias Pearson: Hawthorne and the Ambiguities." *AL*, XXI, 1950.
Gross, S. "Hawthorne's Revision of 'The Gentle Boy.'" *AL*, XXVI, 1954.
Orians, G. H. "Sources and Themes of Hawthorne's 'The Gentle Boy.'" *NEQ*, XIV, 1941.
"My Kinsman, Major Molineux" (*Token*, 1832: "My Uncle Molineux"):
Connors, T. E. "'My Kinsman, Major Molineux': a Reading." *MLN*, LXXIV, April 1959.
Gross, S. L. "Hawthorne's 'My Kinsman, Major Molineux': History as Moral Adventure." *NCF*, XII, 1957.
Lesser, S. O. "The Image of the Father." *PR*, XXII, 1955.
"The Grey Champion" (*New England Magazine*, 1835):
Cohen, B. B. "The Grey Champion." *Indiana U. Folio*, XIII, 1948.
Orians, G. H. "The Angel of Hadley in Fiction: A Study of the Source of Hawthorne's 'The Grey Champion.'" *AL*, November 1932.
"Young Goodman Brown" (*New England Magazine*, 1835):
Cherry, F. "The Sources of Hawthorne's 'Young Goodman Brown.'" *AL*, V, 1934.
Cohen, B. B. *Paradise Lost* and 'Young Goodman Brown.'" *EIHC*, XCIV, 1958.
Connolly, T. E. "Hawthorne's 'Young Goodman Brown,' an Attack on Puritanic Calvinism." *AL*, XXVIII, 1956.
Fogle, R. H. "Ambiguity and Clarity in 'Young Goodman Brown.'" *NEQ*, XVIII, 1945.

Frye, P. R. "Hawthorne's Supernaturalism." *Lit. Rev. & Crit.*, 1908.
McCullen, J. T. "Hawthorne's 'Young Goodman Brown': Presumption and Despair." *Discourse*, 11, 1959.
McKeithan, D. M. "Hawthorne's 'Young Goodman Brown': An Interpretation." *MLN*, 1952.
Miller, P. "Hawthorne's 'Young Goodman Brown': Cynicism and Meliorism." *NCF*, December 1959.
Orians, G. H. "New England Witchcraft Fiction." *AL*, II, 1930.
Walsh, T. F. J. "The Bedevilling of Goodman Brown." *MLQ*, XIX, December 1958.
"The Maypole of Merry Mount" (*Token*, 1833):
Orians, G. H. "Hawthorne and 'The Maypole of Merry Mount.'" *MLN*, LIII, 1938.
"Canterbury Pilgrims" (*Token*, 1833):
Cameron, K. W. "Background of Hawthorne's 'Canterbury Pilgrims.'" *ESQ*, 4th Quart. 1958.
Waggoner, H. H. "Hawthorne's 'Canterbury Pilgrims': Theme and Structure." *NEQ*, XXII, 1949.
"The Ambitious Guest" (*New Eng. Mag.*, 1835):
Cameron, K. W. "Genesis of Hawthorne's 'The Ambitious Guest.'" *Historiographer of the Episcopal Diocese of Connecticut*, 1955.
Cohen, B. B. "The Source of 'The Ambitious Guest.'" *BPLQ*, IV, 1952.
Edgren, C. H. "Hawthorne's 'The Ambitious Guest,' an Interpretation." *NCF*, September 1955.
"The Great Carbuncle" (*Token*, 1837):
Haskel, R. F. "The Great Carbuncle." *NEQ*, X, September 1937.
"Wakefield" (*New England Magazine*, 1835):
Schiller, A. "The Moment and the Endless Voyage; A Study of Hawthorne's 'Wakefield.'" *Diameter*, March 1951.
"The Vision of the Fountain" (*NEQ*, 1835):
Gross, S. L. "Hawthorne's 'Vision of the Fountain' as a Parody." *AL*, XXVII, March 1955.
"The Minister's Black Veil" (*Token*, 1837):
Fogle, R. H. "An Ambiguity of Sin and Sorrow." *NEQ*, XXI, September 1948.
Stiblitz, E. E. "Ironic Unity in 'The Minister's Black Veil.'" *AL*, XXXIV, 1962.
Walsh, T. F. "Mr. Hooper's 'Affable Weakness.'" *MLN*, LXXIV, May 1959.
"David Swan" (*Token*, 1837: "David Snow"):
Gozlan, L. *Une Mission trop secrète*. Brussels, 1854.
"The Prophetic Pictures" (*Token*, 1837):
Cooke, A. L. "The Shadow of Martinus Scriblerus in Hawthorne's 'The Prophetic Pictures.'" *NEQ*, SVII, 1944.
Dichmann, M. E. "Hawthorne's 'The Prophetic Pictures.'" *AL*, XXIII, 1951.
Kane, R. J. "Hawthorne's 'The Prophetic Pictures' and James's 'The Lion.'" *MLN*, LXV, April 1950.
Reed, A. L. "Self-Portraiture in the Works of Nathaniel Hawthorne." *SP*, XXII, 1926.
"Fancy's Show-Box" (*Token*, 1837):
Doubleday, N. F. "The Theme of Hawthorne's 'Fancy's Show-Box.'" *AL*, X, 1938.
"Mrs. Bullfrog" (*Token*, 1837):
Abel, D. "Le Sage's Limping Devil and 'Mrs. Bullfrog.'" *NEQ*, April 1953.
"Dr. Heidegger's Experiment" (*Salem Gazette*, 1837):
Gibbens. "Hawthorne's Note on 'Dr. Heidegger's Experiment.'" *MLN*, LXVIII, 1952.
Hastings, L. "An Origin for 'Dr. Heidegger's Experiment.'" *AL*, IX, 1938.
"Lady Eleanore's Mantle" (*Dem. Rev.*, 1838):
Cherry, F. N. "A Note on the Source of Hawthorne's 'Lady Eleanore's Mantle.'" *AL*, 1935.

"The Birthmark" (*Pioneer*, 1843):

Heilman, R. B. "Hawthorne's 'The Birthmark': Science as Religion." *SAQ*, XLVIII, 1949.

Thompson. "Aminadab in Hawthorne's 'The Birthmark.' " *MLN*, LXX, June 1936.

"Egotism, or the Bosom Serpent" (*Dem. Rev.*, 1843):

Schroeder, J. W. "Hawthorne's 'Egotism, or the Bosom Serpent' and Its Source." *AL*, XXXI, 1959.

"The Celestial Railroad" (*Dem. Rev.*, 1843):

Cronkite. "The Transcendental Railroad." *NEQ*, XXIV, 1950.

"Fire-Worship" (*Dem. Rev.*, 1843):

Bell, M. "Hawthorne's 'Fire-Worship,' Interpretation and Source." *AL*, XXIV, March 1952.

"The Christmas Banquet" (*Dem. Rev.*, 1844):

Davidson, F. "Voltaire and Hawthorne's 'Christmas Banquet.' " *BPLQ*, III, 1951.

"The Intelligence Office" (*Dem. Rev.*, 1844):

Abele, R. von. "Baby and Butterfly." *KR*, XV, Spring 1953.

Cohen, B. B. "Emerson's 'The Young American' and Hawthorne's 'The Intelligence Office.' " *AL*, March 1954.

"The Artist of the Beautiful" (*Dem. Rev.*, 1844):

Davis, R. B. "Hawthorne, Fanny Kemble, and 'The Artist of the Beautiful.' " *MLN*, LXX, December 1955.

Deiaune, H. M. "The Beautiful in 'The Artist of the Beautiful.' " *XUS*, December 1961.

Fogle, R. H. "The World of the Artist: a Study of 'The Artist of the Beautiful.' " *TSE*, I, 1949.

Stein, W. B. "The Artist of the Beautiful': Narcissus and the Thimble." *AI*, XVIII, 1961.

"Rappacini's Daughter" (*Dem. Rev.*, 1844):

Boewe, C. "Rappacini's Garden." *AL*, XXX, 1958.

Gwynn, F. L. "Hawthorne's 'Rappacini's Daughter.' " *NCF*, December 1952.

Male, R. R., Jr. "The Dual Aspects of Evil in 'Rappacini's Daughter.' " *PMLA*, March 1954.

McCabe, B. "Narrative Technique in 'Rappacini's Daughter.' " *MLN*, LXXIV, March 1959.

Price, S. R. "The Heart and Head and 'Rappacini's Daughter.' " *NEQ*, XXVII, September 1954.

Rawls. "Hawthorne's Rappacini." *Expl*, XV, Item 47, April 1947.

Rosenberry, E. H. "Hawthorne's Allegory of Science: 'Rappacini's Daughter.' " *AL*, XXXII, 1960.

Rossky. "Rappacini's Garden or the Murder of Innocence." *ESQ*, Spring 1961.

"The Great Stone Face" (*Nat. Era*, 1850):

Lynch, J. "Structure and Allegory in 'The Great Stone Face.' " *NCF*, XV, 1960.

Pfeiffer, K. G. "The Prototype of the Poet in 'The Great Stone Face.' " *RS*, IX, 1941.

"Feathertop" (*Internat. M.*, 1852):

Kern, A. A. "The Sources of Hawthorne's 'Feathertop.' " *PMLA*, XLVI, 1931.

———. "Hawthorne's 'Feathertop' and 'R. L. R.'." *PMLA*, LII, 1937.

"Ethan Brand" (*Dollar Magazine*, 1851):

Brother, J. "Art and Event in 'Ethan Brand.' " *NCF*, XV, 1960.

Brown, E. K. "Hawthorne, Melville and 'Ethan Brand.' " *AL*, III, 1942.

Fogle, R. H. "The Problem of Allegory in Hawthorne's 'Ethan Brand.' " *UTQ*, XVII, January 1948.

Gross, S. L. "The Origin of Hawthorne's Unpardonable Sin." *BUSE*, III, Summer 1957.

Levy, A. J. " 'Ethan Brand' and the Unpardonable Sin." *BUSE*, V, Autumn 1961.

McCullen, J. and Guilds, J. "The Unpardonable Sin in Hawthorne: A Re-Examination." *NCF*, XV, 1960.
Miller, J. E. "Hawthorne and Melville: The Unpardonable Sin." *PMLA*, LXX, 1955.
Pedersen, G. "Blake's Urizen as Hawthorne's 'Ethan Brand.'" *NCF*, XII, 1958.
Perry, B. "Hawthorne at North Adams: The Amateur Spirit." Boston, 1904.
Reeves, G., J. "Hawthorne's 'Ethan Brand.'" *Expl*, XIV, June 1956.
Reilly, C. A. "On the Dog's Chasing His Own Tail in 'Ethan Brand.'" *PMLA* LXVIII, 1953.
Stewart, R. "Ethan Brand." *SatR*, V, 1929.

Certain of Hawthorne's major tales have not been made the object of individual studies, e.g.: "The Wives of the Dead" (*Token*, 1832), "The Haunted Mind" (*Token*, 1835), "Endicott" (*Token*, 1838), "Drowne's Wooden Image" (*Godey's*, 1844), whereas *Fanshawe* has been paid as much attention as "Young Goodman Brown." As for the minor tales, the following studies may be mentioned:

Cohen, B. B. "The Composition of 'The Duston Family.'" *NEQ*, XXI, 1948.
Gallup. "On Hawthorne's Authorship of 'The Battle Omen.'" *NEQ*, IX, 1936.

THE SCARLET LETTER

Abel, D. "Hawthorne's Pearl, Symbol and Character." *ELH*, XVIII, 1951.
———. "Hawthorne's Hester." *CE*, XIII, 1952.
———. "The Devil in Boston." *PQ*, XXXII, 1953.
———. "Hawthorne's Dimmesdale, Fugitive from Wrath." *NCF*, XI, 1956.
Arden, E. "Hawthorne's Case of Arthur D." *AI*, XVIII, 1961.
Austin, A. "Hester Prynne's Plan of Escape: The Moral Problem." *UKCR*, XXVIII, June 1962.
———. "Satire and Theme in *The Scarlet Letter*." *PQ*, XLI, April 1962.
Barkett, S. S. "The (Complete) *Scarlet Letter*." *CE*, XXII, 1961.
Bouve, C. "Is It the Grave of Hester Prynne?" *Mentor*, October 1938.
Bragman, L. "The Medical Wisdom of Nathaniel Hawthorne." *Annals of Medical History*, New York, 1930.
Carpenter, F. I. "Scarlet A Minus." *CE*, V, 1944.
Cowley, M. "One Hundred Years Ago, Hawthorne Sets a Great New Pattern." Book review, *N. Y. Herald Trib.*, 1950.
———. "Five Acts of *The Scarlet Letter*." *CE*, XIX, 1957.
Darley, F. O. "Compositions in Outline from Hawthorne's *The Scarlet Letter*." Boston, 1880.
Doubleday, N. F. "Hawthorne's Hester and Feminism." *PMLA*, LIV, 1939.
Eisinger, C. E. "Pearl and the Puritan Heritage." *CE*, XII, March 1951.
Fairbanks, H. G. "Man's Separation from Nature: Hawthorne's Philosophy of Suffering and Death." *ChS*, March 1959.
Gerber, J. C. "Form and Content in *The Scarlet Letter*." *NEQ*, March 1944.
Glenkner, R. F. "James's *Madame de Mauves* and Hawthorne's *The Scarlet Letter*." *MLN*, 1958.
Gross, S. L. "Note on *The Scarlet Letter*." *MLN*, March 1938.
———. "Solitude, Love and Anguish: the Tragic Design of *The Scarlet Letter*." *CLAJ*, III, 1960.
Guillace, G. "Peche et Pecheurs dans *La Lettre Ecarlate* et *Le Faune de Marbre* de Hawthorne." *EA*, XV, April 1962.
Hamada, M. "*The Scarlet Letter*, a Tale of 3 Prisoners." *Bunguku-Kai*, Ronsku, Konan Univ., XIII, December 1960.
Hart, J. E. "*The Scarlet Letter*: One Hundred Years After." *NEQ*, XXIII, 1950.
Haugh, R. F. "The Second Secret in *The Scarlet Letter*." *CE*, XVII, 1956.
Hawthorne, J. "The Making of *The Scarlet Letter*." *Bookman*, LXXIV, 1931.
Hoeltje, H. H. "The Writing of *The Scarlet Letter*." *NEQ*, XXVII, 1954.
Johansson, K. "Det Speglade Livet." Stockholm, 1924.
Jones, L. "Mr. Hawthorne's *The Scarlet Letter*." *Bookman*, LVI, 1924.

Levi. "Hawthorne's *The Scarlet Letter*: a Psychoanalytic Interpretation." *AI*, X, 1953.

Maclean, H. N. "Hawthorne's *The Scarlet Letter*: The Dark Problem of This Life." *AL*, XXVII, 1955.

McKenzie. "Lecture sulla Letteratura Americana (Hawthorne e Poe)." Bari, 1932.

McNamara, A. M. "The Character of Flame: The Function of Pearl in *The Scarlet Letter*." *AL*, XXVII, 1956.

Male, R. R. " 'From the Inmost Germ': The Organic Principle in Hawthorne's Fiction." *ELH*, XX, 1953.

Murphey. "Hester in History." *AL*, March 1960.

O'Donnell, C. R. "Hawthorne and Dimmesdale: The Quest for the Realm of Quiet." *NCF*, XIV, 1960.

Raliv, P. "The Dark Lady of Salem," in *Image and Idea*. Norfolk, Conn., 1947.

Reid, A. S. "Rich. Niccols, Sir Thomas Overbury's Vision and Other Sources of The Scarlet Letter." Gainesville, Fla., 1951.

———. "The Yellow Ruff and *The Scarlet Letter*: A Source of Hawthorne's Novel." Gainesville, Fla., 1955.

———. "A Note on the Date of *The Scarlet Letter*." *FurmS*, IV, 1957.

Roper, G. "The Originality of Hawthorne's *The Scarlet Letter*." *DR*, XXX, 1950.

Ross, E. C. "A Note on *The Scarlet Letter*." *MLN*, XXXVII, January 1922.

Ryscamp, C. "New England Sources of *The Scarlet Letter*." *AL*, November 1959.

Sandeen, E. "*The Scarlet Letter* as a Love-Story." *PMLA*, LXXVII, 1962.

Stanton, R. "Dramatic Irony in Hawthorne's Romances." *MLN*, LXXI, 1956.

Stocking, D. M. "An Embroidery on Dimmesdale's *The Scarlet Letter*." *CE*, XIII, March 1952.

Waggoner, H. H. "Nathaniel Hawthorne: The Cemetery, The Prison, and the Rose." *UKCR*, XIV, 1948.

Werner, W. L. "The First Edition of Hawthorne's *The Scarlet Letter*." *AL*, V, January 1934.

OTHER NOVELS

1. *The House of the Seven Gables*:

Abel, D. "Hawthorne's House of Tradition." *SAQ*, LII, October 1953.

Beebe, M. "The Fall of the House of Pyncheon." *NCF*, XI, 1956.

Bogart. "Secret Staircase." *Yankee*, January 1952.

Buitenhuis, P. "*The House of the Seven Gables*, a Serpent Image." *N&Q*, July–August 1959.

Clark. "Another *House of the Seven Gables*? Montpellier, The Knox Mansion at Thomaston, Maine." *Ch. Sci., Mth. Mag.*, 1943.

Dillingham, W. G. "Structure and Theme in *The House of the Seven Gables*." *NCF*, XIV, 1959.

Emry, H. T. "Two Houses of Pride: Spenser's and Hawthorne's." *PQ*, XXXIII, 1954.

Gannon. *Hawthorne and "The House of the Seven Gables."* Salem, Mass., 1955.

Griffith, B. W., Jr. "Hawthorne's *The House of the Seven Gables*." *GaR*, VIII, 1954.

Griffiths, T. M. "Montpelier and 'Seven Gables': Knox's Estate and Hawthorne's Novel." *NEQ*, September 1943.

———. "Maine Sources in *The House of the Seven Gables*." Waterville, Me., 1945.

Havens, E. A. "The 'Golden Branch' as a Symbol in *The House of the Seven Gables*." *MLN*, LXXIV, January 1959.

Labaree, B. W. and Cohen, B. B. "Hawthorne at the Essex Institute." *EIHC*, XCIV, 1958.

Leaf, M. "*The House of the Seven Gables*, by Nathaniel Hawthorne Who had Ghosts in his own Garret." *American Magazine*, CXXI, March 1941.

Levy, A. J. "The *House of the Seven Gables*: The Religion of Love." *NCF,* XVI, 1961.

Marks. "Who Killed Judge Pyncheon? The Role of Imagination in *The House of the Seven Gables.*" *PMLA,* LIII, May 1953.

2. *The Blithedale Romance:*

Abel, D. "Hawthorne's Skepticism about Social Reform, with Especial Reference to *The Blithedale Romance.*" *UKCR,* XIX, 1953.

Crane. "*The Blithedale Romance* as Theatre." *N&Q,* V, February 1953.

Davidson, F. K. "Towards a Re-evaluation of *The Blithedale Romance.*" *NEQ,* XXV, 1952.

Hedges, W. L. "Hawthorne's *The Blithedale Romance*: The Function of the Narrator." *NCF,* XIV, 1960.

Howe, I. "Hawthorne: Pastoral and Politics." *New Rep.,* CXXXIII, September 1955.

Male, R. R., Jr. "Towards The Westland: The Theme of *The Blithedale Romance.*" *CE,* XVI, February 1955.

Marenco, F. "Nathaniel Hawthorne, e il *Blithedale Romance.*" *SA,* VI, 1960.

Murray, P. B. "Mythopoesis in *The Blithedale Romance.*" *PMLA,* LXXV, 1960.

McCullen. "Zenobia, Hawthorne's Scornful Skeptic." *Discourse,* IV, Winter 1961.

O'Connor, W. "Conscious Naivete in *The Blithedale Romance.*" *RLV,* February 1954.

Stanton, R. "The Trial of Nature: An Analysis of *The Blithedale Romance.*" *PMLA,* LXXVI, 1961.

Turner, A. "Autobiographical Elements in *The Blithedale Romance.*" *U. of Texas SE,* XV, 1935.

3. *The Marble Faun:*

Abel, D. "A Masque of Love and Death." *UTQ,* XXIII, 1953.

Brickell, J. "*The Marble Faun* Reconsidered." *UKCR,* XX, 1954.

Brodtknob, P., Jr. "Art Allegory in *The Marble Faun.*" *PMLA,* LXXVII, 1962.

Fogle, R. H. "Simplicity and Complexity in *The Marble Faun.*" *TSE,* II, 1950.

Guilds, J. C. "Miriam of *The Marble Faun,* Hawthorne's Subtle Sinner." *CairoSE,* 1960.

Haselmayer, L. A. "Hawthorne and the Cenci." *Neophil,* XVII, 1941.

Paris, B. J. "Optimism and Pessimism in *The Marble Faun.*" *BUSE,* II, 1956.

Parish, H. "The Sources of *The Marble Faun.*" Unpublished thesis. New Haven: Yale University, 1929.

Peabody, E. "The Genius of Nathaniel Hawthorne." *Atlantic Monthly,* XX, September 1868.

Waples, D. "Suggestions for Interpreting *The Marble Faun.*" *AL,* XIII, 1941.

Wright, N. "Hawthorne and the Praslin Murder." *N&Q,* 1942.

4. *Posthumous:*

Abel, D. "Immortality vs. Mortality in "Septimius Felton"; Some Possible Sources." *AL,* XXVII, January 1956.

Kouvenhoven, J. A. "Hawthorne's Note Books and *Doctor Grimshawe's Secret.*" *AL,* V, January 1934.

Stein, W. B. "A Possible Source of Hawthorne's English Romance." *MLN,* LXVII, 1952.

VI. MISCELLANEOUS

Allen, F. H. Bowdoin College Collection of Drawings and Paintings. 1886.

Arthos, J. "Hawthorne in Florence." *Mich. Alumni Q.R.,* LIX, 1953.

Cook, K. "Nathaniel Hawthorne." *Belgravia,* IX, 1872.

———. "Nathaniel Hawthorne, Man and Author." *Edinburgh Rev.,* CCIII, 1906.

Guido, A. "Le Ambiguità di Hawthorne." *SA,* I, 1955.

Hanigan, D. F. "Nathaniel Hawthorne's Place in Literature." *Living Age,* CCXXXI, December 1901.

"Henpecked Immortals: Hawthorne Censored by His Wife." *Nation,* December 1932.

Higginson, T. W., ed. "The Hawthorne Centenary Celebration at the Wayside, Concord, Mass., July 4–7, 1904." Boston, 1905.

———. "A Precursor of Hawthorne." *Indep.* New York, XL.

Izzo, C. "Un Metafisico della Narrazione: Nathaniel Hawthorne." *SA,* I, 1955.

Loring, G. B. "Hawthorne." In *Papyrus Leaves,* Boston, 1880.

natural).

McCorquodale, M. K. "Melville's Pierre as Hawthorne." *SET,* XXXIII, 1954.

Moffitt, C. "Hawthorne's Optical Device." *AQ,* XV, Spring 1963.

Olivero, F. "Nathaniel Hawthorne." *NA,* CLXVI, 1913.

Peabody, E. "Last Evenings with Allston." Boston, 1886.

"The Proceedings in Commemoration of the 100th Anniversary of the Birth of Nathaniel Hawthorne held at Salem, Mass., June 23, 1904." *EIHC,* Salem, 1904.

Schlefer. "The Italy of Hawthorne." *Nation,* XL.

Spiller. "Closed Room and Haunted Chamber." *SatR,* November 1948.

Stephen, L. *Hours in a Library.* New York, 1874.

Index

471